A LITTLE REVENGE

WILLIAM FRANKLIN

BENJAMIN FRANKLIN

A LITTLE
REVENGE

BENJAMIN FRANKLIN
AND
HIS SON

BY

Willard Sterne Randall

LITTLE, BROWN AND COMPANY

BOSTON   TORONTO

FIRST PAPERBACK EDITION

LIBRARY OF CONGRESS CATALOGING-IN-PUBLICATION DATA

Randall, Willard Sterne.
  A little revenge.

  Bibliography: p.
  1. Franklin, Benjamin, 1706–1790—Family.   2. Franklin,
William, d. 1814.   3. Statesmen—United States—Biography.
4. Statesmen's children—United States—Biography.
5. American loyalists—Biography.   I. Title.
E302.6.F8R18   1984   973.3′092′2[B]   84-15464
ISBN 0-316-73364-4
ISBN 0-316-73365-2 (pbk.)

VB

DESIGNED BY DEDE CUMMINGS

Published simultaneously in Canada
by Little, Brown & Company (Canada) Limited

PRINTED IN THE UNITED STATES OF AMERICA

To the memory of
Catherine Drinker Bowen
who first encouraged
this work

We supped one night in Edinburgh with the celebrated Dr. Franklin. . . . Franklin's son was open and communicative and pleased the company better than his father; and some of us observed indications of that decided difference of opinion between father and son which, in the American war, alienated them altogether.

—ALEXANDER CARLYLE,
Autobiography

CONTENTS

Acknowledgments   xiii

I   MY SON WAS OF MUCH USE TO ME

1.   *We Expect the Enemy Every Hour*   3
2.   *Our Father Was a Very Wise Man*   24
3.   *I Am Too Indulgent a Parent*   40
4.   *We Got Five Scalps but They Got Nine*   72
5.   *The People Happen to Love Me*   100

II   A PARTICULAR SET OF PEOPLE

6.   *One Great Smoky House*   121
7.   *Six Weeks of the Densest Happiness*   152
8.   *I Dislike Family Quarrels*   166
9.   *Yours Till Deth*   185
10.   *I Steer My Little Bark Quietly*   205

III   I HAVE LOST MY SON

11.   *Government Should Have No Passions*   229
12.   *A Man of Letters*   256
13.   *You Are a Thorough Courtier*   275
14.   *The Times Are Greatly Altered*   302
15.   *A Matter of Punctilio*   327
16.   *Adam Had His Cain*   346

CONTENTS

IV NOTHING HAS EVER HURT ME SO MUCH

17.   *With All Due Regularity and Decorum*   369
18.   *It Is Your Turn Now*   388
19.   *A Little Revenge*   428
20.   *I Shall Never See You Again*   461
21.   *My Son Keeps Himself Aloof*   490

Chapter Notes   501
Bibliography   527
Index   549

ACKNOWLEDGMENTS

T HE NUMBER OF PEOPLE I WISH TO THANK FOR HELPING ME is indeed large. First among them is the late Catherine Drinker Bowen, that great biographer, who encouraged me to look at the Franklin family when I was beginning to research the Loyalists. Whitfield J. Bell, Jr., librarian of the American Philosophical Society, which provided the first small research grant for this work, also gave me generously of his time and ideas. Dr. Robert A. East, director of the Loyalist Project for Studies and Publications at the Graduate Center of the City University of New York, invited me to present my first paper on William Franklin at the First International Conference on the Loyalists, and then he and his son-in-law James E. Mooney, former director of the Historical Society of Pennsylvania, frequently offered me advice and guidance. The Honorable Esmond Wright, director of the Center for United States Studies at the University of London, also was helpful. My friend and advisor at Princeton University, John Murrin, has provided many useful insights, as have Lawrence Stone, Arthur S. Link and Stanley N. Katz.

Special thanks go to my editors and publishers at Little, Brown. For his numerous suggestions and his patience as I struggled with myself as well as this book, I must thank Roger Donald, my editor. For willingness to fund unorthodox views of life in America, past and present, I am once again indebted to George Atwater Hall. To

Jean L. Whitnack, much more than a copy editor to me, I owe special thanks. Also providing special assistance were Ellen Panarese, Elaine Richard and Sabina Mayo-Smith. Ray Lincoln, friend, literary agent and sensitive editor, already knows, I hope, how much I owe her in how many ways.

There is a special thank you I wish to extend here — to my son, who has put in hundreds of hours assisting me with all the chores that surround the writing process.

No such project as this is possible without the aid of librarians. In the early stages, the staff of the Cape May County Library in Cape May Court House, New Jersey, exceeded the ordinary demands of a rural library as they tracked down hundreds of books through the excellent New Jersey interlibrary loan system. The staff of the Firestone Library at Princeton University proved solicitous: I wish to thank Stephen Ferguson, curator of rare books; Ann Van Arsdale, Charles E. Greene and Jane Snedeker, in particular. Thanks, too, to Robert Crout of the Madison Papers for his many insightful suggestions. Also helpful were the staffs of the American Philosophical Society Library, the Historical Society of Pennsylvania, the Presbyterian Historical Society and the Lilly Library at the University of Indiana in Bloomington. Personal notes of thanks go to William C. Wright, director of the New Jersey State Archives, and to Albert W. Seaman and Joseph J. Truncer of the Proprietary House Association in Perth Amboy.

A number of timely grants from the following organizations enabled me to carry out this project: the American Philosophical Society, the New York Bicentennial Commission, the New Jersey Historical Society, the Society of Colonial Dames, the New York Authors League and American P.E.N. Among personal friends who have aided this work in a variety of ways are David N. Redman, Mae R. Wilson-Ludlam, Ruth L. King, Donald McKenzie, Bernard Bowman and Nancy A. Nahra.

For permission to quote from papers in their collections, I am grateful to the Lilly Library of Indiana University, the Clements Library of the University of Michigan, the New-York Historical Society, the Massachusetts Historical Society, the New York Public Library, the Historical Society of Pennsylvania, the American Philosophical Society, Princeton University Library, the John Rylands Library of Manchester, England, the Morristown National Historic Park, and Yale University Press for permission to quote from *The Papers of Benjamin Franklin,* edited by Leonard W. Labaree, William B. Willcox and others, 23 volumes. Copyright © 1959, 1960, 1961, 1962, 1963, 1964, 1965, 1966, 1967, 1968, 1969, 1970, 1971, 1972, 1973, 1974, 1975, 1976, 1977, 1978, 1979, 1980, 1981, 1982, 1983 by the American Philosophical Society and Yale University. The spelling, capitalization and punctuation of quotations from eighteenth-century sources have been modernized for twentieth-century readers.

I

MY SON WAS
OF MUCH
USE TO ME

1

WE EXPECT THE ENEMY EVERY HOUR

1755

FOR THE FOURTH ICY JANUARY DAY SINCE THEY HAD LEFT the fortified town of Bethlehem, the Pennsylvania militiamen slogged northwest along the Lehigh River. Hunched under sodden wool coats, they bent into the burning cold wind, their muskets hanging heavily in the hard slanting rain. Aware that the Indians were spying them out, they scanned the thick rocky cover to the left, bushes, boulders and trees to the right. As they trudged along the narrow wagon road, their wet boots slithered and crunched through ice-crusted puddles. They made no more than a mile an hour. Occasionally they glanced up for signals from the officer at the head of the column, then pushed ahead, eager to clear the long gap through Kittatinny Mountain as quickly as they could. If an attack came in this rain, their guns would be useless: they had just learned that eleven of the thirteen militiamen who had left Bethlehem the same day had been killed by Indians when their soaked weapons misfired.[1]

Captain William Franklin, the only seasoned officer on the march, rode the lead horse, his scarlet grenadier's uniform a conspicuous target for Indian snipers. Notwithstanding, he had deployed his 172-man force with an eye to avoiding the fatal mistakes made by General Edward Braddock, whose campaign to Fort Duquesne against the French and Indians last July had ended in disaster at the Monongahela River. (In that tangled wilderness nightmare, British redcoats had paraded in neat ranks into a three-hour cross fire.) Here, the twenty-two cavalrymen were strung out behind Franklin to give the appearance of a much larger force, and behind them marched the infantrymen in single file, Indian fashion, ready to take cover quickly. Ahead, a small contingent of scouts shielded the main body against ambush: they probed thickets and ravines and took each hill as the column approached. Bringing up the rear were the heavy Conestoga supply wagons, each pulled by a plodding six-horse team, and the guard of militiamen. Commander of the expedition was Benjamin Franklin, recently elected colonel of the Pennsylvania militia. Clad in a great blue coat, he rode half-way back in the column with politician friends. Every so often he had to urge the supply teams forward while the rest of the expedition, at Captain Franklin's command, waited for them to catch up.

The men themselves needed no urging. Since Braddock's defeat, all too many of them had viewed the mutilated bodies of relatives and friends, victims of Indian raids along the defenseless 150-mile Pennsylvania frontier. In the last six months, more than four hundred settlers had been killed and an even greater number of women and children dragged west into captivity.[2] At last, on November 25, 1755, the Pennsylvania Assembly had voted the funds to raise a militia for defense. After seven weeks of preparation, the expedition was on its way to build the first of several forts.

The two men leading the grim little column personified the changes sweeping war-torn America as the year 1756 began. Benjamin Franklin, at fifty, had already lived through two wars between the French and the English. His face was puffy and smooth from gout, his body overweight and rounded into the peculiar barrel shape of the once-powerful swimmer too long out of the water. By now his hairline had receded until he considered his brown wig a necessity. His high, convex brow — his most distinctive feature — called attention to his dark, penetrating, unwavering eyes.

Half his age, William Franklin was a smoother, thinner, sharper replica of his father, with the same impressive forehead, the same strong, straight nose apostrophizing the same set jaw and pronounced chin. Both men were tall for their time, Benjamin approaching six feet, William beyond it. Hardened by military service on the frontier, by long canoe trips into the wilderness, William had been at home on horses since he was ten. Acute, whimsical, he was as affable on the surface as his father, but with more elegant manners, more polish.

The older man had, like many successful men, grown vain as he became rich. The younger was already self-assured. He had assimilated easily all his father's hard-bought acquisitions of knowledge, wealth and position, and was determined to find new ways to shape and civilize the world he and his generation would inherit. Relations between the two were unusually close. Together they attacked vehemently any enemy who threatened either of them — as vehemently as they would later oppose each other in their single-minded Franklin drive to prevail no matter what the cost.

In recent years Benjamin had emerged gradually as the pivot of power in Pennsylvania. Neither proprietary hireling nor Quaker pacifist, he had quietly, inauspiciously, entered politics by simply applying for the uncoveted Assembly clerkship. His highly successful publishing business coupled with his increasingly profitable post as deputy postmaster general for the six northern American colonies, had afforded him more and more leisure for scientific experiments, political activities, and an impressive list of civic benefactions, all publicized in his news columns. While climbing politically, he had adroitly handed over lesser perquisites to William. He made "Billy" (as he insisted on calling him) clerk of the Assembly, then postmaster of Philadelphia, then comptroller general of the British-American postal system. William accepted all these posts with enthusiasm. In addition, he acted as his father's secretary on frequent political and postal travels, and as his assistant in most of the electrical experiments; he also lent his skillful pen to his father's political battles.

William's close collaboration with his famous father for twenty-five years and his contributions to his father's activities — political, military and scientific — have been all but forgotten in the two hundred years since the American Revolution. It may have been Benjamin Franklin himself who obliterated his son. One cause of William's almost total obscurity can be found by studying Benjamin's autobiography. The first, incomplete draft was, in fact, addressed to "Dear Son." It was written in the summer of 1771 while Benjamin was visiting friends in the Sussex countryside. At that time he was still close to William: their relationship had not yet become clouded by the Revolution. He stated his purpose clearly: "I have ever had a pleasure in obtaining any little anecdotes of my ancestors. You may remember the enquiries I made among the remains of my relations when you were with me in England. . . . Now imagining it may be equally agreeable to you to know the circumstances of my life, many of which you are yet unacquainted with, and expecting a week's uninterrupted leisure in my present country retirement, I sit down to write them to you." If Franklin had any ulterior motive at this time, it was to inspire his son with the story of his frugal, industrious rise "from the poverty and obscurity in which I was born and bred to a state of affluence." Franklin carried the narrative only as far as 1730, the year in which he took Deborah Read as his common-law wife. He had to stop writing when his vacation was over.

Twelve years passed before he returned to his autobiography. He and his son had become enemies at the start of the Revolution. And as Franklin took up the telling of the next twenty years of his life — the portion that covered so many of his son's experiences as his aide, secretary, assistant in scientific experiments, and confidant in politics — he all but excised William from the narrative. Only once, when writing of the fort-building expedition on the Pennsylvania frontier, did he acknowledge that William was "of great use to me."

Again, Franklin interrupted the work on his manuscript. Five years later, in 1788, he finally finished it. By then he had met with William for the one and only time since their estrangement, and had written his last will and testament, disinheriting him.

If Franklin's best-known piece of writing virtually omitted his son, William's records cannot compensate: they were almost entirely destroyed during the Revolution while he languished in an American prison. His letters to friends and family in England and America, his diaries, journals, ledgers, financial records and manuscripts were all lost in a fire that consumed a British army warehouse containing everything he possessed. Much of what remains he wrote when he was an embittered exile in England. Both father's and son's surviving accounts of each other are therefore self-serving documents written after the breach between them.

Fortunately, scattered through archives in Canada, England and America is enough surviving evidence to permit the resurrection of William Franklin.

In view of the muddled state of Pennsylvania politics in the 1750's, it is surprising that the Franklins' fort-building expedition was ever authorized, even in the face of the French and Indian incursions. By 1756, the Quaker party, for seventy-five years all-powerful, represented only orthodox members of the Society of Friends. Outwardly a solid political bloc, the Friends were actually and hopelessly divided into factions; but though a minority, they managed still to control the German and Scotch-Irish majority by cleverly manipulated election laws. The Quaker party had yielded much influence to the proprietary party, which consisted of friends and hangers-on of the Penn family, the feudal proprietors of the privately owned province. The party was led by William Penn's assertive son Thomas, who lived in London and acted through appointed deputy governors in Philadelphia. He and his brothers had long since ceased to be practicing Quakers and were not averse to war, only to bearing its costs. The third party, rising fast, was the antipacifist and antiproprietary party led by the populist Benjamin Franklin; it was well on the way to taking control of the provincial legislature.

All Quakers agreed on one keystone doctrine: fighting was the deadliest sin. Even self-defense brought expulsion from Quaker meeting. Unarmed, facing its first serious military threat from the Indians, the rich province lay defenseless. All along its borders, the Indians were stirring, aroused by Penn land deals they neither understood nor appreciated. Delawares, Shawnees, the Six Nations tribes — all for the first time were listening to promises of the French Canadians who were fomenting war. In March of 1755, after the latest land sale, Chief Logan, the representative of the Six Nations to the Pennsylvania government, had warned the colonists that "whosoever of the white should venture to settle any land belonging hitherto to the Indians will have his creatures killed first, and then if they do not desist, they themselves would be killed, without distinction, let the consequence be what it would."[3]

While orthodox Quakers opposed war from principle, Quaker

merchants, even if they were willing to be defended, did not want war with the Indians for quite another reason: war would disrupt business. To an increasingly profitable extent, their customers were Indians. In exchange for furs, Quaker merchants sold the Indians English iron kettles and English woolen blankets. They also sold them English-made hatchets, knives and guns.

In the autumn of 1755, the seventy-five-year-long Quaker quandary over self-defense was resolved, at first as silently and stealthily as the fall of maple leaves in the Appalachian forests, then with the ferocity of shrieking, tomahawk-wielding Indian war parties.

When no retaliation came for the defeat of Braddock, the French and their Indian allies sent out small raiding parties to attack solitary targets. Then they became bolder. By October, bands of up to two hundred Delawares were ranging east from Fort Duquesne. On the eighteenth a large party struck the settlement of Penn's Creek on the Susquehanna River within a hundred miles of Philadelphia. The first man in the capital to learn of the attack — from a postrider who galloped in to report the news — was the young postmaster, William Franklin. He, in turn, rushed word to his father, who was chairman of the legislature's committee on defense. The elder Franklin quickly relayed word to London: "Just now arrived in town an express from our frontiers, with the bad news that eight families of Pennsylvanians were cut off last week. . . . Thirteen men and women were found scalped and dead and twelve children are missing."[4] While Franklin was no doubt worried by the raiders' boldness, privately he evinced scant sympathy for the settlers: the raid was "a natural consequence of the loose manner of settling in these colonies, picking here and there a good piece of land and sitting down at such a distance from each other."[5]

Without waiting for help from far-off Philadelphia politicians, forty-five armed neighbors hurried upriver to bury the dead at Penn's Creek. A friendly Indian interpreter warned them of a general attack, urged them to avoid the usual path home. Suspecting a trick, the whites ignored him. Before they could reach their cabins, they were ambushed. Four were wounded fatally; four drowned as they tried to escape across the thin river ice. One survivor hastily wrote Franklin: "I have not yet moved my family, not caring to discourage others. We expect the enemy every hour. I have cut holes through my house . . . and am determined to hold out to the last extremity, hoping for protection from the province soon."[6]

As Quaker leaders rose in meetinghouses and the State House to warn against deviating from pacifist doctrine, Indian raiders razed the cabins of Scotch-Irish settlers within two days' ride of Philadelphia. On October 11, in the first raid east of the Susquehanna, 120 warriors attacked farms just west of Reading. After murdering fifteen men and women, and scalping three children (who survived), they set fire to scores of houses and destroyed large numbers of cattle and horses, quantities of grain and fodder. The terror was intensified when farmers recognized old Indian neighbors among the war parties. One hundred other killings were reported within a hundred miles of Philadelphia. More than forty settlements were burned. Frightened families packed what they could into their wagons and fled east toward Reading. For fifty miles south, the riverfront settlements emptied. Indians once again held dominion over the forests of Pennsylvania.

What William Penn, a political and religious refugee from England, had envisioned as a Holy Experiment, a peaceable kingdom in a new world, by 1755 had become wracked by rigged elections, patronage schemes, land swindles, riots and ethnic prejudice.

The commonwealth of Pennsylvania had taken root well enough: more than a hundred shiploads of immigrants arrived in 1682 alone, lured by Penn's promotion. "The soil is good, air serene from the cedar, pine and sassafras with the wild myrtle of great fragrance," he wrote. "I have had better venison, bigger, more tender, as fat as in England. Turkeys of the wood I had of 50 pounds weight . . . flowers that for color, largeness and beauty excel."[7]

Twice jailed in the Tower of London for his beliefs, Penn spent two decades formulating his plan of government. He consulted John Locke and Algernon Sidney, rewrote his *Frame of Government* seventeen times. The final version embodied a far-reaching expansion of English civil liberties. Not long after Quaker missionaries were hanged in Boston, Penn granted colonists full religious toleration, thereby attracting immigrants of every faith.

The provincial charter called for a legislature consisting of a governor appointed by Penn or his heirs, an upper house, called the Council, and a lower house, the Assembly. The members of the Council were to be appointed by the governor as his advisors; the assemblymen were elected by the people as their representatives. As it turned out, the members of the Council were usually the owners of large amounts of land, men of money and influence who merely rubber-stamped the governor's decisions. The members of the Assembly were given the power to raise taxes, supply the money for government expenses, and decide how the money should be spent. Because the Assembly dispensed patronage and approved the governor's salary, it held more power than any other elective body in colonial America. The Penn family, as owners of the province, reserved the right to sell any amount of provincial land and then to collect from each buyer an annual quitrent for every acre purchased. The Penns could also nullify all laws.

Penn's judgment in appointing governors to rule in his place was less than wise. One governor distinguished himself chiefly as a barroom brawler; with his good friend William Penn, Jr., he severely beat up the town watchman. His successor bickered with the Assembly so regularly they refused to pay his salary. Infuriated, the governor left the province, but not before kicking a judge. Fifty years elapsed, however, before Pennsylvania politicians caused any lasting problem.

In 1737 Penn's sons, hard pressed for land to sell to new German and Scotch-Irish refugees, sought to add to their real estate inventory by negotiating a new treaty with the Indians. They invoked an old treaty promise allegedly made to their father: he could extend his settlements "as far as a man can walk in a day and a half." In the first Walking Purchase, the elder Penn had strolled along with Indian chieftains, pushing branches aside, stopping often for a little wine, smoking the pipe, exchanging pleasantries in their native tongue, and covering fifteen miles, the distance the Delawares expected of his sons.

But the Delawares were now dealing with lawyers. The bargain did not specify exactly which man should make the walk or exactly what route he should follow. The young Penns ordered a wide pathway cleared through the underbrush. They hired and trained the three fleetest couriers in the province, provided relays of horses and riders to take them food, drink and fresh moccasins. Leaving Wrightstown in Bucks County at dawn on September 19, 1737, the whites, heeling and toeing furiously, rapidly outdistanced their Indian escorts. By noon, the fastest woodsman had already covered twenty-one miles and had crossed the Lehigh River. Halting only fifteen minutes for a meal, the Penn runner set off briskly again and duly reached the end of the prepared road. After a short night's sleep he was handed a compass and struck off to the northeast, taking a well-worn warrior path along the Delaware River to the present-day New York border. By the time he dropped at midday, he had covered nearly seventy-two miles and had doubled the Penn real estate holdings.

The Delawares honored their pledge. Slowly, mournfully, resentfully, they began to move farther west.

All parties to the spreading French and Indian War coveted the Walking Purchase lands of the Lehigh Valley, sixty miles north of Philadelphia. To the Delawares, the valley was holy: their birthplace and burial ground. The Shawnees, promised the valley by French agents if they cleared it of English settlers, warned the last remaining unarmed Delawares that they must either daub on war paint and take up the hatchet or expect to be treated as Englishmen. To the French, the Lehigh Gap was the only break in Kittatinny Mountain wide enough to permit the passage of artillery for an invasion of Philadelphia.

Surrounded by a graceful ring of hills, the valley had become the heartland of the Moravian settlements. Even in the drought-ridden mid-1750's it was rich in corn and wheat, thick with dairy herds. The Moravians, German forerunners of the Methodists, had purchased most of the valley from Penn's sons after the second Walking Purchase. They established unarmed towns with Biblical names — Bethlehem, Nazareth — built missions, and preached to the Indian "heathen" a Christian salvation. They alone among the peaceful Pennsylvanians methodically studied the Indian cultures and dialects.

Their unique wilderness community included a hospital, colleges for men and women, woolen mills, shops, grist mills that served surrounding valleys, running water from the first waterworks in America, apothecary gardens, and a cocoonery for growing and producing silk. They were housed in steep-roofed, fieldstone-and-timber dormitories according to age, sex, marital status and occupation. For recreation they loved to sing in *a cappella* choirs, the well-scrubbed women in long black dresses and white caps, the brethren in their starched white linen roundabouts and linen trousers. On summer evenings, violin and French horn, oboe and trombone music floated up the Lehigh River to the windows of Bishop Augustus Spangenberg and the Indians who had come to visit and pray with him.

But on November 25, 1755, there was no music. In the chill early dawn, the residents of Bethlehem were summoned to the church by the doleful tolling of the town bells. The bishop told his people of the massacre at Gnadenhütten, the principal Moravian mission twenty-five miles up the Lehigh River.

Two days before, a company of more than seventy armed Scotch-Irish frontiersmen had dismounted at the Crown Inn, a commodious stone hotel maintained outside the Bethlehem town limits for the segregated comfort of strangers. Tension rose. The Moravians had come to realize that in the eyes of nervous frontiersmen they were suspect because of their Indian guests. For days there had been rumors that hostile Scotch-Irish bands were riding on Bethlehem to destroy it, to wipe out its Indian converts. On this Sunday, the riders assured the Moravians that they meant no trouble: they only wanted to hunt down any hostile Indians they found. A justice of the peace informed the riders that there was no sign of imminent peril from the Shawnees. He would, he said, arrange for them to stay overnight, without charge, if they promised not to cross the river and alarm the townspeople by appearing in the streets with their weapons. He would also provide guides to lead them upriver to the Lehigh Gap. But on Monday morning the frontiersmen marched into Bethlehem willy-nilly, drums pounding, flags flapping in the stiff northwest wind. They wanted to fight the Delawares and Shawnees before a combined French-Indian force of twelve hundred men, now rumored to be on the way, dared any further raids.

Before leading the swarming frontiersmen to the strategic gap, the Moravians insisted on sending ahead an interpreter, David Zeisberger, to warn the mission at Gnadenhütten that a French-Indian force was on the march and that numbers of frontiersmen would be riding through. All the Indians at Gnadenhütten were to remain inside their houses; if they should venture into the woods they might be shot.

The Moravians had built Gnadenhütten on the west bank of the Lehigh River, between the hills and a high bluff where Weissport is today. Besides a church, dormitories, a schoolhouse, an infirmary, stores, mills and barns, Gnadenhütten boasted a large sawmill where oak, walnut and especially fine hemlock were hewn into planks and rafted down the river to build burgeoning Bethlehem. The principal Moravian language school was here also. John Martin Mack had been teaching Delaware and Mohican to young missionaries for the past six years and composing poems and songs in these dialects.

On the east bank the Indians only recently had been given separate quarters in a new village: nineteen substantial stone cottages and a church. About one hundred Indians, mostly women and children, remained in the village that Monday. The older boys and the men were away to the north on the annual winter hunt. Even with the men gone, the mission was crowded. Because of the three-year drought, food along the frontier was scarce and expensive; at the mission it was free.

When Zeisberger reached the new village, just before dark, he handed his instructions to Mack, then turned his tired horse toward the river. He intended to spend the night on the west bank before returning to Bethlehem. As his horse picked its way through the shallow rapids and clattered over the stones, he heard shooting, but dismissed it as signal fire from the approaching frontiersmen.

There were sixteen Moravians at the old mission as the last glow of twilight disappeared. When the bell rang, all but two who were ill — Peter Worbas, in the single men's house, and Anna Sensemann, in the women's quarters — stopped their chores and gathered for dinner in the main room of the mission house. After asking for grace, they began to pass the food around as they talked softly. John and Susanna Partsch, who had arrived only the week before, were eating together. The blacksmith, Martin Kiefer, had taken a place near George Fabricius, a linguist. Martin Nitschmann, six years a missionary, sat with his wife, Susanna. Gottlieb Anders was serving his wife, Johanna, who was nursing their infant daughter. The other single men — John Lesley, John Gattermeyer, Martin Presser, George Schweigert and Joseph Sturgis — were grouped together near the front door.

Seventeen-year-old Sturgis was the first to notice the sounds of footsteps on the crusty ground outside. He went to unlatch the door. As he swung it wide, he fleetingly saw the fierce black-, blue-, brown-, and green-painted faces, heard the first shrieking war cry, saw the flash of muskets. He fell, shot in the face. Another ball hit Nitschmann, killing him instantly.

A dozen screeching Indians burst into the room and fired at the single men. Three were hit and Susanna Nitschmann was wounded as she shoved other women ahead of her up the stairs into the women's dormitory overhead. When she fell, two Indians dragged her outside, she crying out, "Oh, brethren! Brethren! Help me!" The other Indians dragged out the three bleeding, dying men and scalped them.

In the dormitory upstairs, the survivors began to pray. Anna Sensemann sank to the edge of a bed, sobbing, "Dear Savior, this is what I expected!" Johanna Anders wrapped her baby in her apron and bent down over her as the warriors pounded on the trapdoor. All the other women could do was to scream for help through the garret window in the hope of attracting the attention of someone on the other side of the river.

Downstairs, the men who were left looked about for makeshift weapons — they had no guns. Then, suddenly, it became quiet outside. Only the barking dogs made any noise. For a few moments it seemed that the Indians had gone. But when Joachim Sensemann started to hurry back across the compound, he saw that the Indians had surrounded the mission house and with bundles of brush and torches were systematically setting it afire. He ran toward the river, hoping to warn those in the new village.

From a second-story window of the single men's house, Peter Worbas watched helplessly. He saw the Indians drag Susanna Nitschmann away and scalp the three men. His horror increased when he saw a half-dozen warriors ignite the piles of dry wood they had stacked around the building. Some of those inside tried to escape. Sturgis, bleeding from wounds in the face and arm, jumped from a window, landed safely, ran into the woods toward the river. Susanna Partsch jumped immediately after him. She also made it to the woods and hid behind a tree. Fabricius was not so fortunate. As he stepped through the same window, four Indians rounded the building, saw him, fired. He died before hitting the ground. The Indians scalped him, cut out his entrails, reloaded, and fired at the window again.

As the flames burned higher, seven more Moravians died. The twelve Indians stripped the food from the stores, butchered sixty cattle, set the other buildings afire, then cooked themselves a feast as the entire mission burned down in the darkness. Not until midnight did they make off with their plunder and the wounded Susanna Nitschmann.

As David Zeisberger was crossing the river after giving the instructions to John Mack, young Sturgis, bloodied and breathless, burst from the bushes and rushed down the riverbank. Zeisberger helped him on the horse and they hurried back to the new village. Since all the able-bodied Indian men had gone off with the hunting guns, the old men and the women and children were helpless against the attack they were sure would come. Mack told them to scatter. Take to the woods. Hurry toward Bethlehem. Zeisberger wheeled his tired horse and lashed it down the river road.

It was two more days before five survivors — Mack, Sturgis, Sensemann, Susanna Partsch and Worbas — were found by militiamen and brought to Bethlehem. It was four more months before Martin Presser was found and identified by his clothing. He had crawled into the woods, bleeding heavily from the side. He had died lying on his back, his hands folded in prayer.*

On Monday, November 24, the Assembly session was marked by an exasperating deadlock over defense. In the early evening — just as the massacre at Gnadenhütten was launched — the weary assemblymen started home. Ordinarily, as the Christ Church carillon chimed the evening concert, their equipages would roll up the

---

* Susanna Nitschmann died at the Munsee Indian stronghold at Tioga several weeks later. Jachebus, her captor and leader of the twelve-man raiding party, was strangled to death a year later by a Delaware chief who had been baptized by the Moravians.

street in procession, each assemblyman peeling off smartly when he reached his brick town house. But tonight the serene drive home was slowed. The streets were unusually crowded. As Benjamin Franklin threaded his carriage through a side street, he and William could see an unprecedented number of Conestogas pouring into town. The German farmers were not merely bringing their goods to market: they were abandoning the frontier, marching angrily on Philadelphia to demand protection.

When the German immigrants first arrived in Pennsylvania, they found that the valuable bottomlands along the Delaware and Schuylkill rivers had already been taken up. They had to choose between leaving the province for other, less tolerant colonies or settling for cheap, uncultivated land farther north and west on the edge of the wilderness. They chose the latter. In a remarkably short time, through industry and consummate thrift, they prospered.

To learn new customs and to become acquainted with the soil conditions and the climate, many sold themselves for seven years as indentured servants. At the return of their freedom, they were given land as part of the bargain. With hoarded cash brought from Germany and earned from gardening on their own time, they built solid houses and barns of native limestone and dark-red siding. Their kilns turned limestone into fertilizer and whitewash. They spread pulverized lime mixed with dung from their horses and cattle over the newly grubbed fields. In one turn of the seasons, they were ready to join the twice-weekly wagon trains to the Philadelphia market sheds.

The rich rewards of German farming only sharpened other immigrants' envy. By the 1750's, thousands of Scotch-Irish, disgruntled with the high rents in northern Ireland, were swarming over the Pennsylvania backcountry, sometimes expropriating German lands by force. When officials tried to evict them, they often took countermeasures. One German justice of the peace was nearly burned to death by avenging squatters who set his house afire. The cries of one of his children awoke the family, saving their lives. German resentment of the Scotch-Irish still smoldered years later.

There was also growing political unrest. Until 1755, when the Indian incursions began, the Germans who could vote (one in fifty) aligned themselves unquestioningly with the Quakers. Their spokesman, Christopher Sauer, whose powerful *Pennsylvania Berichte* rivaled Benjamin Franklin's *Gazette,* bolstered the pacifism of his readers. As war swept the province, he warned his fellow Germans that Franklin's Assembly party would introduce compulsory military service. All the miseries they had suffered in Germany would be sharpened by the scalping knife. He urged them to oppose Franklin: a vote for Franklin would be a vote for war.

The influx of German farmers could not have been a welcome sight to many Philadelphians. By 1755, the Germans outnumbered the Quakers two to one, and hostility toward them had risen commensurately. A Penn spokesman plumbed the depths of anti-German feeling in an open letter to a London newspaper: "What can be more absurd and impolitic than to see a body of ignorant, proud, stubborn clowns (who are unacquainted with our language, our manners, our laws and our interests) indulged with the privilege of returning almost every member of Assembly?"[8]

Benjamin Franklin shared in the hostility. One of his remarks — a slur that cost him dearly many years later — revealed how lively his prejudice was: the Germans were "Palatine boors herding together." His feeling against them became conspicuous when most of them paid no attention to his plan for an all-volunteer militia. It was further deepened by the failure of the German-language edition of his *Gazette.* The Germans ignored it and continued loyally to support Sauer's paper. Franklin's venture promptly folded. In retaliation, Franklin cornered the newsprint market and then refused to sell newsprint on credit to the German monastics at Ephrata Cloister, who were publishing a German Bible. Whereupon one well-to-do German marched to Philadelphia and plunked down hard cash, something Franklin found impossible to resist.

The Germans were all too aware of the prejudice against them. When the French and Indians continued to burn their barns, slaughter their cattle, and murder their neighbors, they knew better than to expect that the pacifist Quakers would voluntarily protect and defend them. Gathering up their dead and their living, they marched on the capital.

At first, the long line of wagons rolling along the bluff above the Schuylkill River on November 24, 1755, must have appeared like any other bustling market drive toward Philadelphia. Clouds of steam rose from the flanks of the great black draft horses. As the German farmers snapped their bullwhips over the teams, the wagons lurched into a long shuddering line, their barn-red panels blurring into a streak of crimson. Soon, residents of the river towns could see that pieces of furniture and chests of clothing, sacks of food and rolls of bedding were piled on the Conestogas. One alarmed justice of the peace, who had watched the endless cavalcade all day, rushed a message to the governor that there must be a thousand obviously angry German refugees on the march. By nightfall, when the Delawares were putting their torches to Gnadenhütten, the refugees began to bivouac around cookfires on the commons across the street from Benjamin Franklin's house.

Governor Robert Hunter Morris had taken office a year before the German march on Philadelphia. Son of a wealthy governor of New Jersey, he had served as that province's chief justice for seventeen years, during which time he had built a reputation for ruthlessly suppressing land riots and disputing with anyone who had dealings with him. Though he had no military or fiscal experience, he enjoyed the strong backing of the Penn family. The Franklins apparently first met him in 1754 as they were heading for the Albany talks on intercolonial defense.

Pennsylvania governors had quarreled for years with the Assembly, especially over defense. The new governor, Franklin later recounted, "asked me if I thought he must expect as uncomfortable an administration. I said, 'No; you may on the contrary have a very comfortable one, if you will only take care not to enter into any dispute with the Assembly.' " The two men became fast friends. "I was put on every Assembly committee for answering his speeches and messages. . . . Our answers as well as his messages were often tart, and sometimes indecently abusive. . . . One might have imagined that when we met we could hardly avoid cutting throats. But he was so good-natured a man that no personal difference between him and me was occasioned by the contest. . . .

"One afternoon in the height of this public quarrel, we met in the street. 'Franklin,' says he, 'you must go home with me and spend the evening.' . . . After supper, he told us jokingly that he

much admired the idea of Sancho Panza, who, when it was proposed to give him a government, requested it might be a government of blacks. . . . Then, if he could not agree with his people, he
might sell them. One of his friends who sat next me, says, 'Franklin, why do you continue to side with these damned Quakers? Had
not you better sell them? The Proprietor would give you a good
price.' 'The governor,' says I, 'has not yet *blacked* them
enough.' "[9]

The governor soon blackened himself. Benjamin came to consider him "half a madman" when Morris exhorted Quakers to take
up arms and march against the French, and at the same time refused to tax Penn lands, the largest holdings in the province.

For nearly six months, beginning in June of 1755, the Assembly
defense committee met each morning. At noon, the great new
State House bell would somberly summon the rest of the assemblymen to agonize over the province's peril. Each day they were
pulled one way by preachers reminding them "not [to] fear them
that kill the body," another way by the daily litany of the dead, by
the refugees' appeals for arms, food and clothing. Each day
brought, too, the governor's latest attempt to make Quakers pay
for the privilege of war. His policy was more than most assemblymen could tolerate.

Not above exchanging unpleasantries at inopportune moments,
Governor Morris further inflamed resentment the day the emergency session began that followed Braddock's defeat. Immediately
after being called to order, the Assembly sent William Franklin, its
clerk for more than four years, to obtain from Morris the usual au-
thorization to affix the provincial seal to the Assembly minutes.
The governor pretended he did not know that young Franklin was
the clerk. He sent him back, steaming, to obtain official proof of his
position.[10]

Morris soon learned just who William Franklin was. Indeed, it
was William who finally provided his father with the legal means to
trip up the Penn party. In an airy wing on the south side of the
State House was one of the largest law libraries in America, its
glass-covered bookcases containing hundreds of gold-stamped,
calfskin-bound volumes on colonial and British constitutional law.
Here the real work of the Assembly was performed by committees

before the official session convened. As the confrontation between the proprietary and Assembly parties dragged on, William Franklin came to read law in the evening. He analyzed by candlelight every message and document sent down by the governor and ferreted out the legal rulings that buttressed his father's answers on behalf of the Assembly.

In late October and early November, through the early weeks of the crisis, Benjamin Franklin had been confined to bed with a severe cold, thereby increasing William's load. The younger Franklin had to become his father's legs, eyes and ears. Up with most other Philadelphians at five in the morning, he attended committee meetings at the State House, then went back to report to his father and obtain signatures on committee documents. Then back to the State House again. In the afternoon he attended the Assembly session, reported again to his father, made précis of his father's reports and the Assembly addresses to the proprietary. Only then could he tend to his job as postmaster. Hurrying back to his own house, he sorted through the day's post and sent off the penny-post letters throughout the city. In the quiet of the late evening, he again became clerk of the Assembly: he transcribed the day's pile of hastily taken notes and turned them into polished minutes for the record. The long day ended with his poring over lawbooks.

In his third year of studies in a leading law office, William was already gaining a reputation as an astute interpreter of constitutional law. He intended to complete his studies in London once the frontier crisis was over. Meanwhile, since the Assembly did not have a lawyer in its ranks, William acted as such in his capacity as clerk. Now, in analyzing the rulings that exempted the Penns from paying real estate taxes, William thought he detected a flaw in the legal argument. To speak of such a discovery was in itself bold. William knew that Governor Morris was a specialist in land rights. He was a powerful adversary indeed for a young law clerk to take on.

One night, after leaving his father, William found the words he needed in Charles Viner's twenty-three-volume *General Abridgement of Law and Equity*, words that his father could at last fling at the governor. He copied out a long opinion on the duties of landowners and raced to his father's house. Together they composed a strong message for the Assembly to send to Morris — the strongest message to date — and the elder Franklin promptly arranged for a special edition of the *Pennsylvania Gazette* to appear the next day. The front page was devoted to William's salvo, which ended, "Even the King does not claim an exemption from taxes for his private estate, as our Proprietaries do!"[11]

"This," the Franklins declared in a message endorsed by the full Assembly, "is an act of injustice and severity, to defend the Proprietary estates *gratis*. If this be complied with, what would hinder the Penns from insisting that Pennsylvanians be required not only to defend their lands, but to plow them. For this, their lieutenant may allege the usage and custom in Germany, and put us in mind that we are chiefly Germans."[12]

For eight and nine hours a day, all through October and into November, Quaker factions had been huddling around the green baize-covered tables that flanked the State House fireplaces, searching for compromise. On November 19, Assemblyman Franklin introduced a major militia bill before the Assembly.

Once before, eight years ago, when the French had threatened Pennsylvania, Franklin had raised a large volunteer army. Alarmed, Thomas Penn had denounced him from London as a man capable of founding another "military commonwealth" like Oliver Cromwell's. Franklin's activities were "little less than treason. . . . He is a dangerous man. . . . However as he is a sort of tribune of the people, he must be treated with regard." This time, Franklin was not anonymously seeking volunteers. He was demanding a vote to create an official provincial militia.[13]

There was little left for orthodox Quakers to oppose except the entire principle itself. Franklin's bill limited enlistment to three weeks, excused all conscientious objectors and boys under twenty-one, and forbade more than a three-day march from a militiaman's home. In short, the bill made offensive war all but impossible. But orthodox Quakers still did not want war of any kind and almost all the other assemblymen were nominal Quakers who feared defeat at the next year's election.

Israel Pemberton, a Quaker cousin of Franklin's wife and a leading advocate of peace with the Indians, spoke against the Franklin bill. He managed only to defer a final decision by referring the bill into Franklin's committee. Again, the opposing forces caucused late into the night. Early next morning, the bill came out of committee for another full day's debate, even as the Conestogas continued to roll eastward toward Philadelphia.

By the raw morning of November 25, when the courthouse bell clanged for the market sheds to open, the streets were clogged with four hundred wagons. The line of Conestogas was long enough to extend the entire eight-mile distance back to Germantown. Philadelphians attempting to answer the market bell found themselves confronted by eighteen hundred angry, weary, dirty men, women and children, riding toward the residence of Governor Morris. One wagon stopped at the front entrance and a contingent of Germans gently removed the contents. On the sidewalk between the outstretched wings of the house built for peaceable William Penn, they reverently arranged the scalped, mutilated, blackened bodies of a dozen murdered relatives and friends. And then they shouted for the governor to come out.

Morris sent them a message that he would treat with a small delegation inside. Two settlers with good English were ushered into his presence. Grandiloquently, the governor blamed everything on the Assembly and then, for the first time, publicly revealed that the Penns had just authorized him to withhold five thousand pounds from the annual quitrents "as a free gift" for defense. (He did not tell them that the money was to come from uncollectable rents on land in the hands of the Indians.) Further, he promised to sign whatever defense bill the Assembly laid before him. When the delegates repeated his promises outside in German, the crowd shouted "Huzzah!" three times, and replacing the bodies in the wagon, they rolled away, cheering.

The next objective was to display their grizzly cargo at the State House. Once again, they delicately arranged the blood-caked corpses on the sidewalk. As one observer later wrote, "After a loud knocking, the door was opened. . . . There the blame was laid upon the Governor." Although the settlers withdrew after hearing vague words of reassurance from Speaker Isaac Norris, their visit had instant effect. That afternoon, the Assembly broke the ten-month legislative logjam and voted the Franklin militia bill into law, only four Quakers dissenting. Two days later, on November 27, as the

last survivors of Gnadenhütten stumbled into the hospital at Bethlehem and the eighteen hundred Germans rode back home to bury
their dead, the Quaker Assembly voted fifty-five thousand pounds
for "the King's use," their euphemism for war. The Assembly then
created a defense commission to supervise the war effort, to build
forts on the frontier, to draft and arm the provincial militia. The
Holy Experiment was over.

Already Benjamin Franklin and his veteran son had gone far in
recruiting two full regiments of foot soldiers and a regiment of
rangers to fortify the frontier against invasion by the crack twelve-
hundred-man force of French and Indians reportedly marching toward the strategic Lehigh Gap. There was little the governor could
do or say but concur. To his humiliation, he had no choice but to
appoint Benjamin Franklin to the Assembly's new defense commission, which promptly elected Franklin chairman.

2

OUR FATHER WAS
A VERY WISE MAN

1706–1723

To BE BORN ON THE SABBATH IN PURITAN BOSTON WAS THE sign of a great sin. By popular superstition held as sacred as Holy Writ, it was believed that a child born on Sunday had been conceived on Sunday. Intercourse on the Sabbath, even between man and wife, was against God's law. If ever the birth date of Constable Josiah Franklin's new son became public, scandal would spread through the closely knit community, and the infant, Josiah's fifteenth, would be considered a child of the Devil. There was nothing to do but keep the true circumstances of Benjamin Franklin's birth on January 6, 1706, a family secret.[1]

Josiah decided that his new son should be baptized at once, on Sunday, the day he was born. If suspicion was to be averted, they must have him cleansed of his sin in the freezing waters of Christian baptism. When Abiah finished the intricate winding of the swaddling clothes, Josiah bundled little Benjamin under his heavy cape and herded his other children across the twenty yards of icy paving stones into the dank, unheated Old South Church.

After sitting through the three-hour service, the family and the rest of the congregation crowded to the rear to bear witness to the sacrament. The pastor cracked the ice in the baptismal font, and murmuring the words intended to help save the shivering baby's soul, if not his body, splashed him thoroughly with water.

Then Josiah Franklin, prosperous tallow chandler, devoted public servant and devout Puritan elder, led his family and friends in a hymn of joy. This, his tenth son, would be the tithe of his loins, his offering of thanksgiving to God. He would see that the boy studied at Harvard and became a minister of the church in return for all the blessings the Franklins had received in the difficult years since coming to America.[2]

Seventy-five miles north of London, in the center of the Northamptonshire moors, lies the ancient village of Ecton. Shaded by towering oaks, Ecton has produced generations of soldiers, artisans and educators. Ecton first survived the Romans, whose leaders built villas and farmsteads, and left fifty large pottery kilns, which were dashed and plundered by raiding Danes. Next, undaunted Anglo-Saxons laid out their fields in an unusual sundial pattern around a manor house. By the time William the Conqueror's tax assessors visited the village in 1085, forty-one freemen were tilling 480 acres of flat reddish fields.

Long before there were written records of humble families, one Ecton freeman, the village blacksmith, took the name Francklyn (free man). On the forge at the foot of the lane to Ecton Manor, he and his descendants hammered out shoes for the chargers of nobles and the workhorses of neighbors, fashioned latches, andirons, hinges and tools, often of their own original design. In addition to the forge, the oldest of each generation of Franklins held thirty acres of farmland and occupied a long, low-eaved, thatched stone cottage, its ancient sandstone walls burnished smooth gold by the generations.

For centuries life in the village had gone on without apparent change. An uncle of Benjamin's described a boy's life: after long hours of helping in forge, field and cottage, he played ball, hide-and-go-seek and king-of-the-mountain, caught minnows in the stock pond and used them to bait trout in the river. As the boy grew older, he learned to read, dance, sing and play the fiddle. He also learned to tell tall stories as he enjoyed his ale and eyed the village maidens.

Overshadowing the Franklin forge was the square sandstone tower of the Church of St. Mary Magdalen, a symbol of the religious state that ordered and controlled the villagers' lives. Every

Franklin had been christened at the Saxon font. One tenth of all the fruits of Franklin enterprise went into the tithe barn and collection basket to support the clergy, who lived in fine style in the large parsonage opposite the church. After generations as dutiful Catholics, the Franklins, in the sixteenth century, were among the first to rebel against the Church. Despite Ecton's bucolic appearance, growing religious animosity made it what the visiting Dr. Samuel Johnson later described as "an example of a very savage parish."

"This obscure family of ours was early in the Reformation," Benjamin Franklin wrote in his autobiography, "and continued Protestants through the reign of Queen Mary, when they were sometimes in danger of trouble on account of their zeal against popery. They had got an English Bible, and to conceal and secure it, it was fastened open with tapes under and within the frame of a joint stool. When my great-great-grandfather read in it to his family, he turned up the joint stool upon his knees, turning over the leaves then under the tapes. One of the children stood at the door to give notice if he saw the Apparitor coming. In that case, the stool was turned down again upon its feet."[3]

In the mid-1660's, turmoil erupted within the family. Ever since the Puritans had won the decisive battle of the Civil War at nearby Naseby, the Franklins had disagreed over church politics. Josiah Franklin, two of his brothers, and their father, Thomas II, espoused Puritanism; three others, including another of Josiah's brothers, Thomas III, remained faithful to Anglicanism. Their controversy presaged a later struggle in the American branch of the family, when an older Franklin refused to yield to established authority and his son stayed loyal to it. During all the years of civil war, Thomas II must have kept his resentment hidden as he worked at his forge to prepare his Anglican overlord's horses for battle against his Nonconformist friends. Afterwards, when the reconstituted Church of England attempted to stamp out all Puritan dissent, Thomas II refused to submit. Thomas III apparently put enormous pressure on his father to recant. He made life so uncomfortable for the old man that Thomas II took his Puritan sons, abandoned Ecton forever, and journeyed twenty-five miles to the Puritan stronghold at Banbury, where he moved in with a younger son. Thereafter, as they scattered throughout the British Empire, the two camps of Franklins made no effort to keep in touch, a testament to the bitterness of the parting.

Religious attitudes aside, Thomas III was his nephew Benjamin's true precursor. He was the village scribe, a county tax official, and an inventor. To his credit were a set of church chimes arranged to ring out "Britons Strike Home," a drainage system that ended centuries of flooding, and an organ that he played at home. He died without an heir and was buried in the family plot in Ecton.

Old Thomas II, who continued to lash out at the Established Church, was arrested for his scurrilous verses. Eventually released, he died a pauper and was buried in Banbury. After five centuries the Franklin family freehold was sold to the lord of the manor. The Franklin forge was bought by a new blacksmith, and the family home, used briefly as a school, was torn down. The Franklin line vanished from Ecton.

But life for the Dissenters in the family was harder in Banbury. Young Josiah was apprenticed to an older brother, a wool dyer. Eventually, he set up his own shop and married, and three children arrived in rapid succession. He found he could barely sustain himself despite endless fifteen-hour days. The trade, seasonal at best, was stifled by trade laws and foreign competition. Worse, there was no turning to another trade unless he would undertake another unpaid, seven-year apprenticeship. Then, in 1683, Banbury officials again suppressed Nonconformist meetings. Disgusted, Josiah decided to make the drastic step that men all over England were taking that year. He would emigrate, build a new life in a new England.[4]

Soon after twenty-five-year-old Josiah, his wife Anne, and their three small children landed in Boston, the family received another setback. Brightly colored woolens were not in demand; indeed, sumptuary laws discouraged anyone from dressing above his station. Josiah had to find another trade. Luckily, New England law did not require another apprenticeship.

Striding through the thronged streets, he surveyed the town to find a vital trade with little competition. Not one of the overhanging signs he saw offered good hard soap or candles of fine quality;

most of the two thousand families saved their fat and boiled tallow once a year. As he no doubt noticed at a Puritan meeting on a warm day, few bathed. He also noted that reading the Bible was encouraged: he foresaw a ready market for candles. He decided on the career of a tallow chandler.

It was hard, smelly work gathering fat from slaughterhouses and markets amid clouds of flies, hauling it home in a wheelbarrow, rendering it in great wooden vats. The tiny house was filled with a perpetual rancid stench. But among Puritans, the surest road to eternal salvation was the path of diligently pursued business. To four fifths of his fellow townsmen, Boston was a cold place with little prospect of prosperity. The only promising course lay through hard work and election to the Puritan church after a grueling public probation.

How well Josiah fitted Puritanism, how thoroughly he espoused its self-righteousness was to have a far-reaching impact on future generations of Franklins. Josiah taught his children that they would be damned to eternal agony unless they unquestioningly followed the teachings of an unflinchingly stern God. All knowledge, all that was essential to salvation, was found in the Bible and the Sabbath sermon, and was to be obeyed without interpretation. There was a rubric for every good act, a prohibition for every bad one. The Bible was the civil law of Boston; the General Court enforced it. The brother of one Puritan divine anguished over whittling behind a closed door on the Sabbath; young lovers got into trouble for sitting idly under a fruit tree on the Lord's Day.

After giving birth to seven children in eleven years, Anne Franklin died. Josiah, a widower with five surviving children, took little time finding a new wife. His choice was willowy, dark-haired Abiah Folger, a Nantucket girl who lived with her sister in Boston and attended the Old South Church. She was young and as well educated as any woman of her time. An early Nantucket historian wistfully described the qualities Island girls had that proved irresistible to Josiah: "Their dress was moderate and plain, their deportment kind and unassuming. They were satisfied with such habiliments as were comfortable and fitted to the season, disregarding the vain and foppish fashions then prevailing. . . . They were always helpful and careful to make all practicable savings . . . industrious, neat and cleanly."[5]

The Folgers, Protestant weavers for generations, had, like the Franklins, fled England to avoid Stuart persecution. Abiah's father, Peter, had bought a servant girl on the passage over; eventually, they married. One of the first settlers of Nantucket, he became a learned Indian interpreter, surveyor, clerk of the court, miller, poet of sorts — and a rebel.

For surveying the island and soothing the Indians, the other white settlers accorded him only a half share of land, which made him a second-class citizen. Outraged, he refused to record any further court proceedings and declined to turn over the court records. The judge ordered Folger arrested and clapped him into a "place where never any Englishman was put . . . where the neighbors' hogs had layed but the night before . . . in a bitter cold frost and deep snow . . . without victuals or fire."[6] Released, Folger's next escapade was to sympathize with the Indians during King Philip's War in 1676. In one vigorous, signed, 105-stanza burst of doggerel he skewered Puritan leaders, magistrates and Harvard overseers for bringing down the wrath of God on New England by their corruption.

If Josiah Franklin learned any of this, it did not dissuade him from marrying Abiah Folger shortly after his first wife's death. For their ten children, the marriage was a blessing as profound as the curse of Josiah's intensifying Puritanism.

Before election to the Puritan elite of Boston, Josiah had to undergo both private scrutiny and a public display of his piety. It was not enough for him to show diligence in his "calling," as a trade was termed, or faithfulness to his wives. He had to make a public confession of saving grace, admitting his depraved spiritual condition and his willingness to accept God's help. He must also exhibit at the same time peace, joy and hope while somehow displaying a touch of humility. After his formal confession he must demonstrate the thoroughness of the divine hold over him as he poured out his devotion from the long aisle of the Old South Church. Whatever forms of holy violence Josiah demonstrated, he was finally declared a saint in 1694.

To be born the son of a saint was a fearful burden; to be the son of a self-satisfied disciplinarian and a mother brought up by a rebel put Benjamin under immediate strain.

In the twelve years between Josiah's Puritan election and Benjamin's surreptitious birth, Josiah had confidently progressed through the religious ranks until he had become a symbol of stern paternalism for much of Boston. So crucial was the family unit to Puritans, so important was proper child rearing, that officials called tithingmen were elected each March to keep watch over every household. In 1697, burly Josiah — he was built like his blacksmith father — was deemed the ideal choice to enforce church-state discipline over one quarter of the families of Boston. He was reelected a number of times.

Josiah's duty, the law stated, was "to present the names of all single persons that live outside of family government, stubborn and disorderly children and servants, nightwalkers, tipplers, Sabbath breakers by night or day, and such as absent themselves from public worship — or whatever else tending to debauchery, irreligion, profaneness and atheism amongst us."[7] To children he must have been a terrifying specter. Although there is no recorded instance of a child's execution on the public gallows, a linchpin of Puritan theology was Calvin's dictum that "those who violate parental authority by contempt or rebellion are not men but monsters. Therefore the Lord commands all those who are disobedient to their parents to be put to death."[8]

When Josiah Franklin was not checking on the conduct of apprentice boys and servant girls, he was a prominent figure in the Old South Church. Rising from the Franklin pew, he would march down the aisle to poke with his staff of office anyone nodding off or whispering. Carrying more weight than a prod in the ribs was the threat of ostracism: the church was also a social and business club. Exclusion meant exile. Even minor family quarrels could bring fifteen-year terms of probation: fifteen years of the tithingman's visits, of prying questions answered before the full congregation and discussed in hour-long sermons. Even Josiah's children must have done all they could to avoid his censure. Though eligible for sainthood by his father's conversion, Benjamin every day was expected to fall into depravity. His childhood was an unremitting struggle, under so much restraint that it finally made inevitable his long self-imposed exile from the family and affected his relations with his own son.

Benjamin's first images of life were from the hearth of the small rented house on Milk Street, across from the Old South Church in the oldest and poorest part of Boston. To inure him to colds, there was the popular preventive, advocated by the physician-philosopher John Locke, of dipping the baby three times a day in cold water from the well — even in winter, in eastern Massachusetts "hardening off" was the universal custom. Contrasted with this was Abiah Folger's insistence on nursing all her brood. In one of his few direct references to her in his autobiography, Benjamin wrote, "My mother had . . . an excellent constitution. She suckled all her ten children." Indeed, in Benjamin's first seven years of life, there was scarcely a time when Abiah did not have a child at the breast: she spun, wove cloth, sewed, cooked, cleaned, kept her husband's accounts, sang psalms, and taught the children their prayers.

When Benjamin was barely a year old, Josiah Franklin bought a substantial tenement on the northwest corner of Union and Hanover streets in the best commercial district. He moved his tallow business next door, to take it out of the family quarters, no doubt in response to the tragic drowning of his sixteen-month-old son Ebenezer in an unattended tub of soapsuds.[9]

As the years passed, Josiah prospered. In 1703, he was elected constable, with the duties of policing the town by day and commanding the town watch by night. He was not paid for this work, but at least once he sold a considerable number of candles to the watchmen. Despite the fact that Josiah prayed over, preached at, beat, berated, neglected, pampered and menaced his children, the Franklin family still enjoyed what the youngest, Jane, remembered years later as a good if Spartan life. "It was indeed a lowly dwelling we were brought up in, but we were fed plentifully, made comfortable with fire and clothing, had seldom any contention among us. . . . All was harmony, especially between the heads."[10]

Although a prolific writer, Benjamin wrote almost nothing of his parents or of his first ten years of life, but much can be reconstructed. Josiah attended two church services on Sundays and lectures on Thursday afternoons, conducted family prayers morning and evening, and said grace over meals. He was host to evening prayer and discussion meetings in the front parlor. Children were favorite fare for polemic disputation. At night, from the darkness of the room he shared with his older brother, Benjamin could probably hear discussions on saving children's souls.

By the age of four, Benjamin was already resisting his father's grand plan to make him that figure most respected in Boston, a minister. He wanted to be a soldier. As he grew older, he preferred clambering over the cannon on Fort Hill and watching the tangle of ships and the pig-tailed sailors on the waterfront to sitting through boring church services and interminable family prayers. Neither did he relish his father's equally interminable graces before meals, though the presence of a guest offset the ordeal. Already he was opening his eyes at grace, ignoring his father's exhortations, studying maps on the kitchen wall above Josiah's bowed head, dreaming of his escape, wondering where his brother Josiah, Jr., long since run away to sea, was sailing that day.

"At his table my father liked to have . . . some sensible friend or neighbor to converse with, and always took care to start some ingenious or useful topic . . . to improve the minds of his children," Benjamin wrote. But Benjamin was not encouraged to join in. His father subscribed to the standard Puritan dictum "children should be seen and not heard."[11]

By the time he was six, Benjamin was plotting his escape. He fled, first, by reading books. Compared with his father's dull theological tomes, Benjamin found John Bunyan's hero a delightful vagabond. In another year he was writing quatrains to his Uncle Benjamin in England. That year, aging Uncle Benjamin, a widower, came to Boston. He stayed at Josiah's for four years and the two old brothers began a long tug-of-war for the prize of Benjamin's emulation. "Our father, who was a very wise man," Benjamin wrote to his sister Jane many years later, "used to say nothing was more common than for those who loved one another at a distance, to find many causes of dislike when they came together. I saw proof of it in the disgusts between him and his brother Benjamin."[12]

The two brothers had not seen each other in thirty years. Out of respect for his older brother, Josiah moved Benny and James out of the second bedroom to make room for the honored guest. The boys, consigned to the third-floor loft, began the bitter bickering that one day would ripen into hatred. It was not the crowding that kept the house in turmoil during the years of Uncle Benjamin's visit, but the constant tension of opposing philosophies. Whereas Josiah was business first, a religious conservative, tight-lipped, totally pragmatic and authoritarian, old Benjamin, now sixty-three and a chronically unemployed silk dyer, was voluble, speculative, given to endless philosophizing, reading, scribbling of verses — in short, anything but diligent to his calling. His business had failed and he had kept his family poor while he invented a system of shorthand that enabled him to take down hundreds of sermons verbatim. Money needed for capital he had spent on a collection of political pamphlets, which he had to sell for passage to America. (Forty-five years later, his namesake managed to buy many of them back from a London bookdealer.) While Josiah worked hard making soap, Uncle Benjamin taught young Benjamin his idea of poetry. When the boy began to write in Uncle Benjamin's vein, Josiah no doubt reminded Benny that both his grandfathers had served time in jail for poetic barbs at politicians. Even worse, Uncle Benjamin humiliated Josiah at the Old South Church by insisting on singing his own doggerel version of the 107th Psalm.[13]

When, on his seventh birthday, Benny blew a pocketful of coins on a sailor's hornpipe and then proceeded to bedevil the household with its shrill tweeting, he was taught a lifetime lesson about "paying too much for the whistle." There was also the boy's left-handedness. Puritans considered it a sign of the Devil's grip. Josiah administered frequent cuffs to encourage Benny to write with his right hand. And there was Benny's skepticism about long-winded prayers. One autumn day, as Josiah salted away the winter's supply of fish in barrels, Benny asked why he did not say grace over them all right now, all at once, instead of piecemeal at every night's dinner. Josiah saw nothing but the Devil in the remarks, and Benny got the devil for it.

The more Uncle Benjamin agreed with Josiah that the boy should indeed be the tithe of his loins and study for the ministry, the less Josiah liked the idea. Still, Josiah had promised: at eight, Benny trudged off to the Boston grammar school. There he took a back bench and began to learn Latin from Ezekiel Cheever's *Short Introduction to the Latin Tongue.* He moved up rapidly, exhibiting a natural talent for writing prose. He became so proficient in both Latin and Greek that he could render Aesop's fables into Latin verse. By the end of the year, he had overtaken pupils who had started a year before him and he had moved to the head of his class.

Then Josiah took him out of school. The boy must stay home, learn a useful living. He must have a trade. Josiah's trade. He must make good hard soap and fine candles. To the stunned Benny, forced to cut wicks and watch molds all day, it was a cruel, humiliating blow, one made worse by his father's insistence on lying about it. Josiah would not admit that he was disgusted with the prospect of his last son's turning out a financial failure like Uncle Benjamin. Instead, he claimed that with all his children to feed, he was a poor man who could not afford four more years of Latin plus four years of Harvard. But Josiah must have known that many boys went through the Boston Grammar school and Harvard on full scholarships if they wanted to be ministers.

Whenever he could, Benny began to slip down to the docks. His father placed him in an inexpensive one-year school, where he failed in arithmetic. Benny bought books filled with adventure stories, including a set of histories, but he lost interest in school. By his own later admission, he became aggressive and settled arguments with his fists. He longed to run away to sea but realized he was too young. Instead, he taught himself to swim expertly and to sail friends' boats out in the harbor. He also rigged an ingenious kite and used the wind to tow him, naked, across a pond. Other ideas led him into trouble: "There was a salt marsh . . . on the edge of which, at high water, we used to stand to fish for minnows. By much trampling, we had made it a mere quagmire. My proposal was to build a wharf there fit for us to stand upon. . . . I showed my comrades a large heap of stones which were intended for a new house. . . . In the evening, when the workmen were gone, I assembled a number of my play fellows. . . . We brought them all away and built our little wharf. . . . We were discovered. . . . Though I pleaded the usefulness of the work, [my father] convinced me that nothing was useful that was not honest."[14]

By 1718, Benny was the only son left at home. Josiah sorely

needed an apprentice. Yet it was increasingly clear that Benny was bound to run away to sea, like his brother, unless he found a trade suited to him. It would not have occurred to Josiah to ask the boy what he wanted: the boy was only twelve; how could he know? He did take Benny to other workshops and watched for any flicker of interest. Finally it came down to a matter of money. Uncle Benjamin's son had just opened a cutlery shop. There would always be dull blades to sharpen. Josiah would sign the indentures for Benny to work for his cousin Samuel for the next nine years. But Josiah was horrified when Samuel demanded the customary fee. He yanked the boy home again.

To consign Benjamin Franklin to a life of grinding scissors would have been tragic, yet only Josiah's parsimonious nature saved the boy. Once again, the father set out to find his son a position. This time he decided that since the boy liked to read, a printshop would be ideal. Benny's older brother James had just returned from London with type and press. Benny would be his apprentice.

Josiah's adherence to the apprentice system was unusual — it scattered his children and made it necessary for him to seek apprentices of his own. By this time, many parents preferred to educate children in their own work. Even more peculiar was the apprenticeship to a brother, an arrangement guaranteeing friction. What made the papers of indenture almost a prison sentence for Benny were the twin facts that he did not like his twenty-one-year-old brother James, who had mocked him when he was a child, and he still wanted to be a sailor like his oldest brother, Josiah.

The family had all but given up Josiah Franklin, Junior. For nine years no one had heard of him except that he had been seen once in the East Indies. One day, when Benny was nine, Josiah Junior arrived home strong and strange, hair clubbed and face weatherbeaten. All the family gathered to celebrate the prodigal's return. Uncle Benjamin wrote a tasteless poem for the occasion, which probably drew a blank stare from Josiah Junior and a cool look from Josiah Senior.

It was the last time all thirteen of Josiah Franklin's children, from thirty-seven-year-old Elizabeth to three-year-old Jennie, crowded around the old gateleg table in front of the wide fireplace for one of Abiah Franklin's feasts. Samuel, a blacksmith, came up from Providence; Peter, a successful merchant and shipmaster, sailed over from Newport. But young Josiah would not stay. He shipped out as soon as he could. They never heard from him again.[15]

And now Josiah Senior was busily driving his youngest son from the house. Benny was reluctant about his father's choice of a trade for him. "I liked it much better than that of my father, but still had a hankering for the sea," Benjamin subsequently wrote to his son William. The words were flat, emotionless, like those of a condemned man describing the moment of sentencing. "I was to serve as an apprentice till I was twenty-one years of age."[16]

Twelve-year-old Benny packed up his belongings and walked across town to his brother's shop. In return for food, clothes and training as a printer, he was to be in every sense his brother's servant for nine years. He could be worked the clock around and beaten if he complained. He could go home or anywhere else only by his brother's express permission. James quickly made it clear that Benny would receive no special favors. At first, Benny did not quite believe him — probably expecting more of a brother — but a few sound beatings and Benny was convinced.[17]

Between 1719 and 1723, through four years of humiliation at the hands of a brother who could not admit that Ben was better read, a better thinker than himself, Ben remained indomitably proud, always looking for a way to increase his wealth of knowledge and to flaunt it. Denied formal education, he taught himself from books. Because the only public library in Boston had been destroyed when the Town Hall burned, and because he received no pay, he had to borrow books. He admired Cotton Mather's massive history of New England, *Magnalia Christi Americana,* and he talked his way into the great man's library, a stratagem he repeated with other library owners. He also learned to make friends strategically. One, a bookseller's apprentice, slipped him new books at night on condition that he return them unharmed the next morning before opening time. He acquired a formidable knowledge even as he learned to read quickly.

What he read, often fresh from that fleshpot London, scandalized his father, who feared that his son had become a deist, as bad in Puritan Boston as being an atheist. Ben devoured works of Locke and the deists Collins and Shaftesbury, and admired Defoe's *Essay upon Projects.* All through his long, public-spirited life he would think up ways to apply Defoe's civic principles. Since he had to steal hours for reading and writing, he found it hard to spare Sundays for church. His father, the tithingman, noted his absences.

Though James found his brother a trial, he soon saw a use for Ben's literary attempts. When a lighthousekeeper and his family drowned in Boston harbor, James urged the youth to write a ballad about the tragedy. Bostonians snapped it up at a good profit. Ben wrote more, this time bloody-handed quatrains on Blackbeard the pirate, who had recently been killed. Sure he had won his father's approval at last, Ben showed off his verses at home. "My father discouraged me by ridiculing my performances and telling me versemakers were generally beggars."[18]

Ironically, the seventeen-year-old's writing skill saved James's newspaper and gave Ben his freedom. For five years James and his gadfly friends had belittled Boston institutions in the *New England Courant.* In the tradition of small-town yellow journalism, they cared for sensation rather than the truth and were often seriously wrong on major issues. When smallpox decimated the town, far-sighted leaders called for the first mass inoculation in America. The *Courant* stirred the mob against the reformers, even after inoculation proved a success. Cotton Mather, the town's leading Puritan divine, condemned the "wicked printer and his accomplices who every week publish a vile paper to lessen and blacken the ministers of the town and render their ministry ineffectual."[19] For his part, Ben contributed a series of literary hoaxes, signed Silence Dogood, in which he lampooned customs and popular prejudices.

When the *Courant* chided tardy provincial efforts to launch vessels against marauding pirates, the General Court ordered James seized. Ben was hauled before the magistrate for questioning. Loyal to his master, he refused to divulge the source of the provocative story. Privileged under apprentice laws from revealing the trade secrets of his master, Ben was freed. James was ordered jailed. It was left to a boy of seventeen to publish the paper alone. This he did, filling it with his own writings.

When the authorities finally released James, it was with a court order to cease publication altogether. Clever James interpreted this to mean that the paper could continue as long as it was published by someone else. Ben could become the publisher in name and he would be the silent partner. To legitimize the ruse, he signed a release on the back of Ben's articles of indenture and made out a new set. But Ben cunningly realized that James could never show the papers in court unless he wanted to be arrested for contempt.

Now Ben in effect had his passport in his pocket. All during the summer of 1723 he sparred with James. He revealed his authorship of the Dogood papers, which antagonized the volatile older brother even more. At first, because he was the more skillful pleader, Ben won their arguments, which were arbitrated by Josiah. Then he threatened to leave Boston and run away to sea. When Josiah and Abiah heard of this, Ben lost their sympathy completely. His next move — to find another job with his newly acquired skills — was thwarted effectively by James, who asked other printers not to hire him.

Ben's choice was clear-cut: submit or flee. He chose flight. He was tired of his moneygrubbing father — he had recently set a *Courant* ad for a slave sale at Josiah's tenement and another for the return of an apprentice who, discontented with Josiah's treatment, had run away. Even his mother, whom he considered discreet and virtuous, was now firmly with her husband, against Ben. In September, with the help of a friend, Ben stole aboard a ship and lay hidden for three days while his family frantically searched for him. Then he sailed away.[20]

For the next thirty years, Benjamin Franklin reacted strongly to those unhappy Boston years, to his father's fanatical Puritanism, his brother's public sadism. He became all that his father condemned. He strove always to improve himself; he was generous with his time and money in supporting public projects; he was willing always to experiment, unwilling to accept arbitrary authority, religious dogma, the status quo. When he decided to marry, he chose a woman strikingly different from his own mother and sired only two legitimate children by her, preferring to risk occasional dalliances to the encumbrances of a large family.

Franklin returned to Boston once every ten years after his illegal flight. On the first visit, when he was still under twenty-one and subject to imprisonment, he flaunted fine clothes, bought rounds of drinks for his brother's apprentices. He tried to borrow money from his father to set up a press in Philadelphia. His father refused, rejecting him for the last time. For nine years Ben remained silent, virtually lost, never writing a line. Even when he established his own successful newspaper, his parents disapproved. They labeled his writings heretical, their greatest possible curse.[21]

But the long years of rebuff did not dampen Benjamin's zeal for family. He took care of poor and sick relatives in large numbers. When his brother James died, Benjamin agreed to bring up James's son as an apprentice. As Benjamin's business career flourished, he became a silent partner in one family enterprise after another. Until he was an old man he always kept a bright young relative by his side — like Uncle Benjamin rather than Josiah. With his own son, he would not let go, would not send him away. He clung to William, his greatest experiment, until they were pulled apart by politics and became mortal enemies. By then he had become Josiah.

3

I AM TOO INDULGENT
A PARENT

1723–1755

SEVENTEEN-YEAR-OLD BEN FRANKLIN HAD ONLY A DUTCH
dollar and a copper shilling in his pocket when he clambered
down the ladder into the tender of the brig *Beaver* and was rowed
into Philadelphia to make his fortune. Instead, he began seven
years of hard luck that tempered the way he dealt with people for
the rest of his life.

Bright, fast-talking, likable, he had no trouble finding a job with
a printer and a place to live. He rented a furnished room in the
High Street house of the Widow Read — a room down the hall
from the landlady's daughter, a buxom, blue-eyed girl named
Debby — and lost no time in making new friends and ambitious
plans. As soon as possible, he would leave the plodding printer who
had just employed him and set up his own shop.

In May of 1724, less than seven months after his arrival, the tall,
brash young man returned to Boston to make peace with his family — and borrow the money to sail to England to buy his own
printing equipment. His father turned him down.[1] Back in Philadelphia with little money left, Benjamin found an even better solution.
He had been introduced by an in-law to the royal governor, Sir
William Keith. They had talked history over drinks for hours. The
governor glad-handedly promised to appoint the eighteen-year-old
boy the official provincial printer, even give him letters of introduction and credit, if only Ben would sail three thousand miles to

London to buy his own press. Elated, Ben prepared to leave as soon as he could save the money for his passage.

There was one other item of business: for a year, he had been courting the plain, homespun, all-but-illiterate Debby Read: "I had great respect and affection for her, and had some reason to believe she had the same for me." Ben and Debby talked about marriage, but Mrs. Read, who had controlled her daughter's dowry since her husband's death, did not want the youngsters "to go too far" when Ben was about to leave for an indefinite time. Apparently, Mrs. Read also thought Debby could do better than this itinerant young printer's devil.[2]

Undeterred, the two youngsters exchanged promises and Ben sailed off for England, only to discover too late that the governor, a notorious bankrupt, had no credit to offer and, in his cups, had forgotten to send along the proffered letters to London. It was Benjamin Franklin's first bitter lesson in dealing with a British official.

Stranded, a "poor ignorant boy" in the largest, most expensive city in Europe, Ben took two jobs concurrently in leading printing houses — and immediately tried to break a publishing tradition. Printers, he had observed, were usually strapped because they bought beer for each other all day long, beginning with a breakfast eye opener. Ben substituted warm gruel for the beer, pocketed the silver he saved, and preached the virtues of gruel to his fellow printers. Few cared to argue the point with the powerful youth after watching him haul two heavy trays of lead type upstairs and down when most men labored under one.

Making the best of his plight, Ben became the bosom sporting companion of a young Philadelphia poet, James Ralph, who had deserted his wife to come to London. They roared around together, drinking, whoring, going to plays and parties. Ben often magnanimously paid for his friend's adventures and, as usual, wanted full value for his hard-earned money. When Ralph went out of town, Ben expected to partake of the favors of the poet's mistress. He was much taken aback when he was refused.

He also had mixed luck in other affairs. He managed to publish an outrageous pamphlet on metaphysics that he later attempted to buy back and destroy. He tried but failed to arrange an interview with Sir Isaac Newton and had to settle instead for the new secretary of the Royal Society. They chatted about the curiosities of the New World, and Ben managed to sell him one, an asbestos purse, for a handsome profit. Yet with little prospect of accumulating enough money to buy a printing press, Ben foundered in London, never once writing to Debby. For a while he played with the idea of opening a swimming school on the Thames. A number of noblemen had watched him swim the three miles in the rough current from Chelsea to Blackfriars and wanted him to teach their sons.

Then a healthier opportunity appeared. An old Philadelphia Quaker merchant, taken by the engaging lad, kindly offered to make him his clerk, teach him his trade, and pay his passage home. For two years, Ben had not written Debby. He now felt the "cords of love," as he later told a French noblewoman, pulling him to her again. He signed on.[3]

Back in Philadelphia, he received two blows within a few months. Debby had married. Apparently, her mother had urged her to forget the flighty young printer and accept the proposal of a sturdy potter: people always needed pots. Then Ben's new employer died. Ben had managed to learn to sell, to keep books and accounts, but now he was out of luck in love and labor. He had to go back to his former employer and plead for his old printing job. That Ben Franklin was indeed a master printer, too good to turn away, is the only possible explanation for his being rehired.

Four more years followed of drudgework mingled with carousing. There were few ways for a poor printer's helper to acquire the capital to set himself up in his own shop. One was to court a girl with a sizable dowry. Ben certainly tried. He pursued half a dozen eligible young ladies, but no parent with enough money thought much of his prospects, and there were some other girls with the requisite money whom he just would not pursue. "I was not to expect money with a wife unless with such a one as I should not otherwise think suitable."[4]

Another way to wealth, probably his only alternative, was to attract backers. Here he was luckier. The father of one of his good friends offered to finance a new newspaper for his bibulous son if Ben was taken on as his steady, sober partner. They founded the *Pennsylvania Gazette,* but then the father went bankrupt. Unexpectedly, two friends rushed to aid Ben, but only on one condition: he must ditch his hard-drinking friend. Faced with the choice of his own newspaper or an old friend, Ben dropped the friend. At the age of twenty-three, he had his own newspaper.

A ruthless toughness in business dealings quickly became a Franklin hallmark. When his wealthy young friends continued to express doubt that the young publisher could survive in competition with five other printers in a town of fewer than six thousand people, Ben invited them in at mealtime. He took a porridge bowl, filled it with sawdust, stirred in a little water, and then ate the mixture. Word quickly spread throughout Philadelphia that there was a tough new competitor to be reckoned with.[5]

Until his dying day, William Franklin was apparently unsure of the date of his birth, although he always referred to Deborah Read Franklin as his mother. Benjamin Franklin remained silent on the subject and on the question of who William's mother was, even to his own family — a silence that lasted nearly twenty years. Then in 1750 he told his own mother, Abiah, that William was nineteen — when William had already been away from home for nearly four years, including two years as an army officer. It was not a likely story, but Benjamin was clearly ashamed to tell his parents the full truth. All he would ever say about the identity of William's mother was that his common-law marriage to Deborah Read had corrected one of the great "errata" of his life.

Whatever the exact truth of Franklin's deepest secret, on September 1, 1730, a little more than a year after he became the publisher of the *Pennsylvania Gazette,* he "took to wife," as he later put it, Deborah Read. There could be no public ceremony. Legally, Deborah was still married, even if, as the rumors said, her first husband was a bigamist with a wife and child in London and even if he had already, as the scuttlebutt had it, been killed in a barroom brawl in the West Indies. She had no legal proof of either rumor. All she knew was that she could not marry again under Pennsylvania law without being branded a felon, liable to thirty-nine lashes at the public whipping post and imprisonment for life at hard labor.[6]

Why Benjamin Franklin married her is another of the many mysteries about him. The only portrait of her, if accurate, shows a fairly lumpish woman. She was also, like most women of her generation, virtually illiterate. But there was deep in Franklin a guilt he could never excise when it came to Deborah. More than likely they had been intimate before his departure for England, and he would have married her then if Mrs. Read had consented and had paid the dowry of one hundred pounds so that they could have set up shop. There was always a note of pique in dealing with the Widow Read and a note of shame that he had not married her daughter earlier.

But there was more than this to make a man enter a forty-four-year common-law marriage in a moralistic Quaker city. Benjamin had watched Deborah's terrible dilemma for nearly five years. She had obviously once been gay and playful, but then John Rogers the potter used up her money and ran up debts that disgraced her and her family. Even before he ran away, she had refused to cohabit with him. She lived gloomily, trapped in a legal web, a prisoner in her mother's house and shop: "I pitied poor Miss Read's unfortunate situation, who was generally dejected, seldom cheerful, and avoided company." Franklin began visiting the Reads again soon after the potter left, freely gave the Widow Read business advice. "A friendly correspondence as neighbors and old acquaintances had continued between me and Mrs. Read's family, who all had a regard for me from the time of my first lodging in their house. I was often there and consulted in their affairs," Benjamin wrote in his autobiography with obvious pride.

The visits bothered him, though. "I considered my giddiness and inconstancy when in London as in a great degree the cause of [Debbie's] unhappiness, though the mother was good enough to think the fault more her own than mine. . . . Our mutual affection was revived, but there were now great objections to our union." Even if Rogers were dead, another impediment would not fade away, one that could wipe out the precarious existence of Franklin's little newspaper. Rogers "had left many debts which his successor might be called on to pay." Franklin wanted to be paid to marry, not to pay for a wife. He made one last attempt to persuade the Widow Read to raise another dowry with which he could discharge his newspaper debts. She could have mortgaged her house for the money, a proposal he had already made unsuccessfully to another woman's parents. When Mrs. Read refused, Franklin decided to take Deborah to live at common law, renouncing her husband's debts. "None of the inconveniences happened that we had apprehended," he wrote forty years later. "She proved a good and faithful helpmate, assisted me much by attending the shop. We throve together and have ever mutually endeavored to make each other happy."[7]

His narrative poses a few problems. He does not mention one "inconvenience" — his illegitimate son — or how he persuaded Deborah to rear William as her own. Thirty-five years passed before anyone outside their house heard much of the circumstances of William's birth, and then it was clouded in the controversy of a bitter political contest. The best source seems to be the son of a close friend of Benjamin's. All Philadelphia had known for years, he said, that William was born of a disagreeable woman "not in good circumstances," who prevented her maternity from becoming known.[8]

Between Deborah and Benjamin there was little hint of love. Deborah's principal motive for marrying him was apparently gratitude for his rescuing her from the limbo she was living in. Rarely in any of their letters to each other, and never in his autobiography, does the word "love" appear. For him, the match seems to have been a typically Franklinesque measure to solve a number of problems at a single stroke, notably his guilt for his former treatment of her and his strong sexual appetite. Marriage, a thrifty, productive bargain, legitimized "that hard-to-be-governed passion of youth that had hurried me frequently into intrigues with low women that fell in my way which were attended with some expense and great inconvenience, besides a continual risk to my health by a distemper which of all things I dreaded."[9] If ever there was a marriage of convenience, Benjamin and Deborah entered it late in 1730.

There was nothing luxurious about the Franklin family life. Benjamin had an almost spiritual attachment to meager meals served plainly. Deborah helped long hours in the shop, selling legal forms, printing and writing materials, books, spectacles, and Crown soap made by the Franklins of Boston. She ran their house, took care of William, made all their clothes, and destroyed her eyesight by hand-sewing bindings on books and pamphlets at night by candlelight. But even though their prosperity grew, Benjamin still felt insecure and remained almost harshly thrifty. "My breakfast was [for]a long time bread and milk (no tea) and I ate it out of a two-penny earthen porringer with a pewter spoon. But mark how lux-ury will enter families, and make a progress, in spite of principle. Being called one morning to breakfast, I found it in a china bowl with a spoon of silver. They had been bought for me without my knowledge by my wife and had cost her the enormous sum of three and twenty shillings, for which she had no other excuse or apology to make but that she thought *her* husband deserved a silver spoon and china bowl as well as any of his neighbors."[10]

His disapproval of Deborah's profligacy says almost as much about the status of women in the eighteenth century as it does about the newlyweds' relationship, but it was fairly typical of the reformed Franklin. His days of carousing had ended, at least tem-porarily, and he now entered a stage of self-perfection, in which he set out to eliminate all his faults in the best Puritan fashion. In a chapbook he made a chart across two facing pages and under thir-teen headings listed items of personal conduct needing improve-ment. Four examples:

"Temperance. Eat not to dullness. Drink not to elevation." He was in the midst of evolving from a teen-aged vegetarian into a trencherman who preferred old Madeira and kept five of the best French champagnes in his wine cellar.

"Silence. Speak not but what may benefit others or yourself. Avoid trifling conversation." Garrulous among friends, especially in the Junto discussion club of young tradesmen he had helped to found, Benjamin wanted to curb his unbridled tongue. He was also trying to stop his habit of teasing and goading that had earned him so much trouble with his brother James. For his brash challenges he would now substitute Socratic questioning.

"Order. Let all of your things have their places. Let each part of your business have its time." In his boyish attempt at self-improve-ment, Benjamin was living by a strict schedule, much of it dictated by his printing business. But he did take Sundays for himself. He sent Deborah and William off to church while he studied and thought. He was already beginning the process of outgrowing his wife.

"Resolution. Resolve to perform what you ought. Perform without fail what you resolve." As a young man he paid more heed to this heading than he did later as a politician and statesman who had mastered the art of changing position and direction. Even now, however, Franklin learned that new resolutions rarely live to grow old. He soon wearied of his chart, no doubt finding more productive ways to use his time.[11]

It was six years before Deborah bore Benjamin a son of their own — Francis Folger — and then the child's life was cruelly short. As a young apprentice, Benjamin had joined in his brother's gleeful attacks on Cotton Mather's appeals for mass smallpox inoculation. When Frankie was four, he became a victim of the disease after Benjamin hesitated to have him inoculated. For the rest of his life, Benjamin held himself accountable for Frankie's death. To spare others the same grief, he editorialized in favor of inoculation in *Poor Richard's Almanack* and in the *Gazette*. Half a century later, he still had tears in his eyes when he talked of Frankie.[12]

Benjamin Franklin finally found the formula for fame and fortune when he combined equal parts of Yankee wit, native nerve and a touch of plagiarism in a journalistic concoction he labeled *Poor Richard's Almanack*. At the time, the world did not seem to need another almanac: five were already issued each year in Philadelphia. But almanacs had been an American standby from the earliest days. The third book printed in America, in 1639, had been an almanac. Americans crowding into the seaports and spreading out over the frontiers depended on these handy little pocket-sized volumes to tell them the times of tides and when the moon would rise, give them helpful hints for house and garden, and list the dates of market days and court sessions. It was all pretty standard, straightforward fare until Benjamin Franklin decided to inject a little racy humor into it and poke a little fun at his competitors. He had seen, with his romantic couplets and literary hoaxes in Boston, that in the most somber town people will laugh on the smallest provocation. Quaker Phildelphians woke up one morning in 1732 to find in Franklin's *Gazette* an unusual notice advertising a new almanac.

The title was not original — James Franklin was already publishing *Poor Robin's Almanack* in Newport and there was a philosopher-mathematician named Poor Richard in Nathaniel Ames's almanac in Dedham, Massachusetts, in the 1720's — but what caught the eye was the promised table of contents, some of it risqué for gray Quaker Philadelphia. Franklin promised to talk about cuckolds, bachelors' problems and conjugal matters. He also said he would predict the day and hour of the death of the publisher of the leading rival almanac.

The first edition sold out. A delighted Franklin had to run off two more printings. Sales shot up to ten thousand copies a year. The almanac was a runaway best-seller. Not only did the profits establish Franklin as a prosperous printer, they gave him the base for the largest book-distribution business in colonial America. Thousands of copies were shipped to Charleston, Boston, Newport and Williamsburg, and Franklin soon became a celebrity throughout the colonies. People did not distinguish between him and Poor Richard. Much to Benjamin's amusement, they often quoted Poor Richard's homespun sayings to Benjamin to clinch an argument. He did not, of course, advertise the fact that few of the epigrams originated with him. In fact, he combed half a dozen volumes of popular English proverbs, notably James Howell's *Lexicon Tetraglotton* (1660), gleaned what he wanted, and translated it into idiomatic Yankee. Howell's "The greatest talkers are the least doers" became Poor Richard's "Great talkers, little doers." Howell's "The way to be safe is never to be secure" became Poor Richard's "He that's secure is not safe."

Many of Poor Richard's rewritten lines achieved instant immortality and are still attributed to Franklin. He borrowed John Ray's cumbersome epigram "Fresh fish and new come guests smell, by that they are three days old" and shortened it in good Yankee journalistic style to "Fish and visitors stink in three days."

People bought Poor Richard to be amused, but Franklin, increasingly moralistic after his marriage, often wrote and edited with a serious underlying motive. "The vain youth that reads my almanack, for the sake of an idle joke will perhaps meet with a serious reflection that he may ever after be the better for." He preached a workaday gospel of scrimping, saving, going to bed early, and rising before one's neighbors — and, for a while at least, he lived it. "Keep thy shop, and thy shop will keep thee," exhorted Poor Richard. Franklin was often at his press when Market Street merchants opened their shops at 5 A.M. To show that prosperity had not made him too grand, he was fond of donning his leather apron and pushing his wheelbarrow full of paper through the streets, a chore usually assigned to an apprentice. But already he was becoming inventive, and his first and most lasting invention was his own public image.[13]

Franklin found a new passion soon after his marriage, the passion for knowledge. The boy who had failed arithmetic became the man whose methodical studies, first of mathematics, then of languages and philosophy, gave him the solid grounding for his epochal years of experiments in electricity. Along the way he helped bring to his adopted city of Philadelphia a host of civic improvements. Almost every year he introduced another innovation. Working with a small group of artisan friends, he turned the abstract philosophical speculations of the weekly Junto meetings into practical solutions to the city's problems. Typical was his creation of the Library Company of Philadelphia. In London, no doubt, he had learned of circulating libraries set up by subscribers. Most towns in America lacked anything like a public library when Franklin and his friends pooled their annual dues and sent their first sizable book order to London. From the Library Company's books he appropriated the sayings that he transformed into Poor Richard's epigrams, poems and essays. And from his interest in books on natural philosophy came the enthusiastic friendship of correspondents in London who, surprised at the quality of intellect evinced by the books Franklin and his friends ordered, began to send them scientific apparatus.

Each invention brought him greater fame, more customers for his shop, more readers for his publications. In his shop, he branched out into wine, medicines, mariner's instruments, lottery tickets, barrels of cod, sperm oil, even, occasionally, slaves, whom he sold for others or bought as an investment. *Gazette* ads included "a breeding Negro woman about twenty years of age," "a likely Negro wench about fifteen years," "a likely young Negro fellow about nineteen," "two likely young Negroes."

As he earned more money, he hired more people to provide him more time for leisure to devote to reading, thinking and experimenting. All his enterprises began to flourish simultaneously. As he spun off projects that drew on his experiences and as he publicized them through his *Gazette,* he became the catalyst for many civic movements. After the library, he helped found the Union Fire Company, the city watch, the American Philosophical Society, the city hospital, and the Philadelphia Academy for the Education of Youth (the forerunner of the University of Pennsylvania).

His thriftiness was translated into his first serious invention. He hated to see money literally go up in smoke. He observed that most of the benefits of firewood, already a costly commodity, went up the chimney and not out into the room. He tinkered away — he had always enjoyed tinkering — and by 1740 he had a fellow Junto member, whose father owned an iron forge, cast the first Franklin stove, an insert that fitted into a fireplace and radiated the heat outward. "My [living] room, I know, is made twice as warm as it used to be with a quarter of the wood I formerly consumed there," he wrote in the *Gazette.* He offered the idea without charge to the public — a gesture that warmed many readers to Philadelphia's most conspicuous philanthropist.[14]

The secret of all Franklin's multifarious successes lay in his personal magnetism: a mixture of the easy charm, quick Yankee wit and intense personal diplomacy he always employed to make his project of the moment prevail. Whether with a handful of his Junto friends or with scientists in his workshop or with the women of all ages he so needed to brighten his myriad labors he was warm, witty and seductive. A case in point was his wangling cannon from the royal governor of New York. In 1747, he had waged a long campaign, personally and in the press, to persuade the Quaker pacifists that defenses must be provided against the raids by French and Spanish pirates (plantations had been burned within forty miles of Philadelphia). There being no cannon in Pennsylvania, he traveled to New York City and asked the governor to lend him some. "He at first refused us peremptorily, but at a dinner with his Council where there was great drinking of Madeira wine, he softened by degrees and said he would lend us six." Franklin told the governor some more stories. "After a few more bumpers, he advanced to ten. And, at length, he very good-naturedly conceded eighteen. They were fine cannon, 18 pounders, with their carriages, which we soon transported and mounted on our battery."[15]

For seven years, from the death of Frankie until the birth of Sarah, William was an only child. There is no evidence that he was pampered, but if Franklin followed the views on child rearing he expressed years later to a young mother, William was not brought up on a tight rein: "Pray let him have everything he likes: I think it of great consequence, while the features of the countenance are forming. It gives them a pleasant air and, that being once become natural and fixed by habit, the face is ever handsomer for it, and on that much of a person's good fortune and success in life may depend."[16] In 1737, after the Franklins' common-law marriage had lasted seven years, William's birth was legitimized, as British and Pennsylvania law decreed it could be. In every way he would now have the same legal rights as a legitimate son.

As he grew older, he was indeed indulged by his increasingly wealthy father. He was given his own horse, a rare privilege among tradesmen's children, and allowed to choose the school he would attend. When he was eight he was turned over to his first tutor, Theophilus Grew, a mathematician and astronomer who had helped Franklin compile *Poor Richard's Almanack*. (Grew was one of the first to be appointed professor in the College of Philadelphia.) Then, for a year, as if repeating his own boyhood, Franklin sent William to the best school in the city, Alexander Annand's classical academy. There William was enrolled with sons of the Philadelphia gentry. His attendance was short-lived. Franklin's ledgers show payments for only two years. For most of his education, William had to depend, like his father before him, on reading books from his father's and his uncle's bookstores. His readings were solidly classical and almost identical to the curriculum at the Boston grammar school — Roman history, church history, Greek and Latin grammar and literature, including Caesar's *Gallic Wars*, and he mastered *The Education of Young Gentlemen* and *The True Conduct of Persons of Quality*, translated from the French.[17]

Growing up in Philadelphia in William's boyhood meant following the seasons: kite flying in spring, swimming and fishing in summer, skating and sledding in the long winters. He also took part in activities frowned on in the Quaker city: amateur theatricals in a warehouse, horse racing on Race Street. But long periods of boredom intervened, and ships arriving with goods from as far as India made William restless. They came up the Delaware laden with prizes from King George's War, and their crews carried sacks of gold to spend freely in the shops and taverns. It was only a matter of time before William did as his father had done and tried to run away to sea.

Like so many fathers, Franklin was usually too busy during the boy's adolescence to notice subtle changes in him. He was the official provincial printer now as well as the clerk of the Pennsylvania Assembly and postmaster of Philadelphia. When he was not in his printshop or at the State House copying down debates, he was traveling to sort out the postal service or away at night at Junto meetings or Masonic lodge meetings or his Library Company meetings or fire company meetings or attending lectures or working with friends on projects to improve city life. When he was at home, he was often distilling the folk wisdom of *Poor Richard's Almanack*. His conversations must have been given to self-improving aphorisms that rarely probed a boy's problems or even called for an answer. If there were problems in his family, Benjamin Franklin was unaware of them.

As expected of her, Deborah Franklin had worked hard in their shop and hard in their home for years, but by the 1740's she had servants to help with the cooking and housework and with her mother, and always an apprentice or two to do chores and run errands. The family thrived, and if William was guilty of misbehavior occasionally, it was taken in stride. There is no hint of beatings of the kind Franklin had received in his youth, only minor disagreements. He might have been talking about William when he wrote his sister in Boston about her son's complaints of life as an apprentice: "I did not think it anything extraordinary that he should be sometimes willing to evade going to meeting, for I believe it is the case with all boys. I have brought up four or five myself and have frequently observed that if their shoes were bad, they would say nothing of a new pair until Sunday morning, just as the bell rang

. . . or if they knew of anything that wanted mending, it was a secret till Sunday morning. . . . As to going on petty errands, no boy loves it, but all must do it. As soon as they become fit for better business, they naturally get rid of that, for the master's interest comes in to their relief."[18]

Franklin's interest apparently had not come to William's relief by the time the fifteen-year-old absconded. The harbor was full of privateers returned from bloody raids on French and Spanish merchant ships. William knew of openings aboard some of them from his duties as a waterfront newsgatherer for his father's *Gazette*. Franklin hurried from one ship to another searching for him. He could not understand why his son would want to flee from a home where he was treated mildly, fed well, and given the training he would need to provide himself a comfortable living. "My only son," he wrote, "left my house unknown to us all, and got on board a privateer, from whence I fetched him. No one imagined it was hard usage at home that made him do this. Every one that knows me thinks I am too indulgent a parent as well as master. When boys see prizes brought in and quantities of money shared among the men and their gay living, it fills their heads with notions that half distract them and put them quite out of conceit with trades and the dull ways of getting money by working."[19]

Other causes of William's unhappiness did not seem to occur to Franklin. Since Sarah's birth, the women of the household had doted on her and scarcely had time or patience for William. As he grew older, little thought seems to have been devoted to his future. He would work for his father, and since he was well schooled for the town and the time, he would keep the books and read proof for *Poor Richard* and help to supervise apprentices and generally attend to any business his father thought fit for him. There was talk, briefly, even editorials in the *Gazette,* about starting a college in Philadelphia, but it came too late. William's formal education was over. There were no colleges nearer than Yale in Connecticut or William and Mary in Virginia. It never seemed a question of sending William to one of them, even when many of his friends were sent off to England to school.

After Franklin fetched his son back from the privateer, he decided to be more lenient than his own father had been with him.

For William there would be no nine-year sentence of drudgery. If William wanted adventure, let him join the troops enlisting for the latest expedition against French Canada. The privations and discipline of military life would surely make him eager to return to the comforts of a life of trade. Companies of Pennsylvania troops were forming. Let William sign up. As a horseman who could shoot and a man who could read and write well, he would suit as an ensign, an ornament to a fighting force, a messenger between officers and gentlemen.

In November 1745, French-led Indians had attacked and burned Saratoga, New York, killing some of its inhabitants and carrying off the rest. In August 1746, they attacked the provincial capital of Albany, killing hunters and patrols. When Captain Deimer's company of German laborer-volunteers rode north to Albany in September, William, fitted out in a new red uniform, pranced off with them. When Franklin said farewell, he did not expect the infatuated boy to be gone long: he would be back after a taste of danger or a touch of the northern winter.[20]

To Franklin's surprise, William did not hurry back. He thrived on the rigors of military life, on the dangers of frontier war. He learned drill and discipline, tactics and weaponry and fortification, in a hurry. The Pennsylvania troops found themselves surrounded by a large and determined force. Too weak to attack, William's regiment was slowly decimated by wounds, disease and desertion: sixteen men in one of his patrols were killed in one ambush. When the troops marched to Lake Champlain to build Fort Ticonderoga, they suffered heavy casualties. When they sent out patrols from their crude stockade to hunt for food, half the men did not come back. Men who went out to fish were tomahawked. And yet William never complained; in fact, he distinguished himself. The youngest of the Pennsylvania officers, he was promoted to the highest provincial rank: captain. He undoubtedly sent home letters with what little war news managed to get through. Franklin printed the news in the *Gazette*. "We learn that, as forces were marching toward the carry-place [Ticonderoga, about eighteen miles from Albany], one Delamont, a wagoneer, lagging behind, was set upon, shot and scalped."[21]

Franklin's reaction was, in a way, strange. He did not play up the

Ticonderoga campaign in his paper but gave it only short notice on inside pages. On page one he featured, alternately, a little news of King George's War and his own plans to fortify Philadelphia. And even when William was praised in official dispatches for his conspicuous bravery on patrols, even when his son was promoted, Franklin did not mention it in print.

That winter he did visit the army in camp at Fort George. He saw for himself that there was not enough to eat or wear because the Quakers would not decently support Pennsylvania troops. He also saw that the green-wood huts leaked wind and snow and filled with smoke, and he smelled the stench of improper sanitation. Yet despite all this and despite all the deaths from epidemic diphtheria, he saw that William was determined to stay on.

A German visitor to the camp was impressed that the tall grenadier had volunteered to serve with a predominantly German company commanded by a German officer. He reported that the officers of William's unit had been honored for their bravery by being invited to join the officers' mess of the royal governor of New York, George Clinton. It should not have surprised the elder Franklin that William would not abandon this heady life to return to Philadelphia with him. Even when William was ordered back to Pennsylvania to help round up deserters, he did not stay with his parents. After helping his father to organize and drill the Philadelphia Association militiamen in the summer of 1747, William returned to the north for another year's duty. This time he went with his father's blessing and a letter of introduction to the lieutenant governor of New York, Cadwallader Colden, who was a correspondent of Franklin's in the American Philosophical Society. The letter helped William to move easily in New York society. Franklin even went so far as to invest some money in the boy's military education. He ordered from a wholesaler in London a calf-bound, five-volume French translation of the writings of the Greek cavalry general Polybius for William. But when the war was over, he canceled the order.

Captain Franklin's dreams of a military career did not die naturally: they were killed by lack of money. To become a career officer in the British military establishment meant buying a commission from the colonel of a regiment when a post became vacant. When wars ended, there were invariably more officers available than regular army commissions. Even if William had gained personal patronage powerful enough, his father showed no interest in laying out the large amount of cash needed to buy the commission William so wanted. Instead, William returned in his red uniform with its gilt epaulet to gray Quaker Philadelphia, unwilling to resume working in his father's shop, uncertain of what else he could do.[*][22]

He did not have to wait long for excitement. In the idle hours of garrison duty, a friend and fellow officer, William Trent, had filled young Franklin's mind with visions of the fortunes that could be accumulated in the western wilderness. Until the war, Trent had been an active partner in a successful fur-trading company and had made several trips west. Now, a major expedition was being planned to give Philadelphia merchants a monopoly on the trade abandoned by the French. The man in charge was Conrad Weiser, a proprietary official who had admired William's conduct on the New York frontier. Weiser was scouting for men fit to join him on the expedition.

At the cessation of fighting, Indian affairs in the forests from the Delaware River as far west as Detroit were left in turmoil. So hard pressed were the tribes of the Ohio country for arms with which to hunt for food and clothing that in July of 1748 they walked five hundred miles to Lancaster, Pennsylvania, to sue for peace and seek a trade alliance. Official Philadelphia, sensing a windfall of profitable new commerce, mounted up and rode off to Lancaster. Benjamin Franklin, in his dual capacity of Assembly clerk and printer of Indian treaties, and William, the official courier of the provincial land office, went along.

Fifty-five Indian chiefs offered the Philadelphia merchants the exclusive franchise for fur trading, an offer that would open up a thousand miles of rich forests. As the calumet was passed from hand to hand, the Philadelphians eyed the mounds of dark beaver pelts and cream-colored deerskins. When, after five days of formalities, Indians and merchants signed their eternal friendship, Benjamin Franklin noted that "if these Indians and their allies

* He had served 515 days of active duty, for which he was never paid.

prove faithful to the English. . . there will be nothing to interrupt an intercourse between this province and that great river."[23]

The Pennsylvanians lost no time in putting together the men and the gifts needed to clinch the alliance. Once again, official notice fell on Captain Franklin. Conrad Weiser, who was to lead the Pennsylvania trade mission to the Ohio Valley and plant the British flag west of the Alleghenies for the first time, asked the young captain to go along as land office agent. Leaving Lancaster on August 11, 1748, they set a grueling pace on the first day: they rode thirty miles west over the first ridge of hills. By the fourth day out, they had reached the well-worn Tuscarora Indian warpath, northernmost of the great east-west Indian highways. They followed it through mountain gaps for nearly three hundred miles. The hills heaved ever higher, the hot, blistering updrafts turned the rocky slopes slippery with drenching downpours. The rain rotted leather, ruined shoes, soaked gunpowder and supplies.

Captain Franklin's military discipline had hardened him against the discomforts that multiplied as they pushed due west. He was awed by the seemingly endless mountain ranges, by herds of buffalo and white-tailed deer grazing in clearings, by black bear munching leisurely on berries. The prospect of peopling this country stirred his imagination. As the first English officer to carry the Union Jack across these mountains, he could one day expect preferment. He sensed the great promise of this territory and his own place in it.

Nine days and two hundred miles out, the emissaries overtook the packtrain of trade goods sent ahead to placate the impatient Indians: guns, coats, blankets, hatchets, knives, and ten thousand beads of black and white war wampum. Three weeks out, after nearly four hundred miles, they reached the headwaters of the Ohio. Leaving their exhausted horses behind, they rented a large canoe for one thousand black war beads and took off down the river at a furious rate. Making sixty miles in one day, they arrived late at night at a Delaware Indian village where a celebration was in progress. The next morning, Weiser recorded in his journal, they reluctantly wrenched themselves away from their Indian hosts and hostesses, and paddled south along the widening Ohio.

For two weeks, Weiser and Franklin traveled from village to village and feasted on fresh corn and roast venison. More than a thousand Indians rode and walked and rowed with them in a great triumphal progression. While they all waited for the treaty formalities and the distribution of presents, they smoked the calumet in friendship. Franklin had ample opportunity to gather information that one day might be vital to the English. Many young warriors had deserted the more dignified councils of the Six Nations. In all, Franklin and Weiser counted 789 of these renegades and their families, and they were told that the Miamis had a thousand more warriors strung out in twenty towns — a formidable friend or enemy.

Franklin realized that if peace with these unstable remnants of the Delawares and Shawnees was to be maintained, Indian resentment over land dealings must be alleviated and unscrupulous traders must be prevented from selling them rum. At one council fire, Weiser reported that the Pennsylvania Assembly had recently banned liquor sales to the Indians. At a signal, Captain Franklin handed Weiser the appropriate document. "You have of late made frequent complaints against the traders bringing so much rum to your towns," Weiser read, "but it seems it is out of your brethren's power to stop it entirely. You send down your own skins by the traders to buy rum for you. You go yourselves and fetch horseloads of strong liquor. Besides this, you never agree about it: one will have it, the other won't (though very few), a third says he will have it cheaper; this last we believe is spoken from your hearts."

The Indians laughed and Weiser laughed and young William Franklin laughed. The Indians stood by as the whites ceremoniously stove in casks of rum they had confiscated from a trader from a rival province. The warriors consoled themselves with mounds of gifts that had been carefully distributed to each tribe. In the driving, steaming rain of late summer the rum washed away and the talking ended. The Indians scooped up their new guns and hatchets and retired to their huts while the white emissaries began the five-hundred-mile journey home.[24]

William had kept careful notes for his father and for the sponsors of the mission. When he arrived back in Philadelphia, he turned them over to his father. After reading them, Benjamin loaned them to a friend, who lost them.

Young Captain Franklin had returned from the frontier expedition something of a celebrity. Like most fresh veterans who had no idea of what they wanted to do next, he did little but rest between social occasions. He also returned to a city in which, despite his own exploits, his father had emerged as a hero acclaimed for his ingenious defense schemes. Evidently, their regard for each other's martial achievements did little to ameliorate a growing tension between them over the issue of William's future.

"Will is now nineteen years of age," Franklin wrote to his aged mother, "a tall proper youth, and much of a beau. He acquired a habit of idleness on the expedition, but begins of late to apply himself to business, and I hope will become an industrious man. He imagined his father had got enough for him: but I have assured him that I intend to spend what little I have, myself, if it please God that I live long enough, and as he by no means wants sense, he can see by my going on that I am like to be as good as my word."[25]

William must have been surprised by his father's retirement from business at the age of forty-two to devote his full time to scientific experiments. So prosperous had the business become that Franklin decided he could turn it over to a partner, a decision that may have been hastened by William's lack of interest. In retirement Franklin could earn more than a thousand pounds a year from his share of the profits in addition to royalties from the almanac, which he continued to edit.* The move away from the business, away from the Market Street marketplace to a new and quieter rented house on the outskirts of the city was actually to bring the two men into even closer quarters.

When William returned from the West, his father introduced him to Freemasonry, which in Philadelphia was marked by an intense interest in mathematics, astrology and architecture. Many of the most inquiring minds of the time could be found at its gatherings. With Philip Syng and Ebenezer Kinnersley, old friends and

---

* A thousand pounds was equivalent to approximately $125,000 in 1984.

fellow Masons of Franklin's, William was introduced to his father's life away from family and business. It was the realm in which Franklin was more than an American celebrity: he was becoming one of the world's most celebrated scientists.

In William's year away in the army, he missed his father's first experiments with electricity. On a visit to Boston in 1743, the elder Franklin had attended a series of lectures given by a Scottish amateur electrician. Fascinated, he invited the man back to Philadelphia, studied his experiments, then bought his equipment. Later, a London Quaker familiar with Franklin's work on the Franklin stove sent a specially designed glass tube for the Library Company of Philadelphia "with some account of the use of it in making electrical experiments." The account was undoubtedly a *Gentleman's Magazine* article on experiments conducted in Germany.

Thoroughly conversant with Newton's physics and experimental methods, Franklin lost no time in repeating the experiments he had seen in Boston. The blacksmith's grandson liked to work with his hands and took "pleasure in seeing good workmen handle their tools." He said of himself: "I was willing and able to construct little machines for my experiments while the intention of making the experiment was fresh and warm in my mind." Moreover, he had not, as he had grown wealthy, cut himself off from his old leather-aproned Junto circle.

In practicing the European experiments with this group of friends, many of them advanced tinkerers like himself, he soon acquired "great readiness" in performing all the known experiments. He added "a number of new ones. . . . My house was continually full for some time with people who came to see these new wonders. To divide a little this incumbrance among my friends, I caused a number of similar tubes to be blown at our glass house . . . so that at length we had several performers."[26] Unwittingly, he had slipped onto the world stage: nothing in his life would be the same again. Yet, insecure as ever, he did not sense it as he puttered each day in his workroom. The hours and days stretched out to nearly five years of almost total absorption, years that were extremely productive.

William heard about the experiments when he came home from the army on a four-month furlough. He learned his father's theories quickly. He also studied the latest European experiments. From observing his father, from helping him with the heavy laboratory work, and from copying out his father's daily electrical journal, he became conversant with the most recent advances before he rode back to the northern frontier. He took along a glass tube, a gift from his father to Governor Clinton, who was also an amateur experimenter. William personally instructed Clinton in the use of the tube, explained his father's theories and experiments, and left with the governor a copy of his father's journal.

Soon Franklin was sending off to London the first of five long letters reporting his progress. To explain his experiments, he had to coin new terms. A grounded, pointed *conductor* caused a charged conducting body to *discharge* six to eight inches away, he observed. A blunt conductor, however, did not discharge until an inch away, and then a white spark flashed. Astutely, Franklin concluded that "the electrical fire is a real element . . . diffused among and attracting other matter, particularly by water and metals." If a body lost a quantity of this "electrical fire" it was *negative* or *minus.* Moving on to a study of the Leyden jar, he successfully analyzed the properties of this first *capacitor,* which he called "Doctor Musschenbroek's wonderful bottle." He coated the outside with metal and filled the inside with water (he later used shot). Then he ran a wire through an *insulating* cork into the bottle's neck. When he held the jar in his hands to *ground* it, the jar was capable of "holding a vast supply of electricity."

Plus and *minus, charging* and *discharging, —* his letters to London crackled with new terminology as he described new methods of proving the existence of electricity. Soon his theories were being tested in England, Holland, Germany, Italy, France, Sweden. In one paragraph of one letter alone, he reported eleven original experiments. And when he halted after two years because it was hot and stuffy in his workshop in the summer, he still had no idea of the importance of his work. To a London friend he wrote that he was "chagrined a little that we have hitherto been able to discover nothing in the way of use to mankind."[27]

By the time William returned from the West, Franklin was far along in his experiments and the rented house on Race Street was often filled with strange-looking devices and crowds of the curious who had come to look at his tinkerings. To amuse them, he electrocuted turkeys, suspended a young boy from silk threads and sent a current through him, and even accidentally knocked himself senseless for twenty minutes. And he quickly found in the daring William a ready laboratory assistant. No mention survives of William's part in the experiments except by inference: Franklin again was silent on his son's contribution. But much can be deduced. When Franklin traveled, he left instructions "in the family" that electricity from thunderstorms passing overhead should be gathered in great glass bottles. Evidently William eagerly complied. When Franklin was ready to test his lightning rods, someone had to scale the roofs to install them. William obviously was the only volunteer. And when Franklin was ready for his climactic experiment to draw the lightning from the clouds with the aid of a kite and a key, it was William who designed and built the kite and three times raced across a cow pasture in an electrical storm to get the kite aloft while Franklin stood safe in a shepherd's shed nearby.

Indeed, William seemed to love the added element of risk in the experiments. He and his father became a team of laboratory scientists, experimenting boldly wherever they went. In 1755, when they were riding through Maryland on a postal inspection tour, they happened on a small twister in the woods. Eager to test a theory of the causes of tornadoes, Franklin tried to track the whirlwind, but when tree trunks and branches began flying through the air, he abandoned the chase. Not so William. He plunged ahead, spurring his horse deeper into the woods until he overtook the tornado. Only then did he rein in his terrified horse and return to report on the tornado's movements to his waiting father. It was William's style to pursue the whirlwind.

In addition to helping with the post office and the almanac and reading lawbooks, William continued to work as his father's assistant and his contributions became more important. The Franklins' daring kite-and-key experiment had proved that lightning was electricity, something that European scientists had long suspected, but from what direction the current came was a more difficult question.

Benjamin assumed that it came down from electrical storms, but a year later William was able to demonstrate that the opposite was true.

In July of 1753, Benjamin was away in Boston on postal inspections and had left William behind with orders to gather electricity in foil-lined jars inside their house whenever electrical storms passed overhead. On the night of July 8, a heavy dark cloud passed over Society Hill during a downpour. Lightning flashed through a three-story house, blasting out bricks, boring holes in the woodwork, melting lead sashweights, door hinges and glass panes, singeing roofing shingles. At dawn, William was clambering over the roof, prying into every corner of the house, hurriedly taking down notes and making drawings. In a long, excited letter to his father, he offered proof that the lightning had passed *upward.* Courses of brick were knocked out "as if done by a blow of a hammer . . . from underneath." The "[electric] fire" had passed *up* the roof: the thin edges of the cedar shingles were thrown up, the thick edges undisturbed; splinters of wood were driven upward as well, and window frames were shattered from their bottoms up.[28]

Quickly, by return post, Franklin responded from Boston. He was, he wrote coolly, "pleased," but he was sending another experimenter, Ebenezer Kinnersley, older and more experienced, to see William's proofs. A few months later, Franklin wrote to his British mentor a report of progress made. Inexplicably, he gave credit for the discovery not to William but to that other experimenter, Kinnersley.

Franklin had set aside his apparatus and turned to politics before he learned of his recognition as the discoverer of electricity. Others, especially Joseph Priestley, gathered his letters as late as 1769 and gave full credit to Franklin. By that time, it had become known among scientists in England that father and son had carried out experiments as a team: when Oxford University awarded Benjamin an honorary doctorate in 1762, the university overseers voted William an honorary master's degree for his contributions. And in 1802, Joseph Priestley himself wrote to a London newspaper to acknowledge publicly William's role.

As Franklin's political career cut more deeply into his time for scientific inquiry, he decided to give William a share in his political life. When he was elected to the Assembly in October 1751, he turned his paid post of Assembly clerk over to his son. When his political fortunes rose and brought him the lucrative post of deputy postmaster general for North America, he not only appointed William (who was only twenty-three) postmaster of Philadelphia but made him comptroller of the North American postal system, a demanding job that required skill in accounting, tact in collecting money, and patience in making detailed reports. Franklin had won the postal franchise mainly because his predecessor had failed to keep adequate and accurate records. To turn the crucial comptrollership over to William was both a risk for Benjamin and an honor for William. William rewarded his father's trust by excelling in each job.

At the age of twenty-one, William had decided to go his separate way and pursue a legal career. Franklin was not exactly jubilant — his opinion of lawyers was low: "God works wonders now and then . . . behold, a lawyer, an honest man!" said Poor Richard. Yet Franklin now promised his son that when he had completed the customary three-year term of clerkship in the office of a leading Philadelphia lawyer, he would send him to England to study at the Inns of Court. This virtually guaranteed that William would himself one day become one of the more successful lawyers in Philadelphia. Accordingly, on February 11, 1750, he registered by mail in the Middle Temple and enclosed the fee.[29]

It must be noted that neither Benjamin's low opinion of lawyers nor his epigram was original. Poor Richard was rewriting Ben Jonson's recently republished "Epitaph on an Honest Lawyer." On page 213 of *The Life and Errors of John Dunton,* published in 1705, the story evidently appeared for the first time in print: "Ben Jonson . . . was walking through a church in Surrey when he saw a company of poor people weeping over a grave. Ben asked one of the women what the occasion should be? She answered, Oh, alas! Sir, we have lost our precious good lawyer, Justice Randall. He kept us all in peace and from going to law. Certainly he was the best man that ever lived. Well, said Ben, I'll send you an epitaph for his tombstone, which was:

God works wonders now and then,
Here lies a lawyer, an honest man."

According to the editors of Johnson's *Works,* this story had been quoted in the London *Weekly Register* on July 12, 1735. Benjamin Franklin evidently read the newspaper and adapted the epitaph for his almanac.

The days and weeks William spent with his father at political meetings and civic functions, on post office inspection tours, and in the laboratory, did little to ease a growing estrangement between William and the woman he called Mother. Relations between them had become strained after the birth of Sarah. Deborah believed that her husband favored William over Sarah, and indeed Franklin made no secret of his pride in William. He did prefer this tall, polished reminder of his youth almost to the exclusion of other members of the family, who were reminders of a less prosperous time. A young clerk named Daniel Fisher, who lived with the Franklins briefly in the summer of 1755, wrote in his diary that Mrs. Franklin had begun "suspecting Mr. Franklin of having too great an esteem for his son in prejudice of herself and daughter."

Deborah Franklin was never capable of discretion, much less of artifice. She was deeply rankled at having to move from her own house into a rented dwelling away from the center of town. She was constantly irritated by the traffic of artisans and politicians and office seekers, by the infernal jangle of wires and bells when lightning struck the rods on the roof and traveled through the walls. And on that hot June day, her temper flared, unfortunately in Fisher's presence. "Young Mr. Franklin," Fisher recorded, "I have often seen pass to and from his father's apartment upon business (for he does not eat, drink or sleep in the house) without least compliment between Mrs. Franklin and him or any sort of notice taken of each other, till one day I was sitting with her in the passage when the young gentleman came by. She exclaimed to me (he not hearing), 'Mr. Fisher, there goes the greatest villain upon earth.' This greatly confounded and perplexed me, but did not hinder her from pursuing her invectives in the foulest terms I ever heard from a gentlewoman."[30]

Despite Deborah's jealousy, father and son drew ever closer, and what helped to make them confidants was a series of what Franklin considered betrayals at the hands of old friends as his political career brought him more prominence. First to turn against him was his old mentor, Chief Justice William Allen. After joining Franklin's first circle of Masons, he used his powerful connections in England to take control of the Masons in Philadelphia, then openly attacked Franklin's ideas for the defense of Pennsylvania in 1755. The final deserter was the Reverend William Smith. Franklin had encouraged him to create the Academy of Philadelphia, and he was Franklin's closest friend until he saw he could gain control of the academy, a lucrative provost's salary and a rent-free mansion by defecting to the Penn faction.

By late 1755 only one totally trustworthy man was in a position to assist Franklin's last-ditch attempt to save Pennsylvania from invasion. That man was his own son, William Franklin. Together, they rode south to help Braddock round up supplies and transport. William, familiar with an officer's life in camp, made up the list of provisions, rode back to Philadelphia with his father to obtain them, rushed back to Braddock's army, then hurried back again to Philadelphia to rejoin his father.[31]

On the humid morning of June 24, 1755, as Braddock's British-American army labored west to attack the French and Indians, a strange assemblage of Philadelphians filed into an austere new brick building in Norris Alley. After handing in their tickets, government officials, wealthy merchants, carpenters, stonemasons, tavernkeepers and tanners took their places on benches in a spacious meeting room. It was the day of dedication of Freemasons Hall, the world's first building constructed exclusively for use by the society called the Ancient Free and Accepted Masons. For more than a quarter century, the Masons in America had gained strength quietly, their secret organization to a large extent masterminded by Benjamin Franklin. He arrived bedecked in the heavy gold chain of past grand master.

After meeting behind closed doors, the 130-odd Masons, dressed in black suits, white aprons, gloves, stockings and an array of jewels, badges and chains, strutted two by two north through Society Hill to the cadence of a marching band. Leading the procession was the swordbearer, brandishing his saber and followed immediately by six stewards swinging long white wands. Then came the grand secretary — William Franklin — carrying an open Bible on a crimson damask cushion. Behind him marched all the conflicting elements of far-reaching change about to overtake American society. The chief justice and richest merchant, Grand Master William Allen, huffed and puffed as he hauled his great bulk along; Allen had just unseated Benjamin Franklin from the highest post after a long power struggle. Beside him walked Governor Robert Hunter Morris (every governor of Pennsylvania in a generation had been a Mason). Striding confidently behind them came Benjamin Franklin and, behind him, John Penn, the youngest son of the Founder. Stretched out behind them for two blocks were successful artisans and craftsmen, men who would soon shoulder aside pacifist Quakers and hereditary rulers as their self-made city became the capital of a revolutionary new nation.

The day's events revealed the enormous prestige and organizational genius of the man behind the populist movement in America. The fact that his bastard son could play such a prominent part in the proceedings only underscored Benjamin Franklin's self-confident eminence.

As the Masons passed between cheering crowds, a lodge brother's ship fired nine salvos in their honor. To many in the Quaker city the sound of gunfire was startling. Before the year was over, it would become commonplace. That it would take a war to bring about fundamental change came as no surprise to the Franklins, the two men who had organized this symbolic demonstration of money and power that culminated years of careful, quiet planning. The extraordinary number of their successes in civic causes and in political, military and scientific matters helped to explain why they were so confident. They were sure they could quickly pull together the warring factions in time to ward off the French invasion that threatened to destroy all they had accomplished.[32]

On William's part, there was nothing self-conscious about his devotion to his father. Indeed, there had been times when he had had more faith in his father's enterprises than Franklin himself did. When Franklin had failed to kindle sufficient interest in the American Philosophical Society in the midst of a long war with

France, it was William who gathered his young friends together and kept it alive. When Franklin's Junto of debaters drifted apart, William and his young friends formed a new Junto to discuss the burning scientific propositions of their generation. Both organizations survived, thrived, and eventually merged.

Now, when Franklin's political interests were growing, William made one of his greatest contributions to his father's political career. Over the pseudonym Humphrey Scourge, he dashed off polished diatribes that attacked his father's rivals with devastating effect. His first attack came in December of 1755, shortly after the Indian raid at Gnadenhütten assured the passage of the militia bill. The success of providing defense depended on his father's diplomacy in dealing with the proprietary officials, who consistently sandbagged every attempt to raise troops. With two friends, William attacked Governor Morris in a scurrilous pamphlet called *Tit for Tat.* The paper war erupted over the election of militia officers. When Franklin partisans were overwhelmingly elected, Governor Morris ignored the commissions. Pro-Franklin forces demonstrated angrily, burning the governor in effigy. Morris approved some commissions, but denied rank to one of William's coauthors of *Tit for Tat.* William's commission was not disallowed only because he had not been nominated: his father had sidestepped the issue, instead naming William his personal aide-de-camp and secretary to the defense commission.

Officially, William's job was merely to call members together for meetings, keep the minutes, and act as a dispatch rider on urgent commission business. Unofficially, secretly, Benjamin put him to work gathering evidence against the proprietary party and documenting a case which the Franklins now saw they must take to England and lay before Parliament.

Every so often, when the pressures of his complex life built up beyond his forbearance, Benjamin Franklin liked to slip away. As postmaster general he could justify extended trips away from Deborah. On his most recent six-month sojourn in New England in late 1754, he had been introduced to Catherine Ray, the twenty-three-year-old first cousin of his brother John's wife. Caty charmed Benjamin with her elegant manners, her laughter, her youthful beauty and her attentiveness. For weeks, he had found excuses to linger with her in Boston, then accompany her to the Ray farm in Rhode Island. During the seven months after his return to Philadelphia, he received one letter after another from her. One of his replies written on September 11, 1755, in moments stolen from a spate of meetings, reveals how much he enjoyed her adulation: "Begone, business, for an hour at least, and let me chat a little with my Caty. . . . Since I saw you, I have been enabled to do some general services to the country and to the army, for which both have thanked and praised me, and say they love me. They *say so,* as you used to do; and if I were to ask any favors of them, would, perhaps, as readily refuse me, so that I find little real advantage in being loved."[33]

A breathless, reckless letter had arrived in Philadelphia in September 1755 after being lost in the mails for three months. Caty did not know that Franklin had been off in Virginia helping Braddock find wagons for his last campaign. Franklin's failure to answer three of her letters, she said, "gives me a vast deal of uneasiness and occasioned many tears, for surely I have wrote too much and you are affronted with me, or have not received my letters, in which I have said a thousand things that nothing should have tempted me to have said to anybody else, for I knew they would be safe with you. I'll only beg the favor of one line. What is become of my letters? Tell me you are well and forgive me and love me one-thousandth part as well as I do you, and then I will be contented."[34]

This letter brought an ironic reply from Franklin on October 16: "I hear you are now in Boston, gay and lovely as usual. Let me give you some fatherly advice. Be a good girl and don't forget your catechism. Go constantly to meeting or church 'til you get a good husband, then stay at home and nurse the children and live like a Christian. You must practice addition to your husband's state by industry and frugality; subtraction of all unnecessary expenses; multiplication (I would gladly have taught you that myself, but you thought it was time enough and wouldn't learn). When I have again the pleasure of seeing you, I may find you like my grape vine, surrounded with clusters, plump, juicy, blushing, pretty little rogues, like their Mama. Adieu. The bell rings and I must go among the grave ones, and talk politics."[35]

For some time, Franklin had apparently entrusted William with

forwarding the letters addressed to him and arranging safe riders
for his answers. And while Benjamin made little jokes about Caty
to his wife and daughter, especially after Caty guilelessly sent them
a plum pudding she had made, her letters had become so intimate
that they might have embarrassed him, not to mention Deborah,
had they been delivered to his home while he and William were absent on the frontier. Whatever arrangements William saw fit to
make as Philadelphia postmaster, he of course kept them secret.

In the midst of preparations for the fort-building expedition,
Benjamin sent a secret letter to Caty on Block Island:

> You may write freely everything you think fit without the least
> apprehension of any person's seeing your letters but myself. You
> have complimented me so much in those I have already received
> that I could not show them without being justly thought a vain
> coxcomb for doing so. . . . I know very well that the most innocent
> expressions of warm friendship and even those of mere civility and
> complaisance between persons of different sexes are liable to be
> misinterpreted by suspicious minds; and therefore, though you say
> more, I say less than I think, and this letter coolly in the plain com-
> mon form, with only
>
> > Dear Miss
> > Your humble Servant
> > B Franklin[36]

It was a cautiously worded letter that suspicious minds would, as
Franklin said, have trouble using against him, and yet in it he was
clearly encouraging a continuation of the coquetry. He apparently
had no desire to cut off the flow of her affection and looked forward
to the time he would see her again on his postal rounds.

The wonder is not that a man who considered himself "in the
declining years of middle age" would encourage and carry on a
highly flirtatious correspondence with a distant female relative or
even that he would have to draw his only son into the affair to protect evidence of apparent dalliance from prying eyes. What was
truly surprising was that Benjamin would take such risks in mailing
compromising letters to Boston, where his Puritan relatives lived
and his own brother John was the postmaster. Either John or his

wife, Caty's cousin, could have opened the letter accidentally before sending it on to the Ray house on Block Island, where the risk was equally great. These were bold letters for their time, no matter how guarded their language. But Benjamin Franklin was becoming accustomed to taking risks.

4

WE GOT FIVE SCALPS
BUT THEY GOT NINE

December 1755–April 1756

SHORTLY AFTER DAWN ON DECEMBER 18, 1755, FIFTY UNI-
formed horsemen of the Philadelphia first cavalry troop dismounted outside the small red-brick house of Defense
Commissioner Benjamin Franklin. Inside, Franklin was reading the
galley proof of a plea for recruits which was to appear in that day's
Gazette. Summoning an apprentice, he handed him a news item he
had just written: "December 18th: This day the Honourable James
Hamilton, Benjamin Franklin and Joseph Fox set out for the front
in order to settle matters for the defense of the province."[1]

Downstairs in the basement kitchen, Deborah was directing the
servants as they hauled provisions to a waiting wagon. For days she
had marshaled her husband's departure. As his subsequent letters
indicate, she did not want him to go, not only because of the risk
but because he had been ill and would suffer from his weakened
lungs and worsening gout in the wretched, cold wet weather. But
he insisted, so she and her sister-in-law had been cooking and packing.

Seasoned travelers, the Franklins knew the hopelessness of country inns, the unhealthiness of camp rations. They carted along their
own specially stocked kitchen wagon, and Franklin's personal slave,
Peter, cooked for them. Franklin had laid out eighteen pounds for a
cask of good port wine and Deborah was making certain her husband did not want for home cooking. There were roasts of beef and

veal, mince pies, fresh biscuits, jams, tea, cheese and gingerbread to go with their salt pork. Deborah had made sure, too, that her husband's favorite maroon traveling suit, woolen trousers and great blue caped coat were laid out, and his wool flannel nightshirt was packed. William no doubt had his own list of supplies, drawn up with the privations of winter camps during the last war vivid in his mind.

In the weeks since October, when the Indian raids began, Franklin had taken little care to recuperate from recurring pleurisy. He blamed his illness on exhaustion from the rigors of Braddock's campaign and of politicking seven days a week. But now the prospect of doing something about the fate of all he had worked thirty years to build took hold.[2]

That his personable son William was on such good terms with all the factions of Philadelphia society contributed to the success of Franklin's efforts. Father and son did not always share the same views of people. Though Willliam remained dutiful, each year he became less attracted to his father's artisan friends and more closely linked to his father's rivals. One of the latter was James Hamilton, the titular head of the relief mission. Both he and William were Masons and members of Christ Church, and William had spent a number of evenings viewing the art in Hamilton's stately home. He had also played cards with members of the Penn family's social set, and had danced with their wives and daughters.

From his circle of aristocratic young friends, William quickly drew together the best-equipped and best-trained horsemen in Pennsylvania. Men who could afford to outfit themselves for duty away from home, who were familiar with sword, pistol and rifle, and could ride in a group after years of fox hunting together required little additional grooming into a cavalry unit. He also helped his father raise five hundred men from Philadelphia and the surrounding counties, many of them veterans of the last war, to fill out ranger companies.[3] The expedition was made even more a Franklin family affair when Deborah's brother John Read signed on as head of the supply wagons. He had been Braddock's wagonmaster.

Shortly after eight that morning, the Franklin men said goodbye to Deborah and twelve-year-old Sally. At a word from Benjamin, William rode to the cavalry picket post and signaled a bugler to

sound the call to ride out. The Franklins wanted to impress wavering Philadelphians with an ostentatious display of the newly formed
Philadelphia Association militia. The order of march was suitably
colorful: red-coated soldiers out in front; cavalrymen in green-and-
red tunics, with their swords rattling as they pranced on their shin-
ing hunters through the crowd-lined streets; the brightly lacquered
red-and-black Conestogas rumbling behind straining black dray
horses; militiamen marching crisply along with their new muskets
glinting on their shoulders; the flapping white Association battle
flags, their lions rampant.[4] In the midst of this show of arms, the
gray Quaker matchcoat and broad flat beaver hat of Commissioner
Joseph Fox looked decidedly out of place. There had been some
question of his going at all; if he did, he would surely be read out of
Quaker meeting. He went and he was. The two quaintly garbed
Moravian guides, survivors of Gnadenhütten, looked just as incongruous.

Though Benjamin Franklin was merely one of seven men in
charge of defense (he had been denied clear-cut authority by Governor Morris), he always thrived in committee, working early and
long each day, applying sheer weight of time, thought and effort to
the problems at hand. He sensed early that the committee was the
safe, hard core of the new brand of politics, the essence of the Assembly's method of wielding power. Already he had relegated four
of the defense commissioners to minor roles. As the man in charge
of weapons at a time of desperate shortage, he decided who should
be armed and protected. With nearly six hundred trained and disciplined militiamen personally loyal to him, he was conspicuously first
among equals. The superiority of his position was further enhanced
by his control of the postal system: through it, he could monitor the
gathering and transmittal of all intelligence. He also devised a sure-
fire method of accomplishing certain of his aims in the shortest
time: without consulting the other commission members he rented
wagons and paid for firearms with his own money, confident that
his vouchers would be honored by virtue of his hold over the Assembly.[5]

Governor Morris had worked publicly to wreck Franklin's defense efforts. He sent an uncoordinated mass of frontiersmen to
hack away at trees, dig trenches, and build scores of makeshift

stockades that only engendered a false sense of security: the Indians could easily sneak up to the walls and fire directly into the enclosures. Other defenses were poorly linked deathtraps: one Indian attack on a chain of fortified houses left six guards dead and the houses burned.[6] Officers' commissions went unwanted. A cousin of Deborah Franklin's, James Read, wrote that he had the misfortune of being the commanding officer of two of Morris's militia companies. Officers and men marched aimlessly over hills and valleys, running up prodigious bills at taverns. One leading citizen bemoaned that "the people of this country are very willing to join in repelling the invaders but are without order, and many want arms. . . . Before the army will move, officers are obliged to promise to bear their charges upon ye road, and to support them when they stay abroad."[7]

As Franklin gathered arms and men, William's cavalry detachment escorted the supply wagons carrying muskets, rum and blankets to the thousands of refugees. The Franklins' early expectations of a great volunteer army had dwindled, but it was impossible to wait any longer. When Indians attacked Easton, less than fifty miles from Philadelphia, the Franklins received one last desperate plea from the surrounded outpost: "We are now the frontier. Pray do something or give some order for our speedy relief or the whole country will be ruined."[8]

Amazingly, after weeks of stalling commissions to Franklin-backed officers and in the face of the Easton emergency, Morris insisted on leaving the province to attend a governor's conference in New York. Even his staunchest supporter, former Governor James Hamilton, agreed with Franklin that they could not delay until his return. They must reconnoiter, post troops, and lay out a defensive line before it was too late. By now, the Indians were expertly firing long rifles (purchased from Quakers) and were picking off farmers whose antique blunderbusses and inaccurate muskets were no match for them.

With four fifths of Pennsylvania controlled by French-led war parties, even Hamilton, that determined gentleman of leisure, had to leave his carefully landscaped acres to ride toward the uncertainties of the frontier. He was in exceptional discomfort this morning: while working in his gardens, he had contracted poison ivy. When the column halted at the evergreen-lined entrance to Bush Hill, his lavish estate overlooking the city, he mounted a horse and rode off with Franklin and Fox.[9]

Hamilton was all that Franklin was not, all that William admired. Born rich, educated classically in England, he was a great, broad-bellied, well-read, easygoing epicure and a patron of the arts. He astutely subsidized young Benjamin West's studies in Rome and commissioned several works, including his own portrait. Franklin had thought so little of West that he had a copyist try to improve on West's portrait of Sally. Hamilton was famous for his hospitality, Franklin for his parsimony.

When it served his immediate ends, the elder Franklin could convert old enemies into compliant friends. Otherwise intelligent rivals, besieged by the deliberate charm of his conversation, wit and wealth of knowledge and experience, could forget for the moment the caustic encounters with that other Benjamin Franklin, the implacable party politician. Now Franklin literally had everything to lose by unsmiling adherence to politics, everything to gain by drawing others to him.

Franklin and Hamilton were political rivals, but they had been friends for thirty years. Together they had supported Hamilton's father in his efforts to build the State House, the finest government building in colonial America, and when Franklin organized the American Philosophical Society, he had asked the accomplished amateur botanist Hamilton to join its select ranks. First as an assemblyman, then as speaker, Hamilton had sponsored Franklin's appointment as clerk of the Assembly. But recently their political paths had diverged until now they were adversaries. As a rich landowner, Hamilton had allied himself with the Penns in demanding that all quitrents be paid in silver: Franklin, the official printer of paper money, whose business depended on credit, naturally opposed him. But both men had long worked for a strong defense, even if today Hamilton wrote Penn describing Franklin's militia as the "quintessence of absurdity."[10]

With Governor Morris away, Speaker Hamilton was the ranking member of the provincial Council, and as such, acting governor. In theory, with the popular Assembly adjourned, he had dictatorial powers. Had he been more ambitious he could have emerged a popular hero of the French and Indian War. As it was, he rode uncomfortably off to obscurity as the Franklins systematically exploited him and put his proprietary underlings to work for them.

It was an odd little army, typically American, gathering its strength as it marched along. It contained no one press-ganged to serve against his will, no one freed from jail or kidnapped from servitude, no one seeking riches or plunder. All were volunteers who would rather have been in shop, office or field; many were sons and grandsons of strict Quakers. Their doctor, Thomas Lloyd, was a grandson of the Quaker chief justice who had written the rough draft of William Penn's Charter of Privileges; he was related by marriage to the richest families in Pennsylvania. Indeed, the dedication of this volunteer army was enough to astonish an enemy as it quick-marched thirty-five miles over twisting narrow roads on the first day.

That night the defense commissioners found Franklin hospitality agreeable, especially in the filthy little country inn where they had to spend the night. Weeks later, the rigors of campaigning still vivid, Franklin singled out the place in a letter to Deborah: "The woman being about to put very damp sheets on the bed, we desired her to air them first. Half an hour afterwards, she told us the bed was ready and the sheets well aired. I got into bed, jumped out immediately, finding them as cold as death and partly frozen. She had aired them indeed, but it was out upon the hedge."[11] One further inconvenience Franklin did not dwell on, probably because it was so familiar: father and son had to share the bed that night (as the "we" makes apparent).[12]

Long before they climbed South Mountain to stare down at Bethlehem on the afternoon of December 19, the Franklins knew there had been a dramatic change in the once-pacifist Moravian haven since the slaughter at Gnadenhütten: the Moravian elders had finally acted to defend themselves. Even as thousands of refugees flocked south past the Franklin relief column, Bishop Spangenberg had given his orders: "We abide undeterred at our posts, for should we yield, the whole country would become prey to the ravages of the Indians."[13] The bishop, sharply critical of the

Quaker Assembly, had pleaded for a fort to command the Lehigh Gap below Gnadenhütten. If the gutted mission "is left to the enemy," he wrote Governor Morris, "it may prove the ruin not only of all the settlements lying along the Lehigh and the Delaware, but also of Philadelphia."[14]

The murders at Gnadenhütten had finally convinced the Scotch-Irish in nearby valleys that the Moravians were not, after all, Papists in league with the French just because they wore long cowled robes and could speak French. Now the Scotch-Irish crowded into Bethlehem, seeking shelter and food. When aid did not come, the peaceful bishop decided to defend his followers: there were too many old and sick, too many children to evacuate.

It was clear to the Moravian elders that fortifications were needed to seal off the town. The bishop authorized the building of a log stockade to link twelve major stone buildings. While the carpenters were erecting it, paving stones were cemented across the lower halves of all windows on outside walls. Bastions and watchtowers soon rose; the great gates were shut. The peaceful little town of Bethlehem began to look like one of the medieval walled cities of Europe. Nevertheless, Bishop Spangenberg threw himself on his knees before the elders, begging them to give strict orders that, if any Indian invader had to be shot, the guards were to aim low, shoot for the legs, then carry the prisoner to the hospital for the sisters to heal. Furthermore, the bishop would not consent to meet the Franklin war party. He delegated a civilian administrator to talk to the defense commissioners at the Crown Inn.

The next morning, the Franklins decided to move on. The cavalrymen were ferried across the river as the Moravians watched silently. Few brethren believed what their elders had told them: that these strangers with swords, muskets and grim faces were "going hunting."[15]

When the elder Franklin had been a young bachelor setting up a printshop in Philadelphia, one of his Junto debating circle had been a shoemaker-turned-politician named William Parsons. Now a proprietary party official, Parsons had been struggling ineffectually for the past two months to hold together the strategic outpost of Easton. Printer Franklin and shoemaker Parsons had long ago split over politics. Parsons had become the Penns' surveyor general and was sent to lay out Easton, the newest Penn manor. Unfortunately, he had earned a reputation as a coward when a mob of eighty angry frontiersmen smashed his tools as he was carrying out his duties. His timidity did not help when Easton was overrun by Scotch-Irish refugees after the Gnadenhütten massacre. His pathetic pleas had precipitated the Franklin expedition. "Our poor people," he had written Franklin, "have quite expended their little substance and are wearied out with watching. . . . They are moving away as fast as they can. We shall every one of us be obliged to leave the town . . . to the fury of the enemy." Touched, Franklin sent William with guns, blankets and food, "all party laid aside."[16]

When bugle calls announced the arrival of the Franklin force in Easton on December 20, the sound was the only bright note. Below them in the snow and mud the Franklins could see huts and cabins clustered around a crude stone jail, the whole ringed by a rickety stockade devoid of guards. The town appeared deserted. Then Parsons hurried out of a small house to meet them. He was faced with an immediate dilemma: who was in charge — his proprietary superior or his old friend? Franklin never raised the question. He simply deferred to Hamilton.

It was evident to the Franklins that the Delawares were intent on taking back all the land swindled from them by the Penns. To prevent this, they proposed that a line of forts be built on the southern edge of the Walking Purchase, from Easton west through Bethlehem to Kittatinny Mountain. A line of forts would be more defensible than Acting Governor Hamilton's scheme, which was to raise a grand army, retake all the territory that had been recouped by the Indians, and then build forts on the outermost boundaries of the Penn lands. Hamilton, however, was unprepared for the chaos created by fifteen hundred unruly refugees. Nor did he expect the abuse he received when he publicly called for a large volunteer army to fight the Indians. He reported that he had "offered provisions, arms and ammunition to such that would go against the enemy, but none would go . . . insisting on pay as well as subsistence, asking exorbitant prices for food and the transportation of it."[17]

When Hamilton's plan failed, Franklin quietly stepped in and quickly advanced a plan he and William had devised. First, they would fortify a few outposts while setting up a strong defensive base at Easton. Hamilton was forced to yield as Franklin brought in well-armed, well-trained troops loyal to him. For one thing, Franklin was cannier than Hamilton: he knew that farmers who had rented their wagons to Braddock had still not been paid. He and William also argued that troops had a right to be paid, that they should not risk their lives to secure Penn property gratis. William had seen the northern expedition in the last war collapse when the troops were not properly paid and clothed. When Hamilton balked, Franklin decided to pay volunteers out of his own pocket and fight out reimbursement from the government later. In effect, he now had his own private army. But he did not sympathize with the price-gouging farmers who had hauled their goods to safety and wanted high rates from the men who were protecting them. He boycotted them, calling up supplies from Philadelphia, and he banned the sale of rum, thereby putting a stop to the rioting and looting.[18]

As Hamilton sulked, the Franklins smoothly began organizing the defense. First they had to outmaneuver Hamilton and Parsons. Parsons was easily pacified. Among the first commissions Hamilton signed was one for William Parsons, major. While Hamilton drank and wrote self-pitying letters to the Penns, the Franklins began dispatching more than one hundred hand-picked troops to build blockhouses in the Pocono Mountains to the north, where frontier families had been holding out for weeks.

For the defense of Easton, Benjamin called on his expert, William, to form three garrison companies and a town watch, to train sentries to guard approaches to the main streets, to drill rangers and lead them on patrols into the woods. William at once ordered a swath one hundred yards wide cleared around the town, thereby creating a field of fire that would deter Indians attempting to sneak within gunshot. After issuing arms, he worked ten days and nights teaching his men how to look for signs that Indians had approached.

Benjamin also had William draft "instructions" for the newly commissioned Major Parsons. William's military expertise showed through the detailed orders he prepared for Hamilton to sign and give to Parsons (old friend Parsons was never allowed to see that his orders were actually coming from Benjamin Franklin). For his part, Hamilton was unaware that he had been reduced to a figurehead. In only ten days the Franklins had raised and trained nearly eight hundred troops. Now they were ready to ride to Reading, seventy-five miles to the west, to confront proprietary leaders in their stronghold.[19] Leaving half the trained troops with Parsons, they marched.

The sight of the Union Jack flying above the stockaded town of Reading must have heartened the weary troops when they came in sight of the settlement on the afternoon of January 1, 1756. But to the Franklins the flag did little more than underscore the irony of Pennsylvania's plight. Though the royal standard was the symbol of the supposed equality of all British dominions under Crown and Parliament, the two hundred thousand settlers penned up in the southeast part of the province were, to all practical effects, outside the British union. As Benjamin Franklin had said over and over, they had become little more than yoked oxen, vassals of a feudal lord, owned and rented out, each year slipping closer to the status of serfs.[20]

That cheerless afternoon, two columns of men with decidedly clashing points of view bore down on Reading. At the head of forty British redcoats rode Governor Morris, captain general of Pennsylvania, his troops trudging ahead of a long packtrain bearing his personal luggage and a cargo of guns and blankets intended as presents for the remaining neutral Indians on Penn lands. Hurrying from the east came the Franklins, escorted by fifty provincial greencoats and three hundred militiamen, leading a wagonload of guns for the Reading garrison. The governor arrived first and claimed the best rooms in the few inns.[21]

After the governor's pompous declaration about the great army he would bring from New York, the handful of British grenadiers that had shown up only deepened Benjamin Franklin's scorn for the proprietors. The fiasco was typical of Morris. Recently Franklin had written, "The governor, though he spurs with both heels, at the same time reins in with both hands, so that the public business can never move forward and he remains, like St. George-in-the-Sign, always a-horseback and never going on."[22] The Franklins knew that the governor wanted an all-out declaration of war by Pennsylvania against the Indians months before British troops could arrive because his family could expect to grow even richer from the profits of war. One of the leading arms merchants in America was William Walton of New York, whose niece was married to Governor Morris's nephew. Walton not only sold guns to British colonies in America but to the strategic Spanish fortress at St. Augustine, Florida. The guns were then traded to southern Indians who were menacing the Carolina and Georgia backcountry. He was also suspected of acting as an intermediary for the contraband arms traffic through Albany. There, guns were exchanged for the pelts trapped by the French-backed Canadian Indians when they were not raiding New York, New Hampshire and Massachusetts.[23]

In 1755, after the first Indian forays into Pennsylvania, Franklin had rounded up arms in Philadelphia and had sent off an assortment of old firelocks and fowling pieces to Reading. As pleas for arms poured in, he had ordered a thousand pounds' worth of weapons from a New York dealer who was competing with the Walton-Morris firm, thereby touching off the long-smoldering feud with the governor. Morris lost no time in charging the Assembly with infringing on proprietary prerogative by allowing its defense committee to issue arms. He singled out Franklin, accusing him of illegally arming the citizenry and of deliberately waiting to issue weapons until he, Morris, was out of town. It was a serious charge, one bordering on treason in British law, and Morris communicated it to the authorities in London.[24]

The leading official at Reading, the seat of the Penns' new county of Berks, was Major James Read. He was deeply attached to the proprietors. It did not dim his loyalty that Reading, its rough-hewn market town, was, in one visitor's words, "a jumble of a hundred log houses, many with costly decorations on their front, grouped irregularly about an absurdly large and very muddy central square."[25] Read deemed it a proprietary compliment that Governor Morris had chosen to meet the Assembly defense commissioners here.

Like most men who had left behind the comforts of life in the coastal towns to head west, Read had come to Reading to shake off the dead shell of failure. A cheerful, bookish man who loved to translate passages from the classics and correspond with other amateur scholars, he had spent many hours discussing science and ancient literature with the young Benjamin Franklin, who eventually told friends he considered Read "a little crazy." For his part, Read had grown increasingly alarmed over the years as Franklin, the ambitious politician, shouldered him aside, first in politics, then in business. What must have dismayed and surprised him most was Franklin's apparent ingratitude.

When Franklin had first landed in Philadelphia, the Reads were among the first families there. By the time he took a rented room in the Widow Read's house, James's father, who was Deborah's uncle Charles, was already a distinguished alderman. By the time Deborah became Franklin's common-law wife, Uncle Charles was a rich merchant with a fine house overlooking the teeming harbor. Before William Franklin was three years old, James Read referred affectionately to Benjamin as "Cousin Benny." They enjoyed many hours together on market days in front of their adjoining shops: Read's bookstore and Franklin's new printing office.

Young Billy Franklin had been very close to his kindly uncle. From him he had acquired a lifelong love of books and had spent as many hours as his father would allow among the stacks of handsomely bound volumes that Uncle James kept ordering — overordering — from London. The two had studied at the same private school, and Uncle James gave Billy help with polishing his writing style. Though William remained in contact with Uncle James over the years, by the time Major James Read opened the door of his new log home in Reading that first afternoon of 1756, there was little affection left between him and Benjamin Franklin. When Read's credit with a London publisher had run out, Franklin was given power of attorney to collect the large outstanding debt. When Reed's bookstore folded, Cousin Benny enlarged his own book business.

In a last stab at solvency, James Read had lined up proprietary support for his appointment to the clerkship of the Assembly, a post now being vacated by the newly elected assemblyman Benjamin Franklin. As the Reads had long been associated in business with a rival of Franklin's in Philadelphia printing, Franklin apparently regarded the move not only as a threat to his lucrative sideline as Assembly printer but as a piece of family perfidy. He nominated and backed twenty-one-year-old William for the post. With his new power and his ability to call on Association militia veterans, he won the fight for the clerkship. James Read left Philadelphia, a poor man and an enemy.

Any enemy of Benjamin Franklin's was a friend of the Penns. James Read was soon appointed to a row of Berks County offices. As prothonotary, for instance, he collected an array of fees from every new settler. He was soon solvent again, ensconced in a new house and presiding over the county where the defense commission was now convening.

With his good friend Colonel Conrad Weiser, commander of the Berks militia, Major Read managed to ignore Franklin at long range and took few steps to defend the town. Three weeks before the Gnadenhütten massacre, Franklin sent weapons to Reading with detailed instructions for their use. Offering unsolicited advice, he urged Read to instruct ranger parties in using large dogs. "In case of meeting a party of the enemy, the dogs are all then to be turned loose . . . they will confound the enemy a great deal."[26] There is no evidence that Major Read listened to Deborah Read's husband anymore this time than on earlier occasions.

When Franklin arrived at Read's house that afternoon, he fell back on family goodwill, which he often did when he found himself in tight political straits. With him Benjamin brought Deborah's brother, the wagonmaster John Read, who certainly was happy to see his middle-aged cousin once again and to exchange old stories over good food. The tensions of frayed family relations eased when the Franklins and the two Reads ate the hearty fare that had arrived that day from Deborah Franklin's kitchen in Philadelphia.[27]

There was little time for socializing. The defense conference began on January 3 with the arrival of Conrad Weiser, the man who had held panic-stricken Berks County together for two months. Weiser had last seen the Franklins at the first meeting of the defense commission a month earlier in Philadelphia. Not only had he been given the responsibility of stopping the runaway movement from the western frontier, but he was in charge of gathering intelligence from Indian spies. As the Indian agent of Pennsylvania, he knew their strengths and weaknesses, all their warpaths.

Weiser also knew that his role in the defense of the province was vital and that his success would in large measure depend on good relations with Franklin; yet he found it difficult to swallow old political grievances, especially difficult to deal with the elder Franklin's anti-German prejudice. But if Weiser and Franklin were not on good terms, Weiser and the younger Franklin were. The memories of their wilderness adventure to the Ohio did much to smooth Weiser's hackles. Indeed, without the respect William had gained from a number of proprietary officials assembled at Reading, Benjamin's aims might well have been frustrated.

Governor Morris had intended that the conference center around talks with the Indians, but few Indians were willing to venture into a town, especially since two Indian prisoners had been tortured to death at Harris's Ferry. Weiser informed the first session of the conference that he had given up trying to win over the renegades he and William had helped to arm in the Ohio Valley eight years earlier. He did have Indian spies in several villages and had even managed to get one inside Fort Duquesne, the French base. That very day the Indians had brought him intelligence that stunned the conference: from an advance base only fifty miles away, the French had cowed the few remaining neutral Indians. Seven large war parties commanded by French officers were operating in the valleys to the west, just beyond the next ridge of the Appalachians. Each of these war parties contained up to two hundred fifty warriors who could run from Duquesne and back in seven days. The Delawares had rebuffed a direct order from their former Six Nations overlords to stop the killings and were winning over many young Six Nations warriors despite official tribal neutrality. Worse still, these warriors were joining in looting and burning deserted farms and could trigger a general bloodlust insurrection of all northern Indians.

To no one's surprise, Governor Morris's instant reaction was to call for a vigorous counterattack and for building a strategic fort deep inside Indian-held territory. To most of his auditors the lessons of the recent debacle at Fort Duquesne were painfully fresh.

Not only would such a foray be dangerous on its face, with French and Indian forces estimated to exceed twelve hundred men, but Morris was unable to explain how Pennsylvania's militia of only six hundred men could succeed where Braddock's had failed with a thousand British regulars and five hundred militiamen. Moreover, who would defend the exposed frontier in the weeks it would take to build a road needed to haul cannon, ammunition and supplies? And if all the province's meager resources were committed to a single fort, what was to prevent the enemy from ignoring it and striking at defenseless towns, even at unprotected Philadelphia?

When Morris's idea fell flat, the conferees were willing to listen to the Franklin alternative.[28] Benjamin unrolled a sheaf of plans and spelled out the strategy he, his son, and experienced frontier leaders had been devising secretly for weeks. On each side of Kittatinny Mountain, from the New York border southwest to Blue Mountain and the Maryland border, six small forts, each housing fifty or so well-armed and well-trained men, would be built at approximately fifteen-mile intervals. Rangers would patrol constantly between them. Six hundred rangers would be needed, first to build the twelve forts and deliver guns, blankets, rum and food, and then to prevent Indian infiltration.

The Franklins had designed a prototype frontier fort, fifty feet square, armed with swivel guns taken from ships in Philadelphia harbor and defended by sharpshooters firing from platforms and twin blockhouses. In the margins of a thick tome on military engineering entitled *A Short Treatise on Fortification and Geometry,* Franklin had scribbled his calculations.[29] His reasoning was sound. Indians rarely attacked a fortified place, and a log fort, though rickety, was safe against an enemy who had no artillery.

But where should the forts be built? Benjamin said that every frontiersman naturally wanted a stockade built around his house at the taxpayers' expense. He shrewdly deferred to Weiser on this, suggesting that Weiser knew all the strategic sites: the gaps in the mountains that, armed with cannon and riflemen, would block any invasion attempts. Before the debate could continue, a breathless Moravian courier ran in and put a stop to all equivocation: the French and Indians had decided the issue. All along Kittatinny Mountain there had been fresh attacks the day before. More than two hundred fifty warriors had slaughtered the newly posted garrison at Gnadenhütten, scalping and burning Association militiamen in the mission's charred ruins.[30]

Once again, the Lehigh Gap lay open, bleeding.

Conspicuously absent from the Reading conference was Bishop Spangenberg, who had warned Franklin that this would happen. When he and Franklin had conferred in Bethlehem a few days before, he had predicted that a general attack would come the first week of January when the moon was new: the Indians felt they were physically strongest then, safest with the least light at night. Though the bishop had based his prediction on information received from Moravian Indians, Franklin dismissed the warning: perhaps his anti-German prejudice blinded him.[31]

More bad news sped to Reading soon afterward: a second Association militia company, which had been dispatched to rescue the Gnadenhütten survivors, had been decimated by the Indians and driven off. The sensation created when the reporting militia officer brought two fresh scalps into the council room led, on January 3, to the defense planners' first decision. Governor Morris, apparently without opposition, offered a bounty of forty pieces of eight, the equivalent of about two years' militia pay, for each Indian scalp.[32] Scalping wounded warriors had been practiced as long ago as Roman times but in America it was, until Morris's bounty encouraged it, restricted to only a few tribes in New York and South Carolina.

By now, even Benjamin Franklin was willing to admit that the Lehigh Gap must be retaken, and quickly, before French and Indian war canoes swept down the Lehigh River to seize Bethlehem. The Franklins had planned to ride west with the governor to confer with any Indians they could drum up. Seeing himself as the great diplomat, the governor instantly agreed. Unencumbered, the Franklins next called for each defense commissioner to direct the defense of the terrain he knew best: Weiser in Berks County; Hamilton in Lancaster County, much of which he owned. This left all of Northampton County to the Franklins, a region only they were familiar with.[33]

When Benjamin Franklin volunteered, Governor Morris had little choice but to accede. But before he accepted responsibility, Franklin boldly placed a few conditions on his commission as county commander. He must have full power to impose martial law, issue all commissions and administer justice. William drafted a writ of dedimus, which gave Franklin absolute power. No common citizen had ever held more power in America. Quickly, Morris signed.

As his first official act, Colonel Franklin ordered that seven key gaps be fortified in only one month, despite winter conditions and Indian resistance. The first was to be at Gnadenhütten.[34]

Panic is a deadly foe. After a week of Indian attacks, all hopes for defense were threatened by the thousands of refugees streaming over hills, blocking roadways, crowding into settlements. The Franklins knew they must stop this headlong confusion by providing stable garrisons: there was no argument among the defense commissioners on this point. The governor took a detachment of thirty Philadelphia cavalry west to Harris's Ferry to confer with Indian leaders and keep order among a thousand milling Scotch-Irish refugees.[35] As Captain Franklin assembled the remaining provincial cavalry, the irony of his situation must have struck him. Only a half-dozen years before, his father's tightfistedness had quashed his ambitions for a military career. Now his father had called on him to be not only aide-de-camp, courier, legal factotum and confidential secretary, but bodyguard and chief military advisor.

For his part, Benjamin wrote hurriedly and tersely to Deborah to send their rifles. His note must have sent a shudder through his wife when she realized that he and William would be within gunshot range of Indian attackers. Other, more urgent notes summoned all available militia companies to Bethlehem on the double — Bethlehem would obviously be the major target of the French-Indian invasion. Some of these notes Franklin dictated himself; others, drafted and signed by William, he added hasty postscripts to. On January 6, 1756, they left for Bethlehem so quickly they forgot to pay their hotel and bar bills. Two years later, angry tavern owners had forgotten the danger but were still trying to collect.[36]

The Franklins immediately found how fragile the fears of runaway frontiersmen had rendered their power. On January 6, they threaded their way all day through crowds of refugees who were carrying salvaged belongings on their backs, on horses, in carts and wagons. Nothing could stem the panicky onrush. That night the Franklins decided on drastic steps. They must reinforce the militia units, hold the refugees at gunpoint, if necessary, discharge wavering local leaders, replace them with loyal commanders from less-exposed townships. Concurrently, they must popularize the cause of arms in the *Gazette*. That same day, the first of a series of vivid accounts of the latest raids was sent by courier to Philadelphia. To arouse complacent city dwellers, the report underscored the desperate danger of the new French-Indian offensive, and to encourage recruits the Franklins dramatized every act of valor, any hint of disaster: the willingness of the militia to stand against overwhelming odds until ammunition was gone; the selfless courage of a commander rescuing a wounded man; the chicanery of the proprietary arms dealers in supplying faulty weapons. Instances of cowardice were edited out. Brilliant war coverage, stirring propaganda, clever subterfuge, the report was ostensibly intended for the governor, but Franklin sent it to Deborah with instructions to deliver it to the *Gazette* for publication. The governor, like everyone else, had to pay to read it. Then the Franklins rode on through fresh snow toward Bethlehem, arriving there the night of the seventh.[37] The Moravians, who were trying to help hordes of refugees, had crowded every basement, hut, barn and dormitory. More than a hundred refugees had been put up at the Crown Inn alone. After settling in at Justice Timothy Horsfield's stone house, which was to be their headquarters for the next eight days, the Franklins made their first maneuver: they warned Bishop Spangenberg that unless the Moravians and the Scotch-Irish would defend themselves, all troops would be removed, leaving the French and Indians a clear field.

In five years as a popular politician, Franklin had first won the support of Anglicans and Presbyterians against Quakers, then of Quakers against the Anglicans of the proprietary party. At Bethlehem, as he assumed real power for the first time, beholden to no party, he challenged the Scotch-Irish. For thirty years they had been coursing through Philadelphia in a great migration to the

Pennsylvania backcountry. An increasingly troublesome minority, they defied the authority of Quaker and proprietary alike. Their squatting had become such a serious problem that the Penns had resorted to burning down their cabins to drive them off unpaid-for lands. In their hatred of the Penns, the Scotch-Irish had espoused Franklin's Association militia enthusiastically. But now they were foolish enough to make demands on him: he must increase the number of their militia companies, put them on the provincial pay-roll, and allow them to choose their own officers or, as William wrote Governor Morris on January 14, "they would leave immedi-ately, one and all, leave their country to the enemy."[38]

Once before, William had had muskets pointed in his face by un-ruly militiamen: he did not cow easily. He had mustered the best troops in the province and his father knew he could rely on them to break the hold of the Scotch-Irish. The elder Franklin refused all demands. He ordered them to leave Bethlehem and take up their proper post defending the Scotch-Irish settlement on the Lehigh River. The Scotch-Irish backed down. By his second day in Bethle-hem, the Moravians were addressing Franklin as "General Lieu-tenant and Commander-in-Chief."[39]

He and William had to deal with a hundred problems. They des-perately needed weapons. At his own expense, Franklin sent off a rider to New York with an order for muskets, not from Morris's in-law Walton, but from a trusted friend. William meanwhile mus-tered troops, formed and drilled new companies. In one week, after assuming command of only thirty-eight effectives, he had 530 troops under arms. The amazing speed with which the Franklins dispatched their troops to prearranged posts over seventy miles of woods and mountains dazzled observers.

The Franklins had little time or desire to adhere to rank. There never was a question of command. Father and son were inter-changeable. Each helped the other to the utmost in their need to accomplish an impossible task in the shortest time. Almost invari-ably William drafted the letters and orders; the elder Franklin was too busy for more than a hurried signature. The orders commis-sioning a German officer, for instance, were as crisp, as precise, as William himself: "You are to allow every man enlisting and bring-ing his own arms and blanket a dollar for the use thereof." The careful ingenuity with which the Franklins sidestepped supply problems showed through: "You are to keep a diary or journal of every day's transactions and an exact account of the time when each man enters himself with you, and if any desert or die, you are to note the time in your journal." William's military experience, along with his care for complete records and for the courts-martial, was communicated with no wasted words. If either Franklin had a twinge of doubt about scalping, it is not evident: "You are to acquaint the men, that if in their ranging they meet with or are at any time attacked by the enemy, and kill any of them, forty dollars will be allowed and paid by the government for each scalp of an Indian enemy so killed, the same being produced with proper attestation."[40] Colonel Franklin made only minor changes in the draft and signed.

To his considerable surprise, the elder Franklin came to enjoy Bethlehem: Bishop Spangenberg was most deferential, receiving them formally. In a rare visit to church, Franklin listened to the preaching "very attentively": the possibility of dying in the days ahead had taken its natural hold. There was, too, a certain generic resemblance between him and the bishop, a tough, blunt ease of authority each recognized and admired. Undeniably, both Franklins enjoyed being treated as men of rank, flattered in the German fashion.[41]

By Friday morning, January 15, the shipment of guns and blankets had arrived from New York and reinforcements, tough Presbyterian volunteers, many of them veterans of Franklin's Association, had hurried in from Bucks County with their chaplain and their surgeon. Among them was Captain Thomas Lloyd, a great-grandson of one of William Penn's councillors. In his diary is the most reliable record of the march to Gnadenhütten.

By noon, they would have to leave. Benjamin sat down to write Deborah: "My dear child, We move this day for Gnadenhütten." His first concern apparently was that she have enough money. He had paid six months' rent before leaving Philadelphia. Now he gave her instructions for collecting his pay. With surprising candor, considering it was wartime, he attempted to reassure her. "We shall have with us about 130 men."[42]

Colonel Franklin was obviously pleased with his son's performance in the four weeks they worked to buttress the frontier. In his autobiography he was to write, "My son was of much use to me."[43] Colonel Franklin now conferred the post of honor on William, who had already taken personal direction of the march as the only experienced officer. Shortly before noon, the company bugler blew assembly. After the men formed ranks under the gaze of the quiet Moravians, the Franklins passed slowly by in inspection. For days, William had trained his rangers, selecting the best. Now he showed them off. "This day, before we marched," wrote Captain Lloyd, "the several companies were drawn up on a parade and attended with ordered firelocks in the most solemn manner to an excellent prayer and animating exhortation delivered by the Reverend Mr. [Charles] Beatty and immediately after began their march, which was conducted by Mr. William Franklin with great order and regularity."[44]

Captain Franklin had to assume that their every move would be watched, that the Indians would use their favorite tactic, ambush. There were still rumors of a twelve-hundred-man French and Indian force in the area, and two hundred Indians had taken part in the last raid on Gnadenhütten. William would deploy his men so that they could reinforce each other quickly. Mounted rangers, serving as scouts, would fan out in front and on the sides, with Captain Franklin riding on point. As the column advanced, other scouts would ride ahead to the top of each hill to reconnoiter. Next would come a company of twenty-three Philadelphia cavalry and two hundred yards behind them the vanguard company of Moravian pioneers, many of them wrapped in blankets for want of winter coats. In the center would come Colonel Franklin, Beatty, Lloyd, the Moravian assemblyman William Edmonds, seven supply wagons and the Franklin kitchen wagon.[45] A company of armed Moravians, followed by a group of mounted rangers, would bring up the rear.

Advancing northwest along the Lehigh River, they covered roughly six miles that first afternoon. The little force, strung out over a mile, must have appeared unlike any column the French had ever seen: a tree with no trunk to girdle and cut, instead all branches and leaves. It advanced slowly, every man trained to take cover quickly as horsemen flushed hidden Indians. It would take a large force of Indians to surround this snaking, spreading column in the open.

By nightfall they had reached Hay's Tavern at Allen's Town, where the eighteen survivors of the most recent raid at Gnadenhütten were given fresh weapons and joined the line of march. That night, Captain Isaac Wayne and his fifty-three Chester County volunteers caught up with them. The captain had also brought along his ten-year-old-son Anthony. One day Anthony would become a Revolutionary War general. "Much of the evening was spent exchanging the bad arms for the good," Benjamin Franklin wrote to the provincial Council.[46] The next morning the brash little army stepped off to the beat of Anthony's drum and cut northwest over open country as quickly as the heavy Conestogas would allow. They marched twelve miles the second day out. That morning, in the distance, they could see the fog-shrouded Kittatinny ridge ahead: all along their right flank was a sheer hemlock-stubbled bluff, perfect for Indian snipers. As they approached, Captain Franklin kept his rangers far in front and on the right flank as horsemen and wagons hugged the rushing, falling Lehigh River on their left. For the first time in his life, Benjamin Franklin knew what it was like to have enemies sighting down gun barrels at him. The sharp spatter of gunfire reached his ears. Fortunately, the rangers did their work well: no Indian got close enough to hit his target.[47]

By midafternoon, the wind rose to a baleful moan as it rushed through the thousand-foot-high cleft of the gap. The road had become a rutted, muddy slash and the woods hid the riverbanks. So close was the ridge, that the right side of each wide-topped wagon threatened to scrape it. If any attack came, the Franklins were certain it would be right here. As they approached, Captain Franklin slowed the column and the wagons ponderously creaked through the hemlock-lined defile. There was more shooting, but again the Indians failed to come within range. Slowly the wagons wrenched free of the axle-deep mud, lurched through the dangerous pass. Ahead of them, the stone and plank barn of Uplinger's farm emerged from the fog, as reassuring as any fortress. After Captain Franklin posted pickets, Captain Lloyd took out his journal and wrote: "Jan 16th this days march was attended with more danger and difficulty . . . the narrow pass through the mountains made by the Lehigh where the rocks overhang the road on each side . . . render it practicable for a very small number to destroy a thousand."

The rain poured down the next morning. Though it was Franklin's fiftieth birthday, there was little opportunity to celebrate. The men were quickly soaked as they answered the bugle call. Though they sloshed off, they did not get far. Communication between ranger units and commanders was impossible in the thick fog. Marching as if hunched in prayer, unable to see even a pistol shot away, the men were ordered to turn back. The rest of the day they took turns huddling around the cookfires. That evening, firing broke out near the barn. Indian infiltrators, undoubtedly part of a sizable force taking this moment to surprise the sleeping men, stumbled in the dark fog into a sentry post. Quickly, sentries fired at point-blank range. The Indians fled as more sentries rushed up firing.

The next morning it had cleared enough to go on. "Part of our route this day was through the worst country I ever saw," Dr. Lloyd recorded. "Hills like Alps on each side and a long narrow defile where the road scarcely admitted a single wagon. At the bottom of it a rapid creek with steep banks and a bridge made of a single log situated so that the Indians might with safety to themselves from the caverns in the rocks have cut us all off notwithstanding all human precaution. Yet we arrived safe at Gnadenhütten."[48]

The hard march and the harsh weather were obliterated by the sight of the little clumps of scalped, frozen bodies, mounded with fresh snow, that William Franklin discovered as he led the advance guard into the burned-out village. But the dead would have to wait. First, the men had to dig a line of trenches three feet deep at the junction of the Lehigh River and Mahoning Creek. By loading dirt into baskets and binding them together into breastworks, the men were musket-proof within three hours. Using planks carted with them, they then made huts where guns, if not men, could remain dry. All the next day they waited in the huts for their turns on guard duty and patrol.[49] The Franklins did not waste the time. The task would go faster if they unslung the Conestoga bodies and used the wheels to help the horses drag in logs as they were felled. These timbers were eighteen feet long, cut, trimmed and pointed by teams of Moravian axmen.

The fog cleared enough on January 20 to "mark out our fort on the ground and by 10 o'clock begin to cut timber," the Franklins reported. "By 3 . . . the logs were all cut and many of them hauled to the spot. . . . That evening many were pointed and set up."[50] William guarded the workmen and dispatched and led patrols while his father engrossed himself in what, to him, was a fascinating exercise in engineering. The circumference of the fort measured 455 feet, which would require, he calculated, trees a foot in diameter. "Our axes, of which we had 70, were immediately set to work . . . and our men being dexterous in the use of them, great dispatch was made. Seeing the trees fall so fast, I had the curiosity to look at my watch when two men began to cut into a pine. In six minutes they had it upon the ground. . . . Each pine made three palisades of eighteen feet long."[51]

For five weeks, the Franklins had planned, schemed and harangued to get other men to fortify the frontier. In five days they built the key fort themselves. On Friday, January 22, 1756, this puny piece of defiance thirty miles inside enemy lines, little more than a stout wood fence surrounding men standing on a platform to fire through loopholes, was dedicated. Benjamin Franklin, the politician, ironically named it Fort Allen after the proprietary chief justice, who was sitting safely by his fireside in Philadelphia. William Franklin, the soldier, who presided over the ceremony, wrote about it later: "This day we hoisted your flag, made a general discharge of our pieces which had been long loaded, and of our two swivels."[52]

The Franklins had spiked the French winter offensive.

Despite the danger deep inside Indian-dominated territory, the Franklins were in no hurry to return to Philadelphia. Never in all their twenty-five years of collaboration had they been closer than in these seven weeks, when they shared the risks, the camaraderie, the discoveries of life in the wilderness. The experience had been personally gratifying for each man, but in different ways. Trusted with command, William bravely led off work parties fifteen miles to the east and to the west. The green-wood forts they erected would have amused a French military engineer but cowed the Indians, who dreaded frontal assault, and encouraged the settlers to return to their farms. For Benjamin, the direct daily power of a frontier dictator was new and intriguing: no food or weapon or even medical treatment was dispensed in the northern half of Pennsylvania unless the applicant lined up in front of his small headquarters, a hut just inside the front gate of Fort Allen.

To keep morale high, Colonel Franklin shrewdly administered a combination of rum and prayer. "We had for our chaplain a zealous Presbyterian minister, Mr. Beatty," he wrote in his autobiography, "who complained to me that the men did not generally attend his prayers and exhortations." Having seen that the men all showed up punctually for the twice-daily rum ration, he suggested to Beatty, "It is perhaps below the dignity of your profession to act as steward of the rum. But if you were to deal it out, and only just after prayers, you would have them all about you."[53] Beatty complied, and prayer services were henceforth well and enthusiastically attended.

All day the Franklins were busy, William leading work parties and patrols, drilling troops, keeping the muster rolls for every unit under his father's command, carrying out the dozens of duties of a chief of staff and secretary of the defense commission. His father's activities are hinted at in a half-complaining, half-proud letter to Deborah, his first in fifteen days: "Here comes in a number of people from different parts that have business with me." He later would make a lesson of their Spartan life ("there are a great number of things besides what we have that used to seem necessary to comfortable living, yet we have learned to do without them") but he urged Deborah to send nothing more for now. Again he reassured her that she was thought of kindly: "All the gentlemen send their compliments, they drink your health at every meal, having always something on the table to put them in mind of you." As usual, he was careful not to tell Deborah of William's conduct. He mentioned only that they had to sleep side by side wrapped in their capes on the floor of the hut. "We have but one room and that quite public." And he underscored the cool formality between

Deborah and William by adding, "Billy presents his duty to you and love to his sister."[54]

Around the campfire in the evenings, the Franklins had time for long talks. One topic can be surmised. In this fifty-day wilderness foray, the first time the Franklins had faced the frontier together, William began to make his father see for himself what it was that drove him: the vision of indescribable wealth and power derived from western lands. It was a dream of other young soldiers of fortune of William's age and the quest that had brought so many to the New World; now it laid its Midas grip on Benjamin Franklin as well as on his son. They began to build an empire in their minds, to plot their greatest adventure, one that would hold them together even as all other bonds dissolved over the next twenty years. In the long vigilant evenings at Fort Allen, the Franklins turned their minds and their ambitions to the West.

In his 1754 Albany Plan of Union, Benjamin had advocated permanent frontier forts manned by an intercolonial peace-keeping force. He had also suggested a buffer zone of new provinces west of the Appalachians. The plan had been too visionary then and had been defeated piecemeal by each colony. But now the major justifications were once again evident around them. The Quakers would never consent to a standing army. The Germans would never serve in one. Except under direct attack by invaders, coastal merchants would never pay to maintain adequate interior defenses. Stockades, the Franklins knew, were only a frail expedient, an illusion of security to induce frontier settlers to return to their farms, where they blunted attacks on the more populous counties. But if endless warfare was to be averted, endless vigilance was necessary and there were men who, if paid in land and cash, were willing to move west and set up new colonies in river valleys where the rich, unclaimed forests and lush grazing and hunting lands could accommodate thousands of new settlers.

Months later, when the elder Franklin finally grew mortally tired of Philadelphia politics and determined to plead his cause personally before Parliament, he intimated the scope of his and William's ambition in a letter to an old friend, the revival preacher George Whitefield: "I sometimes wish that you and I were jointly employed by the Crown to settle the West. I imagine we could do it effectually, without putting the nation to much expense. . . . What a glorious thing it would be to settle in that fine country a large strong body of religious and industrious people! What a security to the other colonies and advantage to Britain by increasing her people, territory, strength and commerce. . . . Life, like a dramatic piece, should not only be conducted with regularity but methinks it should finish handsomely. Being now in the last act, I begin to cast about for something fit to end with."[55]

Since William was not mentioned in reports to the governor, the inference is left that all his defensive efforts — his brave, successful marches and fort-building sorties — were actually carried out by his father. For years, William had dutifully set aside his own ambitions to work in harness with his father. At the same time, he had interrupted his law studies, had put off courtship, had done little to make a permanent place for himself, always loyally furthering his father's affairs in the apparent belief that what was good for Benjamin Franklin was good for all the Franklins. There had been warning signs: when his father sold his business, when his father told him he intended to spend what he had earned and not pass it on. But William preferred to dismiss these omens good-naturedly. There is no record that he resented his father's building almost exclusively on his military experience and diplomatic skill, and taking full credit for rescuing the Pennsylvania frontier. If the injustice rankled under these slights, he gave no outward sign of it. The chance for a share in a great western empire, for the millions of acres the Penns and their retainers had claimed in just such a situation, was no doubt a powerful inducement to renewed patience, even to a young man of twenty-five.

As always happened when the Franklins found time together, politics intervened to blight their relationship. It was that man Morris again. This time he ignored the plans laid at Reading and called a special Assembly session in which he planned to present not a treaty of peace with the Indians but a plan of war. Worse, Morris had deserted the frontier and had led his troops back to the capital. Furious, the Franklins, at the head of their cavalry troopers, charged off toward Philadelphia on February 4. They rode so hard they had to stop briefly at Bethlehem to have Benjamin's broken bridle repaired and his horse reshod. Covering eighty-five miles of difficult road in less than two days, they clattered into Philadelphia late at night.[56]

When the Assembly was called to order early the next morning, a determined Benjamin Franklin took his seat at the Philadelphia table and William took up his quill. As William's hand moved across the lined foolscap, his father rose to urge the timid Assembly to oppose any further continuation of the folly that had brought their province to the brink of civil war. The proprietary party must be opposed, if necessary by force. Outside the State House, as if to underscore the urgency of Franklin's arguments, two regiments of troops, one loyal to him, the other urged to arms by Morris, maneuvered in the streets.[57] For the moment at least, the dream of a wilderness empire must tantalize from afar. The Franklins must first fight to protect their own freedom in the streets and caucus rooms of Philadelphia. And they were ready.

5

THE PEOPLE HAPPEN
TO LOVE ME

1756–1757

DAY AFTER DAY, BENJAMIN FRANKLIN ROSE IN THE STATE
House to oppose Governor Morris's plan for all-out attack on
the French and Indians even as rival proprietary militia units
formed throughout Pennsylvania. By late February 1756, the
Franklins had become convinced that political action was no longer
sufficient to stop the governor. They must confront him in the
streets in a test of military strength, risking the hangman's noose if
necessary to depose him.

For more than two weeks after the Franklins' return from the
frontier, the governor and the Council had stalled in confirming
commissions in the Franklin forces. Backed by the Quakers, the
Scotch-Irish and the Germans, the Franklins had raised more
troops, this time forming a Philadelphia Association regiment of infantry and an artillery company. Morris, supported by a small number of Anglicans, merchants and proprietary officeholders, refused
them commissions, stalling again as he made a final attempt to buy
off Benjamin Franklin. If Franklin would lead his troops west to attack the French, the governor would make him a general. Franklin
coolly refused.

Even though he had the backing of the Assembly, without
proper commissions signed by the governor Franklin was powerless
to muster city troops. Finally, unexpectedly, Morris ignored the
advice of his proprietary councillors and, on February 24, decided

to commission Franklin a colonel. Yet it was an act of duplicity, for Morris was also issuing commissions to his own men when no regiment could legally have two sets of officers.

Benjamin accepted Morris's commission as colonel, but he ordered William to move fast. In just four hours, Captain Franklin gathered seven hundred armed men and led them to the State House yard. After parading the units past the Assembly, he quickmarched the troops east to the Academy of Philadelphia, where proprietary officers were at that moment forming their own regiment. Franklin troops surrounded the main academy building and shouted for the Penn leaders to come out. Most of the proprietary soldiers were terrified college students: they slipped out the side door and fled.

When the governor's backers still derided the Franklin militia in the next week's papers, William decided it was high time for a show of force that would end all proprietary resistance. He designed a military demonstration such as colonial America had never seen before. After drilling twelve hundred men in heavy snow for a week, on March 14 he led them in a grand review. Preceded by boys playing oboes, fifes and drums, and by a contingent of German axmen in buckskins, the Philadelphia Regiment in red and green uniforms marched past the governor's mansion on Second Street. The governor stayed inside. As the first company reached the specially built reviewing stands on Society Hill, which were filled to overflowing, thousands of spectators began to cheer. On William's orders, each platoon fired a salute and retreated.

To ram the point home, William saved the heaviest firing for last. One hundred smartly maneuvering artillerymen paraded thirteen heavy guns drawn by teams of massive Conestoga horses past the stands, wheeled them, and fired toward the river until the air was thick with merging clouds of smoke. For two hours more, the Franklin troops marched through the streets. At the center of the column, in the post of honor arranged for him by his son, was Colonel Benjamin Franklin. The grand review ended with a swing north past Colonel Franklin's house. When the troops turned and fired one last salute, the electrical apparatus inside his long-neglected laboratory was jarred by the gunfire, fell to the floor, and shattered.

A few days later, Governor Robert Hunter Morris sent a letter of resignation to Thomas Penn in London. Momentarily, the Franklins had won the test of power, at least until the Penns could send out a new governor from England.[1]

Only weeks after returning from the frontier expedition that had brought him so close to his father, William Franklin did something that infinitely complicated their relationship — he fell in love.

As William seceded from his father's political circle, he had drawn closer to the aristocrats of the opposing proprietary party. There is little direct evidence of what he was thinking during this period: none of his papers have survived — or at least none have come to light. Yet his activities can be traced through the records of the organizations in which he was prominent. At a time when he was constantly under his father's domination and hardly got along with Deborah, his voluntary associations show how far he was willing to diverge from his father's views. Indeed, his behavior in Philadelphia at this stage provides insights into his future course of action and underscores the deepening differences of opinion between them.

While his father always eschewed church membership (even if he considered himself a Presbyterian), William had become an active Anglican. He helped to organize a lottery to build the handsome new Anglican citadel, Christ Church. He helped to raise money for its spire, the highest in colonial America, and for its eight chime carillon. Like his father, he was always involved in a variety of projects, often interconnected. As soon as he had returned from the Canadian frontier war in 1748, he also helped to organize the Philadelphia Assembly, the first permanent dancing assembly in America, made up of eighty families of wealthy Anglican merchants, shipowners and landed gentry, the city's rising new elite. In colonial Philadelphia this was a bold act. For years, ever since New Light Presbyterian fundamentalists had padlocked a waterfront warehouse where earlier dances had been held, public dancing had been frowned on in Philadelphia.

To provide an appropriate home for the Assembly balls, William and his friends evidently resorted to a little subterfuge. Many of them were, like William, also members of the Freemasons. William worked hard to bring together three rival Masonic groups so that, with the pooled assets of artisans and gentlemen, they built the new Masonic Hall in Lodge Alley. Here, every other Friday from February through May, the Assembly held its cotillions in rooms obviously designed to accommodate their tastes. It may have been at one of these Assembly balls in the late winter of 1756 that the dashing officer who had led the march to Gnadenhütten became interested in a seventeen-year-old debutante named Elizabeth Graeme.

The ritual of the Assembly balls gave William ample opportunities to see Betsy publicly that winter. On Assembly nights, for six hours at least, Philadelphia's proprietary elite put the dissensions of war and politics aside for the stylized harmony of the minuet and the harpsichord. The ball began promptly at six. As the eight chime Christ Church carillon rang the hour, carriages were already queued up before Freemasons Hall. By 1756, the dancing Assembly, in its eighth year of fortnightly subscription balls, had become the center of Philadelphia social life. In all colonial America, no event could rival its elegant gatherings.

By the time the last couple in line handed in playing-card invitations to the managers greeting them at the door, the preparations for the ball had been going on for days, filling Society Hill's richest houses with a titillation that must have thoroughly scandalized Quaker neighbors. Nothing in William Penn's scheme of a simple life presaged the spectacle of women lining up in chairs at wigmakers' shops for hours of combing, powdering and beribboning, or of ladies sleeping bolt upright in special chairs so that their coiffures would survive until the next night's ball. Certainly it had taken thrifty artisans like Benjamin Franklin a long time to become accustomed to the sight of servants carrying massive silver waiters, bowls and tankards along Second Street as the subscribers provisioned Freemasons Hall with food and drink for the feast that would end the evening.

In the receiving line were scores of Philadelphians who regarded a thriving social life as an integral part of a rising new political and economic order, one based not on birth or religion but on mercantile wealth. Yet men of heraldic rank were still held in higher esteem than men who made their money in trade. Regularly taking their places behind their ladies' brocaded chairs were the brother of

the late Queen Anne's secretary of state, the brother of a hereditary Scottish lord, a former governor, twenty-eight other proprietary officials, and one member of the Penn family. Lavishly
dressed, they stood in clusters around the Assembly room sipping
cider provided by uniformed footmen as they waited for the dancing and the card playing to begin.

It was, to be sure, an odd place in which to find the son of Benjamin Franklin, an enemy of three quarters of the Assembly members, but these were William's friends, men he had gone to school
with, served with, marched and worshipped with. Among them
were former Quakers of shifting principles who had rejected pacifism as they accumulated fortunes in illicit trade with the French
West Indies and with the Indians on the frontier. Tens of thousands of hardscrabble frontiersmen had paid their quitrents in
scarce silver to provide the costly gowns of the members' wives and
daughters.[2]

At precisely six, the ladies took seats along both sides of the
candlelit room with the gentlemen ranged behind them. The manager presented each dancer with a dance card, called a billet, which
contained a number. A duplicate set of numbered cards had been
randomly arranged in a silver basket. The manager then drew one
of the cards from the basket and called off the number. The lady
and gentleman whose billet numbers matched it were paired off for
the evening — all six hours of it. It is most probable that it was
William's good fortune to draw Betsy Graeme at one of these
dances. There could have been few more striking debutantes at the
Philadelphia cotillion that winter than the tall, slender Betsy. Her
portrait shows her with dark hair modestly gathered back and
hanging in long curls, her white gown cut low and weighted with
brocade. William, tall, handsome, ten years her senior, was fascinated by what another of the dancers called "that cat-eyed Bessie."
And there certainly could have been few more romantic settings: as
the dancers stepped to the center of the floor, the fiddlers broke
into the first minuet of the evening and a long and troubled courtship began.[3]

Not everyone had reason to applaud as William and Betsy met
each other to carry out the intricate turns of the contredanses. Al-

though Dr. Graeme, as a member of the governor's Council, had no doubt read enthusiastic reports of the young captain's conspicuous valor on the frontier, he had known the Franklins too long to regard this youth as anything more than an opportunistic extension of his old political foe Benjamin Franklin. Graeme's wife obviously did not share his opinion. She had also known Benjamin Franklin for years, in fact from the first months after his arrival from Boston nearly thirty-five years before. Ann Keith was her name then. She was the daughter of Sir William Keith, the governor of Pennsylvania, and she may have remembered how her father, a historian of some repute, had taken to the brash, articulate young printer, even promising to give him the provincial printing business. There was a strong resemblance between that tall, cocky young Franklin who had ridden in the Keith coach talking history with her father and this handsome young officer with his polished gorget, his braided epaulet. She could not have been at all unhappy with the possibilities.

For William and Betsy, little could distract from the pleasure of the ball. The young couples executed the turning-away, wheeling-past, turning-again-and-sweeping-low maneuvers of the minuet, danced to the concertinos of Corelli, the favorite music of these gatherings. But there was more to interest William in young Betsy than an intriguing face and a light step to the music. Few in the room could have been better educated at a time when the classics were the rage of English society: both had mastered Latin and Greek and delighted not only in music but poetry and sculpture. Betsy would one day become a locally celebrated poet, the leader of the Philadelphia literary salon.

After the last dance ended, the manager announced the buffet supper. The guests filed past the supper tables, where each matron served her specialty: West Indies pepperpot soup, a made dish of gammon, roast suckling pig, duck, chicken, and shamelessly rich desserts — tarts, custards, jellies, syllabub, heavy cream-covered trifle — all accompanied by round after round of punch, porter and beer.

Benjamin Franklin had no time for dinner dances. There is no record that he ever attended an Assembly ball, even if all the rest of his family did. He was not like his lawyer-son, whose training as a professional adversary had taught him to adjourn his emotions until another day in court. In a deadly duel for control of a city-state that had moved from the military stage to intensive behind-the-scenes intriguing, Benjamin was implacably opposed to his former friends.

During his rise to become the most powerful man in Pennsylvania, there had been a number of defections in his personal circle. His wife's cousin, the orthodox Quaker leader Israel Pemberton, was now defying Franklin and the Assembly by openly sending unauthorized Quaker emissaries to negotiate a private peace with the Indians. Not only was Quaker trade suffering, but Quaker missionaries from London had stirred up fervent Quakers to oppose any more bloodshed. Pemberton had also sided with Chief Justice Allen, Franklin's enemy, in opposing Franklin's colonelcy. Once Franklin's mentor, Allen was spinning off fresh intrigues against him on both sides of the ocean. Though biding his time until the new proprietary governor arrived, Allen was secretly working to reverse the Franklin militia law and have Franklin's commission invalidated even as he ordered large quantities of arms for his mercantile firm to profit from by keeping the fighting alive.

One further blow came when another of Franklin's old friends, the Reverend William Smith, took control of the board of the Academy of Philadelphia. After ousting Franklin from the chairmanship and replacing him with a Penn official, Smith busied himself with filling key faculty posts with classical scholars who opposed Franklin's pragmatic program of education. On every front, hostility from the Penn faction was increasing. Benjamin Franklin was learning the tenuous nature of a politician's friendships.[4]

It could not have particularly pleased him to find out that his only son was dancing every week with the daughter of another old friend-turned-enemy. When Franklin's only political job had been as clerk of the legislative Assembly, Dr. Graeme was friendly enough. The two men had worked together to form the first fire insurance company in Philadelphia. But their relations had cooled early in 1756 when the Philadelphia Hospital was opened. Franklin, as president, was empowered to make staff appointments. Instead of awarding the first paid appointment to Dr. Graeme (who had long served as port physician without pay), Franklin hired a younger man. Graeme never forgave him. As a member of the provincial supreme court and of the governor's Council, he was in an advantageous position to retaliate. He attempted to wreck the Franklin party's majority in the Assembly by engineering the expansion of voting districts, and very nearly succeeded. In addition, Graeme was the one who had suggested the Penns' strategic gift of uncollectible quitrents, the ploy that enabled them to avoid taxation of proprietary lands and to blunt the force of the German refugees' march on Philadelphia.[5]

That Betsy Graeme was so strongly attracted to Captain Franklin must have seemed a cruel irony to her father. Dr. Graeme probably had heard the whispers undoubtedly circulated by Benjamin Franklin's onetime confidant, Dr. Smith, that William was a bastard, the baseborn son of a serving wench. Not that Benjamin had any franchise on illegitimacy: all three of Governor Morris's sons were bastards. Moreover, the Graeme family history was clouded: the second husband of Betsy's grandmother, Governor William Keith, had sired at least two illegitimate children who were still living in Philadelphia.

As his letters to her indicate, Dr. Graeme held a special affection for his Betsy. He had lavished a classical education on this intelligent and gifted young girl, and his wealth enabled him to display her talents. Indeed, on the revenues from his wife's estate and his lucrative medical practice the Graemes lived as sumptuously as any other Philadelphians. In the spacious town house on Society Hill and on their fourteen-hundred-acre country estate at Horsham, the Graemes entertained like Scottish lords, which, indeed, their ancestors had been. Dr. Graeme could hardly have wished to admit the bastard of a lowly printer, much less the bastard of an upstart political enemy, into his refined circle.

As William's determination to see more of Betsy intensified, he must have realized the delicacy of his situation: everyone of substance in Pennsylvania knew that the Graeme estate was the stronghold of fashionable proprietary society. As a skilled soldier, Captain Franklin knew he could not take this bastion by frontal assault. He would need a strategy: he began to seek ways to put himself more in the path of Betsy Graeme. There were carefully prescribed rituals to sustain and guide him.

In the winter he could see Betsy at Christ Church on Sundays after the service and at the fortnightly Assembly balls. Another possibility was at tea in one of the town houses on Society Hill — as an eligible bachelor, William could expect invitations from other Assembly members — and on ice-skating parties. Young Philadelphians were proud of their prowess as figure skaters and on Sunday afternoons gathered by the hundreds on the thick ice of the Delaware River. Sleigh rides provided William with yet another opportunity. On midwinter mornings, young socialites were bundled into bearskin robes and driven at a fast clip out the Ridge Road. At an inn beside Wissahickon Creek, they took turns singing and skipping through the paces of high-spirited country square dances to the tunes played by fiddlers brought along for the purpose, and flirted over pewter mugs of hot buttered rum in front of the massive fireplaces. Then they raced back to the city over the snow in time for an evening performance of the latest comedy from London.

But to call on Betsy, to spend time alone with her, William needed a sponsor. Apparently he found one in Mrs. Margaret Abercrombie, the mother of his good friend the curate of Christ Church. Mrs. Abercrombie invited Betsy and William to her afternoon teas in her Society Hill drawing room, where the young couple could talk intimately over innumerable cups of Bohea tea after she excused herself to see to her other chores.[6]

The approach of summer called for a refinement of tactics. Warm weather always aroused a restless hypochondria in William's father, who sought excuses to flee the city. Suddenly Benjamin Franklin was willing to relinquish control of militia and Assembly on the pretext of inspecting postal routes. This summer, the success of his defensive plan and the arrival of a new governor, a seasoned army veteran, made his absence for several months less likely. But if he expected his son and aide to accompany him, he was doomed to disappointment. William declined to go, pleading the press of legal and postal business. As Benjamin must have known, however, William had asked permission of Dr. and Mrs.

Graeme to call formally on their daughter when the family withdrew to its country estate for the summer.[7]

It was a serious step, requiring much behind-the-scenes maneuvering. Betsy's sister Ann, who was married to an ironmaster named Charles Stedman, knew William both as a fellow Dancing Assembly member and as a politician. Stedman was a proprietary member of the city council and was running for the legislative Assembly. Another sister was married to the commissary general of the provincial army, who was just returning from a frontier tour and could speak at first hand of William's winter soldiering. Dr. Graeme could not go against the collective wishes of his family and expect any peace in the isolated confines of his summer retreat. Begrudgedly he yielded. William could call on Betsy but only under the doctor's watchful eye and only if the young man would abandon some of his undesirable political activities.

One particular Franklin insult to the Penns, probably perpetrated by William, must have galled the Graemes that spring and made it necessary for Betsy to put William on especially good behavior. When Benjamin left to ride south, William summoned fifty cavalrymen to escort him, led by officers riding with their sabers bared. It was an honor reserved for governors and kings, one never before accorded in Pennsylvania, even to the Penns. Outraged, proprietary officials once again wrote England to complain of Franklin impertinence.[8]

But a saber's slash could not have cut much deeper than William's words all through that politically tempestuous spring. Under his pen name of Humphrey Scourge, he once again chastised proprietary officials in print. In a letter to the Pennsylvania *Journal,* "Mild Advice to a Certain Parson," William upbraided his father's former friend the Reverend Smith and accused him of currying the favor of the "great ones" in hopes of being appointed "Bishop of America."[9] William took pride in his deliciously scurrilous prose almost as much as the Graemes were outraged by it.

The view ahead as William urged his horse north along Bethlehem Pike toward Graeme Park blotted out the controversies of the city behind him. For a few days, the young captain was escaping the Philadelphia summer, the undrained swamps, the swarms of insects carrying deadly epidemics. Almost anyone who could afford a place in the country fled the city from July to October. More than two hours out, William had to rein his horse left onto a long flat road leading through an oak grove to the entrance of Graeme Park. Here, the trees were set wider. They were groomed and pruned to form an arched approach through pastures speckled with cows, sheep and herds of deer. The carefully arranged pastoral scene must have enchanted William as he aimed his horse toward the red sandstone house at the vanishing point down the long lane. Distinguished by walls two feet thick and by cavernous, outsized windows that allowed the breezes to pass through the rooms, the house must have seemed a cool refuge after the hot ride from the city. Inside, the high-ceilinged parlor, where William, Betsy, and their friends conversed, was a careful classical evocation, with green painted panels, Corinthian columns flanking the fireplace, three gilded mirrors reflecting busts of Roman poets, and a dozen paintings of native birds. This room and the company in it was all that William aspired to.

To pass an afternoon in British colonial society in 1756 required a classical education — conversation was expected to be sprinkled with classical allusions — and a thirst for tea. It was not uncommon for the hostess to refill her guest's cup fourteen, even fifteen, times. When the guest could drink no more, he signaled defeat by placing his spoon across the cup to bar another filling.

The presence of Mrs. Graeme must have helped to alleviate the tension of Dr. Graeme's vigilance. Yet surviving Dr. Graeme's disapproval was essential to William's ambition, which now centered around Betsy. There were long evenings in the moonlight, long, lingering walks through formal gardens and around the millpond and behind the screens of low-hanging catalpa trees. On one of these quiet, unhurried evenings, William apparently found the courage to ask Betsy, not yet eighteen, to marry him.

Betsy accepted, but not, as William soon learned, without conditions. She had no desire for a life pinned between her husband's and her father's political swordpoints. Since Dr. Graeme and Franklin were old enemies, it would be difficult enough for her to win her father over to the idea of having a Franklin for a son-in-law. The only way she could hope to accomplish this was to promise him that

William would never again indulge in factional politics, never again use his pen to attack her father's friends and relatives. The infatuated William agreed.

When Benjamin returned from Virginia, he must have bristled at the news of the engagement. But he had become a politician and was, above all, a practical man. He had refused to support his son or to promise to leave him a substantial estate. The Graemes, of course, could be expected to provide their daughter with a substantial dowry. And the marriage of the most powerful assemblyman's son to the daughter of a ranking proprietary official was more than a marriage: it was a political alliance with far-reaching promise. Soon, as William continued to visit his betrothed, Benjamin began to visit his long-ago friend, her mother.[10]

The distance between William's personal life and his connection to his father closed unexpectedly in the summer of 1756 in a political development that neither man had foreseen. Ashamed and disgusted with a formal British declaration of war against their old friends the Indians and with their own involvement in the bloodshed of recent years, the Quakers of Philadelphia decided to stop compromising their religious ideals and, after seventy-five years in power, resign en masse from the Assembly. Just returned from his southern sojourn, Benjamin Franklin could not restrain his jubilance. "All the Stiff-rumps except one," he wrote a friend in London, "have voluntarily quitted the Assembly."[11]

The resulting power vacuum pulled the Franklins and their proprietary rivals into a climactic swirl that ended only when Franklin took complete control of the State House in the fall elections. To their surprise, Penn partisans found that Franklin had already won the support of many leading Anglicans — men they had expected to fill Quaker seats. One disgusted proprietary man wrote to Thomas Penn, "The Old Churchmen are infected, they are mere Franklinists . . . creatures . . . partisans . . . minions."[12]

In a final effort to win Franklin over, Penn sent instructions with his new governor, Colonel Francis Denny, to take Benjamin aside and offer him a long list of inducements. They came wrapped in the heady praise of British scientists for Franklin's electrical experiments. It was the first that Philadelphia learned he had been elected to the Royal Society and awarded the Copley medal, its highest honor. Even at the presentation banquet politics intruded. "After dinner," Franklin later wrote, "when the company were engaged in drinking, he [the new governor] took me aside into another room and acquainted me that he had been advised by his friends in England to cultivate a friendship with me as one who was capable of giving him the best advice. . . . He said much . . . of the advantage it might be to us all, and to me in particular, if the opposition that had been so long continued to [Penn] measures were dropped. . . . I might depend on adequate acknowledgements and recompenses. The drinkers, finding we did not return immediately to the table, sent us a decanter of Madeira, which the governor made liberal use of, and in proportion became more profuse in his . . . promises. . . . My circumstances, thanks to God, were such as to make proprietary favors unnecessary."[13] Instead, Franklin ran his own hand-picked slate of candidates against the Penn ticket. One of them defeated Betsy Graeme's brother-in-law Charles Stedman.

As long ago as July 1755, when Benjamin and William were rounding up supplies for the ill-fated Braddock expedition, Chief Justice William Allen, the most powerful member of the proprietary party in Pennsylvania, had secretly circulated a petition asking the royal government to take steps against the popular Franklin party. He warned London officials that "if the malevolent party that is opposed to [the Penn] interest and government do not receive a check from England, both their power and estate will be rendered very precarious. . . . There is a conspiracy among the leaders of the opposition to destroy both."[14]

On the day the Franklin Militia Act was signed into law, Chief Justice Allen wrote to London to ask the King to intervene. He labeled the militia law "impracticable and ridiculous" but revealed the real fear of many pro-Penn Englishmen in the province: "One-half the inhabitants of this province are foreigners. . . . They have, in their own country, generally been soldiers. . . . They in the militia bill have the choice of their own officers. . . . They may join the enemy and drive out the English inhabitants." Smith implied that their organizers and leaders, the Franklins, would be at the head of an anti-British army.[15]

For many years, Proprietor Thomas Penn had been growing

more and more alarmed by Benjamin Franklin's ability to gather men about him in emergencies. When Franklin raised the first Philadelphia militia in 1748, Penn ordered his deputy governor to be careful of Franklin because he appeared to be "a tribune of the people." But when the Franklins boldly took control of the city in March of 1756, and then had the effrontery to march with sabers bared through its streets, the Penns could make a strong case before the Board of Trade and Plantations in London that the man was a dangerous republican and ought to be stopped.[16]

Colonial laws could be passed only subject to the approval of the Crown; that is, a powerful committee of noblemen on the King's Privy Council could recommend that the King veto any law at his pleasure. Thomas Penn had powerful connections, including Lord Halifax, the president of the Board of Trade, and the duke of Cumberland, who had little patience with popular movements. It was Cumberland who had bloodily put down the last Scottish rebellion, and he had been instrumental in choosing one of his own officers as the new governor of Pennsylvania. Moreover, as all-out war had once again been declared against France, a controversy raged in England over the use and value of militia. Until the question could be resolved by Parliament, no upstart colonial legislature would be allowed to pass its own militia law.

At a stroke of King George II's hand, the Pennsylvania Militia Act was abrogated. Along the frontier, in the State House in Philadelphia, there was consternation. All commissions from the Assembly, all military and defensive plans, all treaties with the Indians were in jeopardy. Specifically, Benjamin Franklin's commission as commander of frontier troops as well as the defense commission were abolished.

Following up their stunning behind-the-scenes victory, the Penns launched a campaign to punish Franklin for his opposition: they attempted to have him stripped of his lucrative source of income, the deputy postmastership.

It was now abundantly clear to Franklin that he must hurry to London to defend in person not only Pennsylvania's interests but his own, to protect both from court politicians by appealing to Parliament to defend the colony's rights. William, of course, must go along with him to help him prepare the Assembly's case: the marriage with the Graeme girl would have to wait for their return. If the Penns had powerful friends at court, then Pennsylvania must send to London someone intimately familiar with the struggle and one who had strong contacts of his own, to speak for the people of Pennsylvania. No one understood the issues better than the Franklins, especially the Penns' attempt to dodge financial responsibility for defending their lands. It was essential, Benjamin decided, that he explain the problem personally to parliamentary leaders. He must argue for equitable taxes that would support a strong defensive force in order to avoid losing all they had worked for all along the Pennsylvania frontier.

Moreover, he was disgusted with the governors the Penns continually sent out: brawlers, drunkards, that fool Morris, and now this latest governor, Denny. A dilettante, Denny was so effeminate that the Indians declined to talk peace terms with him: they refused to negotiate with a "woman," as they called him. Benjamin intended to see that Pennsylvania was taken away from the Penn family one way or another. He had decided to begin a personal campaign to have the colony made a royal colony under the direct rule of the Crown.[17]

In convincing the Assembly that it was high time to press for reforms, Benjamin had no trouble having himself appointed the Assembly's agent to Parliament and the Crown, and his son appointed the clerk of the mission. But he found it easier to talk the Assembly into paying his way to England at the taxpayers' expense than to cajole his wife and son into his latest scheme. Deborah hated the sea, had no desire to leave her home and her aging mother. And William wanted to know why he should leave the promise of a fine marriage that assured not only his happiness but his success.

To win over William, Benjamin offered to pay the young man's expenses to study law in England. He also wrote a new will, making William his heir and executor. William was to receive a legacy equivalent to five years of his current income, a house, a town lot, his father's extensive library and most of the scientific apparatus. And as executor he was given legal control over Deborah and his sister, Sally. What was an insult to Deborah was the headiest of compliments to William. Further, Benjamin arranged a leave of absence for William from his Assembly clerkship and postal job. By paying for his legal education in London, he assured William's admission to the bar. Under Pennsylvania law, candidates for the bar who did not fulfill the requirements of the Inns of Court in London had to undergo a rigorous oral examination before the provincial governor, the chief justice and his associate justices — a splendid opportunity for political revenge on the Franklins which Benjamin apparently convinced William he should avoid.

All these tempting opportunities proved too much for William. He decided to postpone his wedding until he could return from England a lawyer, a man of parts with high prospects, a gentleman suited to living on an equal footing with the friends of Elizabeth Graeme. But it was not with an easy mind that he left her; she was much too tempting to other men. Indeed, he proposed a secret marriage. But Betsy, apparently afraid to infuriate her father and jeopardize their financial future, declined. Instead, she promised her hand, promised to wait for him, and it was no secret. They happily spread their news throughout the city.[18]

It took fully six months for the Franklins to plan their mission and break away. They could not leave until British forces arrived to take over the defense. The militia outlawed, there was, inevitably, a fresh French-Indian assault that, among other successes, took the garrison of Fort Allen at Gnadenhütten by surprise as the soldiers were carelessly ice-skating on the river. That and other embarrassments led all parties to follow the advice of the pacifist Quakers and meet for peace talks in November of 1756. Benjamin and William rode up to Easton, where Indian leaders, backed by the Quakers, convinced the Franklins that they should add to their list of grievances against the Penns the nefarious Walking Purchase, which everyone now agreed had triggered the bloody Indian warfare.[19]

Before going on to New York to sail with the convoy to England, Benjamin dashed off a hurried note to Caty Ray, lamenting that he would not be able to see her that summer as planned. "I know not now when I shall enjoy that pleasure . . . being about to leave America for some time. . . . I could not go without taking leave of my dear friend. . . . I only wish you well and happy."[20]

And William said his goodbyes to Betsy, writing ever-shorter letters to her through the seven-week delay of waiting for the British fleet to sail. Already he was complaining that his father's constant demands on him made it difficult for him to steal time to write her, but in the same letter he bragged about his evenings on the town with fellow officers.[21] All the letters from Betsy to William were destroyed in the Revolution: his side of the correspondence, however, shows how chatty, witty and charming he could be. On May 5, 1757, he wrote:

> Yesterday I had the pleasure of receiving another letter from you. But where, my charmer, shall I find words to express my acknowledgments for the candid and ingenuous declaration it contains. I will not attempt it. Actions alone can evince the reality of my sentiments on this occasion, and they shall not be wanting.
>
> I dined with Mrs. Abercrombie yesterday on board the Peggy, which lies at anchor opposite the city, about a mile from the shore. Although our friend has been arrived this several days, we have not been able to procure lodgings for her. Every house is crowded with officers. The boat is now sent ashore to take me to breakfast with them this morning.
>
> Parson Campbell and his wife are here. I spent one whole night in her company. This you may say wants a little explanation. You might know then that my father and I were invited to spend an evening at De [Berdt's] where she lodges, in company with several other gentlemen and ladies. We were there informed that Sir Charles Hardy's flag [Hardy was the new royal governor of New York] was to be hoisted by 4 o'clock the next morning and at sunrise to be saluted by all the vessels in the harbor; upon which, as we were all in extreme high spirits, and well pleased with each other, we concluded to sit up and be spectators of the ceremony.[22]

The ocean crossing was all that Deborah Franklin feared it would be: dashing flights from French privateers and a narrow escape from shipwreck off the west coast of England. William wrote from Falmouth on their first morning ashore: "Let the pleasures of this country be ever so great, they are deeply earned by a voyage across the Atlantic. Few are the inducements that will tempt me to pass the ocean again if I am so happy as to return to my native country." His father, not exactly a churchgoing man, sent off a short note to Deborah: "The bell ringing for church, we went thither immediately and with hearts full of gratitude returned sincere thanks to God for the mercies we had received: were I a Roman Catholic, perhaps I should on this occasion vow to build a chapel to some saint, but as I am not, if I were to vow at all, it should be to build a *lighthouse.*"[23]

II

A
PARTICULAR
SET OF
PEOPLE

6

ONE GREAT SMOKY HOUSE

July 1757–July 1759

As the august sun climbed higher, perspiration streamed down Benjamin Franklin's forehead from beneath his new gray wig. For hours he had been marshaling the last preparations for a trip around England and Scotland. William no doubt attributed his father's greater-than-usual urge to get away from London to the greater-than-usual din on this midsummer morning in 1759. Ever since news of the surprising British victory at Minden had arrived, the Tower cannon, little more than a mile away, had been pounding. Their triumphant tattoo mingled in the moist air with the booming salute guns in St. James's Park, the gleeful chiming from Westminster Abbey, and the pealing of a thousand other church bells all over the city.

In the four years since Braddock's defeat in the forests of Pennsylvania, the war news had been almost uniformly bad for the British. In America, India, Europe and the Mediterranean, British armies had faltered and fallen, British fleets had been sunk. Now, in the Rhineland, well-disciplined British infantry had shattered the finest French cavalry, thereby touching off a riotous celebration in London.[1]

Those who could afford to flee the heat and noise were now in full retreat from a late-summer heat wave.[2] All official London had gone north, and the Franklins were following suit. With the law courts adjourned for the summer, there was no work for lawyers, including those who populated Craven Street. It had been William's misfortune to be one of the last barristers to remain at his post.

Both Benjamin and William loved to travel, and now six weeks of riding together through the countryside and visiting lords and gentry opened out before them. As with everything else in his life at this time, William's vacation was under Benjamin's control. Benjamin kept a record of his advances to William as detailed as that for his own expenditures. Some of William's were major, such as the passage to England. Most were routine: meals and lodging along the road, the shoemaker's bill, the tailor's bill (it is worth noting that Benjamin's clothes always ran higher than his son's), the bills for William's handkerchiefs, wine, books, hats, stockings and sword. Evidently, when Benjamin had promised to pay for William's legal education, he meant that he would advance William the money and that William was to pay him back at some future date.

The father had certainly taken the son into account in another sense — in choosing their London residence. As with so many other decisions in his long life, Benjamin Franklin's selection of an expensive and elegant two-story apartment in an outwardly understated red-brick row house at 7 Craven Street, Westminster, served several purposes. Wedged between the fashionable Strand shopping district and the Thames, the narrow sloping street was equidistant from the government offices in Whitehall, where Franklin lobbied cabinet ministers and foreign officers, and the Inns of Court, where William worked over lawbooks all day. William had to ride a horse through the muddy streets, which stank with the effluvia from noblemen's town houses, to dinner-lectures at the Middle Temple while his father drove a carriage that he charged off to his Assembly expense account.

Their London neighborhood bore a remarkable resemblance to their old neighborhood in Philadelphia. From his double windows on Craven Street, Benjamin could look out over the noisy Hungerford Market, the tradesmens' shops of the Strand, the rising and falling ship masts on the river. The hurly-burly of a hundred different hawkers, the cursing of sedan-chair carriers, the rattle and crunch of carriages echoed the din of downtown Philadelphia.

He had also assembled a facsimile family. His landlady, Margaret Stevenson, was a merchant's genteel widow. She had stepped into Deborah Franklin's place. She nursed Benjamin through a long illness, shopped for him uncomplainingly, commanded his servants and hers with a skill and efficiency always somehow beyond Deborah. She initiated Benjamin into the polite art of sipping tea from fine china on good linen that Deborah had never been permitted the expense to learn. Her bluestocking daughter, Polly, a slender, French-speaking heiress remarkably well educated for a woman of the time, had stepped into the slippers of his daughter, Sally, each day growing dearer to him. Benjamin more than once hinted that Polly would make William a gifted wife, a subject William no doubt hoped would not come up on their projected vacation together.

So close had the elder Franklin become to the Stevensons that he often failed to write Deborah. Fully six months after setting up headquarters in London he finally got around to describing their living arrangements: "As you desire to know several particulars about me, I now let you know that I lodge in Craven Street near Charing Cross, Westminster; we have four rooms, furnished, and everything about us pretty genteel."[3]

For father and son, the two years since leaving Philadelphia had marched swiftly even as Benjamin learned painfully the plodding pace of imperial government. Little of their urgent mission had been accomplished. Rebuffed and ignored by the Penns' numerous friends on the King's Privy Council, Benjamin had endured long mornings in noblemen's crowded anterooms, interminable afternoons over tea, long summer adjournments stretching into autumns. He had finally learned that the shortest route to concession from the British rulers was the long, rutted post road around the British Isles. Now, by visiting the great in their country houses and courting others as he went, he could lobby for Pennsylvania with, he hoped, eminent success.

At last everything was ready. Father and son climbed in, Peter mounted the post-horse. They were off for Scotland.

The changes overtaking England since Benjamin's youthful sojourn as a printer's devil were evident as the post chaise swung into the heavy traffic of the Strand. Businessmen like Franklin were clamoring for a place in British society, a fact demonstrated by what the Strand had become. Once a fashionable address for bishops and dukes, it was now almost exclusively the domain of prosperous shopkeepers. The double-leaded windows were crammed with laces and riding habits, rare Morocco-bound books, Chinese Chippendale furniture, Madeira wines, toys, pistols and swords — all vying for the attention of the growing numbers who could afford them. But on every street corner were disabled veterans of the wars with the French: cast-off soldiers and sailors propped against walls, leaning on crutches as they begged. It was they who had purchased these goods so dearly. Today they were puffed up with half-remembered martial airs, momentarily forgetting hardship as they celebrated a great battlefield victory.

At this hour most of the traffic was headed east toward the old city gates, where William's horse usually took him. In the distance, the Franklins could see the Temple Bar with its chilling warning against rebellion and treason. On spikes high above its soot-streaked portal and statues honoring the Stuart king James I and his hapless heirs were the hollow skulls of their last noble retainers, all that remained of three Scottish rebels who had been beheaded for leading the Rising of 1745.

As the Franklin post chaise clattered faster, William was leaving in his wake the brainracking drudgery of the two hardest years of his young life. In one year he had finished his studies for the bar examinations; in the second, he had clerked in a barrister's office, and in afterhours had assembled the longest tome on Pennsylvania legislative history ever attempted, even as he helped Benjamin to counterattack Penn propagandists by sending anonymous diatribes to the London press.

As William had escaped each day from his clerical duties to his law studies at the Inns of Court, he was, unknown to his father, slipping ever farther from the elder Franklin's point of view. To ask William to resist the pull of English law in its heartland probably never occurred to Benjamin until it was too late, but even if he had invoked the folk wisdom of his own *Poor Richard's Almanack,* it is unlikely that William would have emerged from the holy place of English jurisprudence as anything but a staunchly conservative devotee of a strong English monarchy in the time of its greatest resurgence in a century. Indeed, a young man with William's love of history and tradition must have been overwhelmed the first time he walked down Middle Temple Lane into the inner courtyards of the tall, ivy-covered Inns of Court, the six-centuries-old bastion of English law, where barristers labored by the hundreds.

The atmosphere of the Inns of Court instilled a sense of legal rectitude. Students learned the ins and outs of legal procedure and practice not by reading books on the subject — none had ever been written — but by absorbing what was passed along to them by their teachers in cases argued at the dinner table, in after-supper debates, and in moot courts. At the core of the system was the round church called the Temple, a small replica of the Holy Sepulchre in Jerusalem. Here Knights Templar — barons and earls hardened by combat in the Crusades — had dictated terms to Richard the Lion Heart. Now, at this turreted shrine to English civil liberties, William and his young classmates walked past the sarcophagi of ancient legal champions as they took their assigned pews. Facing each other in the richly carved chancel, they read from the Anglican Book of Common Prayer, its phrases bequeathed by Elizabeth I, who had elevated the practice of law to the status of profession. All around him William saw the handiwork of the Queen. She had commissioned the building of the Middle Temple Hall, where meals were served (attendance was compulsory). She had also commissioned the surrounding office buildings and library. Legend had it that in the clothes of a commoner she had come to the hall on the arm of Middle Templar Sir Walter Raleigh to see the first production of Shakespeare's *Twelfth Night,* and that she had applauded as the famous playwright delivered his own lines to the boisterous company of young gentlemen.

William Franklin's impressions as he entered the dining hall on the first day of the 1757 fall term must have remained with him for years. Flickering candlelight threw shadows against the high, hammer-beam ceilings, the stained-glass windows imbedded with the coats of arms of famous graduates, the pennants of great men of the law, the portraits of kings and queens by Titian and Van Dyck. All must have brought home to him his good fortune at being in such a place and engendered in him a craving to belong to this company of gentlemen. As he took his place at a long oak table in the east end of the hall, toward the center (the table reserved for those of lower-class rank), he could see that he was in the company of the best-born men of England, mostly graduates of Oxford and Cambridge.

William did not need to await inspiration from the remote past. Not only had Raleigh and Bacon studied here but virtually every high Pennsylvania official from 1700 on. Among the graduates of William's acquaintance were Sir William Keith, Betsy Graeme's grandfather, and Benjamin Chew, the Pennsylvania supreme court jurist whose learned arguments so infuriated the elder Franklin. Now, William found himself sitting with the sons of some of the most prominent citizens of Philadelphia: Andrew Allen, the son of his father's old nemesis; William Shippen, a friend from the Dancing Assembly; and John Dickinson. Joining them were other young Americans — a Lee and a Byrd from Virginia, a Livingston from New York — almost every colony was represented. Like any new arrival from a provincial city, William had been dazzled by London. After his first three months there, he wrote Betsy Graeme of the "infinite variety of new objects, the continued noise and bustle in the streets." He was even more deeply impressed by the quality of thought and conversation he found at the Middle Temple, by his "frequent engagements amongst politicians, philosophers and men of business."[4]

To aspire to imperial office, William had only to look to the High Table in Middle Temple Hall in the fall of 1758. Seated at a magnificent thirty-foot slab of royal Windsor oak given by Queen Elizabeth sat the highest legal officials of the British realm, all graduates of this same university of the law. In the evenings before dinner, as he stood with other young domus, waiting while the slow procession of King's Benchers in powdered wigs and short black gowns filed through the ornate double doors to their seats, he could see fellow Templars Lord Hardwicke, lord chancellor of England; Lord Mansfield, the chief justice; Sir Arthur Onslow, speaker of the House of Commons; and, undoubtedly, on more than one occasion, flanked by four students assigned for that night's debate, Professor William Blackstone, a man William would certainly meet again when he received his master's degree from Oxford. Blackstone had just finished writing his famous *Commentaries on the Laws of England,* and would read the introductory chapter sixty times as a lecture to law students at Oxford and at the Middle Temple. Already, excerpts from the manuscript had been read privately to the young Crown Prince, the future King George III. Though no record survives to verify the story, Blackstone is supposed to have come to the Middle Temple that very fall to read his manuscript before the domus.

In the early pages of Blackstone's four-volume work were words that would become familiar to every lawyer in the great hall, a legal and constitutional challenge: "The King can do no wrong. . . . The King is and ought to be absolute . . . all-perfect and immortal." These were startling words, a shift in emphasis away from Parliament and back toward the King, a challenge to an age in which rich London merchants and country gentlemen had long controlled a weak central government and, in vying for mastery of world trade, had dragged England through four bloody wars of empire in less than a century. Blackstone was also urging a return to the Tory cavalier virtues of "affectionate loyalty to the King, a zeal for liberty and the Constitution, a sense of real honor and well-grounded principles of religion."[5]

After the evening's readings, after ritual toasts to the health of the King and to domus present and absent, permission was given to smoke, the wine cooler was unlocked, the gambling began. Long, boisterous evenings of freewheeling argument over law, love and politics spilled out into the terraced gardens, to nearby Covent Garden theaters, to the clubs in St. James's Street. It had been during one such afterhours difference of opinion, as Temple tradition holds, that the Wars of the Roses began when the earl of Warwick plucked a white rose, the earl of Suffolk a red rose, and each brandished them at the other. William Franklin, a devotee of the current Shakespearean revival, knew Warwick's challenge from *Henry VI, Part 2*: "And here I prophesy this brawl today, grown to this faction in the Temple garden, shall send between the red rose and the white a thousand souls to death and deadly night." William and his messmates at the Middle Temple would one day divide and draw swords in an even bloodier civil war.

More than learning the law went into the formation of an

English barrister, as William quickly discovered. He was expected to become a gentleman. This was no place for a Puritan. When the old oak floors were replaced a few years later, more than one hundred small yellowed dice were found beneath them, fallen through the cracks. A young gentleman learned to play cards, bowl on the green, swim in the Thames; he became accomplished at dancing, fencing and riding, fluent in French and Latin, possessed of courtly manners, and familiar with the latest court fashions (if he did not always wear them). In a letter to Sally, William showed off by reading her a lecture on the proper style of lace cuffs being worn that year. (She had made the mistake of sending him what was just coming into fashion, late, in Philadelphia.) If, as Ben Jonson put it, the Middle Temple was "the noblest nursery of humanity and liberty in the Kingdom," it was also a cradle of foppery, a fact that would not have delighted Benjamin Franklin if he had known of it.

There were long hours of studying legal terms and precedents and copying out dry writs, but a Templar was not supposed to brag about the wearying tomes in his green leather bag. Sir Walter Raleigh had astonished the crowd at his trial for treason by boasting, "If I ever read a word of the law and statutes before I was a prisoner in the Tower, God confound me." Although he had lost his only case and his head, this quintessential courtier was remembered by Templars in William's time as the model knightly gentleman and may have served as William's model.

But so long as William lived under Benjamin Franklin's roof, he was expected to cleave to his father's mission. He could not stay out late at night, even though he was in his thirties: that would make it difficult for him to rise early in order to tackle his father's lobbying projects and run his errands. As Poor Richard must have reminded him: "Early to bed, early to rise, makes a man healthy, wealthy and wise." No doubt William's duties occasionally included standing in front of the House of Commons distributing handbills urging Franklin views on members.

During his first year in London, William crammed massive doses of law. Besides memorizing the ancient Pandects of the Roman emperor Justinian (which he read in Latin), he had to keep abreast of Blackstone's latest interpretations and add to his store of knowledge by taking notes at major trials in the Court of King's Bench in

Westminster Hall. After the dinners in the Middle Temple, he took his turn the prescribed number of times at debating in moot courts propositions hurled down by the Reader. The debates shaped the would-be young barrister's poise, timing and delivery even as he competed for the notice of legal sponsors who could further his legal, and perhaps his political, career. And in the summers William rode circuit with his preceptor as cases were tried in county assizes across England.

By the end of the autumn term of 1758, William was ready to stand before the Masters of the Bench for a grueling oral examination. Then, on November 10, 1758, after proceeding with his classmates down the aisle of Westminster Abbey, William Franklin, bastard son of a provincial printer, was called to the English bar.[6] He heard the Master Treasurer proclaim the ancient formula beginning, "Omnia praesumuntur rite esse acta": "In the absence of proof to the contrary, the law presumes that you have done everything which ought to be done."

That evening, at Middle Temple Hall, William Franklin, Esquire, took his turn at the dark little table made from a hatch cover of Templar Sir Francis Drake's flagship, *Golden Hind,* and signed the call book. Then he was invited up to the Bench. In every sense, William had become an English gentleman.

England's foremost publisher, William Strahan, described William as "one of the prettiest young gentlemen I ever knew,"[7] as far from his father's plain Boston origins as he could travel. Yet, by this time, Benjamin too had assumed the trappings of English gentility, and hailed by England's burgeoning scientific community as a celebrity because of his widely publicized electrical experiments, he was as popular as his son in the literary circles that revolved around Strahan.

For fifteen years Benjamin Franklin and William Strahan had corresponded between London and Philadelphia. In that time, Franklin became the most successful American book distributor and Strahan the leading English publisher. Among Strahan's authors were Samuel Johnson, Edward Gibbon, Tobias Smollett, Oliver Goldsmith and David Hume; through Strahan, the Franklins came to know them all.

Shortly after Franklin and Strahan finally met, Strahan wrote a letter to Deborah Franklin in which he warned her of one facet of her husband's popularity: "I never saw a man who was, in every respect, so perfectly agreeable to me. Some are amiable in one view, some in another, he in all. Now, madam, as I know the ladies here consider him in exactly the same light as I do, upon my word I think I should come over with all convenient speed to look after your interest. Not but that I think him as faithful as any man breathing, but who knows what repeated and strong temptation may in time, and while he is at so great a distance from you, accomplish."[8] Away from the eyes of his Philadelphia Quaker constituency, Franklin not only flirted with the ladies but he set aside his penny-saved-penny-earned philosophy. He dressed handsomely. His costly London portraits show him in the latest wig and a gentleman's expensive suits, his face full and prosperous-looking. He had Mrs. Stevenson buy the best foods and prepare them for him. He still preferred gruel for breakfast, but in the evenings, when he was not entertaining guests, he habitually ate dinner with fellow clubmen in the best chophouses in London. He belonged to at least six private clubs in addition to the Royal Society.

Less than two weeks after landing in England, Franklin dined for the first time with the Royal Society at the Mitre Tavern on Fleet Street. In all, he attended sixty of its meetings. Science carried much more prestige in England than Franklin may have realized before he arrived, and men of medicine and business were excited about it. Foremost among the so-called philosophical societies in England, the Royal Society counted among its members the finest scientific minds of the day. The gossip over dinner at the Mitre revolved around the latest experiment or innovation in industry. To his even greater delight, Benjamin often found himself the center of discussion. Only one topic was off limits: politics. But Benjamin found he could pursue political conversations privately. Beyond formal meetings, he was frequently invited to dine with Royal Society members in their homes and his circle increased geometrically. He often took his carriage down fashionable Pall Mall on Sunday evenings to the home of Sir John Pringle, a distinguished physician. Here he met scientists, educators, authors and philosophers from Scotland, Europe and America.

To a friend in Philadelphia, he confided, "I find I love company, chat, a laugh, a glass, and even a song."[9] He obviously enjoyed as well the standard club fare: wine and punch, a pipe of tobacco, Welsh rarebit and apple puffs, porter and beer. What he did not advertise was that he intended to exploit his club connections in the summertime as he traveled around Britain lobbying for his special interests.

As a lobbyist on an expense account, Franklin charged nearly everything to the Pennsylvania Assembly. He rented the best available carriage, stocking it with good food and good wine. The carriage rent was more than most of his Pennsylvania constituents and their families had to live on for a year. The man who had broken the journalistic monopoly of Philadelphia by inviting his rival's friends in to watch him eat a breakfast of sawdust and water now spent as much on wine for his days on the road as he had earned in a year as a young printer's devil in London.

With the help of profits from twenty years of promoting thrift in *Poor Richard's Almanack*, Franklin now rightly considered himself an Englishman of wealth. He adopted what he claimed was his family coat of arms, wore it on his ring, sealed his letters with it. He took rides into the countryside to view the old family lands at Ecton: he was considering buying them up and making them the core of his estate. With his son William and his slave Peter, he cleaned off his ancestors' headstones in the churchyard of St. Mary Magdalen and paid the rector to gather information for a genealogy. When he found his English cousins destitute, he gave them food and wine and cash, and took time to sip tea with relatives in towns from Ecton to Birmingham. He showed off his success as unabashedly as any successful immigrant returning to the old country.[10]

But Benjamin saw nothing inconsistent about chastising William for spending too freely when traveling without him on legal business. In August 1758, he wrote to remind William of the tenuous nature of his support. He not only warned him not to spend so much for rooms and meals but told him not to get too attached to English ways. Alarmed, William quickly replied, "I am extremely obliged to you for your care in supplying me with money, and shall ever have a grateful sense of that with the other numberless indulgencies I have received from your paternal affection. I shall be ready to return to America or to go to any other part of the world whenever you think it necessary. [I] have changed [my] lodgings . . . much for the worse, though somewhat cheaper."[11]

By contrast, on their travels together their first year in England, Benjamin's purse had always been open and they had behaved like tourists. They trudged around the Tower of London, where nobles had been beheaded and lions now paced. They crossed the Thames to attend concerts of Handel's latest music at the Vauxhall, went on riverboat rides with Mrs. Stevenson and Polly. Benjamin encouraged William to be kind to Polly.

When Benjamin's old lung malady plagued him that first fall, Mrs. Stevenson had been very solicitous, and after he recovered, he was seized by a fit of generosity to his family — his habitual response to the end of a long illness. This time he sent Deborah a large mug with a picture of a fat serving wench on one side, and a secondhand harpsichord to Sally. He also sent William and Mrs. Stevenson on buying sprees. They rounded up a prayer book and garters, wheels of Parmesan cheese, embroidery floss, shoes, pins, needles, taffeta, gloves, tortoiseshell reading glasses, a candle screen "to save Debby's eyes" as she worked over the silk and patterns he sent along. They were all practical, useful presents.[12] He also sent Debby unsolicited advice: "You are very prudent not to engage in party disputes. Women should never meddle with them except in endeavors to reconcile their husbands, brothers and friends who happen to be of contrary sides."[13]

To William, Benjamin preached a self-discipline he himself had practiced only *after* spawning an illegitimate son. Evidently he espoused to William the religion of self-perfection, an amalgam of his Puritan upbringing and his belief in his own powers of self-restraint. He also preached another virtue he never personally cultivated: contentment. "Security is equal to splendor, health to pleasure," he wrote. Even his attempts at poetry at this time seemed aimed at William:

> I know, dear son, ambition fills your mind,
> And in life's voyage is the impelling wind,
> But at the helm let sober reason stand
> To steer the bark with heaven-directed hand.[14]

If William ever wrote down his reaction to his father's advice, he apparently was prudent enough not to leave it where Benjamin could find it.

Benjamin Franklin's first political mission to England, originally to take six months, was to drag on for five years. The Penns not only had painted him as a dangerous republican to members of the Board of Trade and Plantations, which passed on all colonial affairs, but had even blackened him to members of the royal family.

As soon as the Pennsylvania Assembly had appointed Benjamin its London agent, Richard Peters, the provincial secretary, had written Thomas Penn, "Considering the popularity of his character and the reputation gained by his electrical discoveries, which will introduce him into all sorts of company, he may prove a dangerous enemy."[15] Full of scorn, Thomas Penn had replied, "Mr. Franklin's popularity is nothing here. . . . He will be looked very coldly upon by great people. . . . There are few of any consequence that have heard of his electrical experiments, those matters being attended to by a particular set of people."[16] Penn had reason for overconfidence: he had just enjoyed a long evening's chat with Lord Granville, president of the King's Privy Council. Soon afterward Lord Halifax presented him to King George II.

One London Quaker leader abreast of Benjamin's mission wrote back to Philadelphia in mid-1759 that "Franklin has not yet been able to make much progress in his affairs. Reason is heard with fear: [his] fairest representations are considered as the effects of superior art and his reputation as a man, a philosopher and a statesman only seem to render his station more difficult and perplexing. . . . Great pains had been taken, and very successfully, to render him odious and his integrity suspected to those very persons to whom he must first apply. These suspicions can only be worn off by time."[17]

His first personal encounter with the Penns had been cold. When he refused to address them in writing by all their feudal titles, they refused to meet with him further, and shunted him off to their solicitor. Worse, he received a dressing down from Lord Granville, who had dined with Thomas Penn beforehand: "That nobleman . . . after some questions respecting the present state of

affairs in America . . . said to me, 'You Americans have wrong
ideas of the nature of your constitution. You contend that the
King's instructions to his governors are not laws, and think yourselves at liberty to regard or disregard them at your own discretion.
But those instructions are not like the pocket instructions given to a
minister going abroad for regulating his conduct in some trifling
point of ceremony. They are first drawn up by judges learned in
the laws; they are then considered, debated and perhaps amended
in Council, after which they are signed by the King. They are then,
so far as relates to you, *the law of the land,* for the King is the LEG-
ISLATOR OF THE COLONIES.' "[18]

This on-the-carpet talk rocked Franklin. He retreated to Craven
Street to write down the conversation verbatim and send a copy to
Philadelphia.

The carriage rolled rapidly eastward, past open meadowland: in
those days, cattle grazed a mile from Westminster Abbey. The
travelers hurried past Tyburn Gallows, its bleachers and gibbet
empty today. On the open heath just outside London, the lonely
post chaise was most vulnerable. Highwaymen frequently descended on small coaches, which usually carried noblemen with
bags of gold coins. The road was hard-packed, dusty from a three-
year drought: they careened along quickly. Once they passed
Finchlea Heath and started up the Great North Road, William
could ease down the hammers of the pistols, relax. If ever a young
man needed to relax, it was William Franklin.

Ordinarily, on admission to the bar, a young barrister simply applied for chambers in one of the handsome brick buildings surrounding the courtyards and gardens of the Middle Temple. But
William was too poor to pay the going rent or the fee charged for
affiliating with an eminent barrister's firm. And he was too well
qualified simply to sign on as a clerk and copy out writs. As usual,
he was put in an awkward position by his father's parsimony. When
the elder Franklin was bedridden for months with the lung ailment,
William had, more than ever, been needed to keep the Pennsylvania mission alive.

Soon after arriving in London, he had met the man who would
have the profoundest effect on his future, a dashing bachelor named

Richard Jackson. Several of Jackson's friends, Dr. Samuel Johnson included, had bestowed upon him the nickname Omniscient because of his encyclopedic font of ready, if often erroneous, information. Omniscient Jackson was as engaging as Benjamin Franklin, as experienced and as popular, but he was better schooled — a graduate of Cambridge and a respected Bencher of the Inner Temple. He was also a rich, landed gentleman with sizable estates and a coterie of accomplished friends, and he was delighted to introduce William to them.

Jackson had a penchant for taking the mineral waters at the fashionable Tunbridge Wells health spa with his good friends Dr. Johnson, Mrs. Thrale, and the Shakespearean actor David Garrick. Along the Flemish-tiled Upper Walk they window-shopped for the latest European fashions and mingled with members of the nobility. Between cups of the mineral water — it had a strong iron taste — they took carriage rides to historic country estates nearby.

William enjoyed the company of the most illustrious conversationalists in England. Jackson and his friends were delighted with the handsome, witty young barrister. Despite his father's sometime disapproval, William's fortunes and those of Jackson would interlock for many years. Jackson was the most astute observer of American colonial policy in England. Long before meeting him, Benjamin Franklin had written to seek his advice on governmental affairs. Jackson the barrister knew charter rights and privileges; he was equally acceptable to the King's ministers and to the populists. Shortly after reaching London, Franklin hired him to gather evidence that would knock down the Penn claims before the Privy Council. It soon occurred to Franklin that all parties could benefit if William had the run of Jackson's chambers: William would have a rent-free office; Jackson would have the benefit of William's voluminous Pennsylvania Assembly and defense committee files, and Benjamin would have an entrée to the inner circle of English government and an expert to help in their most ambitious joint project, publishing a hefty book that would lay out the Assembly's case against the Penns.

It was a secret venture, a typical Franklin committee effort. The plan was to expose the proprietors' abuses of the fundamental rights guaranteed the citizens of Pennsylvania in Penn's charter of

1701 and in a series of enactments over the past fifty years. The method was to print the documents chronologically with a connecting commentary. The exact editorial arrangements were never made known. Apparently, Benjamin hired Omniscient Jackson to write a foreword that would lend the weight of a British expert on American affairs to the project. Jackson would dedicate the book to a fellow Templar, Sir Arthur Onslow, speaker of the House of Commons — a gesture to demonstrate that the book was not aimed at the general public. Under Jackson's supervision and certainly in his office, William was to assemble and edit the documents and write the commentary. Benjamin was to stay in the background, merely arranging the printing and writing an anonymous introduction.

When William was beginning his work on the manuscript, two long letters were published under pseudonyms in several of the London newspapers. The authors claimed that the Quakers had not been willing to spend any money to fortify the frontier and that American militia were weak, cowardly and unwilling to defend their rights and homes. The letters appeared at a time when British newspaper readers were looking for scapegoats to blame for British military blunders. William could remember the cowardice and confusion of Braddock's British army as vividly as he recalled the tightly disciplined, all-American fort-building force he had led into enemy gunsights at the Lehigh Gap only two winters before.

As William later wrote home to Colonel Philip Schuyler, his former commanding officer, the letters were malicious lies that hurt the cause of American arms at a critical time. "They [make] the provincial forces in particular, and the Americans in general, appear in a very ridiculous, nay hateful, light to the Mother Country. It would therefore have been unpardonable if none of the Americans on the spot where these aspersions were published had not stood up on behalf of the colonies and shown how egregiously facts had been misrepresented."[19]

Despite his pledge to his fiancée to avoid politics, William the officer and gentleman saw it as his duty to expose the falsehoods. His letter of September 16, 1757, to the London *Citizen* countered the Penn propaganda: "The scalping of the frontier inhabitants by the Indians is not peculiar to Pennsylvania but common to all the colonies. . . . The inhabitants of the frontiers of Pennsylvania are not Quakers. . . . The disputes between the late and present governors and the Assembly of Pennsylvania were occasioned and continued chiefly by new instructions from the proprietors to those govenors. . . . Though Quakers have scruples against bearing arms, they have granted large sums for the King's use."[20] He ended with a detailed catalogue of the forts, men and arms mustered at Quaker expense by his father and himself. His letter was never refuted.

Instead of hiding behind a pseudonym, the literary convention of the time, William boldly signed his name to establish that the author had been an officer and an Assembly official on the scene. The letter, to his delight, was promptly reprinted in the *Gentleman's Magazine* and made him somewhat of a celebrity.

He then returned to the task of knitting together the case against the Penns. From all that can be deduced, William completed his work on the book in a little more than three months, finishing before the start of his legal studies in October. The result was an unusually strong and carefully developed attack on prerogative, privilege and the use of arbitrary power.

The foreword supplied by Jackson addressed the highest officials of the realm with a studied combination of familiarity and respectful persuasion. Jackson pointed out that Pennsylvania's problems applied to all the American colonies. For his part, Benjamin Franklin could contribute little to the project because he was seriously ill with his lung ailment throughout the fall. When he was able to, he wrote an introduction filled with smooth, polished aphorisms: "Liberty, it seems, thrives best in the woods. . . . We love to stare more than to reflect." And an old line he had used before with considerable success as the wagons of the dead had rolled into Philadelphia that tense morning four years earlier: "He who would sacrifice essential liberty to obtain a little temporary safety deserves neither liberty nor safety."[21]

The work was published in June 1759, under the accurate but cumbersome title *An Historical Review of the Constitution and Government of Pennsylvania,* and its printing and binding costs were charged by Franklin to his Assembly expense account. There is no record that either William or Richard Jackson was directly paid for his efforts, although Jackson immediately afterward assumed more of the paid legal work for the province and was promised the Assembly's lucrative agency business when Franklin returned to America.

The anonymity was well advised. In many ways, the *Historical Review* was an incendiary work that verged on libel and sedition. Neither Franklin ever claimed it; indeed, they both treated it as an unacknowledged, illegitimate literary child. To prevent a libel suit, they blurred their identities. Each gave the other or Jackson credit for the compilation. William, for instance, wrote to Joseph Galloway on June 16, 1760: "My father has been much occupied of late with putting together the materials for the work against the [proprietors], but Mr. Ralph is engaged to see it through the press, as he does not wish to appear in the affair."[22] Benjamin wrote: "Billy afforded great assistance and furnished most of the materials." And in the same letter, he pointed to Jackson as the author: "It is wrote by a gentleman said to be one of the first pens in England, and who interests himself much in the concerns of America, but will not be known."[23] He wrote Hume expressly to deny writing the book. To others he gave out conflicting versions, probably to throw off suspicion. To his trusted political lieutenant Joseph Galloway in Philadelphia he wrote: "The publication of the Defence of the Province, mentioned in mine of Sept. 2 [1757], will probably be one of the first acts of hostility on our side, as being necessary to prepare the minds of the public in which the proprietors will be gibbeted up as they deserve to rot and stink in the nostrils of posterity."[24] To Issac Norris, the speaker of the Assembly, with whom he had long clashed, he officially denied having anything to do with the project: "The book relating to the affairs of Pennsylvania is now published. . . . The proprietor is enraged. He supposes me the author, but is mistaken. I had no hand in it."[25]

Franklin was clearly pleased by the effort. He shipped five hundred copies back to Philadelphia for sale in his bookstore and then had William pack several dozen specially bound presentation copies into the portmanteau on their post chaise for distribution to influential politicians throughout England and Scotland.

In the five months after he arrived in England, William wrote to Betsy Graeme only once — on the day he landed. He finally sat down to write her a long letter on December 9. But the day before and three thousand miles away, the first words of William's to reach her in all that time appeared in the news columns of the *Pennsylvania Gazette:* a reprint of his counterattack on the Penns in the London *Citizen.* Evidently no word of William's to prepare her for his decision to break his promise to refrain from partisan politics ever reached her. How he could have neglected his fiancée for so long and allowed her to learn of what must have seemed a betrayal in such a callous way is incomprehensible. He may have written her, of course, but if he did, the letter must have been lost at sea or intercepted by her father. No word of explanation on his part survives. There is only Betsy's angry reaction: she called him "a collection of party malice."[26]

William was stunned. As his reply to her on October 24, 1758, reveals, he felt that he was every bit as much the aggrieved party. Had he not, if not politically, been personally faithful to her for a year and a half in a society filled with temptations? "I looked upon myself as engaged to you during that time." He felt more than ever torn apart by his loyalty to his father. He had had no other choice but to return to the newspaper wars: someone who knew the truth had to answer the Penn party's lies. It was her father's friends who had broken the truce as soon as the Franklins were out of town. The quarrel between his father and his father's enemies had become, William feared, "the bane of my future happiness." But if she truly loved him, she should understand all that.

He believed the rift between them had begun because he had failed to write her. Unquestionably, he had neglected her shamefully. Too late, he now made a feeble excuse: "I was ever a bad correspondent. England has made me much more so." As he wrote on, he obviously became more annoyed with her, more self-righteous. "Love might at least have shown indulgence. But how great the reverse! You must be fully sensible from the whole tenor of my latest letter that my affection was in no way abated. You must, you cannot but know the contrary."

William had grown weary of the cross fire between his father and Betsy's family. Her words seemed to confirm to him that she had too little love left to understand the bind in which his father's politics had placed him once more. His infatuation with her — it cannot have been much more than that — had obviously faded, and while he professed his constancy to her, he may have become interested in someone else. His final words to her were a strange combination of self-pity and dejection: "Forget the man who in all probability could never have it in his power to be so happy as to contribute to your happiness. I, only I, have to learn forgetfulness."[27]

In William's mind he had broken their engagement, but not in Betsy's. Whether she continued to write him is not known, but apparently he never wrote to her again. Three years later, when William returned, married, to America, she still considered herself betrothed to him. She became a recluse at first, despondent, then went to England for a year, to avoid and forget him.

On the first afternoon of their vacation, the Franklins evidently turned their post chaise off the Great North Road for a brief visit with John Stuart, third earl of Bute. To gain access to the houses of the noblemen Franklin wanted to court that summer, he needed letters of introduction that would produce invitations. He had obtained a few from his friend Sir John Pringle, but only Lord Bute could have opened some of the doors he and William passed through in the next three months. As with so many Franklin dealings, the stopover at Luton Hoo, Bute's estate in Bedfordshire, was a carefully guarded secret. Its occurrence can only now be deduced from a close study of the Franklins' movements during their fifteen-hundred-mile odyssey through England and Scotland.

Blocked by the Penns and their protectors, Granville and Halifax, Franklin had turned to Prime Minister William Pitt. Busy running a world war, Pitt repeatedly declined to see him. Angered, Franklin next sought out Lord Bute, Pitt's rival, a man every bit as secretive and insinuating as himself.

As the Franklin carriage rattled up the driveway of Luton Hoo, the Franklins could congratulate themselves on a successful series of maneuvers. While the Penns had been busily courting the favor of noblemen around the aging George II, the Franklins were looking to the imminent day when the old King would die and his grandson, the Prince of Wales, would succeed to the throne. Already, young Prince George was surrounding himself with his future ministers, men of his mother's choosing whom he trusted as much as he despised the ministers of his ailing grandfather. Foremost among them, in the eyes of the Prince and his mother, was Lord Bute.

The twenty-one-year-old Prince dared trust few men. His father, Prince Frederick, had trusted too many. For twenty years he had lived in raucous dissipation and meddled in European military affairs. As if in spite the old King had outlived his son and heir. Frederick died of heart failure from overexertion on the tennis court.

The man who had been closest to Prince Frederick was Lord Bute. He had come to influence at the court by a quirk of royal caprice. It was raining one day as Frederick, his princess and their entourage rode out to the Egham races. After the races, during a downpour, Bute was summoned to the royal tent to make up a whist party. He so impressed the Prince and Princess that he became a fixture at their court. He made the Prince laugh with his wit, his easy charm, his amateur theatrical productions. In turn, the Prince appointed him a lord of the bedchamber. Bute also became the man closest to Frederick's widow. Dowager Princess Augusta, the homely mother of seven, was carrying another child when her husband dropped dead. Her intimacy with Bute fed London gossip for years. To avoid scandal, Bute left her boudoir by a secret exit, but little could be kept from the servants. At Frederick's death, Bute smoothly transferred his allegiance to the young Prince George and became the Prince's personal tutor and intimate friend.

Their relationship reveals all the weaknesses of the favoritism, influence-peddling and deference that dominated the reign of the man who inherited the world's richest empire and managed to alienate and lose much of it. Ironically, the Dowager Princess, the cause of scandal herself, detested the moral corruption she saw in others all around her. She was determined to keep her tall, immature, introverted son chaste. Though not a likely-looking rakehell — he had inherited the ancestral weak chin, hooded eyes and florid complexion — the Prince was nonetheless a prince, and he was beset by women. He delighted his mother by rebuffing most of them. Indeed, besides his mother, Bute was the only human being he liked or completely trusted.

He repeated and espoused ardently all that his mentor taught him. His letters to Bute gushed with pathetic self-abnegation and boyish pledges of self-improvement. When he was eighteen, in an age when eighteen normally constituted manhood in every sense, George wrote to Bute: "I will employ all my time upon business, and will be able for the future to give you an account of everything I read!"[28] What he read and admired led him to see himself as the reincarnation of King Alfred the Great. In an essay he penned for Bute, he summed up King Alfred's ninth-century virtues: "He examined into everything himself, impenetrable in his secrets. . . . He got rid of the incorrigible . . . and formed new subjects . . . to raise his own glory. . . . No good and great Prince born in a free country and, like Alfred, fond of the cause of liberty, will ever despair of restoring his country to virtue, freedom and glory, even though he mounts the Throne in the worst corrupted times."[29]

Bute also instilled in George a deep aversion to the perpetual European wars that had made the Prince's Hanoverian cousins rich at British expense, and he weaned George from an attachment to Germany. George genuinely wanted to make Britain great. Unlike his German-speaking grandfather, he considered himself a Briton. It is entirely possible that his education included readings from the Franklins' *Historical Review*. Many passages seem intended for his eyes and ears. One in particular suited Bute's purposes: "We are at present so lost in the military scramble on the Continent next us, in which it must be confessed we are deeply interested, that we have scarce time to throw a glance towards America, where we have also much at stake, and where, if anywhere, our account must be made up for at last."[30]

Generally disapproving of everyone save "Mama" and "my lord Bute," George had been schooled to favor revolution from the top — the conservative position. He listened eagerly as Bute read aloud from Blackstone's manuscript the stirring call to "affectionate loyalty to the King, a zeal for liberty and the Constitution, a sense of real honour and well-grounded principles of religion." Most of all, George was learning to hate his grandfather's friends and love his grandfather's enemies. In a school of politics where revenge was the chief motive and kings were expected merely to reign, not rule, George eagerly rejected his grandfather's bloody-handed Scottish policies. By defiantly making a Scot his chief advisor, by refusing to remove him even at the old King's request, George was taking a slap at the majority of Englishmen, who looked down on the Scots as gutteral-speaking, provincial savages.

Yet Bute and the increasing Scottish population of London could never forget the wave of hatred after the Highlanders invaded England and came within one hundred miles of London in 1745. When news reached the capital that Bonnie Prince Charlie's army had been crushed at Culloden, mobs surged through the streets seeking out Scotsmen to finish off. Several leading Scottish expatriate writers had been in a London coffeehouse when the news of Culloden arrived from the north. Alexander Carlyle recorded in his diary that he had been nursing a hot toddy with the Scottish novelist Tobias Smollett and other friends when word of the bayonet-wielding Hessian victory in a Highland glen had been shouted through the tavern door. "London all over was a perfect uproar of joy," Carlyle wrote. When he and Smollett set out for their homes, they found themselves in the midst of rioting mobs. "We were glad to go into a narrow entry to put our wigs in our pockets and take our swords from our belts and walk with them in our hands not speaking a word, lest the mob should discover our country."[31]

It was ironic how quickly the Scots had turned their defeat into political victory, so much so that Franklin now felt it expedient, even necessary, to court the favor of Bute's faction.

The steps a responsible businessman takes to cast aside all he is bred to believe in, to risk losing all he has earned, to become a plotter and a rebel against the established order, are steps not taken lightly or quickly. For Benjamin Franklin, nearly fifteen years of growing disenchantment with the British Empire began that summer of 1759. But so far from rebelling against British rule was he at this time that he actually wanted to enhance royal control over Pennsylvania where all his wealth and political power resided. It had not been many years since New Jersey had been taken over by the Crown from inept proprietors. The precedent was clear.

For the man who controlled the Pennsylvania Assembly almost singlehanded and who had himself been, as postmaster general, a ranking British colonial official, it was not too great a stretch of his imagination to see himself in line for preferment as royal governor of Pennsylvania once the Penns were ousted. Equally within the realm of his thinking was the possibility of patronage for his son. For Benjamin, coldly infuriated by the studied snubs and insults of the Penns and their British friends, the motive was unmistakable: revenge.

To carry off the feat of stripping the Penn family of nearly ninety million acres and putting them under the actual control of the Crown but the virtual control of the Franklins might seem to have been ludicrously difficult, but actually it had come down to a simple matter of influence. The family that had the strongest and highest connections in the royal fray could expect success in an age when influence-peddling was approaching perfection. Shrewdly, instead of marching in frontal assault on St. James's Palace to win their case, the Franklins took the long march around England and Scotland that summer, lining up the support of men of influence against the day when Bute and his royal patron came to office and power and could deliver an entire province into their hands.

Their quest for connections with the heir apparent could begin right next door to their Craven Street residence in the shop of a wine merchant named Caleb Whitefoord, a close friend of Bute's. As Benjamin Franklin knew, the surest way to a businessman's friendship is to put money in his pocket. Four days before the Franklins left for Scotland, Franklin's expense journal shows that he settled his longstanding wine account in full and charged the total to the Pennsylvania Assembly. His visit to Whitefoord put a substantial sum in the wine merchant's purse and must have put him in a good mood to write letters of recommendation to his friend Lord Bute.[32]

Franklin's records indicate that no sooner had he recovered from his unsuccessful meetings with the Penns than he began to make substantial purchases from Whitefoord, each visit to the wineshop evidently giving him another excuse to talk with the man. Yet, as Franklin had learned from earlier London experiences, he needed surer ties to Bute. His maneuvering was discreet, clandestine. He learned that his friend Dr. Pringle was physician to the earl of Bute and the Prince of Wales. And he soon discovered that Bute was keenly interested in the Franklins' electrical experiments and had carried out a few of his own. Accordingly, the visit with Bute at Luton Hoo on the afternoon of August 8, 1759, offered considerable common ground for conversation.

Six months earlier, without fanfare, Benjamin had received notice that he had been awarded an honorary doctorate in philosophy by the University of St. Andrews. It was not the most signal of honors: St. Andrews, once the premier university of the British Isles, now numbered only a handful of students in a few moldering ruins on the North Sea coast of Scotland. But Benjamin coveted academic honors. At the height of his military success in Philadelphia, he had dropped his battles with the Penns and the Indians long enough for a lightning visit to Virginia. Under the guise of post office business, he had also called at the College of William and Mary to receive an honorary degree acknowledging his electrical experiments.

Actually, Franklin wanted an honorary degree from Oxford, but when he arrived in England, he had found that the Penns' minion, the Reverend William Smith, who had earlier received just such an honorary degree, had cast doubt on the originality of Franklin's discoveries in a libelous letter to some of the Oxford dons. Thwarted, Franklin was more than eager to accept a St. Andrews degree.

At this time, he was on familiar terms with only one St. Andrews graduate — Dr. Pringle. Almost certainly, Dr. Pringle had recommended him for the honor and had written to Bute to ask him to write letters of introduction for the Franklins. It was natural then for Benjamin also to call on Dr. Pringle's influential patient, and as was the custom of the time, ask him in person for letters of introduction (no doubt prepared in advance) to ranking men of science and government along his way.

As all who knew him quickly learned, Lord Bute was mercurial. One week he would greet visitors in riding pink and spurs, and would refuse to sit down, an unmistakable message that visitors should only stay a few minutes. At other times, he took long rides with his guests around Luton Hoo, conversing volubly. Just how Bute received the Franklins is unknown, but not all the letters of introduction the Franklins needed seem to have been ready. Three weeks later, on August 29, Benjamin wrote Deborah: "I am not certain whether we shall continue our route to Scotland but I expect letters at Lancaster."[33]

Before they left Luton Hoo, there was no doubt time to indulge William's interests, to view the famous Beauvais tapestries of the King of China, an incomparable collection of porcelain, a Rembrandt, a Titian. Bute had also something to show the Franklins that both father and son could appreciate: reputedly the largest collection of scientific apparatus in private hands in England. By the time the Franklins bowed themselves out they assuredly had enough letters of introduction to warrant their continuing their country-house tour.

As Benjamin wrote candidly to a Philadelphia ally, the trip was not to be an idle time. "I have been much in the country, traveling over a great part of the kingdom, partly to recover my health, and partly to improve and increase acquaintance among persons of influence."[34] Part journalist, part scientist, Benjamin was forever making a point of his ramblings. He was convinced that all he saw would somehow, someday, become useful. Father and son usually kept journals. The Franklins could not merely travel: they had to indulge their heightened powers of observation en route to justify their expense accounts. On this trip they noted local trade regulations and postal arrangements, and studied the output of mines, forges and factories; the behavior of underground elements; the effects of tides in rivers; traffic, wealth, harbor defenses.

During the skirmishing with the Penns in the London newspapers, William Franklin had returned to the subject of his grand scheme to win for the Franklins a vast patrimony in the American wilderness. In his long, signed letter to the *Citizen,* he had introduced the possibility publicly for the first time in such a way that a careful reader could not overlook the opportunity for speculation. William wrote glowingly of the prospect of large numbers of land-hungry English subjects, regardless of religion or politics, pushing ever westward "beyond the narrow bounds of three islands to a continent larger than all Europe and to a future empire as fully peopled, which Britain may probably one day possess in those vast Western regions."[35] When the article was reprinted in American newspapers late in 1757, it was a signal to friends in England and America that the campaign for a charter for a vast new British colony, far more ambitious than any land scheme of the Penns, was beginning.

Nothing, not even political schemes or dreams of empire, could mitigate the wrenching, jarring, bone-wearying ordeal of traveling the Great North Road. About twenty-five feet wide in most places, up to one hundred feet wide in others, the road was dirt, caked hard and rutted in the summer, except for a four-foot-wide strip in the center. This was paved with stones, but by 1759 it had worn down into a trough. One traveler actually measured ruts four feet deep. Horses tired quickly. Axles snapped and carts broke down, blocking traffic. So bad was the road that stage coaches, though capable of making good time in the south of England, could not pass other vehicles here. The Franklin post chaise had to plod along behind packtrains of horses hauling coal, milk and food north to the new factory towns of the Midlands, the Franklins' driver, the slave Peter, doing his best to dodge ruts and potholes. It seemed that all England was on the road, cursing, crawling, waiting to pass.

Worsening the congestion were farm families on foot or in their carts. Dirty, dusty, forlornly escorting their belongings to the next town, they were looking for day wages, their faces reflecting the worry of men cast off the common lands that their ancestors had shared with their neighbors since Anglo-Saxon times. In the towns to which they migrated, the Industrial Revolution was beginning. In the fields they left, the enclosure movement was, in the name of scientific progress, turning thousands off the land at the precise moment when the new machinery of the Industrial Revolution needed men, women and children for mines and mills.

To consolidate lands and profits, some two thousand private bills were introduced into Parliament authorizing the fencing of common grazing lands into enclosures that would accommodate larger herds. By 1759 much of twenty-eight counties was fenced in. At the same time, rents for land and cottages were increased to pay for improvements. As it was, a tenant farmer could barely eke out a living. He had kept his livestock on the common, cut his fuel there. When the common lands were broken up and the landlords demanded cash for fencing, the tenant had no alternative but to give up his leasehold.

At first, the new system did not seem too bad. He could hire himself out for wages. But what he earned was not enough to pay the rent for the same cottage, the price of firewood, food and clothing. He could no longer raise animals, have a little meat, weave cloth. By 1759, the sturdy yeoman class was also suffering from enclosure. Heavily taxed, too poor to pay day wages and too proud to accept them, they were selling their land to rich neighbors. In little more than a century after the Glorious Revolution of 1688 supposedly guaranteed every Englishman's rights, one fourth of the farmers of England lost their land. So volatile was the situation that, by the late 1750's, the slightest attempt to introduce any further innovation in farming methods met with violent opposition. When a Lancashire farmer tried for the first time to mow wheat with a scythe, his laborers deliberately spoiled his crop.

Thousands were deserting England. In America, a day laborer earned two or three times as much as in England. If he saved, he could one day buy his own land. For years the Franklins had watched the flow of immigrants through Philadelphia to the west country.

What the Franklins now saw at first hand along the Great North Road fortified their conviction that, given enough cheap land on the American frontier, many more Englishmen would desert their crowded, cash-poor homeland and migrate to new American provinces where enterprise, not birth or even religious convictions, would decide a man's degree of success. By the end of their trip, their dream had become an obsession, one they both shared until the days of the American Revolution.

For the present, however, years of Indian raids were channeling the flow of the dispossessed, not to ports of embarkation, but to the burgeoning industrial towns of the Midlands.

Whenever the Franklins passed through Birmingham on summer vacations, they were "continually on the foot from one manufactory to another and were highly entertained in seeing all the curious machines and expeditious ways of working."[36] This time, they bustled around for two days. Here Benjamin could actually see hard at work the new order he so heartily endorsed. Here men aspired, as he had, to rise in a single generation to wealth and power. Here, as in the other blooming Midland towns, science was being harnessed in tandem to a growing work force and abundant capital, and a great number of important industrial innovations were being brought to bear all at the same time. As expansion of the British Empire ensured more orders for steel, textiles and hundreds of other products, more men and women were needed to run power smelters, looms, machinery. The Franklins talked with the new capitalists, men with whom Benjamin felt instinctively at home, men whose sons, like William, could expect to live as gentlemen and cultivate their own broad acres.

They visited the great Soho ironworks, the button factories, the workshops where mass-produced silks were printed on presses. Then they rode on to Derby, the hub of English porcelain production, of lead and iron mines. Here they saw the first true factory in England, one employing two hundred people in a six-story mill. They navigated the twisting road to the Derbyshire iron forges and, once again, William went down into the dark, wet workings of a mineshaft to gather material for his father. Seven years later, an anonymous pamphlet attributed to Benjamin was published under the title *A Derbyshire Working Miner*. It was apparently based on William's observations.

Another day's ride brought them to Manchester. Everything about the "greatest mere village in England" underscored the clash of industry and agriculture. The population had multiplied tenfold in half a century as surrounding farm counties drained manpower into the city. Livestock jostled with the hundreds of horses hauling hides, coal and textiles from outlying villages where a thousand families produced piecework goods for a single clothier. The Franklins had trouble sleeping in the noisy downtown inn and hurried west toward Liverpool. There Benjamin dashed off a hasty note to Debby: "We have been out now almost three weeks having spent some time in Derbyshire among the gentry to whom we were recommended. We shall set out today for Lancaster. The journey agrees extremely well with me and will probably be many ways of use to me. Billy presents his duty."[37]

By early evening of August 29, as they braked before the white-washed Castle Inn overlooking Morecambe Bay, they had the precious letters they needed to assure a rewarding visit to Scotland, its low foothills now beckoning through the haze.

The Great North Road from Lancaster to the Scottish border traverses one of the most beautiful stretches of highway ever to awe a traveler, yet if either Franklin was impressed by the natural beauty around him, no hint of the fact survives. For two days as they passed through the Lake Country they were apparently engaged in a growing debate over what they had seen. From William's letters to Philadelphia and other writings before the trip, and his differences with his father when they reached Edinburgh a few days later, we can infer that Benjamin by now had elevated colonial expansion to a personal religion. Like his son, he saw the great world war for empire still engaging the powers and colonies of Europe as a necessary bloodletting to drain off the pressure of French encroachment on the western American frontier, to open the immense valleys west of the Alleghenies to a land rush from the overcrowded coastal colonies. At the same time that both men were using their influence to secure a niche in this new land for themselves, Benjamin wanted to fill it with men as tough and determined as the zealous Presbyterians who had fought with them in Pennsylvania, men of his own tongue and principles who were willing to fight to defend what he was lobbying to obtain.

By this time, however, the Franklins had developed two distinctly different views of what they had seen. Benjamin always thought of himself as an American; William considered himself an American-born British subject. Benjamin consequently viewed with alarm increasing British restraint of American trade and expansion. Moreover, in England he saw heavy taxation of the small landowner class from which he had come. William, like other eighteenth-century students of law and history (including Rousseau and Montesquieu), saw that the English enjoyed the broadest civil liberties of any European people.

Neither, apparently, could see the ultimate collision of their views. Where William fundamentally differed from his father was the way he chose to obtain his ends. He saw no harm in living in grand style, no sin in reaping the social status that naturally results from wealth. He had boundless faith in the final triumph of the

British system. Indeed, he favored perfecting the English constitution by moving closer to the old landed aristocracy, where hereditary transfer of land and power curbed the rising threat of the mob. The bastard craved fine company, noble trappings, the appearances of legitimacy. He garbed his reasoning, his vision of himself as the landed lord of a great forest empire, in a romanticized idealism sharply opposed to his father's earthy pragmatism. Benjamin saw land as a way to wealth, to a family dynasty, and secretly sought it. William saw land not only as the basis of money but of social acceptance, influence, refinement and leisure.

It took three torturous days to cover the rugged twisting road from Carlisle to Edinburgh. At last, on the afternoon of September 3, after twenty-seven days on the road, the Franklin post chaise reached the summit of Soutra Hill and they could see, through the perpetual acrid cloud of smoke, the view that had invited English invaders for centuries. Almost before they could look out over the walled city of Edinburgh, they could smell it. Stench and all, Edinburgh boasted the finest minds in Europe, and during the summer of the Franklins' visit it was the gathering place for the men who were on the way to controlling the destiny of the new British Empire.

7

SIX WEEKS OF THE DENSEST HAPPINESS

September–October 1759

CELEBRATED THROUGHOUT EUROPE FOR ITS UNIVERSITY, hospitals, philosophers and historians, the walled city of Edinburgh was, in September 1759, crowded with fifty thousand people crammed into a few noisy, foul-smelling square miles. Homes, shops, churches and Parliament buildings flanked the two main streets, which ran up a sharp incline from the twelfth-century Holyrood Palace to the equally venerable Edinburgh Castle. Branching out from the city's spine like ribs were courtyard-squares surrounded by roughhewn stone tenements eight to fourteen stories high. The lands, as these early apartment houses were called, contained fashionable shops on the lower floors, the town houses of earls and lairds on the middle floors (their coats of arms were emblazoned above the doorways), and many of the city's poor on the upper floors, to which they had to lug their coal, food and water.

Edinburgh attracted visitors every summer, but it was hardly a tourists' haven. As usual, the Franklins could find only wretched accommodations on their first night in the city. The next morning they hastened to look up a printer, who recommended to them the best boardinghouse in the city. This was Mrs. Cowan's flat, halfway up an eight-story tenement on Milne Court.[1]

The next ten days were packed with unexpected pleasures. In a surprise ceremony, the Franklins received the city's highest honor, the Freedom of the Burgh, enjoyed only by its most distinguished citizens and visitors. On Wednesday morning, September 5, after the city herald sounded his trumpet at the market cross in Parliament Square, a proclamation in the Franklins' honor was read and they were escorted in a colorful parade to the Guild Hall. The Franklins followed assorted baillies and old baillies, deacons, and just ahead of them, the lord provost of Edinburgh himself, Sir George Drummond, who marched serenely in his vast wig and billowing robes, his heavy ebony staff tapping out the cadence. Four other dignitaries, including Lord Bute's friend Lord Lyttleton, a member of the King's Privy Council, and his son, joined them at the Guild Hall, where they were to be admitted as members that day. Beside the Lyttletons sat the soapmaker's son and his bastard while baillies straightfacedly debated the day's point of law: "Whether the daughters of burgesses shall lose their freedom if they are not reputed virgins." The issue remaining unresolved, the Lord Provost moved "to admit and receive Benjamin Franklin of Philadelphia, Esquire, and [William] Franklin his son, to be burgesses and guild brethren of this city in the most ample form."[2]

To venture into Scotland in the mid-eighteenth century, to seek alliances relying on the influence and loyalty of its lords and intellectual leaders, was a dangerous business. To be pursued without harm, it required some knowledge of the treacherous crosscurrents of religion and politics. As long ago as Queen Elizabeth's reign in the sixteenth century, British nobles had worried that Puritanism, especially the dissenting Presbyterian form set up in opposition to the Church of England, carried within it the seeds of democracy, of the innate downfall of monarchy. James I complained that "some fiery-spirited men in the ministry . . . finding the taste of government sweet, began to fancy a democratic form. . . . I was calumniated in their sermons not for any vice in me but because I was king, which they thought the highest evil."[3] When James's son Charles I and his grandson Charles II reigned in England, they did their utmost to break the power of the Scottish kirkmen, who retaliated by rallying the faithful against *their* descendants.

Through it all, the clergy of Scotland kept alive a representative democracy of sorts. In fact, behind the facade of autocracy flourished the only democratic form of government in Europe. The members of each parish elected parsons who, in turn, elected representatives to control the Kirk, and thereby Scottish life, at every level. In long-winded General Assemblies each summer in Edinburgh and Glasgow, the clergy exercised great power. Indeed, the Scottish clergy claimed divine inspiration, and therefore infallibility, in all matters of faith and morals. They assumed control of private and public lives in much more vigorous fashion than the lax old Catholic clergy they had overthrown. If Catholics burned heretics, Scottish Presbyterians made life a living hell for anyone who disagreed with their views. Not satisfied with berating fornication and adultery, they banned the theater, pursued witches, then paid for the firewood to burn them.

Yet above all, the Presbyterians of Scotland hated bishops and their costly, showy way of living. All bishops had long ago been ordered to cease being bishops and apply for admission to the Assembly as simple ministers. At the same time, Scottish parsons coined the one-sided doctrine of separation of church and state, limiting the effectiveness of government while extending their own influence. Clerics could meddle in state affairs, but the state must keep out of church politics.

One English king, himself Scottish-born, saw that this could lead to the overthrow of monarchy. Sensing that his brother Scots would one day try to bring down the kings of England, James I had decreed that the Kirk could not excommunicate anyone without state approval. When the presbyters persisted, James executed four of them. Hard-core dissidents fled into exile. But the Scots persisted. Anonymous pamphlets blackened the kings of England, ballads proclaimed their tyranny, housewives cursed them to hell's fire. Worse, thrifty Scots paid less and less into the King's tax coffers. Finally, James had to give the Kirk a separate charter, restoring all its powers, abolishing all bishops, allowing exiles to come home in triumph. One of them, John Knox, called the King "God's silly vassal" and then he declared bluntly: "There are two kings and two kingdoms in Scotland. There is Christ Jesus and His Kingdom, the Kirk, whose subject King James is. . . . Not a King, nor a head, nor a lord, but a member."[4]

The fractious Scots fought not only the King, they quarreled fiercely among themselves. In parsonages all over Scotland, fires of religious disputation smoldered, breaking into conflagration at the General Assembly each summer. In 1759 the issue was the Scottish Enlightenment. At first breaking out at the University of Glasgow and then at Edinburgh, an intellectual revolt against Kirk repression had been gathering momentum for a generation, fueled by the writings of David Hume (who was labeled by the Kirk an atheist), and by the lectures of Adam Smith and the Reverend Doctor William Robertson, regent of the University of Edinburgh and the celebrated author of the best-selling *History of Scotland.* When Robertson took power in the university and the Kirk, his free-thinking was challenged by a severe young dominie from Paisley. The Reverend John Witherspoon wrote and preached against decadent ministers like Robertson, who drank, bowled on the green, went to plays, and learned to speak English. So acrimonious had the General Assemblies become that one noted controversialist ended an impassioned speech by keeling over dead. The debate raged on uninterrupted as his body was carried out.

The Franklins had known for years of the Scottish Enlightenment. Benjamin had bought his first electrical apparatus from a Scot, Dr. Adam Spencer, and his printing partner was Scottish-born. Despite their defeat by the English in battle, the Scots dominated British jurisprudence under a Scottish-born lord chief justice. Moreover, most of the best books published in England were consistently written and published by Scots.

The Franklins were wined and dined every evening of their stay, but one invitation was particularly memorable. It came from none other than Dr. Robertson himself. The Franklins had met him in London at William Strahan's and knew that around him revolved the most influential men in Scotland. Late on the appointed afternoon, they set out, with a leather-bound copy of their *Historical Review* to present to their host. The post chaise edged out into the uphill current of the Canongate, up the steep grade past rows of gray, turreted houses and half-timbered shops and swung right to the Cowgate for the half-mile ride through the city. The streets were alive with hundreds of black-garbed kirkmen, looking like a legion of crows come to town to pick over the latest steaming morsels of religious disputation. Just inside the west gates, the Franklin post chaise reined in before a tall Elizabethan house.

Inside, they were ushered into the company of genius. Dr. Robertson, small, round and whimsical, introduced them to David Hume, the philosopher; Lord Kames, a master of British law; William Cullen, physician and pioneer chemist; three other distinguished members of the medical faculty of the university; Adam Smith, the economist (in from Glasgow); Sir Alexander Dick, the foremost physician of Scotland and an intimate friend of Lord Bute's; the philosopher-historian-poet-clergyman Adam Ferguson, who had recently been appointed professor of natural philosophy at Edinburgh; William Strahan, the publisher (up from London); the Reverend Alexander Carlyle — nicknamed Jupiter because of his classical good looks — a freethinker and president of the Edinburgh Philosophical Society; and Carlyle's brother-in-law, a Dr. Wight, whom the Franklins had already met by chance at breakfast on the Great North Road.[5]

William and Ferguson evidently took to each other at once. As the only soldiers in the room, and competent ones at that, they had ample to talk about. In any event, they became good friends in later years. Ferguson was known far and wide as the fighting chaplain of the Black Watch Regiment. Broadsword in hand, he had led troops at the battle of Fontenoy against the French. Not long after the evening at Dr. Robertson's he published a pamphlet on the militia and a book on the principles of warfare. Of special interest to the Franklins was his close friendship with Bute's secretary, John Home. He was also the tutor of Bute's sons.

The guests of honor found themselves drawn into a discussion of the war. Shortly before their visit Jupiter Carlyle had published a satirical pamphlet applauding the Pitt administration for seeking to expand the war in Europe until England could win an all-out victory over the French. But Carlyle was dubious about the wisdom of pouring more men into the frontier war in America.[6] Yet it was William's argument that the only thing that could ensure the success of the attack on Quebec was sufficient manpower. All that prevented victory over the French — William had argued the point in a long letter only a few weeks before — was the decision to attack too many targets at once, thus spreading British forces too thin.[7]

Evidently, when William argued that British victory in the West Indies was more important than many British leaders believed, his father contradicted him. It was Benjamin's view that the sugar islands of the Caribbean were relatively unimportant. William no doubt surprised his father by disputing him. He was convinced that, with prudent management, they would prove a very valuable acquisition. He also doubted whether Britain would be invaded by the French, a view opposite to that of his father, who had pointed out on their travels several areas of the British Isles that were especially vulnerable. As William made his points to the delight of the other guests, Benjamin lapsed into a sullen silence. If William noticed this, it did not deter him. Not every day did he have such an intelligent, appreciative audience. The more he talked, the farther Benjamin receded.[8]

Benjamin probably had turned his thoughts to the purpose of their visit and how these men could be useful to him. There was no point in arguing openly with his son. The flavor of the evening was decidedly Tory, he could see. Dr. Robertson was on good terms with Lord Bute. Prince George could depend on Robertson to uphold monarchy in his popular historical writings. In fact, most of the men at dinner tonight staunchly supported Bute and his royal student.

Soon enough, the talk turned from politics to science. Predictably, even this discussion took the form of disputation, something William had mastered after the dinners at the Middle Temple. But Benjamin always despised disputation, preferring the Socratic pose of the humble questioner. "Persons of good sense, I have observed," he wrote subsequently in his autobiography, "rarely fall into it except lawyers, university men and men of all sorts that have been bred in Edinburgh."[9]

The evening was memorable for several of the company. Strahan wrote to Benjamin's printing partner in Philadelphia, himself from Edinburgh, that the Franklins had been "most cordially entertained . . . in the most genteel manner imaginable. . . . I am sure they will never forget their reception or cease to think highly of the conversation of our countrymen."[10] But Dr. Alexander Carlyle, a perceptive observer of character, took home another impression. Years later, he wrote in his memoirs that there had been a certain unpleasant undercurrent in the room. "Franklin's son," he recalled, "was open and communicative and pleased the company better than his father; and some of us observed indications of that decided difference of opinion between father and son which, in the American war, alienated them altogether."[11]

The number of invitations rose each day as the last night's festivities provided yeast for the next. On a tour of the city, the Franklins strolled down narrow College Wynd to the university. Unbeknownst to them, James Boswell was a student there at the time. They also visited the city hospital and the medical Chamber of Rarities. Then, before leaving for St. Andrews, they spent a few days in Glasgow with Adam Smith at his invitation.

Benjamin was enamored with Glasgow from the start (he had sometimes found himself uncomfortable in Edinburgh). The thoroughly commercial city was his idea of paradise. The marks of mercantile success were everywhere: in the stately rows of homes built with the profits from trade in slaves, tobacco and rum, and from building the ships to carry them.[12] The down-to-earth intellectualism, too, was more to his taste. In the university quadrangle worked as many inventors as professors, as many aproned artisans as red-gowned students. On the debit side, the Franklins could not avoid seeing the knots of hungry men and women willing to sign on as ballast in the empty ships headed for America, where they dreamed of exchanging their poverty for a plantation on the frontier.

At the core of the commercial ferment was Professor Adam Smith. Only seventeen when he had imbibed Hume's liberating *Treatise on Human Nature,* Smith had attended Oxford on a scholarship and returned to Scotland to give lectures on literature and poetry to the young elite of Glasgow. He had delighted their anti-English sentiments by boldly declaring that Shakespeare wrote "some good scenes but never a good play." He expounded in his classes the broad principles of economics and free trade which, by the time of the Franklin visit, had become the basis for a book he was writing: *The Wealth of Nations.* Nurtured by other intellectual Scots — in 1752 Hume had published his inspirational essays on the balance of trade — Adam Smith preferred conversation that turned on import duties, currency exchange rates and the problems of labor. In Glasgow, as man and boy studied the thought and writings of Adam Smith, he studied them, making the marketplace his laboratory.

At dinner in his home on Professor's Court, in leisurely strolls on the gravel walkways of the professors' garden and on a bench in the shade, the Scottish economist and his American guests eagerly exchanged data on trade. Not only did Dr. Franklin and Professor Smith have similar economic theories underpinning their views of a successful life, they both proclaimed a universal optimism about the course and destiny of human nature. Only a few months earlier Smith had published his briefly popular *Theory of Moral Sentiments,* in which he attempted to reduce to reason the origins of human feelings.

Everywhere the Franklins traveled that summer, they saw the raw scar tissue of religious warfare, of the thousands of killings in the name of God. In this superficially peaceful mountain realm, they found the bitterness that had impelled more than one hundred thousand Scots to leave their homeland. The Franklins began to understand the waves of Scottish religious refugees who, once arrived in America where they believed they were out of the reach of oppressive authority, were willing to fight anyone who dared attempt to impose upon them even the slightest trace of the old country's austere rule.

After every abortive uprising, more Scots fled the cross fire of hatred and conflicting loyalties. At least fifty thousand Presbyterian Scots cross the Irish Sea to take up lands emptied by the purges of Catholics in northern Ireland. When they began to win Irish elections, nervous Anglican bishops and English overlords barred them from public office, hiked rents and taxes. Rather than submit, thousands embarked for America with an undying bitterness against things English, especially Anglican. Another fifty thousand were deported to America after the defeat of the Highland clans at Culloden.

As the Franklins hurried north along the western shore of Loch Lomond, they saw one Scottish laborer after another swinging his pick or mattock in rhythm to a song of grief for his wife and children bayoneted in the glens. After following the narrow dirt road west a short while, they faced the grandeur of Inverary, where the infamous dukes of Argyll, hereditary leaders of the Clan Campbell, lived in regal majesty. Few settings promised more peace than the promontory between the River Aray and the eastern shore of Loch Fyne, a great blue slash of the Irish Sea that cuts deep into Scotland's side. Here, the Clan Campbell had lived and plotted since at least the thirteenth century.

The Campbells of Argyll and their rivals, the MacDonalds of Glencoe, had feuded for centuries. In 1689, when William III came to the British throne and decreed that all Highland clans take an oath of allegiance to him, the ruling MacDonald reluctantly agreed to submit to the duke of Argyll, the King's agent in Scotland. The proof of MacDonald compliance was suppressed by the duke, who lied to the head of the Campbell regiment sent to force submission. Marching to Glencoe, the Campbell at first accepted the hospitality of the MacDonald, dining and playing cards with him while their soldiers ate and drank in the barns. But at five the next morning, the Campbells rose and fell upon the MacDonalds in their sleep. Up and down the glen, MacDonalds died before sunrise, their chief shot through the heart, his wife raped and left to die, some thirty-eight other clan leaders left to bleed to death, and their herds of cattle, horses and sheep driven south.[13]

The leading Campbell at the time of the Franklins' visit was Archibald, the third duke. A boy of ten when his uncles returned from their savage raid, he had become a symbol of cruelty in his own right when he systematically annihilated the Highland clans. As the Franklins knew, this particular Campbell, as well as being Lord Bute's uncle, was a member of the King's Privy Council, a man who would sit in judgment on their plans for America and the one who controlled the Scottish bloc in Parliament. He was by far the most important nobleman in Scotland. After the Franklins bent their knees and kissed his ring, they presented him with a handsome calf-bound copy of their *Historical Review*.

Leaving Inverary behind, they hurtled north, then east, and at last climbed down wearily at the King's Arms Tavern in Dunkeld the night of September 29. The next day, they made the obligatory side trip to Scone Palace, the summer home of Lord Mansfield, the lord chief justice of England, and another privy councillor and Middle Templar. After paying their respects, they were shown to the spot where Scottish kings had come for hundreds of years to be crowned on the Scottish Stone of Destiny before it was carted off to Westminster Abbey to help prop up the English monarch's throne at every coronation. "Who knows," Benjamin remarked, "but St. James's [Palace] may some time or other lie in ruins as Scone does now."[14]

Their arrival at St. Andrews on the North Sea coast on October 1 did not alleviate the sadness of their Highland tour. They wandered through the hollowed ruins of the once-great cathedral-fortress, where the Scottish Reformation had been wrought with the dagger, the cardinal archbishop of St. Andrews murdered and his body pitched into a dry moat. The town, built on a sheer red bluff to stave off invasion by Norsemen, had fallen finally from within. All that remained in 1759 was the gaping, twin-spired shell of the finest cathedral in Britain, its empty windows staring down at the houses and moldering university buildings made of its stones. Once filled with the chanting of monks, it now howled with the fierce north wind.

The University of St. Andrews was down to twenty students, who were attending classes in seedy, unheated halls. The members of the faculty were nearly as numerous as their pupils. From visits with William Strahan, the Franklins already knew the mathematics professor, David Gregory, who had helped to arrange the honors. Faculty and students filed into the library and sat on benches that flanked great leaded windows. Outside stood the dark thorn tree planted by Mary Queen of Scots at an earlier commencement. William joined the students as his father, garbed in the black gown of a doctor of laws, knelt on the graduation stool. The citation was read aloud in Latin by the president of the university: "Whereas the ingenious and worthy Benjamin Franklin has . . . by his ingenious inventions and successful experiments enriched science . . . and more especially . . . electricity which heretofore was little known . . . we grant to him all the privileges and honors which are anywhere granted to Doctors of Laws."[15] The president touched the head of the Boston grammar school dropout with the square black cap once worn by John Knox, draped the scarlet hood over his shoulders, and bade him to rise Dr. Franklin. Off to the side, William looked on as his father received recognition for their long and dangerous experiments. If he bore any resentment at being excluded, he did not register it.

For three days the Franklins lingered at St. Andrews. Each day away from city smoke in a place where Benjamin enjoyed receiving the attention of fellow scientists reinvigorated him. Yet despite more than one thousand miles of awful roads in scarcely two months, he was soon eager for the road again. Lumbering off toward Edinburgh, the Franklins returned to the capital for another brief round of visits before journeying south.

The mail forwarded to them at Mrs. Cowan's boardinghouse informed them that the King's Privy Council, acting on Benjamin's petition, had agreed to adjudicate the claims of the Delaware Indians against the Walking Purchase. And every British subject had reason to celebrate that week. Just as the Franklins returned to Edinburgh, an exhausted messenger dismounted at the market cross to read a dispatch from London. On the Plains of Abraham outside Quebec, the British army — including valiant Scots officers leading kilted Black Watch regiments — had crushed the French and seized the capital of French Canada, effectively ending the French and Indian War for the domination of America.

For the Franklins especially, it was good news. Peace with the Indians, peace with the French, would remove the long threat to the Pennsylvania frontier, to all of the fifteen-hundred-mile frontier of English America. Once again, settlers could surge across the Appalachians to stake out lands William had first seen as a young British flag-bearer more than ten years before. The men who controlled that land, who collected the rents and fees from subdividing a forest empire, would be exceedingly rich. With their new and powerful connections, the Franklins were in an excellent position to stake out for themselves a dominion greater than any their old rivals the Penns had enjoyed.

As veterans who had contributed much to the British effort, the

Franklins were more in demand than ever at dinner. They stayed on until October 6 in a flurry of invitations and then in a flurry of farewells. On the way back to London they stopped off for a visit at Prestonfield, the country seat of Sir Alexander and Lady Dick.[16] Built of stone in the Flemish style in the seventeenth century, Prestonfield was known to be the most fashionable house in Scotland. The Franklins duly admired the white-stuccoed exterior, the stepped roof, the grapevine motif of the papier-mâché ceiling moldings, the black and white tiled floors. William was so impressed that he imitated a number of these features in his own house many years later.

After a hearty dinner the talk inevitably turned to American scientific affairs. This time Benjamin shone. Sir Alexander and all the guests knew of his work. At length the company adjourned to the gardens to sit in the shade of centuries-old yew trees. Local legend has it that while William took a crack at lawn bowling with Sir Alexander, Benjamin sat on a worn gray bench once owned by Mary Queen of Scots' mother, the Queen of France, exchanging epigrams from *Poor Richard* for bits of poetry with Lady Dick and her nine-year-old daughter.

The Franklins' last stopover in Scotland was with Lord and Lady Kames, and again they were treated royally. Lord Kames was an esteemed authority on jurisprudence known for his toothless, hawk-nosed leer as he pronounced the death sentence. He was a fitting target for a favorite Franklin hoax. After dinner, as was her custom, Lady Kames called for her Bible for the evening's reading. When she had finished, Benjamin sent William to fetch his bifocals and *his* Bible. He read what he introduced as the parable of Abraham and the stranger: "When Abraham saw that the man blessed not God, he said unto him, 'Wherefore dost thou not worship the most high God?' . . . And the man answered, 'I do not worship the God thou speakest of . . . for I have made to myself a God which abideth always in mine house.' . . . And Abraham drove him forth with blows into the wilderness. . . . And God spake again unto Abraham, saying, 'For this thy sin shall thy seed be afflicted four hundred years in a strange land!' "[17]

Benjamin's listeners supplied their amens. It was another day before they looked into their own Bibles and failed to find the parable. Benjamin had concocted a chapter of his own, had it set into type and bound into his Bible, all to make a point against religious intolerance. As usual, he had made his philosophical protest charmingly among strangers. He instructed William to make a copy for Lady Kames. One year later, William finally complied.

Eventually, Lord Kames drove them in his own splendid carriage across the border into England. In January 1760, Benjamin wrote back to his lordship, still glowing that "on the whole, I must say, I think the time we spent [in Scotland] was six weeks of the *densest* happiness I have met with in any part of my life."[18]

Familiarity breeds content among British aristocrats. By the summer of 1760, the Franklins had called at enough country houses, bent their knees often enough, to become trusted by many of those in power. They had learned that it was public opposition, not opposition itself, that infuriates the British establishment.

In his first three years as agent for Pennsylvania in London, the elder Franklin had submitted nineteen provincial laws for confirmation by the King. By skillful lobbying, the Penns had obtained vetoes of six of them. Franklin had prevailed in thirteen, of which the most important by far were those concerning taxation of Penn lands for defense, the main objective of Franklin's mission to London.

As he and William walked into Whitehall Palace on August 27, 1760, they saw that they were among friends. In the Cockpit hearing room they recognized around the long table facing them such new-found friends among the King's privy councillors as Lord Lyttleton, who had paraded through Edinburgh with them, and Lord Mansfield of Scone. After two days of wrangling, Lord Mansfield caught Benjamin's eye. "Beckoning to me," Benjamin wrote later, "he took me into the Clerk's Chamber while the lawyers were pleading and asked me if I was really of opinion that no injury would be done the proprietary estate in the execution of the [tax] act. I said, 'Certainly.' " Calling in the lawyers for both sides, Lord Mansfield got them to agree to sign a bond, then led them back out to the public hearings. "When Lord Mansfield returned to the Council Chamber, finally the law was allowed to pass."[19]

The Franklins had won the first round of their five-year battle against the Penns.

It was now apparent that the Penns, alarmed at the Franklin inroads, were prepared to fight even harder to keep their colony. They sent John Penn to govern the colony personally, thereby dealing a severe blow to the Franklins' strategy of charging them with neglect of the province. It would be years before the Franklins could win their struggle for power in Pennsylvania, if ever.

William was growing tired of his father's perpetual plotting, and was decidedly beginning to lose his awe of his father. The relatives of a great man often fail to see his achievements as clearly as they see his everyday failures, flaws, hypocrisy, pettiness, selfishness. Whatever fate held for Dr. Franklin, his son knew he could no longer thrive and grow in his shade: he must seek the light, give himself room. His dream of empire, he feared, was fading in the rush of his father's attention to his own interests and hatred of old enemies. He must, whatever the cost, cut free, even if it meant openly espousing views quite opposed to his father's, even if it meant leaving his father's comfortable nest on Craven Street and going back to America alone to seek his own fortune. William was liked and respected for himself. Before middle age set in he had to take control of his own life. And he did.

8

I DISLIKE FAMILY QUARRELS

1760–1762

O N THE NORTH BANK OF THE THAMES IN THE WESTMIN-
ster district of London stood Northumberland House, the
winter home of the Percys, one of the most tempestuous ducal families in England. Atop its ornate Tudor facade, a great lead lion
strutted defiantly westward toward the government offices in
Whitehall. The neighboring commercial bustle of the Strand and
the prim town houses of Craven Street were in every sense beneath
it.[1]

In the year since the Franklins had returned from Scotland, as
victorious armies brought home to London the spoils of a great
new empire, William had gradually drawn away from his father's
middle-class influence and spent more and more time with his new
friends at Northumberland House. Next to a direct royal summons
to the Court of St. James, an invitation to Northumberland House
at this time of resurgent Tory power was a sure sign of the King's
favor, of a young man's chances to rise in the new imperial society.
To judge from the number of engraved cards William was receiving,[2] he could hope for a substantial post in the expanding colonial
service as soon as the intrigue surrounding the new King subsided.

Old King George II had died at last on October 25, 1760. His
collapse ended nearly seventy-five years of Whig-Protestant-busi-
ness control of the Crown. Even before his death was announced,
the scramble for power had begun. Carriages of cabinet ministers

streaked to Whitehall. Notified of his grandfather's death, twenty-two-year-old Prince George, the heir apparent, wrote immediately to Lord Bute, "I am coming the back way to your house."[3]

The young King began his reign by forcing the popular wartime prime minister, William Pitt, to wait in an anteroom two hours while he conferred with Bute in the Closet. In the ensuing year, Bute and his prince would steadily force Pitt and his old order out of power, and Bute would be installed as the prime dispenser of royal patronage. The new King revolted against all his grandfather had done. George II had won an empire and held it together by favoring a strong coalition government, a policy that had made him appear deceptively weak. By contrast, George III exalted himself, appointed mediocre ministers (every one of them Tories), and set about dismantling much of what his grandfather had won and maintained.

The young Bostonian John Hancock wrote home from London: "The Prince of Wales was proclaimed King through the city with great pomp and joy. . . . His coronation I am told will not be until April."[4] In colonial America, the newspapers heaped adulation on the virtuous young King, who reportedly rose at five every morning, lit his own candle, went to chapel at six, and remained "remarkably respectful and loving" to his mother. But to closer observers at court, another side was becoming apparent. Bute was allowed to put up Tory members for traditionally Whig seats in the House of Commons even as the young King made a brash speech against the "bloody and expensive war" that still dragged on in Europe. In the eleven months before he was crowned, he not only dismissed his grandfather's ministers, but took into his own hands the immense treasury and used it to buy control of Parliament. Then he proclaimed in a speech from the throne that "born and bred in this country, I glory in the name of Briton."[5] Not Englishman, but *Briton* — that is, including the Scots. This Bute-inspired remark, taken as a slap by the public, set off riots in London that made it dangerous for Bute to venture out of his house without bodyguards.

Despite official mourning, Tory society, now restored to power, celebrated jubilantly, and at no place more conspicuously than at Northumberland House. There, Lady Percy, a descendant of Charles II and now a lady of the bedchamber to the new Queen, convened her own court and proposed her own hand-chosen favorites for office to her dear friend Bute, who recommended them to the King.

After William Franklin gave up the idea of marrying Elizabeth Graeme, he joined wholeheartedly in the society of Northumberland House, where he apparently had been introduced by Scottish friends. As was their wont, the Percys flattered William, competing for his presence with other hosts and hostesses almost as eagerly as he courted their favor. An avid student of English history, William was no doubt familiar, from the writings of Hume and Robertson, with the Percy family's Tory tendencies. Since the eleventh century, Percys had helped English monarchs onto the throne and off. They fought William the Conqueror; they made and broke Richard II; their quarreling with Henry IV was immortalized by Shakespeare; their heads rolled for loyalty to Mary Queen of Scots. Percys guarded the children of the beheaded Charles I, yet counseled moderation during the Stuart Restoration. Bastards, as William must have known, were no strangers to their line: the Percys, like Bute, were descended from illegitimate sons of Charles II. By the 1760's they no doubt considered themselves, and with reason, more durable than the royal family. For the son of a Whig dissenter to align himself with the notoriously quixotic, Tory, High Church Percys was a serious step for William to take, one that was bound to lead to trouble with his father.

The leader of the Percys at this juncture was Lady Elizabeth Seymour Percy, duchess of Northumberland. The Whig diarist Horace Walpole described her as "mischievous under the appearance of frankness, generous and friendly without delicacy or sentiment, and a fond wife without curbing her Lord's amours, or her own."[6] She was a glamorous woman in her early forties when William met her, a woman intimate with some of the handsomest young men in England.

To be a courtier in London, while it certainly did not require morals, demanded the utmost discretion. A man was not welcome in the salon of a duchess if it became known that he took notes. When James Boswell published letters about his visits to Northumberland House, he was ostracized and lost any chance for an officer's appointment. William Franklin took no notes. Though discretion was *de rigueur,* wealth was not. According to Boswell's journal, it cost only a good suit of clothes and the right connections to attend the Percy court, and Benjamin had bought William a new suit when he was admitted to the bar. William would follow a pre-scribed routine, as Boswell described it:

"I had called once or twice and left my name. I now received a card of invitation. . . . This raised my spirits, gave me notions of consequence and filled me with grandeur. . . . In the evening, I went to Northumberland House to the rout, which was indeed magnificent. Three large rooms and the gallery (a prodigious one) were full of the best company, between three and four hundred of them. The gallery is richly adorned. . . . The King and Lady Northumberland are exhibited in full-length portraits in their robes.

"As I was standing in pleasing reverie in the gallery musing on the splendid scene around me and joining with that the ancient ideas of the family of Percy, My Lady came up to me with the greatest complacency and kindness: '. . . I am very happy to see you. How do you do? I hope you are come to settle among us. I was very sorry that I was not at home when you called. I gave positive orders that you should be admitted whenever you called.' This put me into the finest humour. I thanked her sincerely. I chatted easily. She then carried me to My Lord, who was very glad to see me and very civil to me. This is indeed a noble family."[7]

Coming home to Mrs. Stevenson's plain-faced boardinghouse on Craven Street was a prospect less and less appealing as William progressed in Lady Percy's favor. Indeed, evenings at Northum-berland House surrounded by daringly dressed women were enough to madden a virile young man. Young courtiers often stopped off on the way home to patronize ladies-of-the-evening or, if they had the money, took mistresses. The Strand was a vast out-door brothel at night, where a half crown bought a young girl fresh from the country for a quick sortie to a tavern or behind the bushes in St. James's Park.

A less transient relationship was at the very least safer. In the winter of 1759, following the errant path of his father, William Franklin had a brief affair that led to the birth of another bastard Franklin. Who the mother of William's son was remains a mystery.

There is a hint of it in a frantic flurry of pleas from a milliner just before the Franklins left on a vacation. She wanted help in setting herself up in a business. Benjamin did come across with an uncharacteristic loan to her, but the evidence stops there. The news of William's sexual adventure momentarily disturbed the elder Franklin's settled life on Craven Street, but he could only look back on his own youthful escapades and realize that unless he had legitimized William he would have had no surviving son of his own.[8]

At the age of twenty-three, in a tightly knit small town in America, Benjamin had felt the moral pressure of a Quaker community and openly admitted his greatest erratum by adopting and giving his name to William. Now, at fifty-four, a careful politician in a large metropolis, he apparently was opposed to William's following suit. Neither did he favor a marriage: it might mar William's chances for a government post. At the same time it could prove even more scandalous to abandon the child: the laws of England were quite clear on the responsibility of a father to support a bastard. Of course, arrangements had to be made for wet nurse, doctor and the mother's support. Evidently in an effort to make a generous settlement without his father's help, William turned to Strahan, who provided him with twenty pounds and later helped him rear the child and keep the fact of its existence secret.[9]

More than ever, Benjamin was now determined that his son should marry someone acceptable like Polly Stevenson and settle down. He wrote Deborah, "You cannot conceive how shamefully the mode is here to a single life. One can scarce be in the company of a dozen men of circumstance and fortune but . . . eleven of them are single. The great complaint is the excessive expensiveness of English wives."[10] To Franklin, bred in Puritan Boston where bachelors were presumed guilty of immorality and fined, it was a lesser evil to marry and commit adultery than to avoid such hypocrisy and simply remain unmarried at William's age.

On many occasions he had urged a match with Polly Stevenson, a frail young spinster with a mind as sharp as her face. She had been sent to a London suburb to live with a rich maiden aunt who had more money than time left to spend it. William was decidedly cool to the idea: Polly was known to London society as "Virgin Mary." Yet Benjamin persisted. He told Polly that William would eventually come around. If William went for a stroll in St. James's Park and Polly was not in town at the time, Benjamin wrote to her, reporting that William had missed her. If Polly knew of William's nocturnal activities, it was not from Benjamin. Ten years passed before she was told that the child called "Master Temple" was William's son. Benjamin, who in his time had resisted parental manipulations, was fond of the outdated notion of arranged marriages. He had actually proposed marriage between his daughter and Strahan's son before the two were in their teens. Strahan was rich, Benjamin pointed out to Deborah. He would hardly have been more subtle with his own William, caring little to ask whether William had someone else in mind for a wife.[11]

Officially, Benjamin Franklin's mission to England had ended in August of 1760, when it became evident that he could do no more in his fight against the Penns. Yet he was reluctant to go home. Although he missed his friends, at times his wife, yet he basked in the hospitality of his London clubs and societies. He stayed on for two more years and traveled restlessly to Europe in the summer of 1761.

At no time in his life was Franklin less sure of himself. Adrift without the compass of his mission, he did not know what course to chart for a life he often felt was over. Though he was honored for his inventions and discoveries, his sojourn in England had been inconclusive. His personal vendetta against the Penns had discredited him in many British eyes and had damaged his reputation. Dr. Johnson, for one, lumped Franklin with other Americans as "a race of convicts [who] ought to be thankful for anything we allow them short of hanging. . . . Their numbers are, at present, not quite sufficient for . . . greatness . . . but by Dr. Franklin's rule of progression, they will, in a century and a quarter, be more than equal to the inhabitants of Europe. When the Whigs are thus multiplied, let the princes of the earth tremble in their palaces. But let not our boldest oppugners of authority look forward with delight to this."[12]

So deep was Franklin's infatuation with the rising Tory government that he was more than ever determined to stay in London while he worked to take Pennsylvania away from the Penns and place it under direct royal rule. His lingering absence from Philadelphia made him a lightning rod for rumors that sped across the ocean and disturbed his family and friends. "Some people here enquire," wrote one Philadelphia Quaker friend, " 'Do you know what Benjamin Franklin is doing? We hear so little.' " Others, however, heard more than Benjamin wished, and upbraided him over "the station of thy Debby and Sally, who ardently wish for thee." For years, Deborah had put up with "thy long absence with a more resigned and Christian spirit than could be expected."[13]

But there were persistent rumors that Franklin had all the female company he needed on Craven Street. After Deborah's mother fell into the kitchen fire and died horribly, Deborah could suffer in silence no longer. She wrote to complain of her loneliness, of her husband's neglect. Finally, Franklin was forced to write her. "I am concerned that so much trouble should be given you by idle reports. . . . Be satisfied, my dear, that while I have my senses, and God vouchsafes me his protection, I shall do nothing unworthy the character of an honest man, and one that loves his family."[14]

Deborah apparently was satisfied but there was good reason to doubt his pompous protestations.

On a visit to London a few years later, Deborah's tenant in her mother's old house gathered graphic evidence of Franklin's infidelity. The artist Charles Willson Peale, a teacher at the Academy of Philadelphia and a close friend of William's, visited Craven Street to ask the elder Franklin for a letter of recommendation. As he later told the story, Peale found the front door unlocked and let himself in. On reaching the second floor, he found the door to Franklin's apartment ajar and looked in. There was Franklin with a young girl on his lap, kissing and fondling her as she caressed him. Peale tiptoed downstairs and quickly sketched the scene, then loudly banged on the front door.[15]

The doubts about Franklin's fidelity while he was away from home were amplified by his unusually strong attachment to Polly Stevenson. He had assured her that he could make her into a woman of science. He proposed a correspondence with her, and over the next two years they exchanged at least one hundred thirty letters, far more than he wrote to his wife and daughter.[16]

Despite the years of Deborah's open antagonism, William could not accept his father's unnatural second family. The domestic arrangements on Craven Street became an increasing source of friction between them. Whenever he could, William avoided Craven Street. But soon his own domestic difficulties opened him up to his father's meddling.

The daughters as well as the sons of wealthy colonials were sent to England to be educated, polished, and matched to the well-born. They came to live with aunts and married sisters, to be introduced at Assembly balls and promenaded at Bath and Tunbridge Wells until they attracted suitable mates. It must have been at one of the endless parties in one of the fashionable houses clustered around the approaches to the Court of St. James that William was introduced to a golden-skinned, languidly gracious woman of thirty, a frail, aristocratic beauty named Elizabeth Downes. The spoiled daughter of a Barbados sugar planter, she had been reared in luxury in a houseful of slaves, and she had been educated in music and literature with the object of bringing a great name to a great fortune. Elizabeth was in many ways similar to that other Elizabeth whom William had once loved. And again, his suit was frustrated by lack of money and position. Despite his military bearing, courtly manners, good looks and intelligent conversation, to Elizabeth's family William was the penniless son of a retired printer, hardly the husband they had envisioned for their daughter when they established her in her married sister's house in London.[17]

At first William had to content himself with dancing with Elizabeth at Assembly balls in London, at Tunbridge, at Bath. Now that his ties to Betsy Graeme were broken, he began to think of acquiring a wife to match his tastes and talents, despite his father's opposition. But the elder Franklin's insistence on taking his increasingly ineffective lobbying on the road in the summer continually set back William's marital plans. Stuck in steamy London for the Pennsylvania tax hearings in the summer of 1760, William had to settle for a short stay in Bath with his father after a whole month of visiting businessmen, scientists and hospitals from Birmingham to Worcester. All they did invariably concerned his father's interests. There is no record of their seeing anyone who might advance the western-land schemes or promote William's chances for a government job.[18] To a not-so-young man anxious about his future, the uprooting from his own circles, from his own attachments, began to rankle.

It probably did not occur to Benjamin that William should be given the opportunity as well as the money for a grand tour of Europe with others of his age and station. His father always had to go with him, pay the bills, control the travel arrangements.

A marriage to a woman with a dowry and the prospect of a sizable inheritance must have appeared to William as the only way to break free of his father. Although he had his law degree, he knew his suit would not be easy. Since he did not have money, he must bring prestige to a marriage. His campaign would require a two-pronged assault: he must apply pressure on well-connected friends for a suitable government post and win Elizabeth at the same time. And he must be careful to avoid disturbing his father further: if angered, Benjamin could insist on an untimely return to America, thereby ruining everything.

At the death of the old King, all government posts had to be surrendered. All new appointments awaited the coronation. Yet nothing delayed courtship, and while he had to wait for his political fate to be decided, William eagerly followed the route prescribed for winning the hand of a London lady of fashion. In eighteenth-century English aristocratic society, the steps were more intricate than the ritual dances William had learned on Society Hill in Philadelphia.

When long winters of cribbage and the minuet gave way to spring, he and Elizabeth could join the rush outdoors to one of London's magnificent public parks. Then as now, London was a city arranged around its parks. William's and Elizabeth's favorite was St. James's. They could take afternoon strolls along tree-lined Pall Mall, over Birdcage Walk, along broad gravel walkways past Charles II's elaborate artificial canal. They could feed flocks of clamoring geese and wild ducks, hold out handfuls of gingerbread to the fallow deer. And everywhere they could see and be seen by the same people they nodded to at the Chapel Royal on Sunday mornings, or at Shakespearean plays starring Garrick at Covent Garden, or at the mineral springs and cotillions of Bath and Tunbridge Wells, or at the levees of Lady Percy at Northumberland House.

By the spring of 1761, as all England seemed to angle for the favors of the new court, William Franklin and his tawny escort had become fixtures in Tory society. By now William was on easy terms with Lady Percy's son, who had studied at Edinburgh with the closest friends and advisors of the remote Lord Bute. In the summer, whenever William could break away from his father and from London, he visited Elizabeth and her family at their country house near Bath. It did not hurt his ambitions that Elizabeth's merchant brother-in-law had been personally recommended to rent the place from the first lord of the admiralty, who in turn was an in-law of the lord chief justice, a Middle Templar and the decisive vote on the Board of Trade and Plantations.

Benjamin Franklin responded characteristically to his son's love affair by tearing him away from it, taking him on a long holiday. On August 10, 1761, he wrote to Polly Stevenson, "We are set out this week for Holland, where we may possibly spend a month, but plan to be home again before the coronation. . . . I could not go without taking leave of you."[19] As their traveling companion, the Franklins took Omniscient Jackson.

Benjamin's account of the tour to Deborah in Philadelphia is terse except for a little gossip about the old friends he met along the way. William's version contrasted sharply. "I kept a sort of journal," he wrote Sally. "When I have the happiness of seeing you we will read it over together. In general, we saw all the principal cities and towns in the Dutch and Austrian Netherlands. . . . At Brussels we were at Prince Charles of Lorraine's, in whose Cabinet, which is full of art and nature, we saw an apparatus for trying my father's experiments in electricity. . . . In all these towns there are English nunneries. . . . We went and saw the nuns. . . . Indeed they did not look very inviting but on the contrary appeared like cross old maids who had forsaken the world because the world had first forsaken them. . . .

"At Leyden, we visited Professor Musschenbroek, who first discovered the electrical bottle [Leyden jar]. He was extremely glad to see my father. . . . At the Hague we received great civilities from

Sir Joseph Yorke, our ambassador there, with whom we dined in company with most of the foreign ministers. We dined also at Count Bentinck's, who is at the head of the nobility in Holland. . . .

"The most disagreeable circumstance I met with in Holland was their continual smoking of tobacco. I don't recollect that I saw more than one Dutch man without a pipe in his mouth, and that was a fellow who had hung in chains so long that his head had dropped off. . . . But what surprised me most of all was the seeing at one of the houses a man of ninety drag out his partner and dance a minuet smoking most solemnly a long pipe during the whole time.

"Our passage over to Holland was pleasant enough, we having fine weather and the whole cabin to ourselves. But our return was as disagreeable as possible, having hard blowing contrary winds and upwards of fifty passengers of different nations in a small sloop, who not being able to stand the deck on account of the weather, all crowded below. Here we soon became most seasick, and however it might be with the lading of other vessels, I can assure you that on board ours, there was no such thing as *inside contents unknown.* For my part, whatever I might have been formerly, I think I must now be one of the best natured men living, as old Neptune . . . took that opportunity of depriving me of every bit of [gall] I had in my body. I resisted as much as I could, and would fain have saved a little for my enemies. . . .

"Though we landed sixty miles farther from London than we expected, yet we made shift to get there time enough for the coronation, for which we had engaged places. . . . I, however, did not make use of mine, having a ticket given me by which I was enabled to see the whole ceremony in [Westminster] Hall, and to walk in the procession quite into the Abbey."[20]

As this open, hearty, affectionate letter to his sister reveals, William Franklin had finally emerged a self-assured man with a high degree of sophistication combined with a penchant for understatement. Typically, he had the good grace not to trumpet the fact that his influence at court was now greater than his father's. He had received from one of his powerful friends, probably Lady Percy, a place in the royal procession itself and a seat inside Westminster Abbey. Benjamin Franklin was able to obtain tickets only for a booth overlooking the coronation parade route. William's personal quest for his own station was almost over, his clashes with his father just beginning.

With the ambitious egotism of the educated young, William thought he could combine all his ripening talents and bring them to bear on improving the administration of colonial law in America. At thirty-five, he had become the opposite of his born-rebel father. Formally schooled, elegantly mannered, easy of speech and wit, he was a government man, one who believed deeply in the majesty of British law and was determined to uphold it. He now set his sights on public office.

In October of 1761, three weeks after the coronation, Prime Minister Pitt resigned. Lord Bute instantly took his place as first minister. Elated, William believed it was now only a matter of waiting for the proper billet in the American service under the new Tory government. On every possible occasion, he gave high British officials an opportunity to notice him. In his way, Benjamin cooperated by using William as his stand-in on errands of agency business before the Board of Trade. The secretary of the board, John Pownall, already knew William well for his passionate antiproprietary pamphleteering, often in defense of Pownall's brother, who had formerly served as lieutenant governor of New Jersey. William did have competition. With the war over, aristocratic sons had returned and were looking for government jobs. Many of them were as well qualified for office as William, though few had better connections. Fortunately for William, an event of minor consequence and a powerful friend intervened.

In New York, North Carolina and New Jersey, a controversy was brimming over the manner of appointing judges to colonial supreme courts. The Franklins' old nemesis, former Governor Morris of Pennsylvania, had long ago received a commission as chief justice of New Jersey "during good behavior" (that is, he could not be dismissed from office without good cause). All commissions expiring at George II's death, Governor Josiah Hardy proposed to reappoint Morris, again "during good behavior," but London informed him that it would have to be "during pleasure," that is, the pleasure of the Crown. It was a sore point with Lord Bute. As the new secretary of state, he insisted on this precise wording. After a long clash over prerogatives involving Scottish judges, Bute was determined to break the hold of colonial assemblies, to bring judges throughout the empire under the direct control of the new King. Chief Justice Morris objected vehemently and the New Jersey Assembly threatened that unless Morris's commission was made to read "during good behavior," they would not appropriate any funds for the chief justice's salary. Governor Hardy gave in, in spite of Bute's instructions. Learning by letter on March 18, 1762, of this "premeditated and unprecedented act of disobedience," the Board of Trade immediately recalled Hardy "as a necessary example to deter others." Such summary punishment of a royal governor without a hearing was in itself virtually without precedent, but before the dazed governor could protest, Lord Bute replaced him. As a courtesy he first offered the post to former Lieutenant Governor Thomas Pownall. Pownall declined and before the vacancy became known in official London, Bute sent a note to the Board of Trade recommending the appointment of none other than William Franklin.[21]

For five years Benjamin Franklin had waited impatiently while friends at Oxford tried to overcome the blackball of his old enemy William Smith of Philadelphia. This, coupled with a bad investment of Pennsylvania funds placed in his charge, had clouded Benjamin's last years in England. It came as a surprise, then, when in February of 1762, Oxford finally granted him an honorary doctor of laws degree, and at the same time bestowed on William an honorary master of laws degree in recognition of his assistance. The two, thrilled, went careening off in their rented carriage to receive the honors at the April commencement.[22]

As usual, the enjoyment of father and son in each other proved brief. Although William certainly had accomplished all that his father had wished and more since they had come to England, Benjamin was growing deeply dissatisfied with William's aristocratic tendencies. Whether or not there was an actual showdown between the two men, Benjamin obviously did not approve of his son's choice of a career, a wife or a political party. Shortly after their mission to England was capped at Oxford, the Franklins parted company. Benjamin left England abruptly, refusing even to wait a few weeks for his son's wedding and his investiture as a royal governor. In numerous letters to Polly Stevenson, to his sister Jane and other friends and relatives, he made his displeasure with William clear.[23]

Yet for once William did not yield. He had resisted his father's attempts to make a match for him with "Virgin Mary" Stevenson instead of the expensive daughter of a rich planter. And he actually applied for a low-ranking royal office in South Carolina near the plantation of Elizabeth Downes' brother. William was determined to have his own life, to express his independence rather than return to Pennsylvania, where he would need his father's patronage.

By the spring of 1762, William's suit after the wealthy Elizabeth Downes and the dowry she most probably brought with her were as certain as his place in the expanding imperial service. His Oxford degree could only help his case with her older brother, Jonathan, an Anglican priest and a Fellow of Cambridge University. And William's own powerful connections at court no doubt impressed the Downes family that he had a distinguished political future.[24]

Even as early as 1760 William had become bold enough to begin publicly challenging his father's political judgment. During that year Benjamin published a brilliant pamphlet summing up the military and political ramifications of the British plan for administering French Canada. William was annoyed that his father chose to dedicate it to William Pitt, who had ignored the Franklins. On June 16 he wrote candidly to his old legal preceptor Joseph Galloway in Philadelphia that he objected to his father's posturing toward Pitt "to make him look more favorably on America. If it has that effect, I shall be glad. But I hate everything that has even the appearance of flattery." He also criticized his father's feuds with Pennsylvania politicians: "Public business can never be well carried out where private animosities are suffered to interfere."[25] A friend in Philadelphia informed Benjamin of William's brash words. What the elder Franklin did about them has not been recorded.

On August 20, 1762, Lord Bute informed the Board of Trade that King George III was "pleased to appoint William Franklin, Esq., to be Governor of Nova Caesarea, or New Jersey. . . . I am to signify His Majesty's pleasure, that you should prepare draughts of a commission and instructions for him."[26] They were ready for the King's signature in five days.

For the rest of William's life, it was his glory that he was, in his own words, the first royal governor appointed by the new King. And his own son, Benjamin Franklin's first official biographer, made clear the point that obviously mattered so much to William. In his *Life of Benjamin Franklin by His Grandson*, William Temple Franklin wrote unequivocally that his father "was appointed through the influence of Lord Bute and without any solicitation on the part of his father as Governor of New Jersey."[27]

Indeed, for the first time William's connection to his father almost thwarted him. Instead of his appointment being confirmed routinely by the Privy Council, despite Lord Bute's patronage William was hailed before the Board of Trade and Plantations. In an unprecedented, grueling session, he was interrogated by the president, Lord Halifax. Temple Franklin wrote that his father was grilled "closely" by the minister of American affairs on "account of his colonial birth and youth." Lord Halifax, considered the father of American trade, had other reasons as well for resisting the appointment of young Franklin. He despised the father's upstart republicanism, as he had told Benjamin in their first encounter five years earlier. He was also the loyal friend of the Franklins' mortal enemies, the Penns. Evidently, William once again made clear that his views varied considerably from his father's, for Lord Halifax changed his mind after the hearing and quickly ratified William's appointment.

But by this time, the hour of his son's greatest triumph, Benjamin Franklin had left England without him. As early as the preceding March, Benjamin hinted in a letter to Deborah that he was coming home. On July 20, as his son's affairs soared toward success, Benjamin, eclipsed, wrote to Strahan that he had made up his mind to leave with the next troop convoy for America: "I feel here like a thing out of its place, and useless because it is out of its place. How then can I any longer be happy in England? You have great power of persuasion, and might easily prevail on me to do anything but not any longer to do nothing. I must go home."[28]

Franklin had another reason to leave before he could attend

William's investiture. He was worried that his own political power base had eroded in his five years away from Pennsylvania. He must stand for election to the Pennsylvania Assembly in October and he was being sharply criticized because of the expenses of his mission and the fact that he had accomplished more for himself than for Pennsylvania. "I cannot find that his five years' negotiation at a vast expense to the province hath answered any other purpose with respect to the public than to get every point that was in controversy determined against them," wrote his former friend James Hamilton. "Yet what is this to Mr. Franklin? Hath it not afforded him a life of pleasure and an opportunity of displaying his talents among the virtuosi of various kingdoms and nations? And lastly hath it not procured for himself the degree of doctor of laws, and for the modest and beautiful youth his son, that of master of arts from one of our most famous universities? Let me tell you, those are no small acquisitions to the public, and therefore well worth paying for!"[29]

Before Franklin left England, he went on a round of goodbyes. Methodical as ever, he made a list first. Last on the list he put "Miss Downes."[30] By now, William had asked Elizabeth to marry him and she had accepted.

Benjamin never recovered from his disappointment that William had spurned Polly Stevenson. Early in August, as William hurried around London preparing for his wedding and oath-takings, Benjamin gathered up his belongings, ordered Peter to pack them in the chaise, and rode off to Portsmouth to take ship. To "my Polly" he poured out his sadness in a brief letter from a crowded wharfside inn: "It will tell my Polly how much her friend is afflicted, that he must perhaps never again see one for whom he has so sincere an affection joined to so perfect an esteem whom he once flattered himself might become his own in the tender relation of a child. Adieu, my dearest child. I will call you so. Why should I not call you so since I love you with all the tenderness, all the fondness of a father? Adieu. May the God of all goodness shower down his choicest blessings upon you and make you infinitely happier than ... marriage to William could have made you. Adieu."[31]

Shortly before noon on September 4, 1762, Elizabeth Downes was escorted down the long aisle of fashionable St. George's

Church on Hanover Square, where her brother waited to officiate at her marriage to William Franklin. That afternoon, William sent a note to Strahan. "Your friend," he wrote hastily, "is this moment arrived at the land of matrimony and, to continue the seaman's phrase, hopes to get safe into harbour this night. I know you and good Mrs. Strahan will sympathize with Mrs. Franklin (for so I am now happy to call her) and me in the unbounded joy this long wished-for event occasions. If you mention it in this evening's Chronicle, don't style me Excellency, as I think it not quite so proper, as I have not yet kissed hands. . . . I am to do it for certain on Wednesday."[32]

With his bride of less than a week, William was ushered into the presence of the young King and Lord Bute at St. James's Palace. Five years earlier, William had arrived in England too insignificant to come into the palace and presence of a British monarch. Now, bending his right knee, he took the King's hands into his own white-gloved hands and kissed them, then rose to receive his commission and recite his oath of office.

The news of his appointment left for America soon after he and Elizabeth backed out of the King's presence. As Governor Franklin and his wife rode off to a late summer vacation at her family's home near Portsmouth, copies of the London *Chronicle* were stuffed into pouches at the Pennsylvania Coffeehouse along with letters carrying the reactions of others to William's good fortune.

Omniscient Jackson's brother-in-law, Thomas Bridges, dashed off the news to Connecticut: "The young gentleman took unto him a wife, I will not leave you to guess who, for you cannot suppose it to be any other than his old flame in St. James's Street. We think the lady has great luck on her side to get a smart young fellow for her husband and the honour of being a governor's lady."[33] And Strahan echoed this opinion of Elizabeth: "The lady is, in my mind, as good a soul as breathes, and they are very happy in one another. She is indeed a favorite with all who know her."[34]

Yet there were other views, ones that promised a stormy reception in America for the young couple. Former Governor Hamilton told Thomas Penn that William "is, perhaps, a man of as bad a heart as I ever was acquainted with. . . . He would certainly make wild work without his father's experience and good understanding to check and moderate his passion." Cannily, Penn wrote back to assure him that William's appointment "would serve to make Benjamin more tractable — the son must obey royal instructions, and what he is ordered to do, the father cannot well oppose."[35]

Unfortunately for William, the news of his bastardy became public knowledge at the moment of birth of his political career and touched off more heated controversy than he could have expected. Forty years later, John Adams still echoed the outrage of staunch Puritans: "Without the supposition of some kind of backstairs intrigue, it is difficult to account for that mortification of the pride, affront to the dignity and insult to the morals of America, the elevation to the government of New Jersey of a base-born brat." John Penn wrote from Philadelphia: "I am so astonished and enraged at it that I am hardly able to contain myself at the thought." And as if to guarantee William a troublesome administration, the governor of Pennsylvania wrote to a member of the New Jersey Council: "If any *gentleman* had been appointed it would have been a different case. . . . I make no doubt but the people of New Jersey will make some remonstrance upon this indignity put upon them."[36]

No one, it is evident, learned of William's appointment from his own father. Benjamin Franklin's disapproval was cold, silent. He did not even bother to write his favorite sister of his son's accomplishments: she read about them in the Boston newspapers. When she wrote to Benjamin of her surprise at his omission, he responded without emotion in a stiff note: "As to the promotion and marriage you mention, I shall now only say that the lady is of so amiable a character that the latter gives me more pleasure than the former, though I have no doubt but that he will make as good a governor as husband, for he has good principles and good dispositions, and I think is not deficient in good understanding."[37]

Before leaving England, William wrote a will to provide for his wife and his illegitimate son. He asked his good friend Strahan to take care of Temple but to keep the boy's identity secret awhile longer, until William was established in his new position. The bills were to be sent to William in New Jersey. The passage to America was marred by winter storms at sea followed by a freezing one-hundred-mile ride in an open carriage in a raging snow squall. But the reception given the governor and his lady raised their spirits. Apparently, Benjamin had decided to capitalize on William's new post for his own political ends. He rode down with a troop of William's old cavalry unit to meet the couple and take Elizabeth home in his coach. No sooner had William thawed from the voyage than he rode with his father to New Jersey for his investiture in each of the province's two capitals.

To all appearances it was a powerful political alliance that straddled the Delaware River, and neither man dispelled the illusion as they clattered over the frozen roads into the Jerseys. Their journey carried them, first, to the western capital at Burlington and past the house where Betsy Graeme had come to grieve with friends at the news of William's marriage. She had read of it in the newspapers and would always maintain it was the first hint she had ever had that her engagement to William was broken.[38] The Franklins rushed on, escorted by a cavalcade of sleigh-riding ladies and gentlemen and the Middlesex troop of horse in plumes and capes with their sabers drawn and crooked beside them.

On the icy, bitter-cold morning of February 25, the elegant young governor shrugged off his bearskin robe and mounted the steps of the old stone courthouse in Perth Amboy before a shivering crowd of loyal subjects. Even his father had to be proud of him this day, of his first official act. After relieving the old governor and hearing his new commission read aloud, William gave a mercifully short speech and led the way down the street to the nearest tavern for a hearty dinner and a round of toasts.[39]

9

YOURS TILL DETH

1763–1769

As homesick as Benjamin Franklin professed himself while in England, no sooner did he arrive in Philadelphia and hang portraits of the new King and Lord Bute in his dining room than he began to long again for London. It did not help that his close friend Dr. John Pringle wrote, "Our friends continue to meet at my house on Sunday evenings. I suspect they would not be so punctual if they did not hope for your return."[1]

Although reassured of his political potency by the Philadelphia election returns, Franklin nonetheless was troubled to learn that Lord Bute, unpopular with the people and disgusted with the compromises of public office, had resigned. (As yet it was not known that he would keep on as the King's confidential advisor.) The Penn party, both in England and Pennsylvania, was immediately reenlivened. Without Bute's conspicuous protection, Franklin was once more under sharp attack.[2] His postal job was threatened and he was beginning to worry that he had only a few more years' income from his partnership in the *Pennsylvania Gazette*. Once again, spurred by each letter from friends in London, his mind turned to moving to England.

"If you were determined before to return to England," Dr. Pringle wrote, in advising him of Bute's fall, "you will now see a good reason for hastening your departure."[3] Unfortunately for Franklin, Deborah flatly refused to go. She was stubbornly rooted in Philadelphia and she wanted a decent home of her own. In twenty-five years of common-law marriage she had lived either in crowded rooms above the store or in a house her husband had rented on the edge of town. Though he had done more than any man alive to improve the quality and safety of living, their quarters had never been fitted out with his improved fireplaces or one of his ventilation systems or any of the host of gadgets he had invented.[4]

The question of Deborah's crossing the ocean was evidently settled quickly, if not peacefully. Only a few months after Benjamin's return, William was writing to Strahan in London, "My mother is so entirely averse to going to sea that I believe my father will never be induced to see England again. He is now building a house to live in."[5] In postwar Philadelphia, the building trade was booming. Franklin was rich enough to hire the best architect and the best builder, but he had to wait. Work on the house — a three story, brick structure thirty-four feet square, set deep in a large lot — moved along, annoyingly, at a snail's pace.

Benjamin Franklin never was very good at staying home. He was possessed by an immense restlessness. When he was not embroiled in some political or scientific controversy, he wanted to travel, to run away from domesticity, to escape. Consequently, when he returned to plainly provincial Philadelphia in 1762, he soon invented ways to leave it again. In fact, he spent eight of the first twelve months at home away from home. After traveling to New Jersey for William's investiture, he waited impatiently for the roads to thaw, then set off south on one of his long, leisurely inspection tours of post offices — Virginia ever seduced him in the spring. Home again in Philadelphia, he stayed only three weeks, scarcely long enough for Deborah and the servants to do his laundry and reload his chuckwagon. Then he rode off again for six months of travel through the New England summer and fall.[6]

This time he had a new traveling companion, his nineteen-year-old daughter. Sally had been vacationing with her brother William at his riverfront house in Burlington. William welcomed his father, and they reminisced about other trips. Sally played Scottish airs on the harpsichord while Benjamin accompanied her on his armonica. He sat through a ceremonial dinner in his son's honor, then moved on north with Sally, now his new favorite. Deborah never would go to Boston to meet her husband's relatives, but Sally was eager enough.

Benjamin warmed daily to this stout, hearty girl. At nineteen, she much resembled her mother at the same age, except that she had been taught to read and write — her father had seen to that. She had also learned French, had mastered the harpsichord, and had begun to play the flute. She was, if somewhat homely, a vivacious, intelligent young woman and this was her proud debut in Boston. Benjamin introduced her thoroughly, leaving her with relatives. Then he went happily off to Rhode Island to visit his old friend Caty Ray, now married and the mother of two children. He wrote back that he had been thrown from his carriage, and he had to stay for weeks with Caty, who nursed him affectionately.[7] He only tore himself away in time to return to Philadelphia for one of the great personal and political crises of his life, one that shaped not only his own destiny but his son's for the rest of their troubled lives.

News of the peace treaty ending the French and Indian War reached the French and Indians last. In the summer of 1763, French commanders deep in the Mississippi Valley goaded their Indian allies into a great uprising all along the English colonial frontier. Once again, accounts of scalpings and brutal killings flooded the State House; once again, pacifist Quakers vacillated as the tempers of German settlers and Scotch-Irish squatters in the bloody valleys one hundred miles to the west began to flare.[8]

Thousands of these rough-cut new settlers had crowded across the Allegheny Mountains, where they were poised for the final surrender of the French and the chance for a great land rush. Sent reeling by Indian raiders into rickety stockades, they were looking for scapegoats. High on their list of grievances was the fact that pacifist Quakers and Moravians still sheltered hundreds of Indians who had supposedly converted to the Christian religion. The settlers claimed that these Indians, in turn, harbored, fed and abetted young warriors. Their anti-Indian fervor first led to the forced resettlement of 130 Moravian Indians of the Conestoga tribe. They were taken from their village just west of the Lehigh Gap, where they had been installed after the 1755 Gnadenhütten massacre, into settled country where they could be watched: at the Penns' Conestoga Manor, near Lancaster.

During the night of December 14, 1763, fifty-seven riders, armed with long Pennsylvania rifles, cutlasses and tomahawks, gathered in Lancaster. At dawn they surrounded the huts of the Indians, most of whom were away for the day. "Only three men, two women and a young boy were found at home," Franklin wrote in *A Narrative of the Late Massacre,* "the rest being out among the neighboring white people, some to sell the baskets, brooms and bowls they manufactured. These poor defenseless creatures were immediately fired upon, stabbed and hatcheted to death! The good Shehaes [who had signed the last treaty with William Penn] was cut to pieces in his bed. All of them were scalped and otherwise horribly mangled. Then their huts were set on fire."

Franklin was horrified, and in his strongest and finest journalistic outpouring, he angrily lashed out with uncharacteristic emotion at the "barbarian" Scotch-Irish, calling on his fellow citizens, in a pamphlet he paid to publish himself, to form together into armed associations to safeguard the remaining peaceful Indians as well as the honor of Pennsylvania. His outcry came too late to save the last fourteen Conestogas, who came home that night to discover the charred remains of their relatives. Taken to the Lancaster jail for their own protection, they were there attacked two weeks later by a hundred Scotch-Irish, who stormed the jail and slaughtered the Indians while they prayed for mercy. Stunned, Franklin and his political allies in the Assembly brought the Moravian Indians under armed escort to Philadelphia, finally herding them off to the city pesthouse and placing them under guard.

Franklin was uncompromising in his criticism of the frontiersmen. "All good people everywhere detest your actions," he wrote of them. *"Cowards* [he underscored the word] can strike where they are sure to meet with no return, can wound, mangle and murder, but it belongs to brave men to spare and to protect. . . . The only crime of these poor wretches seems to have been that they had a reddish brown skin and black hair, and some people of that sort, it seems, had murdered some of our relations. If it be right to kill men for such reason, then, should any man with a freckled face and red hair kill a wife or child of mine, it would be right for me to revenge it by killing all the freckled red-haired men, women and children."[9]

Franklin's indignant slaps at the Scotch-Irish did little to cool emotions. Thousands of Philadelphians, including a surprising number of young Quakers, closed ranks behind him, forming six companies of foot, one of artillery, two troops of cavalry. All day Sunday, February 5, 1764, as outlying officials rushed word to Philadelphia that hundreds of "Paxton Boys" were riding on the capital to kill the Indian refugees, the church bells tolled the alarm. That night, as Franklin wrote later to his English friend John Fothergill, Governor John Penn "did me the honour . . . to run to my house at midnight, with his counsellors at his heels, for *advice,* and made it his headquarters for some time."[10]

Penn offered Franklin the command. Franklin preferred to be the first citizen to enlist as a private in Penn's defensive army. Once again, he took down his rifle and rode off. Along with church leaders, he parleyed with the Paxton leaders at their camp in Germantown, warning the marchers that the city was prepared for bloodshed. Astonished that the cityfolk would risk their lives to save Indians, the frontiersmen agreed, at Franklin's urging, to prepare a petition of grievances, send a deputation to the Assembly, then disperse. "And within four and twenty hours your old friend was a common soldier, a counsellor, a kind of dictator, an ambassador to the country mob and, on their returning home, *Nobody* again."[11]

Peace proved short-lived. The double-dealing Penn faction not only refused to prosecute the murderers but put together a powerful new political alliance with the Scotch-Irish in return for their votes to unseat the Franklin-Quaker "old party" from the Assembly. In a city known for its crude electioneering, new depths of dirty politicking were plumbed that autumn of 1764. In one scurrilous broadside, Penn penmen revealed William's bastardy by accusing Benjamin of brutally mistreating the scullery maid who allegedly was William's mother. "Her recent death," a bard recounted, "lately deprived him of the mother of EXCELLENCY."[12]

Red-faced, the Franklins both counterattacked in print. The young governor of New Jersey literally rolled up his sleeves and stumped door to door for votes for his father in Germantown. But Benjamin's prejudices had hurt him badly. His thirteen-year-old, anti-German slur about "Palatine boors herding together" brought out one thousand resentful Germans. Despite William's efforts, despite Benjamin's keeping the polls open all night and hauling in stretchers and wagons filled with the aged and infirm to vote for him, Benjamin was beaten by a coalition of bitter Scotch-Irish Presbyterians and grumbling Germans. From speaker of the House of Assembly, Benjamin fell to private citizen once again.

But only momentarily. Benjamin could not stand defeat. He must always counterattack. The fault was not his own prejudice, it was those vile Penns again. Within five weeks, he was on his way back to England. Bent on revenge, he manipulated friends in the Assembly, urging them to write petitions to Parliament to have Pennsylvania taken away from the Penns and made a royal province under the King. In spite of criticism that what he really wanted was to be the first royal governor, he again won an appointment as the agent for the Pennsylvania Assembly to the Crown to present the Assembly's petitions and legislation to the King. Leaving behind a deeply depressed Deborah and their unfinished town house, he sailed down the Delaware to the boom of borrowed cannon. In his newspaper, he made a pompous farewell: "I am now about to take leave (perhaps a last leave) of the country I love, and in which I have spent the greatest part of my life. I wish every kind of prosperity to my friends, and I forgive my enemies."[13] Indeed, he would never see many of his friends, or his Debby, again.

In Benjamin's last two years at home, William had seen him perhaps a dozen times. Yet, in September 1764, they were still so closely in tandem that, when Benjamin sent Assembly resolves to London for Strahan to print, William wrote a postscript on his father's covering letter.[14] The longest time the Franklins evidently had together was a week in the spring of 1764 in Burlington. That they once again discussed William's grand scheme for a great western settlement seems evident from Benjamin's letters to friends in England. William plainly saw Benjamin's latest mission as an opportunity that in many ways could benefit him.

But the flare-up of Indian hostilities soon took up much of the young governor's time until his father's departure. Indian raiding parties had come down from northern Pennsylvania and plundered frontier settlements in New Jersey. William hastily proclaimed that the Indian raiders "no longer deserve to be considered as in the scale of human beings." Then an Indian prisoner was beheaded by settlers, and two Christian Indian women were murdered in reprisal. William reversed himself. He ordered two white men arrested, jailed and tried. After further incidents, he ordered the execution of two Scotch-Irish Indian killers and invited Indian leaders to witness the hangings. By giving justice to the Indians, he earned the cumbersome title Sagorighweyoghsta, "Dispenser of Justice," and a place as a trusted negotiator at later peace talks with the Indians.

He encouraged, moreover, the settlement of the first Indian reservation in America at Brotherton, near Burlington, and ordered the planting at province expense of three hundred apple trees to give the Indians a cash crop as a medium of barter. "Not only humanity, but sound policy and common sense," he said, "dictate that we should give all the encouragement and protection in our power to those who show themselves our friends."[15]

If William's attitudes toward Indians echoed his father's at this stage, so did the results. Civilized men viewed him as a statesman, but thousands of Indian haters never forgave him his stand.

His first few years as a royal governor were relatively tranquil. He was not controlled by his father, as his enemies asserted he would be, but began to gain more self-confidence, to demonstrate the independent spirit that he had acquired in London. Indeed, William so pleased most of his constituents that he won an unheard-of concession, a handsome pay raise from the Assembly, which controlled the purse strings and annually voted his support. One reason was his choice of an official residence. The eastern capital, Perth Amboy, was a hated symbol of the landed aristocracy that lived there. The western capital, Burlington, was the power base of Quakers and owners of smaller freeholds. William made himself popular with the majority by basing himself at Burlington. He rented a house on the river from a Quaker grandee until he could build his own handsome, three-story brick waterfront mansion, paid for in part by a generous housing allowance from the legislators. The western capital was also more convenient to Philadelphia. William took his bride to Assembly balls and horse races, and visited Deborah and Sally often, even if he and Elizabeth usually stayed with William's former law teacher and closest friend, Joseph Galloway.[16]

Though born to the opulence of a tropical sugar plantation and accustomed to the latest London fashions, Elizabeth Franklin tried valiantly to adapt to the dour Quaker capital of Burlington. She decorated her sycamore-shaded town house in brilliant Georgian crimsons, golds, pale yellows. She imported an English maid to supervise the servants, even as her husband instructed his coachman in the planting of elaborate formal gardens. When provincial politicians convened each spring, Elizabeth entertained the leaders and their wives lavishly. On Sundays she brought up the train of a stylish procession into St. Mary's Church, gliding into the royal governor's pew on her husband's arm. The Anglican socialites kneeling to her left admired her courtly bearing, delicate manners, modish attire. The ladies of the colony looked to her leadership in arranging rounds of teas, parties, dinners, church benefits. Wearied by the strain of incessant entertaining, Elizabeth was often ill for long spells. Indeed, she had never been strong and probably suffered from acute asthma, a fact that cropped up again and again in William's letters to their old friends, the Strahans, in London. On their honeymoon voyage to America, William had confided, he "had much to do to keep up poor Mrs. Franklin's spirits." Yet Elizabeth's tenacity, he added, was "much beyond my expectations." Having to live in rented rooms while their first house was prepared for them depressed her again. She longed for England, but eventually, William wrote, became "pretty well reconciled to America and has her health, I think better than when in England."[17] Even so, she was seriously ill three times in a single year, her asthma aggravated by heavy humid summers, by windy waterfront winters.

Only the occasional semiofficial jaunts to the manor houses of New York aristocracy, to the Assembly balls in Philadelphia, and the annual autumn legislative pilgrimage to elegant Perth Amboy, fifty miles closer to the invigorating social climate of New York City, seemed to revive her. Perth Amboy boasted a cosmopolitan mixture of music, bright talk and intelligent company that reminded her of England, of home, and she wanted to move there.

As usual, her gregarious husband made many new friends, even of expected enemies. London gossips had predicted social rejection of the bastard governor and his bride by Robert Hunter Morris, Benjamin Franklin's old enemy from Pennsylvania who had long been the leader of proprietorial society in the Jerseys. But Morris, as so many knew, had at least three illegitimate sons of his own. In any event, he soon dropped dead at a Christmas ball, thereby removing the Franklins' chief social obstacle. The governor's other expected rival was William Alexander, the pretender to a Scottish earldom and an in-law of the Penns. But William's affable blend of flattering attention and storytelling and his military service with the New York Livingstons, who were Alexander's relatives, soon resulted in an invitation to spend half a summer at the Alexander country estate. For the moment, Lord Stirling, as Alexander called himself, saw no serious threat from the young Franklin. At his Basking Ridge summer retreat, the Franklins met and mingled with the highest British military and civil officials and their wives.[18]

The Franklins used the power of their position to create a circle of the unusually accomplished and talented. One was Samuel Smith, the historian of colonial New Jersey and a Quaker grandee who served on the New Jersey Council. William lent Smith his own books on architecture, interior design and scientific farming, and when Smith brought out his classic chronicle of the colony's first one hundred years, William sent copies of it to high British officials.[19] He also welcomed into the Franklin coterie a hulking, humorous young Princeton graduate named Jonathan Odell, who was something of a poet. William sponsored him for Anglican orders, recommended him to his father in London, proposed him for elevation to become first bishop of America.

For more than a decade, the Franklins' richly laid table was graced by visiting British generals, lords and ladies, American artists and, as was the custom, untold numbers of weary travelers. Among the latter were Colonel George Washington and his stepson Jack, who were en route to New York where Jack would enroll in King's College. Some of the guests were out-and-out freeloaders. One of these was diminutive Francis Hopkinson, up from Philadelphia. A dandified little would-be poet and perennial office seeker, he was the first American to compose for the harpsichord. No doubt he charmed the ladies with his trilling renditions of his most popular piece, "My Days Have Been So Wondrous Free." The words of the song title were an apt description of the parasitic habits of so many Franklin guests. Hopkinson, whose father had helped William's father form the Junto discussion group and many other civic organizations in Philadelphia, amused the governor and his guests with his wit, his music, even his florid allegorical Indian poem "The Treaty." Somehow, Hopkinson's version of an Indian conference, "Give me the bubbling fountain's mossy side / In contemplation sweet to lull my mind,"[20] did not quite square with William's recollection of extended orgies. But their cheerful conversations undoubtedly turned after dinner to the Indian sports they had both witnessed at each treaty signing, to the ball games and archery contests, to war dances and stupendous bouts of drinking.

When Hopkinson left Burlington to ride back to the city, he did not fail to send thoughtful presents to Elizabeth. In one of the governor's letters of thanks, he wrote that Elizabeth "has deputed me to acknowledge the very acceptable present of fruit. Miss D. and Mr. P. happened to be with us when it was brought from the wharf. . . . As the watermelon was cracked, owing to a fall it had received on board, and bound round with a piece of spun yarn, Nancy insisted that you were inside, and begged that we would not stick a knife into it for fear of cutting you in two. However, upon knocking several times on the outside, and calling to you without hearing any answer, I ventured with a larger carving knife in my hand to pass the [Rhine]."[21]

From the veranda of his house in Burlington, Governor Franklin could look out over broad lawns to the sycamore-lined river and ponder the persistent problems plaguing all colonial governors: insufficient currency, almost no foreign exchange, smoldering feuds over land titles, no legal way to pay official salaries without groveling before the pinchpenny Assembly, made up mostly of thrifty farmers. He thought he could see an answer to this last and most vexing problem. In the Delaware River between New Jersey and Pennsylvania were unclaimed islands with rich farms on them. It occurred to him that this land might be annexed by the Crown, rented back to the farmers, and the income earmarked to pay his salary. He sent off his scheme to the authorities in London at once. Ominously, the Board of Trade and Plantations in England ignored his idea, leaving the Franklin administration at the mercy of the Assembly.[22]

But minor problems are often absorbed, disappearing inside greater ones, and both Franklins found their chief political concerns quickly obliterated by the Stamp Act riots. On March 22, 1765, two months after Benjamin arrived in London, Parliament passed a tax act that required American colonists to pay sizable taxes on paper, as the English had for more than half a century. The act would go into effect on November 1. Items to be taxed included bills of lading, dice and playing cards, mortgages and liquor licenses, printed pamphlets, newsprint and newspaper advertisements, almanacs, calendars, surveying documents, college degrees. At a time when cash was sparse and unemployment high, the taxes must be paid in silver or gold. Some were outrageously steep. The stamp for a college diploma cost four pounds sterling (about two hundred dollars today) at a time when half the students at Harvard were studying for the ministry on scholarship.

The British government, faced with immense war debts, reasoned that Americans had profited most from the war that had rid them of the French menace and that they should pay a fair share of the pile of bills.[23] Unfortunately, the news of the passage of the act reached America in May of 1765 and coincided with a serious postwar slump in America. A New Jerseyan named James Parker summed up conditions throughout the colonies in a letter to Attorney General Cortlandt Skinner: "There is such a general scarcity of cash that nothing we have will command it and real estates of every kind are falling at least one half in value. Debtors that were a year or two ago responsible for £1,000 cannot now raise a fourth part of the sum. . . . There is an entire stop to all sales by the sheriffs for want of buyers, and men of the best estates amongst us can scarce raise money enough to defray the necessary expenses of their families. . . . Under the insupportable distress we are now called upon for many thousands of pounds sterling to be paid by a stamp duty."[24]

As unemployment soared and families had less and less to eat, conditions were ripe for riot. That Benjamin Franklin at first misread events is evident from his recommendation of close friends as stampmen and from his letters to British friends. "I am not much alarmed about your scheme of raising money on us," he wrote his old friend Richard Jackson, a member of Parliament who had voted the tax.[25] William confided his true feelings to no one and revealed them only by his adroit actions.

Setting the pattern for the other colonies, all the lawyers in New Jersey met on September 19, 1765, in Perth Amboy and agreed not to conduct business requiring the obnoxious stamps, which in effect meant that no legal business could be conducted in the colony. By the time they met again in February 1766, many were suffering hardships from their resolves, and all were under pressure from a new radical group, the Sons of Liberty, who showed up eight hundred strong in case the lawyers wavered.

All over New Jersey and up and down the Atlantic coast, there were violent protests. When the hated stamps arrived off New York on HMS *Royal Charlotte,* Governor Franklin, on the advice of his trusted councillor William Alexander, refused to let them be landed. On the entire coast there was no safe place in which to store them. The stamp commissioner, who had been recommended for the job by Benjamin Franklin, had resigned before the law could take effect, thereby forfeiting a £3,000 bond.* He had been refused the rental of a house unless he could guarantee that it would not be pulled to pieces by a mob. He could not, of course, provide such a guarantee, especially in view of what had happened in other colonies. In Boston, mobs had destroyed the homes of the lieutenant governor and the stamp commissioner; in New York City, an inebriated throng had sacked the house of the British major who had tried to prevent the seizure of the stamps stored in Fort George. The New Brunswick Sons of Liberty followed the New Jersey stampman when he left for Philadelphia and forced him to take an oath never to sell the stamps. Other stamp agents recommended for their jobs by Benjamin Franklin had no better luck. In Connecticut, mobs forced William's old London friend Jared Ingersoll to forswear his oath, and in Philadelphia laid siege to the house of the Franklins' close friend John Hughes, which broke Hughes's health and terrified his family.

* About $375,000 in 1984.

Nothing had prepared any of the royal officials in America for the ferocity of the riots. Governor Franklin exhibited uncommon shrewdness during the crisis. When he refused to let the stamps be landed, he pleaded that he had received no clear instructions for their disposition in such an emergency, and then arranged to send his problem out of the colony. He alerted a British contingent of troops in New York, then had the stamps transferred to HMS *Sardoine,* which was anchored in the harbor between Perth Amboy and Staten Island. Unfortunately, the captain objected: he had to have the vessel put into drydock and stripped of her guns for the winter. Governor Franklin stalled him off and appealed to the governor of New York for permission to store the stamps at Fort George. The answer was a refusal. The fort was already crammed with troops and supplies, the governor replied; there was no room left, not even for a small trunkful of stamps. William turned back to the captain of the *Sardoine* and persuaded him to keep the stamps with the ship's stores for the winter. He cogently reasoned that the citizens of one colony would not think to seize the stamps of another.

When he finally wrote to his father of his role in the affair, William was sharply critical of the tax measure and its official handling. "Governor Bernard [of Massachusetts] and Governor Colden [of New York] by an unnecessary officiousness have made matters much worse in their governments than they otherwise would have been." He also displayed a strong instinct for survival, which he would often demonstrate in more personal crises later. "It is best at all times, but more especially in times of ferment and confusion, for a man to *lower himself* a little, rather than let others lower him." A canny political realist, he refused to attack the radicals or endorse British policy: "Indeed for any man to set himself up as an advocate for the Stamp Act in the colonies is a mere piece of Quixotism, and can answer no good purpose whatever. And if he is an officer of government he not only becomes obnoxious, but is sure to lose all the authority belonging to his office. It seems to me that we might legally go on with business in the usual way, as much as if the stamps had never been sent or had been lost at sea, seeing that no commission or instructions have been sent to anybody."[26]

As the day the Stamp Act was to go into effect approached, Philadelphia was near civil war. Mobs were assembled at night by muffled drums. Only the existence of another, pro-Franklin mob of eight hundred tradesmen and mechanics ensured the protection of Deborah Franklin and Benjamin's old friends.[27] On September 22 1765, she wrote him: "I was for nine days kept in one continued hurry by people to remove. Several houses [were] threatened to be pulled down. Cousin Davenport come and told me that more than twenty people had told him it was his duty to be with me. . . . Towards night, I sed he should fetch a gun or two as we had none. I sent to ask my brother to come and bring his gun also, so we made one room into a magazine. I ordered some sort of defense upstairs such as I could manage myself. I was very sure you had done nuthing to hurt anybody nor I had not given any offense to any person. . . . Billy come again to ask us up to Burlington. I consented to Sally going, but I will not stir."[28]

Far from creating the stamp crisis, as his foes charged, Benjamin Franklin did more than any American to alleviate it by giving key testimony before the House of Commons that helped to hurry its repeal. From July 1765 to May 1766 he lobbied relentlessly against the measure and soon maneuvered himself into the position of prime spokesman among the sixteen American agents in London. "I never in my life labored any point more heartily than I did that of obtaining the repeal," he wrote to Daniel Wister. Under an assortment of pseudonyms, he bombarded London newspapers with letters, distributed hundreds of copies of a cartoon he had had drawn depicting a dismembered British Empire against a backdrop of idle ships. "I was extremely busy attending members of both Houses, informing, explaining, consulting, disputing, in a continual hurry from morning to night."[29]

But it was his firsthand knowledge of British industry and commerce and of their leaders, which he had gained in his years of travel through the English countryside, that gave him special leverage: all over England men like him were suffering from the American boycott of their goods. Working closely with other merchants and agents, he circulated petitions from trading towns, then arranged for a hearing before the Commons on the ill effects of the act. On February 13, 1766, he was summoned before Parliament. Ten days later, he testified.

The questions had been carefully planted, to be asked in rapid, lucid succession so that no unfriendly line of questioning could obtrude. There were 174 in all, but the heart of the questioning was laid bare quickly enough:

Q.—Do you think it right that America should be protected by this country and pay no part of the expense?

A.—That is not the case. The colonies raised, clothed and paid during the last war near 25,000 men and spent many millions.

Q.—Do you not think the people of America would submit to pay the stamp duty if it was moderated?

A.—No, never, unless compelled by force of arms.

Q.—Can anything less than a military force carry the Stamp Act into execution?

A.—I do not see how a military force can be applied to that purpose.

Q.—Why may it not?

A.—Suppose a military force [is] sent into America, they will find nobody in arms; what then are they to do? They cannot force a man to take stamps who chooses to do without them. They will not find a rebellion; they may indeed make one.

Q.—If the act is not repealed, what do you think will be the consequences?

A.—The total loss of the respect and affection the people of America bear to this country, and of all the commerce that depends on that respect and affection.[30]

The Stamp act was repealed in March of 1766.

When word of Benjamin Franklin's tour de force reached America, the celebrating was jubilant. William, aged somewhat by the ordeal, admitted that he had feared his house would be "pulled down about my ears and all my effects destroyed."[31] Vastly relieved, he led the victory celebration in Burlington with Elizabeth, and joined a public festival at which he fired off two small cannon on his lawn and offered eighteen toasts.

From Philadelphia, Sally Franklin wrote her father joyously: "The bells rang, we had bonfires. . . . Indeed I never heard so much noise all my life, the very children were distracted."[32] Benjamin celebrated by sending Sally fancy negligées and petticoats, two dozen pairs of gloves, and four bottles of lavender water. For Deborah's new house there were damask tablecloths, curtains, an Oriental rug for the dining room. And for William: a note chastising him for meddling in Pennsylvania politics in his absence.

For the first time in their correspondence, William wrote back as an equal: "It is impossible for you at so great a distance to be acquainted with every circumstance necessary to form a right judgment of the expediency or inexpediency of particular transactions. I have all the evidence the nature of the case will admit that they [the proprietary party] had taken their measures so effectually with the Presbyterians and the Sons of Liberty in this province that, had it not been for the paper I published . . . I should have had my house pulled down about my ears. . . . All my friends in every part of the province have approved my conduct, and I have ever since experienced the good effects of it. . . . For my part, I always think it best to nip in the bud every report which may tend to hurt a man's character."[33]

With the gifts Benjamin had sent Deborah came an enticing line: "I send you also a box with three fine cheeses. Perhaps a bit of them may be left when I come home."[34] Soon, Deborah hoped, she would have her Benny to herself. The great man would be home, in a home of her choosing.

He did not come. Newspapers arrived with accounts of his celebrated words, and friends by scores came to congratulate her. But he still did not come. He returned to his vengeful fight with the Penns, heady with his new influence, sure of himself as never before. His next letter (they came almost predictably once a month) was short, hasty, saying he was well, mentioning nothing of his intentions. May passed, and then in June, he wrote that he had been ill, was feeble in fact, but that he was well enough to leave the next day on a long and arduous trip to Germany with Dr. Pringle, the Queen's physician. He had become "used, as you know, to make a journey once a year. . . . We must be back at farthest in eight weeks."[35]

Deborah began to grow gloomy, her notes full of the sickness and death of friends. She seemed on the point of despair. Even her new house did not cheer her; Benjamin would have to write a letter prying details from her. Six months passed before she heard from him again, and then his letter was full of instructions about dealing with a proprietary neighbor who resisted the privilege of having a sewage drainpipe laid through his property from the Franklin house. He was curt with her, demanding to know if she had paid for a new parcel of land. "I have several times asked this question and received no answer." And what post office money had she received? "Pray send me the account directly, without delay." He was still unsure when he would come home. "I have fixed in my mind, God willing, to return homewards . . . but as yet something may happen. . . . I would have you continue writing as if I were to continue here. Let me know how your tenants pay, and what rents you receive . . . whether you have insured the house."[36] But nowhere did he ask how *she* was.

She was not doing well at all. Her melancholy was drifting into a quiet madness, her memory lapsing and fading. The accounts she felt obliged to keep were erratic, sporadic, sometimes listing items but no prices. The house she so long coveted quickly became her prison, an unfinished prison set back nearly one hundred yards from High Street, solitary, square, somber. Benjamin may have attributed her condition to the tension all around her, the riots, the alarms, but her letter of October 6, 1765, would have warned a more sensitive man that something was amiss, that he should cut short his travels, immediately abandon his clubs and his politics, and go home.

When she described the house and the move to it — as he had pointedly asked her to do in his last letter — her sadness came through without her realizing it. She was incapable of sarcasm: "I took all the dead letters and papers and put them into boxes, barrels and bags and I did not know in what manner you would have shelves in your room. Now this I did for several reasons once as it did imploy my mind and keeps me verey busy. . . . Now for the room we Cale yours. . . . As to Curtains I leve it to you to due as you like your self or if as we talked be fore you went. . . . All these things air be cume quite indifrent to me att this time."[37]

For weeks, in letter after worse-spelled letter, Deborah had poured out her loneliness to him: "I have wrote several letter to you one almoste everey day but then I Cold not forbair saying sumthing to you [about] publick afairs then I wold [destroy] it and then begin a gen and burn it a gen and so on. . . . All is well att home. . . . No body but my self at home. . . . As ever yours till Deth, D. Franklin."[38]

When Benjamin had not returned by April of 1767, Deborah had to face a major decision alone, risking his displeasure. She had reason still to smart over his criticism that she had spent far too much for a lot that neatly squared off their parcel of land. She was obviously timid, then, about raising the subject of Sally's choice of a husband. "I am obliged to be father and mother," she wrote in a long letter she labored over for a week. She treated Sally's suitor as a friend, she wrote, "and shall while I am alone for I thinke he deserves it" and she wisely worried that if she acted otherwise, Sally, twenty-four, mature, deeply in love, would only see him anyway.[39]

Not that Benjamin would approve of Sally's other friends. They were the sons of Penns and Allens, the daughters of merchants from the proprietary camp, and they rode across the river ice to visit William's wife, who had taken charge of Sally's courting, even though William did not approve. William had said as much in a confidential letter to his father. Sally's lover, Richard Bache, was a "mere fortune hunter," William warned, "who wants to better his circumstances [by] marrying into a family that will support him. . . . If Sally marries him they must both be entirely dependent on you for subsistence. . . . Do burn this."[40] Benjamin did not burn the letter. He kept it in his papers where Sally could one day see it.

To Deborah he wrote: "I must leave it to your judgment to act in the affair of your daughter's match as shall seem best. If you think it a suitable one, I suppose the sooner it is completed, the better.

"In that case, I would only advise that you do not make an expensive feasting wedding, but conduct everything with frugality and economy, which our circumstances now require to be observed in all our expenses; for since my printing partnership with Mr. Hall is expired, a great source of our income is cut off; and if I should lose the Post Office . . . we should be reduced to our rent and interest of money for subsistence, which will by no means afford the chargeable housekeeping and entertainments we have been used to; for my own part I live here frugally as possible not to be destitute of the comforts of life, making no dinners for anybody, and contenting myself with a single dish when I dine at home."

Deborah must have been reeling by now: no Benjamin to give away *their* daughter, the daughter whose expectations he had so greatly raised. And then came this lecture instead of his badly needed presence: "When people's incomes are lessened, if they cannot proportionably lessen their outgoings, they must come to Poverty." Poverty! She no doubt remembered it vividly. The years of gruel and hand-sewing bookbindings, the rented quarters over the shop, the rooms crowded with relatives, apprentices, boarders.

"I know very little of the gentleman or his character," the letter went on. "I hope his expectations are not great of any fortune to be had with our daughter before our death. . . . At present, I suppose you would agree with me that we cannot do more than fit her out handsomely in clothes and furniture."

As for when he was coming home, he merely wrote, in passing, "It seems now as if I should stay here another winter."[41]

To his future son-in-law, who had recently sustained severe business losses, Franklin also wrote that he was "truly sorry to hear of your misfortune. But a few years of industry and good management" would replace the losses. Meanwhile "your own discretion will suggest" that it would be wrong to marry. "I love my daughter perhaps as well as ever a parent did a child, but I have told you before that my estate is small, scarce a sufficiency for the support of me and my wife who are growing old."[42]

Franklin had advice enough left over for Sally. She could live at home to save rent. She should be "not too proud" to open a shop, learn accounting, copy letters for a little cash, nurse her mother: "indeed, it seems to be your duty to attend her as she grows infirm."[43]

In reply to William's confidential letter warning that Bache was a fortune hunter, Benjamin took him to task. Disgusted, William fired back: "I am very sorry that you think I am too apt to listen to whisperers and makebates, and that there is any danger of my being concerned in a family quarrel. It is not at all my disposition; on the contrary, I can safely say it has been the constant endeavor of my life to avoid all such quarrels."[44]

Sally Franklin bravely went ahead and married Richard Bache, though neither her father nor her only brother attended the wedding. And she was not too proud to open a dry goods store to help rescue the man she loved, something her father coldly refused to do. She learned from her mother that her father, instead of coming home for her wedding, had gone off to Paris for six weeks, where he dined in the presence of royalty, bought a new bag wig that made him look twenty years younger, and was proud to have it said that he had chatted with the King and Queen of France. He was always impressed by royalty.

He did not see fit to write these details directly to his wife and daughter. Instead, he wrote them to Polly Stevenson. And when Polly married soon afterward, he stood for her in church and he walked *her* down the aisle. Then he wrote home to tell Deborah all about it.[45]

10

I STEER MY LITTLE BARK QUIETLY

1765–1771

A VISITATION FROM GOVERNOR WILLIAM FRANKLIN'S RAP-
idly receding youth rode up the sycamore-lined lane to the
royal governor's Burlington mansion one November afternoon in
1765. Colonel George Croghan, a companion of Franklin's on that
long-ago expedition into the Ohio Valley, had come for a clandestine meeting that would begin two years of secret negotiations on
western lands. Like his host, Croghan had grown prosperously
heavier in the eighteen years since their wilderness expedition.
Carving an ever wider swath through the forests, he had built a
reputation as a master palaverer-trader. Into the bargain he had accumulated a vast, heavily mortgaged personal estate, which included many of the best acres he had officially superintended as the
Crown's second highest Indian agent in America.[1]

Franklin knew from the newspapers that the glib-tongued colonel had recently returned a celebrity from a six-month mission to
Indian country. In covering nearly five thousand miles by foot,
packtrain, birchbark canoe and sailing vessel, he had survived tom-
ahawking and capture by the Indians. He had talked his tormentors
into releasing him and, as a suitable gesture of repentance, into
welcoming supply trains sent out by his secret Philadelphia trading
partners to frontier outposts just vacated by the defeated French.

The talk that day of mineral rights to gold, silver and copper, of
the annual harvest of beaver, fox and otter pelts, of endless corn-

fields and profitable royal bounties, may seem flamboyant to a later generation. But among hundreds of cash-poor aristocrats on the fringe of an immense unclaimed continent, it was a serious business that winter all along the crowded Atlantic seacoast. In Virginia, land-speculating Lees and Washingtons were organizing French and Indian War veterans and clamoring for massive land grants in the Mississippi and Ohio valleys. In the New England backcountry, colonels of militia and Puritan divines conspired with British officials to lay claim to entire Indian-occupied river valleys in the name of the Great Jehovah.

In the cleavages of the Appalachian Mountains, a new and classless democracy of the land-hungry was forming. Buckskinned younger sons of tidewater aristocrats mingled with threadbare clerics and runaway debtors, with restless, Indian-hating frontiersmen and penniless Scotch-Irish immigrants — all waiting (and just as many not waiting) for the signal from the British government to fill one thousand miles of virtually unpopulated forest all the way west to the Mississippi.

Despite carefully groomed appearances, William Franklin was as broke and desperate as any other debt-ridden provincial aristocrat who was being gobbled up by runaway postwar inflation (prices had tripled during the French and Indian War), unfavorable exchange rates with British creditors, the frustrating refusal of the British home government to allow the colonies to coin their own money.[2]

The youthful governor and his style-conscious wife had not exactly been following the penny-wise platitudes of *Poor Richard.* William's letters to London friends were full of orders for perfume, fancy fabrics, the best teas, fine furniture, half a dozen pairs of shoes at a time. One British traveler mentioned red damask bed curtains in his room. When parsimonious assemblymen refused to build Franklin a suitable governor's mansion with an adjoining chapel, he turned in the chapel sterling the King had given him and applied the credit to a tea service made by the King's goldsmith.

On his dining room walls were hung oil portraits of his father and the King. He had gone down to Philadelphia and borrowed large numbers of handsome leather-bound books from his father. He prided himself on maintaining a complete run of Strahan's

London *Chronicle*. If there was a new book or pamphlet written about America, he promptly ordered it for his growing historical library.[3] He had, since the age of ten, had a weakness for horses. He bred them and raced them in Philadelphia, and his carriage, a rarity among the New Jersey farm carts, stood out conspicuously against the farmscape. He was also contributing generously to the support of Anglican missionaries by ordering hymnbooks, prayer books and silver for new churches, helping to found a fund for the relief of ministers, widows, orphans.

Occasionally, he betrayed a touch of his father's frugality. Most of his fine furniture and his silver flatware and china he bought cheap from a British governor general called home. He also took pains to run a Spartan public administration. For years he answered all his own mail himself, researched and wrote his own answers to legislative measures sent him by the Assembly, to instructions sent him by the Crown. He often spent long hours in the saddle visiting not only his privy councillors, as he was expected to do, but also potential rivals in the popular Assembly, whom he won over gently to the Crown's latest instructions by the constant application of his smile, his courtly good manners, his easy, anecdotal wit. He had seen enough of aloof, high-handed behavior among Pennsylvania officials. He was determined to dignify the office, to be the best governor in all His Majesty's service.

New Jerseyans were startled to find they had a successful, shrewd governor, one unafraid to compromise in order to uphold the Crown's prerogative, but at the same time one who used his good judgment to advance the interests of the colony. In pushing badly needed reforms past bullheaded assemblymen, he introduced a pioneering welfare plan to feed and clothe destitute farmers. He proposed a law outlawing prison for debt. He espoused a second college, campaigned successfully for more and better roads and bridges built with the proceeds of public lotteries, launched an eleven-year battle with London authorities for a loan office to alleviate the cash shortage and self-liquidate government expenses. As one New Jersey historian has observed, "Governor Franklin's endeavors for the prosperity and welfare of the province were earnest and unremitting. . . . Had Franklin been governor of New Jersey a decade earlier, there is no reason to doubt that his administration would have been far more successful than it was."[4]

As fiscally sound as Franklin's administration continued to be, he never managed to solve his own chronic cash shortage. Three times the New Jersey farmer-legislators, citing the heaviest per capita war debt in America as the reason, refused requests for raises. Passed over twice for promotion to the more lucrative governorship of Barbados, his wife's native country, William unhappily was sliding deeper each year into his father's debt. Benjamin agreed that William must maintain a proper standard as governor, but he kept track of every farthing he advanced on his son's London account. He was especially careful to bill William for all the expenses of maintaining "Master T." with a governess until the boy would be old enough to join his grandfather on Craven Street.[5]

Despite Governor Franklin's generosity, he was shrewd enough to realize why his old acquaintance, Colonel Croghan, had come to visit him. He knew that Croghan and his Philadelphia Quaker merchant-backers wanted to use him. The state of their affairs was well known. For years, even as the firm of Baynton, Wharton and Morgan supplied both British garrisons and Indian tribes, it had been demanding reparations from the British government for goods allegedly seized or destroyed during the French and Indian War by vengeful Indians as well as irate white settlers. Only the year before, the Whartons had paid Croghan's expenses to London to press for cash or lands to settle their claims. Croghan rushed back empty-handed to report both to the merchants and to his superior officer, the Indian superintendent Sir William Johnson, that "half of England is now land-mad and everybody there has their eyes on this country."[6]

The colonel had heard rumors that a land company was forming to petition the King for a huge grant to the Illinois country, a vast, thinly populated French province that stretched west from the forks of the Ohio River. The merchants needed little coaxing. What they lacked was influence at court. They quickly thought of the Franklins. The governor of New Jersey must have strong ties to the nobility: how else could a young bastard seize such a prominent position and hold it without opposition? And Benjamin Franklin? Well, all America was abuzz at the way he had tilted British politics to his point of view on the Stamp Act. Besides, Franklin prestige could act as a magnet for other investors.

In Benjamin's vendetta against the Penns, he had relied on the large Quaker family of Wharton more than once. Young Wharton had gone door to door in Philadelphia to obtain signatures on Benjamin's petitions to oust the Penns. Now, to satisfy what they apparently considered a double quid pro quo, the Whartons sent Colonel Croghan to New Jersey to entice the governor into persuading his father to represent their claims surreptitiously at court. On the surface, the colonel was to ask to see the elder Franklin's correspondence about British plans for reparation payments. Moreover, Croghan had set his sights on his old friend William as a new source of credit. William must be rich: there were few finer houses in America. He would make a valuable ally indeed.

Governor Franklin had overcome most of the objections to his illegitimate birth and had won widespread respect in his early years in office by holding himself aloof from the usual bribes and gifts from favor-seekers that made up the run-of-the-mill opportunities for official corruption. Like his father, he placed relatives wherever possible in patronage jobs. He even appointed his mother's cousin to the New Jersey Council. Nepotism was never a term of misconduct in the Franklin lexicon. He took only what small emoluments were legally his, chiefly fees from the sale of land warrants and the three-shilling charge for a marriage license, which he personally signed. But he had carefully avoided the blandishments of a rent-free palace at Perth Amboy and large gifts of land from the hated East Jersey proprietors, whose blatant greed had, not long before, brought on riots. In fact, in a disreputable profession he appears to have been so honest a governor that no one believed him when he said he needed money.

But his career was clearly stagnating. His father's expense accountings grew ever longer, ever more insistent. His need for money pressed him hard. The opportunity to become fabulously rich, to be independent at last of his father, fired his old dreams of landed wealth. Many officials saw inside trading in lands not as a crime but as one of the few inducements to an otherwise thankless job. If William had any misgivings he quickly swept them away and decided to capitalize on his position for the first time. Colonel

Croghan reported to the Whartons that Governor Franklin was eager to join them in a vastly larger land scheme than even they had envisioned.

In a six-month series of private meetings with Croghan, the Whartons and their friends, William secretly conspired to win a western empire before any likely competitor got wind of the dealings. There was already enough competition. Fully twenty years earlier, second-rung Virginia aristocrats had petitioned the Crown for settlements at the forks of the Ohio. Young George Washington had been on his way to protect these claims when he had met his first defeat by the French at Fort Necessity. But the Virginia claims, while older, lacked the powerful backing in London that Franklin connections guaranteed. Indeed, the new Philadelphia partnership had an inside track through American channels just because Croghan's boss was the Indian superintendent. Sir William Johnson was a man with an avowed taste for land speculation (eventually he would accept gifts of more than 150,000 acres from the King and from Indian clients). His approval of the Wharton-Croghan-Franklin plans was not just desirable, it was necessary. The Indian country was, after all, still in the control of the Indians. Only Johnson could bring them to terms.[7]

In visit after visit to Philadelphia across the frozen river that winter, William ostensibly called on Deborah and Sally and carried them in his coach to the Assembly balls, but he was clandestinely dickering for a fortune. As usual, he and Betsy — as everyone called her — stayed at the home of Joseph Galloway and his wife, Grace. Galloway, William's best friend, was now the Franklins' closest political ally as well as speaker of the Pennsylvania Assembly. William enlisted him as a shareholder — they were already partners in a silver-mining venture — knowing that Galloway was married to the richest heiress in Pennsylvania.[8]

No doubt in a meeting at Galloway's mansion on High Street, William took over direction of the land venture. While the Whartons were willing to settle for a mere 250,000 acres of western Virginia hill country, the governor had an even bolder scheme in mind. He let it be known that he had long studied the matter. He thought the Whartons' claim impractically conservative. Why not ask for an entire new colony from the Wisconsin to the Ohio, from the

Wabash to the Mississippi — something more like 1.2 million acres? The French must soon leave their stockades and trading posts in the Illinois country. The Indians would need supplies: all they had to barter was wilderness land. The French would jump at the opportunity to sell cheaply the titles to the all-but-empty tracts they would otherwise lose outright to a military occupation. And the British, just so they did not have to pay any hard money, would certainly allow the Whartons to establish a trading monopoly in Illinois to supply far-flung British garrisons. It was as bold a scheme as any in the speculation-crazy new British Empire.

And, William needed to know, had they considered the form of government of this new colony? It should not be a military government such as the French had fostered in the province of Quebec and which the British were thinking of continuing. Instead, it should be a civil government, free to tax, govern, finance, and defend itself. It must be free of all old political alliances. It must have an experienced governor at its head. His meaning could not have been lost on his new partners. Again, the partners agreed. The Articles of Agreement of the Illinois Company were signed on March 29, 1766.[9]

In only a few months, the Illinois scheme had come to embrace officials in several colonies as well as senior British officials in the Indian establishment. Emboldened, the partners invited the British commander in chief in America, Sir Thomas Gage, to join them. He declined. He was against westward expansion. As head of all British frontier garrisons, he had to sign the Indian department pay orders and knew that land development could be a dreadfully expensive business. Besides, he wanted to pull his troops off the frontier and concentrate them along the seacoast in case there was more trouble with rioters.[10]

But Sir William Johnson, in the process of building an opulent forest mansion in central New York, was less squeamish. He was in a position to decide what areas could and could not be settled by whites and then treat for the land with the Indians. But his department had sizable contracts with the Whartons. Croghan offered to keep Johnson's name out of the official papers "till the success of our plan is known."[11] Invariably a bit short of cash, Sir William quickly yielded to Colonel Croghan's insistent "half of England is now land-mad." He agreed to be a full partner, to do all in his considerable power to advance the venture, but he agreed that his involvement should be kept secret: "It would answer better that I recommend it in general terms, as an affair I had heard was in agitation."[12]

In late March of 1766, Governor Franklin, brushing aside the stack of routine business, drew on his knowledge of British law to draft articles of agreement for the private partners of the Illinois Company. Then he moved on swiftly to write a long, eloquent panegyric to the King, extolling the merits of his company's claims and the wisdom of the Crown in favoring it over all other conflicting applications. His "Reasons for Establishing a Colony in the Illinois" was a masterpiece of subtle economic persuasion. It demonstrated clearly that in addition to learning law at the Inns of Court, William had absorbed a great deal of his father's clever technique of appealing to the innate British love of the blessings of commerce instead of wasting time on patriotic appeals: "The Country of the Illinois on the Mississippi is generally allowed to be the most fertile and pleasant part of all the Western Territory now in the possession of the English. The lands produce tobacco of a much superior quality to any raised in either Maryland or Virginia, and rice and indigo equal to the best in Carolina. But what is of the utmost consequence to Great Britain, no country in the known world is better adapted than this for the raising of hemp, flax, and silk. . . . Great Britain might also be furnished from thence with cotton, copper, iron, potash, wine, salt-peter." William knew of Britain's great balance-of-trade deficits, and he drove his points home.

Such a frontier colony, he continued, would also act as a military buffer against incursions from French and Spanish operatives across the Mississippi. Grants of one hundred to twelve hundred acres would be given according to rank to each veteran of the Indian wars who actually settled in Illinois. "From the Illinois we might likewise carry on a more extensive and advantageous fur trade with the numerous Indian Nations . . . supplying them with British manufactures. . . . Nor will the French be able to rival us in this trade, as we can transport our goods . . . to that country much cheaper than can be done from New Orleans . . . *against the stream* [the Mississippi]." He underscored the words: it was a key point.

"A question arises — What will be the most efficacious means of supporting these posts. . . . It is answered — a colony at the Illinois, under a good civil government. . . . Let the first Governor be a person experienced in the management of Indian affairs . . . who has given proofs of his influence with the savages."[13] William could point to his wilderness mission at eighteen, his treaty role at twenty-six, his summary judgment of murderers of Indians at thirty-five, his years as a skillful, smooth governor in New Jersey. Casting his broad hint all the way to London, but wording it so carefully that every other partner could see himself as the candidate, he sent the prospectus off to Sir William Johnson.

Governor Franklin did not, however, evidently feel comfortable enough about his interest in the proposed colony to declare it openly to the British government or to subjects closer at hand in America; he must have known that it created a possible conflict of interest or could, at the very least, be construed as inside dealing. Although his name appears first on the list of the private articles of agreement among the partners, it is absent from the list of signatures on the formal public petition. Evidently, Sir William wanted his 150,000-acre share of the grant badly enough to quiet any qualm. He endorsed the plan in a long letter to the King, but like Franklin he did not openly sign the petition.[14]

On June 6, 1766, William secretly drafted for the Whartons a letter of transmittal to Sir William Johnson, again omitting his own signature as well as Colonel Croghan's. It was signed by all the other shareholders. Enclosing his unsigned *Reasons for Establishing a Colony,* William asked the Indian superintendent "to transmit and recommend our proposals to his Majesties Ministers."[15] Sir William knew of the younger Franklin's involvement, of course. On July 10, he wrote to Benjamin Franklin that he had approved the plan and had agreed to become a private shareholder. Then, in the name of the shareholders, he invited the elder Franklin to join them. "I now enclose you a scheme proposed for establishing a colony at the Illinois. . . . I have accordingly sent it under a flying seal and must request you to forward it as addressed."[16] A seal was attached, but the letter was left open. Franklin was to read the contents, seal the letter, and send it on to colonial officials in Whitehall.

William had broached the subject of Croghan's claim for lost traders' goods to his father. On December 17, 1765, he had urged Benjamin to lobby for a large grant of land for his old friend.[17] But that Benjamin did not at first know of this vast new scheme is evident from William's personal letter to him of June 30, 1766, which was not written until more than a month after the articles of agreement were signed. When William finally sat down to write the letter, he broached the subject with studious diffidence. First, he lavishly praised Benjamin for his success in the Stamp Act repeal; then he answered Benjamin's criticisms of William's continued meddling in Pennsylvania politics. Finally, he turned to the subject of the land scheme, coolly commenting that "a few of us have formed a company to purchase of the French settled at the Illinois such lands as they have a good title to and are inclined to dispose of. But as I thought it would be of little avail to buy lands in that country unless a colony was established there, I have drawn up some proposals for that purpose, which are much approved of by Col. Croghan and the other gentlemen. . . . The company shall consist of 12 now in America, and if you like the proposals, you will be at liberty to add yourself and such gentlemen of character and fortune in England as you think will be most likely to promote the undertaking."[18]

This plan of William's, the culmination of so many years of travel and thought, the child of the Franklins' long journeys together, obviously electrified the usually cautious Benjamin. In a rare burst of enthusiasm, he wrote to William the day after the mail packet reached London that he had already set the plan in motion. He had immediately mailed the letters and "Reasons," and he had already begun to approach key British ministers. In a rare compliment to his son, he commented, "The plan is, I think, well drawn." He would, indeed, be agent for the Illinois Company. "This is an affair I shall seriously set about."[19]

He, too, had been worrying lately, although unnecessarily, about money. His Philadelphia printing partnership would expire at the end of the year. His deputy postmaster-generalship was again under political attack in England. He had recently formed a joint venture and had won a land grant on the mainland of Nova Scotia, something on the order of twenty thousand acres of forest.[20] But if his calculations were correct, he wrote excitedly to his son, the Illinois Company was not talking about one million acres but sixty-three million! Most certainly he wanted to be a shareholder. "I thank the company for their willingness to take me in, and one or two others that I may nominate. . . . I wish you had allowed me to name more. . . . By numbers we might increase the weight of interest here." He also wrote to Sir William Johnson the same day : "I shall not fail to use my best endeavors here in promoting it and obtaining . . . the necessary grants."[21]

Benjamin wholeheartedly threw himself behind the land scheme, but it is a pity that he and William sullied the effort by pursuing their joint fortune while they still held office as British officials. For years, as Assembly officers in Pennsylvania, they had railed against just such undertakings by the Penns and their minions. For William, it was an even greater piece of corruption: using his position within the colonial service to deal secretly in British-owned lands. But it is fruitless to hold men of one age accountable by the standards of another, even if both thought fit to keep their involvements in the scheme secret. At the very least it made them hypocrites, little different from their old archrivals, the Penns.

Their years of working together for the Illinois land grant once again brought them closer together. A new, evenhanded tone crept into the elder Franklin's letters to the younger. Each letter overlooked the revolutionary events surrounding them and blotted out the danger signs with the latest news of their personal, conspiratorial quest for a family fortune.

When the first session of Parliament since the repeal of the Stamp Act was convened in the autumn of 1766, Benjamin Franklin summoned his carriage around to Craven Street and drove into Westminster to call at the morning levees of cabinet ministers. His letters to William stressed the critical problems he as a lobbyist faced. Under King George III, cabinet shuffles of the same handful of ministers were becoming so frequent that the inner circle of government had become a repertory theater of the absurd. "There are such continual changes here," he wrote William on September 12, "that it is very discouraging to all applications to be made to the ministry. I thought the last [cabinet] well established, but they are broken and gone. The present set are hardly thought to stand very firm and God only knows whom we are to have next."[22] On Bute's resignation his cousin Grenville came to power and bored the King with long dull lectures. After thoroughly bungling the stamp crisis, Grenville resigned at the King's insistence, thereby making way for the ailing warlord Pitt to patch together a frail coalition. The old lion put in charge of the American colonies a trusted young lieutenant of his, the earl of Shelburne. A dashing army veteran, Shelburne had a progressive view of empire; he was bent on reorganizing the system of governing and taxing America even if it meant bucking his peers. Unfortunately, as a planner he was unimaginative.

Franklin took instantly to this young secretary of state. He had never completely extinguished the idea, first kindled on the war-torn Pennsylvania frontier, of granting lands in a new western colony to battle-seasoned Dissenters. As was his wont when meeting new government officials, he searched for common ground with Shelburne and found that they were both Dissenters, both amateur naturalists and economists. "I have mentioned the Illinois affair to Lord Shelburne," he wrote William later in September. "His Lordship had already read your plan . . . and said it appeared to him a reasonable scheme, but he found it did not quadrate with the sentiments of people here. I fancy but am not certain that his Lordship meant Lord Hillsborough who, I am told, is not favorable to new settlements."[23]

Indeed, few Americans knew the imperious Lord Hillsborough, who was one of the largest absentee landholders in Ireland and a man who would do as much as anyone to touch off the American Revolution. With large crops of flax and hundreds of poor Scotch-Irish cottagers on his lands to provide cheap labor, Hillsborough was deeply involved in developing the Irish linen industry. Understandably he was alarmed at the number of his tenant farmers who were leaving for America. He had no desire to foster any further movement to cheap lands in the American West. As a leading member of the Board of Trade and Plantations, he took a hard-line view of America. Laws had been on the books since 1660 to regulate American trade and industry so that it would supply and enrich British commerce, not compete with it. Hillsborough rightly saw expansion into the American West as a serious threat. He enunciated his fears in the board's first report on the Illinois scheme: "The expense on the [overland] carriage of [British] goods would oblige the people manufacture for themselves. . . . It would be difficult to defend [Illinois] and to govern it. . . . It may lay the foundation of a power in the heart of America. People [are] wanted here in [Great Britain] . . . none could be spared for a new colony."[24]

It did not help, either, that the Whartons had chosen this moment to attempt to put the friendly Lord Shelburne's undersecretary of state in their collective pocket. They offered him a kickback on a contract to supply British garrisons in Illinois if he would advance their interests to his lordship. Whether Franklin actually transmitted the Wharton offer is unclear — records of such dealings are rarely put into writing — but the undersecretary, calling the proposal "a bribe," said he nevertheless would not hold it against the Illinois venturers.[25]

Franklin was undaunted by initial ministerial objections and he again lobbied before Lord Shelburne. What clearly encouraged him was his own appointment by Lord Shelburne to an advisory committee to examine the ministry's proposed "Plan for the Future Management of Indian Affairs."[26] Shortly thereafter, he wrote William that he had found the opportunity for several more private meetings with Shelburne. William knew how his father operated. He must have guessed that Benjamin went into these meetings well prepared, with a marked copy of the ministers' forty-three-point program under his arm and a list of priorities in his head. No moment, no word touching ever so slightly on the Illinois venture was wasted. Yet, when he learned of the details of these meetings, William undoubtedly was surprised by his father's agreement to one article, one that would work against his partners Sir William Johnson, Colonel Croghan and the Whartons: "The [Indian] agent and his deputies and the commissaries are not to trade."[27]

"Should it not," Franklin asked Lord Shelburne, "be a part of their oath that they will have no concern in such trade directly or indirectly? Private agreements between them and the traders for a share of profits should be guarded against. And the same between them and the purchasers of lands from Indians."[28] Apparently, Franklin either saw no inconsistency in his and his son's involvement or wanted to avoid any suspicion of double-dealing by his partners. It is doubtful, on the face of this evidence, that he had admitted the Franklin interest in the Illinois proposal either to Lord Shelburne or the ministers of trade. One of Franklin's unquestionable skills was his ability to keep to his self-set priorities.

His letters to his wife and daughter dwindled in number even as his missives to William became more frequent. Every two weeks now, he sent off fresh news to his son. "I was again with Lord Shelburne a few days since," he wrote on October 11, "and said a good deal to him on the affair. . . . He was pleased to say he really approved of it, but intimated that every new proposed expense for America would meet with great difficulty here, the Treasury being alarmed and astonished at the growing charges [for defending and administering the new American frontier]."[29]

By the next mail Franklin related another good omen. His son's old friend Omniscient Jackson, now a member of Parliament and counsel to the Board of Trade, not only had become an Illinois shareholder but "the ministry have asked his opinion and advice on your plan of a colony. . . . He has just sent me to peruse his answer in writing. He warmly recommends the plan. He corroborates what I have been saying and . . . appears less to be suspected of some American bias."[30]

This particular piece of intelligence, indicating an amazing inroad into the ministry by two artful lobbyists, should have thrilled William, but the delays worried him. It was never his nature to be as patient as his father. In his letters he bridled at ministry objections to his plan. He was indignant at what he considered British blindness to the true nature of the frontier problem. Although Secretary of State Shelburne saw the inevitability of westward movement and was willing to risk his office to carry the point over Lord Hillsborough, it worried William that Lord Shelburne was a relative by marriage of Thomas Penn's, that this fact might somehow be bringing about delays. Was not the only pertinent question whether a separate government should be formed *at once* in Illinois before "it is become the residence of a numerous and lawless banditti"?[31] William, too, evidently saw little self-interested pleading in his outburst. By now he regarded himself as an imperial statesman, an impartial advocate of a sane and sensible frontier policy.

Little can be more cruelly tantalizing than sporadic encouragement of great success to a man drowning slowly in debt. Worsening money problems made William increasingly desperate. The paper colony began to yellow and curl in its cubbyhole in Whitehall even as hundreds more families of squatters trudged through mountain passes and settled on Indian hunting grounds. William must have fairly screamed at his father's latest letter in the spring of 1767: "Great changes being expected keep men's minds in suspense and obstruct public affairs of every kind. It is therefore not to be wondered that so little progress is made in our American schemes."[32]

At the start of summer, when William again brought his mother and sister and brother-in-law for a two-week vacation to Burlington, the elder Franklin was leaving for another Paris vacation. He wrote briefly: "The Illinois affair goes forward but slowly."[33] He had succeeded in winning a second major land grant of twenty thousand acres on the Nova Scotia mainland. By the time he returned to London late in the year, even he was becoming exasperated. "The confusion among our great men still continues as great as ever. A melancholy thing it is to consider that, instead of employing the present leisure of peace [to] extend our commerce, pay off our [national] debts, secure allies and increase the strength and ability of the nation to support a future war, the whole time seems wasted in party contentions about power and profit, in court intrigues and cabals. . . . Some are professed adversaries to America, which is now made one of the distinctions of party here. Those who, in the last two sessions have shown a disposition to favor us, [are] called by way of reproach *Americans*."[34]

At three thousand miles' distance, after not seeing each other for three years, the two Franklins seemed, in their intimate, even dangerous, exchanges more closely allied than ever. When Benjamin could not send encouragement, at least he sent William long, chatty anecdotes of his London observations — a spicy scandal or a memorable vignette to pass along to their mutual American friends. He had been keeping a London journal (now lost) detailing the antics of British society. Too revealing to print, he sent it to William. "I was highly entertained with the perusal of those few pages of your journal which you were so obliging as to send me," William wrote. "You may rely that the contents will be kept an inviolable secret."[35]

In the wrong hands, the pages could have hurt Benjamin badly, especially one mocking passage. "At the beginning of this session in the [House of Commons]," Benjamin wrote, "Mr. Grenville [author of the stamp tax measures] had been raving against America as traitorous, rebellious, etc., when [a] firm friend [of America] stood up and gravely said that in reading the Roman history he found it was a custom among that wise and magnanimous people whenever the senate was informed of any discontent in the provinces, to send two or three of their body into the discontented provinces to enquire into the grievances and report to the senate what mild measures might be used to remedy what was amiss before any severe steps were taken to enforce obedience. That this example he thought worthy our imitation in the present state of our [American] colonies . . . that it might not be supposed he was for imposing burdens on others that he would not be willing to share himself, he did at the same time declare his willingness, if the House should think fit to appoint them, to go over thither *with that honourable gentleman* [Grenville].

"Upon this, there was a great laugh which continued sometime, and was rather increased by Mr. Grenville's asking, 'Will the gentleman engage that I shall be safe there? Can I be assured that I shall be allowed to come back again to make the report?' As soon as the laugh . . . subsided . . . Mr. Onslow could be heard again, 'I cannot absolutely engage for the honourable gentleman's safe return, but if he goes thither upon this service I am strongly of the opinion the event will contribute greatly to the future quiet of both countries.' "[36]

The Illinois colony seemed, by late 1767, stillborn of neglect, another victim of British postwar efforts to reduce property taxes in England by making her colonies self-supporting. Yet Benjamin always reacted well under such pessimistic pressure. When William had all but lost hope, he tore open a thick envelope from Craven Street.

"Last week I dined at Lord Shelburne's and had a long conversation with him and Mr. Conway (there being no other company). [Henry Seymour Conway was a friend to America, a military-minded secretary of state.) I took the opportunity as one means of saving expense in supporting the outposts that a settlement should be made in the Illinois country. I mentioned your plan . . . the readiness and ability of the gentlemen concerned to carry the settlement into execution with very little expense to the Crown. The Secretaries appeared finally to be fully convinced. There remained no obstacle but the Board of Trade, which was to be brought over privately before the matter should be referred to them officially. Communicate nothing of this letter but privately to our friend Galloway. I am your affectionate father."[37]

The day after returning from his 1767 vacation, Benjamin again wrote hurriedly to William: "Just now heard that the Illinois settlement is approved of in the Cabinet Council. The Board of Trade are to consider it next week."[38]

A suspenseful month passed before William slit the seal of the next franked envelope from London. "The King in Council referred the proposal to the Board of Trade who called for the opinion of two merchants. Mr. Jackson and I [the two merchants] were present and answered in the affirmative unanimously. We shall know in a few days."[39] They were now so close.

But soon another cabinet shakeup stymied Franklin plans. Pitt, ailing, was out again. A wobbly successor, in an attempt to shore up his coalition, asked anti-American nobles to join his administration. A new secretary of state, the wily Lord Hillsborough, superseded Shelburne. Benjamin wrote William in March of 1768 that he knew too little of this man Hillsborough to predict the outcome of the Illinois colony. Gloomily, he noted that "the purpose of settling the new colonies seems at present to be dropped."[40] But before this news could reach him, William had already plunged into his most reckless real estate scheme.

He had become involved, in fact, in the largest piece of inside real estate dealing in colonial American history. In July, in anticipation of the opening up of the vast new British territories between the Appalachian Mountains and the Mississippi River, Sir William Johnson summoned the governors of eight colonies and the leaders of the Six Nations tribes to a conference at Fort Stanwyx, New

York. Johnson had pressed the British for a new and realistic boundary line that took into account the incursions of white settlers and allowed the Indians to sell their lands before squatting by frontiersmen triggered more bloodshed. What Johnson had in mind, however, was not exactly a public land sale: it was a gigantic piece of wheeling and dealing by government officials and their cronies.

William Franklin and a few hand-picked friends met with Galloway, who was representing Pennsylvania, and they wended their way through the New York forests to Johnson's sumptuous estate on the Mohawk River. In the wilderness clearing, they found preparations in progress for the largest Indian conference in many years. Fort Stanwyx had been cleaned up for the occasion, arbors built for shade from the late summer heat. Herds of cattle complained noisily as they were led into pens to await slaughter to feed the multitude. Boatloads of rum were placed under guard alongside chests of Spanish silver dollars to pay for the land. Three thousand Indians soon squatted in the clearings to hear Sir William open the grand sale.

But first, a few side deals: Governor Franklin and his Burlington neighbors bought 30,000 acres of land in Albany County, New York. The Indians trusted this governor, again calling him Dispenser of Justice. They even overlooked the fact that he was not always willing to join their rituals. Years later, Benjamin Rush, the son-in-law of William's friend Stockton, wrote that William "offended an Indian family by declining to eat some broth made of venison that had maggots in it. The Indian rebuked him by saying, 'Eat it, young man, it is good enough to be made into———.'"[41] By the tenth day of eating and drinking and speechmaking, the Indians agreed to sell their rights to 1.8 million acres of wilderness land to satisfy the Whartons' claims for goods destroyed in the Indian wars. Then the Six Nations ceded 104,000 acres more at the site of present-day Cooperstown, New York to Governor Franklin, Croghan and their partners without asking why his silver prospectors were interested in such rocky, desolate hill country.

If the acreage involved so far seemed staggering, it was but a prelude to the main transaction, the sale of 2.5 million acres along the Ohio River. As if by magic, the boundary between the English territories and the Indian hunting preserves shifted seven hundred miles west. The western Pennsylvania lands forced upon the Delaware and Shawnee tribes after the infamous Walking Purchase were now wrested away from them by the arbitrary stroke of a quill pen.

At the end of the two-week trading session, Sir William opened the rum casks wide and ladled out £10,000 in silver coins to pay the Indians for a total of more than four million acres of land. The Indians went on a binge only rivaled by the speculative spree of William Franklin and his cronies. They all left Fort Stanwyx certain they were rich men. Nothing more remained except for the formal ratification of the sales by Lord Hillsborough.

William and his cronies were, of course, only rich on paper, and shortly after his return to New Jersey, William's luck went from bad to worse. He was land rich but cash poor, and when nervous Burlington neighbors pressed him to pay a large debt or put up his lands as collateral, he tried to collect from his old friend Croghan. But Croghan was now hiding in the backwoods of Pennsylvania, his assets already attached by other creditors. So worried did William become that the following winter he traveled back through heavy snows to Albany to have his lands surveyed and recorded so that he could sell them to pay his debts. He now had debts equal to at least three years of his governor's salary.

In a rare moment of sharp trading, William exchanged two thousand acres of unsurveyed land on Lake Otsego (the site of present-day Cooperstown), for an established farm in Burlington County, New Jersey.[42] Located on a high knoll known as Strawberry Hill that overlooked Rancocas Creek only fifteen miles northeast of Philadelphia, the farm absorbed William's excess energies between 1770 and 1773. He acquired 525 choice acres and a spacious Georgian house and made them over into Franklin Park, a showcase country estate.

A wide fieldstone house, Franklin Park stood, as William later wrote, "on a fine healthy spot." Betsy would be happier here. The house had symmetrical fireplaces and clustered chimneys at either end, random-width hardwood floors, heavy doors and brass fittings. William added on a wing and installed a new roof. He imported an English gardener and they laid out a formal garden, a deer park and orchards. He also had the fieldstone house painted dead white, in the latest English fashion. With "an exceeding good dairy, stables, barn stalls, and sheds for cattle," Franklin Park was as opulent as any tidewater plantation. The house looked out over "an exceeding good grazing farm" with "a large range for young cattle, several fields of upland meadows and about thirty acres of banked meadow, which yield a considerable quantity of good hay. The whole is in good fence, and divided into proper fields, having upwards of 20,000 cedar rails with a park containing about 175 acres in which there are between thirty and forty deer." Along "several pleasant shady walks, particularly in a young grove of pines," the governor and his lady led their guests, often including his sister Sally and her husband and assorted Franklin cousins.[43]

William was proud of his cattle, his sheep and his hogs, his goats, chickens, horses and oxen. He unabashedly sent home-cured hams from the little wharf on Rancocas Creek across the ocean to members of Parliament, to old friends from schooldays in London, and he fairly clucked over their appreciative comments. But each year William had to write to his father to beg patience over his latest expense account for Temple "till I have got my land [in New York province]."[44]

The elder Franklin's letters to his son became rarer and now often contained long accounts of advances on William's behalf. One in particular annoyed William. He protested against "Remarks on Benjamin Franklin's Account Against William Franklin dated April 20, 1771." William was always better at spending money and keeping track of his debts than his father was. He pointed out that he had repaid some of the items before; and he had accepted prints, Franklin stoves and books on consignment or as gifts for relatives, and should not be charged for them. Ever honest with his father, William also pointed out that he owed him one hundred pounds for "Master T.," now in an expensive London boarding school, and seven pounds, ten shillings, for a plow for his new farm. (Benjamin always sent him farm implements quickly, luxuries at a more leisurely pace.) A great deal of their disagreement hinged on Benjamin's double billing for nine pounds of Lapsang Souchong tea. The accounting also demonstrated that William had generously loaned money to relatives, including Deborah.[45]

Now redoubling his quest for an El Dorado, William helped organize yet another New York land company and acted as go-between for Sir William Johnson, Colonel Croghan and a Burlington syndicate of investors. At least once a month he wrote Johnson until the baronet wearied of the business. It did not help that Johnson had already learned of Lord Hillsborough's outrage at the private land deals at Fort Stanwyx and of his lordship's blocking the new boundary line. This ploy effectively quashed all sales and completely frustrated the Illinois scheme as well.

It was characteristic of Benjamin Franklin that, once he latched onto an idea, he turned it over in his mind until it caught the light. If the Illinois plan was fizzling, maybe it was not grand enough. A larger venture, involving more high-level sponsors, was needed. This time, he himself would exert control.

The assemblage of British dignitaries he summoned to the incorporation meeting on December 27, 1769, at the Crown and Anchor Tavern in Fleet Street was a masterpiece of Franklin invention. The new shareholders of the Grand Ohio Company included three Walpoles who were nephews of a former prime minister; the brother of the secretary of the Board of Trade; the lord chamberlain; the lord chancellor; two members of the Privy Council; William Strahan (now an MP); one director of the East India Company; the postmaster general; the leader of the landed gentry in Parliament; the secretary of the treasury and his undersecretary. Omniscient Jackson took his seat beside Franklin, who was chairman of the meeting and proxy for the American partners. The key members of nearly every agency and jurisdiction needed to smooth the path of a 2.4 million–acre land grant plunked down two hundred pounds each for a share of the Franklins' wilderness empire.[46]

The gathering was also a stunning testimony to Benjamin Franklin's lobbying expertise. When a committee of delegates paid its first official call on Lord Hillsborough at Whitehall, he was momentarily overawed. Why, he asked, should they doubt the Crown's willingness to sell land? As Benjamin wrote William, Hillsborough "thought their best plan would be to purchase a tract of land sufficient for a separate government, a new colony. Indeed, why not apply for, say *twenty* million acres?[47] Benjamin was suspicious, the others puzzled, but they amended their petition to a twenty million–acre grant of all the territory from the Appalachians west to the Mississippi River, from the Pennsylvania border southwest to the Kentucky River. The new company would buy out all rival claimants and pay all the expenses of the Fort Stanwyx treaty, even pay the Crown rent for every acre of cultivated land. It was a thoroughly sensible plan. Only one week later, the lords of the treasury tentatively approved it and sent it over to Whitehall to Lord Hillsborough.

III

I HAVE LOST
MY SON

11

GOVERNMENT SHOULD
HAVE NO PASSIONS

1771-1773

B Y THE TIME BENJAMIN FRANKLIN PRESENTED HIS NEW
commission as agent for the Massachusetts Assembly to the
colonial secretary on January 16, 1771, he was beginning to harbor
unpleasant thoughts about Lord Hillsborough. In a letter to
Thomas Cushing of Boston, he described Hillsborough as "proud,
supercilious, extremely conceited (moderate as they are) of his political knowledge and abilities, and inimical to all who dare tell him
disagreeable truths."[1] Franklin evidently came to dislike Hillsborough when his lordship, as one of the postmasters general, tried
to oust him from his lucrative postal sinecure. According to
Franklin, Hillsborough considered him "too much of an American" to hold high imperial office. Hillsborough's unavowed policy
of delaying the Illinois grant only added to Franklin's irritation. By
that time, Boston leaders who for years had thought Benjamin too
much of an Englishman could see the wisdom of making him their
London lobbyist. The stage was set for a confrontation that led to
Benjamin's deepening disgust with the British ruling class. He later
wrote a memorandum to send back to Boston which graphically
describes that first formal meeting with Hillsborough:

> I went this morning to wait on Lord Hillsborough. The porter at
> first denied his lordship, on which I left my name and drove off. But
> before the coach got out of the square the coachman heard a call,
> turned, and went back to the door. . . . The porter came and said:
> "His Lordship will see you, sir.". . . Several other gentlemen were

there attending, with whom I sat down a few minutes, when Secretary [John] Pownall came out to us and said his lordship desired I would come in. I was pleased with this ready admission and preference, having sometimes waited three or four hours for my turn; and being pleased, I could more easily put on the open, cheerful countenance that my friends advised me to wear. His lordship came towards me and said: "I was dressing in order to go to court, but hearing that you were at the door, who are a man of business, I determined to see you immediately."

I thanked his lordship and said that at present my business was not much; it was only to pay my respects to his lordship and to acquaint him with my appointment by the House of Representatives of Massachusetts Bay to be their agent here, in which station if I could be of any service — I was going on to say, to the public, I should be very happy; but his lordship, whose countenance changed at my naming that province, cut me short by saying, with something between a smile and a sneer:

L.H.—I must set you right there, Mr. Franklin. You are not agent.

B.F. —Why, my lord?

L.H.—You are not appointed.

B.F. —I do not understand, your lordship. I have the appointment in my pocket.

L.H.—You are mistaken; I have later and better advices. I have a letter from Governor Hutchinson; he would not give his assent to the bill.

B.F. —There was no bill, my lord; it was a vote of the House.

L.H.—There was a bill presented to the governor for the purpose of appointing you . . . to which the governor refused his assent.

B.F. —I cannot understand this, my lord; I think there must be some mistake. . . . Is your lordship quite sure that you have such a letter?

L.H.—I will convince you of it directly. (*Rings the bell.*) Mr. Pownall will come in and satisfy you.

B.F. —It is not necessary that I should now detain your lordship from dressing. You are going to court. I will wait on your lordship another time.

L.H.—No, stay; he will come immediately. (*To the servant.*) Tell Mr. Pownall I want him. (*Mr. Pownall comes in.*) Have you not at hand Governor Hutchinson's letter mentioning his refusing his assent to the bill for appointing Dr. Franklin agent?

Sec. P.—My lord?

L.H.—Is there not such a letter?

Sec. P.—No, my lord. . . .

B.F. — I thought it could not well be, my lord, as my letters are by the last ships, and they mention no such thing. Here is the authentic copy of the vote of the House appointing me, in which there is no mention of any act intended. Will your lordship please to look at it? (*With seeming unwillingness he takes it, but does not look into it.*)

L.H.—An information of this kind is not properly brought to me as Secretary of State. The Board of Trade is the proper place.

B.F. —I will leave the paper then with Mr. Pownall to be —

L.H.—(*Hastily*) To what end would you leave it with him?

B.F. —To be entered on the minutes of that Board, as usual.

L.H.—(*Angrily*) It shall not be entered there. No such paper shall be entered there while I have anything to do with the business of that Board. The House of Representatives has no right to appoint an agent. We shall take no notice of any agents but such as are appointed by acts of Assembly to which the governor gives his assent. . . .

B.F. —I cannot conceive, my lord, why the consent of the governor should be thought necessary to the appointment of an agent for the people. It seems to me that —

L.H.—(*With a mixed look of anger and contempt.*) I shall not enter into dispute with *you*, sir, upon this subject.

B.F. —I beg your lordship's pardon; I do not presume to dispute with your lordship; I would only say that it seems to me that every body of men who cannot appear in person where business relating to them may be transacted should have a right to appear by an agent. The concurrence of the governor does not seem to be necessary. It is the business of the people that is to be done; he is not one of them; he is himself an agent.

L.H.—(*Hastily*) Whose agent is he?

B.F. —The King's, my lord.

L.H.—No such matter. He is one of the corporation by the province charter. No agent can be appointed but by an act, nor any act pass without his assent. Besides, this proceeding is directly contrary to express instructions.

B.F. —I did not know there had been such instructions. . . .

L.H.—Yes, your offering such a paper to be entered is an offence against them. (*Folding it up again without having read a word of it.*) No such appointment shall be entered. . . .

B.F. —(*Reaching out his hand for the paper, which his lordship returned to him.*) I beg your lordship's pardon for taking up so

much of your time. It is, I believe, of no great importance
whether the appointment is acknowledged or not, for I have
not the least conception that an agent can *at present* be of any
use to any of the colonies. I shall therefore give your lordship
no further trouble.[2]

The irate colonial secretary took Franklin's last words as a personal affront. Franklin reported to Boston a month later: "He calls
[my words] extremely rude and abusive. He assured a friend of
mine [probably Strahan, now the King's official printer] that they
were equivalent to telling him to his face that the colonies could
expect neither favor nor justice during his administration. I find he
did not mistake me."[3]

Franklin's clash with Hillsborough evidently startled this pragmatic London lobbyist into taking a long look at the shifting relations between George III's government and the American colonies.
For the first time he was forced to think of himself more as an
American than as a British subject. A man who often reacted
quickly, hotly, to personal challenge, Franklin was growing increasingly outraged by the blatant condescension of Lord Hillsborough
and his ilk.

As a lowly tallow chandler's son who had grown rich in business,
he was no doubt accustomed to the upper-class British scorn for the
lowborn, yet it obviously rankled him. His exchange with Hillsborough and his letters about it over the next year show a profound
change in his attitude toward the British. For five more years he
would publicly remain the obsequious imperial bureaucrat in his
dealings as agent for five American colonies, but privately he began
more and more to speak and write as an American.

Indeed, for the first ten years of the reign of George III, he had
seemed blandly royalist in his reactions to the stirrings of popular
protest against the new high Tory regime. As year followed unstable year and cabinets came and went in chaos, Franklin remained
unsympathetic to English radicals who had aligned themselves
against his friend Lord Bute and Bute's faction of the King's
friends.

"This capital," Franklin had written in amazement in May of
1768, "the residence of the king, is now a daily scene of lawless riot

and confusion. Coal-heavers and porters [pull] down the houses of coal merchants that refuse to give them more wages, sawyers destroying sawmills, sailors unrigging all the outward-bound ships and suffering none to sail till merchants agree to raise their pay; watermen destroying private boats and threatening bridges." He went on to say that officials had belatedly responded. He lamented the necessity of soldiers' firing into the crowds of rioters and killing men, women and children, "which only seems to have produced a universal sullenness that looks like a great black cloud coming on, ready to burst in a general tempest. What the event will be God only knows. Some punishment seems preparing for a people who are ungratefully abusing the best constitution and the best king any nation was ever blessed with."[4]

What Franklin undoubtedly did not know was that, as the turmoil dragged on, the young King had grown to hate not only the mob, but any vestige of democracy or republican spirit. On more than one occasion he personally called out the redcoats to fire into the crowds. As he railed impotently against his recalcitrant children in England, he became even more vituperative in punishing his distant and, he thought, weaker subjects in America. For nearly ten years, he was able to hide his personal involvement in repressive anti-American policies behind a screen of trusted advisors, thereby creating the impression of royal benevolence betrayed by wily ministers. But after the popular prime minister William Pitt had a mental breakdown in 1767, the exasperated King gave power to three avowedly anti-American nobles: Townshend, Hillsborough and North.

Amid all the jubilation in America over the repeal of the hated Stamp Act, few colonists, not even Benjamin Franklin, had heeded a clause in the bill repealing the act: that Parliament, by right, shall have jurisdiction over America "in all cases whatsoever."

At this point, Franklin was, as a letter to William shows, just beginning to consider deeply the quarrel over who should rule America: the mother country through Parliament, the colonies themselves through their chartered assemblies, or both. Franklin had just finished reading *The Farmer's Letters,* which had been published anonymously but actually written by the pro-Penn Philadelphia lawyer John Dickinson. "I am not yet master of the idea these and the New England writers have of the relation between Britain and her colonies," he wrote William. "The more I have thought and read on the subject, the more I find myself confirmed in opinion that no middle doctrine can be well maintained. Something might be made of either of the extremes, that Parliament has a power to make all laws for us, or that it has a power to make no laws for us."[5] In any case, Benjamin did not foresee an intensive struggle over the disclaimer at the tag end of the repealing clause of the Stamp Act.

To veteran London observers, the Declaratory Act, as it became known, seemed at first a *pro forma* face-saving declaration, having no weight because colonies had always had the right to make their own laws and then submit them to the King for ratification. But as the next few years rolled by like the constant menace of a gathering storm, it became evident that the new high Tory regime was attempting to abridge rights as venerable as the oldest colonial charter.

For at least a century, since an earlier Tory king had imposed systematic mercantile regulations on America, there had been latent tension over the colonies' rights to trade and manufacture. But British efforts at enforcement had always been haphazard. Indeed, when the Whigs returned to power in 1715, they had ignored the trade laws and encouraged American trade that often involved Britain's commercial rivals under an unspoken policy of "salutary neglect." Great fortunes such as the Hancocks' of Boston and the Whartons' of Philadelphia had developed around illegal trade with the French West Indies.

In peacetime, British merchants reaped a ready market for overpriced, often shoddy goods in the American colonies; in wartime, the British navy was assured crucial supplies of naval stores — wool, cotton, hemp, timber, flour, rum — and supposedly could rely on colonial troops to defend the frontiers against French and Spanish attacks.

Considered mainly a backwater, the American mainland colonies were of less importance to British lawmakers than a few small, sugar-rich Caribbean islands, of even less worth than British strategic bases on Gibraltar and Majorca that figured in the endless wars for European domination. Ironically, for years both Franklins had been vocal in urging England to stop her preoccupation with ancient power struggles in Europe and instead turn her attention to her rapidly growing American interests. It was America, Benjamin argued over and over, that one day would hold more people and generate more commerce than all the other British possessions combined. And now, after a century of neglect, England was turning toward America, belatedly and belligerently.

The most contentious problem was that, in the worldwide struggle that produced the Seven Years' War and continued for more than fifty years, Britain found herself the winner of a large and costly empire. With no precedents as guides and a paucity of hard money with which to sustain herself, she began a long and painful period of experimentation. At first she concentrated on trying to make each colony pay for itself. This might have been possible even if the obvious advantages of trade had not been figured into the calculations; but debt-ridden British landowners were growing increasingly resentful of having to pay heavy land taxes to cover the high costs of defending the new American borders. Aligned with Whig merchants and the King's newly appointed anti-American ministers, they enthusiastically pushed through Parliament sweeping customs reforms that threatened to price American goods out of European markets.[6]

As each colony began to encounter more difficulties with British officials sent to enforce the new regulations, colonial legislatures hired London agents familiar with court officials and procedures to attempt to protect American interests. But, as Benjamin had learned from Lord Hillsborough, the British government viewed Americans as troublesome children who must be punished into obedience. Indeed, Lord Hillsborough had already begun to administer his discipline. In October of 1768, at the request of nervous Crown officials in riot-prone Boston, he had ordered two regiments of grenadiers, the new British garrison forces in America, quartered in Boston. Not long after they marched up Long Wharf and bivouacked on Boston Common, the first serious flare-up occurred. A local butcher taunted one of the soldiers, who knocked him down. The commanding officer applauded the "lesson." Fined by a local justice, the British soldier refused to pay up and slashed the constable attempting to arrest him. When British troops built a guard box on private property, the owner led a crowd that attacked with sticks, bricks, stones. Two soldiers were seriously injured.

Then local nonimportation laws were extended and some pro-British merchants balked. They were blacklisted by name and denounced as traitors in a broadside. One merchant dared to publish a letter complaining that he was being deprived of his livelihood in the name of liberty. A crowd of young boys responded by mobbing his store. A sympathetic neighbor tried to tear down their placards. The boys chased him home and threw rocks through his windows, injuring him, his wife and a daughter. One older member of the mob pounded on his door, shouting, "Come out, you damn son of a bitch, I'll have your heart out!" From an upstairs window the merchant fired a round of birdshot into the crowd, fatally wounding a thirteen-year-old boy.

Insults quickly produced more injuries. A soldier was walking past a rope yard when a voice called out, "Soldier, will you work?" "Yes," the soldier replied. "Then go and clean my shit house."[7] The soldier, gathering thirty comrades armed with cutlasses and clubs and headed by a tall black drummer, attacked the workmen, who took up the heavy wooden tools of their craft, counterattacked, and drove them off. The soldiers vowed that revenge would occur three nights later.

Under a full moon on the night of March 5, 1770, only two months after Franklin exchanged insults with the colonial secretary, sailors and young boys gathered near the Boston Customs House. A young boy taunted a sentry. He struck the boy with his gun. The boy fetched a sizable crowd of tough young men and pointed out the sentry: "There is the son of a bitch that knocked me down." From the crowd came shouts, "Kill him, kill him, knock him down." More troops were called. A larger crowd, led by a giant mulatto workman, Crispus Attucks, pressed in. They pelted the retreating soldiers with chunks of ice, hard-packed snowballs, oyster shells, cudgels. The troops loaded their muskets. The crowd drew closer, lashing out with cutlasses and clubs, screaming at the guards, "Come on, you rascals, you bloody-backs, you lobster scoundrels! Fire if you dare, God damn you! Fire and be damned! We know you dare not!"[8] The troops fired point-blank. Attucks and two others dropped, dead. Six others were dragged away, bleeding on the frozen snow.

Benjamin Franklin was one of the first to see where the confrontation could lead: it could lead, he was now writing, to "a total disunion of the two countries. . . . The resentment of the people will, at times . . . , burst into outrages and violence. . . . This naturally draws down severity and acts of further oppression. . . . The more the people are dissatisfied, the more rigor will be thought necessary. Severe punishments will be inflicted to terrify. Rights and privileges will be abolished. Greater force will then be required to secure execution and submission. The expense will become enormous. It will then be thought proper, by fresh exactions, to make the people defray it. Thence the British nation and government will become odious, and subjection to it will be deemed no longer tolerable. War ensues, and the bloody struggle will end in absolute slavery to America or ruin to Britain by the loss of her colonies. The latter [is] most probable from America's growing strength and magnitude."[9]

If Franklin had any hint that his path was taking him away from his only son, he did not show it now. In the next few months, he poured out a stream of letters to William. At William's request, he wrote the opening of his autobiography during a long country-house vacation. He began with the words "Dear Son." His letters were full of solicitude (William had been ill), advice (William needed exercise). "Several of the foreign ambassadors have assiduously cultivated my acquaintance, treating me as one of their corps. . . . [They] begin to hope Britain's alarming power will be diminished by the defection of her colonies."[10]

What he did not add was that he was involved in another controversy, this one over his electrical theories, a feud with political overtones that made it difficult for him to leave England. A rival with ministry ties had attacked Franklin's pointed lightning rods, declaring that round tips were more efficacious. Apparently afraid that the entire body of his scientific work might be discredited, Franklin took the threat seriously. His connections in the Royal Society lined up behind him; his political enemies aligned them-

238 I HAVE LOST MY SON

selves with his antagonist. The preposterous debate raged in the
Royal Society for five years. In the process he threw more logs of
resentment on the fire of his hatred of Tory politicians. They now
opposed him categorically, even down to the points on his lightning
rods.

The news from London for years had been almost uniformly bad
for William. He had struggled to maintain a delicate balance between being his father's son and a dutiful royal servant. As early as
1767, when Lord Hillsborough apparently assumed that William
was collaborating with his father in writing *The Farmer's Letters,*
William had been singled out in Parliament by the former prime
minister George Grenville for "disobeying the orders sent" him
"to give an account of the manufactures carried on in the respective
provinces."[11] Actually, William had taken longer than the allotted
time to assemble a voluminous and detailed report of the colony's
resources, and when he had finally sent it, it had been lost.

The incident had given Hillsborough a pretext to write William
and complain hotly about "your conduct in so many instances" and
to demand an "explanation of the motives of your conduct." Hillsborough alleged that William's failure to control the New Jersey
Assembly gave him grounds to lay the legislature's proceedings before the King. The Assembly's actions and William's role in them
"cannot but give His Majesty great dissatisfaction."[12]

Hillsborough's menacing note had thoroughly shaken William.
It had come at a time when he realized that Hillsborough, not his
father, had control of his destiny, not only as colonial secretary but
as the British official who would decide the fate of his Illinois land
scheme, his only chance for financial independence from his father.
Clearly, Hillsborough was attacking Benjamin through him, but
just as clearly he was attacking William himself, who was far more
vulnerable. It was not William's nature to ignore or downplay criticism of his conduct. In a thirty-page letter his father probably
would not have advised his writing, William denounced Hillsborough's charges as "unmerited" and said it was "in my power to
prove them so to every impartial person." Then, in a defense he
made public, he insisted that, until that time, he had never questioned Parliament's authority either "openly" or "privately."

But then he had proceeded, in a strong defense of American rights that could have cost him his governorship, to declare that every assembly in America "believes that the Parliament has not a right to impose taxes for the purposes of a revenue in America." Hillsborough's use of troops to protect the tax collectors, he said, was also ill advised.

"Men's minds are soured," William warned, "a sullen discontent prevails, and, in my opinion, no force on earth is sufficient to make the Assemblies acknowledge by any act of theirs, that the Parliament has a right to impose taxes on America. As long as this temper continues [America's legislators] will do all in their power, in their private capabilities, to prevent the consumption of British manufactures in the colonies, that the mother country may thereby lose more in her commerce than she can possibly gain by way of revenue." Not only was it a boldly honest criticism of Hillsborough's policies, it was an accurate prophecy of the nonimportation agreements that soon were to be signed by merchants from Boston to Virginia, and it went further than any of his father's declarations on American rights.

But Hillsborough evidently had not believed that William wrote from conviction, from genuine fear for the future of an empire whose mismanagement increasingly troubled the distant governor. William was, he professed, deeply wounded by the thought that doubt of his "principles" reached even higher than the colonial secretary. If his principles were questioned by his monarch, "nothing I can say or do will be of any avail. . . . Nothing could affect me more sensibly, as I have long valued myself on a strict performance of my duty, and the strongest attachment to my sovereign."[13]

As the American crisis had deepened, William from this time forward passed up no opportunity to prove his loyalty to the King, even as it increasingly required that he must separate his political destiny from his father's. But he already feared it was to prove a painful process, that Hillsborough was unable to distinguish between the two Franklins. "The truth of the matter is," William wrote to William Strahan in June of 1771, "having been disappointed in his late attempts to injure my father, [Lord Hillsborough] is now endeavoring to hurt him through me. He has no reason (other than the natural connection between us) to imagine

that I entertain the same political opinions with my father with regard to the dispute between Britain and America.

"My sentiments are really in many respects different from those
which have yet been published on either side of the question." He
did not elaborate on the differences, but went on to say that, given
the mood of each of the parties, he did not expect anyone to listen
to an individual, even a royal governor. "I for the most part [have]
kept my sentiments to myself, and only endeavored to steer my little bark quietly through all the storms of political contest with
which I [am] everywhere surrounded." But that did not mean he
had retreated from his duty as he saw it. "I have on no occasion
given up a single point of the Crown's prerogative, nor have I ever
attempted the least infringement of the people's privileges."[14]

As the confusion over American affairs thickened, it became
even more difficult for William to delineate his interests from his
father's in the eyes of the Hillsborough administration. Actually,
this was partly William's fault. While he could send messages
through trusted American friends to Strahan and Hillsborough, a
practice he now initiated, he had taken, for a royal governor, the
unusual step of sending all his official London correspondence first
to his supposed rival, the agent of the New Jersey Assembly: Benjamin Franklin. He often wrote out more than one version of a letter to the Colonial Office or the Board of Trade and sent them
unsealed to his father, which allowed Benjamin to choose the version he considered more suitable to the politics of the moment. He
intended to make it easier for Benjamin to advance and defend
Franklin interests but, in addition to strengthening Benjamin's hold
over him, William managed to further infuriate Lord Hillsborough. His lordship not only was bribing a mail carrier to intercept Benjamin's mail before it reached Craven Street but he was
aware that, after William's letters eventually reached Benjamin, it
was Benjamin who was sending them on to Whitehall.

When Hillsborough complained to the governor, William shot
back: "Besides being my father, he is an agent appointed by the
Governor as well as by the Assembly. . . . It may be necessary for
him at times to appear in behalf of one as well as the other."[15]

But by then, Benjamin, the most conspicuous American agent in
England, was beginning to be regarded by Tory ministers as a

symbol of American resistance. In April of 1772, Strahan wrote William that Benjamin "could not stir in the Illinois business as he is not only on bad terms with Lord Hillsborough, but with the Ministry in general. Besides, his temper is grown so very reserved, which adds greatly to his natural *inactivity,* that there is no getting him to take part in *anything.* Of this, he himself is so sensible that I once heard him at my house propose to Mr. Wharton to strike his name off the list, as it might be of prejudice to the undertaking. *But all this to yourself.* My sole motive for writing you thus freely is to *put you upon your guard* and to induce you to be as circumspect in your conduct as possible, as it is imagined here that you entertain the same political opinions with your father, and are activated by the same motives with regard to Britain and America."[16]

As if to prove the ministry wrong, to prove decisively that his first loyalty lay to the King and on the very issue that had provoked Benjamin's darkest clash with the colonial secretary, the question of an agent's commission, William insisted that the New Jersey Assembly submit to a clause in its annual support bill allowing the governor's signature on his father's commission. William felt so strongly that he must uphold the royal prerogative in the case that he actually went without his own annual salary until the Assembly backed down.[17] And then, after the deed was done, William informed his father. This had become his pattern in important dealings where it was almost certain his father would disagree if consulted first.

"I have had a very amicable session," William wrote Benjamin, "contrary to the expectation of everybody, and indeed contrary to the intention of most of the members of the Assembly." For the first time, William was pulling away from the popular Assembly. "I have carried two points, of great difficulty with which I suppose the Ministry will not be a little pleased. One is for the supply for British troops." The other was to leave out controversial wording in the annual government-support bill which Lord Hillsborough felt gave the Assembly the sole right of appointing an agent. "This last, however, I suppose you will not be altogether pleased with."[18]

How could Benjamin possibly have been pleased? For twenty years, since he had first entered Pennsylvania politics, he had upheld the right of popularly elected assemblies to pay and dispatch their own representatives to the King in Parliament. For fifteen years, he had been just such an agent. William knew that his father would never have acceded to giving the Penns power over Benjamin's commission. Yet William had now determined, even if it meant antagonizing his father, to follow Crown instructions in all cases. And Benjamin did not disappoint him. He threatened to resign as New Jersey agent. But William would not yield. It was Benjamin who finally backed down.

William's conduct apparently pleased Hillsborough, if only because he must have enjoyed anything that discomfited Benjamin Franklin. The governor had made it clear, shortly after Benjamin's clash with Hillsborough, that he held views entirely different from those of his father. In what Benjamin would have undoubtedly considered a singular piece of disloyalty by his son, had he known of it, William had covered himself against Crown retaliation by sending word of his private position with Wharton to England to deliver to Strahan, who was close to Hillsborough. Undoubtedly, Strahan delivered the message, for when the chief justice of New Jersey, Edward Smyth, paid court to Hillsborough in the midst of his feud with Benjamin, Hillsborough said he was sympathetic to William.

Bluntly, William wrote his father that "Lord Hillsborough wrote so complaisantly to me" and "he has besides spoke handsomely of me to our chief justice . . . and said at several other times that I was a sensible man, made a good governor and wrote well. He likewise told [the chief justice] of the civilities he had shewn to you in Ireland, and the invitation he had given you to visit him in London, but that you had called to his house but once since your return and that was at a time when you must have been morally sure of not seeing him, though you knew he had a day in every week set apart for seeing the agents and gentlemen from America. However, he said that he looked upon you as a man of great abilities, and of uncommon knowledge in American matters, and that he liked to hear you talk on the subject, tho' you differed from him in sentiments respecting some particular points."[19]

Benjamin did not write again to William for some time. His silence came when William felt all but abandoned by the Crown after ten years of treading water in backward New Jersey. He deeply resented the fact that in all those years of faithful service, even as prices doubled and tripled, he had received only one raise from the Assembly. He was the lowest-paid royal governor in America. He saw his father's feud with his immediate superior, the colonial secretary, the only man who could promote him, as the cause of his problems. When he learned at dinner with the governor of Pennsylvania, Richard Penn, that another governor of Barbados had died, he wrote to his father that he wanted the job and wished his father would help him obtain it. But he was sure he stood "no chance for any promotion or enlargement of my salary" while the ministry "is so much displeased with your conduct, tho' I am now the oldest governor [in years of service] in all His Majesty's American dominions."[20]

William did, indeed, need money. Despite inflation and a frozen salary, however, he had not curbed his taste for luxuries, as his father no doubt noted. In the same letter asking for help to obtain a better-paying job, William requested that his father order twenty custom-made mahogany side chairs for his parlor at Franklin Park, an indication of the scale of entertaining he carried on. Moreover, Benjamin must have resented his son's pointing out to him in the same letter that he had dined with a Penn, whom he had become "very sociable" with. Sarcastically, Benjamin answered, "I am glad to learn that you and your neighboring governors are so sociable."[21]

Almost every letter from Craven Street mentioned the money William owed his father. Unsympathetically, Benjamin pressed William harder for the sums he claimed his son had owed him for ten years. William once again patiently went over accounts with him, pointing out that the amount in dispute included £330 for furniture he had purchased secondhand when he became governor; he had long ago repaid the loan. William also pointed out that he was still due £259 from his old job of post office comptroller, a job he had left fifteen years before. It was bad enough that his father would not help him, worse that his father's accounting, often slipshod, should be trotted out against him.[22]

For a moment it appeared that Benjamin would soften. In the first draft of his next letter, he offered William the use of his own back salary as New Jersey agent. He wrote that he had enough cash on hand for the next three years. But at the last moment he scratched out the paragraph and rewrote the letter without the offer.[23] William must have known by now that he could expect little help from his father, who had grown to despise the thought of a relative in British service and wanted his son to quit the governorship and stick to farming. William probably saw, on one of his frequent visits to the Baches, the letter Benjamin had written to Sally when Bache had asked for help in gaining a government post: "I have advised [Richard] to settle down to business. I am of opinion that almost any profession a man has been educated in, is preferable to an office held at pleasure, as rendering him more independent, more a freeman, less subject to the caprices of superiors."[24] And when William tried to help a down-at-his-luck cousin, Josiah Davenport, get a customs appointment in Burlington, Benjamin refused to intercede for him.

For all of 1771 and most of 1772 — a crucial period — Benjamin Franklin talked no more of the problems of troubled Boston with the only man in the British government in a position to alleviate them. Only once did Hillsborough appear willing to bend. In the autumn of 1771, Franklin took another long vacation tour of the British Isles. He had planned the trip with William years before; he took it with their friend Omniscient Jackson. After a resounding welcome by the Irish Parliament, they met Lord Hillsborough inadvertently in Dublin. "He was extremely civil," Franklin wrote to William on January 30, 1772, "wonderfully so to me whom he had not long before abused to Mr. Strahan as a factious, turbulent fellow, always in mischief, a republican, enemy to the King's service, and what not."

The next day Franklin's coach had to pass Hillsborough's country house, and Franklin felt obliged to pay a social call. He was "detained by a thousand civilities from Tuesday to Sunday"; the colonial secretary was "attentive in everything that might make my stay in his house agreeable and put his eldest son, Lord Kilivarling, into his phaeton with me to drive me a round of forty miles that I might see the country . . . covering me with his own greatcoat lest I should take cold."

Benjamin was not deceived, he wrote to William. He felt he was being cultivated for use as a tool to convince Americans that Hillsborough was ready to throw his mantle of paternalistic protection over them. He had already reported to Boston his shrewd assessment of Hillsborough: his lordship had sensed "an approaching storm" and wanted to reduce "the number of his enemies he had so imprudently created. But if he takes no steps toward withdrawing the troops, repealing the duties," Franklin reassured Bostonians, "I shall think all the behavior I have described is meant only, by patting and stroking the horse, to make him more patient while the reins are drawn tighter and the spurs set deeper into his sides." Franklin's assessment of Hillsborough's latest ploy was no doubt correct.

On his return to London, he attempted further fence-mending with Hillsborough. "I waited on him to thank him for his civilities. . . . The porter told me he was not at home. I left my card, went another time, and received the same answer, though I knew he was at home, a friend of mine being with him. After intermissions of a week each, I made two more visits and received the same answer. The last time was on a levee day, when a number of carriages were at his door. My coachman drawing up, alighted, and was opening the coach door when the porter, seeing me, came out and surlily chided the coachman for opening the door before he had inquired whether my lord was at home; and then, turning to me, he said, 'My lord is not at home.' " I have never since been nigh him, and we only abuse one another at a distance."[25]

Nearly six years had passed since William Franklin and his partners had first enticed English aristocrats with the lure of vast wilderness landholdings. For all those years, Hillsborough, both at the Board of Trade and the Colonial Office, had blocked the plan. But his power was declining. Many Englishmen thought he had pushed the Americans too far.

Customarily, the Board of Trade and Plantations, of which Hillsborough was president, decided all matters affecting colonial policy. His recommendations were accepted routinely by the King's Privy Council and the King himself. But a powerful faction on the Privy Council was out to break Hillsborough. In April 1772, the

Board of Trade was finally forced to issue its report on the Illinois grant. Instead of accepting the board's recommendation, however, the Privy Council's Committee for Plantation Affairs refused to endorse the report. The committee chairman, Lord Gower, and one other member, Lord Rochford, both stockholders in the Illinois Company, exercised their prerogative and called for full public hearings.

On the day of the hearings, five other stockholders — Benjamin Franklin, George Mercer (representing Virginia interests), the London banker Thomas Walpole (now president of the land company), and William Franklin's old cronies William Trent and Samuel Wharton — rode to Whitehall. Wharton had been chosen as spokesman. At least this one member, a speculator by trade, appeared to have no conflict of interest. In a brilliant one-hour discourse, Wharton presented his arguments against the Hillsborough-inspired Board of Trade report. But brilliance was unnecessary. The committee had already made up its mind. A majority of the members present were stockholders of the Illinois Company. They voted overwhelmingly to overturn the board's finding and instead recommended the Illinois land grant to the full Privy Council and the King.

Hillsborough raged. On July 1 the committee formally released its report and urged the immediate creation and settlement of the new colony. Hillsborough threatened to resign rather than implement the report. A cabinet crisis ensued. On August 2, Hillsborough submitted his resignation to the King. To his surprise, the King accepted. Hillsborough's brother-in-law, Prime Minister North, managed to cling to his high office only by deserting his brother-in-law and choosing a stepbrother, Lord Dartmouth, as the new colonial secretary. Ten days later, the full Privy Council approved the creation of the new colony, to be named Vandalia in honor of the German birthplace of Queen Charlotte. And then the whole matter was turned back to the Board of Trade for the formalities of drawing up a charter.

Benjamin Franklin had every cause for jubilation. He and his son and all of their friends on both sides of the ocean would soon without doubt be rich. A quick computation of each member's profits at prevailing land prices was, in today's money, at least three million dollars. But Benjamin had been around London bureaucrats too long not to learn a measure of skepticism. In a letter to William a week later, he took no credit for Hillsborough's downfall: "The truth is that all his brother ministers disliked him extremely and wished for a fair occasion of tripping up his heels, so seeing that he made a point of defeating our scheme, they made another of supporting it to mortify him, which they knew his pride could not bear. The King, too, was tired of him. He had weakened the affection and respect of the colonies for a royal government. I used proper means from time to time that his Majesty should have due information."[26]

Yet Franklin did not foresee a speedy disbursement of the lands. Nearly a year later, as he had predicted, the new charter still had not passed the seals. Hillsborough left friends behind who had attacked the legal questions raised by conflicting land claims. "The affair of the grant goes on, but slowly," Franklin wrote to Galloway. "I do not yet clearly see land. I begin to be a little of the sailor's mind when they were handling a cable out of a store into a ship, and one of 'em said, 'Tis a long heavy cable, I wish we could see the end of it.' 'Damn me,' says another, 'if I believe it has any end, somebody has cut it off.' "[27]

As a form of solace, Benjamin assured William that his appointment as governor of New Jersey was safe under the new colonial secretary, Lord Dartmouth. On November 3, 1772, Dartmouth had held his first levee. "I said I was happy to see his lordship in his present situation. . . . I begged leave to recommend my son to his protection, who, says I, is one of your governors in America. The secretary [John Pownall] put in, *And a very good governor he is.* Yes, says my lord, he has been a good governor, and has kept his province in good order during times of difficulty."[28]

But words, even of praise, are little comfort for a man desperate for money. William decided, despite his father's objections, to appeal to the Crown not only for a raise, but for an end to the insecurity of depending each year on Assembly approval of his salary. He wanted his name added to the Civil List of officials paid directly by the King. It was a controversial request. Popular control of a governor's salary was a right sacred to the colonists. In Massachusetts, when Lord Hillsborough had ordered the payment of judges by the Crown to remove them from control by the people, there had been protests at a Boston town meeting that this was a dangerous abridgment of colonial liberties.

In January of 1773, William wrote to Lord Dartmouth that while "others in my station have made considerable fortunes, been promoted, or received considerable honors and rewards, my own private fortune has been really lessening." He asked that his position be made known to the King, "from whose goodness and justice I have not the least doubt I shall then either receive an increase of my salary or a promotion to a better government." His claim that he needed money was no doubt accurate. The salary he received in 1773 was the same as his father's income from printing alone in 1757, equivalent to about $125,000 in 1984 currency. As William told the colonial secretary, New Jersey was a "great thoroughfare between the two cities of New York and Philadelphia which subjects [the governor] to the entertainment of numbers of officers and gentlemen who call upon him on their way from one to the other."[29]

On the same day, he wrote his father to put in a "word or two in my own behalf."[30] But Benjamin was adamant in his refusal to take any step that in his opinion would inflame the question of salary with the New Jersey Assembly. He kept William waiting three months before answering: "I saw Lord Dartmouth about two weeks since. He mentioned nothing to me of your application for additional salary, nor did I to him, for I do not like it. I fear it will embroil you with your people."[31]

In July 1773, William decided that his last hope of keeping his farms was to travel to Albany and arrange to take over tracts of land from his defaulted partners, then hope he could sell the tracts to pay his debts. With the second mortgages in his hand, he could satisfy his own creditors a little longer while the Illinois charter was drawn. He had, by the eve of the Revolution, been unsuccessful in almost every aspect of his intricate land schemes. He did succeed in gaining control of his insolvent partners' acreage in Tryon County,

New York, and in fact cornered most of the land in what became Franklin Township, but he had little luck selling the land, and by the summer of 1773, five months before the Boston Tea Party ended the era of land speculation in colonial America, he was more deeply in dept than ever.

Benjamin had encouraged William to gamble heavily on using his office and legal knowledge to garner a wilderness empire because Benjamin had no intention of leaving any of his estate to his son and heir. To be sure, on paper William could still look forward, if all went well, to one day owning 313,142 acres of Illinois land, worth at least £35,000 sterling, the equivalent of twenty years of his government income. This was a fortune to reinvest by any standard, and he could reasonably expect to become governor of this vast new territory, again if all went well.

But all did not go well. No one could foresee a bloody nine-year revolution, of course, but even in the short term, William was so strapped for funds that he must move immediately to sell or rent Franklin Park to raise cash. To find a suitable buyer or tenant, he and Elizabeth visited New York City that summer. They just managed to rent the place — to an in-law of the royal governor of New York, but then he failed to pay the rent. Totally distracted, William, past hoping that his father would extricate him, dashed off a brief note to Benjamin on July 29, just in time for the mail ship. He was not only worried about his own affairs, but had a disquieting feeling about his father's activities after talking with royal officials and friends in New York: "Our Chief Justice [of New Jersey] is just returned from Rhode Island [where he had been investigating radical activities as part of a government commission]. . . . He tells me that Governor Hutchinson [of Massachusetts] is made very unhappy by the publication of his letters . . . and the consequently harsh treatment he has received. He talks of going to England. It is said by some that you sent the letters . . . [that] you went so far as to advise them [to insist] on their *Independency.*" The idea was so abhorrent to William, so new and revolutionary to this moderate British constitutional lawyer, that he heavily underlined the word as if in disbelief. Surely Benjamin would write back this time to reassure him that this was not true,

that it was only the vicious talk of more of his father's many enemies![32]

It is possible that Benjamin Franklin would never have returned
to America, would never have become a revolutionary, had he not
been publicly and searingly humiliated before his English friends.
As the troubles in America had dragged on, he had settled ever
deeper into sedate domesticity. His ostensible reasons for being in
England had fallen away as time went by. Each year found him further from favor with the British government. Consequently, there
was no chance for him to carry out his scheme to get rid of the
Penns by bringing about a change in Pennsylvania's form of government. Britain's new Tory rulers would not wrest private property away from proprietors against their will, especially in the face
of popular pressure. Indeed, Franklin had only retained his agency
business because of the enduring strength of the political machine
he had left behind him in Philadelphia. Characteristically, he never
admitted that his vindictive fifteen-year-long campaign against the
Penns had been a failure. Ignoring defeat, he pitched into the
larger struggle of British-American relations, projecting the impression that he had transcended to the sphere of America's unofficial ambassador to the Court of St. James. He loved his easy access
to courts and kings.

For three summers, in the lull before the final storm broke over
the Anglo-American Empire, Franklin stayed with Lord Le Despencer at his vast estate in Buckinghamshire. In his youth a notorious rakehell who was one of the founders of the Hell-fire Club and
a host to its diabolical revels, Lord Le Despencer was now Britain's
premier baron and a joint postmaster general. Together, his lordship and Franklin, without the slightest encouragement from the
Church of England, were abridging the Book of Common Prayer,
and Franklin clearly enjoyed the experience. In a letter to William
in 1773, he indicated for the first time that he intended to remain
permanently among his friends in England. He probably would return to America for no more than a brief visit to put straight his
business affairs. That would mean two more ocean crossings, all he
thought his aging body could withstand, but he intended to return
finally to London.

By now, home had become London. Deborah and his Philadelphia family had receded into the past. His perfunctory, dutiful, all-too-occasional letters should have made that clear. After ten years of pampered living in the exciting capital of the English-speaking world, why should he ever hanker after narrow, provincial Philadelphia. Did he not have all that home had to offer? His landlady of fifteen years, Mrs. Stevenson, directed her servants to cook the delicacies Deborah and William seasonally shipped from America. His agencies and postal jobs paid well, even if he complained to William of the double expense of homes in London and in Philadelphia.

Moreover, he had constructed yet another family around him. An English niece, bearing his daughter Sally's name, came to live with him, fetch for him, run errands around London for him until she left to marry and wait on another man. This English Sally Franklin was a companion to William Temple, by now thirteen years old, when he was on vacation from his English boarding school. Benjamin had his surrogate family — his Billy, Sally, Deborah.[33] He even had a printing shop across Craven Street, where he could indulge his nostalgia by setting the type and pulling the proofs of his latest pamphlet. From his press came a steadily increasing torrent of pro-American propaganda guaranteeing that Dr. Franklin was the center of attention at every gathering of men of science, of philosophy, of politics. By the year 1774, he was more than America's unofficial ambassador, he was the personification of America in the minds of his English friends and enemies.

The Franklin his friends saw was a well-dressed man of powerful physique for his age, a man in thick businesslike spectacles, usually smiling, a man of great economy of speech and appearance. He had let his gray hair grow and had stopped wearing a wig, a gesture of plainness that marked him with a peculiar distinction, a studied plebeian in powdered and periwigged official London, someone who had lived remote from cultivated society as the British knew it.

His circle of friends, most of them scientists or those with scientific interests, was widening to include men on the fringes of Whig politics. His new Whig friends were, like himself, controversial men of dissent, especially the teacher–preacher–part-time scientist Joseph Priestley. Benjamin used his influence to win jobs for friends like Priestley at the very time he berated William for seeking patronage jobs for needy relatives. The elder Franklin interceded with Lord Shelburne, who hired Priestley as his private librarian. The well-paid post gave Priestley money and leisure for experiments that led within the year to his discovery of oxygen.[34]

Franklin's associations were increasingly secretive. He frequented Masonic activities, and among his cronies at the Thursday night dinner meetings of the Club of Honest Whigs were Unitarian religious revolutionaries as well as a schoolmaster, electrical experimenters, a composer, an editor, a merchant, three physicians, the secretary of the Royal Society, the keeper of the reading room in the British Museum and, occasionally, the playboy-diarist James Boswell, when he wanted to escape a boring play on nearby Drury Lane. "We have wine and punch upon the table," Boswell recorded. "Some of us smoke a pipe [Franklin never did], conversation goes on pretty formally, sometimes sensibly and sometimes furiously. At nine, there is a sideboard with Welsh rarebits, apple puffs, porter and beer. Much is said . . . against Parliament."[35]

Benjamin Franklin was still ambivalent about his choice of friends. His vanity was obviously flattered by the attentions of high and mighty lords and ladies, but his evolving view of the inevitable rise of the burgeoning middle class often made him more at home with intelligent men of achievement regardless of their social status. Even as he lost favor with the British government, the Whigs were beginning to win out with him. He gravitated toward men who approved of his republican opinions; he relaxed with men of similar tastes.

As with clubmen everywhere, he and his friends worked to advance mutual interests and causes. The foremost American scientist since his election as president of the American Philosophical Society, Franklin worked to get his English friends into the American society, his American friends into the British Royal Society.[36] If he seemed a bemused, benevolent old codger to his friends, his ever more strident defense of American rights, coupled with his incessant attacks in print on British colonial policies, had made him the scourge of Whitehall, the unpopular embodiment of a hairshirt colonist. Considered by many Tory ministers as a commoner who had been at trade, a man of little social standing who lived in rented rooms and displayed neither money nor style, he was shunned by the highest levels of Georgian society.

He sometimes felt this keenly. To William, he complained when the prime minister, Lord North, ignored him at a country-house weekend at Lord Le Despencer's. "Displeased with something he said relating to America, I have never been at his levees. Perhaps he has taken that amiss. He seemed studiously to avoid speaking to me. I ought to be ashamed to say that on such occasions I feel myself to be as proud as anybody. We dined, supped and breakfasted together without exchanging three sentences."[37] It was ridiculously peevish — a lowly colonial agent snubbing a prime minister. It was just as silly for Britain's first lord to return the insult. But the tension between the leading Briton and the most conspicuous American was highly symbolic. Benjamin Franklin had come to think of Americans as the equals of Britons, whether commoners or nobles. He considered himself in every way a representative American. For their part, Lord North and the councillors closest to the King were tired of trying to placate these upstart colonials. The King's men were spoiling for an opportunity to administer a lesson in submission to Parliament and Crown. Lord North could never forget his friend Hillsborough's disgrace in the Illinois Company affair. There were many in power who suspected that Benjamin Franklin had engineered the coup. If true, his accomplishment meant that far too much power had collected in the hands of an American. They were waiting to trip up this Dr. Franklin.

He did not keep them waiting long.

In America, nearly four years had passed without political incident. But there was rarely any peace in the turbulent politics of Boston, where anti-British agitation was kept alive. Massachusetts, like every other colony, had by this time two distinct political factions roughly paralleling the political parties in England: Whig and Tory, country party versus court party. But a sinister element made the factional infighting in Boston especially unpredictable and virulent: the popular leaders now had at their bidding well-organized mobs. Given the slightest hint of marching orders, they roared in from the South End and the North End, chasing down the first customs official they could find, igniting their torches and heating a barrel of tar under the Liberty Tree. They stripped their terrified quarry and lowered him into the scalding resin, sprinkled him with goose feathers and jostled him in agony on a sharpened fence rail through the streets.

Primed with too much rum, they could not be controlled at all. No British governor could ever forget the sack of Governor Hutchinson's house. During the Stamp Act crisis, a mob composed of many unemployed waterfront toughs who blamed Britain for all their woes, polished off the rum provided by radical merchants, then surged uphill to Hutchinson's mansion. Breaking in as he fled with his family, they proceeded to shred the priceless collection of rare books and documents he had gathered for his history of Massachusetts, then shattered his fine furniture and china and cut down or uprooted every tree and shrub in his formal garden.[38]

The popular party did not like Thomas Hutchinson despite the fact that he was a native-born, Harvard-educated expert on constitutional government who had served selflessly as an official for forty years. Many of the patriots could not explain why they detested him. They just instinctively blamed him, as the figurehead for Britain, for the succession of ever-harsher controls placed on what had once been a comparatively freewheeling way of life. Indeed, there was no solid evidence that Hutchinson was guilty of anything more than doing his job of carrying out royal instructions. That is, not until a ship arrived from London early in 1773 bearing a packet of letters for the speaker of the Massachusetts House of Assembly from its London agent, Benjamin Franklin.[39]

The leaders of the Assembly were expecting a letter from Franklin. Earlier in the year, a British revenue cutter had run aground off nearby Rhode Island. Its captain had been seized and shot by a crowd of one hundred Sons of Liberty, and the ship set afire and burned to the waterline. As could be expected, the British tried to indict the ringleaders. In London, the Privy Council declared the attack on a British warship an act of high treason, punishable by hanging, drawing and quartering. Suspects were ordered brought to England for trial. The King offered a large reward and appointed a royal commission, which included the Chief Justice of New Jersey, but "they could obtain no evidence," William wrote to Benjamin.[40]

In London, the colonial secretary decided that justice had to be taken out of American control. According to Hillsborough's plan, implemented first in Massachusetts, the justices of the supreme court and superior court in each colony would henceforth be paid by the Crown directly, thereby ending accountability to colonial legislatures. Under the circumstances, so too would Governor Hutchinson be added to the Civil List. Massachusetts radical leaders demanded the right to retain some control over Hutchinson, who ignored popular opinion unless a purse of gold was dangled before him at annual appropriations time. The Massachusetts Assembly petitioned the Crown to strike Hutchinson's name from the royal payroll. Agent Franklin was instructed to take the petition to the colonial secretary at Whitehall for forwarding to the King.

Indeed he did, and his handling of the petition led to his first great miscalculation. It embroiled him in a controversy that led to his public disgrace in England, completed his conversion to the American revolutionary movement, and hastened the final breach between England and her colonies.

12

A MAN OF LETTERS

1773–1774

B ENJAMIN FRANKLIN HAD SUCH A TENDENCY TOWARD VEN-
detta that he sometimes lost all his objectivity. His hatred for
Lord Hillsborough and British aristocrats like him, as much as any
set of deeply held first principles, led him more and more to blame
England for all the colonies' grievances. He apparently had not
considered the possibility that the ministry's repressive tactics not
only had been brought on by American extremists, but were actually favored by some Americans. He evidently did not believe the
visitor to Craven Street who told him that Americans, not
Englishmen, had asked British officials to send in the troops to
Boston, to use greater force to collect taxes, protect officials, take
the instruments of the law out of local hands and move them to
London beyond the intimidating reach of the Boston mobs.

In 1768, not long after the American crisis had first erupted into
riots in Boston, Thomas Hutchinson and his friends, victims of the
mob, had opened a long and secret correspondence with Thomas
Whately, who was a member of Parliament, a former undersecretary of the treasury and a coauthor of the Stamp Act legislation.
Hutchinson's own letters to Whately were riddled with slashing
charges against "the licentiousness of those who call themselves
sons of liberty." He accused Boston leaders of passing a number of
"very criminal laws," and he reported them in detail. "The government . . . has been so long in the hands of the populace," he went

on, "that it will be a work of time to bring the people to just notions of the nature of government. . . . There must be an abridgement of what are called English liberties." In other words, force must be used to restore order so that the magistrates could break the power of the radical junta controlling the seaport, put a stop to smuggling, and allow collections of customs duties without fear of reprisals.[1] The Hutchinson letters were of value only as a weapon in the wrong hands, as an instrument to stir up further trouble in Boston to mortify and possibly dislodge Hutchinson. Everyone ever connected with them, however, eventually regretted their existence.

To the day of his death, Franklin never did reveal who told him that there existed in London, in private hands, a number of letters alleging that Americans, not Englishmen, had requested Hillsborough's repressive policies. It was probably his old friend Strahan, somewhat of a court gossip, who told him, but the evidence is murky. Strahan visited Franklin twice at the time, but it is hard to believe that as dedicated a Crown official as Strahan was would jeopardize his job to steal letters for anyone, even an old friend, in such obvious disfavor as Franklin, or that Franklin would allow him to. Franklin evidently asked an American-born courtier named John Temple to purloin the letters.

From his earliest misadventures in Pennsylvania politics, Franklin had disliked the influence of royal governors. He was willing to believe the worst about them, even about Hutchinson, who was probably the keenest legal mind among Britain's appointed colonial officials. In choosing Temple as the purloiner, Franklin may have allowed his loathing for royal governors to blind him to a number of unsavory facts. First, John Temple, a longtime friend of William Franklin's and the son-in-law of a leading Boston radical, had been fired from the American board of customs in Boston because of his pro-American conduct, which included exceeding his authority by appointing a distant Franklin cousin as a customs collector. Second, if Hutchinson were somehow embarrassed and removed at public insistence, Temple was, as lieutenant governor of New Hampshire and scion of a powerful English family, a leading contender for the job. One cousin was Whately's former boss, George Grenville; another, Lord Temple, was a privy councillor to the King. In any case, a packet of seventeen letters was taken from the home of

Whately's brother shortly after Whately's death. It would have been an easy matter for Temple, a man who moved easily in this circle, to gain a few moments alone with Whately's correspondence, and Temple later complained bitterly when Franklin did not help him win a job in Boston, presumably for his part in the affair.

Not only was Benjamin Franklin's political judgment questionable, but he conveniently set aside his ethics at the very time he was condemning British agents for opening letters to him from his son. If he were as truly interested in reconciliation as he claimed to be, he would never have risked arousing the Boston mobs. They had come close to killing Hutchinson and his followers before. To reveal that Hutchinson had secretly courted the British and invited the troops was to place Hutchinson's life in peril. Of much smaller consequence, though of course reprehensible, was the misuse of private letters by the highest-ranking British-paid postal official for America.

Franklin's behavior is hard to explain except in the light of his admitted failure in his first important confrontation with Lord Dartmouth. In August of 1773, when he received the Massachusetts Assembly petition, he immediately delivered it to Whitehall. Dartmouth was shocked by its tone and summoned Franklin for a conference. He was cordial but he proved to be velvet over Sheffield steel: smooth, sincere, unbending in his support of royal privilege. He would not, he informed Franklin, accept the petition on behalf of the Crown. He urged Franklin to return it to Boston for further consideration.[2] Perhaps both men, sensing the crisis of the moment, hoped that a respite would relieve tensions. If so, Dartmouth offered nothing more than delay. And Franklin, in giving way, inadvertently helped him throw away any hope for future colonial peace.

Back at his Craven Street desk, he immediately wrote a report to the Massachusetts Assembly. His lordship had insisted, he said, that "presenting [the petition] at this time could not possibly produce any good, that the King would be exceedingly offended. . . . I hope my conduct will not be disapproved." Then, as if to ameliorate his failure to press the Assembly's case, he went on quickly, in the next sentence: "On this occasion, I think it fit to acquaint you that there has lately fallen into my hands part of a correspondence that I have reason to believe laid the foundation of most if not all our present grievances. I am not at liberty to tell through what channel I received it. . . . I have engaged that it shall not be printed, not any copies taken of the whole or any part of it."[3]

Franklin sent off the originals. He did not name the authors, but their identities were unmistakable to Boston politicians who had corresponded with Hutchinson and his lieutenants during many embattled legislative sessions.

To John Adams and his fellow radical leaders in Boston, it was inconceivable that Benjamin Franklin would send such incredibly revealing letters if he did not intend them to be made public. "Bone of our bone," Adams stormed when he read them. "Born and educated among us! Vile serpent! Cool thinking deliberate villain!"[4] The letters were published in the Boston *Public Advertiser* on August 31, 1773, and laid before the Massachusetts Assembly.

If British officials thought for a moment that the citizens of Massachusetts, stirred to renewed fury by the Hutchinson letters, would cease pestering the King with petitions, they were gravely mistaken. To Puritan Bostonians, the right to pay their civil magistrates was a deeply troubling issue involving legal rights as old as the Magna Carta. When Lord Dartmouth refused to take their petition of grievance to the King, he was, in the King's name, tampering with their rights and nullifying the ancient contract between them and the Crown. It was the Crown, not they, who was making dangerous innovations, the Bostonians believed, and they said so, loud and clear, in a series of open meetings, first in Boston, then in towns all across the Bay colony.

The resulting new document, a declaration drafted by the Boston town meeting in February of 1772, enunciated a revolutionary theory of government, one not new to British rulers, but one they had long chosen to ignore: John Locke's theory of a social contract between King and subject. By averring that the King had broken his social contract with his people, the freemen of Massachusetts were declaring the contract dissolved and themselves in an original state of nature, where there were no kings and no subjects, where all men were created equal, where all men had the right to revolt against anyone who usurped their natural and inalienable rights.

Like all men, Massachusetts men were entitled to enjoy their lives, their liberties and their property.

It was the especially important right of the citizens of Massachusetts to control the magistrates' powers by tightening the purse-strings. No faraway legislature of men not of Massachusetts' own choosing could pass laws for them or pass sentence, thereby substituting foreign wisdom for that of men on the scene. No body of foreigners with conflicting beliefs and interests could regulate their commerce, tax them, or in any way usurp their rights.

The angry Bostonians went even farther. The King had exceeded his prerogative by appointing customs officers, an action unauthorized by the Massachusetts charter granted by an earlier English king. Ordering troops to Boston in peacetime and forcing the people to house them and feed them was also unconstitutional. The King had also broken constitutionally guaranteed covenants by issuing illegal writs of search and seizure, and secret instructions to governors that countermanded the wishes of popularly elected officials. He had authorized the transport of prisoners to England for trial by men who were not their neighbors, their peers. Even worse, the Bostonians smelled a Tory plot to displace their Puritan ways of worship with an established Anglican episcopacy, which they must pay to support. Their ancestors had left England for less.

Once again, the unpopular Hutchinson accurately saw and described what was taking place around him. The Boston town meeting had issued nothing less than a "declaration of independency." By setting up a committee of correspondence and sending its declaration to other Massachusetts towns and urging them to take similar action, the citizens of Boston had taken an irrevocable step into open resistance to British authority.[5] The gauntlet was down: all along the Atlantic seacoast, stunned Americans watched and waited for the certain response. When Franklin opened and read the declaration of the Boston town meeting, he did not flinch from presenting it to Whitehall.

This time he went even further than his instructions. He prepared the declaration for publication in the London press and he wrote a strong preface to it. He certainly could not be accused of cushioning the impact of Bostonian rhetoric. His opening lines were a slap on the other royal cheek: "All accounts of the discontent so general in our colonies have of late years been industriously smothered and concealed here, it seeming to suit the views of the American minister to have it understood that, by his great abilities, all faction was subdued, all opposition suppressed, and the whole country quieted."[6] For full effect, Franklin withheld the provocative publication until official London returned from vacation, but he sent off advance copies to Boston. Probably for the first time, Bostonians learned from his preface of the intent of the British to unload huge surpluses of tea on the American market. His preface almost certainly planted the idea to resist the forced sale of tea in America.

Off again in August to Lord Le Despencer's for a country vacation, Franklin wrote a trio of essays, which he mailed off to London newspapers. The first, carried in the *Public Advertiser,* called for a return to the *status quo ante* of ten years earlier, before King George III's controversial policies had begun to unfold. The second, appearing in the same paper three days later under the title "Rules by Which a Great Empire May Be Reduced to a Small One," was a satire intended to make British readers see the crisis through American eyes. He quickly followed it up with an elaborate hoax he called "An Edict by the King of Prussia." His cleverest piece of writing, it built on substantial British fears that the aggressive German monarch was considering sending troops to London to safeguard the English monarch from mobs. Benjamin was delighted when a guest at Lord Le Despencer's rushed in and read the piece aloud. The elegant gathering took the spoof at face value, believing that Frederick the Great had actually inflicted a series of outrageous restrictions on England just as England had on America.[7]

"Such papers," Franklin wrote to his son later that fall, "may seem to have a tendency to increase our divisions, but I intend a contrary effect, and hope that by comprising in a little room and setting in a strong light the grievances of the colonies, more attention will be paid to them by our administration and that, when their unreasonableness is generally seen, some of them will be removed, to the restoration of harmony between us."[8]

Benjamin Franklin could not comprehend that his actions were about to unleash not only the Boston mobs but the British forces increasingly eager to smite them. He was refining his beliefs to the point where he no longer was willing to concede sovereignty to King and Parliament. As his political philosophy fed on the controversy, he came, first, to deny the right of the King to the ownership of unsettled lands in America, and then to decide that Americans were not subjects of the British but were subjects of the King, thus denying the sovereignty of Parliament. Franklin had not settled on just what to do to consolidate all his new opinions, but he was also quickly coming to believe that the King's authority over Americans only went so far as the colonists themselves wished it to extend.

On July 14, 1773, he did reveal to his son for the first time that he had rationalized their western-land dealings, that he now thought it foolish to apply to the King for confirmation of an Illinois grant already approved by the Privy Council. The land could be and had been bought from the Indians. Its owners could therefore either accept the sovereignty of some foreign prince, like George III, or "they may erect a new government of their own. My opinion, as being somewhat of a civilian, goes a little farther than that of those great Common Lawyers" — a sneer at the Crown legal experts who were tying up the purchase — "for I think that it is the natural right of men to quit when they please the society or state, and the country in which they were born, and either join with another or form a new one."[9] This was radical doctrine indeed. Franklin was aligning himself with the leading young American revolutionaries. Among the "great Common Lawyers" was undoubtedly William Blackstone, who had stated flatly that the King owned all the territories taken by British arms. That a man has the right to quit society and country whenever he wants to and start new ones was a radical ideological breakthrough. Franklin had become a revolutionary, and he was declaring his radical beliefs to his son, a constitutional lawyer, a Tory, and a man whose training and instincts could only make him bridle at his father's arguments.

While keeping William abreast of land grant developments and his own reactions to them, Benjamin's ideas sailed across the sea, not to his son, but to the Boston leaders, and mingled with theirs until little distance remained between them. Governor Hutchinson could charge with accuracy that Benjamin Franklin was now the "director" of the Boston radicals. This convergence was nowhere more evident than after a series of town meetings that effectively unleashed the revolution in Massachusetts.

The British Empire, largely won in a glorious year of victories over France, was still in its adolescence in 1773. Its foreign policy was clumsy and immature, with one bungler succeeding another in advising the King on the delicate juggling act of balancing the recurrent crises that plague all nations. Far from familiar with America's problems or even interested in them at this stage, England was distracted by the irksome difficulties of the moment in other equally remote reaches. The Carib Indians were rebelling on St. Vincent Island. Canada needed a new form of government. The armies of Frederick the Great, made strong by British subsidies only a decade earlier, were moving to the French frontiers and stirring fresh war scares in Europe. And closer to hand, the disastrously corrupt fiscal policies of the East India Company were jarring the British economy and absorbing the interest as well as the capital of London.

As Franklin wrote to his son in February, "The continued refusal of North America to take tea from hence has brought infinite distress on the company. They imported great quantities in the faith that that American nonimportation agreement could not hold, and now they can neither pay their debts nor dividends. Their stock has sunk, annihilating near £3,000,000 of their property [something like $550,000,000 in 1984 American dollars]. . . . Government will lose its £400,000 a year [subsidy] while their teas lie upon hand.

"The bankruptcies brought on partly by this means have given such a shock to credit as has not been experienced in fifty years. And this has affected the great manufacturers so much as to oblige them to discharge their hands. . . . Thousands of Spitalfield and Manchester weavers are now starving or subsisting on charity. Blessed effects of pride, pique and passion in government, which should have no passions."[10]

Six weeks later, he renewed this theme in his next letter to William: "The ideas of the court may change, for I think I see some alarm at the discontents in New England and some appearance of softening in the disposition of government on the idea that matters have been carried too far. But all depends on circumstances and events. We govern from hand to mouth. There seems to be no wise regular plan."[11]

By May, the House of Commons, in thrashing about for ways to refloat the economy, decided to amend the tea laws. It was no secret that Americans consumed about one million pounds of smuggled tea a year. Smuggled tea was cheaper. The mercantile law forced the East India Company to ship its cargoes to England, unload and reload them, thereby increasing the retail price. Now, the tea laws would permit direct shipment to America from India, which would lower the price to the consumer and presumably price smuggled tea out of the market. The foundering company would be saved from bankruptcy and the stockholders would avoid nasty losses. (Many MP's held at least one share of stock in the East India Company — one share cost a thousand pounds — and were understandably interested in protecting their investment.)

The new colonial secretary, Lord Dartmouth, himself a stockholder, was equally eager that the declaration from Boston should not complicate matters further by reaching Parliament in its present mood. Meeting with Franklin privately in early May, he appeared willing to begin reconciling British-American differences despite the fact that he had just seen the inflammatory declarations of the Boston town meeting. "What can be done now?" Dartmouth asked Franklin. "It is impossible that Parliament can suffer such a declaration to pass unnoticed."[12]

At this late date, it appears that Franklin's role as revolutionary was still equivocal. With a British lord he played the imperial bureaucrat, his words to the colonial secretary far more conciliatory than his letters to the Boston radicals. "In my opinion," he said, "it would be better and more prudent to take no notice of it. It is words only. Acts of Parliament are still submitted to [in Boston]. No force is used to obstruct their execution. And while that is the case, Parliament would do well to turn a deaf ear and seem not to know that such declarations had ever been made. Violent measures against the province will not change the opinion of the people." Dartmouth agreed to delay submitting the declaration, yet he worried aloud that "our divisions must weaken the whole, for we are yet one Empire, whatever may be the sentiments of the Massachusetts Assembly."[13]

Franklin remained secretive about his role. A thorough search of his correspondence with his son reveals that he did not tell William of his secret dealings with Boston leaders until after William independently learned of them from friends. Benjamin's letters to his son remained infrequent and filled with old business, chiefly the Illinois land affair. He did not mention the Hutchinson letters until William wrote to him that he had learned during a visit to New York that the radicals of Boston were "elated on receiving some letters from you."[14] William apparently refused to credit rumors that his father was advising Bostonians to insist on independence. William nevertheless fired off a pair of letters to Benjamin after hearing persistent rumblings from Boston of his father's complicity. In one of the letters, since lost, he apparently demanded to know what the Massachusetts town meetings hoped to accomplish with their rebellious resolutions. By September 1, 1773, Benjamin, about to leave on his latest country vacation, felt compelled to explain crisply his actions to his son for the first time:

"I think the resolutions of the New England townships must have the effect they seem intended for, namely to show that the discontents were really general and their sentiments concerning their rights unanimous and not the fiction of a few demagogues, as their governors used to represent them here." This was his first veiled hint that he had seen the Hutchinson letters. He insisted that he believed Massachusetts claims would ultimately be heard and heeded by Parliament, which had passed the Declaratory Act, the basis of the tea duties, only to avoid further Parliamentary resentment against the King's ministers for failing to make the stamp tax stick. "I remember Lord Mansfield [the chief justice of England] told the Lords, when upon that bill, that it was nugatory." Then, in a venture into legal philosophy to his lawyer son, he added, "To be sure, in a dispute between two parties about rights, the declaration of one party can never be supposed to bind the other."

As was his fashion, Benjamin sent William more political gossip about legislation pending before Parliament, gossip that had little bearing on the real purpose of his letter, before he turned abruptly to the matter of the Hutchinson letters:

"It is said here that the famous Boston letters were sent chiefly, if not all, to the late Mr. Wheatly." Benjamin may have deliberately misspelled the name, one he knew well from helping Whately obtain five thousand acres of land in western Pennsylvania. He had cleared his throat, however, and now he went on in a clear voice: "They fell into my hands, and I thought it my duty to give some principal people there [in Boston] a sight of them."

It was the first time Benjamin had admitted his part in the affair to anyone. Having confided in his son, he then put him under the obligation of concealing his complicity. "In Boston, they concealed who sent them [over from London] the better to conceal who received and communicated them. And perhaps it is as well that it should continue a secret."

Evidently, Governor William Franklin had already read the letters when they were reprinted in the Boston papers and had written his father that he did not see what all the resentment against Governor Hutchinson was about. He was therefore lectured as if he were ignorant of Boston politics: his father still could not conceive that William might have another view of the American crisis than his own. "Being of that country myself, I think those letters more heinous than you seem to think them. But you had not read them all."[15]

It was an amazing letter in many ways, especially considering that the Hutchinson letters were now the *cause célèbre* of two continents. Franklin had long been aware that his correspondence with his son was opened by the ministry, and yet here he was admitting his role in a major scandal, which he still could not believe was significant.

In December 1773 news of the Hutchinson affair broke into the London newspapers. Whately's surviving brother, also a member of Parliament, blamed John Temple for stealing private letters and exchanged insults with him, first in print, then in person. Early one December morning, William Whately and John Temple and their seconds rode west from Westminster to a corner of Hyde Park and took their places with pistols at the ready. Temple refused once again to reveal who stole the letters. The duelers were placed back to back and they walked and wheeled and fired. Whately dropped, badly wounded in the leg. But he had not had enough: he again challenged Temple. He meant to fight him to the death.[16]

On December 22, Benjamin Franklin sent a letter with the customary one-guinea gold piece to the editor of the London *Public Advertiser,* who immediately had the notice set in type for the Christmas Day edition: "Finding that two gentlemen have been unfortunately engaged in a duel about a transaction and its circumstances of which both of them are totally ignorant and innocent, I think it incumbent on me to declare . . . that I alone am the person who obtained and transmitted to Boston the letters in question."[17]

On December 16, a week before Benjamin Franklin confessed publicly in the press that he had purloined the Hutchinson correspondence, a crowd of one thousand men gathered for a mass meeting at the Old South Meetinghouse in Boston. Then, shortly after dark, they marched to Griffin's Wharf and cordoned off the area. A select group of fifty men armed with hatchets and pistols, and wrapped in blankets with their faces painted, gave a war whoop and boarded three ships bearing English tea. It was a cold night, but they were warm with wrath. Tea had become a hated symbol: the tax on it — a matter of £7,000 — would be used to pay Governor Hutchinson, the judges and the customs commissioners. Leading the raiders over the decks and into the holds were several tea smugglers, including John Hancock. For three hours, ignoring all other cargo, they hauled 342 lacquered crates of tea topsides, smashed them open, and threw them into the harbor.

The customs officers vanished. No shots were fired. The crowd dispersed before troops could be called from their fort in the harbor. No suspects were ever arrested.

Similar incidents all along the Atlantic coast apparently were prompted by anonymous letters sent from London to every seaport in America where the tea had been consigned. Some of the letters were written in Benjamin Franklin's unmistakable style.

News of the destruction of property so valuable to British interests reached London on January 20, 1774, even as Franklin pre-

pared for a hearing on the Massachusetts petition to remove
Governor Hutchinson. America finally had Britain's full attention.
No one, least of all Benjamin Franklin, was prepared for the result.

Franklin had made the two-mile trip through Westminster to
government offices in Whitehall so many times that his coachman
needed little direction, except to be told that this afternoon's hearing was to be at the Cockpit. Every Londoner knew where this
was: here King Henry VIII had once indulged one of his favorite
blood sports, cockfighting. In Franklin's day, the Cockpit was
where hearings were held before the King's Privy Council.

The hearing on the petition to remove Governor Hutchinson
had been bottled up by John Pownall, secretary of the Board of
Trade, himself a former governor of Massachusetts, until just before Christmas. When Franklin was called to appear before the
Committee on Plantation Affairs on January 11, 1774, for a preliminary hearing, he had expected to argue that Hutchinson had
become inimical to the people of Massachusetts and therefore
should be recalled. His strategy was simple enough: go over the
grievances point by point, show Hutchinson, not the King, to be
the cause of all the troubles, thereby demonstrating that the only
solution was to extract this thorn from the side of the people so that
order and harmony would be restored. Such tactics had worked before, in fact against Hutchinson's predecessor.

To Franklin's surprise, however, what was supposed to be a debate between Assembly agent Franklin and the agent for Hutchinson was being viewed by the Crown as a far more serious matter.
Dr. Franklin had been advised to retain counsel, as if the proceeding were a trial instead of a hearing. He had been granted a three-
week postponement until January 29 to prepare his defense.[18]

Even more of a surprise was Hutchinson's counsel: none other
than Alexander Wedderburn, solicitor general to the King. The
notorious Wedderburn, a former friend of Lord Bute's, had found
it expedient to leave his native Scotland after insulting the presiding
judge in open court. He had practiced hard to lose his native Scottish burr and just as diligently dropped his unprofitable Whig politics when Tory leaders in Parliament found him such a vituperative
opponent they bought him off with the solicitor-generalship. It was

Wedderburn who, irate at Hillsborough's ouster, had blocked the Illinois land grant by two years of legal nitpicking. Franklin knew he could be a fierce adversary who justly deserved his reputation for mixing wit, oratory and abuse.[19]

As his attorney, Franklin retained the man Wedderburn had replaced as solicitor general. John Dunning was sharp-tongued and a staunch Whig, a Middle Templar who had angered the ministry by successfully defending the radical John Wilkes, first as his lawyer, then by opposing the vote to unseat him in Parliament.[20]

Franklin should have been more apprehensive than he was. Since the arrival a week earlier of the first report of the Boston Tea Party, friends had been warning him that the Crown intended to make something more than a mere hearing on a petition out of Franklin's appearance before the Privy Council. A few days later, shortly after the London *Chronicle* published a long account of the tea raid, Dunning informed Franklin that their principal line of attack had been ruled inadmissible. There was no evidence, no witnesses to support the charges against Hutchinson, only Franklin's own biased hearsay arguments.

But Franklin remained unconcerned. Not only did he have good lawyers, he was also distracted by a suit William Whately had brought against him in Chancery Court over the Hutchinson letters. And he was considered so far out of favor after his admission of leaking the letters that no friend at court had warned him that he was, in effect, to stand trial, not simply as Massachusetts agent on the merits of the petition, but in place of the unindicted radicals of Massachusetts. So far indeed had Franklin's stock fallen at court that his fellow Illinois shareholders had asked him to write a public letter of resignation so they would not suffer from association with him. He had complied, but privately he remained a secret partner.[21]

That morning, he selected a favorite blue suit of Manchester figured velvet, ate quietly, sent Peter for the carriage shortly after ten. Soon, the carriage was rolling through Whitehall Gate toward the Cockpit.[22] In more than twenty years of attending hearings and pleading petitions, Franklin had never seen such a crowd there. As he alighted, he met his radical Whig friends Joseph Priestley and Jeremy Bentham. Shouldering through the crowds, they spotted their good friend Edmund Burke, a member of Parliament. The less fortunate stood tight-packed in surrounding rooms, craning, whispering, pointing at Dr. Franklin as he passed. Franklin's friends sent in for passes — they got front-row seats.

In the minutes before his three lawyers arrived, Franklin was surprised to see so many ladies of the court, the wives of privy councillors, as if at an entertainment. The lovely Lady Elizabeth Montagu, an acquaintance of his from Lord Le Despencer's country house, sat on a gold-trimmed red-velvet chair on the right side of the lofty chamber. She was half-turned, talking with her intimates: the duchess of Rutland, Lady Falmouth, Lady Hardwicke, the countess of Coventry and the countess of Marchmont. Ladies of lesser rank peered down from the galleries.

Wearing a scarlet cape and a full white wig, Lord Gower, chairman of the Privy Council, entered and took his place on a small throne under a scarlet canopy. Above him loomed the carved royal coat of arms; below him, the long council table and the crowd. Though Lord Gower was a stockholder in the Illinois venture, he was known to be generally unsympathetic to America. Filing in from a long meeting on the crisis in Boston, some thirty-five of the King's councillors, an unusually large number, noisily arrayed themselves in gilded chairs around the green baize-covered council table. If indeed under British law, a man was tried by his peers, here were the peers in quantity — though not Franklin's.

Franklin stood near a great fireplace off to the left and surveyed the King's advisors. Just in front of him sat the corpulent lord of the King's bedchamber, the earl of Denbigh, described by Horace Walpole as "the lowest and most officious of the court tools." Beside him was Lord Parker, one of half a dozen fellows of the Royal Society in the room. To his right was Lord Le Despencer, and next, Lord Sandwich, first lord of the admiralty and a joint postmaster general who did not believe an American should hold high office.

Friendlier to America but one of several East India promoters on the council with financial reasons for resenting the agent of the Boston patriots was a former prime minister, Lord Rockingham. Lord Jeffrey Amherst, who opposed the Franklins' Illinois scheme, was flanked by two other former soldiers: Lord George Germain and the marquis of Granby. Lord Rochford, an Illinois Company stockholder who only the week before had asked Franklin to resign, was seated beside another major land speculator, Lord Rodney. Franklin knew Rodney as a "complete slave to women and to play."[23] He could also see his enemy Lord Hillsborough.

Protocol demanded that Franklin stand in front of the council table throughout the hearing. As he walked up to take his place, he saw that Lord Dartmouth, too, was watching him. Benjamin could expect little but formal courtesy from Dartmouth, who had no doubt read the intercepted letters that Franklin had been sending to Boston radicals, advising them to remain resolute. Others in the room had seen and bristled at Franklin's words: "You cannot have it both ways. If you choose to have it without our consent, you must go on taking that way and be content with what you can so obtain. If you would have our free gifts, desist from your compulsive measures, acknowledge our rights." To these berobed peers, the hereditary rulers of England, the words, coming as they did from this son of a Boston candlemaker, were supreme impudence.

Benjamin Franklin himself wrote the most complete record of the next ninety minutes. He never forgot his hour of humiliation before the people he had cultivated for so many years. When he was deeply hurt and angry, he grew cold, silent, at best, terse. His account, written to Thomas Cushing a few days later, is exceptionally succinct: "The hearing began by reading my letter to Lord Dartmouth enclosing the petition, then the petition itself, the resolves [of the Boston town meeting], and lastly the [Hutchinson] letters. Our counsel then opened the matter, and acquitted themselves very handsomely."[24] Chief counsel Dunning, ill with a sore throat, hoarsely made the point that this was a hearing of a suit at law, not Hutchinson's impeachment. The Massachusetts Assembly was appealing to the King, as a favor, to remove the governor in order to quiet unrest.

Standing beside Lord Sandwich at the Privy Council table about twenty feet from Franklin, was Solicitor General Wedderburn. As he began to speak, he leaned forward dramatically and began tapping his hand on the table to underscore his point that this hearing was "of no less magnitude than whether the Crown shall ever have it in its power to employ a faithful and steady servant in the administration of a colony." Then, gesturing abundantly for the benefit of the audience, he launched into a highly colored history of the last ten years in Massachusetts as seen through the eyes of his client, Governor Hutchinson. Wedderburn ended with the assertion that there had been no complaint against the governor until Dr. Franklin had stolen and published the governor's private correspondence.

If Franklin was surprised when no lawyer at the table objected that the solicitor general had strayed from the point at law and brought up the entirely separate legal issue of Franklin's conduct, he did not show it. Under the rules of procedure, once he retained counsel he had no more right than a felon to speak in his own defense. He had, as a friend noted later, composed his face and stood, head cocked slightly, almost quizzically, to one side, face impassive, hands clasped lightly behind him.

"They owe therefore," Wedderburn went on about his clients, the governor and councillors of Massachusetts, "all the ill will which has been raised against them to Dr. Franklin's good offices in sending back these letters to Boston." Unchecked, Wedderburn became louder, his voice more scornful. "Dr. Franklin therefore stands in the light of the first mover and *prime conductor* [here and there in the chamber there were snickers at this electrical pun] of the whole contrivance against his Majesty. . . . By the help of his own special confidants and party leaders, he first made the Assembly his agents in carrying on his own secret designs. He now appears before your lordships to give the finishing stroke to the work of his own hands."

As Franklin's enemies quietly exulted, Wedderburn revealed the special reason for his personal attack. Whately had been his intimate friend. He knew Whately had been extremely careful with his letters. "Nothing, then, will acquit Dr. Franklin of the charge of obtaining them by fraudulent or corrupt means, for the most malignant of purposes, unless he stole them. . . . I hope, my lords, you will mark and brand this man. . . . He has forfeited all the respect of societies and of men. Into what companies will he hereafter go with an unembarrassed face. . . . Men will watch him with a jealous eye. They will hide their papers from him and lock up their *escritoires*. He will henceforth esteem it a libel to be called *a man of letters.*"[25]

The lords and ladies laughed at Wedderburn's sally and overlooked his unprecedented fist-pounding on the council table.

He then read aloud the letter in which Franklin took full responsibility for purloining Hutchinson's correspondence. Franklin's letter was "impossible to read without horror." The lords thumped loudly with their canes: only a few of Franklin's friends winced for him. One of his lawyers wrote later that Wedderburn was "pouring forth such a torrent of virulent abuse on Dr. Franklin as never before took place within the compass of my knowledge, his reproaches appearing to me incompatible with the principles of law, truth, justice, propriety and humanity." Another wrote to the *Public Advertiser* that the Crown lawyer summoned up "all the licensed scurrility of the bar. . . . The approving smile of the board clearly showed that the coarsest language can be grateful to the politest ears." Joseph Priestley recorded: "At the sallies of Wedderburn's sarcastic wit all members of the Council, the president himself included, frequently laughed outright."[26]

Franklin himself later reported only a little of the rising resentment that held him erect, silent. In a letter anonymously printed in the Boston *Gazette,* he said he had "stood the butt of Wedderburn's invective and ribaldry for near an hour. . . . Not a single lord checked and recalled this orator to the business before them, but on the contrary, a very few excepted, they seemed to *enjoy highly* the *entertainment,* and frequently burst into *loud applause."* They came to the Cockpit, he wrote bitterly to a friend, "as if to a bullbaiting. I made no justification of myself, but held a cool sullen silence, reserving myself to some future opportunity."[27]

The hearing ended with Wedderburn's diatribe. Dunning's feeble response was ignored. The Privy Council immediately issued its report, obviously formulated and written earlier, and dismissed the charges against Hutchinson. Disgusted, Franklin gathered his papers and walked slowly from the hearing room. As his friends hurried up to him and they worked their way through the crowd, Franklin bumped up against Wedderburn. Under the rules of the hearing, he had not been able to speak out. But now he could. He looked icily at Wedderburn, spoke to him slowly, so that those around him could clearly hear him: "I will make your master a little king for this."[28]

Two days later, the ministerial ax fell. A courier pounded on the door of 7 Craven Street with a letter for Dr. Franklin. At the insistence of the ministry and over the heads of two of the three joint postmasters general, Benjamin Franklin was dismissed as deputy postmaster general for North America. For the next two days, as the Boston mail packet rocked at anchor on the Thames, Benjamin furiously fired off letters to radicals in Massachusetts, to political allies in Philadelphia. Finally, he dashed off a hasty note to his son:

Dear Son:

This line is just to acquaint you that I am well, and that my office of deputy postmaster is taken from me. As there is no prospect of your ever being promoted to a better government, and [the office] that you hold has never defrayed its expenses, I wish you were settled in your farm. 'Tis an honester and more honorable because a more independent employment. You will hear from others the treatment I have received. I leave it to your own reflections and determinations upon it, and remain,

Your afffectionate father,
B Franklin[29]

13

YOU ARE A
THOROUGH COURTIER

February 1774–April 1775

ENJAMIN FRANKLIN KNEW AS LITTLE ABOUT THE CONDI-
tions in most of the American colonies as his son did of
England's hardening attitude toward her colonists. "Happily New
Jersey is out of the question,"[1] he wrote to his old Quaker friend
James Kinsey, speaker of the New Jersey Assembly — by which he
meant that New Jersey was free of riots and rebellious ideas.
Franklin had not asked his son if this supposition was actually true,
and as agent for New Jersey, he must have looked silly in Kinsey's
eyes. In addition, he still did not question his firm belief that his son
was in every way his dependent, that William's career was inextricably tied to his own political fortunes. On February 18, 1774, two
weeks after his Cockpit ordeal, he sent a second letter of advice,
confused and contradictory, to William: "Some tell me that it is
determined to displace you likewise, but I do not know it as certain," he wrote. "I only give you the hint, as an inducement to you
to delay awhile your removal to Perth Amboy, which in that case
would be a trouble and an expense to no purpose." He had apparently paid little attention to the seriousness of William's financial plight. He had also ignored the pressing personal reasons for
William's decision to move the capital from Burlington to Perth
Amboy and make the Proprietary House there the official and permanent governor's residence. Moreover, Benjamin would not real-

ize for nearly another year that he had also badly misjudged William's reaction to his public disgrace.

"Perhaps they may expect that your resentment of their treatment of me may induce you to resign and save them the shame of depriving you, whom they ought to promote. But this I would not advise you to do. Let them take your place, if they want it, though in truth I think it scarce worth your keeping since it has not afforded you sufficient to prevent your running every year behindhand with me." (Benjamin could not resist in every letter some insensitive dig about William's tardy accounts with him.) "But one may make something of an injury, nothing of a resignation."[2]

When William wrote hastily to his father in January 1774, he undoubtedly had just learned of the Boston Tea Party and as yet had little grasp of its importance. He certainly had no idea of his father's involvement or pillorizing by the ministry. Their letters crossed. William devoted most of his letter to talk about presents of barrels of pork and apples from the farm he was now forced to sell, only remarking parenthetically that he was "at present a good deal engaged" with the New Jersey Assembly.[3]

Indeed he was. The engagement was more along the order of a running battle that had placed him at sword's points with a tough new breed of rebellious New Jersey legislators. Even in this rural province of gardens and orchards, there were more men every year bitterly opposed to every symbol and representative of the established imperial order.

The issue that finally separated William Franklin from the popular party seems almost trivial, but at the time it was deeply symbolic of old antagonisms that were becoming inflamed in every American colony. For generations, settlers had paid quitrents, small but galling annual payments in hard cash to the holders of the original proprietorial shares in the province. It was as if a man were perpetually buying his land over and over again, though he had paid a purchase price to begin with. Even as the population surged, as thousands of Scotch-Irish squatted in the northwest frontier hill country and transplanted New Englanders filled up the river valleys, even when the land changed hands again and again, these payments came due every year, as if they were private and duplicate taxes. And every year their recipients were hated more by men who found it hard to come up with silver coins in a debt-ridden barter society. It was irksome that the man who also collected the taxes, the provincial treasurer, was one of these landed proprietors. It was downright infuriating when the treasury chest containing an entire year's tax receipts for the province was stolen from his mansion in Perth Amboy as he supposedly slept upstairs.

The theft of the New Jersey treasury forced William Franklin for the first time to take sides in the smoldering feud between the rich landlord class and the smallholders — usually farmers and mechanics. He chose not from instinct but from conviction, from a deep knowledge of and insistence on the law. And when his legal judgment was vigorously challenged for the first time, he sided with a close and trusted friend in the contest, who just happened to be the treasurer himself, Stephen Skinner. (Their wives were also best friends.)

The violent clash between Governor Franklin and the Assembly began innocuously enough. The Assembly passed a resolution expressing its faith in the treasurer's good character. But there were those who preferred to believe that the official had rigged the theft with the help of hired accomplices. They saw the case as an excellent way to embarrass the aristocratic Perth Amboy group both in the Assembly and on Governor Franklin's Council. The next session they mustered enough votes to demand an investigation. The committee of inquiry, while absolving the treasurer of stealing the money, found him negligent for keeping the money unguarded in his house and ordered him to repay the entire sum, with interest, as a fine. The governor, who had berated the penny-pinching Assembly for ignoring his reform programs and being in a lethargic stupor, now had reason to wish that the farmer-lawmakers would doze off again.

New quarrels irritated raw nerves on both sides. Because of its strategic location athwart the main road between Philadelphia and New York, New Jersey had traditionally been forced to feed and maintain British troops in large barracks. Now the uproar over quartering troops in Boston spilled over into New Jersey and gave radical politicians a fresh issue with which to test their strength. The governor finally arbitrated the matter. He reduced the demands of the British troops and induced the tightfisted lawmakers to acknowledge that free-spending soldiers also were good for the colony's shaky economy. But now another layer of tender scar tissue had been added. When the Assembly reopened the treasury case, demanding the treasurer's resignation as well as full restitution despite the treasurer's plea of innocence and his assertion that he could not afford the fine, William stepped in angrily. Accusing the Assembly of usurping his executive power to make appointments and ask for resignations, he declared hotly that "no consideration whatever shall induce me to give up that right but the King's express commands."[4] Then he launched his own full-scale investigation and discovered evidence that a sizable gang of counterfeiters with connections in the radical party had actually stolen the treasury. Identifying the men by name in a proclamation after county justices refused to indict them for the theft, William offered a large reward to anyone willing to bring the men to the capital for trial. Not only did no one rise to his bait, but a mob broke into the Morris County jail, where three men were awaiting trial on the counterfeiting charge, and freed them.

William Franklin had no patience with mobs. He had already sat by nervously as rioters, resenting high legal fees, had taken over some of the county courts. On that occasion he allowed the local magistrates to settle the dispute. But now, when jailbreakers, thieves and counterfeiters roamed free, he called in dilatory sheriffs and judges to a Council meeting and dressed them down. Then he turned them over to the Assembly for legal action. The breakdown of law, the refusal of a grand jury to act in the face of clear evidence, thoroughly alarmed William. In his eyes an open rebellion was unfolding when a mob decided to break down jail doors and release felons politically favorable to their cause while at the same time the Assembly refused flatly to try the treasurer so that he could clear his name. This William could not tolerate. The last straw was the action of William Livingston, the leading radical lawyer in the province: he came out of retirement to write a legal opinion denouncing Governor Franklin's handling of the case and insisting that the treasurer resign. William's patience ended. Early in 1773 he joined the emotion-charged battle on the side of the wealthy Perth Amboy proprietors. At a time when it seemed that all laws were being challenged, he decided, by instinct as well as by education, to remain a legal conservative.

William ignored his father's recent letters of advice. He did not resign. And he accelerated his move to Perth Amboy, where he would at last be closer to like-minded advisors in the deepening crisis. In mid-September of 1774, he visited the Proprietary House in Perth Amboy with Lord Stirling, a member of the Council. Ten years earlier, when he had deliberately avoided taking up official residence in the palatial house built for the governor's use by the rich landed gentry of Perth Amboy, he had chosen instead the simpler life of Burlington. Over the years he had drifted closer to the East Jersey aristocrats. As early as 1770, he had been wined and dined at one land-rich proprietor's house in the company of the leading merchants and landowners of both New York City and New Jersey. His new alliance could not have been less popular. For years the East Jersey proprietors had evicted countless squatters who now were flocking to the Whig standard. But by now, William Franklin was ready for a profound change.

The minutes of a meeting of the East Jersey proprietors record that the Franklins, with several of the proprietors, visited the mansion, the hated symbol of proprietary quitrents and taxation, on September 21, 1773. He and Elizabeth toured the mansion and its grounds with new friends who were offering to repair the house, build stables, and generally fix up the place without charge. The rent was modest: the Franklins could have the splendid mansion for the meager housing allowance (sixty pounds) provided with the governor's salary.[5]

William climbed the tiered marble steps with Elizabeth, crossed the eighteen-foot-wide marble hallway, wandered through the marble-mantled ballroom, the study that would house his library, and up to the spacious bedrooms and dressing rooms. It was one of the finest houses in America, the rival of any other royal governor's residence. In his own hand, he sketched the plan for papering each wall in the latest London patterns to match Elizabeth's furniture and decorations. The pièce de résistance of the redecoration, "if it won't add much to the expense," was to be black-and-white murals: "the Falls [of] Passaic and Cohoes" on the walls of the main hall and "the Falls of Niagra [sic]" on the wall of the staircase.[6]

Even with a revolution breaking around him, Governor Franklin was determined to maintain a high royal standard. As the proprietors sent agents to scour the shops of New York to meet the governor's requests (the merchant John Roosevelt submitted twenty-eight patterns for the governor's study alone),[7] William went to Philadelphia to say goodbye to his mother and sister while Elizabeth began the long process of packing and crating.

As soon as they had hung the gilt-edged portraits of King George and Queen Charlotte in the great parlor, William sat down to write Benjamin, asking him to bring William Temple, now fourteen, to Perth Amboy to him. "I hope to see you and him in the spring and that you will spend some time with me at Amboy, where I am now happily settled in a very good house and shall always have an apartment at your service."[8]

In the weeks between revealing his responsibility for the Hutchinson affair and his dismissal from office, Benjamin Franklin wrote a letter to his son that showed he felt he had righted the injuries of his actions by his candor and that he was not afraid of the consequences. The entire episode "has drawn some censure upon myself, but as I grow old, I grow less concerned about censure." That he was deeply wounded, deeply bitter, about his handling by the Privy Council, was evident, not only in his defensive pamphlets published at his own expense and his series of letters to the newspapers of England and America but certainly in his stiffening attitude toward his son in 1773 and 1774.

Benjamin had begun to reveal his changing political thinking to William months before the Cockpit trial, even as he denied he had urged Bostonians to hold out for independence. He had also insisted that he had urged the leaders of Boston's radicals to avoid confrontation. His letter to William of October 6, 1773, was quite the opposite of his apparent inflammatory rhetoric in anonymous tracts and in his signed preface to the Boston resolves. But Benjamin *was* beginning to acknowledge to William his change of sentiment toward King and Parliament: "From a long and thorough consideration of the subject," he wrote, "I am indeed of opinion that the parliament has no right to make any law whatever binding on the colonies. That the king, and not the king, lords and commons collectively, is their sovereign; and that the king with their respective parliaments [here Benjamin clearly meant the assemblies of each colony] is their only legislator. "I know your sentiments differ from mine on these subjects. You are a *thorough government man,* which I do not wonder at, nor do I aim at converting you. I only wish you to act uprightly and steadily, avoiding that duplicity which, in Hutchinson, adds contempt to indignation. If you can promote the prosperity of your people, and leave them happier than you found them, whatever your political principles are, your memory will be honored."[9]

William had not exactly kept his father abreast of his own changing thinking during the political struggle, even if his letters and legislation partly explained his views. He believed that his old friend Strahan, now a member of Parliament, had advised him wisely: that it was better for him to make it clear to the ministry that father and son were not one and the same in their beliefs. It was not entirely a case of wishing to protect his job. He sincerely believed that his father was wrong on a number of counts. Nevertheless, ministerial rumors that William was to be removed from the governorship were actually planted in the New York newspapers shortly after the Cockpit trial. They stopped a few months later when Thomas Hutchinson reached London and told authorities that to his knowledge Governor Franklin did not approve of his father's conduct. In his diary Hutchinson recorded that "Governor Franklin had wrote a letter to William Strahan, the King's Printer, in which he condemns his father's whole conduct in the affair of the letters."[10]

In the three months following the elder Franklin's disgrace in England, William actually wrote nothing to his father. When he finally broke the silence, on May 3, 1774, he wrote cautiously that he was visiting his mother in Philadelphia and "I have it not in my power to write particularly by this opportunity." (He evidently meant he could find no safe channel.) Once again, he concealed his personal feelings from his father, only commenting, "It seems your popularity in this country [America], whatever it may be on the other side, is greatly beyond whatever it was." That night, in fact, as William was writing his letter, the effigies of Wedderburn and Hutchinson were burned in the streets of Philadelphia. "But *you* may depend when you return here," he continued, "on being received with every mark of regard and affection." He added that he was no longer worried about his own political security: a wealthy New York landowner who was a close friend had journeyed to England and talked to friends in the ministry and had just written him that Lord Dartmouth's "sentiments respecting my conduct . . . [have] made me easy as to my office." He would not resign his office but would act carefully from now on. "I am determined not to give any just cause of complaint, so that if, after all, I should receive any injury from that quarter, I shall be at no loss what to do."[11]

That William knew exactly what he was doing is revealed by records in British as well as New Jersey archives. Coincidentally, on May 4, 1774, the day after he wrote that he would not step down out of any sense of familial loyalty to his dismissed father, a letter was addressed to him from Lord Dartmouth at Whitehall which cryptically indicated that the King would continue to favor the younger Franklin. William's appointment of his close friend Richard Stockton as an associate justice of the New Jersey supreme court was confirmed by the King. This was a mark of royal favor that probably would not have been made if William's tenure were at all in jeopardy.

That same month, William took the fateful step of opening a "secret and confidential" correspondence with Lord Dartmouth. In a long letter, written on the thirty-first, he in effect set himself up as a royal advisor and offered himself as the instrument of what he hoped would be Anglo-American reconciliation. The letter indicates that he had decided on this course after studying the harsh act of Parliament that had closed the port of Boston in punishment for the Tea Party. He warned that some merchants and farmers were organizing aid to the people of Boston. Their assistance would neutralize the effect of the Royal Navy blockade. But William doubted that other colonies would set off another round of nonimportation agreements. Thus, he said, Britain had little to fear from America's principal weapon, a boycott on trade. On the contrary, many merchants, fearing an embargo, "have ordered much greater quantity of goods than is common to be sent out by the next fall ships from England."

He then informed his lordship that "a Congress of members of the several Houses of Assembly" had been called for the autumn of 1774, and each assembly was to vote on sending a delegation. He had stalled off the New Jersey vote for three months — a longer time than any other colony — but neighboring New York had then voted a delegation and New Jersey, "not wanting to appear singular," had followed suit. He called such an unauthorized intercolonial congress "very absurd if not unconstitutional." The assemblies, he said, could be dissolved at any time by their governors, rendering their committees and delegations illegal, a step he declared he was prepared to take if necessary.

"His Majesty may be assured that I shall omit nothing in my power to keep this province quiet," William pledged. "Let the event be what it may, no *attachments* or *connections* shall ever make me swerve from the duty of my station."[12]

Benjamin still did not know of William's decision when he wrote again, on June 30, to report the news from Boston: a full-scale, nonimportation agreement was intended by Boston radicals. "If it is general, and the Americans agree in it, the present ministry will certainly be knocked up," Benjamin wrote. He spoke to William as if they were coconspirators against a common enemy, as if William would still be a party to such an anti-British agreement. The lag in mails left Benjamin unaware of William's change of course, but William's next two letters to England, sharply at variance with his father's view of him, underscored Benjamin's total lack of comprehension of his son's thinking.

On June 28, Governor Franklin sent to Lord Dartmouth a set of documents: the resolves of a meeting of rebellious citizens of Essex County, New Jersey, the onetime center of anti–Stamp Act resistance. Many of the protestors were relocated Massachusetts men. Several were large landholders, graduates of Princeton and Yale. Indeed, most of New Jersey's future revolutionary leaders had attended the meeting. A comparison of drafts of the resolves reveals that the Essex meeting had taken on the shape of an illegal assembly, called without the governor's sanction as required by law. Indeed, the clerk of the gathering drew a line through the word "meeting" and replaced it with the much stronger phrase "members of this assembly." These revolutionary resolves, as sweeping as those of the Boston town meetings, announced that the Essex County radicals were making "common cause" with Bostonians, were entering and enforcing a total embargo of British goods and were urging other New Jersey counties to send delegates to the general congress in Philadelphia. Finally, the Essex organizers had summoned a New Jersey congress.[13]

Not only did Governor Franklin maintain in his report that he was powerless to stop such meetings, since he had no police and no troops, but he went further than any American had gone thus far in attempting to bring about peace between the two opposing camps. He urged the Crown to outmaneuver the radicals by calling its own congress. "If properly authorized by His Majesty and consisting of the several governors and some members of the Council and Assembly in each province," he wrote Lord Dartmouth, such a legally sanctioned imperial congress would produce "the most beneficial consequences to the British Empire in general," especially if "assisted by some gentlemen of abilities, moderation and candor from Great Britain."

As the constitutional lawyer William Franklin pointed out, there was ample precedent for sending a royal commission to meet with American leaders to "settle matters of far less importance." The present crisis, he stressed, was "worthy of more attention and consideration than anything that has ever before concerned Great Britain." His plea went beyond any suggestion sent so far to the ministry. It also directly opposed his father's outraged advice to radicals to stand their ground. The King must act with equal moderation before less thoughtful men prevailed and managed to gain control of what to William was now an obviously fast-spreading conflict. "There is no foreseeing the consequences which may result from such [an unsanctioned] Congress as is now intended," he warned Lord Dartmouth.[14]

A few days later, even before he knew whether Lord Dartmouth still trusted this particular Franklin, Governor Franklin received proof that he had gambled correctly. The letter was dated July 6 from Whitehall: "I should do injustice to my own sentiments of your character and conduct in supposing you could be induced by any consideration whatever to swerve from the duty you owe the king."[15]

If Benjamin still thought that William was on his side in the growing controversy, William just as obviously believed that Benjamin, since he had been ousted from office, would be more willing to come around and join with *him*, that his father had somehow moderated his views since his dressing down before the Privy Council. "There is no foreseeing the consequences which may result from such a Congress," William wrote his father — the identical words he had penned to Lord Dartmouth. Then, for the first time, he clearly revealed how far from his father's way of thinking he had journeyed in their years apart, how total his transformation from impecunious young office seeker to conservative middle-aged man of influence and property.

The Boston Tea Party was an illegal attack on property, he wrote. Restitution must be made. Nothing else would do. "I cannot but think it very extraordinary that neither the Assembly of Massachusetts Bay nor the town of Boston have so much as intimated any intention or desire of making satisfaction to the East India Company and the officers of the customs," William wrote. "By doing these two things, which are consistent with strict justice, and by declaring that they will not hereafter attempt to hinder the landing at Boston of any goods legally imported, they might get their port opened in a few months."

William was lecturing his father, the architect of Boston resistance to the tea duties, and advocating surrender to the very demands contained in the ministry's coercive Boston Port Act! And he was making it seem the only rational and legal alternative. "If they are to wait for this until the Congress meets, and until the Grand Question is settled between the two countries, they may as well never have their port opened, for by that time all their trade will have got into another channel. Besides, they ought first to do justice before they ask it of others." William, not totally unsympathetic to the Whig cause, added that in his view apologies for the tea raid would help the radicals win redress of their just grievances "and do credit to their cause."[16]

When Benjamin Franklin read this letter, he immediately fired off a long, angry reply to William, methodically attacking each of his son's arguments: "In my opinion, all depends on the Americans themselves. If they make and keep firm resolutions not to consume British manufactures 'til their grievances are redressed and their rights acknowledged, this ministry must fall and the aggrieving laws be repealed." Gratuitously, he added, "This is the opinion of all wise men here." He dismissed his son's proposal for an imperial congress with a single line: "I hear nothing of the proposal you have made." And then he swung his full powers of political reasoning into refuting his son's arguments, numbering each point as if in a legal brief. "I do not, so much as you do," he began sarcastically, "wonder that the Massachusetts have not offered payment for the tea." What guarantee was there the British would keep their word and reopen the port? And what sum should be paid? And what would satisfy the customs men who were in the King's power?

"As to doing justice before they ask it, that should have been thought of by [Parliament] before they demanded it of the Bostonians. They have extorted many thousands of pounds from America unconstitutionally under color of acts of Parliament and with an armed force. Of this money they should make restitution. They might first have taken out payment for the tea and returned the rest. But you, who are a thorough courtier, see everything with government eyes."[17] It was Benjamin Franklin's most radical statement on the proper responsibility of the British to Boston. It was, moreover, his worst imaginable insult: to equate his son with the venal and corrupt courtiers he had so lately come to despise and loathe.

Another month, another mail ship, and he continued in a calmer tone, this time arguing for an all-American congress without British intervention. One British jurist, he said — a man whom William respected — had declared "he would give half his worth in the world to be present at the debates of such an uncorrupted body on so important an occasion. . . . I often regret that I did not leave this country in time to have been there myself." The letter ended with the old irritating refrain: William was behind in his remittances.[18]

A man of remarkable patience, William had endured his father's dressing downs for more than thirty years. He had learned how to control his temper. He did not now throw more paper on the fire between them. He did not answer his father for three months, a full year after the Cockpit hearing, and then he wrote only because he had to. His letter gave Benjamin a far more personal reason to wish he had returned to America sooner.

Honoured Father,

I came here on Thursday last to attend the funeral of my poor old mother, who died the Monday noon preceding. Mr. Bache sent his clerk express to me on the occasion, who reached Amboy on Tuesday evening, and I set out early the next morning, but the weather being very severe and snowing hard, I was not able to reach here 'til about 4 o'clock on Thursday afternoon, about half an hour before the corpse was to be moved for interment. Mr. Bache and I followed as chief mourners. . . . Several other of your friends were carriers, and a very respectable number of the inhabitants were at the funeral. . . . Her death was no more than might be reasonably expected after the paralytic stroke she received some time ago, which greatly affected her memory and understanding. She told me, when I took leave of her on my removal to Amboy, that she never expected to see you unless you returned this winter, that she was sure she should not live 'til next summer. I heartily wish you had happened to have come over in the fall, as I think her disappointment preyed a good deal on her spirits.[19]

Then William softened for a moment. His father, he must have sensed, would be stricken enough by the letter. Benjamin had just kept putting off his return, he knew. As long as two years before, Deborah had written to her husband, "I find my self growing very febel verey faste." For nearly a year she had not been able to write at all. But Benjamin had been too absorbed in his own affairs to notice. He wrote her only short impersonal notes, one of his to every three of hers: promises of returning, excuses for delaying. There was no sense affixing blame. Benjamin should have known from the pathetic letters, the feeble handwriting, that Deborah was pining away without her Benny, that she had been failing steadily since a partial stroke five years earlier. But now was not the time to recriminate. It *was* time to get him to come home. The rest of the letter was only the pleading of a son for a father, nearing seventy, to rejoin his son after a ten-year absence: "It gives me great pleasure to find that you have so perfect an enjoyment of that greatest of blessings, health. Notwithstanding you are sensible that you cannot in the course of nature long expect the continuance of it, yet you postpone your return to your family."

The courier for this sad strong letter was none other than their trusted old mutual friend John Pownall, secretary of the British Board of Trade. Pownall told William face to face of Benjamin's implacable private and press warfare with the ministry; how his three petitions against the closing of Boston port had been rejected by overwhelming majorities in both houses of Parliament and by the King himself; of the utter hopelessness of Benjamin's campaign; and arrest for sedition if he further antagonized the government by plotting with opposition leaders to reverse anti-American legislation. Benjamin, he knew, had actually been denounced on the floor of the House of Lords, called little less than a traitor by noblemen who were amazed that he was still allowed to remain at large on the streets of London.

Worried by all that he had heard, William added to his letter, "If there was any prospect of your being able to bring the people in power to your way of thinking, or those of your way of thinking's being brought into power, I should not think so much of your stay. But as you have had by this time pretty strong proofs that neither can be reasonably expected and that you are looked upon with an evil eye in that country, and are in no small danger of being brought into trouble for your political conduct, you had certainly better return while you are able to bear the fatigues of the voyage to a country where the people revere you and are inclined to pay a deference to your opinions. However mad you may think the measures of the ministry are, yet I trust you have candor enough to acknowledge that we are no ways behindhand with them in instances of madness on this side of the water. However, it is a disagreeable subject, and I'll drop it."

There is no letter or memoir to reveal whether Benjamin mourned his wife of forty-four years. He merely noted that he would have to clear up his business in London quickly in order to return home and assume the personal management of their financial affairs. But it was nearly three years before he commented on her death: "I have lately lost my old and faithful companion, and I every day become more sensible of the greatness of that loss, which cannot now be repaired."[20]

In his first days as a self-sure young governor fussing over the furniture, Governor Franklin had dealt mostly with wealthy West Jersey Quaker farmers and rich Anglican land barons of East Jersey, many of them absentee landlords who were also active in New York politics and society. But in the ten ensuing years, even as most Quakers withdrew from politics to avoid further tests of their scruple against warfare, Presbyterian newcomers rushed in. From their twin power bases of Elizabethtown in the north and the College of New Jersey at Princeton in the south, they quickly became a major political force, challenging the Anglican proprietors at every turn. The rise of these plain Presbyterian men, most of them only a generation or two removed from the Lowlands of Scotland, must have seemed ironic to William.

As a young boy, he had witnessed the fervid, writhing crowds moaning and shouting out at the fire-and-brimstone preaching of George Whitefield and his disciples during the Great Awakening religious revival. The revival had filled the streets of Philadelphia, closed the Assembly balls, and bolstered the ranks of the Indian-fighting militia with tough soldiers. Although the elder Franklin had rarely taken a public stand on religion, he had nonetheless led the movement to build a meetinghouse for New Light Presbyterians when they were barred from holding services in other Philadelphia churches. In the editorial columns of his *Pennsylvania Gazette* he had openly supported zealous Presbyterian missionaries based in New Jersey. He had dreamed aloud of peopling new western colonies with Presbyterians. A generation later, the revival had matured into an educational movement. Presbyterians had formed the University of Pennsylvania and the Indian college of Dartmouth while the Awakeners of New England vigorously proselytized Yale students who were trying to study in their rooms. They had brought about renewed religious fervor all over America as converted collegians returned to preach in their home colonies. But the heart of the Presbyterian movement remained the College of New Jersey at Princeton.

As *ex officio* president of the Princeton trustees, William Franklin evidently concurred in recruiting from Scotland the fieriest and most articulate of the Presbyterian reformers, the Reverend John Witherspoon, a beetle-browed, bombastic orator who had become famous for his attacks on the performance of the first Scottish plays. By 1774, Witherspoon had turned the infant college into a mecca for strict anti-English Presbyterians from all over colonial America.

William must have remembered his long-ago Scottish tour, when the fundamentalist preacher was busily defending his radical attacks on Anglican backsliding. Nonetheless, in Witherspoon William had welcomed another literate man to rural New Jersey. He had sponsored him for membership in the American Philosophical Society. In his turn, Witherspoon included the Franklins' electrical experiments in his lectures at Princeton and duplicated William's design for the kite.[21] But by the 1770s, as the pace of revolutionary events quickened, students at Princeton, undoubtedly with Witherspoon's knowledge, quite possibly with his consent, were in the forefront of open resistance to British policies. They burned in effigy merchants, governors and members of Parliament, broke into the college storehouse, and destroyed a large quantity of tea at the appropriate moment. With Governor Franklin on the dais, they showed up for graduation in homespun American garb instead of imported academic gowns to dramatize their embargo of English goods. Even valedictory addresses, delivered in Latin, were defiant diatribes on patriotism. One was delivered by President Witherspoon's own son. If Witherspoon had disapproved in the slightest, immediate expulsion would have resulted.

Among Witherspoon's devoted alumni were young merchants and lawyers at the core of the radical movement in Essex County. By 1774, Witherspoon himself, still denouncing the clergy's participation in politics from the pulpit, was secretly campaigning for independence among delegations to the Continental Congress in Philadelphia when he was not meeting at the Hudibras Tavern in Princeton with fellow members of one of the New Jersey radical political committees based there.

While Governor Franklin watched apprehensively, a new element of unyielding grassroots politicians slowly took power, squeezing out Quakers and lukewarm patriots in county after county until radicals all but controlled the New Jersey Assembly. Without troops, there was little the governor could do.

The most widespread lawlessness was the smuggling. The royal customs officials were but a feeble check on a large and well-organized industry. The bulk of what today would be approximately $200 million in goods smuggled annually into Philadelphia from the West Indies passed through booming New Jersey contraband ports. Long wagon trains rumbled through the Pine Barrens day and night under heavily armed escort. Customs officers daring to interfere received harsh treatment. One unsuccessful royal collector complained to the governor that ships were being unloaded and that untaxed wagonloads were hauled right past his window: the governor could only add the man's complaint to the stack on his desk. When the collector and his two sons tried to seize a smuggler's shipload of claret, they were beaten off and then robbed by the smugglers. Persisting, he dispatched one of the sons to Philadelphia for reinforcements. There the youth was pursued by a mob, dragged out of a house, tarred and feathered, then beaten with sticks as he was dragged with a rope around his neck through the streets. After several hours of being further abused in a pillory, he was finally thrown into the river. Miraculously, he survived.[22]

Adding a special virulence to the mob's hatred of Britain was a strong element of religious prejudice, which had been exploited for fifteen years by Samuel Adams in Boston, William Livingston in New York, and Witherspoon wherever he went. The radical Puritans raised the bogeyman of popery, trying to confuse the ignorant and deliberately blurring the distinction between the Church of England and the Church of Rome, or "the Whore of Babylon," as Boston bigots preferred to call both. Religious prejudice had been mixed with fear of Catholic Canada and its baptized Indian raiders since the foundation of the American settlements. The radical leaders in the Continental Congress received timely assistance in stirring the coals of religious hatred from the bungling and insensitive North ministry in the weeks just before the Continental Congress convened.

For fifteen years, conquered Canada had been ruled by martial law. At this exquisitely inopportune moment, North, Dartmouth and their advisors decided that since they were rewriting American colonial policy anyway, they should draft a new charter for the province of Quebec. Intended as a model of its kind, the Quebec charter created a highly centralized government. It was to be ruled by a governor and a council entirely appointed by and serving at the pleasure of the King, with *no* representative elective lower house. Taxes were to be voted by Parliament in London. All laws were to be subject to Crown veto. The rights, religious and civil, of the French Catholic majority were to be guaranteed. Since most Canadians were Catholic, the guarantee, in effect, made Catholicism the state religion. The courts were to follow French law, which did not admit trial by jury. Moreover, the French-Canadian fur traders were rewarded by the extension of the provincial borders south to the Ohio River, thus wiping out the land grants not only of the Franklins but of the Lees, the Washingtons, the Whartons, and other land-hungry speculators from Massachusetts to South Carolina. Parliament had created "an arbitrary government on the back of our settlements dangerous to us all," as Benjamin Franklin described it. To the radicals as well as to Franklin it was obvious that Britain intended to subdue Puritan New England, then bring it under just such a popish, Parliament-controlled government.[23]

The prospect of French traders and Catholic priests roaming — no, *owning* — the Ohio backcountry did more than anything else to convince frontier Scotch-Irish as well as New England Puritans that the Catholic Stuarts were once again ascendant and about to invade America from the north. Sam Adams was able to tell the Boston mobs with sincerity what Benjamin Franklin had concluded when he first read the Quebec Act in London. As the Congress met, moderate southern leaders, driven into the camp of the Boston radicals by the destruction of their chances for more lands to support their topsoil-depleting crops of tobacco and cotton, joined in vehement chorus against this latest intolerable transgression by the Tory ministry.

The anti-British movement was spreading throughout New Jersey by the summer of 1774. In little more than the month following the Essex County resolves, some seventy-two radical delegates from every county gathered to reject the Boston Port Act as "repugnant to the common principles of humanity and justice." They voted unanimously to dispatch five delegates to the Continental Congress in Philadelphia. William immediately informed London of their action.[24]

The delegation was led by William Livingston, the squire of Liberty Hall in Elizabethtown, who had for years packed the coffeehouses and taverns of New York City with noisy debaters as each weekly installment of his magazine, *The Independent Reflector,* came off the press. Promulgating radical and Puritanical political theories, he attacked the established provincial government, the tax laws and, most especially, the Anglican Church. One early and eager subscriber had been the printer Benjamin Franklin, who evidently first imbibed Locke's doctrine of the right to revolution by reading distillations of Scottish political philosophy as they came from the pen of Livingston.

After retiring to the idyllic life of a country gentleman from a law practice stunted by his time-consuming radical writings, Livingston announced his return to politics by issuing a long legal opinion attacking Governor Franklin's stand in the case of the New Jersey treasurer. As radical leaders from all over British America headed for the Continental Congress, he then maneuvered to emerge as the head of the New Jersey delegation.

William Franklin could foresee that the swirling revolution would soon spill over with blood. His suggestion for a British-sponsored congress unanswered, he made a fresh attempt at reconciliation. He urgently requested that Lord Dartmouth convince his peers that Americans, if they were to be taxed and regulated by Parliamentary law, should be given seats in Parliament. Again he had to wait, even though he knew that time was running out. Then, in the summer of 1774, as revolutionary committees planned the strategy for the Continental Congress, William crossed the Delaware River to meet frequently with his old law teacher, Joseph Galloway, who had held the Franklin party together through the long years of Benjamin Franklin's absence. Together, they worked hard to revise and modify the Albany Plan of Union, which Benjamin Franklin and Thomas Hutchinson had presented in 1754 at the Albany Convention to counter the French offensive. That plan had called for a union of colonies under a president-general ap-

pointed and paid by the Crown. A grand council elected by the colonial assemblies (each colony to have from two to seven delegates)
was to have legislative power subject to approval by the president-
general and the Crown.

More recently, Galloway had drafted a letter from the Pennsylvania committee of correspondence to the Massachusetts committee of correspondence proposing union between the American
colonies and England similar to the merger between Scotland and
England in 1707.

When William Franklin and Joseph Galloway met at Trevose in
Bucks County, Pennsylvania in early September, they each apparently had drawn up resolutions to submit to the Continental
Congress when it met later that month. Their proposals differed
slightly not only from Benjamin's plans of twenty years ago but
from each other's.

The Franklin-Galloway Plan of Union called for a grand legislative council to be elected triennially by the legislatures of all the colonies and to meet annually. Only its president was to be appointed
by the King. Whereas Benjamin's plan had merely called for a
union of all the colonies to facilitate defense against the Indians and
arbitrate land claims, the Franklin-Galloway Plan went much further: the American legislature was to be connected to Parliament,
and would send delegates from America to sit in the House of
Commons. This particular provision, proposed by William, would
provide virtual representation of Americans in Parliament, the lack
of which had done so much to provoke the unrest of the 1760's.
Furthermore, either Parliament or the American colonies could
propose laws to govern the colonies, but the underlying principle
behind the Franklin-Galloway Plan of Union was that no law could
bind America without her consent.

The only other major difference between William's and Galloway's provisions were characteristic of the two men themselves.
Galloway's called for another humble petition from the Congress to
the Crown; William wanted the Continental Congress to send the
plan to each colonial legislature, which in turn could legally pass on
it and then present it to the Crown. William's approach was not
only the more constitutional of the two, but it was the more Whig-
gish, honoring the authority not only of Parliament but of the colo-

nial legislatures. It was a statesmanlike difference which, if it had been adopted, could have helped to avert the Revolutionary War. It also anticipated in many ways the British Commonwealth of Nations, adopted by Parliament a century and a half later.

The version printed and presented to the Continental Congress by Galloway, Pennsylvania's chief delegate to the Congress, was supported by moderates in South Carolina and New York as well as in the Middle Colonies. In 1774, it was all the congressional radicals could do to keep it from winning adoption. Patrick Henry saw it as the ruin of all his plans if it were to pass. The radicals stalled for time. They moved to table the plan for further consideration, polling only one more vote than the moderates in the crucial motion to table.

As Galloway complained to William in a letter William transmitted to Lord Dartmouth, the radical faction then went skillfully to work "out of doors." Part of its success came from the well-concerted activities of the Philadelphia radicals. Soon after Galloway's compromise plan was shelved, he received a strong hint to withdraw the plan from consideration. A box was delivered to his mansion containing a hangman's noose and orders to use it himself or else a mob would. Also in the box was a torn insurance policy. William reported to Lord Dartmouth that Galloway abruptly withdrew his motion and decided not to submit William's plan in its stead. Galloway then retired to his farm.[25]

The Congress had agreed in advance to make all its votes unanimous to protect individual members. The Galloway Plan of Union was unanimously withdrawn. Then the Congress voted unanimously to instruct its secretary to expunge the motion entirely from the minutes.

William Franklin's compromise plan never was presented to the Congress. When Galloway anonymously published his plan a few months later, calling the Congress an "illegal, motley" gathering inciting "a Presbyterian plot for independence from England,"[26] William sent it without comment to Lord Dartmouth.

When he was not funneling Galloway's reports of the debates in the Congress to England, Governor Franklin was trying to keep order in his own province. For him the key test of his ability to maintain royal authority in New Jersey came two months later. In January 1775 the Assembly convened to consider whether it would follow the recommendations of the Continental Congress by endorsing the Association, a total boycott of British imports and exports, and send cash and supplies to the inhabitants of blockaded Boston. William knew that several populous New Jersey counties were strongly opposed to the radicals and had voted delegates to the provincial Assembly with instructions to block involvement in what they considered a Massachusetts quarrel. William clung to the hope that he could keep New Jersey neutral. If he failed, there would probably be open hostilities in those counties where radical committees of observation and inspection had been trying to stop all trade with England by searching out and destroying goods owned by increasingly resistant pro-British merchants.

Earlier that winter, the Essex County grand jury, siding with Boston, had boldly sent a warning to the province's second highest Crown official, its chief justice: "No fawning servility . . . no hopes of future preferment will induce any man to damp [his] . . . patriotic ardor nor lend his helping hand to . . . riveting those chains which are forging for us."[27]

At the same time, New York newspapers circulated in New Jersey warned that the radicals were "elated with power, new and unconstitutional." One asked bluntly in a headline, "What Think Ye of Congress Now?" and scolded, "These men arraign the highest authority on earth, insolently trample on the liberties of their fellow subjects, take from them their property, grant it to others and expose them to the vilest injuries."[28]

Hoping for peace and compromise, William Franklin tried to remain in the middle of the road in this struggle. But he felt increasingly isolated and skeptical of the courage of like-minded men around him to resist the incessant pressure of the Congress party, of the mob. He had gradually ceased being the passionate Whig who, only five years earlier, had railed at the incompetence and arrogance of Lord Hillsborough's bungling anti-American policies.

"Few have the courage to declare their disapprobation publicly," he wrote confidentially to Lord Dartmouth. "They well know, if they do not conform, they are in danger of becoming objects of popular resentment." And, he bemoaned, "It is not in the power of government here to protect them." He was even beginning to worry for his own safety, for that of his wife. "Indeed, the officers of government [except at Boston] have but little or no protection for themselves."[29] He was bitter that the Congress had failed to propose some compromise such as his plan of union. He knew that such a union between England and Scotland had, earlier in that century, helped to end a millennium of conflict. Without compromise, he was certain England must, as a point of honor, punish her upstart American colonies. Passing along a copy of the suppressed Galloway-Franklin Plan of Union, he turned gloomily to prepare what he knew could be his most important speech.

To prevent violent legislative reaction to the news of the Boston Port Act, William had stubbornly refused for nearly a year to call the Assembly, as was his lawful prerogative. He knew that to call the Assembly was to risk legitimate legislative endorsement of the proceedings of the extralegal Continental Congress. Yet there was also a thin chance that doing so would provide a forum in which he could make his appeal to avoid war with England.

On January 11, 1775, Governor Franklin climbed the steps of the old stone courthouse at Perth Amboy and entered the chamber where he had taken his oath of office on just such a frozen blustery morning twelve years earlier. After the thirty assemblymen and the twelve executive councillors and provincial officials filed to their places, William rose, tall, grave, confident. Arranging his carefully prepared text on the lectern before him, he looked up to face these men, many of them old friends, but so many of them strangers. In his clear commanding voice he welcomed these "gentlemen of the Assembly." This was to be the keynote address of their most important meeting, and the governor's speech left no doubt that he expected them to uphold royal authority, that he intended in every way to "prevail on you to exert yourselves" to prevent further "mischiefs to this country." But he also made it clear he was holding to his decided course of careful neutrality and would tread lightly on their prerogatives.

"It is not for me to decide on the particular merits of the dispute between Great Britain and her colonies, nor do I mean to censure those who conceive themselves aggrieved for aiming at a redress of their grievances. It is a duty they owe themselves, their country, and their posterity.

"All that I would wish to guard you against is giving any countenance or encouragement to that destructive mode of proceeding which has been unhappily adopted" (every member knew his sympathies now) "by some" (and they knew some of the most radical were sitting in this chamber) "in this colony." William paused often, spoke slowly, ominously. "If you, gentlemen of the Assembly, should give your approbation, you will do as much as lies in your power to destroy that form of government of which you are an important part, and which it is your lawful duty to preserve."

There was, moreover, absolutely no need for the freeholders of New Jersey to imperil themselves, their families, their estates so hard-bought and prospering. If they had any grievances of their own or proposals for the Crown, "I can assure you from the best authority" — and here every man must have known his meaning, his direct personal link to the King through Lord Dartmouth — "that such propositions will be properly attended to and certainly have greater weight coming from each colony in its separate capacity than through a channel the propriety and legality of which there may be much doubt."

He had not once mentioned the word "congress," denying it a legal part in these proceedings, refusing to acknowledge its existence. Yet every assemblyman knew that what his excellency was proposing was in fact their outright defiance of the Continental Congress. He was proposing a separate peace between this single, small colony in the middle of America and the British Empire, in spite of the concerted acts and opinions of all the other colonies.

"You have now pointed out to you, gentlemen, two roads — one evidently leading to peace, happiness and a restoration of the public tranquillity — the other inevitably conducting you to anarchy, misery, and all the horrors of a civil war. Your wisdom, your prudence, your regard for the true interests of the people, will best be known when you have shown to which road you give the preference."

And then William Franklin concluded as he had once before, ten tumultuous years earlier during the Stamp Act crisis. "Every breach of the Constitution, whether it proceeds from the Crown or the people, is, in its effects, equally destructive to the rights of both.

It is a most infallible symptom of the dangerous state of liberty when the chief men of a free country show a greater regard to popularity than to their own judgment."[30]

No sooner had Franklin confidently left the council chamber at the end of this sobering speech than the radical leaders in the Assembly began arguments that lasted for days. They brought in William Livingston and Elias Boudinot, who urged the moderates not to stand alone but to adopt the measures of the Congress as their own and to do it quickly, to set an example for the neighboring New York Assembly, deadlocked in the same debate. *Do not stand alone*, they warned. *Act quickly* before the governor has time to dissolve the Assembly. The debate raged off and on for three weeks. Finally, the two houses voted. The upper house, the Council, its members for the most part personally appointed by Governor Franklin over the past decade, sided unanimously and openly with the governor: "Your Excellency may be assured that we will exert our utmost influence, both in our public and private capacities, to restore harmony."[31]

But the Assembly argued down to the last moment of its longest session in years. A majority of members finally folded under the pressure of what the governor denounced as radical "caballing." The Franklins' old political ally, the Quaker Assembly leader James Kinsey, tried to push through the governor's plan for a joint British-American legislature, but had to withdraw it under intense radical pressure. Furthermore, the radicals again would not allow any trace of dissent. Seven assemblymen had voted against complaining to the King. They were lectured on the need for unanimity. Again a vote was taken, and again, and again, until there were no nays. In a last-ditch effort to block the petition, and as a signal to the governor, to London, that slavishness to the wishes of the radicals was not total, the speaker of the Assembly refused to sign the petition. Again, the radicals forced the issue. The members would decide whether he was to sign or not. The vote was tied. The speaker cast the tie-breaking vote. He was not forced, this time, to put his name on a document complaining about the abridgment of civil liberties.[32]

Wavering a moment, the Assembly then indulged in some classic fence-straddling. Declaring themselves "His Majesty's loyal subjects," they nevertheless approved the grievances drawn up by the Continental Congress. To placate their governor, they sent the petition, not through the Congress, but separately to the King, asking for relief from grievances "under which your American subjects have been so long laboring . . . although the grievances do not immediately affect the people of this colony."[33] Angrily William refused to forward the petition. Instead, the Assembly sent it to Benjamin Franklin, its London agent, to present to Lord Dartmouth. William did send Lord Dartmouth a long letter damning these "demagogues of faction [who] oppose everything which may have even the remotest tendency to conciliate matters and omit nothing which may widen the breach."[34] And he named Livingston and the other radicals, in essence accusing them of treason. By mid-1774, as Lord Dartmouth's papers reveal, he was gathering evidence of treason by American radicals.

One month earlier, Lord Dartmouth and his fellow privy councillors had conferred with Crown lawyers and decided that the radicals were in open rebellion against the King and were therefore to be "treated as rebels and traitors."[35] Now, William took from his desk a royal order he had kept pigeonholed for four months. He had objected as loudly as any American to British regulations on smuggling. He had ignored the appeals of British customs officials for more rigid enforcement because he had considered the laws ill advised, unworkable, provocative. But now he took his own position as a British official seriously, as if for the first time. As captain general as well as governor, he ordered all customs officers and sheriffs to search out and seize all arms and ammunition the radicals smuggled into the colony. He would no longer shield New Jersey from royal rules. He would henceforth govern his colony despite the displeasure of the radicals.

All through the tense winter and into the spring of 1775, William heard nothing from his father. No reaction to Deborah's death, to the resulting confusion of family matters, to his own serious problems and proposals to the Crown. His financial plight had improved slightly, but his land speculations were in ruins. The Illinois grant had been comatose since his father's disgrace. Virginia had sent an army to seize the Forks of the Ohio as signs of war appeared everywhere.

William still clung to the hope that one day his father would return, if only so that Benjamin could see the "glorious public virtue," as he called it from afar, that every day beset William in America as he tried to keep the forces of discord from tearing his province apart. He was, his father would see, succeeding so far as anyone could in steering the narrow neutral course of peace with all parties. But his hope for compromise diminished drastically at dusk on April 25, 1775, when a weary rider whipped his panting horse down the Great Post Road and turned off at Elizabethtown. Pounding on the door of Elias Boudinot's house — Boudinot was the chairman of the committee of safety for Essex County — the exhausted courier handed the radical leader a countersigned letter from Massachusetts. Fighting had broken out in a little village just outside Boston.

14

THE TIMES ARE GREATLY ALTERED

May 1775

FOR THREE DAYS IN EARLY MAY OF 1775, AS IMPETUOUS young militiamen marched and countermarched across New Jersey, Governor Franklin had been preparing a "secret and confidential" report to Lord Dartmouth. At any hour he expected the arrival of a trusted dispatch rider who would spirit a pouch of letters and papers to a waiting warship in New York harbor. "The accounts we have received from Massachusetts Bay respecting the proceedings of the King's troops and the late engagement between them and the inhabitants," he wrote, "have occasioned such an alarm and excited so much uneasiness among the people throughout this and the other colonies that there is danger of their committing some outrageous violences."[1]

Ten days earlier, William had read a special broadside edition of the *Pennsylvania Gazette*. "I have taken up my pen," the Boston correspondent had begun offhandedly, "to inform you that, last night, about eleven o'clock, 1,000 of the best troops in a very secret manner embarked on board a number of boats at the bottom of the Commons and went up the Cambridge River and landed. . . . From thence they marched to Lexington, where they saw a number of men exercising. . . . They ordered them to disperse and immediately fired on them, killed eight men on the spot. This alarmed the country so that it seemed as if men came down from the clouds."[2]

Governor Franklin put the copy of the *Gazette* in the packet for Lord Dartmouth with the other, more secret documents, then turned his criticisms to the British military. The ministerial policy of disarming Massachusetts at gunpoint had been a singular piece of stupidity, coinciding as it had with Lord Dartmouth's attempts to reduce tensions before they reached the point of irreversible hostilities. The clash at Lexington had become inevitable so long as Lord North, the prime minister, ordered his field commander to use force if necessary and concurrently allowed the Colonial Office to negotiate toward a peaceful settlement.[3] For six months beginning in October of 1774, even as their delegates sought intercolonial support in the Continental Congress, the people of Massachusetts had stood sullenly by, watching while columns of redcoats marched out of Boston into surrounding towns to seize the arms and ammunition the local militia had stockpiled. Thousands of farmers turned out quietly, and openly drilled on town commons. It was amazing that fighting had not broken out sooner.

Coolly, Massachusetts radical leaders had taken advantage of the British commander's obvious lack of clear-cut marching orders. First, the radicals constituted themselves a provincial congress, in open opposition to the royal government; other colonies quickly followed suit. Then they formed a committee of safety and took control of existing militia companies. When pro-British officers would not take oaths to the new Continental Congress, they were forced to resign their commissions and new officers were elected who were faithful to the radicals. At the core of rebel fighting strength were crack units of minutemen, each unit seventy strong, who were especially trained to respond quickly to each fresh British alarm. One of these units, warned by radical leaders in Boston, had drawn up on Lexington green as the first British troops appeared in the pale dawn light, quick-stepping toward Concord to seize radical leaders and destroy their largest supply base before the rebellion could spread any further.

In the confused aftermath of the clash, few knew that the raid had taken place against the express orders of the one ministry leader still trying to avert bloodshed. The colonial secretary, Lord Dartmouth, had instructed General Thomas Gage, the military governor of Massachusetts, to round up and punish "the ringleaders of the riots at Boston" as well as the "destroyers of the tea," and prosecute them all in the colonial courts, thereby reversing Lord Hillsborough's provocative British policy of sending such miscreants to London for trial. It was a major concession on the ministry's part, aimed at reducing the sting of British punitive measures.[4] But Gage had disregarded the Privy Council's orders. Three hundred sixty-six men lay dead or wounded. The British had suffered galling casualties of more than twenty-five percent, which shook the British myth that American militia would not stand and fight against regular troops. Worse, one day of fighting had rendered all but useless the fragile attempts of Lord Dartmouth and William Franklin to introduce a plan for compromise into troubled America.

"It is greatly to be regretted that the late skirmish happened at the time it did," Governor Franklin wrote gloomily to Dartmouth. "It has, in its consequences, proved one of the most unlucky incidents that could have occurred in the present state of affairs. It will not only be a means of retarding, if not entirely defeating, the wishes and measures of His Majesty for a happy reconciliation, but will endanger the lives and properties of every officer of government in the King's colonies." Clearly, William was apprehensive about the risks of functioning any longer as a royal governor. "What renders the situation of American governors more difficult and dangerous," he went on, "is the publication of their correspondence with His Majesty's Ministers." And yet if a governor's report "does not [square] with ideas these men [the radicals] may afterwards choose to have entertained of their conduct, the governors are sure to be held up as enemies to their country and every undue means taken to make them objects of the people's resentment."[5]

By sending these intelligence reports to London, William saw himself carrying out a vital function of his commission as a royal governor. He was in charge of maintaining law and order in his colony: the radicals were, in British government eyes, engaged in a widespread general conspiracy against the constitutional, established and legitimate government. They were rebels, outlaws. It was William's uncomfortable duty as an American-born British official to gather and transmit evidence against them. But William still held out hope for settling the dispute between England and America somewhere short of state trials, executions and martial law. Most of all, he dreaded leaving the solution of the crisis to British military commanders.

To him, the reports he wrote to Lord Dartmouth provided the opportunity to state fairly the nature and scope of the conflict. He limited the blame to a handful of conspirators and to agitators on both sides. To rebel leaders trying to give the impression of invincible, unanimous American opposition to all British measures, any voice speaking out against that of the Congress had to be silenced. In their view, William's letters made him an enemy of American liberties, a spy. They were doing all in their power to stop his letters and, as soon as they dared act, to stop him.

In the sheaf of letters and newspapers in the mail of May 10, 1775, William found a letter in his father's handwriting. There had been no mail from him in more than six months, not since William had written that Deborah Franklin had died. The fact that this letter had come from Philadelphia was in itself a surprise. It was William's first hint that his father had finally slipped home from England.

Ten years. It seemed such an unnaturally long time to be away, for a father and son once so exceptionally close to be so far apart. Oceans of time and experiences had engulfed their increasingly conflicting careers, their interchanging places in American affairs. After thirteen years in office, William Franklin was now the senior royal governor in America: Benjamin, stripped of his post as deputy postmaster general, deprived of his income and his place in royal society, was returning to America an old man of controversy, despised by most British, a generation older than most Americans. Still, how good, indeed how urgent, it was for William to see his father, to talk with him at last.

"I don't understand it as any favour to me or to you" — Benjamin's hand was firm, large, obviously angry — "being continued in an office by which, with all your prudence you cannot avoid running behindhand if you live suitably to your station. While you are in it, I know you will execute it with fidelity to your master. But I think independence more honourable than any service, and that, in the state of American affairs, which from the present arbitrary measures is likely soon to take place, you will find yourself in no comfortable situation and perhaps wish you had soon disengaged yourself."[6]

What was this letter? The first words of a father whom he had not seen in so many years? Another diatribe about William's past-due bills? Or a hint that his father, as William dreaded, had decided in favor of independence and needed to know now, without further pleasantries, if his son had chosen unalterably which side he would take in the civil war now impending.

Whatever the implications, it was obvious from the tone of the terse note that Benjamin, too, had seen the latest *Pennsylvania Gazette,* and after his previous and ever-more-strident letters of advice to William to step down as governor, was firing off a furious reaction to his son's latest published attempt at peacemaking and continued adherence to the Crown. William, of course, had already made up his mind long ago. He must finish his dispatch to Lord Dartmouth. His father would know, soon enough, how he felt.

"Every day, new alarms are spread, which have a tendency to keep the minds of the people in a continual ferment, make them suspicious and prevent their paying attention to the dictates of sober reason and common sense." The day the news of combat at Lexington had raced south through New Jersey, he went on, hundreds of Essex County farmers had formed into militia companies. At Princeton, nearly half the students turned out to enlist, were issued arms, elected their own officers, paraded. In one day, a hundred young men in the small village formed ranks and prepared for war. And only the other day, when a rumor raced from town to town that a British man-of-war had come to Perth Amboy to seize the provincial treasury, thirty homespun militiamen followed their committee of safety fifteen miles over the wooded Middlesex hills to inspect and protect their tax money. They passed menacingly near the governor's mansion, "flags flying, fifes and drums playing," and did not march home until they were satisfied that the British had not landed.[7]

Just across the harbor, in fortified New York City, British officials were no safer. In the first week of May, radical leaders in New York and Connecticut had gathered 360 armed men and ridden on

Manhattan. After surrounding the Customs House, they had demanded its keys from the collector of the port and padlocked it, effectively closing the port of New York in retaliation for the closing of Boston harbor. Then, "with the pride of a dictator,"[8] as an eyewitness, one of William's friends, put it, the rebel leaders closed the polling places in the city and mobbed the governor's councillors, accusing them of inviting the King's troops into the city.

"I am convinced that matters are now carried so far," William told Lord Dartmouth, "that the Americans in general are disposed to run the risk of total ruin rather than suffer a taxation by any but their own immediate representatives." Moreover, he warned, there was little chance for a change in American opinion. Once again he expressed his worry for his own safety: "There is no defending ourselves. We must patiently submit. All legal authority and government seems to be drawing to an end here and that of the congresses, conventions, and committees establishing in their place."[9]

On April 25, the day William learned of the disastrous British foray to Lexington and Concord, Benjamin Franklin was still in the mid-Atlantic. The sea had been remarkably smooth, the winds following and strong, the ship making a near-record passage from England to Philadelphia. Since they had set sail from Plymouth, Benjamin had been cooling down from the rage that had fueled his final days in London. Even as ministry lawyers pondered his arrest, he had fumed when he heard a member of Parliament boast over dinner at Sir John Pringle's that, given a thousand British grenadiers, he would march from one end of America to the other, gelding all the males "partly by force and partly by a little coaxing."[10]

For more than a year since his discharge from the post office, Benjamin had endured abusive anti-American speeches in Parliament, in the homes of friends, in the newspapers. His firing had cast his affairs into turmoil, and his finances were in a shambles as well. His partnership in the *Pennsylvania Gazette* had long since expired. Because his income from the post office had been cut off and neither Massachusetts nor Georgia had paid him his agent's salary (Georgia was four years in arrears), he had been unable to pay the legal fees for his defense at the Cockpit hearing. He was also being sued in civil court for stealing the Hutchinson letters. Worse, he was all of four years behind in his rent to Mrs. Stevenson. Not that she was pressing him: in fact, she lent him money until he could return to America and settle accounts that had been left in confusion by Deborah's death. Without influence at court, without official business to keep him in England, Benjamin could not, at first, accept these facts.

When old friends, Quakers, insisted it was his moral responsibility to try to bring about reconciliation, he evidently saw a chance to redeem his tarnished reputation and emerge as the great British-American statesman. In November of 1774, nine months after his dismissal, he was asked by intermediaries who were supposedly working for Lord North just what, exactly, the Americans wanted. Although the British were apparently aware that Franklin had no authority to bargain for the Continental Congress or for any colony, they began a round of negotiations with him. He clearly was better acquainted with issues on both sides of the Atlantic than any other American in England.

Lord North, however, was not interested in any suggestions from Benjamin Franklin. After one lord demanded in a speech in Parliament why Franklin was still at large in London, Franklin discovered that the negotiations were being used as a device to keep him in England while Solicitor General Wedderburn and other Crown lawyers prepared warrants for his arrest.

Infuriated, Franklin broke off the talks and wrote one last bitter attack on the ministry, which he never sent. Only the advice of two friends in Parliament — that it would be considered an affront to the entire English nation and would cause "considerable danger to your person" and almost certain arrest for treason — made him refrain from firing off his parting shot. Thoroughly alarmed, he took Temple out of school and hastily prepared to board the first fast ship to Philadelphia. He left England on March 20, so quickly that he was unable to pack most of their clothes and books, and his scientific apparatus. Temple did not even have time for farewells. It would be six months before their things were sent after them. And poor Mrs. Stevenson did not know what to tell Temple's friends. Benjamin gave the wrong date for his departure and instructions to say that he would be back in a few months, after he settled his wife's affairs. But to his closest friend, the Dissenter-inventor Joseph Priestley, he confided, in tears, that he was sure he would never live to see London again.[11]

After ten years of lobbying for America in the mother country, Benjamin Franklin set his face and his mind toward home. He would make his private peace with his family, his remaining friends, the sons of his old friends already gone. He did not need this rotten old state, as he increasingly called his so recently beloved ancestral home. And neither did his son. He would make some provision for William, bring him around, prove to him that he had made every reasonable effort toward peace, but that now they must cut loose the draglines or be pulled under.

Once on shipboard, he began a letter to "Dear Son" that took him six weeks to write and consumed 196 pages of paper.[12] He set forth in detail his version of his recent attempts at reconciliation and his rejection by the British government. He was certain that when William was faced with the depth and weight of the narrative, he could not fail to be convinced of the rightness of the American cause. He would be turned into a formidable ally once again, especially now that he had doubtless resigned his post.

On the evening of May 5, 1775, Benjamin Franklin, Temple and the slave Peter were rowed ashore in Philadelphia. Next morning the news of their arrival flashed through the town, and before the day was out Franklin had been elected a member of the Pennsylvania delegation to the Second Continental Congress. That day, he wrote to a friend in Parliament his first reaction to the clashes at Lexington and Concord: "You will have heard before this reaches you of commencement of civil war. The end of it perhaps neither myself, nor you, who are much younger, will live to see. I find here all ranks of people in arms, disciplining themselves morning and evening, and am informed that the firmest union prevails throughout North America."[13] That day, also, he was placed at the head of the Philadelphia committee of safety. Once again, he was in control of the defense of the capital. It was the third day home before he dashed off his terse and angry note to William decrying William's continuance in office. By now, he was clearly becoming deeply disturbed by reports of his son's vigorous pro-British activities. Even his sister, a refugee from British-occupied Boston, had written him from Caty Ray's in Rhode Island that she had heard the "hored lies" about William.[14]

Benjamin sent off the brief, brusque note, but he did not post the long letter he had written William at sea. He wanted Galloway to see it, and maybe a few others; and Bache wanted to make a copy. Besides, William would come, soon enough, to fetch Temple. He would give it to him then.

In his seventieth year, Benjamin Franklin was two generations older than many delegates to the Second Continental Congress, a generation older than most. Thomas Jefferson, newly elected by the Virginia provincial congress, was thirty-two; George Washington, sitting near him, forty-three. Most of the men who had sat with Franklin in this room in the State House through a score of sessions of the Pennsylvania Assembly were dead of old age. Franklin found himself "a stranger among strangers." The old friends and allies who still lived were mostly opposed to these proceedings. The pacifist Quakers had grown to abhor all thought of war and the political processes that abetted it. The Quakers, the Moravians, the German pacifist sects and most of the Anglican merchants constituted a silent majority opposing nonimportation agreements and military resistance to the Crown. Only Benjamin Franklin, of all the "old party" leaders, was, by his presence, declaring openly for resistance.

Many influential radicals, in fact, did not trust Benjamin Franklin. Chief Justice William Smith of New York, for one, believed that Franklin was trying to engineer a peaceful settlement with opposition members of Parliament in order to get revenge for his humiliation in the Cockpit. "I have heard of Dr. Franklin's arrival with extreme anguish," Smith wrote his old confederate William Livingston. "I dread this event and his influence upon your councils. . . . It can never be Franklin's wish to preserve a set of men in office who have deplumed him and who detest him."[15]

Franklin's silence during his first six weeks in the Congress had even led Samuel Adams to suspect him of being a British spy. And when Franklin wrote to David Hartley, a member of Parliament, that he would provide him "authentic" intelligence on the state of British-American affairs and expected Hartley to reciprocate, the letter was probably read by Sam Adams before it left Philadelphia. The radicals now controlled the mails.[16]

Even as Benjamin took his place at the Pennsylvania table in the Congress, an element of religious persecution surfaced in several colonies: Presbyterian mobs besetting Anglicans. By May 1775, the leading Anglican divine in America was preparing to leave for England, heartily disgusted. The Reverend Thomas Bradbury Chandler had warned his coreligionists a year earlier in the pamphlet *What Think Ye of Congress Now?* that American actions would bring on British vengeance. For his candor he had been repeatedly threatened by the Sons of Liberty until he finally felt compelled to flee Elizabethtown in Essex County, New Jersey, with only a few "articles of necessary apparel, hiding from the turbulent faction which was determined to pay me a visit in the home of New York's attorney-general." He slipped aboard a British man-of-war at night and sailed for England. Joining him en route to exile were the president of King's College, a retired Royal Navy captain, and one of the leading landowners of New Jersey. All of them, in the Reverend Chandler's words, had been "proscribed for their loyalty."[17] In Massachusetts, mobs followed up the Lexington alarm by systematically driving three thousand Loyalists into Boston.

As a radical reign of terror accompanied the calling of the Second Continental Congress, as far south as South Carolina those loyal to Great Britain were leaving their homes. The Reverend John Bullman, curate of St. Michael's Church in Charleston, left for England after berating his charges from the pulpit. "We pry into our neighbor's secrets, that we may censure and find fault, and are exceedingly rash and precipitate in passing judgment. . . . Every idle [person] who cannot govern his own household or pay his debts presumes he is qualified to dictate how the State should be governed and to point out means to pay the debts of Great Britain. Every silly clown and every illiterate mechanic will take upon himself to censure the conduct of his prince or governor."[18]

While many loyal subjects of the King shared Bullman's view, it gave a distorted image of the men who called themselves the Patriots and had traveled to Philadelphia to meet in the Congress, and when Bullman's description was forwarded to Lord Dartmouth, it only added to the British misunderstanding of the nature of the contest. There were, to be sure, a few men of marginal literacy in the tall Windsor chairs around each delegation's green-covered table in the State House. One had been a shoemaker and two were plain farmers. And there certainly were some firebrands whose rhetoric had incited to violence. But the great majority of the delegates were men of substance and education who had prevented the quarrel between Britain and the American colonies from degenerating entirely into a class revolution. In fact, some of the richest men in America participated in the Second Continental Congress, including nine wealthy plantation owners and five rich merchants — all men of hereditary landed and mercantile fortunes. There was a country doctor, a former governor, a law professor and a judge. The greatest proportion were men trained in the law, men who had served in legislatures and on high courts, men who had helped write the charters of hospitals, colleges and counties, men who were not intimidated by the idea of writing a new constitution for a new government. Five were graduates of the Inns of Court. Among the Yale graduates was one who had led his class all four years; others were graduated from Cambridge, Harvard, Pennsylvania, William and Mary. And one was a self-educated retired printer from Pennsylvania.

There were, to be sure, men with old scores to settle. Samuel Adams, reputedly the man who had stirred up the Boston Tea Party and many other mob activities, had seen his father's fortune destroyed by British currency regulations. But the motives of most of the delegates were more complicated than revenge. Some were the second sons of second sons, raised in hereditary comfort and then stripped of it by British laws of primogeniture and entail: they sought reform. Others were successful southern planters whose methods of cultivation required huge amounts of fresh acreage in order to raise tobacco and corn and cotton, crops that quickly wore out the soil. By cutting off expansion to the west, British land policies promised to make the planters' sons poor. They were fed up with British factors who manipulated prices and paid them bottom dollar for their crops, then charged them top prices for goods that were often too shoddy to sell to Englishmen.

Men who had been educated for the Puritan ministry saw the specter of Roman Catholic power under British military rule in Canada and a costly, haughty Anglican episcopacy growing within the colonies: the Catholic Stuarts and their persecutions were only two generations away in memory. Merchants who had traded freely with England found that with the enforcement of the customs laws it was more difficult for them to earn a living, particularly when the American colonies were forbidden to manufacture so many kinds of goods and wares. Every American could see how British regulations and taxes had proliferated since George III, with his notions of an imperial monarchy, had come to power. Many could no longer abide the roughshod treatment of a country which not only needed them, but treated them haughtily, as if they were a conquered people.

Benjamin Franklin was silent during the first weeks of the congressional session. It seemed to colleagues that he was more a spectator than a participant. Even at home he felt himself a stranger among strangers. His daughter was his only link to his past home-life. Fortunately, since Sally looked so much like Deborah and could cook and sew and receive guests, Franklin eventually settled in. The oldest Franklin chuckled at the two youngest, when his grandsons shouldered toy muskets and mimicked militiamen drilling beyond the tenant houses on Market Street.[19]

He soon became intimate with one of the former occupants of these houses, which Deborah had so long rented out to support the family. Charles Thomson had been a young Ulster immigrant when Benjamin had taken him in, found him a teaching job at the Academy of Philadelphia and a cheap place to live. The young man and William had become friends. Together they had kept the Junto debating society and the American Philosophical Society alive while the elder Franklin was abroad and had run political errands for him. But in recent years Thomson had outgrown the house and the chores. He had married a rich widow and had earned a justifiable reputation as the "Sam Adams of Philadelphia." At the time of the Stamp Act, when Benjamin lamented that the "sun of liberty is set," that it was "time to light the lamps of industry and economy," Thomson replied characteristically: "We shall light torches of a different sort."[20] By 1772, his Presbyterian party had trounced Benjamin Franklin's and Joseph Galloway's "old party" at the polls and ousted it from power.

In 1774 he and Bache organized the local protests against the British blockade of Boston (suitably announced by Paul Revere, who had raced to Philadelphia with the news of the British intent). Typically, Thomson worked so feverishly on that occasion, sleeping only one hour out of two days and nights, that as he stood on a table in a crowded waterfront coffeehouse haranguing three hundred partisans, he quite dramatically passed out. His next feat, later that year, was to protest Governor John Penn's refusal to call a congress of all the colonies. Thomson turned out more than eight thousand of the city's twenty-three thousand people for a mass protest on the State House lawn. And it was no doubt Thomson who sent the noose and the note to Galloway.

Understandably, Benjamin Franklin spent much time in his first weeks back in America cultivating the company of this young leader who claimed the support of the workmen, the mechanics, the artisans, the sailors. Ironically, the man who had destroyed Franklin's old power base now offered to share his new party, the radicals, freely with Franklin. But Benjamin did not commit himself. He could easily see that the radicals were still very much in the minority. New York was holding out stoutly, as were Maryland, Delaware and New Jersey, for neutrality. This was Boston's problem, not theirs: why risk British invasion? Benjamin realized it would be impossible to resist the British unless the colonies could be unified. More and more, he uttered the line that became his watchword: "We must hang together or we most assuredly will hang separately."[21]

His strategy presented itself naturally. Two old Franklin lieutenants held the keys to the control of the Quaker majority in Pennsylvania, New Jersey and Delaware, needed to keep the radicals in the northern and southern colonies in close communication. Even after Galloway's defeat in Philadelphia politics and despite his intimidation into retirement, he was still the manager of Quaker power. He was married to the daughter of the richest merchant in Pennsylvania, and he was firmly in control of Bucks County, a Quaker stronghold that had disproportionate control over the Quaker arm of the Assembly. On the day after Franklin's return to

America, Galloway, who had acted as the whip hand in the Assembly through all the years of Franklin's absence, wrote a cordial note of welcome and offered to send his carriage whenever Franklin wanted to come into the country and talk politics at Galloway's estate, Trevose, in Bucks County.

The second man Franklin obviously needed was his own son. The greatest coup he could deliver to consolidate his power in the divided Congress was the conversion of William, who had become an embarrassing reminder of royal power. In his time-honored way, Benjamin went about accomplishing a number of important aims with a single stroke. He would meet William and Galloway on the neutral ground of Trevose. He would present to them the history of his efforts in England as the preface to declaring his plan of action in America. Once William heard the complete details, he would surely come around.

Father and son had met briefly in early May, when William rode to Philadelphia to pick up Temple and take him to Perth Amboy. Benjamin Franklin had changed. William saw that as soon as he laid eyes on his father. The old man's teeth were gone, his cheeks were hollowed, his heavy-rimmed spectacles more prominent, his clothes darker, plainer. His barrel chest had lost some of its roundness. Even so, there must have still been power in his handshake.

The meeting was not a success. Benjamin was still smarting from his son's criticism of his treatment of Deborah, and to arrive home and find that William had stubbornly refused to heed his advice and resign as governor had affronted him further. He refused to discuss politics at all. Instead, they focused on Temple, a slim boy of fifteen, who had been an infant when his father had last seen him. Their talk concerned Temple's schooling, which they had long disagreed about in their correspondence. Benjamin had come to like the boy more at each vacation, and he agreed with William that it would be useful for Temple to be trained in the law so that he could assume the status of gentleman.

Since the age of five, Temple had attended one of the more controversial British boarding schools, Elphinstone, run by William Strahan's brother-in-law. The Elphinstone plan of education offered a shift away from the classics, instead meting out a diet of writing and mathematics — the practical fare given Benjamin after his own father removed him from the Boston grammar school. Elphinstone had its critics. The Reverend Alexander Carlyle, who had discoursed broadly with William during the Franklins' Edinburgh tour, denounced it as a "Jacobite seminary where the mind and body both starve." But Benjamin favored the school. Besides, it cost only twenty-five pounds a year for room, board and tuition. Even when William was running in arrears, he could see to it that Temple had drawing, riding, dancing and fencing lessons in addition. Apparently, money had much to do with William's early acquiescence in the choice of the school, but as his views diverged more and more from his father's he came to share Dr. Samuel Johnson's verdict on Elphinstone: "I would not put a boy to him whom I intended for a man of learning, but for the sons of citizens who are to learn a little, get good morals and then go to trade, he may do very well." Benjamin and William had finally agreed to keep him there.

That is where agreement ended. Benjamin and William had conflicting definitions of "gentleman." As usual, Benjamin wielded his power of the purse. William wanted his son prepared at Eton and Oxford before studying law at William's alma mater, the Inns of Court. In letter after letter, Benjamin challenged William's plans on the grounds that he could not even keep up the tuition payments for Elphinstone, which cost only one-eighth the tuition at Eton. Never once did Benjamin offer to share the expense, only the control.

He meddled again when William, exasperated, asked him to bring Temple to America. As second choice he would enroll Temple in King's College in New York. Benjamin opposed the new Anglican-influenced college. As a trustee of the more austere Academy of Philadelphia, he thought Temple should attend this less expensive school, which was only a few blocks from the Franklin house, where he could board. Could William afford otherwise while he was so far behindhand in his account with his father? He could not.

And so, after the civilities of their brief reunion marked the end of eleven years of separation, the Franklins settled into a frosty tug-of-war over Temple. Benjamin was throwing his weight on the side of money and politics: living in New York cost more than living with him; King's College was notoriously high Tory. And William, just as certainly, wanted his son at *his* side, as *his* companion, away from the influence of the Congress, away from his father's radical friends.

As usual when money was involved, William lost. He could not pay his debts to his father, as his father knew, until his lands and his houses were sold. Benjamin had been dunning creditors ever since his return, as his ledgers show, and his first note to his son makes clear that he made no exception of William. What else could William do but cede on Temple's schooling until he could afford to send him to England himself? Temple would live with Benjamin during the winter, with William at Perth Amboy in the summer, starting now.

Was Temple ready? He had only a few trunks and his pet Pekingese, Pompey. And then they were off to present Temple to his childless stepmother. It was a tense ride back through the troop-filled streets. Hostile faces no doubt turned toward them often as they rattled by, oblivious, talking. They had so much to talk about.[22]

Governor Franklin was, he well knew, engaged in the most urgent battle of his political career. In July 1774, radical committees from every county in New Jersey followed Massachusetts' lead in convening a revolutionary provincial congress. He countered by calling a special session of the Assembly. He still believed there were enough reasonable men sufficiently alarmed by the shocking course of events to insist on reconciliation, but was apparently unaware that, by his own indiscretion, by writing candidly to his friend Galloway in Pennsylvania of the behavior of the New Jersey lawmakers during the past stalemated session, he had lost vital political support. He had frankly described the Quaker leader Kinsey as "weak enough" to be the "tool" of Livingston's radical junto. This same letter moreover revealed the depth of William's opposition to the radical-dominated Congress, especially "to the Whigs, as they call themselves." Further, he praised Galloway for upholding "the supreme power of Parliament over all the Dominions." Unfortunately for both men, William's letter was not delivered to Galloway for two weeks. Intercepted, it was diverted to Philadelphia, copied, then sent on its way. William's blunt appraisal of Kinsey's weakness lost him the friendship of many New Jersey Quakers and further alienated his father, who evidently read the intercepted letter. By the time Governor Franklin convened the Assembly in Burlington, that revolutionary May, the radical faction was so confident they had gained the upper hand that they promptly submitted "a string of furious resolves" against him. Worsening William's position was the timing of the Assembly session. It closely followed the publication in American newspapers of purported excerpts of another of his confidential letters, this one to Lord Dartmouth, in which William named radical leaders. It had apparently been copied by a Colonial Office clerk at Whitehall, sold to Almon's *Parliamentary Register,* printed in London, then reprinted in American newspapers with alterations by the radicals out to discredit him.[23]

Yet William felt more than a match for his radical opponents. The reason for his renewed self-assurance was the arrival of the first solid British proposal for reconciliation. William realized, when the governors of neighboring colonies refused to call their assemblies in the worsening crisis, that he was the only royal governor still willing to risk radical wrath by openly taking the side of the Crown. Penn had faded in Pennsylvania; the governor of New York refused to try.

The British proposal had stunned Americans loyal to England by going farther toward meeting radical demands than any radical would have dared to hope only a few years earlier. While Parliament again declared its right to tax America, the plan advocated by Prime Minister North promised to "forbear" taxing any colony that would contribute its fair share of the cost of imperial defense. The North plan would have earmarked customs revenues collected in any province to pay the military, judicial and civil government costs for that province. The money would be collected by the British, remitted to London, and there credited against that colony's account.

In effect, the North plan would have been a clear-cut victory for both sides. Parliament could have satisfied its clamorous supremacists by maintaining nominal authority and America could have escaped taxes on such imported English goods as tea, thereby returning British-American trade relations to their status before George III. But the times had changed too rapidly in the two years Lord North had taken to meet the demands of the Boston town meeting. Too many lives had been lost on the road to Lexington, too much national pride was at stake for instant American approval of even the most generous British concessions, as William discovered when he laid the North plan before the New Jersey Assembly for its first official American reading.

Every American legislator had no doubt seen the North scheme in the newspapers by this time, but "scarcely any have seen it in its proper light," William told them. He had received the customary secret instructions from the Colonial Office along with the proposal, and while he was not at liberty to reveal them, he could not think of any more "essential service" he could render his countrymen than to attempt to explain and elucidate Parliament's position so that "you and the good people you represent will be enabled to judge for yourselves how far you ought or ought not to acquiesce."[24]

William looked around the crowded Assembly chambers. He saw lawyers, merchants, clergymen, farmers, all but a handful of them part-time politicians with an extremely narrow knowledge of the world outside the province. He saw confusion, concern, indecision; he saw worry, resentment, open hostility. He spoke simply but without condescension to them now, saddened by the knowledge that many of them were unsophisticated, peaceful men who only wanted to mind their acres and keep government expenses down, men who must feel trapped now between the awesome might of the British and well-organized radical mobs only a few miles away across the Delaware River in Philadelphia. He was somber as he continued his carefully prepared speech, and even his bitterest critics in the assemblage must have been disarmed momentarily by his open sympathy for their dilemma, his fairness to both sides. William Franklin later admitted that at this moment he saw both sides all too clearly to be fully in accord with either party, either extreme, but this day he rose to represent the ancient English concept of King-in-Parliament, the heart of the English constitution, by which all Americans were still ruled.

The King wanted reconciliation "by every means," but "without prejudice to the just authority of Parliament, which His Majesty will never suffer to be violated." The Parliament *is* the people, *all* the people of the entire empire. The King obviously believed that his offer to withhold taxing obedient colonies "forever" was a firm step toward easing the crisis. His Majesty could not conceive that a civil war would be allowed to tear asunder a great empire made up of men of the same stock and language and common heritage over the right of some men to tax themselves to pay for their own government.

Clearly, the King, his ministers and the majority of Parliament considered their American subjects "unfortunately misled" by a handful of riot-rousing, treasonous radicals, William Franklin declared, looking out over a room half filled with such men. And who should his subjects believe in this unprecedented crisis, these self-appointed rulers of questionable wisdom, or the King of England, of all the British Empire supported by the Lords and the Commons. Furthermore, what of their sense of duty? Could any of them ever forget "the benefits they have received from the parent state"? Could they ever forget "the expense of blood and treasure" that they owed England for "that security which hath raised them to their present state of opulence and importance"?

Little more than ten years earlier, the colonies had cowered in the bloody-handed shadow of warlike French Canada and its perennial Indian raiders until British money and arms poured into this and every other colony to help crush the common enemy. Could they now so ungratefully cast off their benefactor, now refuse to pay for their own share of the burden of upholding *their* empire? "Justice requires that you should, in return, contribute according to your respective abilities to the *common defense* of all the empire."

And what, after all, was their alternative?

"I must tell you, His Majesty considers himself bound *by every tie* to exert those means the Constitution has placed in his hands for preserving that Constitution *entire,* and to resist with firmness every attempt to violate the rights of Parliament, to distress and obstruct the lawful commerce of his subjects, or to encourage in the colonies ideas of independence." But there *was* "no design of oppression." Even the King's Privy Council had decided that the hot-headed General Gage (the father-in-law of one of the councillors in the room) had gone too far and must be recalled to England.

"We have now, thank Heaven, a happy opportunity of getting entirely rid of this unnatural contest" by merely doing what every reasonable man would concede was "our indispensable duty." Once again, William looked into the faces turned upward toward him, then concluded sadly but emphatically. "There is so much truth in the observation that mankind generally act, not according to right, but according to present interest, and most, according to present passion. There are no difficulties but what may be easily surmounted, if men come together, *sincerely* disposed to serve their country."

And, in case any of them missed the meaning of his appeal, he added wisely his personal offer of peace: "Who has been most in the right or most in the wrong can never be satisfactorily decided. Many things will ever happen in the course of a long, continued dispute which good men of both parties must reflect on with pain, and wish to have buried in oblivion. In the present situation, we should only look *forward*, and endeavor to fall on some expedient that may avert impending danger."[25]

To the thumping of canes, the governor left the Assembly to its deliberations. Once again, he thought he had cause for hope. But he was almost certainly unprepared for the resounding rebuff the radical faction managed to inflict on him over the next three days. Brushing aside all William's attempts to rouse the moderates and Quakers, the Livingston faction dismissed the British tax allocation plan as "nothing new," and instead succeeded in focusing attention on the governor's remark implying that they were acting from self-interest and passion. For three days, charges and counter-charges filled the chamber as supporters of the Congress overrode the supporters of William Franklin and the royal government he represented.

In his final message of the emergency session, William Franklin wearily resolved to allow the radicals to take the question out of the Assembly's hands. "I have done my duty," he told them plainly. "The times are greatly altered. I lost no time laying before you propositions for an amicable accommodation." And he was not at all impressed by their argument that there was nothing new in the North Plan. The radicals were obviously stalling, unwilling and afraid to discuss the King's peace offer seriously until the Second Continental Congress considered it. Finally, William could not resist upbraiding the moderate legislators for their impotence. He was now, he indicated, embarrassed that he had brought the King's peace proposal to them first among all American representative governments. "I could have no suspicion that you did not think yourselves competent to the business," and needed "to wait the determination of another body. It was but last session that you assured me you would not 'suffer any of the rights vested in you to be wrested out of your hands by any person or persons whatsoever.' I shall forbear to point out your inconsistency."[26]

There was no point in going on. William gathered his papers and left old friends and new enemies to pack off their ever unanimous petitions to the Congress. He knew by now that, besides insulting him, the Assembly had once again been pressured by the radicals into stamping out all hint of dissent from its proceedings, from the radical point of view. As William promptly reported to Lord Dartmouth, the speaker of the Assembly, Cortlandt Skinner, was not allowed to record his dissent to the radicals' decision to refer the King's petition to the Continental Congress on the minutes of the Assembly.[27]

The next day, as he prepared to go to Philadelphia to rally opposition to the radical party, William received a letter from a friendly New Jersey delegate to the Congress who informed him that, despite his failure to secure a direct negotiation between his province and the Crown, William had succeeded "too well" in raising the doubts of many fence-sitting members. Not surprisingly, the "violent party" in the Congress was terribly angry at him, the letter warned, for sponsoring the North plan, for forcing it officially into public view where it could not be expunged or any longer ignored. It would, of course, be unwise for William to come to Philadelphia under the circumstances.[28]

Governor Franklin's efforts to keep the peace in the chaotic months between the outburst of violence at Lexington and Concord and the first full-scale battle at Breed's Hill have been all but totally obscured, undoubtedly because the Franklins, like many other prominent Americans, kept their thoughts and actions in late May of 1775 more carefully concealed than at any other period of their lives. But their conversations must have often turned to the terrible choice between loyalty to King and ancestral homeland and loyalty to a new, illegal, untried and unfounded collection of colonies with no head and only the vaguest outline of a form. In the eyes of the British government, the only established authority over America, the issue was a question of treason. Few men contemplating the hangman take notes that can be used later as fatal evidence. The memory of hangings, drawings and quarterings after the last Scottish uprising only thirty years earlier was still all too vivid for tens of thousands of immigrant English and Scottish Americans. For the Franklins, the sight of rebel skulls moldering on spikes, providing nests for starlings, atop the Temple Bar entrance to London was even more recent, more graphic. It was a time of making painful choices that involved not only physical survival and financial uncertainty but also that most frustrating of decisions, family loyalty. Old allegiances of all sorts were breaking down. Furtive conversations, hasty alliances made necessary by the runaway momentum of revolution, led to suspicions, doubts, and animosities that lingered for a lifetime.

Still, there were men fighting for peace. The atmosphere of secrecy and intrigue that William Franklin encountered when he arrived in Philadelphia on May 21 radiated from the Second Continental Congress, which met behind closed doors and windows in the State House. Once, William had been in constant attendance here; now, he was more than unwelcome: he was barred from entrance. All members of the Congress had sworn to keep the proceedings secret. It was a promise Benjamin Franklin, who preached the importance of a united, anonymous front, scrupulously observed. Not only were the debates locked up inside the airless, horsefly-infested chamber — if publicized, they might have revealed the extent of internal discord — but comments on after-hours meetings were to be avoided. Most congressmen realized the potential price of loose tongues, telltale letters. A few, nonetheless, kept diaries as well as draft copies of their speeches, notes and memoranda, which are only now, more than two hundred years later, being published. Combined with the often misleadingly terse official congressional journal, heavily edited and published a quarter century later by the secretary, Charles Thomson, it is possible to trace through them the crucial activities and arguments of rival leaders.

That William Franklin actually risked the wrath of radical leaders by driving into Philadelphia to press Lord North's peace plan privately on the more moderate congressmen is verified by an entry in the diary kept by a Connecticut delegate. Silas Deane's notations for May 23 show that a vehement debate went on all that day on the question of opening peace negotiations with England. More delegates spoke out against reconciliation than in favor of peace, Deane reported. There is a gap in his reporting before he abruptly ends his entry: "finally, at five o'clock, the motion passed agreeable to all."[29]

In his diary, Deane indicates that John Dickinson of Pennsylvania presented a carefully reasoned strategy to satisfy both hawks and doves. A rich Philadelphia lawyer who dressed in lavish Quaker-gray silks and white hose, Dickinson was known throughout the empire as "the Farmer," the author of the first major published assertion that Parliament had no right to tax America in any form. A leader of the Penn proprietary group and an old and bitter enemy of the Franklins, he had joined forces in the Congress with the conservative New York lawyer John Jay to urge the Congress to petition publicly for peace as a cloak to hide an undeclared policy of rapid military preparation.

The unanimous vote to bear the olive branch with one hand and carry a concealed sword with the other had been made virtually inevitable by a dispatch rushed to the Congress only four days earlier. "In the name of the Great Jehovah and the Continental Congress," a small raiding party led jointly by Ethan Allen and Benedict Arnold had seized Fort Ticonderoga, the key British stronghold on the New York–Canadian frontier. As another delegate wrote home to his brother in Virginia, the attack had not been authorized by the Congress and was certain to arouse a British invasion of New York from Canada.[30] Thousands of British redcoats had died to wrest Ticonderoga from the French in two wars. The day William arrived in Philadelphia, the Congress was drawing up a secret letter of advice to New York radical leaders, urging them "to make provision for carrying their women and children into the countryside and to remove their warlike stores" from Manhattan before the arrival of British troops. At least thirty thousand Americans were now under arms between Boston and Philadelphia. There was no more time to decide for war or peace. While the Congress faced the prospect of war, its members appointed a committee, which included Colonel George Washington, "to consider what posts are necessary to be occupied in New York" and passed an after-the-fact resolution to justify the seizure of Fort Ticonderoga. The fort had to be taken because "there is indisputable evidence that a design is formed by the British ministry of making a cruel invasion from the province of Quebec." Just what evidence there was never has been made clear. The congressional resolution stated that, at the very least, "some inhabitants residing in the vicinity of Fort Ticonderoga" were nervous enough to take the fort away from its sleeping garrison, apparently not worrying for a moment that they had alienated *their* nervous neighbors to the north, the Canadians.[31]

Some moderate congressmen were deeply troubled by these rapid developments, by the choices they were hurriedly being forced to make. In his personal notes prepared before his longest speech advocating simultaneous peace overtures and armaments, John Dickinson recorded the misgiving of Americans that the King's ministers, too, might be capable of deception. Lord North's motion might have had "two objects." The first was "to divide." The other, "to render the measures of administration still more popular in that kingdom by holding up to the people there the appearance of humanity, condescension, forbearance and I know not what other gentle, generous virtues." Dickinson reflected the agony of every thoughtful man when he foresaw the hazard of not at least talking peace, of not taking the North Plan as seriously as William Franklin had. "While Great Britain is silent from notions of dignity and America from notions of firmness, each rushes on, blind with their respective passions, to the destruction of the other."[32]

A majority of congressmen, if not all of the delegates as Thomson recorded, shared Dickinson's ambivalence that day, and whether it was through prudence or calculated duplicity, the Congress voted for war and peace, rekindling the hopes for peace of moderates such as William Franklin, who almost certainly knew of the congressional mood by dinnertime that evening. As Silas Deane confided to his diary, that night he and other key members of the Congress "dined with Mr. Moore, Governor Franklin, etc."[33] Deane's et cetera may well have included both Dickinson and Governor John Penn, who had volunteered to take an olive-branch petition to the King. The "Mr. Moore" of Deane's diary was probably Charles Moore, a member of the Pennsylvania Council, a rich and outspoken leader of the proprietary party, and the son of a man who, for at least a quarter century, had been an enemy of the Franklins. That William would dine with him and with Dickinson at such a moment indicates that he had decided to go around his father, to join forces with the Penns in his quest for peace, a fact he publicly revealed in hearings in England fully ten years later.

As a member of the committee of safety in charge of gathering intelligence in the city, Benjamin Franklin would know almost instantly of his son's dinner engagement. What must have enraged him was the fact that this Mr. Moore was an in-law and a political ally of Benjamin's longtime nemesis, the Reverend William Smith, president of the Academy of Philadelphia. That William had not only openly advocated negotiating with his father's enemies in the British ministry but now was pressing his case with old personal enemies in Philadelphia was enough to compel the elder Franklin to break his guarded silence and finally confront his son. On May 24 he evidently decided that they must meet. But it must be on neutral ground. William later wrote that his father was embarrassed to meet him in Philadelphia. So Benjamin finally accepted Joseph Galloway's three-week-old invitation to meet William twenty miles away from the Congress at Galloway's country seat in Bucks County.

15

A MATTER
OF PUNCTILIO

May–June 1775

I N ALL BRITISH AMERICA, THERE WERE FEW MORE ELEGANT
expressions of hereditary wealth and entrenched political power
than Trevose, the Bucks County estate of Joseph and Grace Galloway. A chestnut-lined lane circled in front of a fieldstone manor
house five windows wide, which was flanked by two-story dining
and stable wings connected to it by colonnades. From this hilltop
retreat, the Galloways surveyed a domain that reached nearly five
miles down Neshaminy Creek through orchards with thousands of
apple trees, past herds of fattening livestock, to one of the most
important ironworks in colonial America. The Durham Iron
Works produced a new fortune almost every year. Hundreds of
barges carried its pigs of iron down the Delaware for shipment to
England.

The estate was the creation of Grace Galloway's grandfather,
Joseph Growden, who had been one of Penn's privy councillors.
The Growden family had gradually come to dominate Quaker politics in Pennsylvania. Before he died, Joseph Growden became
speaker of the Assembly as well as serving on the provincial supreme court. He passed his political mantle to his son, then to his
son-in-law, both of whom became speakers of the Assembly. His
granddaughter Grace eventually inherited the Growden fortune
and turned it over to her lawyer-husband, Joseph Galloway.

After the last Indian invasion, the Quakers had chosen to withdraw from the Assembly rather than deny their consciences further by voting for war. They put their considerable power, including voter registration in the most heavily represented counties in Pennsylvania, into the hands of a few trustees, chiefly Galloway and Franklin. Franklin more than ever needed Galloway and his Quaker constituency: without Quaker gold, Quaker crops, Quaker iron, without the Quakers themselves and their pacifist allies, half a million of the richest and most respectable Americans would be lost to the revolution and to the new nation. He needed to convince both Galloway and William that Americans must rise together and shake off the yoke of British rule or become slaves.

William's mood was more difficult for him to gauge. New Jersey radicals had formed an extralegal provincial congress, which was attempting to collect taxes and train troops, even while the legitimate New Jersey Assembly was preparing to convene. Because many moderates had been elected to the provincial congress, its proceedings were deadlocked and its delegates to the Continental Congress were gathering support for reconciliation with England. By late May 1775, when William rode from Burlington to Trevose for the meeting with Galloway and his father, there was even a possibility that he could lead a drive to have New Jersey secede from the Continental Congress and negotiate a separate peace with Parliament. Without the Middle Colonies, New England and the South would find war virtually impossible. After his talks with conservative leaders in Philadelphia, William surely was aware of the growing strength of his position.

Both younger men, Benjamin knew, were polished orators, trained debaters. He himself was a poor speaker, and he always preferred to compose his thoughts, write them down before important meetings. There could be few more important meetings than this. Unfortunately, if he did write down the points he wanted to make, they have not survived. Most certainly, though, he brought along the lengthy, undelivered letter he had written to William on shipboard. From his viewpoint it said everything.

For William, the meeting was critical in another sense. He must learn his father's intentions. He must try to dissuade him from the self-destructive course he was almost certainly pursuing. William no doubt had carefully run over the arguments he must now make with his father, as carefully as any legal brief, as any political speech. There was so much he could tell his father about the motives of the men usurping power all around him. If only they could come together, bury the past for a few hours, listen to each other and forget who was right and who was wrong. So much depended on this evening, and he must have sensed it.

There is no complete record of what was said that night. Galloway subsequently told Thomas Hutchinson that Benjamin argued long and late with him and with William. The editors of the papers of Benjamin Franklin at Yale University have recently concluded that Benjamin read aloud about three quarters of his 196-page letter to William that he had written on his homeward voyage, thereby giving his listeners his version of the London negotiations. If and when William argued with him can only be conjectured, but it is known that they quarreled at this time, that father and son parted bitterly, and that months passed before they had any further contact. Furthermore, what William said and how he felt on the exact same issues immediately before and after the confrontation at Trevose are known from his letters and speeches. It is possible, therefore, to reconstruct the events of that climactic evening.

At the outset, Benjamin said to his old political lieutenant, "Well, Mr. Galloway, you are really of the mind that I ought to promote a reconciliation?"[1] Unfortunately, Galloway did not record his response. He and William no doubt wanted to take the field, to thrust their plans of union upon Benjamin, but both would have deferred to the older man. Also, both were careful lawyers who knew how to wait patiently, to listen for the holes in the opposing argument.

In the autumn of 1774, during the recess of the last Parliament, Benjamin began, the opposition to the North ministry saw in the "violence" of anti-American measures such as the Stamp Act riots and the Boston Tea Party "a hazard of dismembering, weakening and perhaps ruining the British Empire" unless a coalition brought down Lord North. "I took some pains to promote this," Benjamin confided. "I beseeched and conjured [members of Parliament] most eagerly not to suffer, by their little misunderstandings, so glorious a fabric to be demolished by these blunders." The opposition, he noted, had "frequent doubts of the firmness and unanimity of America." He then dropped this subject and hurried on: "From the time of the affront given me at the [Privy] Council, I had never attended the levee of any minister. I made no justification of myself. . . . I made no return of the injury by abusing my adversaries, but held a cool sullen silence, reserving myself to some future opportunity. Now and then, I heard it said that the reasonable part of the administration were ashamed of the treatment they had given me. . . .[2]

"They began, as it seems, to think of making use of me. . . . But it was too humiliating to think of applying to me openly." (As a matter of record he was consulted by ministry intermediaries both high and low late in 1774 and early in 1775, in a series of secret negotiations that William and his friends could not have known about. To William, a high royal official, the involvement of his father, recently dismissed by the British government, could only have seemed far-fetched.)

"When I came to England in 1757," Benjamin continued — and must have looked at William as he did so — "you may remember I made several attempts to be introduced to Lord Chatham [Pitt, who had since been elevated to the peerage], but without success. He was then too great a man. I afterwards considered Mr. Pitt as an inaccessible. I admired him at a distance."[3] (William no doubt recollected otherwise. His father had been rebuffed by Pitt and had proceeded to court Pitt's enemy Lord Bute.)

Late in August of 1774, Benjamin went on, a mutual friend of his and Chatham's told him that Chatham wanted to see him. The next morning "that truly great man Lord Chatham received me with abundance of civility." His lordship asked about American affairs, "spoke feelingly about the severity of the late laws" against the Bostonians. Benjamin said he had warned Chatham that "countries remote from the seat and eye of government" had always "been oppressed by bad governors."[4] Benjamin had never concealed his distaste, even disgust, at his son's chosen career, much less displayed family loyalty in the matter. Here he showed himself to be more impervious to his son's feelings than ever.

Much of what he was reading had been argued by the two

Franklins before. So much of it was what Benjamin considered William's "wrong politics"; yet he had been careful to inject a tantalizing lure by reviving the western land schemes — if only Lord Chatham and his party were restored to power. Indeed, he reported, Chatham liked the idea of "extending our western empire, adding province to province as far as the South Sea." Even here Benjamin had come to consider himself the author of the land venture: Chatham favored "my idea of extending the empire"; it was "worthy of a great, benevolent and comprehensive mind."[5]

Then Benjamin quickly dropped the subject: Chatham had also worried that America "aimed at setting up for itself as an independent state." (So even Chatham, though a leader of the opposition in Parliament, shared the ministry's fear that all the petitions and grievances were only justifications for independence, a mask over the radicals' true intentions.) Benjamin had kept his own mask firmly in place at Lord Chatham's: "I assured him that, having more than once traveled from one end of the continent to the other and kept a variety of company, eating and drinking and conversing with them freely, I never had heard in any conversation from any person drunk or sober the least expression of a wish for a separation."[6]

Could William believe his ears? Had his father managed to say this to his lordship straight-faced? Obviously, he had. The only possible explanation was that Benjamin had been away from America so long that it had seemed the truth to him at the moment. Had he not, in his letters disapproving of William's and Galloway's plans of union, called continued ties between Britain and America "coupling and binding together the dead with the living"? But Benjamin apparently did not notice the obvious contradiction. Lord Chatham had expressed "much satisfaction in my having called upon him. . . . He should be glad to see me again."[7]

It had been a year since a British noble had done anything but insult Benjamin Franklin. If Chatham's graciousness had turned the head of a vain old man, the attention of one of England's most elegant socialites had completely seduced him. Three months after that first meeting with Chatham, Benjamin was cryptically invited through an intermediary in the Royal Society "to visit a certain lady who had a desire of playing with me at chess." The lady turned out to be the sister of Admiral Lord Howe. "I had not the least apprehension [of] any political business," Benjamin insisted.

When he finally met Lady Howe, she asked him, "What is to be done with this dispute between Britain and the colonies? I hope we are not to have a civil war?"

"They should kiss and be friends," said Franklin. "What can they do better?"

"I have often said," Lady Howe remarked, "that I wished Government would employ you to settle the dispute for 'em. I am sure nobody could do it so well. Don't you think that the thing is practicable?"

"Undoubtedly, madam, if the parties are disposed to reconciliation, for the two countries have really no clashing interest to differ about. It is rather a matter of punctilio which two or three reasonable people might settle in half an hour."[8]

(Both the younger men must have laughed. A matter of punctilio indeed. All that ever obstructed reconciliation was the wounded pride of men on both sides of the argument. Perhaps, after all, the elder Franklin had kept silent so long because he did indeed favor peace!)

The chess matches had led to talks with Lord Howe, a Whig member of Parliament, as well as to talks with two leading Quakers supposedly acting on private instructions from Lord North. No high-level official in the Tory ministry would meet personally with Franklin, yet Franklin was certain, when one low-level intermediary asked him to submit a written plan for reconciliation, that Whitehall would read it. His resulting fourteen "hints," as he called them, were enough to stun both his son and his old friend Galloway. Boston must pay for the destroyed tea, as William had suggested; Benjamin himself would pledge ten thousand pounds for reparations. But in exchange England must repeal the Tea Act, return all taxes collected under it, submit all existing British laws governing America to the legislature of each colony for ratification or repeal. Every one of the old grievances of the Boston town meetings must be met even as all powers to legislate America's internal affairs were to be disclaimed by Parliament.[9]

The British intermediaries could not have been more shaken by

Benjamin Franklin's intransigent "hints" than his own son that night at Trevose. It was a staggeringly one-sided list of demands that first disarmed by pledging reparations for the insult of dumping British tea into Boston harbor, then quickly added fresh insults by demanding British capitulation on a host of constitutional issues. Any British-trained barrister — and both Franklin's auditors were such — must have known just how outrageous these ingenuous "hints" were. It was certainly clear to William that his father's ten thousand pounds were safe: he had left little room for further negotiation.

Worse still, it seemed that his father was determined to insult everyone about him at a time calling for great personal tact and diplomacy. Benjamin once again lumped all royal governors together, this time derisively as "men of no estate or principle who came [to America] merely to make fortunes and had no natural regard for the country they were to govern." They were, he added, men of "rapacious and oppressive dispositions."[10]

What came next doubtless jolted William again: his father had actually been asked if he were willing to serve as one of three British peace commissioners along with his old friend John Pownall, secretary of the Board of Trade. But he refused even to consider it "because there was little likelihood that either of us should be so employed."[11] So the old man had lost all faith in the possibility of reconciliation! He had turned down the nearest thing to a personal invitation from the prime minister to negotiate peace. Instead, he had decided to send the congressional petition of right not through the proper channels to the King but to Lord Chatham, the out-of-power enemy of Lord North. "[Lord Chatham] received me with an affectionate kind of respect that, from so great a man, was extremely engaging," Benjamin went on.[12] There could be little doubt in William's mind that his father knew full well that as an agent he was empowered only to lay the petition before Lord Dartmouth, and that he was deliberately using the American crisis as a device to revenge himself on his enemies in the ministry by aligning himself with their popular rival Lord Chatham. Indeed, Franklin stated clearly that he had been delighted when Chatham had promised to draw up legislation and personally introduce it into Parliament.

There was something almost admirable about the way Benjamin Franklin could blandly sit there that night reciting how he had coaxed the Great Commoner, an old man terribly crippled with gout, out of his bed for one last battle even as Benjamin methodically rebuffed the overtures of the ministry to reconsider his demands. He now revealed that Howe had promised "that I might with reason expect any reward in the power of government to bestow." This, Benjamin said he had dismissed as "what the French call 'spitting in the soup.' "[13]

When Lord Chatham duly introduced his peace plan into Parliament, Benjamin now related, "Lord Sandwich arose and in a petulant, vehement speech opposed its being received at all and gave his opinion that he could never believe it the production of any British peer. That it appeared to him rather the work of some *American,* and turning his face toward me, who was leaning on the bar, said he fancied he had in his eye the person who drew it up, one of the bitterest and most mischievous enemies this country had ever known."[14] Chatham's motion, receiving no second, died. Lexington and Concord had seen to that.

Benjamin's meetings with Chatham had continued, culminating in one at Craven Street. "He stayed with me near two hours, his equipage waiting at the door. . . . It was much taken notice of and talked of. Such a visit from so great a man on so important a business flattered not a little my vanity. . . . The honor of it gave me the more pleasure as it happened on the very day twelve-month that the ministry had taken so much pains to disgrace me before the Privy Council."[15]

All along, Benjamin Franklin had been negotiating in bad faith. His refusal to compromise, his rejection of reconciliation except on his own terms — even after the ministry's repeated offers to make amends for his dismissal from office — were themselves nothing better than "spitting in the soup." When he proffered to pledge security to pay for the destruction of the baneful tea, it had given the negotiations new life. But when he reversed himself after the failure of the Chatham proposals and said he would not pay for the tea until all the radicals' demands were met, he singlehandedly scuttled all efforts toward an immediate peace.

Now he launched into a slashing tirade against the entire House

of Lords, "these hereditary legislators. . . . Their total ignorance
. . . prejudice and passion . . . willful perversion of plain truth . . .
gave me an exceedingly mean opinion of their abilities and made
their claim of sovereignty over three million virtuous sensible people in America seem the greatest of absurdities. . . . They appeared
to have scarce discretion enough to govern a herd of swine."[16]

The ease with which Dr. Franklin and Mr. Galloway, as they
still insisted on calling each other, urged their ideas upon each other
was something William had to admire. For all his consummate skill
at personal politics in his years as governor, once he departed from
carefully prepared arguments he tended to become painfully blunt.
Now he knew that, while he must be tactful, he must nonetheless
tell his father straightforwardly how he felt about the crisis between
America and England. He must not allow either Galloway or his father to forget what he had told the assemblymen of New Jersey so
recently, even if his words would now irk his father as they had the
radical faction in his province.[17] As politely as he could, William
must have interrupted his father. That was not at all how he perceived the ministry's attempts at conciliation. The House of Commons was wisely and humanely trying to restore peace between
Great Britain and her American possessions. Their mutual welfare
depended on it. The contest between the Continental Congress and
Parliament was an unnatural contest among men of the same language, laws, traditions, beliefs and blood.

At this hour and time, it was too late to argue about past differences. Who was most in the right or most in the wrong could never
be satisfactorily decided anyway. In the course of this long and
angry dispute many things had happened that good men recalled
with pain, that both sides must wish to bury. Both sides must look
ahead and see a peaceful solution to avoid all the horrors of a civil
war. Both must seek some ground for accommodation.

All attention should be given to the tenor of the ministry's proposals. It was clear from their tone that His Majesty and his ministers had nothing more at heart than to secure the liberties of the
people without lessening the necessary power and dignity of Parliament, which is the people of all of the empire.

As William knew, the North Plan called primarily for each British colony to contribute only its fair share to the cost of imperial defense in war or peace. This demand had been brought about by the huge British deficit, much of it on the ledgers for fifteen years, ever since the Great War for Empire had driven the French from British America. The British debt stood at £42 million, a staggering sum to which the maintenance of ten thousand troops in America was each year adding £375,000. The North Plan asked each colony to "make provision according to conditions and circumstances."[18] It was reasonable and fair. Money was to be raised by colonial tax collectors: no legion of British publicans would invade the provinces. Each colony was to judge how to make up its share. It was an equitable answer, William believed, to an old imperial problem. He was sure his father remembered the tumult over taxation to defend Pennsylvania against Indian raids not so long ago.

Benjamin, however, had quite a different view of Lord North's proposition. Its terms demanded that the colonies should grant money until Parliament agreed they had given enough. To Benjamin Franklin, a Pennsylvania assemblyman for twenty-five years who had chronically fought what he considered corrupt governors, to a businessman who resented British taxation and to an agent who had seen the squandering in England of money raised by taxation in America, the North Plan was nothing more than a blank chit to pay any and all British expenses without having to justify them to the most prosperous people in the British Empire, the Americans. It was an insane surrender of the most basic English rights. In fact, Benjamin was correct in his view of the bad faith of North and North's henchmen.

As the debate went on, William's interpretation of every facet of the North proposal differed widely from his father's. The difference, as it no doubt became apparent to both men, arose from years on opposite sides of legislative interest. As a royal governor who had studied Blackstone's interpretations of the English constitution, who for thirteen years had wooed, cajoled and fought part-time politicians mainly interested in holding down taxes, William had come to think of most colonial assemblymen as ridiculously one-sided. To him, the North Plan would end the degrading annual spectacle of every royal official bickering for his salary. And it would pay the bills of government out of the taxes on merchants and householders who could most afford them instead of by levying taxes on the entire population.

It must have seemed to Benjamin that William had seen and always expected nothing but the best from the British government. To William, it could only have appeared that Benjamin had observed and experienced the worst. That the gap between them had become wider and deeper than either of them had supposed it was must have come home to them both. When the discussion inevitably turned to the alternatives to American submission, William evidently felt he must show his father why the British, with their victorious armies and invincible navy, would, in the end, win the field.

If all Lord North's terms were met, Parliament would forgo all internal taxation of America forever. Parliament was not even any longer requiring the people of America to make any formal acknowledgment of Parliament's right of taxation, just so long as America should perform its part of the compact. However, if America did not yield the point, as he had told the New Jersey legislature, His Majesty was making it quite clear that he considered himself bound to exert every power at his command to preserve the constitution entire.

If the North Plan was accepted, all would be well. But if Benjamin and his friends in the Congress totally rejected it or something similar to it, if it was not at least made the basis of negotiation, only one conclusion could be reached: the Americans were actually plotting to throw off all dependence on Great Britain — to foment a revolution.

The rights of Parliament. The lawful commerce of loyal subjects. William's interpretation of the words was a resounding slap to Benjamin's lifelong and cherished concept of the rights of his people. His own son was espousing the parliamentary view and actually threatening without personal reservation to inflict it on his own country! He was indeed a thorough government man, as much a King's man as any lord of the bedchamber. He really did believe in American subservience to Parliament and he furthermore was urging that America's best interest lay in sending its own representatives to sit in a corrupt British Parliament as the best protection of American interests.

No, William did not agree with his father any more than he had agreed fully with Mr. Galloway's plan of union. He had his own solution to the imperial crisis. He did not believe that imperial reform had to end with the North Plan, nor did he believe it the best and final answer to a number of America's problems. He believed that America should indeed have a congress, but that it must be sanctioned by the King, exist as a lower house of the English Parliament, and be presided over by the King's appointed high commissioner for America. The congress should send representatives to Westminster, just as Scotland had since its Act of Union with England in 1702. Scotland had flourished in trade and government, and he was convinced that such a union between England and America was the best scheme for true and lasting peace and prosperity in both countries.

There would be, William was willing to concede, some inconveniences. The cost of living in England was high, the representatives would often be unable to gain any outside income, but American merchants were already sitting in Parliament, and other men of substance were willing to serve. Some inconveniences attend every plan. At the same time, enlightened members of Parliament would no doubt establish more equal representation for the people of both England and America. Such an amicable, peaceful extension of representative government would soon lead to general reforms in Parliament that would end much of the corruption of which Benjamin so frequently complained.[19]

But what would all this unprecedented largesse on the part of Parliament cost America, other than her freedom, her dignity, her right to tax and govern herself? What guarantees were there of anything but more taxes, more demands? And was not all the talk of reconciliation and reform meaningless so long as there were British troops occupying Boston as if she were a captive nation, stifling her trade, holding her people hostage, depriving them not only of their rights but of food and firewood? Was not every consideration overshadowed by the ability of British men-of-war to shell and destroy all the possessions of thousands of Americans like Benjamin Franklin, whose estate lay within easy gunshot range?

The struggle would never come to open warfare, William was sure — unless Americans provoked it. If Americans would only stop demanding, only stop declaring to Parliament, and instead petition King-in-Parliament in the time-honored manner. And what of the colonists' duties, of the loyalty and honor demanded by their ties to King and countrymen in England? These were matters that weighed more heavily with William than rights. How could any American forget either history or recent memory? All that England asked was to preserve her honor and dignity in the eyes of the world. It was to the advantage of all her possessions to show her a proper regard. And who would protect the colonies if they did not honor their just debts to England? What would their word be worth?[20]

By now, Benjamin must have been heartily disgusted with his son's thoroughly British turn of mind. The debate had gone on for hours. Neither man was about to yield to the other's arguments. They had grown too far apart for accommodation in a single evening. But it was time that each man at least know where the other would stand in the worst eventuality. As Joseph Galloway years later told Thomas Hutchinson, "The glass having gone about freely, the Doctor, at a late hour, opened himself and declared in favor of measures attaining to independence."[21]

Whatever preamble Benjamin attached to his personal declaration, by now it should have come as no surprise to his son, but to hear it actually said would still have been a profound shock: Benjamin knew as well as his listeners the possible consequences of his words. In reporting the conversation to Thomas Hutchinson, Galloway noted that Benjamin "exclaimed against the corruption and dissipation of the kingdom, and signified his opinion that, from the strength of opposition [in Parliament] and the want of union in the ministry, [and] the great resources in the colonies, they would finally prevail."[22]

What measures the Congress had in mind Benjamin probably did not say. All three men knew that a declaration of independence was the necessary precondition for securing foreign aid from

France and her allies, and for trading with them, as well as for the formation of a confederation of independent American states ruled by the Congress. Benjamin asked once more that Galloway take his elected place in this Congress and vote with him. Galloway declined.[23]

William made Benjamin listen to one more remark before he left the room that night. Four years later, Galloway still remembered. "The son said to him, he hoped that, if he designed to set the colonies in a flame, he would take care to run away by the light of it."[24]

William rode off to New Jersey the next morning as Benjamin left for Philadelphia, all indecision and vacillation gone from them both. The evening's confrontation had coalesced their thinking, and each now acted on the ideals he had enunciated and been forced to defend. For William, there was little he could do but watch nervously as the provincial congress took further steps to establish its power by forming its own militia and raising troops. William also watched for word from Philadelphia that the moderates had seen the wisdom of accepting Lord North's peace overture.[25]

But Benjamin became more active than at any time since his days as a young printer. No longer attempting to placate and unify factions opposed to him, he threw all his efforts into the revolutionary cause. Rising at five every morning as he had when a young man, he called early-morning meetings of congressional committees and of the committee of safety, and attended as many as four of these meetings in the morning before driving to the State House for eight hours of debate. He solicited and won appointment to eleven key committees, among them committees to create a new post office department, to draft a final olive-branch petition to the king, to manufacture gunpowder.[26]

The first committee he poured his time into was the panel to consider Lord North's plan. The day after the Trevose meeting, Charles Thomson, the secretary of the Congress, received a resolution from the New Jersey Assembly. Actually, it was a copy of the North Plan presented in this roundabout form to avoid raising the question of acceptance or rejection. The Congress handled the document just as gingerly, voting only to receive it and refer it to committee. The moderate president of the Congress, Peyton Randolph of Virginia, had gone home ill. He was replaced by the radical Boston financier John Hancock. Hancock immediately appointed Benjamin Franklin to receive and study the plan in committee. Franklin bottled it up for the next nine weeks, thereby successfully thwarting the ministry's peace initiative. He also, quietly and skillfully, intercepted and blocked his son's attempt to force the ministry's proposal before the full Congress.

The talk of civil war in America ceased to be a matter of abstract possibility and became inescapable fact three weeks after the Franklins' meeting at Trevose. Massachusetts radicals learned from informants inside besieged Boston that the British were planning to seize the high ground overlooking the town, fortify it, and thus free enough troops to march to the provisional capital of Cambridge and arrest the entire Massachusetts Assembly.

At a secret meeting on the night of June 15, 1775, Dr. Joseph Warren, a Boston physician and politician who was president of the provincial congress, won the approval of militia leaders from Connecticut and New Hampshire for an immediate and fateful offensive. What had been a local uprising of Boston-area radicals now became, in this first American council of war, a full-scale rebellion involving all of New England. The rebel leaders voted unanimously to occupy and fortify Bunker Hill, the highest of three hills on the Charlestown peninsula, before the British could. For some odd reason, the small force dispatched to dig entrenchments marched past Bunker Hill and instead fortified Breed's Hill, which was lower and indefensible.

Like so many battles that followed it, what became known as the battle of Bunker Hill did not have to happen. The Americans were ill prepared, had few cannon and no skilled artillerists, little ammunition, poor communications, no chain of command, no reinforcements or escape plan. They were, however, an army of zealots prepared to take on the British who had bullied them for so many years and now reportedly were about to attempt to crush them finally in an all-out invasion of Massachusetts. For all their handicaps, the Americans had officers seasoned by many of the same battles in which the British leaders had learned their tactics in two wars against the French. And they had surprise on their side.[27]

With about one thousand frontiersmen and farmers, Connecticut and Massachusetts leaders set off from Cambridge on the night of June 16 and marched on the double to Breed's Hill. The hill was seventy-five feet high and flanked on the east by an impassable swamp. From its summit shells could be lobbed down into Boston harbor and into the town of Boston itself. The Americans marked out a small redoubt roughly 130 feet on each side. At midnight they began digging and ran the east wall, a breastwork, one hundred yards down the hill to the swamp. Expecting that the British would try to outflank them, they deployed two hundred Connecticut frontiersmen and two small cannon behind a stone fence two hundred yards behind the redoubt on a line running down to the Mystic River. In front of this they quickly constructed a zigzag rail fence and covered the space between the fence and the wall with fresh hay taken from a nearby field. Then, joined by four companies of riflemen from the New Hampshire frontier, they ran a high stone wall down across the beach to the water's edge.[28]

At the same time, eight hundred rugged farmers were busy digging a square hole five feet deep, piling the excavated dirt into a six-foot-high wall around it. They laid wooden platforms along the insides of the redoubt to stand on when firing. Then they pierced the front parapet and the side walls with six gunports for their small cannon.[29]

At dawn, the British forward observers were startled to find that the rebels had fortified the entire hill overnight. General Gage called a hasty council of war. There was to be an immediate attack before the Americans could entrench the other hills and cut off Boston from the mainland. Major General Sir William Howe, brother of the Howe who had only weeks before talked peace terms with Benjamin Franklin in London, was to lead the best troops. The officers decided on a quick and classic textbook assault on the rebel positions. Their decision showed their scorn for the lessons of Lexington and Concord, and for the Americans facing them.

As Bostonians hurried into their houses, crowded into windows and scurried onto rooftops for a better view, British men-of-war maneuvered closer to shore, anchored, and sent their flatboats ashore even as their cannon began sending shells crashing into the hillside in front of the redoubt. As noon neared, British grenadiers marched through the streets and down to the bank of the Charles

River to wait for their landing craft to ferry them across. American snipers with long rifles posted in the deserted houses of Charlestown began peppering them. Most of their shots fell short. Then the British fleet lowered its guns and shelled the town, setting it ablaze. Soon, smoke could be seen twenty miles away. The British landing boats had to wait for the tide and by the time they inched up onto the beach at two in the afternoon, the sun was high and hot. The regulars wore their only uniforms, of heavy wool, and carried 125 pounds of weapons and gear, a week's rations and cooking implements on their backs. Their orders were to roll over the peninsula and march right on to Cambridge and beyond if necessary to break up the rebellion before it spread any further.[30]

From the start, things went badly for the British. Their field artillery mired down in the muddy fields. The advance grenadier guard, trotting down the beach on the right, stumbled into the new rail fence and a withering fire. According to all the military textbooks, now was the time for a bayonet charge. But the Connecticut sharpshooters were firing in rotation. There was no pause in which to rush them as they reloaded. Row on row of redcoats — most of them shot in the legs and groin at close range with buckshot so they would never fight again — pitched into the fresh-mown hay as they tried to clamber across the fence, their heavy gear throwing them off balance.

When the first flanking effort fumbled, General Howe called for reinforcements, this time unleashing twelve hundred men up the steep rough hillside over fallen trees, tangles of blackberry and blueberry, through tall grass toward the strangely silent earthworks. Behind the long, low breastwork, an old man thanked God for sparing him to fight this day, and Colonel Israel Putnam of Connecticut, cutlass in hand, lectured his sharpshooters: "Men, you are all good marksmen. Don't one of you fire until you see the whites of their eyes." This was the American secret weapon. Europeans did not believe in aiming at a specific man: they laid down a field of fire impersonally. To aim was, in the view of British officers and gentlemen, to commit murder.

At one hundred yards the redcoats fired a volley. Too high, too far away. At fifty yards, they fired again. Again, too high. Up they trudged, their bayonets glimmering, until the Americans could make out the brass matchboxes on their coats. At fifteen yards, the earthworks roared, flashed. Three long scarlet ranks of Britain's best troops crumbled, pitched into the tall grass, thrashed and screamed.

Only the best American marksmen had fired, sighting in on the crossed white sashes of the redcoats where they intersected at the belly. Behind the earthworks, young boys rammed home rusty nails and double-charged buckshot and bits of glass and lead balls and cloth wadding and handed them up to the sharpshooters on the parapet. Wave on wave of British died — casualties reached ninety-five percent in some companies — before the British commander allowed them to strip off their heavy gear and charge over the low breastworks and get at these vicious bloody rebel bastards with their bayonets.

By now, British artillery had pounded holes in the crude fort, sending shells through the useless little sally port and killing defenders with iron bombs that detonated as they skittered along the ground, shearing off arms and legs. Suddenly, the little fort had turned into a deathtrap. As careful as the sharpshooters had been to conserve their precious powder, it had been profligately wasted by untrained artillerymen and was almost gone. The last two cannonballs were cut open, the gunpowder divided among the marksmen.

Sensing victory, the decimated British ranks now regrouped, charged through the ragged fire, surrounded the ramparts, stormed over them. There was no way out, no escape route, provided for the slowly retreating, surrounded Americans. The British quickly made the fort their own, firing down into the mass of stumbling, running, yelling Americans. Dr. Warren, president of the Massachusetts Congress, was shot in the head as he fled. A British grenadier refused to spare him, ran him through with his twisting bayonet. In the cross fire, one hundred fleeing Americans died, one hundred fifty were wounded and taken prisoner. By late afternoon, the British held all of the Charlestown peninsula.

Proportionately, it was the costliest victory in all British military history: 1,054 killed and wounded out of 2,000 troops engaged. Among the British dead were old friends of William's: James Abercrombie, in whose home William had courted Betsy Graeme and who had sailed to England with him; and Lord Percy, son of Lady Percy of Northumberland House.

Yet both sides claimed victory. The Americans were certain now that, given enough gunpowder, time and men, they were the match of the best soldiers in the world. The radical cause skyrocketed. Inside barricaded Boston, even as they slaughtererd their horses to get fresh meat, the British high command declared, as carts of moaning wounded rumbled over the rough rutted streets, that they had fallen short of totally destroying the rebellion only because they lacked adequate manpower. Gage demanded thirty thousand fresh troops from London. The Revolutionary War had begun.[31]

Shortly after Benjamin Franklin learned the news of the battle, he sat down in his study in Philadelphia and wrote his old friend William Strahan in London:

Mr. Strahan:

You are a member of Parliament and one of that majority which has doomed my country to destruction. You have begun to burn our towns and murder our people. Look upon your hands! They are stained with the blood of your relations! You and I were long friends. You are now my enemy, and I am

Yours,
B. Franklin[32]

16

ADAM HAD HIS CAIN

June–September 1775

IN THE TENSE TWO MONTHS FOLLOWING THE SAVAGE BATTLE at Breed's Hill, the differences between the advocates of war and the advocates of peace in British America became virtually irreconcilable, even if most people still could not comprehend that a long and bitter civil war had started. For ten weeks Benjamin and William Franklin exchanged not one line, not one word: neither man seemed capable of reaching out across the ninety miles separating them.

As Benjamin Franklin approached the age of seventy, he seemed to work with increasing vigor and intensity. Almost compulsively he drove himself and his revolutionary colleagues in eighteen-hour days as they dismantled the old colonial order and invented in its place a new form of government, a radically new nation. His only son was just as busily trying to keep alive the British provincial establishment. He was thwarting the revolutionaries of New Jersey and their attempts to usurp his authority, take over the militia, assess taxes, and divert treasury funds for military purchases. Powerless without troops or even a single British warship, Governor Franklin nevertheless continued to preside precariously, insisting on carrying out what he deemed his sworn duties of holding meetings, keeping courts open, signing licenses and deeds, conferring almost daily with his few trusted councillors. In his own words, he was "providing a semblance of royal authority" until the British army and peace commissioners arrived to prevent the spread of rebellion.[1]

In each letter to the authorities in London, William depicted the changing attitudes of Americans on both sides of the imperial conflict. His reports were candid and remarkably balanced. In early June, a week after the clash with his father at Trevose, he wrote Lord Dartmouth that "the present leaders of the people" did not evince "the least symptoms of a disposition to promote conciliatory measures." Even before the battle of Concord, he had already been braced for the defeat of the North Plan in the Congress. "What their determination will be respecting it, I cannot say, but I have reason to think they will not comply with the resolution at present, if ever."[2]

By early August, six weeks after the shock of Breed's Hill, William reported that the rebellion had moved beyond the stage of a constitutional quarrel, beyond the boundaries of New England. One result was that all around him a strong conservative reaction was setting in. "There is indeed a dread in the minds of many here that some of the leaders of the people are aiming to establish a republic. Rather than submit . . . we have thousands who will risk the loss of their lives in defense of the old Constitution. [They] are ready to declare themselves whenever they see a chance of its being of any avail."[3] It was the first hint that William saw himself in the vanguard of a Loyalist army resisting the rebellion and physically opposing his father's revolutionary party.

In a letter to General Thomas Gage in Massachusetts, William sharpened the point. Many loyal New Jerseymen would "show themselves if they had a chance of doing it in safety — fight to preserve the supremacy of Parliament and their connection with Great Britain until some constitution should be formed for America."[4] In the long run William still foresaw the need, even the success, of a new imperial constitutional union. For the moment, he bemoaned the fact that there was not one British warship off New Jersey to encourage resistance to the rebels.

Governor Franklin's continuing correspondence with British leaders was, it itself, an act of defiance of the rebels surrounding Perth Amboy. Using secret couriers, he provided his superiors with a comprehensive view of the growth of the conflict even as he kept up the pressure for peace. He pointed out in his official dispatches that forces under Benedict Arnold had invaded Canada, that radicals were inciting French Canadians against the British. He also asserted that the outburst of fighting at Lexington and Concord had, as the Americans maintained, been provoked by General Gage and his officers. From the ninety sworn depositions smuggled to him by Loyalists (he could send off only four to Lord Dartmouth), he drew a startling picture of the fighting, a view he was sure Gage would not present to his superiors in London. A farmer from Lexington swore that when the British officers shouted, "Disperse you rebels immediately!" the American militia "dispersed every way as fast as it could, and while they were dispersing, the regulars kept firing at them incessantly." The British had fired first. Another witness, this time a British soldier, testified: "I never heard any of the inhabitants so much as fire one gun." A British officer wounded and taken prisoner at Concord swore that the British had also fired first at Concord Bridge: "I myself was wounded at the attack of the bridge and am now treated with the greatest humanity" (by his American captors.)[5]

One of William's principal sources of information was the newspapers. He continued to receive them from all over America, England, the West Indies and Canada. In the summer of 1775 he began sending Dartmouth accounts of both British and American attacks. One detailed letter, written by an intermediary in Cambridge, Massachusetts, on May 26, raises the possibility that he actually had at least one highly placed spy inside rebel headquarters: the letter reported an unsuccessful British foraging raid which demonstrated that Americans would burn their crops and barns rather than support the besieged British garrison in Boston.[6]

In sending intelligence reports to London, William saw himself as carrying out a vital function of his post, but to rebel leaders trying to give the impression of invincible, unanimous American opposition to all British measures, any voice other than that of the Congress had to be silenced. To them, William's letters made him an enemy of American liberties, a spy. They were doing all in their power to stop his letters and, as soon as they dared act, to stop him.

Each month that passed without help from England found William more apprehensive. He was dismayed when close friends and neighbors in Perth Amboy allowed themselves to be elected members of county committees, then as delegates to the provincial congress in nearby New Brunswick. But gradually he rationalized their participation in the rebels' shadow government: "It is perhaps best that gentlemen of property and sense should mix among these people. They may be a means of preventing their going into some extravagances." He had cause to fear "extravagances": one Perth Amboy revolutionary was urging that the homes of all Tories be burned.

Even before Breed's Hill, William was plainly worried that he was about to be arrested. "The public officers from the highest to the lowest are now only free on sufferance," he wrote Lord Dartmouth on June 5. "I have no doubt but it is their intention, in case General Gage should get the better in any engagement with the provincials, to seize all the governors and make them hostages for the release of prisoners."[7] Shortly after the battle he asked his wife to pack her things, go to New York, take the first British ship to London, and live with her relatives there until the civil war was safely over. She refused. She would stay by William's side, she insisted. Running away, for her, would be a signal of weakness in the face of the rebels. She would help William carry on the duties of government, a symbol of resolution that might give others courage.

Late in August, William was heartened to learn from London just how seriously the King's ministers were taking his attempts to mediate between Crown and Congress. Lord Dartmouth reassured him that all future dispatches would be "communicated only to the King's most confidential servants." Dartmouth was aware, he said, that publication of William's earlier dispatches had compromised him and had stirred up resistance to his conciliatory efforts, but publication had been necessary nonetheless, to kindle support in Parliament, even if it hurt one faraway royal governor. Dartmouth urged William to keep up his reports. "The present state of North America makes every intelligence of that sort more and more important. . . . Your continuing to transmit it to me is considered as a mark of your duty and attachment to the King." He did not mention in his letter that William was the last royal governor to perform such a dangerous function, and praised him for his futile opposition to the Congress, whose actions "could not have been prevented by any measures in your power."

Dartmouth's letter, which had been written on June 5, was a good illustration of the fatal lag in British communications. He obviously did not know, then, about the slaughter at Breed's Hill. As late as three months after the battles of Lexington and Concord, they were still being discounted in London as fabricated "with a view to create alarm."[8]

Just how perilous William's situation was as he sat in his study looking out over an empty British barracks he made clear in his unusually terse reply to Lord Dartmouth on July 4. His account was unsparing and offered no hope for an early peace. "Ever since the Lexington affair, hostile measures engross the attention of the whole continent. . . . I cannot hear of any steps taken or likely to be taken, towards an accommodation. . . . Everything gives us a prospect of the direct reverse."[9] Indeed, the rebels in his province were making no attempt to conceal their activities. Two companies of Princeton students and teachers had escorted General Washington, the new Continental commander in chief, through New Jersey to the New York border when he was on his way to Boston in June. Crowds of rebels and curious Tories had lined the streets or rode escort with the general and his staff. And in New York City, the crowds turned out twice in one day, first as Washington and his staff rode through, again as the new British military governor of New York, Sir William Tryon, arrived with a squadron of ships from England.

One thousand New Jersey militiamen, recruited by the extralegal provincial congress in the wake of the fighting at Breed's Hill, had been ordered to march to New York to join Connecticut troops on a sweep of heavily Loyalist Long Island. There they were to disarm potential enemies and arrest anyone refusing to take an oath of allegiance to the Congress. From frontier forests and valleys from Pennsylvania to Virginia, thousands of rough-cut Scotch-Irish frontiersmen with long rifles rushed to reinforce Washington. "I am informed that three hundred riflemen are to march this day from Philadelphia to join the New England army at Cambridge and that they are to be followed by five hundred more," William went on. His report was amazingly accurate, obviously based on intelligence leaked by a member of the Congress. It dovetailed exactly with congressional authorizations for that date. Evidently worried that his report might be read by unfriendly eyes, William added, "I know nothing of the proceedings of Congress except what are published."[10]

Though William's mail was being intercepted by this time, he still managed to have his letters to Lord Dartmouth dispatched. He sent multiple copies of each letter by various routes, but two out of three never got through. For its part the Colonial Office was responding by sending as many as half a dozen copies of each document on separate warships to New York. William's London newspapers served as a cover, and a young Perth Amboy neighbor acted as courier. Inside New Jersey, even a member of the Council could not safely send a letter directly to the governor. One of William's longtime advisors feared that the rebels would carry out their threat of invoking *lex talionis,* the eye-for-an-eye law of revenge, on all royal officials if rebel prisoners taken at Breed's Hill were harmed. Councillor Daniel Coxe, a leading Quaker landowner, wanted Governor Franklin to implore General Gage to treat prisoners leniently or be aware of the "certain consequences." But he felt forced to write to Attorney General Cortlandt Skinner "as less suspicious," and ask him to pass his "apprehensions" on to William. No doubt Skinner, now William's closest confidant, took the letter directly to the governor. William had it copied and found a way to transmit it, without comment or contradiction, to New York, where it was routed to Boston and London by way of Halifax, Nova Scotia. The letter told how many of William's friends in Perth Amboy felt: "Such is the present infatuated temper of the times, the minds of men daily increasing in madness and frenzy, that they are ready to enter upon the most daring and desperate attempts. What then have men of property not to fear and apprehend, and particularly those who happen and are known to differ in sentiment from the generality? They become a mark at once for popular fury, and those who are esteemed friends to government devoted for destruction — they are not even allowed to preserve a neutrality — passiveness becomes a crime — those who are not for us are against us, is the cry."[11]

Coxe's grim warning crossed the next dispatches from London on the high seas. Not until July 5 did Lord Dartmouth answer William's first report of Lexington, sent two months earlier, and it took nearly two months more for the letter to reach William. At last Dartmouth was crediting the rumors of war. William's presentation of the North Plan was "very highly approved of" in London. Dartmouth was about to resign in despair when the King's more militant ministers drafted declarations of rebellion and war, but he now commiserated with William and agreed that William's proposal for a conference of royal governors with the British peace commissioners and leaders of the Congress might have averted bloodshed, that Gage's attack at Lexington had been an "unfortunate event," that the "happy moment of advantage is lost."

Instead of reconciliation, "all America is in arms against Great Britain, and committed in rebellion that menaces to overthrow the Constitution. In this situation, then, it is the King's firm resolution that the most vigorous efforts should be made both by sea and land to reduce his rebellious subjects to obedience." The words were enough to send a cold thrill down William's back. His lordship confided the ministry's plans in considerable detail: reinforce Gage, deploy British naval squadrons off New York, Delaware Bay, the Chesapeake, the Carolinas. All American shipping except that of "friends of government" was to be seized. All intercolonial trade was to be obstructed by blockade.

The captains of men-of-war were ordered "to receive on board and give protection to any officers of the Crown who may be compelled by the violence of the people to seek such an asylum."[12] This arrangement for protecting royal governors was a relief to William, especially since he had learned the fate of one royal governor, his friend Major Philip Skene. In Philadelphia, Skene had been hooted and jeered at when he arrived from England in July to take over as the new military governor of Fort Ticonderoga. He had been jailed by the Pennsylvania committee of safety, Benjamin Franklin presiding, when the Congress found that Skene carried orders authorizing him to raise a Loyalist regiment in America. Moreover, Benjamin must have known that Skene was William's neighbor and friend from their New York land dealings as well as William's intermediary to Lord Dartmouth. Skene was sent under heavy guard to a prison in the rebel stronghold of Hartford, Connecticut. William immediately reported his seizure to Lord Dartmouth.[13]

William's orders from Dartmouth were to coordinate his actions with British military commanders, but the final instructions were what must have electrified him: "It is His Majesty's express command that you do exert every endeavor and employ every means in your power to aid and support him . . . in all such operations . . . for carrying the King's orders into full execution and restoring the authority of His Majesty's Government."[14] The letter was an unequivocal command to resist the Congress and his rebellious brother Americans. It also put to rest William's anxiety that the British government had not once and for all made the distinction between him and his father — an anxiety that had plagued him ever since his father's disgrace in England. The British government now considered William a trusted subject and a high royal official in good standing. Rebels like Benjamin Franklin were to be treated as traitors; as early as 1774, in fact, Dartmouth had sought copies of the elder Franklin's Boston correspondence as evidence of treason.[15]

By late summer, when William had heard nothing from Benjamin in the more than two months since their quarrel at Trevose, he decided to break the unnatural silence. His letter, now lost, was evidently ignored, as his next attempt makes clear: "I wrote to you by the stage [but] I have not heard from you."[16] Benjamin's continued silence obviously worried William. He knew his father was often most secretive when immersed in covert governmental operations. What he could not learn of his father's activities from informants inside the Congress he could readily enough surmise by recalling his father's *modus operandi* in their political activities against the Penns. Benjamin Franklin had always sought and won control of supplies and munitions as the first step to taking and dispensing power.

Actually, as early as June, Benjamin had dispelled suspicions of his loyalty to the revolutionary cause. He had gained enormous leverage in the business of preparing America for the expected British onslaught. William must have seen a copy of the deceptive Olive Branch Petition drafted by John Dickinson's committee with member Franklin's tacit support, but he probably did not know it was a deliberate ruse; nor did he likely know the contents of the very next congressional resolution, which was passed on July 5, 1775, the same day the peacemaking petition to the King was unanimously authorized.

"As it is very uncertain whether earnest endeavors by this Congress to accommodate by conciliatory measures will be successful," Secretary Thomson recorded, troops were to be systematically recruited, armed, and trained immediately.[17] Benjamin was serving on a committee to procure gunpowder, on another to encourage the home concoction of saltpeter, on yet another to seek and smelt lead ore for bullets, and on a fourth as a commissioner to the Indians on western lands. When George Washington was given command of the rebel forces outside Boston and made the highest-ranking American general, Benjamin Franklin was placed at the head of the committee to draw up Washington's orders, plan in detail the structure of his military chain of command, and write the declaration Washington was to read to the troops when he formally assumed command.

As Franklin wrote Priestley in July, he was as busy as he had ever been in his life. His days began at six in the morning with a committee of safety meeting, and from nine to four he sat in the Congress.[18] The early morning meetings evidently reinvigorated his inventiveness. The committee needed to tackle the bayonet problem. British bayonets had been devastating at Breed's Hill, and because the barrels of American rifles were octagonal, bayonets could not be affixed to them. As a countermeasure, Franklin came up with the pike, a short-handled spear used by naval boarding parties. Next, he championed the reintroduction of the bow and arrow to mitigate the acute shortage of muskets and gunpowder. (This particular inspiration never caught on.) If his ideas seemed unconventional, it was because, as he grew ever more implacably opposed to all accommodation with the British, he looked more and more for chinks in the armor of the superior British forces.

His knowledge of military engineering found full expression in building up the naval defenses of Philadelphia. First, his committee ordered the construction of twenty-five row galleys — fast, maneuverable fifty-foot boats powered by two dozen stout oarsmen. With auxiliary lateen-rigged sails, they could hurry up to larger ships and intercept their landing boats by sweeping them with shot from bow- and stern-mounted swivel guns, which Franklin had first seen on his last tour of Scotland. But it would take something more than rowboats for America's first navy to stop huge British men-of-war carrying sixty or more heavy cannon plus contingents of marines. Franklin had just the thing in mind, and his early-morning colleagues must have been stunned when he unveiled it.

The rebel capital lay nearly one hundred miles up the heavily shoaled Delaware River from the sea and was also protected by islands in midriver that made it difficult for men-of-war under full sail to rake the Philadelphia waterfront with broadsides. To enhance these natural defenses, Franklin suggested planting underwater obstacles just below the surface of the water. Similar defenses had ruined a British attack on France three decades earlier, as his Scottish friend Hume, secretary to the admiral of the ill-fated expedition, may have told him. Benjamin designed a series of chevaux-de-frise — huge submersible wooden barricades bristling with large iron-pointed spikes to pierce the hulls of unwary invaders' ships. Over the next year, nearly five thousand men became involved in fabricating, assembling and laying three grand lines of these underwater defenses. In all, 239 hemlock timbers, extremely tough and from fifteen to twenty inches thick, were cut and rafted to the site three miles south of the city, then lashed together and covered with two-inch-thick deck planking caulked on bottom and sides. Protruding from these giant open-topped boxes, each sixty feet long, were pointed timbers capped with sharp iron spikes that could pierce and rip the bottom of a ship passing over them. The tips of the spikes remained submerged six or seven feet beneath the surface. The massive defense project deeply impressed the rebels and further allayed their fears of the British. Franklin's genius was once again acclaimed.[19] (Ironically, the chevaux, while the marvel of military science of the day, never damaged a British ship and only managed to impale a friendly French ship at the war's end. Tory guides who had watched the entire project helped British captains elude the defenses.)

Each month, Franklin's power multiplied. In June he was commissioned to oversee the engraving of Continental money to replace British coins bearing George III's likeness. By late July, he was able to appoint his son-in-law congressional commissioner of the first American mint. As his conspicuous efforts for American resistance won him the favor of more and more congressmen, Franklin moved to advance old designs as well as new. He dusted off his twenty-one-year-old Albany Plan of Union, revised it slightly, and proposed that the delegates sign articles of confederation uniting the colonies in a "perpetual union . . . to continue firm till the terms of reconciliation proposed in . . . the last Congress" were accepted by the British. He demanded reparation for Boston's commercial losses and for the destruction of Charlestown, and insisted on the removal of all British troops from America. He also read a cryptic clause into the articles that would give the Congress charge of the "planting of new colonies." Benjamin received no opposition on this obvious allusion to the Illinois land scheme: more than one congressman was involved in western land speculations.[20]

But the majority of congressmen were still more moderate than Franklin, still not ready for the tacit vote for independence implied in signing articles of confederation. Franklin did not press the issue: he had attracted key support and he was willing to bide his time.

On July 31, 1775, a few days after the North Plan was thunderously rejected, the most powerful politician in America was appointed postmaster general of America at a salary of one thousand dollars, the highest salary at congressional disposal and double that of General Washington. As Franklin's ledger reveals, he was also given the customary expense account. Like Washington he turned back his salary to the new government to help the war effort, but not his expense account. The appointment also gave him control of the gathering, transmittal and interception of all intelligence. And when the Second Continental Congress adjourned on August 1, 1775, Benjamin Franklin was placed on its most powerful committee: the standing committee to rule until a new congress could be elected. As William should have realized by now, his own father was the King's most resourceful, formidable and pervasively rebellious subject in all America.

Through the feverish weeks of Benjamin's rise to power, he did not write once to his son. It was William who finally broke the three-month silence on August 14, 1775.[21] He had received an encouraging letter from two members of Parliament who were secret partners in the Illinois scheme. The missive is now lost, probably destroyed by Benjamin himself, but William used it as an excuse to communicate with his father and forwarded it along with his own letter, which survives. His tone was conciliatory. He expressed regret for the rancor of their meeting at Trevose and attempted to pull at the only thread that to him seemed still to connect them: money. The letter also revealed, despite the widening breach between them and the danger of the times, how much William was still willing to trust his father. "As you were so kind to say that you had no objection to do anything for me that might be in your power respecting the lands," he began tentatively, "I send you enclosed a copy of the letter on that subject." The letter was unsealed. In his old intimate way, William asked his father "after perusal, please to seal and deliver [it]." With a war breaking around them, William believed it was not too late to discuss their real estate dabblings. Indeed, the records of the Illinois partners reveal that both men were still clinging, however tenuously, to hope for a bonanza in the West after peace was restored. William pointed out that the British partners, hard as it was to believe, were hopeful of the outcome: "since you left England, they have received the *strongest assurances* that as soon as the present great dispute is settled our grant *shall be perfected.*"[22] The partners' letter also revealed a lack of understanding of how deep the imperial struggle was, and it showed, as well, that Benjamin Franklin's old friends were worried enough about his treasonable involvement in the rebellion, and their own sub rosa connections with him, to ask that their continued partnership with the Franklins be "kept *as private as possible,* for should it be known on their side of the water, it might rather prejudice us than do us any service."[23]

But William was not quite so naive as his father's old British friends. "I think it proper therefore to say, just to you," he confided, "that, in my opinion, it is hardly likely that such a transaction will be kept so secret as they think necessary."[24] With civil war breaking out and Benjamin's enemies in England in power, William was sure that sooner or later the ministry must learn of Benjamin's continued, if silent, partnership in the Illinois venture. As William was so painfully aware, no land grant openly involving

Benjamin Franklin was ever likely to win the blessing of the King. Yet he no doubt clung to the hope that he would one day be rewarded by a grateful monarch for his unswerving loyalty during the colonial crisis.

More immediate hope of settling William's debts to his father rode on the second mortgages he had taken on properties of former land company partners now beyond his reach on the western Pennsylvania frontier. William referred his father to the business agent in Philadelphia for his bankrupt partners, Croghan and Trent. He asked Benjamin to use his influence to help collect his debts from them so that he could square his accounts with his father: what was owed William was exactly what he owed his father. He apparently still thought that much of his father's cold silence toward him was connected to their longstanding money problems.

In signing off with "your ever dutiful son," William added a postscript, in case the point was not already clear enough: "I should be glad to have a line from you by the post to let me know if I may expect to see you here — whether you approve of my coming to Philadelphia — and when it will be proper. Billy [Temple] should be there in order to go to the college. The above and the enclosed were copied by him."

Whether or not his father approved, after the carnage at Breed's Hill and the rejection of the King's peace terms it was no longer safe for so notorious a British sympathizer as William Franklin to ride through the streets of Philadelphia. Even as the Congress deliberated in the State House early that August, a mob demonstrated across the hallway in the chambers of the Pennsylvania supreme court just how dangerous it had become to represent the British viewpoint in the rebel capital.

A dry goods merchant had been caught selling British cloth in defiance of the nonimportation embargo. He went to court to try to get his goods back. In the crowded courtroom the merchant's lawyer, Isaac Hunt, was seized by a mob, dragged outside, and dumped into a horse-drawn cart. Taken from intersection to intersection as an impromptu fife and drum corps played the "Rogue's March" (usually reserved for men condemned to die), he was forced at every stop to apologize for speaking out against the Congress and was stoned as he spoke. Years later his son, the poet Leigh Hunt, wrote in his autobiography that "one of the stones thrown by the mob gave him such a severe blow on the head as not only laid him swooning in the cart but dimmed his sight for life."[25]

The elder Franklin may well have thought that William had become a Tory of necessity, not conviction, a man who had lost all hope of financial security except from continuing royal favor. Perhaps he was convinced that William's impassioned pleading for Lord North's peace plan was only a lawyer's pleading, that the true source of the rift between them was only one of money. A check with the agent for their former land company partners, as William had suggested, would more than confirm William's inability to repay his father or even to survive without some regular source of income.[26] It was also readily discernible that, in the unsettled atmosphere of the times, no one was willing to pay William what he needed for his farms or his town house. If he could be offered a new salaried position, he might be won away from the royal standard.

When Benjamin had drafted the legislation creating the Continental postal service in July of 1775, he had created two paid posts. The second highest, the office of comptroller general, was to pay $320 a year, slightly less than one third of Benjamin's salary and only one fifth of Governor Franklin's. But it was one of the few paid congressional patronage jobs and the one Benjamin could most readily justify: it was William's old job and he had been good at it. There would, of course, be an expense account allowing William to charge off much of his cost of living and working to the Congress. And Benjamin could offer other inducements: relaxation of debt payments, help with Temple's schooling, the certainty of eventual wealth as his son, executor and heir. He even had papers drawn up to give one half of his Nova Scotia land grant to William, despite the fact that the grant had just expired and was in British hands. Confident he had the ways and the means to bring William back to his side, Benjamin set off for Perth Amboy at the end of August.

The cost of the entire trip he charged to the post office department. The tab came to ten pounds, as much as a schoolteacher was paid in a year.[27] Once again, Benjamin was living well and traveling stylishly at government expense. But most of all, his activities along the way made a mockery of his son's edict against importing arms.

Benjamin's surviving correspondence from the taverns he visited en route shows that he was busily pursuing his revolutionary activities. At Trenton, he met with the New Jersey committee of safety and gave orders for a wagonload of gunpowder bound for New York to be returned to Philadelphia. He met with New Jersey revolutionaries again at New Brunswick. They informed him that four wagonloads of arms and ammunition had just been smuggled into the colony at a cove not fifteen miles from Perth Amboy, in defiance of Governor Franklin's express executive order. The munitions were already on their way to New York rebels.

Benjamin not only huddled with rebel leaders about arms but he also discussed William's behavior with William's avowed enemies, the Livingston faction. A letter he wrote to Robert Morris, a fellow member of the Philadelphia committee of safety, mentions the meeting and reveals that he was losing no opportunity to broadcast just how ineffectual his son, the royal governor, had become.[28] William would have been hurt and angry had he known of his father's open disloyalty to him.

The letter also casts a sidelight on a tactic of Benjamin's, learned long ago in another war: to make a decision without consulting the other committee members. If the committee disagreed with him about the wagonload of gunpowder, he wrote, he would personally pay for it, then worry about reimbursement. Of course, no one disagreed with Benjamin Franklin. That he intervened in revolutionary activities affecting two other colonies only underscored his confidence in his own power.

Franklin never had felt welcome in Perth Amboy. When he had first visited the town in 1724, he had been a runaway printer's apprentice seeking a day's labor and a dry place to sleep before pushing on to Philadelphia. Unable to find lodgings, he had been hounded as a common vagrant to the town limits by a constable.[29] Now, on August 30, 1775, though his ride into Perth Amboy was more comfortable than on the previous occasion, he found that the place had become a royalist bastion. In the words of Charles Pettit,

William's secretary, Perth Amboy was "almost the only spot in America where a friend to American liberty is a disgraceful character."[30]

A tradition persists in Perth Amboy that, during Benjamin's later visit, he and his son argued frequently and loudly. During their longest quarrel, which took place during a walk through the town, many residents overheard snatches of the conversation. Undoubtedly the Franklins argued.[31] During the three-day visit, apparently no notes were taken, but William's letters to his father afterward indicate that they discussed their land ventures (William gave Benjamin his proxy to vote at meetings in Philadelphia) and other aspects of their financial dealings. That Benjamin made William the offer of the postmastership of Philadelphia and the comptroller-generalship of the fledgling American postal system if he would resign as governor is also evident: Benjamin waited to offer the post office job to his son-in-law until after his visit with William. Nearly thirty years later, a London magazine reported that Benjamin even offered to sign over his entire estate at once to William if he would come over to the revolutionary side.[32]

If William did not immediately reject his father's offers, his reaction seems to have been carefully controlled disdain. He would have slipped back twenty years into the job and status of his youth. Once again he would be at his father's bidding, be thoroughly humiliated and degraded in the eyes of his friends, constituents, business associates. Moreover, he would have to return to his farm; he knew how miserable his wife had been there. For the first time in their thirteen years in America, Elizabeth was happy. She had made a few close friends of like background and breeding. He could not tear her away, turn her again into a farm wife. What Benjamin clearly saw as a last generous gesture to help his wayward son return to solvency from the brink of self-destruction, William could only interpret as a ridiculous offer that would undercut his entire way of life. Besides, William believed that, as the senior British governor still at his post, he stood an excellent chance to serve as the chief conciliator between Great Britain and her colonies when the British peace commissioners finally arrived in America.

Benjamin could argue very persuasively. He may have even confided his confederation plan as he had proposed it to the Congress, the old Albany Plan of Union that William knew so well, and in effect offered William a stake in the new nation. Who would govern New Jersey? Why should William step down? He had been a good and popular governor. There were, to be sure, obstacles. William had recently offended, indeed endangered, the leading revolutionaries by denouncing them to Lord Dartmouth. But if Benjamin could only make assurances that William would, at the very least, stay quiet in the contest, Benjamin could probably bring William's enemies around. There was a precedent: Governor Jonathan Trumbull of Connecticut had kept his governorship while transferring his colony from the royal to the revolutionary standard.

That summer Benjamin Franklin was fond of saying that the British had just paid two thousand lives in two months to gain two hundred yards, that the Americans had lost only one hundred and fifty lives while sixty thousand more Americans had been born. William would not argue with such spurious logic. America had great resources, to be sure, but they were potential; those of Britain, the most powerful nation on earth, were real and immediate. America, William was sure, could not win an all-out war against an aroused and resolute British nation, especially since he believed that a majority of Americans did not want war with the mother country. America's only hope was to reconcile its differences with Parliament before the British fleets arrived in the spring to punish the rebels, before innocent victims were caught between the armies. Then and only then could Americans convene a just and legal congress willing to work for the peace and prosperity so much in everyone's interest.

There was no point to arguing further. Both men felt keenly the depth of the impasse. William was not willing to resign, not willing to accept his father's largesse. He would do nothing more than attempt to vindicate his handling of the North Plan and try to undercut rebel complaints that he had officially accused them of traitorous conspiracy in his correspondence with Lord Dartmouth. Accordingly, he would provide Benjamin with a complete set of Assembly minutes for the past year as well as a copy of his original letter to Dartmouth of May 6 and his refutation of rebel charges against him. This appeared to satisfy Benjamin that he would eventually succeed in winning over his son. He was sure enough of

William's conversion to make plans that presupposed William's remaining pro tem in office in Perth Amboy. He arranged to bring Jane Mecom, his last remaining sister, away from the warfare in New England to what he considered the sanctuary of Proprietary House in Perth Amboy. Then he cut short his stay, hurried Temple along with packing for college, said goodbye to his son and daughter-in-law. But he did not rush to Philadelphia without making a few stops, notably one in Princeton to visit the Reverend John Witherspoon. And he began the trip with a visit to a tavern in Perth Amboy. Apparently, when he and Temple left, he was somewhat less than clearheaded. A few days later, William wrote to him: "Yesterday evening, Thomas [William's steward] found the enclosed letter in the bar of one of the taverns in this town." William sent the letter along, evidently unopened, as well as the copies of all the documents he had promised his father. He signed off as he always used to: "I am ever your dutiful and affectionate son."[33]

In October, when the Second Continental Congress reconvened, Benjamin Franklin was sent on an inspection tour of the Massachusetts battle area. In meeting with General Washington to arrange the payment of the troops in the new Continental dollars, he saw at first hand the devastation around the town of his birth. The shock of the sight wiped away any trace of hope he might have nurtured for an early peace. Both sides were obviously digging in for a long war.

The Franklin family had already suffered its first war casualty. Jane Franklin Mecom had lost her son Josiah on Breed's Hill in extraordinary circumstances. When last seen, he was fighting hand to hand with a British redcoat — the man who had married the widow of his brother John. Josiah was never seen alive again.

"Oh how horrible is our situation," Jane bemoaned to Benjamin, "that relations seek the destruction of each other!"[34]

Franklin finished his business at Cambridge headquarters, bought a carriage, and hurried south to Caty Ray Greene's house in Rhode Island to fetch his sister. After a few days' rest with his dear friend, he bundled Jane and Caty's son Ray into his carriage and headed for Perth Amboy.

In the two months since Benjamin had left William to ponder his course — loyalty to his father or to his King — the Revolution had come to a virtual standstill in New Jersey, despite the utmost efforts of the rebels and a number of key defectors from the governor's Council. The ebb of events only served to confuse William Franklin further. "What step is best to take in this critical situation is difficult to determine," he wrote Lord Dartmouth on September 5. "I am loath to desert my station, as my continuance in it is a means of keeping up some appearance of government. . . . Matters may possibly take such a turn as to put it in my power to do some service. On the other hand, it would mortify me extremely to be seized upon and led like a bear through the country to some place of confinement in New England, as has lately happened to Governor Skene."[35] He had asked General Gage to dispatch a vessel so that he could send his personal papers and valuable possessions for safekeeping on shipboard. Gage ignored him. Then William thought of "sending some things on board the *Asia* at New York." But since that ship had recently fired on the city, the radicals would not allow a boat to leave the Jersey shore. They were "constantly on the watch."

William went on to report that his authority was steadily deteriorating, but then, so was that of the New Jersey congress. "The provincial congress have taken upon them the entire command of the militia." Yet many people were resisting the new military tax: "Some absolutely refuse to pay any part of it." William expected to see his salary cut off in the fall: "What [are] the officers of government supposed to do?" he asked Dartmouth. He expected the Continental Congress to complete its takeover by cutting off payment of all provincial license fees and, at Benjamin Franklin's suggestion, payment of all land rents. Moreover, he foresaw the seizure of all Crown lands and assets so they could be sold by Congress "under pretence of making good the damage done by the King's forces to the people."[36]

Notwithstanding his official impotence, William was "extremely concerned" that the King was "having recourse to a military force to secure his dominions." A bad peace, he believed, was always preferable to the most justifiable war. "I was once in hopes that all differences would have been settled in some amicable way. . . . Had the actions of the leaders of the people in this country corresponded with their repeated professions, such must have been the happy consequence. Were the people, even now, left to judge for themselves and the avenues of information not obstructed, I have no doubt but their good sense would prevent their engaging in support of the present hostile and destructive measures." In the interests of averting the catastrophe of civil war William felt justified in giving words of advice to his superiors. He now dared to advise the King's Privy Council. Unless Great Britain displayed the political maturity to "condescend, for the sake of peace, to make other [proposals] . . . to bring the dispute immediately into . . . negotiation," there was little chance of counteracting the "pernicious designs of many of the leaders [of the Continental Congress]."[37]

At this point, even the smallest encouragement braced him. In January Lord Dartmouth's praise of his last speech to the Assembly had inspired him to keep the courts open. But he could not find replacements for the vacancies on the Council. He brooded that unless the Continental Army's attacks on Canada and Boston were repulsed, "the inhabitants in general will implicitly follow the Continental Congress in all their extravagances," including "an entire separation from the mother country."[38]

The new provincial congress was more radical than the last because it was led by militant Presbyterians close to the Reverend Witherspoon of Princeton. The radicals were tightening their grip: an attempt to land arms for Monmouth County citizens loyal to the King had been quashed when their sloop was intercepted as it came ashore from a British man-of-war. The provincial congress was also trying to raise two battalions of New Jersey troops, but the frugal farmers refused to pay for them. The radicals, embarrassed, had to appeal to the Continental Congress for funds. Their failure only provoked harsher revolutionary measures. No longer satisfied with passing resolutions, the provincial congress now considered itself legally constituted and empowered to pass laws, its authority for the first time derived from the people, even if not a clear majority of them, instead of from the Crown. One of the first ordinances decreed that tax payments were compulsory, to be collected at gunpoint if necessary, even against the will of neutrals and Quakers. If taxes were not paid, property, including furniture and other goods, would be seized and sold.

That the rebels felt compelled to use force finally led William to end his long months of wavering. In October of 1775, while his father was traveling through New England, William received a letter from Lord Dartmouth that raised his spirits. Dartmouth had read William's reports, speeches and provincial records carefully and had concluded that William was, despite his doubts, close to succeeding in his efforts to bring about a separate peace between New Jersey and the Crown. "They feel the force of your arguments and only withhold their concurrence from the fear of the consequences that would follow from the appearance of separating from the other colonies," he wrote.[39]

Slowly, William had been drifting toward the most difficult decision of his life. Now, the British government's trust in him and the openhanded confidence Dartmouth had shown in letter after letter heartened him. Far from resigning, he would raise the royal standard, thereby setting an example for other hesitant royal governors. William prepared to convene the New Jersey Assembly and present the King's final offer for peace.

When Benjamin Franklin returned to Perth Amboy on November 7, he had his answer.

Early the next morning, he hurried his sister and Caty's boy into the carriage: he would not stay another day in "this Tory house."[40] On the trip home he evidently made several decisions. William would no longer be his son and heir. Bache would, instead, be the first comptroller and secretary of the Continental post office (he and Bache had the same views — they would work well together once Bache learned his duties). The Bache family could live free in Franklin's house, and Franklin would see to it that the children were well educated, that Sally and her husband would one day inherit all he had planned to leave to William.

As with Deborah's death, years would pass before Franklin revealed how deeply he had been affected by the parting from his only son. In a letter to Bache he confided, obliquely, the extent of his alienation from William: "I have lost my son."

IV

NOTHING HAS EVER HURT ME SO MUCH

17

WITH ALL DUE REGULARITY AND DECORUM

January 1776

FROM HIS STUDY WINDOW, GOVERNOR WILLIAM FRANKLIN could see, above the bare winter-black branches, the rebel soldiers on the distant hillside. Small, nondescript figures, even in the brilliant winter sunlight they were dark in the garb of poor farmers and backwoodsmen. They shouldered ancient family firelocks as they trudged back and forth, trying to drill in the chill January air outside the commandeered British army barracks. Last fall, there had only been a few dozen of them when, unopposed, they had marched into Perth Amboy, seized the empty garrison, then paraded through the streets past the governor's front gate. This morning early in 1776, there must have been more than one hundred of them, and they appeared to be well disciplined. William no longer could ignore them. He began to write what could well be his last official dispatch to the colonial secretary in London.

It had become extremely dangerous to smuggle out his official correspondence to the King's ministers. The rebels had every road and ferry blocked. Their boats patrolled the seacoast, cutting off all communication with New York. As William had already reported to London, his mail was being opened there. Each month the atmosphere of terror intensified, fueled by espionage and betrayals on both sides. In November of 1775, William had taken the enormous risk of forwarding to Crown officials a copy of a secret intelligence report written by Dr. Benjamin Church, surgeon general of the

Continental Army, a former delegate to the Continental Congress and a trusted rebel leader in Massachusetts. Dr. Church, desperate for money, had been receiving a retainer from the British commander for spying on his comrades-in-arms and sending encoded messages through the lines. His most detailed report, enumerating troop strengths, the names of rebel officers, and the disposition of cannon and supplies had been intercepted. Church was in jail in Connecticut.[1] William somehow obtained a copy from one of the rebel committees of a neighboring town, and bundled it off to Lord Dartmouth as proof that "the scheme of independency was no new thing among the members of the Congress."[2] As William was to learn later, his letter made its way to the King himself.

In December, he had time only to dash off a hasty covering note to Dartmouth, but his official dispatch pouch brimmed with reports of a legislative struggle — Loyalists versus rebels — in the New Jersey Assembly. In the last days of 1775, Governor Franklin tried to pull off a separate peace between the people of New Jersey and their King, as Dartmouth had urged him to do. Rarely had an American colony seen such political maneuvering as in this two-month test of nerves.

Although the town of Burlington had effectively ceased to be a royal capital when Governor Franklin received Crown permission to move his government to Perth Amboy, under its ancient charter it was still such. William decided to make use of the fact in convening the long-delayed legislative session. His timing was critical. The Continental Congress had decreed compulsory military service for men between the ages of eighteen and forty-five, and the New Jersey provincial congress was already busy collecting the military tax assessments. Antiwar sentiment had swept New Jersey in response. Now was the moment to act. William could depend heavily on Quaker pacifism — Burlington County was its heart. Pastoral letters had arrived from Quaker leaders in London reminding the Society of Friends in America that they could not in conscience support a revolution. Since no legitimate government existed, they must therefore tacitly support the established order. Already confident of widespread support in Perth Amboy and surrounding counties to the east, William called the Assembly to meet in Burlington, only fifteen miles from the deliberations of the Continental Congress.[3]

Rebel leaders took no immediate action when William announced the session in Philadelphia and New York newspapers. Every other royal official in America had declined to risk arousing rebel wrath by calling a public meeting. Governor William Tryon of New York had actually received Crown permission to go aboard a British warship.[4] Other royal governors had followed suit as far south as the Carolinas. Governor Franklin, without a ship to protect or shelter him, had actually moved closer to the heart of rebel power and now was convening the most successful legislative session of his thirteen years in office.

Apparently stunned by his audacity, the rebels did not attempt to prevent the New Jersey legislature from convening, but instead tried to boycott the session. On the first two days, six rebel members stayed home. Without a quorum no business could be transacted by the Assembly. Yet Governor Franklin had expected such an obstacle. In a round of personal diplomacy he diligently persuaded every Loyalist, Quaker and neutral to attend. By the third day, he had his quorum, even without the six rebels.[5] He coolly summoned the New Jersey Council and Assembly into the council chamber on the second floor of the old stone Burlington County courthouse. In his scarlet robes of office and powdered wig, and with the British coat of arms above him, His Excellency William Franklin, Captain General, Governor, Commander in Chief, Chancellor and Vice Admiral of New Jersey, faced down both his old friends and many of the leading revolutionaries of the colony. Heading off another perennial objection of colonial assemblies to royal prerogative, he broke with tradition and read directly from his latest private instructions from Whitehall. It was as stern a speech as Governor Franklin ever gave, the indignation of the British sovereign coming unfiltered through William's usual diplomacy: "His Majesty laments to find his subjects in America so lost to their true interests as neither to accept the resolution of the House of Commons . . . nor make it the basis of negotiation. It would have led to some plan of accommodation. . . . As they have preferred engaging in a rebellion which menaces to overthrow the

Constitution, it becomes his Majesty's duty . . . to reduce his rebellious subjects to obedience. . . . The commanders of His Majesty's squadrons in America have orders to proceed, as in the case of a town in actual rebellion."[6]

William put the royal proclamation of rebellion forcefully, directly. Once again, he was the first American to declare the royal will. No other royal official in America had faced his people and read to them, in the name of the King, the King's actual words bluntly announcing the consequences of further resistance. Others merely had published them and fled. There were men in the room who would hang one day if the proclamation were enforced. The words were now his:

"The King's officers in this province have not as yet met with any insults or improper treatment. Yet such has been the general infatuation and disorder of the times that, had I followed the advice of some of my best friends, I should ere this have sought (as other of the King's governors have done) an asylum on board of one of His Majesty's ships." William was sure that he had the welfare of the people at heart. "I am so unhappy to differ widely in opinion with their representatives."

He was equally sure that "our retreat would necessarily be attributed to either the effect, or the well-grounded apprehension, of violence, and of course subject the colony to be immediately considered in actual rebellion. Let me, therefore, gentlemen, entreat you to use *your* influence with the people that they may not, by any action of theirs, bring such calamities on the province. No advantage can possibly result from the seizing, confinement or ill treatment of officers of government. If you should be of a different opinion, and will not or cannot answer for our safety, all I ask is that you tell me so in plain, open language. It is high time that every man should know what he has to expect."[7]

The effects of William's words were immediately apparent. As he had hoped, the warning shook the weaker members of the rebel's five-man delegation to the Continental Congress. Two resigned. A third asked leave of absence from the Assembly session. He told no one where he was going, but he undoubtedly galloped off to Philadelphia for emergency instructions from the Congress.

The rebels once again tried to bring the session to a standstill by staying home on the third day. Angrily, William, with the concurrence of the House, sent sergeants-at-arms after them over the weekend. Three of the six were brought to Burlington, deeply angered to have to apologize publicly for absenting themselves.[8] When the Assembly resumed its business, William showed that royal government still could function as usual, despite an imperial crisis. An act was passed, for instance, to prevent "rams from running at large at certain seasons of the year."

There was also important business. For more than a year the governor had pleaded for reconciliation. Now, it seemed he was finally gaining support for his daring rearguard action against the rebel advances. Assembly radicals were voted down when they attempted to rekindle the smoldering issue of his letters to Lord Dartmouth. Instead, the radicals found themselves faced with a strong protest against their incendiary tactics. Thirty-four Burlington County farmers and merchants packed the small Assembly chamber to petition their representatives to stop the drift toward war. The petitioners lamented that "either country should dwell so much on their own dignity." They were "greatly alarmed at the sentiments of independency openly avowed by too many people." They dreaded "the destruction of the whole British Empire," foreseeing "a perpetual bar to every door of peace and reconciliation." The ministry and Parliament could be opposed without changing the constitutional form of government. "Your petitioners have not the least desire that the union of the colonies should be broken." Instead, they wished to petition the King directly, modestly setting forth the "reasons we cannot accede to the [North Plan]," at the same time declaring "our desire of a perpetual union, and our willingness to contribute our just proportion of the support of the whole Empire."

In solemn tones that stirred the assemblage and echoed William's arguments during the past three embattled sessions, the Quaker yeomen of New Jersey, frugal, hardworking men who had conserved the freeholds their fathers had purchased from William Penn and made them prosper, now denounced the rebel movement for distorting the authority they had given their representatives to the Continental Congress. They declared it "never was our intention to vest any Congress or body of men" with the power to "change the form of government by law established." After generations of persecution for their religious beliefs, the British government had granted the Quakers a generous domain with unprecedented freedom in America. They did not want to see what they had gained washed away in the blood of a civil war. They pressed the Assembly to "make such resolves as may discourage independency."[9] They urged the legislators to pass bills immediately in support of the established royal government. Their orderly protest delighted the governor and his adherents. He moved quickly to consolidate his gains.

For eleven years, he had crusaded against Crown restrictions on currency. He had jeopardized his job by battling Lord Hillsborough in an attempt to end the shortage of specie in the colony. Eager now to bestow a conspicuous mark of royal favor on New Jersey for its listening to the royal side of the quarrel and trying to drive a wedge into the Middle Colonies that might break up the Continental union, the new colonial secretary, Lord George Germain, sent the King's approval for the issuance of paper money. For three months, William had held his trump card close to his vest. Now he played it.

The radicals were furious. To them it was a bald-faced bribe. But the pacifist majority gratefully responded by renewing William's salary and funding the royal government for another year. There were dissenters: the men he had ordered hauled to the session voted to cut his pay. But they were outvoted.[10]

When William turned to the issue of the safety of Crown officials, a majority of the Council for the first time turned against him in public. With great irritation the Council took him to task for even thinking aloud that he and other royal officials were in any imminent physical danger. "Your Excellency's safety we apprehend to be in no danger," wrote William's longtime friend Francis Hopkinson for the Council. Moreover, Hopkinson said he knew "of no sentiments of independency that are, by men of any consequence, openly avowed. We have already expressed our detestation of such opinions. We really deserve to be exempt from all suspicion."[11]

Despite his friendship with Hopkinson, William was not fooled by him. The poet-composer was now closely attached to his wealthy father-in-law, a member of the rebel committee of safety.

When Hopkinson expressed amazement at the governor's fear of arrest, William could not resist calling Hopkinson's protestations "extraordinary." If, as Hopkinson said, the only safe refuge a British subject always had was in the laws of England, then the Council and the Assembly would not mind petitioning the provincial supreme court to grant a writ of habeas corpus whereby British officers illegally confined by unlawful authority would be released. Then he chided Hopkinson for publicly declaring that no one of consequence secretly favored independence. "I sincerely wish that you and I may, ere long, have the happiness to see those who either openly or privately avow independence *made* men of no consequence."[12]

Five days after Governor Franklin revealed the King's assent to printing provincial paper money, the Assembly, evidently convinced that the Crown was genuinely seeking to solve America's problems, formed a committee to draw up a new petition. This time, as William had requested seven months earlier, it was to be sent directly to the King, not through the Continental Congress. In asking the King "to prevent the effusion of blood," the committee pleaded for "a restoration of peace and harmony with the parent state on constitutional principles." Resolutions were also passed restricting the conduct of the Assembly's delegates to the Continental Congress: they were admonished against "any propositions that may separate this colony from the Mother Country or change the form of government thereof."[13]

The governor's hold over his colony resurging, his defiance of the Continental Congress became complete. He moved to seize the property of the ranking revolutionary officer in New Jersey — William Alexander — for back taxes.

Even before William Franklin had first taken office in New Jersey, William Alexander, who called himself Lord Stirling, had threatened to become the governor's chief rival. William Franklin had worked assiduously to make peace with Alexander, who not only was president of the New Jersey Council but also president of the Proprietors of East Jersey and surveyor general of the province.

A large, hard-drinking, two-fisted spender who at various times had owned iron and copper mines and forges, numerous farms and at least thirteen thousand acres, Alexander had squandered three fortunes: his mother's, his fugitive Scottish father's, and one he had made selling munitions to the King's troops during the French and Indian War. For a good many years Alexanders had dominated the elite and the legal profession of New York and had been the foremost land speculators in New Jersey. Yet fifteen years after inheriting one of the largest fortunes in colonial America, William Alexander faced sheriffs' sales for back taxes on his lands in at least three New Jersey counties. He was so desperate he attempted to sell his lands in a notorious five-year lottery. Most prominent Americans bought at least a handful of tickets and received nothing in return but embarrassment. Not only had the New Jersey Assembly legalized the lottery, but Governor Franklin sent tickets to his father in London to sell through friends, only to be informed that private lotteries were outlawed in Great Britain. Even cagey George Washington lost six pounds on the drawing and went whistling for the prize of two hundred pounds he won.[14] By 1775, only orders from the Continental Army for round shot, grapeshot and cannonballs from Alexander's near-bankrupt ironworks in northwestern New Jersey saved him from having to sell his New York town house as well as his lavish country seat in New Jersey. His familiarity with provisioning and his ability to supply heavy munitions to the rebels made him a prime candidate for a commission in Washington's army. But what really clinched his appointment as colonel of the First New Jersey Regiment was his reputation for toughness. He and a neighboring ironmaster had quarreled over the supply of firewood for their furnaces. Lord Stirling had personally led sixty-five of his brawny ironworkers in bloody brawls — stout clubs were wielded — with the hired hands of his rival.

After Lexington, many New Jersey militia officers resigned their royal commissions to take new appointments from the provincial congress. William Franklin had been powerless at first to stop them. When the Continental Congress decided that pacifist New Jersey must begin to arm itself, their first choice, Cortlandt Skinner, refused the colonelcy. The Congress then offered it to Lord Stirling. He quickly accepted.[15]

Reluctant to confront Governor Franklin at the council table in

Burlington and face in person the charge of betrayal by an old friend, Stirling sent his excuses. William could never resist reminding hypocrites of their own words: it was a lifelong failing. On October 3, 1775, he wrote a public letter to Lord Stirling. It struck him as incongruous that a man who called himself an earl, who had spent five years and a fortune to have a Scottish court recognize his claim to an earldom, should now declare himself a rebel against all the nobles of Great Britain. William reminded Stirling of his frequent statements that "a man ought to be damned who would take up arms against his sovereign."[16] Their bitter correspondence ended only when Governor Franklin fired Lord Stirling from the New Jersey Council for accepting the commission. To add financial injury to public insult, the governor's party in the Assembly moved to collect the heavy tax arrears on Stirling's lands and set up a committee to investigate his financial dealings.

This public assault on the pocketbook of one of their colleagues finally roused the rebel leaders. When Governor Franklin attempted to convince the Assembly to bypass the Continental Congress by petitioning the King directly, the rebel faction, which included the ranking officers of the radical provincial congress, took control of the key committee of correspondence. Over the governor's objections, they sent to Philadelphia for the most persuasive orators in the Continental Congress to dissuade New Jersey from bolting the Continental cause.

Recognizing the threat of William's stratagem clearly now, congressional leaders, including Benjamin Franklin, carefully studied Governor Franklin's tactics and the makeup of his supporters. They chose their emissaries wisely. The leading radical, Samuel Adams, led the delegation to Burlington to meet with New Jersey radical leaders. To address the legislature came the famous "Farmer Dickinson." The Congress also sent the New York lawyer John Jay, a rich conservative related by marriage to more than one of the Perth Amboy aristocrats in the Assembly chamber. To sum up the Continental argument was the most brilliant constitutional lawyer in America, George Wythe of Virginia. It was as dazzling a group as ever entered the old Burlington courthouse.[17]

All William's exhaustive efforts to talk the Assembly leadership out of allowing this extralegal intrusion into New Jersey's affairs failed. He could not convince them that a congressional delegation had no legal right to speak to the Assembly. Even the governor himself was barred by law from entering the Assembly chamber when the House was in session. Only taxpaying citizens of the colony were entitled to appear. But William's closest friend, speaker Cortlandt Skinner, finally yielded to the intense pressure and stepped down to allow the Assembly, sitting as a committee of the whole, to hear the emissaries from Philadelphia.

Skinner took careful notes of Congressman John Dickinson's opening address: "He began with informing the House that the Congress, alarmed at the reports of the House going to petition the King, had taken the matter into their serious consideration. The result was that he and his colleagues were deputed by Congress.

"He then began with the first Congress ... their humble petition and declaration of rights, which was approved by all America, particularly this House. . . . But the petition was rejected, and Britain prepared for war. She had been taught to believe we were a rope of sand and would not fight — to divide us the [North] resolution was sent out. In the spring, General Gage without cause put to death some Americans, but in the end was forced to retreat shamefully. Had the Congress then drawn the sword and thrown away the scabbard, all lovers of liberty, all honest and virtuous men would have applauded him, but they again humbly petitioned. . . .

"But it was necessary to convince Britain that we would fight, and were not a rope of sand. Therefore an army was formed. [There was an] expedition against Canada. Success attended us everywhere. The savages, who were to be let loose to murder our wives and children, were our friends. The Canadians fought in our cause, and Canada, from whence [so long came] armies to overrun us, is conquered in as few months as it took Britain years. We have nothing to fear but from Europe, three thousand miles distant, but a country so united cannot be conquered. The eyes of all Europe are upon us. Britain has natural enemies, France and Spain. Should we be unsuccessful in the next campaign, France will not sit still and suffer Britain to conquer.

"He then bragged of our success and courage — said nothing would bring Britain to terms but unity and bravery — That all

Britain wanted was to procure separate petitions which we *should avoid.* It would break our union. We would become a rope of sand. — He repeated, as if to frighten, that neither mercy nor justice was to be expected from Britain . . . and entreated us not to petition, but rest on our former petitions, and that of United America."[18]

In a typically long and carefully constructed speech, as important as any he had delivered in his brilliant career, the artful Dickinson had used every lawyer's device, including deliberate distortion: America was not united then. Only one county in all of Georgia, for example, had sent a delegate to the Continental Congress. At least five other colonies were resisting the congressional policies of taxation and conscription. New Jersey did not stand alone. All the moderate Middle Colonies — the people of New York and Pennsylvania, Delaware and Maryland — were watching the outcome of this Assembly. As New Jersey went at this moment, so would go the hopes of the radicals for continued Continental union against the British.

Nevertheless, William Franklin and his neutralists were swept away by a tide of national fervor that carried their ideas of law, reason and prudence before it. The British were three thousand miles away; the forces of America were rising everywhere against the British, and they menaced little New Jersey for daring to stand alone. No distant power of England's could arrive in time to save them, and now they must choose.

There was no single vote, but the next day, after Governor Franklin pleaded with the Assembly to reconsider, to ignore the advice of strangers and demagogues, to petition their King as they had planned, they decided, by a narrow vote, not to petition, not to seek a separate peace.

The last royal Assembly of New Jersey ended badly for Governor Franklin in other ways. He had to postpone two urgent items of business: his long-needed pay raise and funds for building or buying suitable government buildings, even though both had been conditions of the King's approval of the paper money bill. The timing was all wrong now for talk of money. He also had to defer further action on the investigation of Lord Stirling until the next Assembly.[19] But at least he had forced the debate over the North peace plan into the open, and he had more than kept up the semblance of royal rule right under the guns of the rebels. He had even managed to make it much more difficult for a rebel army to be recruited in New Jersey. In the last hours of the Assembly, he had signed into law a bill that enabled creditors to crack down more effectively on debtors who were seeking refuge in the rebel militia. Lord Stirling's correspondence with the Continental Congress indicates that, by the end of the session, rebel recruitment had all but stopped. Many New Jersey soldiers were arrested and imprisoned for "very trifling debts."[20]

As 1776 began, William returned to Perth Amboy, riding right past rebel troops wrapped in old British blankets. He found he could no longer trust enough of the other members of the New Jersey Council to summon them for the private meeting necessary to convene the Assembly. As he began to prepare his most urgent message to London, he was totally isolated. Marking it "Secret and Confidential," he detailed his attempts to hold New Jersey for the King.[21]

William underscored the fact that both New Jersey and his native Pennsylvania were "greatly averse to independency, and if they could be convinced that their present leaders have such intentions, would immediately unite to oppose them." But the royalists were totally disunited, with none of the discipline and superb organization the rebels had achieved over the past three years. Not one unbiased newspaper was left in either colony. In New Jersey, since only rebel-controlled newspapers circulated, sent in by the thousands from New York and Philadelphia, most of the yeomanry read only what the rebel leaders wanted them to. "The danger seems to be that [their] design will be carried on by such degrees and under such pretenses as not to be perceived by the people in general till too late for resistance."

Enclosing the Assembly minutes, William went on to tell Lord Germain of the congressional delegation's "great haste" to come to Burlington and "harangue the House," and he sent along a copy of Skinner's notes as evidence. He told matter-of-factly of his failure to carry off his plan for negotiating a separate peace. "It was this part which alarmed the [Continental] Congress and occasioned them to take so extraordinary a step to prevent [the petition's] being sent, they being of opinion that no colony ought to presume to make separate proposals, but to leave the whole to their management."

He held back nothing now. In naming the names of the congressional emissaries, he realized fully the consequences of identifying them if their revolt failed. And he was obviously bitter about his betrayal by members of the New Jersey Council. He recited the details of their "very unexpected attack," even if he did not report their names. To say who had opposed him would also give away those who still remained loyal. "The truth is, as I have reason to believe, three of the leading members of the Council favor the measures of the Congress. The rest have a leaning the same way, except two or three at most. . . . Even these think it necessary to their safety to observe a kind of trimming conduct, a seeming difference with the Governor. My situation is not a little difficult, having no more than one or two among the principal officers of government to whom I can speak confidentially."

His fear for his safety and that of his wife grew by the day and he made no attempt to hide it. "Notwithstanding the declarations of the Council and the Assembly with regard to the perfect safety of the officers of the Crown, less than a fortnight after the session was over, two judges and one justice of the peace in different counties have been seized. One of them is a member of the Assembly. What is to be their fate I know not." He did not mention that the daily alarms of rebel depredations had left his wife ill and made a gloomy nerve-wracking time of Temple's Christmas visit. William always kept his personal life out of his dispatches.

As for the gathering and transmission of intelligence, so long as William remained governor, he was duty-bound to continue them. The King's proclamation of August 8, 1775, stipulated: "We do accordingly strictly command all officers civil as well as military, and all other our obedient and loyal subjects, . . . to disclose and make known all treasons and traitorous conspiracies . . . to transmit to one of our principal secretaries of state . . . due and full information of all persons who shall be found carrying on correspondence with, or in any manner aiding or abetting the persons now in open arms and rebellion against our government." But now William apologized for his inability to gather intelligence as effectively as he

had a few months earlier. "Since correspondence by letter is become so precarious and indeed dangerous, I obtain very little intelligence of public matters than what is to be found in the
newspapers."[22] For this dispatch he could come up with only the
following tidbits:

He advised the ministry for the first time that the Continental
Congress had "well-grounded assurances of assistance from France
if not Spain." It was his father's best-kept official secret: Benjamin
would have been furious to know that his son was reporting
American strategy directly to London. More damaging was his
next revelation: according to his sources, "the French Ambassador
in England has immediate and full intelligence of whatever passes
in the Privy Council and the Cabinet and conveys the same to persons in London connected with America. They [the Congress] are
determined to apply for foreign aid if they find government likely
to apply foreign troops against them. They meet with little difficulty getting powder, etc., from the French islands, I have reason
to think with the connivance of the French governors. A French
fleet is expected in the St. Lawrence [as] early as the season will
admit. We have certain intelligence of a considerable body of
French troops being arrived in the West Indies."[23]

The powder was smuggled in through numerous coves all along
the seacoast. William named the smugglers and coves so that the
traffic could be "prevented by the King's ships."[24] As he told Lord
Germain, he had no illusions about the arrival of the British ships in
time to help him personally. He knew he was defenseless. He could
not even control the countryside a scant ten miles away: "In Sussex
County in this province there are, I am told, a considerable body of
people who are called Tories." It was a new use of an old word to
him — Tories. In the seventeenth century, under Charles II, it had
been used by Puritans as a term of loathing for the supporters of
the House of Stuart. Now, it was being applied to any American
who opposed or even disagreed with the Congress and its measures.
"It is said [the Tories] have lately been furnishing themselves with
arms and ammunition. The Committee of Safety are to meet next
Tuesday at Princeton to consult on measures for disarming
them."[25]

As if his dispatch were not devastating enough, his selection of newspapers for the ministry's private reading was even more revealing. The Congress was attempting to blockade even the shipment of newspapers to England, for reasons that William's transmittal to Lord Germain made obvious. The first issue of the New York *Journal* for the new year showed that the suppression of Tory dissent, once kept deliberately at the level of ostracism and intimidation, now had become cruel, systematic and ritualistic.

Thomas Randolph, a cooper in nearby Piscataway, "had publicly proved himself an enemy to his country by reviling and using his utmost endeavors to oppose the proceedings of the Continental and Provincial Conventions and Committees in defense of their rights and liberties." His sentence: tarring and feathering (he was not an important enough person to warrant a severer sentence). The ritual of tarring and feathering was by now familiar to every good Son of Liberty. In the freezing December weather Randolph's clothes were stripped off. A fresh barrel of pine tar was broken open and heated in an iron cauldron until it was bubbling hot and thin enough to spread. It was then applied to Randolph's head and face and body and arms and legs and groin and feet with ladles and brushes until all of his writhing squirming skin was covered and beginning to shrivel and blister and give off a rancid steam into the crisp winter air. He must have screamed and prayed and pleaded for mercy. Then they slit open his mattress with their knives and, dancing and cheering around his strange-looking form, sprinkled soft white feathers all over his roasting stinking flesh. If, as usual, a few of the feathers were ignited by the sizzling tar, they could be beaten out readily enough, even though, by this time, the slightest touch made Randolph scream again. So that every damned Tory could witness his punishment and every good patriot hear him recant, Randolph was "carried in a wagon publicly round the town," as the New York *Journal* reported. "He soon became duly sensible of his offense, for which he earnestly begged pardon and promised to atone, as far as he was able." After a half hour of this, Randolph was released and suffered to return to his house. . . . The whole was conducted with that regularity and decorum that ought to be observed in all public punishments."[26] (No account was given of the aftermath, but cleaning the tar from Randolph's body could have been the worst part of his ordeal. As a rule the skin, hair and flesh clung to the tar as it was peeled off. Infection was almost inevitable.)

Newspaper accounts of the spreading persecution of Tories became more and more frequent. The December 28, 1775, issue of the *Journal* gave some idea of its scope. "Last Tuesday, about four hundred of the militia of this county assembled and proceeded in good order and regularity in quest of Tories, a considerable number of whom had entered into a combination and agreement not to comply with any Congress measures. About forty, we hear, are taken, most of whom have recanted, signed the Association and professed themselves true sons of liberty, being fully convinced of their error. Two or three who remain incorrigible are to be sent to Congress to be dealt with."[27] The day's hunt had been conducted with all due regularity and decorum by two rebel colonels, both members of the provincial congress.

The secret strategy of the Congress must have been abundantly clear to William Franklin by this time, as his dispatches to the King's ministers show. And it was obvious now why few assemblymen were willing to travel to Perth Amboy for the reconvened legislative session. Most of all, it should have become clear to William Franklin just what he, the last active royal governor at his post in colonial America, could expect.

Governor Franklin needed nearly all day January 5, 1776, to gather newspapers and petitions and minutes to send to the Colonial Office. After stuffing everything into two large packets, he arranged for a courier. He had one more letter to write and he evidently wrote it himself, without summoning his secretary. Not that he did not trust Pettit. Pettit was, after all, a kinsman. William had sponsored him for an assortment of minor posts to help make up an income for the man. He had never questioned where his confidential secretary stood on the matter of loyalty to King and country.[28] He had made a judgment on the man long ago and trusted him implicitly. For many months, Pettit had avoided the subject of loyalty, keeping especially secret his correspondence with his stepbrother-in-law, Major Joseph Reed, who was General Washington's private secretary and a thoroughgoing rebel.[29] "I have more than once been told," Pettit confided in one of his letters to Reed, "that a person avowing the sentiments I do ought not to hold an office in government, and it is not improbable that I may be told so by Authority [Governor Franklin] before many months."[30] He admitted to Reed that the part he was playing was one he despised and that he was being pressed by rebel friends "to lay an anchor to windward with the Congress for the offices I now hold."[31] No record has come to light of any promise to make him either a paid informant or a rebel official, but he emerged from the next six months of turmoil and duplicity as a full colonel in the Continental Army; he retained all his provincial offices and in less than two years assumed the lucrative post of assistant quartermaster general of all the Continental forces. On that evening in January, his moment of opportunity arrived. He was the only man other than the governor who was in a position to know the exact contents of the dispatch pouches, the identity of the rider and the precise timetable of the rider's movements.

William never did divulge the name of his most trusted courier, but the man was probably Heathcote Johnston, the dashing young son of a Perth Amboy shipping magnate. His frequent business trips to New York City for the Johnston firm provided an ideal cover. He was also second-in-command of the Perth Amboy militia contingent, a fact that ordinarily would put him beyond suspicion. And he was Charles Pettit's brother-in-law. There was, in consequence, every reason for Johnston and Pettit to discuss in detail the governor's arrangements in advance of the secret mission. By late in the night of January 5, Pettit would have had all the information he needed for delivery to rebel headquarters at Elizabethtown, sixteen miles north of Perth Amboy.[32]

William was especially careful in choosing the courier's route. Instead of taking one of the two ferries from Perth Amboy to Staten Island, the courier was to ride north through rebel Elizabethtown to the northernmost ferry crossing at Elizabethtown Point, where he would be least expected to go. Besides the routine dispatches and other correspondence, William gave the courier a separate and smaller packet, which he asked the man to hide on his person.

The rider was off. To avoid arousing suspicion he made no sign that he was in a hurry. He took the coast road at a leisurely pace, following the fringe of Raritan Bay. By noon he reined in at the ferry tavern in Elizabethtown Point. But before he could dismount he was surrounded by a troop of rebels. Captain Joseph Morris, a man he had known socially from childhood, was pointing a cocked pistol at his head. A trooper grabbed his reins and wheeled his horse around. In a matter of minutes the rebels were shoving their prisoner through the front doorway of Lord Stirling's headquarters.

Stirling had reason to be pleased. For four months, while rounding up Tories all over New Jersey, he had anticipated this moment. Since the day the governor had publicly insulted him by questioning his commission from the Congress, he had sought a way to trip up William Franklin. It would have been so easy to bag the unprotected governor while he was presiding over the Assembly at Burlington. Stirling had even ridden into the town and held an illegal meeting of the committee of safety across the street from the courthouse where Franklin was showing the British flag. But he had awaited orders from the Congress.[33]

Until the fall of 1775, the policy of the Congress toward arresting royal officials had remained ambiguous. Then, on October 7, after a debate lasting the entire day, a resolution was passed which recommended that each provincial congress "arrest and secure every person whose going at large may, in their opinion, endanger the safety of the colony or the liberties of America."[34] John Adams's diary further records that during the debate Governor Franklin's status came up. He was declared "not dangerous."[35] Whether this conclusion was reached after consulting the wishes of the most prominent member of the Congress, Benjamin Franklin, can only be conjectured.

By the end of the year, all along the seacoast, there was evidence that the Loyalists were preparing to rise and, with the leadership of royal governors and the support of British ships and men, to fight against the rebels. On January 2, Stirling received new orders. All "unworthy Americans" who, "regardless of their duty to their Creator, their country and their posterity have taken part with our oppressors" were to be disarmed, and the more dangerous among them either kept in safe custody or bound with sufficient sureties to their good behavior."[36] Stirling at once ordered all royal mails intercepted, and snared a compromising letter from Attorney General Cortlandt Skinner to his brother in the British army. In the nick of time Skinner fled in a rowboat to the sanctuary of a man-of-war, leaving his wife and thirteen children behind.[37] As for Governor Franklin, all that Stirling needed was evidence strong enough to warrant his arrest.

Now he had it. He did not wait for a direct order from the Congress. As he immediately wrote to the president, John Hancock, he had had "particular reasons," unquestionably provided by the governor's own aide, to suspect that the governor's courier would be carrying "dispatches of importance for the ministry of Great Britain." His men "this moment have brought back the messenger with the enclosed two packets to the Earl of Dartmouth, which I think it most proper to send you unopened in order to be laid before Congress." Stirling was about to seal his message and send it off to Philadelphia when it occurred to someone in the room that the courier might be carrying something else of value. Ordering the man thoroughly searched, Stirling received another pleasant surprise. He promptly shared it with the Congress: "P.S. After sealing the above, I found on the messenger some private letters to *Mrs. Gage,* which I have forwarded. The handwriting of one of them I knew to be that of a most dangerous man, and for very particular reasons I was induced to open it. I now send it to you."[38]

Of course, the governor was sending messages through Mrs. Gage. She was both the wife of the British commander in chief at Boston and the daughter of a leading New Jersey family whose summer house Stirling could see from the windows of his own country seat. And a private letter to her would seem innocent enough, especially if it carried no return address. For thirteen years, Stirling had seen these unmistakably bold flourishes of the royal governor's handwriting. Jubilantly, he scanned the long, detailed intelligence report to Lord Dartmouth before sending off the day's catch to the Congress under heavy guard. Just as quickly, he issued the order for his second-in-command to take one hundred of his best men and march to Perth Amboy to arrest Governor Franklin.[39]

18

IT IS YOUR TURN NOW

January–July 1776

T HE RESOUNDING BATTERING ON THE GREAT DOUBLE doors of Proprietary House started William and Elizabeth Franklin awake. The noise terrified Elizabeth and sent the governor fumbling out of the bedcovers and rushing to the front window. In the pale moonlight he could make out the dark forms of some fifty militiamen armed with muskets. William had seen them marching into Perth Amboy just before dusk, and had sent his man Thomas to ask what they wanted. Thomas had been told that they would call on the governor on "particular business," but not until the next morning. Instead, Stirling's orders were to wake them in the middle of the night. He had done this deliberately!

William tried, unsuccessfully, to calm his hysterical wife. Always frail, she had become ill from anxiety during the last weeks as reports of terror in the countryside had poured into Perth Amboy. Now she could not be reassured. William finally had to leave her to deal with the rebels. Stirling had sent him a note: "I have hints you intended to leave the province if the letters that were intercepted should be sent to the Continental Congress." Then Stirling *knew* that William had learned of the capture of his courier! There was more: Stirling was demanding his parole of honor, actually demanding that a royal governor, the King's own representative, give "your word and honour that you will not depart this province till I know the will and pleasure of the Continental Congress."

Outraged, William wrote out a hasty reply. He had no choice but to stall Stirling, appease him until help arrived. His intercepted letters "contained nothing but what was my duty as a faithful officer of the Crown." They were merely reports of "public transactions." He had not "the least intention to quit the province" unless "compelled by violence." To act otherwise would not be "consistent with my declarations to the Assembly nor my regard for the good people of the province."

The governor's answer seemed to satisfy the rebel officer. He ordered some of his men to form guard stations at the front gate, the rest to march off. Shortly after dawn all but one sentinel were withdrawn. In the morning William learned that the rebels had also surrounded the house of Cortlandt Skinner during the night, forced their way in, and searched for him without avail. Skinner was already safely aboard a British ship. The search party was led by Skinner's former law clerk.

Despite the interception of his earlier dispatches, late that night William once again poured out to the colonial secretary in considerable detail the narrative of his plight. The rebel lieutenant colonel who had placed him under house arrest had sent his letter to Lord Stirling and was awaiting further orders. "He has just assured a servant of mine who met him in the street that he was extremely concerned for the disturbance he gave me and Mrs. Franklin at such an improper time of the night, but that he could not avoid it, his orders being positive to send [Stirling's] letter to me at that time. So that it seems I have nobody to blame but Lord Stirling for that transaction. I find it is conjectured that the Congress will order me to be seized and sent to the interior part of the country, that I may not have an opportunity of transmitting any more intelligence to your lordship. This has occasioned me to make another copy of the letter which was intercepted." William also had gathered copies of other documents and newspapers. He wanted to send them by special messenger to New York for transshipment, "but as I find there are sentinels placed at all the ferries" it was impossible "to trust him" with a copy of his earlier intelligence report. Only a single letter would get through. He concluded:' "Whatever may happen, I am determined that nothing shall influence me to swerve in the least from that loyalty and duty which I owe his Majesty, which has been the pride of my life."[1]

Just what to do with William Franklin now that Lord Stirling had placed him under house arrest was the dilemma that finally forced into the open the disorganization of the New Jersey radicals. As Lord Stirling's aides rushed word of the governor's activities and his arrest, first to the committee of safety in Princeton and then on to the Congress in Philadelphia, Stirling's officers marched once again from their barracks in Perth Amboy and Elizabethtown to Proprietary House to demand that William sign a parole.

Deciding to have no part in what he considered an illegal proceeding, William refused even to discuss the arrangements of his house arrest with the rebels. As he later reported in still another smuggled letter to Lord Germain, "I absolutely refused to give my word and honor to Lord Stirling. . . . I wrote him a letter commanding him to remove the guard placed about my house, as he would answer the contrary at his peril." Stirling's second-in-command was, William recorded in his diary, "ordered by Lord Stirling to seize my person and send me under a strong guard to Elizabethtown. Accordingly, I was made a prisoner by a party of about one hundred soldiers headed by four or five officers, it not being in my power to make the least resistance."

But while William was preparing to go with them, the provincial chief justice, now the senior British official still at liberty, rode up to Proprietary House. Frederick Smyth was still trusted by the rebels.* They let him pass to talk to the governor. Smyth, who lived in Perth Amboy, was, William later recalled, "greatly alarmed at hearing of my being made prisoner and apprehensive for the ill consequences that would ensue to the province in general and to this town in particular should I be demanded by one of the King's ships now stationed at New York." It was not an idle fear: a British man-of-war had just shelled New York City to deter an attempt to seize that colony's royal officials.

---

* Not to be confused with William Smith, chief justice of New York.

The chief justice requested that Stirling's officer in charge of the Perth Amboy barracks countermand Stirling's orders. William wrote later: "I expressed myself perfectly indifferent whether I was sent to Elizabethtown or not, and that I should consider the insult I had received equally the same. I certainly had no inclination to be taken from home, especially as I must leave Mrs. Franklin in so dangerous a state as she had been thrown into by her fright. Yet, as they had presumed to come with an armed force and make me a prisoner, I was determined to ask nothing that should have the appearance of a favor to myself, nor would I at all interfere in the matter, but should be ready to go in a quarter of an hour wherever they might think proper to take me." William's captors agreed to wait while the chief justice rode to the barracks. William went on with his preparations.

"After waiting about an hour, finding that the officers seemed uneasy that [Smyth] did not return, and having particular reasons why I wished not to delay the journey longer if I was to undertake it, I told them I was ready to set out. They desired me to get into my coach, then waiting at the door, and I set out accompanied by Mr. Stephen Skinner [Cortlandt Skinner's brother], one of His Majesty's Council, whom I had desired to go with me in order to be my witness to what might pass between me and Lord Stirling." (For five years, William had stood by Stephen Skinner while the Assembly accused him of stealing the East Jersey treasury from his own house. Now Skinner remained loyal to the governor.) "But I had not gone above two or three hundred yards before I met the chief justice, accompanied by one of [Stirling's] officers who directed my guard to stop." Smyth brought permission for the governor to remain at Proprietary House while Smyth rode to Elizabethtown to persuade Stirling to countermand his orders.

"I was accordingly brought back to my house. I told them that, as to sending to Lord Stirling, I desired they would remember that it was a matter entirely between themselves, for I considered myself in illegal confinement and should therefore neither approve or disapprove the measures." As William almost lightheartedly summarized the events two months later in a dispatch to the Colonial Office in London, "the result was that the chief justice went to

Lord Stirling, the guards were soon after his return removed from my house, and I have continued unmolested ever since." For the moment at least, William apparently thought he was out of danger.[2]

In a letter to his son, William laid the blame for the entire affair on Lord Stirling: "We have been most abominably used by a most abominable ------- ."[3]

On January 9, the day after William Franklin's arrest became known, the New Jersey committee of safety hastily convened. With one leading royal official fled, the other under guard, and the Assembly prorogued indefinitely, radical leaders now believed they could consolidate their power. From their farms and law offices the rebel committeemen hurried toward Princeton. Several of them rode all night over icy wagon tracks to swing down cold and exhausted from their saddles at Hudibras Tavern in Princeton late the next morning. After thawing before the fire and reviving themselves with hot rum, the nine committeemen went about the business of setting up a provisional government. They must remove the opposition — they would put the more adamant Tories on trial — and try to find some way to arouse the Jersey farmers to active rebellion. The first levies of militiamen had been Scotch-Irish riflemen who had marched north to the Canadian frontier months earlier; few others were now willing to desert their farms in the face of the British invasion expected any day. Opposition to war was so general throughout the colony that efforts to arm the scant one hundred rebel soldiers still remaining was lagging abysmally. And so moderate were the most radical New Jersey provincial congressmen that the radical leaders of the Continental Congress were bypassing them: they could no longer act without clearing every step with Philadelphia. Decrying the "defenseless condition" of New Jersey, Benjamin Franklin asked the Pennsylvania committee of safety to ship in gunpowder and urged the New York committee to send arms for the few militiamen available.[4]

For days, the New Jersey committeemen champed and waited in the crowded tavern. The Continental Congress may have been busy attending to New Jersey military business, but it was obviously ducking the embarrassing problem of what to do about its most powerful member's Tory son. A substantial bloc in the Congress, as many Jerseymen knew, disapproved of Governor Franklin's conduct in provincial affairs, but they believed he would eventually come around and make a valuable addition to the American side. At the same time, his devastating dispatches to London could not be ignored, now that the British offensive was heating up. At almost the exact moment that Lord Stirling's aide delivered to the Congress the two compromising packets from Elizabethtown, a courier from Virginia pounded on the State House door with the first report of the shelling and burning of Norfolk by British navy gunners under the direction of, no less, the provincial royal governor. Royal governors were becoming more and more a menace.

As usual when the congressmen could not decide what to do about a touchy matter, they referred it to committee. Disgusted, one New Jersey delegate reported to the committee of safety, still waiting in the Hudibras Tavern in Princeton, that "nothing was done regarding Governor Franklin."[5] The frustrated committeemen could only adjourn and head for home, and the Revolution once again sputtered to a halt in pivotal New Jersey.

Enormously gratified, William reported the breakdown to Lord Germain in London: "I have heard, indeed, that many of the members of the Continental Congress disapproved of Lord Stirling's conduct toward me, though they have not as a body censured him on that account. It is in a great measure owing to this circumstance that I have not yet experienced any further effects of his resentment.

"On the whole, I should have been better pleased that the Chief Justice had not interfered between us (though he probably did it from the best motives) as the Congress, had I remained a prisoner at Elizabethtown, would have been under a necessity of giving some orders respecting me. I much wanted to see how they would have behaved. They, or some of them at least, want to have the King's governors quit the colonies that they might have a pretense for forming them into separate republics. My language has constantly been, '*You may force me, but you shall never frighten me out of the province.*' "[6]

William Franklin might have suffered no worse fate than to sit out the Revolution in elegant comfort had it been his nature to acquiesce. All over colonial America natural opponents of the republican rebellion were moving to their country houses and keeping quiet. One of William's neighbors, the privy councillor James Parker, had taken to the hills of Hunterdon County. Many leaders of the proprietary party in Pennsylvania, as well as his old friend Galloway, were living silently if sullenly in stylish serenity in the countryside.[7] But William stayed quiet only briefly, fulminating at his isolation, his inactivity. At first there was little more he could do, but before many weeks passed he began to turn his mind to the steps he would need to take as soon as the King's ships finally hove into sight around Sandy Hook. Constructive thinking was difficult: all the news reaching Perth Amboy had been uniformly bleak. Another friend, the Anglican preacher Jonathan Odell, was arrested in Burlington after hiding for weeks in the priest's hole in William's old riverfront house.[8] William's income had sagged also: the tenant of his Rancocas farm, a brother-in-law of the royal governor of New York, failed for the second year to pay any rent.[9]

On the same day the Continental Congress learned of William's arrest, the first copies of a scorching political pamphlet, printed at Benjamin Franklin's suggestion, came off the press: Thomas Paine's *Common Sense*. The firebrand best-seller was read in front of tens of thousands of American hearthsides that winter, making fence sitters shake their heads, Loyalists fume, radicals demand independence. Such words had never been seen in print before by a mass readership and would have been censored in any other country. The King of England was referred to as "the royal brute." Monarchy was "exceedingly ridiculous." The ancient ties between America and England "sooner or later must have an end."[10]

The impact of *Common Sense* was intensified when that week's newspapers printed the King's address at the opening of the current session of Parliament. *All* America was in rebellion, he declared, and would be punished "by the most decisive exertion." To accomplish this, he threatened to hire mercenaries — he had received the "most friendly offers of foreign assistance" from German princes eager to sell the services of their troops.[11] William feared, after reading Paine's tract, that the King's speech would surely drive the Continental Congress into the waiting arms of France.

He also read, obviously with more relish, a script forwarded by Temple: John Trumbull's patriotic play "M'Fingal." Disgusted with the revolutionaries' egalitarian promises to the poor and to debtors, William openly cheered M'Fingal's disbelief that the Revolution would wipe away class differences. Any honest man could see that the Revolution had been taken over by rich planters, financiers, businessmen and Whig landholders. In thanking Temple for the script, he showed in his answer that he was trying to remain objective despite his wearing confinement. "I like pieces that are well wrote, let them be of what side the question they may, especially when they abound with wit and humor, as is greatly the case in that performance."[12]

Benjamin Franklin had not written William since storming out of Proprietary House three months earlier. He had apparently not told Temple or Sally of William's arrest: a letter from Temple written six days after Benjamin learned of the attempt to imprison William did not mention it. When William answered by the next week's mail, he told Temple how worried he was about Elizabeth. Her "spirits continue so agitated that the least sudden noise almost throws her into hysterics and I am really apprehensive that another alarm of the like nature will put an end to her life." William was bitter that Temple had heard nothing about their fate from his father: Elizabeth had come to rely on Sally, her social protégé and sisterly companion of many summers. If Elizabeth felt neglected, what exacerbated her anxiety was that William's family "do not at present seem disposed to give themselves any concern about her, omitting even those inquiries and outward forms of complaisance and civility which she daily receives from strangers."[13]

Temple's answer checred William and Elizabeth. At least their *son* had not deserted them. Temple's note was full of apologies for not knowing of their plight, full of concern for his mother. William wrote back that he "could not imagine that any of our friends could have been ignorant of what the whole country rang of, or I might have acquainted them with it."[14] Sally's preoccupation with childbirth explained her seeming neglect. Early in February, Elizabeth received another lift, a letter from Sally full of chat about her new baby girl. Gratefully, Elizabeth wrote back, telling her sister-in-law how they had been "scandalously treated." Perth Amboy had been "a very agreeable place till within these four weeks, but everything is now changed and, instead of these joyous social evenings we used to pass with each other, we only meet now to condole together over our wretched situation."[15]

The letters from Philadelphia were not filled with news of Benjamin's activities in the Congress. They did not mention, probably on his instructions, that he had resigned from the Pennsylvania committee of safety to devote all his time to planning a secret diplomatic mission to Canada. In the last two months of 1775, invading American forces had captured Montreal but had been beaten back bloodily at the gates of Quebec. Benjamin was asked to lead a delegation north to try to win over the French Canadians to the Continental cause. For obvious reasons he did not write William about the mission. Indeed, he made all the arrangements for the New Jersey leg of the journey with William's mortal enemy, Lord Stirling. The Franklin entourage passed by Perth Amboy on its way to Canada but did not stop at Proprietary House. When William learned who was in the train of carriages and wagons, he wrote to Temple that he was alarmed for his father's health, traveling to Canada in the winter at his age. He would have told his father so, had he "any reason to think it would have been to any purpose."[16]

In one sense William must have been relieved that Benjamin was gone for a while. Temple had been under enormous pressure, living in a revolutionary household and attending a rebel-dominated college. He wrote to William that he was worried about what would become of him without his influential grandfather's protection. The boy was still so conspicuously English that Philadelphia's more ardent rebels considered him a high Tory.[17] "Your situation will not be so agreeable in his absence," William wrote to counsel his son, "but let it not be your fault if it is not. However others may behave to you, be careful that your conduct to them is as polite, affectionate and respectful as possible."[18] Though he was willing to provide advice that no doubt raised Temple's expectations, William refused, two weeks later, his son's request for additional pocket money. Temple had obviously spent all the money William had deposited with Bache for the boy's allowance. In his tense and irritable state, William forgot how he had once resented his father's tightfistedness and homilies: "Every necessity being found you, you can only want money for trifles. You have much greater allowance than I had at your age, and I believe more than nine tenths of the boys at college have. However, when you have occasion for anything that may be useful, or for promoting your learning, I shall not begrudge the expense." How much like his father William sounded as he, in his turn, began to alienate his own son. "But I cannot afford you money to fool away. Nor would I if I could, as it would only be furnishing you with the means of going into excesses that would be productive of the ruin of your constitution, hinder your growth, and make you miserable hereafter."[19]

Temple had failed to send the political pamphlets his father ordered and instead had written back to defend his expenses as necessary. William insisted on an accounting and berated his son for his improvidence. Temple was told to see that he sent along the newspapers as well as a dozen copies of a pamphlet attacking Paine's *Common Sense* (although he did not say where Temple was to get the money to pay for them). In a postscript he added, "You need not let anyone know you send these." Whether he was trying to save Temple from embarrassing questions on the boy's account or whether he was consciously using his son as a messenger to gather material he would eventually use as intelligence to send to the British is unclear. In either event, he chose this inopportune time, when he most needed Temple's affection, to lash out at him. Ten more days passed without a reply from the boy. He wrote again: "If you are not more punctual in obeying my orders, I must find some person that will." And he took Temple to task for not walking a few blocks to buy a newspaper "if it is not too much trouble."[20]

The exchange did not deter Temple from coming to Perth Amboy in April for his spring vacation. He found the governor and his lady still trying to keep up appearances, and by the time he had to return to Philadelphia for classes, he was eager to go, especially since his father this time generously advanced him ten weeks' allowance so he would not have to be dependent on Bache. (The money was gone in less than three weeks.)[21]

Despite his ill-timed outbursts, William missed his father and son acutely. The gloom that normally settles over a household when a son returns to school replaced the usual promise of spring in the country. It was a season of turmoil for William, churned by each week's newspapers. The rebels were everywhere gaining ground, the King's loyal subjects stymied at every attempt to preserve the imperial union. The fighting had spread from New England north to the Plains of Abraham, south to the Carolinas. In western North Carolina, Scottish Highlanders pulled their claymores from hiding places, donned their tartans, and marched behind their skirling bagpipes down from the high country for a rendezvous with a British fleet on the coast. On February 27, in the morning mist over Moores Creek, they charged across a narrow bridge to break through rebel lines. But the rebels had taken up the bridge rails, smeared the runners with bear grease. As the Highlanders gave their fierce cry and tried to pick their way across in the half-light, they were cut down by round after round of grapeshot fired at point-blank range. It would be years before southern Loyalists attempted another rising.[22]

Indeed, the largest concentration of Loyalists in America fled the country early in March. Washington's overnight fortification of Dorchester Heights left the British garrison in Boston facing the prospect of a devastating artillery barrage from a hilltop too high for British naval guns to reach. The British officers decided at a hasty council of war to abandon the city and sail for Halifax until proper reinforcements arrived from England. One thousand Loyalists from all over New England crammed British troop transports, leaving their homes and often their families to the fury of the Yankee mobs they so hated and feared. All over colonial America, men and women had to choose between loyalty to a distant King and his laggard armies — or allegiance to a new country flushed with a year of victories.[23]

For William Franklin, the time, heavy time, actually made him physically ill. His confinement at Proprietary House stretched into months. He had only the most meager assurances of assistance from British superiors. A stray spring transport brought a brief note from Lord Germain that the King had seen William's reports, "approves your zealous endeavors for his service and relies upon a continuance of them under all the difficulties which surround you."[24] Despite his confinement William still felt it his duty to continue sending his detailed intelligence reports. The King must be told that all America had not gone mad with revolution, even if Thomas Paine's hugely successful propaganda had inflamed the colonies with debate over the question of independence. "A great number of people" had been swayed by this "most inflammatory pamphlet in which that horrid measure is strongly and artfully recommended," William wrote Lord Germain in March. But there had been a reverse effect for many others. It had "opened the eyes of many people of sense and property who before would not believe that there were any persons of sense or consequence either in or out of Congress who harbored such intentions. Those are now alarmed — see their danger — and begin to express their fears and apprehensions."[25] William sent along copies of pamphlets rebutting *Common Sense* even as he reported the retreat of Continental forces across the Canadian border with heavy casualties.

In this, the last letter that William was able to smuggle out to London, he informed the ministry in an angry postscript: "I have just heard that two of the delegates (Dr. Franklin & Mr. Chase) have passed through . . . this morning in their way to Canada."* The two Franklins, never to see each other again in America, each in his own way had now exchanged unspoken insults. Benjamin had left his only son in the charge of an unpredictable personal enemy, left the country an old man without saying goodbye. William had responded with the most vindictive weapon at his command. He had put his father on report in an official communication to the King, singling him out of the anonymous rebellious multitude as a traitor exporting revolution across the frontiers of His Majesty's dominions.

The British abandonment of Boston after an eight-year occupation left behind not only a horde of brass cannon, military stores, food and clothing desperately needed by Washington's army, it left thirteen British-American colonies in the hands of the rebels without out a single redcoat to claim them for the Crown. A tremendously heartening victory for the Continental forces, the precipitate British withdrawal nevertheless foreshadowed a vengeful British offensive as soon as the King's new levies arrived off America's

---

* Actually, three delegates were sent by the Congress to Canada: Benjamin Franklin, Samuel Chase and Charles Carroll.

unprotected seacoast aboard the spring fleet. All Americans waited apprehensively for the British onslaught. With more than one thousand miles of coastline to defend, George Washington, Benjamin Franklin and the leaders of the Congress puzzled over the most likely landfalls. They were sure the British would seek bases where they had the strongest Loyalist support: New York and Charleston.

Even before moving into the deserted shambles that had been Boston, Washington began peeling off companies of riflemen and shipping them south. He ordered Lord Stirling to take charge of building the defenses of New York City. He sent one thousand militiamen to disarm the Tory farmers of Long Island, who were estimated to make up more than three-fourths of the population, and to secure their vital food supplies for his army. The congressional decision to fortify New York made more embarrassing than ever the presence of Governor William Franklin of New Jersey and his royal establishment less than twenty miles from the new Continental headquarters. The radicals decided to isolate the Loyalists and deal with them once and for all. They set up a new provisional capital at Princeton, which had become the center of revolutionary activity.[26]

By May of 1776, revolutionary leaders were exasperated that New Jersey, a certain British target in the American heartland, stayed largely neutral, its stubbornly conservative farmer-freeholders unwilling to do anything voluntarily to jeopardize their prosperity and drag themselves into the war. Most of New Jersey's early rebels had by this time withdrawn from active politics and had been displaced by a more radical faction centered in Princeton. A large percentage of the new revolutionaries were either former students or trusted political allies of the Reverend John Witherspoon. One Witherspoon protégé had taken over the Middlesex militia at Perth Amboy, another was Washington's adjutant general, still another, his mustermaster of troops. Other Princeton graduates who had imbibed his philosophy from his lectures — Aaron Burr, Light Horse Harry Lee — had early joined the struggle as staff officers with Continental forces from Charleston to Quebec. Princeton students were ardent Whigs and all ninety of them in 1776 considered themselves revolutionary officers.

President Witherspoon for many years had inveighed against ministers involving themselves in politics and he kept his political views out of his pulpit, even if every American and British official had a pretty clear idea of where he stood. Since his youth in Scotland, he had betrayed little loyalty for the Hanoverian Kings of England. As a young cleric, he had raised a corps of militia and led them into battle on the side of Bonnie Prince Charlie in the Rising of 1745. After escaping from prison, he organized the anti-Anglican popular party within the state church of Scotland. He espoused hard-line orthodox Calvinism, attacking reforms made in church and civil life by more moderate clergymen. He demanded a separation of church and state, and outspokenly opposed the influence of the Anglicans. While still in Scotland he had been arrested, convicted, and fined heavily for delivering a defamatory sermon in which he accused backsliders by name from the pulpit. He was technically jumping bail when he emigrated to America to take charge of the fundamentalist New Light Presbyterians and become president of Princeton.

For many years he kept silent on the widening rift between England and America. "When I first came into this country, nothing was further from my expectation than the contest that has now taken place," he wrote in May 1776.[27] Yet for five years he had also written sharp criticisms of the ignorant English in Scottish and American newspapers and magazines under a variety of assumed names. A natural conspirator capable of giving an appearance exactly the opposite of his true beliefs, he planted turnips for his students even while he lived in an elegant country house a mile from the campus, lavishly entertaining visiting trustees, fathers of prospective students and American political leaders. One private feast showed how flexible was Parson Witherspoon's standard. On August 27, 1771, he was host to sixty trustees and their friends at the annual meeting of the college. He provided them, according to receipts in the Princeton archives, with twelve double bowls of punch, seventeen quarts of beer, twenty-one bottles of port, sixteen bottles of Madeira and six bowls of hot toddy.[28]

Each year, he carefully and secretly involved himself ever more deeply in the fabric of revolutionary influence. He increasingly opposed the establishment of the Anglican Church in America.

Through his missionary graduates, whom he sent along the frontiers from Pennsylvania to Georgia to spread his version of the Gospel, he counterattacked the London-based missionary Society for the Propagation of the Gospel in Foreign Parts, whose leading supporter in the Middle Colonies, where it was making its deepest inroads, was Governor William Franklin, a director of the Anglican organization. By the outbreak of the Revolution, Anglican missionaries were working hard to win over Dissenters, and more than one hundred Princeton-trained fire-and-brimstone missionaries were waging a holy war to win over Americans who had come to think of Puritanism as too rigid. New churches of both denominations were being built in almost every modest-sized town. Many of the Anglican missions were endowed with silver plate, prayer books and altar linens donated by Governor and Mrs. Franklin.[29]

As long ago as 1759, when the Franklins visited Glasgow, Witherspoon was enunciating his central theme: "There has been a struggle from the very first dawn of the Reformation between Presbytery and Episcopacy."[30] In the early days the struggle had meant turning out legions of black-garbed Presbyterian troops to fight for Cromwell against the Anglican Stuarts. Now, in 1776, it was time to renew the struggle left unfinished one hundred years ago. It was time now, Witherspoon said, to complete the holy civil war.

At each turn of the Revolution, Witherspoon spoke out more boldly to radical leaders passing through Princeton: Benjamin Franklin, George Washington, John Adams and Samuel Adams. After a three-day stopover, John Adams found him "as high a son of liberty as any man in America."[31] Whenever the Congress was in session, Witherspoon went to Philadelphia to lobby quietly for his position. His words inspirited the rebels when he revealed to the politicians his private messianic vision: "The *people* have a natural throne in their consciences to give warning and pass sentence against the King as a tyrant. Earthly princes lay aside their power when they rise up against God."[32] A decadent aristocracy's subjects "ought rather utterly to defy them than to obey them."

It galled Witherspoon that, for nearly ten years, he dared not speak out against the arch-Anglican Governor Franklin when Franklin argued that the right to resist, which Witherspoon was sanctioning, leads to anarchy. Privately, Witherspoon argued that "to refuse this inherent right in every man is to establish injustice and tyranny and leave every good subject without help, a tame prey to ambition and rapacity. There are many instances of rulers becoming tyrants, but comparatively few of causeless and premature rebellions."[33] But publicly he still had to defer to this illegitimate son of a printer.

Even as late as Bunker Hill, Witherspoon managed to keep his political views out of sight, out of his sermons. For public comsumption he said he had "not the most distant thought of subverting the government or of hurting the interest of Great Britain, nor the least desire of withdrawing allegiance from the common sovereign."[34] But to fellow members of the Somerset County committee of safety he said otherwise. Even as Governor Franklin preached reconciliation and tranquillity and warned the Assembly against "all the horrors of a civil war," the Reverend Witherspoon countered: "We are firmly determined never to submit, and do deliberately prefer war with all its horrors, and even extermination itself, to slavery riveted on us and our posterity."[35]

These two clashing symbols of authority — the governor in his carriage, the parson in black on his dark steed, as they crisscrossed New Jersey — gave colonists a clearly defined choice: established power and wealth, cultural refinement and an easy, pleasant religion, or the austere, self-sacrificing if politically untested republican virtues offering their rewards later, perhaps entirely, in the afterlife. Witherspoon had long labored to make plain the choice between sinful luxury and godly self-denial.

In the lingering spring of 1776, it was time for Jerseymen to make their final choice between the messianic Reverend Witherspoon and the high and mighty Governor William Franklin. Witherspoon made his first open bid for power in April. He placed unsigned advertisements in New York and Philadelphia newspapers, and then called a mass meeting of revolutionary delegates from every county in New Jersey without the authority of either the Continental Congress or the provincial congress. After also calling, as a cover, the stated annual meeting of the Princeton board of trustees, he slipped away on the second day and rode to New Brunswick for the secret meeting.

On their way home from the trustees' meeting, two Princetonians happened to stop off in New Brunswick for lunch in a tavern. There they learned of the mass meeting, were told that Witherspoon was not exactly following the advertised agenda of discussing ways to promote home manufactures to offset British imports. Witherspoon had been forced to acknowledge that it was he who had placed the advertisements calling the convention. He said he "wanted to consider the peculiar situation of the province" and "the propriety of declaring a separation from Great Britain and forming an independent constitution for ourselves."

Elias Boudinot, who attended the meeting that afternoon, recorded in his diary: "Dr. W. rose and in a very able and elegant speech of one hour and a half endeavored to convince the audience of the absurdity of opposing the extravagant demands of Great Britain while we were professing a perfect allegiance to her authority and supporting her courts of justice. The character of the speaker, his great influence among the people and the artful manner in which he represented the whole subject had an effect on the assembly that astonished me. There appeared a general approbation of the Doctor's scheme."[36]

As leading Presbyterian, Boudinot resented the way Witherspoon had overlapped the meetings, thereby making it appear that the Presbyterian leaders in Princeton endorsed independence. "I never felt myself in a more mortifying position. It altogether looked so like a preconcerted scheme to accomplish the end [independence] that I was at my wit's end to know how to extricate myself, especially as the measure was totally against my judgment." Boudinot disliked being swept along against his will. "I determined at all events to step forward. No one had spoken in opposition until I rose and, in a speech of about half an hour, endeavored to show that [Witherspoon's] plan was neither founded in wisdom, prudence nor economy." Boudinot's opposition was "wholly unexpected by the Doctor," who appeared "a little disconcerted" with "the great attention" the crowd paid to Boudinot. "But he soon recovered himself and began a reply. Two or three gentlemen of the audience came to me and desired that I would inform the Doctor that if he proceeded any farther, they would not be answerable for his safety." Someone whispered to Witherspoon. "He directly stopped — informed the chairman that he found he was giving offense — he would say no more on the subject, but hoped the committees would return to the respective counties without coming to any determination. To this I objected." Boudinot demanded a vote. Contradictory versions of the debate must not be reported around the colony. "The Doctor was a good deal out of humor and contended warmly against [it]." But a large majority of the meeting insisted on one. "Out of thirty-six members, there were but three or four who voted for the Doctor's proposition, the rest rejecting it with great warmth. Thus ended this first attempt to try the pulse of the people on the subject of independence."[37]

But John Witherspoon was never daunted by a single setback. He now openly organized opposition to reconciliation with Great Britain in a campaign that made ample use of William Franklin's confinement. Under a series of pen names, he launched a crusade in print against the notion of restoring peace. "No alternative is left," he wrote, "but either to go with ropes about our necks and submit ourselves not only to the king but to the kingdom of England to be trampled underfoot or risk all the consequences of open and vigorous resistance."[38]

Sending personal word to Lord Stirling that he was ready to cooperate in forcing the takeover of New Jersey from the moribund royal government, he then recommended to the Continental Congress through his trusted Presbyterian colleague William Livingston that the Congress nudge lukewarm citizens by declaring a solemn day of fasting and prayer throughout America to accompany news that the Congress was about to take up the final debate on a declaration of independence.[39]

On the appointed day, Whig ministers took to their pulpits and Anglicans hid or were urged by mobs to stay home. In at least one instance, sharpshooters were stationed in the congregation to fire at the first word favorable to the King. In Princeton, the Reverend Witherspoon marched into the simple red-brick Presbyterian meetinghouse and climbed into the high pulpit. His stocky form loomed over his parishioners, who noted that he was not wearing the traditional white wig but letting his close-cropped gray hair show unadorned.

"You are all my witnesses that this is the first time of my introducing any political subject into this pulpit. At this season, however, it is not only lawful but necessary, and I willingly embrace the opportunity of declaring my opinion without any hesitation that the cause in which America is now in arms is the cause of justice, of liberty, and of human nature." He told the anxious farmers and college boys, the sturdy local squire and his wife and daughters, that he had long studied the struggle for signs of sinful "pride, resentment or sedition" but found only "a deep and general conviction that our civil and religious liberties" as well as "the temporal and eternal happiness of us and our posterity depend on the issue." He called on them to bow their heads with him and he pleaded with them for holiness and for concern for their own salvation in these trying times. He then called on them all to join him in the struggle against Parliament's "usurped authority." He emphasized that they all must fight this holy war for far more than taxes or judges' salaries: their continued religious freedom, that most sacred of issues, was at stake. "There is not a single instance in history in which civil liberty was lost and religious liberty preserved. If we yield up our temporal property, we deliver the conscience into bondage."

For a Presbyterian sermon, his message was short, but it was bristling with bellicose biblical references to illustrate the fates of those who had submitted and the glory of those who had resisted despite the ultimate cost. "The blood of martyrs was the seed of Christians; the more abundantly it was shed, the more plentifully did the harvest grow." And to stiffen the resolve of listeners worrying about the immense British fleet bearing down on their shores, he compared their circumstance to the attack of the Spanish Armada on Protestant England less than two hundred years earlier. "And it pleased God so entirely to discomfit it by tempests that only a small part of it returned home, though no British force opposed it at all."

He concluded by pronouncing inseparable the two issues of "true religion" and the struggle for freedom from domination by the English Parliament, and prayed that his people would stand up

and fight for both as "uncorrupted patriots" and "invincible soldiers."[40]

By May 1776, William Franklin knew the long lull was over and
that full-scale warfare must break over America unless, by some
miracle, it could be averted. The Continental Congress had passed
two critical resolutions after weeks of bitter debate. One resolution,
passed on May 15, supported by the South and New England but
adamantly opposed by the moderate Middle Colonies called for an
end to royal government. Authority under the Crown "should be
totally suppressed and all powers of government exerted under the
people." On June 7, the companion resolution declared that the
colonies "are and of right ought to be free and independent
states."[41] The Congress sent delegates home for new instructions:
to break the year-long impasse they needed a directed vote for independence.

A general election of new provincial congresses was set. The
revolutionaries went to work in the swing states of New Jersey,
Pennsylvania, Delaware, Maryland, and New York. To counteract
the conservative majority in the Middle Colonies, special oaths
were required of all voters that they no longer gave their allegiance
to the King or Great Britain but pledged their fidelity to the Congress. Tories, suspected Tories, or anyone formerly accused by any
rebel committee were barred from voting. Moreover, the very fact
of an oath was against the religious beliefs of nearly half a million
nonjurors from more than two hundred religious sects, predominantly Quakers and Moravians. It is one of the shameful ironies of
American history that just when a new nation dedicated to freedom
and personal liberty was being created, the nonjuring majorities in
the Middle Colonies were deliberately disenfranchised.[42]

William Franklin was well aware of congressional tactics and he
knew that he must make a last-ditch attempt to give what he considered a majority of the people of his province a clear-cut choice
between independence — which meant certain civil war — and
continued union with Great Britain. His decision to stand alone
among the royal governors in calling his Assembly without the
protection of troops or even bodyguards was the central act of
bravery of his life. At the moment when he had to make the deci-

sion to stand alone, he was sure he would be at least tacitly supported by large numbers of the peaceful people with whom he had
lived for so many years. There was also the possibility that some
not-so-peaceful Loyalists would arm themselves and take his part
until the King's ships arrived.

Early reports of the balloting in rural New Jersey riveted the attention of the Continental Congress. Sam Adams noted in a letter
home that "the Jerseys are agitating the great question."[43] Radical
leaders in the Congress were apprehensive. On May 15 New Jersey's five-man delegation voted against resolutions calling for an
end to royal rule and for the establishment of independent states.

It would be two years before William Franklin could record the
outcome of the election, but the voting was, he reported to Germain, extremely light: "A twentieth part of the electors attended
the election in any county, and in some not a hundredth part."[44] In
the Quaker counties of Burlington and Gloucester, scarcely fifty
men — all rebels — voted: the Quakers were conscientiously
barred, and even if they had ignored their beliefs, a second test oath
made it impossible for them and for Jews and many other non-
Christian sects to hold seats in the Congress. In three other eastern
counties around Perth Amboy, there were heavy Loyalist turnouts.
In several other counties, known Tories were actually elected
to the rebel congress, eleven out of the sixty-five seats falling to
them.

William Franklin had all the encouragement that time would
permit him. He decided to call the Assembly to meet him in Perth
Amboy before a new provincial congress had time or reason to declare an end to his authority. Two days after the general election,
the readers of New York and Pennsylvania newspapers circulated
in New Jersey were surprised to read Governor Franklin's announcement that, despite the fact he was under house arrest, he felt
compelled by "matters of great importance" to convene the last
royal assembly in all America into emergency session on June 20.[45]
This, his boldest stroke, was calculated to force an open confrontation between the New Jersey Assembly and the Continental Congress.

Both he and the congressional leadership knew that if he succeeded in driving a wedge into the middle of the union, the Conti-

nental Congress could splinter before the British arrived. The wording of the congressional edict empowering establishment of provincial congresses stated clearly that they should usurp royal authority only where "no government sufficient to the exigencies of their affairs" remained. William intended to deny the rebels legal grounds for their Congress. As the last royal governor at his post in America, he hoped to convene peace talks on Staten Island "before the Congress could take any measure to prevent it."[46]

He had long ago given up any idea of persuading the New Jersey assemblymen to break ranks with the Continental union, but "he was convinced" that an early peace conference would prove to wavering Americans the King's "kind intentions to remove every reasonable cause of complaint" and would thus pave the way for direct negotiations between Crown peace commissioners and the Continental Congress. Then, if Congress refused to negotiate, the New Jersey Assembly would no doubt consider itself "absolved from holding any further connection with the Congress."[47]

But William's dramatic move reckoned without John Witherspoon, who anonymously urged radical assemblymen to ignore the summons to Perth Amboy and instead rush preparations for the provincial congress. By June 9, rebel leaders from nearby counties began arriving in the old royal capital of Burlington, where only six months earlier William Franklin had challenged the Congress. On the tenth, a heated floor fight took place when there were insufficient members present to make up a two-thirds quorum. The newly elected congressman Witherspoon was unswayed by moderates' arguments that to proceed without the absent members, many of them Loyalists who had deliberately boycotted the session, was to make the entire session illegal. Putting out the word that it was time to "throw the neutrals overboard," the Witherspoon faction managed to have the rules changed: one-half attendance now constituted a legal quorum.[48]

On the first day, with all the proceedings closed to the public, the provincial congress began debate on independence. Again, the respected moderate leader Elias Boudinot took to his feet and denounced the idea as premature for a wide variety of reasons. For one, "as soon as we declare for independence, every prospect of peace must vanish in ruthless war." In bloody detail, Boudinot sketched his vision of the holocaust. If Britain won, her terms were sure to be severe. Even if she lost, she would resentfully "parcel out this continent to European powers. But supposing once more we were able to beat off every regiment that Britain can spare or hire, destroy every ship she can send, that we could beat off any other European power that would presume to intrude." And then he voiced the fear of many middle-class Americans, the fear so often avoided in congressional debates: "A republican form of government will never suit the genius of the people or the extent of the country. The Americans are properly Britons. They have the manners, habits and ideas of Britons." And in a telling conclusion he warned that the cost of a republican American government would far outweigh anything they had ever seen as British subjects. "Where the money is to come from to defray this enormous expense I know not, unless some one of our warm ones for independence has discovered the philosopher's stone."[49]

All Boudinot managed to do was to slow down Witherspoon's juggernaut for three days. By Friday, June 14, many more radicals had arrived from outlying counties to swell the rebel majority and Witherspoon lieutenants had been elected to all the key congressional posts. The provincial congress set aside the question of independence, for the moment turning to the more pressing question of what to do about the royal governor. As William subsequently related, Sam Adams rode over from Philadelphia to bolster their determination and urge Witherspoon to depose and arrest him. By a vote of 38 to 11, the congress that afternoon passed the first of a series of motions to overthrow the governor. Then came a motion to outlaw the New Jersey Assembly. Included was a reference to William Franklin as "the late governor" and a warning to Jerseymen that he henceforth "ought not to be obeyed."[50] The motion passed in a dramatic rollcall vote.

The next morning, in a rare Saturday session, the congress received petitions from citizens of Perth Amboy and Shewsbury "praying that the government not be changed."[51] They were ignored. The congress swept on, declaring by the same wide margin that William Franklin "has acted in direct contempt" of the Continental Congress.[52] Some of the more moderate members had already left Burlington in disgust by the time the next motion was read, which declared that "William Franklin, Esquire, has discovered himself to be an enemy to the liberties of this country and that measures ought to be immediately taken for securing the person of the said William Franklin."[53]

The relentless resolves left the provincial congress seriously divided when the next item of business was introduced. The lieutenant colonel ordered to implement the will of the congress refused to carry out his commission and resigned. He was immediately replaced by a tavernkeeper from Middlesex County, Colonel Nathaniel Heard, who had already earned himself the appellation of "Tory hunter" for his brutal tactics in rounding up and disarming nearly fourteen hundred Loyalists on Long Island. To the tune of "Yankee Doodle" they bitterly sang:

> *Colonel Heard has come to town*
> *In all his pride and glory;*
> *And when he dies he'll go to Hell*
> *For robbing of the Tory.*

For weeks he had pursued some of the leading lawyers, doctors and judges of New York State and members of the New York legislature like wild animals through woods, pine barrens, and valleys to bring them to bay and force them to take oaths to the Continental Congress. Several had been shot down, or had been bayoneted when his militiamen prodded for them in haystacks and hollow trees. The more important Loyalists had been marched off to the remote Connecticut hill country, out of reach of the King's ships.

In handwritten orders empowering Heard to seize William Franklin "with all the delicacy and tenderness which the nature of the business can possibly admit,"[54] he was handed a blank parole which offered the governor his choice of three places of confinement: Princeton; his former friend Hopkinson's farm at Bordentown; or his own farm at Rancocas, where he was to live "upon his honor. . . . But should he refuse to sign the parole, you are desired to put him under strong guard and keep him in close custody. We refer to your discretion what means to use. . . . You have full power and authority to take for your aid whatever force you may require."[55]

Their muskets gleaming in the early summer sunlight, the patriot troopers fanned out around Proprietary House shortly after nine o'clock on the morning of June 17, 1776. Aides steadied the horse of the portly Colonel Heard. Soon the boots clattered up the marble steps and Thomas ushered in the colonel and his aide-de-camp, Princeton-educated Major Jonathan Deare. Before William could come out of his study, the officers and a squad of their men crowded into the room. Colonel Heard gruffly told the governor he was under arrest. He showed William the written resolutions of the Congress and handed him the parole form. The governor was to fill in the blank for his site of confinement and then sign.

William could no longer restrain his anger. As he later re-counted: "In terms suitable to such unmerited provocation [I] rejected the parole with the contempt such an insult deserved from one who has the honor to represent His Majesty."[56] According to Heard, the governor "forbid me at my peril to carry the order into execution" and told him, "It is your turn now, but it will be mine another day." Heard was thoroughly nonplussed. Accustomed to immediate compliance by quavering Tories, he was reluctant to proceed without more detailed orders. He posted a strong guard and hurried back to the barracks to write for them forthwith. In doing so, he advised the congress that in his opinion the governor would never consent to sign. A courier rushed the letter overnight to Burlington. Direct orders, unanimously authorized, sped back at once: "Sir — It is the desire of Congress that you immediately bring William Franklin Esquire to this place under such guard as you think sufficient."[57]

The congress sent concurrently a full report to John Hancock in Philadelphia. It was the first word to reach the Continental Congress of New Jersey's decision to unseat the governor. The New Jersey congress "beg leave to submit to the consideration of the Congress whether it would not be for the general good of the United Colonies that Mr. Franklin should be removed to some other colony. . . . Congress will easily conceive the reasons of this application, as Mr. Franklin, we presume, would be capable of doing less mischief in Connecticut or Pennsylvania than in New Jersey."[58]

When Secretary Thomson opened the message and turned it over to Hancock, Benjamin Franklin was not in his usual seat at the

State House. He was home, as he wrote Washington three days later, recovering from the effects of his unsuccessful mission to Canada.[59] He had suffered severe attacks of gout and pleurisy and had twice been forced to halt his journey home to lie in bed for several days. But he had kept abreast of fellow committee member Jefferson's drafts of the Declaration of Independence.[60] It is difficult to believe he was not informed of his son's arrest and the urgent request for congressional action.

Hancock evidently did not wait long to inform the Congress of the crisis across the river. The radical southern faction was delighted. Fully two weeks before, Richard Henry Lee had written a colleague in Virginia that William, by defiantly calling the Assembly, "is endeavoring to bring himself under the notice of Congress . . . I believe he will effect it now."[61] A North Carolina delegate had been waiting day by day for word "of that governor's being seized, which I think ought to have been done many months ago."[62] In Elbridge Gerry's opinion, "Jersey has behaved nobly with Governor Franklin."[63] John Hancock sent a message to George Washington at his New York headquarters of New Jersey's action. Continental troops could now be sent in.

For the first time the Continental Congress as a whole had been publicly confronted by the Loyalism of a relative of one of its members. The division in the Franklin family was by no means unique. John Adams and John Hancock had in-laws who were outspokenly loyal to the King. George Washington had Tory cousins. Indeed, Washington's first love had married a Fairfax, one of the leading Loyalist families of Virginia. The brother and father of one Maryland congressman fled to England rather than submit to the authority of the Congress. Delegates from New Jersey and New York — William and Robert Livingston, James Duane and John Jay — were related by marriage to active Tories. "All families are liable to have degenerate members," declared the New Jersey delegate William Livingston when his nephew was arrested. "Even Adam's had its Cain. Among the twelve Apostles, there was at least one traitor."[64]

But whether Benjamin Franklin was so circumspect will probably never be known. Always secretive, he was especially so on this subject, and who was to question him about it? To Washington he pretended to be ignorant of the affair. On June 21 he wrote Washington that gout "has kept me from Congress and company almost ever sincce you left us [June 4], so that I know little of what has passed there."[65] But the leaders of Congress could hardly have ordered the incarceration of the son of one of its most celebrated members without that member's knowledge and consent. To Benjamin, it was the hour of his family's deepest disgrace. The effects of the secret congressional debate on William's fate could only have prolonged his illness at home.

The debate was short, decisive. On June 19, the same day the Congress received New Jersey's request for instructions, John Hancock sent the courier to Burlington with emphatic orders: "Proceed on the examination of Mr. Franklin and if upon such examination they shall be of opinion that he shall be confined, to report such opinion to Congress, and then Congress will direct the place of his confinement."[66]

As at so many other critical times of his life, William instinctively took up pen and paper while two congresses pondered his fate. Just as the Continental Congress had for so many months officially ignored his existence, he still insisted on ignoring the Congress. He addressed himself to the defunct New Jersey Assembly in a message he obviously intended to have read to its members if and when they convened, and to the New Jersey Council that had, almost to a man, betrayed him.

Facing the bitter reality of his circumstances, he began to write an address that he now doubted he would ever be allowed to deliver in person. Matter-of-factly describing Colonel Heard's visit, William copied out each document himself. The words appearing under his hand stung him: "To be represented as an enemy to the liberties of my country (one of the worst characters), merely for doing my duty to their future happiness and safety was, as you may imagine, sufficient to rouse the indignation of any man not dead to human feelings."[67] William's one hope, he must have known, was an emotional appeal to his people to resist the pretensions of the Congress. "To you, gentlemen, to every individual in the province, can I safely appeal to vouch for me." He had never, he insisted, done anything to harm the colony. From the beginning of the imperial struggle, he had "uniformly" worked for "negotiation and treaty from a full conviction that America might thereby obtain a fixed constitution which would afford every reasonable security for enjoyment of British liberties."

He resented being made a prisoner: to bar the Assembly's meeting was enough. His seizure only proved that "they meant a personal affront to me or designed to wound the dignity of the Crown through my person. Even were the charge of contempt of Congress true, as governor it surely could not be any crime in me, nor justify such treatment as I have received and am likely yet to suffer."

"But the fact alleged is false," he argued, pointing out that there was no need to dismantle the Assembly, that neighboring colonies had convened their assemblies since his arrest, that he was willing to dissolve the Assembly if it was the wish of its members and the majority of their constituents. But he had not abdicated, appeared in arms against his people, or neglected to call a meeting. Exhaustively, William contested every charge as if before a jury, even berating his enemies for the "meanness" of cutting off his salary, calling it "unworthy treatment of a man who has done his duty faithfully during a thirteen year administration." He could not choke down the fact of his arrest: "As you, gentlemen, at our last meeting intimated your desire that I would not quit the province and as I flattered myself that by remaining quietly here I might be of some service when His Majesty's Commissioners should arrive, I have never attempted to remove myself, though the insult I received [his house arrest] soon after that session would have fully justified me."

Even as he wrote, he felt there was little hope. "This, gentlemen, I well know, is not language to the times. But it is better, it is honest truth flowing from a heart that is ready to shed its best blood for this country. A real patriot can seldom or never speak popular language."

He ended with a personal lament: "I shall take my leave of you and the good people you represent — perhaps for the last time.

Permit me, before we part, to recommend it to you to defend your constitution in all its branches. Let me exhort you to avoid, above all things, the traps of independency and republicanism now set before you, however tempting they may be baited. Depend upon it, you can never place yourselves in a happier situation than in your ancient constitutional dependency on Great Britain. No independent state ever was, or ever can be, so happy as we have been, and still might be, under that government."

For three days, William waited; he was allowed no visitors. "Even the doctor and ladies of the place, who wanted to visit and comfort Mrs. Franklin in her distress, were refused admittance."[68] On the afternoon of June 19, Heard returned with a troop of cavalry. William was told to get his things. He had only a few moments to embrace Elizabeth for the last time. With an armed escort of sixty-four men, they hurtled west toward Burlington, spending the night in New Brunswick. The guards were abusive and insulting, he later charged. The inn was squalid, the June night tepid, the noise of the guards and the flies incessant. William got "not one wink of sleep. . . . I was guarded so close as not to be allowed to quit the room I was in at the tavern, even upon a pressing call of nature, forcing me to make a most humiliating submission."[69]

By the time the cavalcade covered forty miles of dusty roads and reached Burlington late on June 20, William was sick with worry over Elizabeth, ill with fatigue, hunger, anxiety. The New Jersey congress had already adjourned for the night. Under heavy guard, he was taken past his gardens and his empty riverside mansion to the small house of his cousin Josiah Franklin Davenport, the town postmaster. William had once persuaded his father to employ this cousin; now he was his cousin's ward (Davenport later put in a bill for reimbursement by the Congress for William's room and board).[70]

William Franklin resented above all the rough treatment he, a royal governor representing the King, had received. Indeed, as he was escorted into the supreme court chamber next morning, he castigated the thirteen members of the revolutionary tribunal as rebels. They were trying to destroy what he believed to be the finest form of government. In its place they themselves wanted to rule—these county justices of the peace, Presbyterian ministers, farmers, most of them new to office and power. To William they were a totally illegal tribunal.

Presiding was Samuel Tucker, the president of the Congress. Once an ardent Anglican, he had been charged with graft and corruption in his post as sheriff of Somerset County. He was flanked on his left by the close-cropped William Paterson, secretary of the congress and a faithful adherent of Witherspoon's. Paterson had graduated from Princeton while William was out of the province for six months on his personal real estate transactions in New York. Unable to establish a law practice without William's signature on his license, Paterson had drifted into poverty and ran a country store until revolutionary politics rescued him. He was still so obscure that William evidently mistook him for a Presbyterian clergyman.[71] On Tucker's right sat the man William was now finally certain had undermined his government and engineered his arrest, the Reverend John Witherspoon.

William was later annoyed with himself for taking the proffered seat within the bar — "a civility I was afterwards not quite satisfied with myself for accepting" — but he was too fatigued to refuse even if he meant by every means to express total disapproval for the makeshift court and its proceedings.[72] As President Tucker repeated the instructions from the Continental Congress, every man in the room must have studied the ousted governor. Witherspoon's official biographer learned from a witness, his own father, of the strange combination of sadness and admiration that stayed with some of the congressmen for years. "At best, the examination of the Governor could have been little more than a form. Even had he been able to make out a case for himself, his official usefulness was at an end. He was well aware of his predicament, but he faced his doom unflinchingly, maintaining to the end the bearing of an undaunted and loyal officer of the Crown.

"Beneath the surface there was something very sobering and almost pathetic in the scene, for it marked the final passing of an old established order with all its historic associations, its power, and its rich prestige. The confrontation of this splendidly representative figure of a British colonial governor — William Franklin was

marked as one of the handsomest men in America — by a hetero-
geneous body of humbler and homelier persons bent on freeing
themselves from the government he represented meant that, in his
person, once more the world was to see a mighty empire brought to
bay."[73]

This remarkable description by the son of John Witherspoon's
closest friend was written with the hindsight of many years. At the
time, however, John Witherspoon and many of his revolutionary
followers were more infuriated than reflective. Faced with an extraordinary grilling by men he considered criminals, William refused to answer any questions. Tucker tersely recounted William's
conduct later that day to John Hancock: "He refused to make any
answer, for two reasons: first, because we were an illegal assembly
which had usurped the government of the King; secondly, because
we had not treated him as a gentleman. We had resolved that he
was an enemy to this country, which we knew to be false. We had
made him a prisoner and had robbed him, having deprived him of
part of his salary, and now, do as you please, and make the best of
it."[74]

President Tucker considered William's behavior "gross and insolent." John Witherspoon was beginning to turn purple with rage
as he huddled with Tucker at the table, deciding what to do. The
Continental Congress had sanctioned the interrogation. They
would proceed with the questions whether or not Mr. Franklin
concurred.

"Did Mr. Franklin issue the proclamation of the 30th of May
last calling the Assembly of New Jersey, a copy of which is presented in the several newspapers, or one to that effect?"

William did not answer.

"Did Mr. Franklin at that time know of the resolve of the Continental Congress of the 15th of May last, directing that all authority
under the Crown of Great Britain should be totally suppressed?"

Again, William remained silent. He had stood before the bar of
Parliament, sworn his oath to the King, kissed His Majesty's hands.
He would not dignify this gathering of rebels.

"By what authority did Mr. Franklin undertake to call the Assembly?"

The question was almost laughable to William. He controlled himself, again refusing to speak.

"With what view did he undertake to call that Assembly, and what important business had he to lay before them?"

This very day, William was to have read his royal instructions, his assurances that there was still hope for reconciliation, before the King's Assembly in Perth Amboy: he would not answer here. The business must lie buried for now. He again stayed silent.

"Did Mr. Franklin write letters to the Ministry of Great Britain, encouraging them to proceed in their designs against this country?"

Silence again.

"And did he undertake to point out to that Ministry the means of distressing this country, particularly on the seacoast of New Jersey?"

Clearly this was the charge that had most embittered his enemies, but again William maintained his cool, aloof silence. John Witherspoon glowered at William fiercely from beneath overhanging gray eyebrows. He always tugged at them when he was excited. He fairly pulled one off now. This insolent Franklin was trying to make them all look foolish. With difficulty, Witherspoon, too, held his silence as the president of the congress went on, ever louder and more annoyed.

"The Congress being informed that Mr. Franklin dropped some threatening expressions to Colonel Heard, such as 'it is your turn now, but it will be mine another day.' They would be glad to know what he meant by them?"

The answer was self-explanatory: the governor did not acknowledge it. He sat stonily. If he would not respond to these formal questions, they must proceed to dispose of his case. Unexpectedly, William Franklin stood up. Denouncing the tribunal as a "parcel of ignoramuses" for arresting him, he insisted that Colonel Heard be brought into the courtroom to testify to his exact words.[75] The assembly fell silent as Witherspoon, Tucker and Secretary Paterson huddled. "This occasioned a little debate among them," William later reported, "which I was sorry did not last a little longer, as it was the only amusement I had had for some days."[76] The huddle broke up. Oddly enough, Witherspoon moved that Heard be brought in, but the congressmen were unwilling to turn a hearing into an unauthorized trial and the motion was voted down. Suddenly, the Reverend Witherspoon exploded with wrath. Franklin's denunciation of the tribunal had been more than he could bear. He launched into a venomous personal attack that only the Scotsmen in the room could fully understand. So thick was his burr that for several minutes the secretary was unable to take down what he was saying. "The Doctor's aspect was truly awful," Congressman Jacob Green observed,[77] and Colonel John Mehelm, a member of the tribunal, wrote that "Dr. Witherspoon rose up and shook his wig and said, 'You can't expect to receive that polished treatment from a parcel of countrymen that your distinguished birth and refined education might entitle you!' "[78] Congressman Green's version of these words was slightly different: the Doctor "ended his tirade with the sarcastic fling, 'On the whole the governor's performance was worthy of his exalted birth and refined education.' "[79] Every man present could understand this: the Reverend Witherspoon had called the royal governor William Franklin a bastard to his face in front of the congress.

The hearing, a shattering affair for all involved, was over. Amid an uproar, William Franklin was ordered to be taken immediately back to his cousin's house while the provincial congress decided his future. Sheriff Bowes Read, a brother-in-law of Charles Pettit and a distant cousin of William's, escorted him out to his coach. No time was lost sending the Continental Congress a full report of the interrogation. After the formality of voting, Secretary Paterson quickly took down the verdict: "As the said William Franklin by this and his former conduct, in many instances, appears to be a virulent enemy to this country and a person that may prove dangerous, therefore, it is *unanimously resolved,* that the said William Franklin be confined in such place and manner as the honorable Continental Congress shall direct." President Tucker and Congressman Witherspoon sent along their recommendation "that for many reasons we think it highly proper that Mr. Franklin should be confined. The place and manner of his confinement we cheerfully submit to the Continental Congress." Just so long as it "shall be out of this colony.

"Only one thing we beg leave to add, that in our opinion, the sooner the Continental Congress take him in charge the better."[80]

From the moment of William Franklin's birth, his timing had always been bad. His luck did not improve as he sweltered in his cousin's house surrounded by guards, chafing while the Continental Congress decided his case. It was late Friday afternoon before the Jersey dispatch rider dismounted at the State House in Philadelphia. The parent Congress had adjourned for the weekend. William's fate must wait.

The deposed governor did not idle away the time. He obtained pen and paper and wrote a postscript to his long letter to the Assembly that he had begun in Perth Amboy. He had lost none of his nerve: he sent Thomas with the missive to the King's printer in Burlington. He still hoped to take his case before the people in an open letter to the old Assembly. The printer, however, declined his business. "He at first gave me expectations that he would do his duty," William wrote that Saturday. "He was afraid of offending the provincial congress. . . . He did not doubt but he should be killed if he should print it for me. No argument could prevail, and he returned the copy. I have since heard that he (contrary to my express orders) communicated it to the congress, who passed a resolve this day prohibiting the printing [of] anything for me. Poor men! They can no more bear the light of truth, it seems, than owls can endure the light of the sun!"[81]

His authority, if not his spirit, obviously at an end, William learned on Tuesday, June 25, the outcome of Monday's deliberations in Philadelphia. Before the full Continental Congress, Secretary Charles Thomson read the dispatches from Burlington. At that moment Benjamin Franklin apparently *was* in his Windsor chair at the Pennsylvania table. He had recovered enough by June 21 to write Washington of his two-week illness as if it were over. But he left no mention of what his feelings were at that dark hour. After nearly ten years elapsed without his exchanging a word with his son, he acknowledged to William that "nothing has ever hurt me so much."[82]

The full transcript of William's hearing was "laid before Congress and read." Secretary Thomson did not note which delegates were present and which absent. The journals of the Congress matter-of-factly recorded the usual unanimous vote after the motion to depose William was made. Thomson only reported the resolution: "that William Franklin be sent under guard to Governor Trumbull who is desired to take his parole, and if Mr. Franklin refuses to give his parole, that Governor Trumbull be desired to treat him agreeable to the resolutions of Congress respecting prisoners."[83] Although Thomson omitted recording the name of the author of the resolution, it is impossible to escape the suspicion that Benjamin Franklin himself eased congressional embarrassment by requesting William's incarceration. At the end of the Revolution, William revealed to a leading Loyalist historian that his father had indeed made the formal request.[84] That the elder Franklin also had some say about the place of William's confinement can only be surmised, but he must have remembered William's popularity in the Pennsylvania German countryside. The only other Continental prisoners outside Connecticut were being held at Lancaster, where William's career as a British representative had begun nearly thirty years earlier as an eighteen-year-old ensign and flagbearer on that first royal mission to the Ohio country. In any event, William was sent to Connecticut.

William was ill by the time the order of imprisonment was read to him by Colonel Read, his onetime partner in real estate speculations. In finishing his letter of farewell, William complained bitterly that the Congress had attacked him personally rather than his office to "show how all sufficient their present power is and thereby intimidate every man in the province from giving any opposition to their iniquitous proceedings." But "I have, thank God, spirit enough to face the danger. *Pro rege et patria* was the motto I assumed when I first commenced my political life. I am resolved to retain it till death shall put an end to my mortal existence."[85]

It was to be nearly a year before this message reached a Loyalist printer and was published. By then, British troops had recaptured New York and William's suffering had become a lingering scandal. Late in the afternoon of June 25, William sent off what he might well have thought was his last letter to his only son:

Burlington, June 25, 1776
Dear Billy,

I was ordered this day to set out on a guard to Princeton, on my way, I hear, to Connecticut; but, as I had a pretty high fever on me, their Low Mightinesses with great difficulty were persuaded by some friends of mine to postpone my departure till tomorrow morning, when I must go (I suppose) dead or alive. Two of their members, who are doctors, came to examine me to see if my sickness was not feigned. Hypocrites always suspect hypocrisy in others.

God bless you, my dear boy; be dutiful and attentive to your grandfather to whom you owe great obligations. Love Mrs. Franklin, for she loves you, and will do all she can for you if I should never return more. If we survive the present storm, we may all meet and enjoy the sweets of peace with the greater relish.

I am ever your truly affectionate father
Wm. Franklin[86]

On Saturday morning, former Governor Franklin climbed into the post chaise and began the rattling, bone-wrenching ride over back roads leading north. Three days later, when the party reached Hackensack, the young daughter of the former militia colonel who had resigned his commission rather than arrest the royal governor noted in a letter to a friend that William was "looking very dejected."[87] But he apparently was not too ill to give up thinking of making another stand: as soon as one becomes a prisoner, the thought of escape begins. In a last attempt to remain in New Jersey, William persuaded the captain of his guard to allow him to stop long enough to send a final appeal to the Continental Congress. He was now willing to give his parole. He also sent what indeed proved to be his last letter to Elizabeth, hinting strongly that there was still time to organize a relief party. He had somehow convinced himself that "something will turn up to make my removal improper, and at any rate, to gain time will be of advantage."[88] Once again, his incipient plans were foiled by the careful surveillance of his enemy Stirling, whose intelligence network intercepted William's letter and rushed it to Washington's headquarters in New York.

The commander in chief was in no mood to tolerate delays. He had just survived a plot to assassinate him. That same day he had hanged one of his own trusted bodyguards for taking part in what was alleged to be a widespread conspiracy involving the Tory governor of New York and the mayor of New York City. It was rumored that as many as five hundred Loyalists planned to blow up the powderhouse adjoining rebel headquarters, kill all the staff officers including Washington, and at the approach of the British armada seize the passes leading into the city.

Nervous about a general Tory rising as the British fleet approached, Washington sent a stern warning to William's escort: "It is not for you to hesitate on frivolous pretenses. . . . Set forward on your journey with Governor Franklin. . . . Make all possible dispatch for the place you are ordered to."[89] And just in case the governor's guards could not be trusted, Washington authorized the Essex committee of safety to place the governor under a strong guard and speed him to Connecticut without further ado. William Franklin had been escorted into office by sleigh-riding aristocrats in a winter snowstorm. Now, heavily armed minutemen in hunting shirts hurried him out of the province in a heat wave.

After a harrowing two-hundred-mile ride along the Hudson highlands and through the Berkshire foothills, he arrived, exhausted, in Hartford, the rebel capital of Connecticut. The *Constitutional Gazette* reported his passage through the city: "Governor Franklin of New Jersey passed . . . on his way to Governor Trumbull at Lebanon. . . . A noted Tory and a ministerial tool, [he] has been exceedingly busy in perplexing the cause of liberty." A detailed catalogue of William's crimes against the new state followed. And in case the connection had escaped anyone: "he is son to Doctor Benjamin Franklin, the genius of the day and the great patron of American liberty. If his excellency escapes the vengeance of the people, due to the enormity of his crimes, his redemption will flow not from his personal merit but from the high esteem and veneration which this country entertains for his honored father."[90]

On July 4, 1776, as his honored father read the first proofs of the Declaration of Independence in Philadelphia, William Franklin was led by his guards into a small shingled outbuilding, the Connecticut War Office, near the house of Governor Trumbull. From his stone mansion, the rebel governor, surrounded by bodyguards, stepped quickly through a short underground tunnel to his office. There, he called to order the Connecticut council of safety, examined the commitment papers of the newest Tory prisoner and asked William if he was willing to pledge his word and parole of honor as a gentleman.

As he had feared since the arrest of his friend Philip Skene the year before, William had been "led like a bear through New England," a prominent prisoner on display, shunted through an assortment of expensive, bug-infested roadside inns with no time to rest, no clean clothes. But now he was determined to muster his little remaining strength to argue for a parole to Perth Amboy. In an unprecedented legal challenge before the council of safety and the rebel governor, he filed a written appeal, demanding that his parole be extended to New Jersey and questioning the right of the Continental Congress to limit his parole to Connecticut. He faced not only former Puritan minister-turned-merchant prince-turned-governor Trumbull, but the Connecticut council of safety, made up of Harvard and Yale graduates. On the council sat the determined core of the rebellion in Connecticut. The surviving minutes are terse, exasperated. The council was accustomed to summary proceedings with prisoners. "Said F. moved by letter for alteration and liberty to return on his parole . . . took up most of the forenoon."

In the seven-year course of the war, there were twelve hundred such meetings in the little shingled war office in Lebanon. But William insisted on taking his captors through the legalities and constitutionality of all the proceedings and papers from the Continental Congress: "Many letters from Congress, etc. considered and good deal discussed. . . . Finding he could not be returned to New Jersey, [William] moved by the officer to have leave to go to Stratford."[91] And if he could not return to New Jersey, William at least wanted parole in a town where he might find a friendly reception. Stratford was heavily Anglican and Loyalist. It was also the home of an old friend and former agent in London, William Samuel Johnson, son of the founder of the King's College in New York. But Eliphalet Dyer, a member of the council, was also a close friend of Johnson's, and evidently suspected a Tory plot. Stratford was declared off limits to William.[92]

The next step was for two officers to persuade William of the folly of his course. Dyer called in the ranking officer in Washington's army in this region, Colonel Samuel B. Webb, a youthful veteran of Breed's Hill, a son-in-law of Silas Deane and an aide to General Washington. Colonel Webb had just herded to Connecticut a number of leading Tory prisoners allegedly involved in the New York plot. He was not prepared to waste his time on this one. He took William aside and evidently painted for him a sharply detailed picture of the alternative.[93] If he refused to give his unconditional parole to live quietly under house arrest without trying to escape or to get in touch with the enemy, he must go to prison. William was no doubt aware that to be in prison anywhere for any length of time, as he was sure to be, was tantamount to a sentence of death. Already, the few county jails in Connecticut — wretched squalid structures meant only to hold a man until he came to trial and execution — were overcrowded with Tory prisoners. For months the Loyalists of Pennsylvania, New York, Massachusetts and Connecticut had been force-marched into the Connecticut hill country out of reach of British navy rescue parties. In those days, a prisoner in Puritan New England was usually whipped or fined promptly, then released; or he was hanged. There was no attempt to rehabilitate or reform, no need for penitentiaries. The few crude county jails had been augmented by the first Continental prison, an abandoned copper mine in the mountains north of Hartford. Simsbury Mine was being filled with Anglicans, outspoken Loyalists, deserters from Washington's army, prisoners from the fighting around Boston — all mixed in with the worst convicted felons: murderers, counterfeiters, robbers. A man led down into Simsbury Mine might never come back up alive.[94]

In his latest orders accompanying Loyalists marched into Connecticut, General Washington had written that gentlemen "might have every accommodation and indulgence, have a respect to their rank and education, consistent with safety."[95] Certainly, William could now evaluate the choices: a rented room in a revolutionary's house, a crude, crowded and loathsome-smelling cell in a county jail or — the Mine.

Exhausted, filthy, seriously ill, William Franklin signed the parole. He was marched outside to his coach. The destination was

Wallingford, just east of New Haven. On the way, he was allowed to dine with British officers on parole in Middletown, and two days later he arrived at the private home where he was to be a paying guest-prisoner. The owner, a Continental officer, signed the body receipt and led the deposed governor to the room assigned him. At last, William Franklin could rest.[96]

19

A LITTLE REVENGE

July 1776–November 1778

NO ONE WAS MORE SHOCKED THAT THE SON OF THE CELE-
brated Doctor Franklin was under arrest and on his way to
prison in Connecticut than his own sister Sally and his son Temple.[1] Apparently ignoring the wishes of Benjamin, who was studiously ignoring the subject of William, the family rallied as best it
could without its patriarch and decided to try to comfort Elizabeth.
Sally had been distracted in recent weeks not only with her new
baby, but with the arrival of her Aunt Jane and little Ray Greene.[2]

When Benjamin *was* home, it was with a crowd of political
comers and goers, messengers and committee members. Mostly he
was at the State House and Sally was left to manage a houseful of
family and guests. She was no doubt embarrassed for all the Franklins to learn that the woman who had once taken her away to safety
from the rioters of Philadelphia was now alone and helpless, especially this woman who had always dreaded more than anything
being left in this strange land with no relatives of her own to turn
to. Sally promptly invited Elizabeth to come and live with her and
Temple.[3]

Stunned by his ill father's letter of farewell, Temple was unable
to learn for weeks whether William had survived the journey.[4] As
soon as he could arrange it, he went off to Perth Amboy to help his
stepmother as his father had wished. He left in such a hurry that he
forgot his favorite waistcoat as well as the razor he had lent John

Adams. He managed to get his grandfather's permission to go and borrowed from him sixty Spanish dollars to take to Elizabeth for food and other expenses. After William's salary was cut off, he had been unable to make adequate provision for his wife. His friends evidently helped him raise "several hundred" pounds sterling, which he took along into captivity.

Elizabeth seems to have succumbed to an acute depression when William left. All she could do at first, she said, was "sigh and cry."[5] To do her justice, much of her behavior — the planter's belle, fainting and crying to get attention — was due to genuine illness. Her asthma seems unquestionably to have been aggravated by the months of anxiety she had endured, the unremitting alarms and confusion. Now, however, she seemed to rally. She took her dear friend Elizabeth Skinner and most of the thirteen Skinner children into Proprietary House with her and busied herself with her teenage son.

Before Temple left Philadelphia in early August, his stepmother wrote him a letter that only partly prepared him for what he could expect in Perth Amboy, just a summer before a place where people laughed and danced away the evenings. "Our little town now swarms with unruly soldiers, and more are pouring in every day." As soon as William's royal establishment had been overturned and the new provincial government shifted to Princeton, General Washington had rushed in fully eight thousand men. He made Perth Amboy a "flying camp" for the reserves surely needed against the day when British troop ships now beginning to appear off Staten Island began the invasion of New York City. These raw militia, mostly unruly Scotch-Irish frontiersmen, as well as eight companies of Pennsylvania Germans (authorized by the once anti-German Benjamin Franklin), were openly unsympathetic to the plight of the Tories remaining behind the lines in the Loyalist town. "They have been extremely rude," Elizabeth wrote Temple, "and have terrified me almost out of my senses. But the day before yesterday, General Mercer* sent two of his officers down to acquaint me that he had given strict orders that none of his men should for the future come down to my house or treat any of my

---

* General Hugh Mercer, commandant of the American militia and a close friend of George Washington's.

family with disrespect. Yesterday the orders were obeyed, but today a party of them came down and plucked all the green apples off the trees and threw them about the orchard, and was going to steal your dog."[6]

Without William's usual cash crop of hard apples for the New York market and for Elizabeth's winter table, she was even less certain of sustaining herself. She had apparently already received, and declined, Sally's kind invitation to live in Philadelphia with the Baches and Benjamin Franklin. "It is certainly disagreeable living here at present, but I cannot think of removing. In the first place, I have no house to remove my family to [she would not consider living under Benjamin's roof] and if I had, I could not move so much furniture as we have without being at a vast expense and running the risk of having great part of it shattered to pieces, as it must go by land. Therefore, I am resolved to stay, and trust to the Almighty God for protection."[7]

It would take swift intervention from Providence to ease the tension at Proprietary House. Washington was worried as early as July 4 that the thousands of redcoats already "marching about" nearby Staten Island "are leaving no arts unassayed to gain the inhabitants to their side." The "disaffection of that place [Perth Amboy] is exceedingly great and unless it is checked and overawed it may become more general and very alarming," he wrote. Already many of the men of fighting age had slipped away at night to join Cortlandt Skinner, who was forming a Loyalist regiment on Staten Island. "It is not unlikely that in a little time they may attempt to cross to the Jersey side."[8] Washington ordered in a thousand men to arrest the chief justice, Frederick Smyth, and other leading Loyalists and march them to Princeton.

One of the men herded off was the town doctor. On July 8, Elizabeth wrote a letter on behalf of the women of the town, petitioning that he be allowed to return. "They apprehend fatal and melancholy consequences to themselves and families and to the inhabitants in general. . . . His attendance is hourly necessary to several patients now much indisposed, who will be left helpless if he be removed." It was a week before Elizabeth learned that her doctor would not be returning. The president of the provincial congress informed her, "Unhappily, madam, we are placed in such a situation that motives of commiseration to individuals must give place to the safety of the public. . . . Dr. Lawrence has fallen under suspicion of our generals."[9]

Elizabeth could find little comfort in church as she usually had. The service at St. Peter's had changed. The Sunday after independence was declared revolutionaries took the rector outside and, according to local legend, pointed a pistol at his head. They suggested that he drop the prayers for the King and the royal family. He complied. Besides, the church itself was beleaguered. A British brig of war was anchored only a hundred yards offshore and earthworks to protect an American eighteen pounder were under construction in the churchyard. When shots were exchanged, the British cannonballs broke off headstones in the parish cemetery. Occasionally, British marines on board the brig sniped at Virginia troops that marched tauntingly along the beach just out of musket range. Each day, too, more earthworks were thrown up along the waterfront, more cannon implanted. By the time Temple arrived, Perth Amboy was the fortress closest to the largest expeditionary force Britain had ever sent against any enemy.[10]

Word of William's safe arrival in New Haven reached Elizabeth when the newspapers reached her, but it was weeks before she learned anything more of him. The note Temple brought from her father-in-law reminded her that many others were suffering more than she was. At this point she decided finally against going to Philadelphia. In her reply she said she considered the money he had sent her a loan that she would repay "as soon as Mr. Pettit settles his account with me." She also told her father-in-law that her troubles were "really more than so weak a frame is able to support" and sharply reminded him that "it is generally in your power to relieve them."[11] Why could not William be allowed to take his parole and permitted to live at home?

Benjamin did not reply. There is no record that he tried to change the order of the Congress. He began a series of letters to Temple, each one more insistent than the last, in which he attempted to prevent the boy from going to William or staying on with Elizabeth. The old man was understandably nervous as the fighting around New York increased. He considered Temple his last hope for creating a Franklin dynasty now that William was in disgrace. He obviously had allowed Temple to go to his mother only to keep the boy happy. By the time Temple arrived in Perth Amboy, there had already been heavy artillery duels across Arthur Kill Sound, often with casualties. A Philadelphia soldier was killed by one cannonball, a Loyalist prisoner in the jail up the street, by another.[12]

On August 25, Temple saw the spectacle that would have shaken Benjamin if he had known how close Temple was to the war. Thirty thousand British and Hessian troops were in resplendent motion on Staten Island. They were visible through a spy glass from the roof of Proprietary House. Nearly two months earlier, on July 4, as Philadelphia militia had fired off jubilant salutes to the new nation and William was led off a prisoner, the British fleet had arrived silently, its sails as thick as a flight of snow geese crossing the windows of Proprietary House. Inside two weeks, 479 ships disgorged ordnance, supplies, and thirty-four thousand of the world's toughest troops — Highlanders, Irish veterans, Hessian jaegers, cavalrymen — into a sprawling city of tents on Staten Island. They were spoiling for combat after months at sea.

Crossing over to Long Island, at three in the morning on August 27, picked troops under General Henry Clinton began a five-hour march around Washington's main army on Brooklyn Heights. The Americans were expecting another of Sir William Howe's frontal attacks, like the one at Breed's Hill. They did not realize until too late that the main British attack was coming from behind them. British grenadiers with bayonets and Hessian mercenaries with rifles gave no quarter at the battle of Long Island. The Hessian jaegers pursued the rebels through the woods and into a swamp, where hundreds of men from Pennsylvania and New Jersey drowned in a deep black creek. The decimated rebel army was saved from annihilation only by the dogged rearguard action of Lord Stirling's heroic troops, a fog that lasted three days, Howe's vacillation and Washington's bold escape by boat.[13]

On both sides there were men who considered the rebellion over. Most important of them was Lord Howe, who had the odd historical distinction of being, at once, the admiral of the huge punitive naval force and the leading peace negotiator. Instead of swiftly following up the British victory, he wrote to his old chess rival Benjamin Franklin to propose that they parley over peace terms. Howe was not empowered to negotiate with the Congress. That would constitute recognizing not only the Congress but an independent nation. What he proposed was that he meet privately with some key congressmen before his brother's army struck an even more compelling blow. The Congress selected Benjamin Franklin, John Adams and Edward Rutledge of South Carolina as negotiators. Franklin wrote back to propose a meeting either at Proprietary House in Perth Amboy or at Howe's headquarters on nearby Staten Island.

Avoiding "that Tory house," they stayed at a crowded tavern at the Perth Amboy ferry. Benjamin and his mission accepted the admiral's invitation and took his private barge across to Staten Island, where they marched through a double file of saluting Hessians in blue uniforms and powdered pigtails to debate with Howe for more than three hours.

The talks were inconclusive. The negotiators hastened back to Philadelphia (Franklin had no time to stop at Proprietary House on the way) and reported to the Congress that Howe had no authority except to grant pardons if America would submit. Swiftly, the Howes drove home their arguments by invading Manhattan four days after the peace conference. As Washington called a general retreat, a mysterious fire broke out, destroying nearly one third of the city. Cut off by the British, the main American force escaped only by picking its way quietly through a peach orchard while Howe and his staff stopped nearby to have tea.

A few days after returning to Philadelphia, Franklin received a letter from Temple. He wanted to visit his father in Connecticut and take him a vital letter from his mother along with some cash and badly needed supplies. Replying as coolly as he knew how in a long letter to his latest "Dear Billy," Benjamin said he had "considered the matter and cannot approve of your taking such a journey at this time, especially alone, for many reasons which I have not time to write." It was one of William's tricks, Benjamin was sure, and he would head it off. "If your mother should write a sealed letter to her husband and enclose it under cover to Gov. Trumbull, acquainting him that it contains nothing but what relates to his private family concerns," Trumbull would forward it. A letter would have to do. Benjamin would not even tell Temple or Elizabeth exactly where William was being held. "I hope you do not feel any reluctance in returning to your studies," Benjamin went on, quickly changing the subject. He launched into a lecture on Temple's need "to lay foundations" for his "importance among men. . . . If this season is neglected, it will be like cutting off the spring from the year." Bache would soon deliver Temple's forgotten clothing to "that Tory House," as Benjamin could not resist calling it even as he sent "my love to your good mama and respects from her friends in the family. . . . They desire I would express more particularly their love to Mrs. Franklin."[14]

When Temple did not drop, but strengthened, his appeal to go to his father, Benjamin fired back a sterner reply: "You are mistaken in imagining that I am apprehensive of your carrying dangerous intelligence to your father, for while he remains where he is, he could make no use of it were you to know and acquaint him with all that passes." Benjamin was, he said, hurt that Temple had not given him credit for "a little tender concern for your welfare" because of the long journey, "your youth and inexperience, the number of sick returning on that road with the infectious camp distemper, which makes the beds unsafe, together with the loss of time in your studies." But he was unquestionably suspicious: to take such a journey "to avoid being obliged" to Governor Trumbull "for so small a favor as forwarding a letter seems to me inconsistent with your mother's usual prudence." He stopped short of implying that Temple was complicit in any plotting. The boy's idea came, he told him, from "your inclination to a ramble and disinclination to return to college, joined with a desire to see a father you have so much reason to love."[15]

It was almost cruel, the way Benjamin exerted influence over Temple and then pointed out Temple's deep devotion to his father in this way: as usual, Benjamin Franklin must stay in control. He closed by arranging to send franked envelopes for Elizabeth to use in sending letters back and forth to William — but they must pass through Benjamin's hands in Philadelphia. "It will make but two days' [difference]."[16]

When Temple did not write again and did not come back, Benjamin wrote a more urgent letter on September 28: "I hope you will return hither immediately, and that your mother will make no objection to it, something offering here that will be much to your advantage if you are not out of the way."[17] Postmaster Bache must have personally delivered the cryptic note to Temple with a whisper of the nature of Temple's advantage. His grandfather had been appointed minister plenipotentiary to France. Temple was to go to Paris with him and be his paid personal secretary.

Just such an offer from Benjamin to his impressionable son had once lured William away from his fiancée to London. Now, Benjamin's willful blandishments turned Temple's head away from his suffering parents. Temple no longer needed to be convinced of his own poor prospects if he stayed behind in America without his grandfather's influence and generosity. He hurried back to Philadelphia to pack and went off to France without breaking stride long enough to write for his father's permission or even to tell William that his visit to Connecticut was not to be. In this final bout of the eighteen-month-long tug-of-war for Temple's loyalty, Benjamin controlled both ends of the rope. He later defended his action in a letter to Bache on October 22, 1779: "I have rescued a valuable young man from the danger of being a Tory." But there was also the plaintive note of an old man fearing death. "If I die, I have a child to close my eyes and take care of my remains."[18]

William learned of his latest loss in the first letter to reach him (under Benjamin's frank) four months after his arrest. He gathered the best grace that remained to him and wrote back to Elizabeth: "If the old gentleman has taken the boy with him, I hope it is only to put him in some foreign university." Doubtless, he would have said more if he could have risked his father's wrath, if he were not, even now, dependent on his father for mail to his wife. As for Elizabeth, she was disgusted with her son's performance, for promising to visit his father in prison and then going off without even remembering the vital letter she was trying to get through to William. In her last letter to Temple, she bemoaned being "truly miserable indeed to be here in a strange country without a friend or a protector."[19] It was as if she knew she would never again see her father-in-law or the boy who had so briefly been her son, and was beginning to realize that she might never be reunited with her beloved William.

William's treatment under parole was at first lenient. As was the custom, he had to rent rooms at inflated rates, first in the house of an officer in Wallingford. A guard was placed at the door. He had to pay for everything, and there were no bargains for Tories, even when Thomas was able to find anything for his master to eat.

One piece of great good fortune unexpectedly came William's way as soon as he reached Connecticut. On hearing of his arrest, his old Illinois land partner Thomas Wharton wrote to another wealthy Quaker in Connecticut: "During his residence in Connecticut, thou'll let him have what sums he may want, and take his draft on me for the sums, which shall be cheerfully paid."[20] William's longstanding support of the Quakers coupled with his land speculations came through at this moment to save his life when his own family was unwilling or unable to do so.

William did not abuse Wharton's generosity. He sent his horses and carriage back to Elizabeth and instructed her to sell them, along with his other horses, to raise some money for herself.[21] One week after reaching Wallingford, he appealed to Governor Trumbull for permission to have his parole shifted to Middletown, a picturesque old town north of Hartford on the Connecticut River and the most prosperous smuggling port in all New England. It had become the chief place of confinement for high-ranking British prisoners, including two other royal governors and several senior British officers. It was here he found his old friend Skene and his family, recently kidnapped by New York rebels. The prisoners had formed a committee of refugees to help find food and housing for more destitute Loyalists. There was also the added succor of the only functioning Anglican church in the region. William welcomed its services and the bold Anglicans it attracted. Trumbull's Puritan Council apparently feared, however, that William might try to stir up trouble by organizing the Loyalists even further. In granting William's request to move to approved lodgings in Middletown, the rebel governor declared the town off limits to prisoners on parole in surrounding towns.[22]

William rented lodgings one block from the crowded waterfront in the home of Jehosaphat Starr, a leading merchant. Starr was a supplier of war materials to the rebel army and was Colonel Webb's trusted quartermaster. By early August, William had settled into a comfortable routine of sorts, as a letter from a New Haven merchant reveals. On August 7, a Tory merchant named Ralph Isaacs wrote to William in care of his captor-landlord: "I had the pleasure to forward you a case of [whale] oil [for lamp and stove] and a pound of green tea. I wish I could have procured you better, that was not in my power." He had also located "half-dozen of stockings which are coarse, if they will do. Be so kind as to let me hear by the bearer. . . . I beg you will be so kind as to let me know if Lady Franklin is coming this way. I shall esteem it a particular honor to wait on her."[23] The letter also contained heartening news: the British fleet had finally arrived.

Defiant rituals of green tea and an occasional dinner with fellow prisoners made coarse Yankee underwear more bearable. When one British victory followed another, William and his friends organized a celebration in Middletown that irked their rebel captors and ended up before Trumbull's court. Toward the end of November 1776, the town watch was summoned late one Saturday night to Governor Franklin's lodgings, where, according to their sworn deposition, there was much "hallooing and shouting." The governor and his friends were "roaring out a catch about 'King George's health, and it shall go round,' and a song with a chorus to the effect that Howe was a brave commander." The noise could be heard "forty rods off." A political argument ensued. As the British historian George Trevelyan described it, "Franklin and his friends called the American soldiers cowards, cursed the colony and those who governed it, prayed that the Hessians might soon be there to cut all their throats, and uttered the most terrible oaths ever heard, introduced into almost every sentence." One prisoner told a Puritan guard that he could not get to heaven anyway, as he had "nothing but Continental paper money with which to pay the expenses of the journey. . . . Blows followed words, and in the end the whole party were marched off to the guard room."[24]

The Connecticut war records corroborate the incident and make plain Governor Trumbull's displeasure. But they omit any hint that rebel officials looked behind the noisemaking and the crowd of Tory revelers to discover William's real purpose. In late November and throughout the winter months, William Franklin was undoubtedly carrying on a bold scheme of gathering intelligence and passing it to the British, and obtaining and issuing official British "protections" for thousands of Tories. His intelligence-gathering skill, honed in New Jersey during long years of prerevolutionary unrest, now stiffened the morale of Tories in Connecticut, New York and New Jersey. Indeed, wherever British and Hessian troops advanced that winter, landowners sympathetic to the Crown were able to brandish small pieces of paper signed in the flowing hand of a royal official daring to assert his authority behind rebel lines.

Even the innocent-looking request for William's business by the New Haven tea peddler may have been a cover for crucial military information. American censors, in reading a letter to the former governor, would, more than likely, stop long before the wordy commercial solicitation got around to its real purpose: to report British positions and strengths in such a way that Tory volunteers could coordinate their movements with the British invasion. As the weeks passed, too, hundreds of houses throughout Connecticut, apparently following some prearranged plan, sported black-and-white stripes on their chimneys to indicate they should be spared by British raiding parties.

William evidently carried on his espionage without any moral compunction. Even though he had signed a parole of honor pledging to carry out no warlike activities in exchange for his mild treatment and the privilege of traveling by horse or carriage within a six-mile radius of Middletown, he clearly considered the pledge worthless and obtained under duress. Further, he had always insisted that Loyalist prisoners were not civil prisoners but were, like American officers taken by the British, actually prisoners of war. As such, it was both his right and his duty to do all in his power to hinder the enemy and plot his escape.

On November 30, as the battered rebel army reeled backward across New Jersey, the Howes issued a proclamation from their

New York headquarters. Every American, rebel or Loyalist, was given sixty days to "appear before the governor or any other officer in his Majesty's service" to swear an oath: "[I] promise and declare that I will remain in a peaceable obedience to his Majesty and will not take up arms in opposition to his authority." All oath-takers were to receive "full and free pardon of all treasons."[25]

British military successes and Continental Army failures led men all over America to have second thoughts about independence. Nearly one thousand lined up at British headquarters in New York City the first day alone. In a little over a month, 5,620 "protections" had been issued. In New Jersey, the proclamation dried up the supply of rebel militiamen Washington needed to slow the British onslaught and swelled the ranks of rapidly forming Loyalist regiments. In Connecticut, where it was more difficult to find a British officer, William obtained copies of the pardons and began issuing them to the stream of Loyalists who visited him daily. His own captors may have hedged, never knowing when the British regulars would turn and attack them. At least one fourth of Connecticut was secretly loyal, one leading Loyalist scholar has recently reported.[26]

Apparently passing information and distributing money, food and clothing through his servants, by released British prisoners going back into New York City for exchange, and with the aid of the Anglican clergy, William was able to supply the King's protections to loyal subjects as far away as New Jersey and Long Island. As a consequence, when British columns sacked and burned rebel homes and farms all over the Middle Colonies and Connecticut during the next year, the homes of Tories were almost always spared.

It was as risky to pay a call to William as it was for him to carry on his intelligence-gathering. One visitor was shot at and mobbed on his way home, and even Captain Abiathar Camp, a well-known rebel officer, was hauled before the Connecticut General Assembly on suspicion of Tory leanings for visiting William too frequently. The charges were brought by an in-law of Camp's who was William's warder, Captain Starr: Camp had "till lately very frequently visited at my house, but since Governors [Montford] Brown and Franklin have been in town, his visits seem . . . confined to them and others esteemed unfriendly to the liberty of America.[27] Starr omitted to say that he, too, had visited these prisoners as a go-between for their purchases from Ralph Isaacs.

As the months passed and Temple still had not come, William wrote to Elizabeth to send "necessaries which I shall want for winter, if I stay here."[28] A prisoner has difficulty surviving without two fundamentals, and William further enlivened his routine with both: the hope of early release and a legal appeal. Even as he carried on intelligence-gathering, he kept sending appeals to the Continental Congress for his exchange. He apparently was unaware that his friends were seeking his release. On Staten Island, within days of the first British landing, Cortlandt Skinner had arranged a dinner and horseback ride with two British generals, their aides and Ambrose Serle, the influential private secretary of Lord Howe. "Mr. Skinner informed me much of Governor Franklin's situation," Serle recorded in his diary. The governor "appears to be, as I have long since had good reason to think him, a steady honest man and really attached to Great Britain. His father is and has been every way his misfortune. Upon his account, [William] has been suspected at Home [England], and is too well known for his integrity to expect any favor here. There has long been a rupture between him and his father, who seems to have thrown off all natural affection for him. The Governor was seized by the rebels and is now confined somewhere in Connecticut. The rebels, knowing the domestic breach, show him no favor upon account of his father."[29]

By early August of 1776, word of William's seizure reached England in a letter from General Howe which was published in the London newspapers. "Governor Franklin, who for a long time maintained his ground in New Jersey," Howe was quoted, "has been lately taken into custody." William's old friend William Strahan, now a Tory member of Parliament, printed the news in his *Chronicle,* and presented it in person to "people in power, in case it might eventually be in their way to administer him some relief."[30]

Encouraging war news buoyed William's morale. As one British army smashed south from Canada, recapturing Crown Point and destroying Benedict Arnold's makeshift flotilla, the main British force was driving Washington north from New York City. The Continental Congress began to entertain petitions for prisoner exchange. William was considered of equal rank with a rebel general taken in Canada. His chances improved markedly on November 16, when 2,818 rebel prisoners were taken at the capitulation of Fort Washington on the Hudson River. Two days later, the British invasion of New Jersey began.

Within the week, the Congress resolved that "General Washington be directed to propose to General Howe an exchange of William Franklin, Esquire,"[31] for the rebel general, William Thompson. On December 1, Washington sent the offer through the lines to British headquarters as Howe's infantry pursued the "shattered remains of the rebel troops, a set of naked, dispirited fugitives," across snow-covered North Jersey. The British concentrated their forces at Perth Amboy.[32]

Elizabeth Franklin's hopes soared that her husband would be home before Christmas, but John Hancock again sent a message to Washington, rescinding the offer. Philadelphia was in turmoil, he wrote. The Congress was about to flee to Baltimore. Rebel troops were rounding up Quakers and known Tories to prevent a general Loyalist uprising in Washington's rear. It was feared no doubt that William would all too likely raise and lead the Loyalists against Washington. "In the present state of the army and situation of our affairs, an exchange of Governor Franklin might be prejudicial and attended with some bad consequences."[33]

With hundreds of wounded and sick rebel prisoners packed into unheated sugar warehouses and abandoned churches in New York City, the Connecticut rebel government prepared to surrender. The General Assembly "actually appointed and empowered a committee of their body to proceed to New York to make submission to the King's Commissioners to ask a restoration to the King's peace and, if possible, to preserve their charter from forfeiture, their estates from confiscation and their persons from attainder [for treason]," recorded Thomas Jones, chief justice of New York. "So far did Connecticut look upon the contest with Great Britain as over that, in December 1776, the Great and General Court released every prisoner in their power — except Governor Franklin, who was detained and most inhumanely treated, and that at the request of his father, the arch rebel, Dr. Franklin."[34]

All through December 1776, William must have foreseen

clearly, only days or weeks away, the time when he would return triumphantly to New Jersey to resume his office. But he was thwarted on Christmas night when Washington led his ragtag army back across the Delaware into New Jersey, encircled the Hessian outpost at Trenton, and captured or killed nearly one thousand startled mercenaries. After winning a second victory at Princeton a little more than a week later, Washington chased the British back toward their base camp at Perth Amboy. Once again, the rebels controlled New Jersey. In the next few months, Washington learned of William's daring duplicity. It cost him when Washington found out.

The first high-ranking rebel to suspect that William was brazenly attempting to act as a royal governor in captivity was his successor in New Jersey, the rebel William Livingston. The second governor to learn was Trumbull. He was thoroughly embarrassed and surprised. Even as Washington's army fought fiercely around Princeton on January 6, 1777, William Franklin again petitioned Trumbull to be allowed "to return to his family as has been allowed to some other gentlemen." The Connecticut Council, noting how William was "remonstrating in terms more sharp than decent against Gov. Trumbull's neglecting an answer to a former letter," unanimously advised Trumbull to refuse William's request "at this time of distress" in New Jersey. Moreover, the Council ordered the arrest of Ralph Isaacs, William's merchant-messenger, and had him deported to the frontier.[35] On March 23, William's name came up again before the Council. In a major investigation of Loyalist activity in New Jersey during the British occupation, Governor Livingston had found evidence that William Franklin had sent protections into New Jersey to be distributed by, among others, William's physician, Dr. John B. Lawrence. Livingston sent copies of the compromising pardons to Washington, who wrote to warn Trumbull of William's actions.[36]

Trumbull found William's involvement hard to credit. He wrote to Livingston that he found his complaint unbelievable. But when more reports reached him, Trumbull sent them to the Congress and asked for instructions. Congressional debate was acrimonious in the extreme. Roger Sherman, a Connecticut delegate, wrote

Trumbull that unquestionably William Franklin had put one over on his Connecticut warders. "The gentleman who gave information of Gov. Franklin's misbehavior and the inattention of our government to prevent it," Sherman wrote to Trumbull, was Lord Stirling's son-in-law, Congressman William Duer of New York, who was a member of the congressional committee overseeing treatment of prisoners and the man in charge of counterespionage in New York. To obtain the damning evidence, Duer had laid a trap.[37]

Suspecting that William Franklin was issuing protections, Duer sent Robert Betts of Jamaica, Long Island, to solicit one from an Anglican clergyman who was working with William. According to a deposition Betts gave before a Philadelphia justice of the peace that was later presented to the Congress, he received a protection on January 20, 1777, "delivered to him by the Reverend Mr. Servas of Middletown in the State of Connecticut to whom he had applied to speak in his behalf to William Franklin, Esq., late Governor of New Jersey, that he might take the benefit of the proclamation, issued by Lord and Gen. Howe . . . that the said William Franklin had granted near three thousand certificates in the State of Connecticut."[38]

William's activities became the subject of congressional debate on Friday, April 18, when the Reverend John Witherspoon returned from investigating at first hand the British campaign in New Jersey. Witherspoon's college had been plundered by both armies, shelled by rebel artillery. It was in ruins. The Congress was hushed as Witherspoon described Princeton, "the fences destroyed, the houses deserted, pulled in pieces or consumed by fire, and the general face of waste and devastation spread over a rich and once-well-cultivated, well-inhabited country." The recitation was long, explicit and absolutely devastating to William's chances for lenient treatment. Witherspoon omitted no detail: there had been "many instances of rape and vengeance against particular persons." Witherspoon's own farmhouse had been plundered, part of his library used as kindling by Hessian troops. His narration of Princeton's agony listed the destruction of the homes of two members of Congress, Richard Stockton and Jonathan Dickinson Sergeant. A Tory guide had pointed out Sergeant's house for destruction. Above all, "places of worship, ministers and religious persons of some particular Protestant denominations seem to have been treated with the most rancorous hatred. . . . The inhuman treatment of those who were so unhappy to become prisoners" included four days "without food altogether" and "the utmost distress from the cold, nakedness and close confinement. . . . Multitudes died in prison." Witherspoon did not have to remind his listeners of the vicious bayoneting of the fallen General Mercer or of his nine-day ordeal before dying. He did tell of a Presbyterian minister from Trenton "massacred in cold blood" and of "the lust and brutality of the soldiers in abusing of women." Witherspoon's committee had "authentic information of many instances of the most indecent treatment and actual ravishment of married and single women."[39] In a bloodlust rage as Witherspoon concluded, the Congress adjourned for the weekend.

The first item of business on Monday morning was William Franklin's abuse of parole by issuing protections to the Loyalists of New Jersey. The vote was unanimous: he had brought unnecessary suffering on his former subjects and now he must pay. He was sentenced to solitary and indefinite confinement in prison.[40]

On April 30, an express rider dismounted at the war office in Lebanon, Connecticut, to deliver the unanimous resolve of Congress. Governor Trumbull was informed that William Franklin "has sedulously employed himself in dispensing . . . the protections of Lord Howe." William was ordered "into close confinement, prohibiting to him the use of pen, ink and paper, or the access of any person or persons."[41] The surprised Governor Trumbull wrote to Hancock that "Mr. Franklin is without question highly inimical to the rights and liberties of the United States and disposed to do everything in his power to injure them." But Trumbull had enemies in Congress, too: he disbelieved that the conspiracy was as pervasive as one of those enemies, William Duer, had made out. There had even been whispers that Trumbull had turned a blind eye to William's issuance of pardons. The rumors were, Trumbull insisted, "perfectly false and injurious. I have no knowledge that [William Franklin] has ever given out one certificate of that kind, though there is reason to believe that he has," Trumbull wrote Washington. "Whatever has been done, has been under the cover of secrecy." William had "been treated with civility." His "conduct has been carefully watched with a jealous eye." Moreover, "sundry of his letters have been intercepted," but they seemed to Trumbull to contain "no very material things."[42]

That very day Trumbull received the first reports of a daring British raid on Danbury. Military supplies had been the target, but as they were burned, the fire had spread to engulf the homes of rebels and Loyalists alike. Scores of Loyalists had joined the retreating British as they marched back to their ships. William Franklin must be moved beyond the reach of such raids, as far into the backcountry as possible, where he could not be rescued.

On May 2, William Franklin was in his rented room in Middletown when the sheriff's party dismounted noisily in front of the Starr house. As he came out to see what was causing the uproar, one of the deputies raised his musket and fired at him. The shot whizzed by "only an inch" behind William's head. The deputy later claimed that his gun had gone off accidentally; he never explained whether he had also cocked it accidentally. Far from apologizing, the sheriff ordered William seized and immediately taken inside. William was to speak to no one.

After the sheriff read aloud the resolve of Congress that William had been "sedulously employed in dispensing protections and otherwise aiding and abetting enemies of the United States," William was prodded up onto a horse before his servant could bring him any of his clothes. "They hurried me away about forty miles to Litchfield," William wrote later. As soon as he could learn where he was being taken, he had some hint of his fate. Litchfield jail was a notorious prison, already crowded with Loyalists condemned to death. In William's own words, it was "the very worst jail in America."[43] Even to sympathetic Americans, William's fate seemed certain. General Philip Schuyler, commander of the northern army, told William Smith of New York that William Franklin was sure to be hanged.[44]

As the grim cavalcade hurried west and climbed the rough road into the Berkshire foothills, the neat frame houses surrounded by farms gave place to raw cabins with rotted stumps still studding the clearings. By the time they reached Litchfield late that afternoon, William was thoroughly shaken. He could expect little sympathy from the townspeople: scores of young Litchfield men had died in British prisons in New York City in recent months.

Litchfield jail was a long, squat log building of two stories, almost obscured when he first saw it by a huge elm tree on the edge of the town common. The tree, he would learn, was the whipping elm. The houses they passed were mostly wood, only a few more than a single story, most of them unpainted. There were a few substantial residences: Oliver Wolcott, a delegate to the Continental Congress, lived here, but the dominant building was the stark, towering, white Congregational church. The jail seemed a crude contrasting adjunct to the church's unforgiving elegance. The starkest sight of all stood beside the jail: Litchfield's great gallows.[45]

There was little chance to take in the sights. William was delivered at once to Sheriff Lynde Lord. He saw from Lord's manner that he could, indeed, expect no conversation here. The sheriff ordered his men to take the governor quickly up to the death cell on the second floor. The smell hit him first, then the darkness. There was only a small window with bars, the floor was covered with straw long since matted with the wastes of earlier prisoners. There was no chair to sit on, no bed to lie on, no toilet facilities.

The cell was almost too small for William to stretch in, the dark, hard walls and the filth instantly depressing, but the worst horror, as William was to learn, was the strange combination of noise and silence that was his particular punishment. He was to speak to no one except the sheriff. He was to write to no one. He was to have nothing to read. At the same time, there was the noise, the sounds of the suffering of his fellow Tory prisoners, the loud shouting and roaring and laughter of the guards. His cell was directly over the guardroom, which evidently also served as a tavern.

William had been under arrest for sixteen months now, but on this, his first official day behind bars, he was beginning to discover that there is no bottom to the depths of a prisoner's despair.[46]

Elizabeth Franklin left no surviving record of her first reaction to her husband's conviction for parole violation or his harsh treatment at Litchfield. Word of his imprisonment prompted Joseph Galloway, who had fled his Pennsylvania farm to join the British, to visit Elizabeth early in May. He found her "very unhappy on account of her husband."[47] Elizabeth was caught up in endless pleadings for help for William, for herself. Perth Amboy had become a crowded, dirty, run-down British garrison town. British troopers stabled their horses in the Presbyterian church. Hessian soldiers stripped fences and porches and carted off woodpiles and hacked down trees from lanes and orchards to warm themselves. Proprietary House had been turned into the British headquarters and was constantly full of booted officers clanking across the bare floors. With her friend Betty Skinner and all the Skinner children, Elizabeth lived in the upstairs rooms, the servants bringing what food they could buy up the back stairs at mealtimes.

Then, as abruptly as they had come, the British announced they were abandoning Perth Amboy. New orders from the ministry called for British offensives from Canada south through New York and up the Chesapeake Bay through Maryland, Delaware and Pennsylvania. The rebel capital was to be captured to cut off the food-producing southern colonies from the New England colonies, which were to be raided and scourged by land and sea. This new policy of dividing and conquering caught the Loyalists of New Jersey unprepared. Faced with the prospect of bitter reprisals from rebels eager to repay injuries suffered during the British occupation, they obviously must leave.

Elizabeth waited in anxiety for weeks before she was told that she would be taken along with the official British party. She had only a few days to see that all her husband's hundreds of books, maps and manuscripts were packed into barrels and their furniture, rugs and bedding piled into army wagons. As the accumulation of fifteen years of marriage jostled off, scraping and rattling before her, with her silver and clothing stuffed around her, she took Thomas's hand and climbed into the sulky and joined the Loyalist retreat into New York City.[48]

There she rented rooms in a Loyalist merchant's house on Great Dock Street in a neighborhood already overcrowded with refugees. The furniture and other effects were stored in a British army warehouse. The strain of the move was more than she had strength for. On June 9, another refugee wrote to William that she was so weak she could not hold a pen.[49] Dr. Lawrence, who had also managed to flee Perth Amboy, presently came to see her but his visit had to be short: Loyalist refugees were dying of dysentery at an alarming rate and he was needed.[50] As he left Elizabeth's bedside, Dr. Lawrence summoned Thomas. Mrs. Franklin appeared to be dying. He must get word to the governor. Sure she would never see her husband again, she had given up — that was the only explanation. Only a visit from her husband could save her: there was nothing in Dr. Lawrence's bag that could help her now.

Somehow, Thomas got a message through to Litchfield. It must have gone by way of Governor Trumbull: Thomas knew that only the rebel governor could now approve a letter for the Loyalist governor. By July 22, 1777, William had received permission to ask for pen and paper from Sheriff Lord.

Brushing aside the flies, the vermin, ignoring the stink, the heat and the noise for a few hours, he scrawled a letter to George Washington. His wife was on the point of death. Could he be paroled only long enough to journey through the lines to New York to see her this once more. Other prisoners, British prisoners, had been accorded similar courtesies. Moreover, Washington knew Elizabeth Franklin, had enjoyed her hospitality on Rancocas Creek. William did not need to remind him of that.

But when he received the message, Washington was still angry at William Franklin for what he considered a blatant violation of his parole. He was not about to disregard a direct order from the Congress for all the personal sympathy he might feel. "However strong my inclination to comply with your request, it is by no means in my power to supersede a positive resolution of Congress, under which your present confinement took place."[51] He sent this note back to William and forwarded William's request to the Congress along with his personal recommendation that the appeal be granted. William's "situation is distressing and must interest all our feelings, as I have no doubt of the great indisposition of this lady. I should suppose, after his solemn assurances and being laid under such further restrictions as Congress may judge necessary to impose upon him, that he might be indulged to see her." Furthermore, Washington wrote, "Humanity and generosity plead powerfully in favor of his application." Washington knew how Congress stalled unpopular decisions: "If it is granted, he should have the earliest notice, or the end and views of Congress may be disappointed in the death of Mrs. Franklin before his arrival."[52]

It took another week before the letter reached Philadelphia and Congress decided to consider the request. No such powerful personal endorsement of Washington's could be dismissed out of hand, even by William Franklin's most suspicious and unforgiving enemies. On July 28, the Congress finally debated and denied the request. "After such a violation of so sacred a tie as that of honor, [the Congress] cannot think it consistent with the safety of the States to permit him to have an opportunity of conferring with our open enemies under any restrictions whatsoever."[53] The congressional decision was transmitted to Washington the next day. By the time it reached him, Elizabeth Downes Franklin, born forty-three years earlier on a Barbados plantation, first lady of New Jersey for fifteen years, was dead.

From all over New York City, her friends gathered the next evening to walk through the streets behind the wagon that carried her body to a funeral in St. Paul's Chapel of Trinity Church, just off Wall Street. She was buried in the churchyard. Five days later, *Rivington's Royal Gazette* noted that her funeral procession had been "attended by a number of the most respectable inhabitants of this place," and added that Elizabeth Franklin had been "a loving wife, an indulgent mistress, a steady friend . . . affable to all."[54]

Several days after the funeral, Thomas Parke rode into Litchfield with permission to visit his master. No account of their brief meeting survives. Elizabeth had, William subsequently wrote, "died of a broken heart occasioned by our long separation and my ill-treatment."[55]

Ten years later, from his exile in England, he commissioned a large plaque to be erected in her memory in Trinity Church. He still treasured his memories of her. "Sincerity and sensibility, politeness and affability, Godliness and charity were with sense refined and person elegant, in her united. From a grateful remembrance of her affectionate tenderness and constant performance of all the duties of a good wife, this monument is erected by him who knew her worth and still laments her loss."[56]

For more than a year William had feared that his stand would cost Elizabeth her life, but this hardly lessened the impact of her death. That his fear had been justified only added guilt to his grief. He plunged into a deep and morbid depression. "Anxiety I was long under on account of the distressed situation of my dear wife, whose death I was convinced would be expedited by the intelligence she would necessarily receive of my cruel treatment, and the affliction with which I was overwhelmed on the news of the actual death of the best of women, has brought such a dejection of spirits, attended with an almost constant fever, that my life has become quite a burden to me."[57]

In fact, William's physical health had deteriorated markedly by the time the grim news reached him. A portrait of him, posing for the King's painter in London before sailing to America, shows a hardy, ruddy, healthy William with a high hairline, a strong jaw and, obviously, a full set of his own teeth. A few years later, when the finished portrait still had not arrived, William joked that the painter had better add quite a few pounds to his frame, as he had gained weight. He was strong and yet overweight before he went off to captivity. By the time he emerged, there is graphic evidence in a sketch by Benjamin West that he had aged rapidly and prematurely in prison. He had lost his hair and his teeth and there was little of the old stockiness through the chest and shoulders that marked him as a Franklin.

William had been in Litchfield Jail for four months before he learned of Elizabeth's death. He had endured the rising noise, the insults of his guards, the bugs that shared his cell with him. He had choked down the bad food he had to buy from his jailer, swatted at the horseflies that seemed to crowd through every opening. It had bothered him terribly that he could learn nothing of the war that was not couched in the boasting of his scornful guards, bothered him almost as much as the smell of his own body, which he could not wash, and of his underwear, which he could not wash, mend or change.[58]

At first, he had been sick from the food and the stench and the worry about Elizabeth. He had begun to lose weight from lack of exercise and malnutrition, and now that he knew she was gone he often could not bring himself to eat. Elizabeth, Temple, his father — all were gone from him. He received not one word from his sister, who must have learned of Elizabeth's death from the newspapers. The only news to reach him from the outside was bad. He undoubtedly surmised that the rebels were renewing their persecution of Loyalists because he could hear and occasionally see the signs of their fury. Other prisoners were marched into Litchfield and hounded by the guards. David Mathews, the mayor of New York City, was there, sentenced to death for conspiring to blow up Washington's headquarters the year before. On one day in the summer of 1777, one hundred fifty Loyalists were herded up to the crowded jail at the end of a forced march of more than a hundred miles from the coast, where they had been collected after kidnapping raids on Long Island. William could probably not learn all the details, even if he succeeded in bribing the guards, but he surely heard the gunfire when three of the new prisoners broke and ran and were shot down outside the jail.[59]

Thomas Parke stayed on in Litchfield to do anything he could to help his master. How he managed to live in the rebel stronghold of Litchfield without being stoned or run out of town is an unanswered question. In any case, he and Joseph Galloway were in communication. Six weeks after William learned that Elizabeth had died, Galloway got word to Thomas that he was about to leave New York and had no way to care further for the Franklins' belongings.

After languishing in solitary confinement for nearly six months, William's tone in writing to Governor Trumbull was subdued. He was "under a necessity of requesting your permission to send my steward, Thomas Parke, to New York, to assist in taking care of [Elizabeth's] effects and to bring out some linen [underwear and shirts] of which I stand in great need and which I cannot procure here for money. There are, besides, some papers and accounts in which my father is interested and which I would willingly transmit to him or his attorney in Philadelphia before I die, an event that I am convinced cannot be far off unless there should be some speedy relaxation of the unparalleled severity of my confinement. I feel myself in a sensible decline and am already so much reduced in size and become so weak and relaxed as to render it extremely improbable that I shall ever recover my health and strength again. In short, I suffer so much in being thus buried alive, having no one to speak to day or night, and for the want of air and exercise, that I should deem it a favor to be immediately taken out and shot — a speedy or sudden death being every way more eligible than such a miserable lingering, though equally sure, [death] as I seem at present doomed to."[60]

William believed that relief would only come from Governor Trumbull if he could somehow make a case that he had not violated his parole. Even in his weakened state, the lawyer in him sought another appeal. He was sure, he told Trumbull, that he could vindicate himself, if only he could be allowed more pen and paper and be granted the peace and quiet to compose his thoughts.

His cell, he explained, "is directly over the common sitting room of the tavern, in which there is generally so great a noise as to render it almost impossible for a man to collect and digest his thoughts on any subject." Certain that whatever the outcome of his appeal to Trumbull he was soon to die, William asked to be transferred to a house nearby long enough to write his father and his son to settle his business with them. He still could not reconcile himself to "my father's total neglect and inattention, notwithstanding, as I was informed, that the American Party had sent him an account of my sufferings, requesting his interference in my behalf."[61]

That "Governor Franklin was in actual custody shut up in a nasty, dirty jail," as the Loyalist chronicler Thomas Jones put it, was a scandal that eventually brought censure on Benjamin Franklin. It mystified William Strahan how Benjamin could have let Elizabeth's death come about, and he rebuked his old friend for his attitude toward William. Strahan was one of those who believed that the Presbyterians and Puritans were treating William with undue harshness because he was "the son of the old sinner." It was still unclear to Strahan as late as 1778, two years after William's arrest, "what may have brought upon him this severe treatment." Strahan, as a member of Parliament and a journalist, was in a position to know how William's treatment compared with that of other prisoners of equal rank and he could not condone Benjamin's complicity in such harsh tactics. "Whatever his demerits may be in the opinion of the reigning power in America," Strahan wrote Benjamin in an attempt to appeal to his old friend's vanity, "the son of Dr. Franklin ought not to receive such usage from them." Strahan obviously refused to believe that Benjamin Franklin could be to blame for his son's harsh treatment.[62]

Other old friends brought up to Franklin the question no one in America evidently dared ask. To Jan Ingenhousz, he felt compelled to write, "You enquire what has become of my son. As he adhered to the party of the king, his people took him prisoner and sent him under a guard to Connecticut, where he continues, but is allowed a district of some miles to ride about, upon his parole of honor not to quit the country."[63] Benjamin gave Ingenhousz no intimation of his acquiescence in William's arrest.

Franklin was more than mildly concerned with the welfare of prisoners at this time. He was preoccupied with the subject almost from the time he arrived at Versailles to begin laying the groundwork for a Franco-American alliance against the British. As British prisons in England filled with captured American privateersmen, Benjamin began a two-year correspondence with another influential old friend in Parliament, David Hartley. In at least thirteen letters he prevailed on Hartley to help alleviate "all the horrors of imprisonment" for these Americans.[64] Hartley and Benjamin's Whig friends raised money by subscription even as Minister Franklin supervised attempts to organize a prisoner exchange. French jails, too, held hundreds of British seamen captured after France joined the worldwide war. Indeed, Benjamin Franklin appears to have been completely in charge of what had become a potent diplomatic weapon: the treatment and exchange of prisoners. And he, as usual, concerned himself with every detail. He expressed abhorrence "that our people are not allowed the use of pen or ink, not the sight of newspapers, nor the conversation of friends," the same treatment meted out to his own son.[65]

Franklin's years in France are replete with such ironies. He was worshipped by the court even as America's endless demands for loans impoverished the royal family to an extent that helped bring them to the guillotine in their own bloody revolution. He was, in his own words, a "vogue": "Few strangers in France have had the good fortune to be so universally popular."[66] He was mistaken for a Quaker in the marten hat and simple black traveling suit he had worn ever since the Paris crowds decided, on first seeing him, that this was what all American republicans looked like.

He was more indulgent in every way with Temple than he had been with William. Even as Benjamin packed Sally's son Benny off to Geneva — "I intend him for a Presbyterian as well as a republican"[67] — he allowed Temple to become a libertine. All he asked of the youth was to dance attendance on him, to perform the duties of aide and private secretary. But he also led Temple to believe he would one day inherit Benjamin's mantle as America's premier diplomat, and he outraged other American envoys by sending Temple on sensitive errands.

Temple's list of duties ran from delivering calling cards and copying letters to helping his grandfather arrange prisoner exchanges. The Reverend John Witherspoon's second son was captured on a secret diplomatic mission at sea (the oldest had been beheaded by a cannonball at the battle of Brandywine) and sent to the Tower of London as a traitor and a spy. Franklin put Temple to work, advancing Benjamin's own money to young Witherspoon, forwarding his father's letters to him, interceding through diplomatic channels as Benjamin wrote "to procure your son's liberty" and to put him on a ship home to America. Yet when Temple made an attempt to help his own father, Benjamin was quick with a rebuke.[68]

Benjamin's life in Paris was far from frugal. To his dear old friend Caty Ray Greene, he wrote, "I live here in great respect, and dine every day with great folks."[69] Yet when his daughter Sally wrote to request that he send her some French linen, some long black pins, lace and feathers, Benjamin told her, "It disgusted me as much as if you had put salt into my strawberries." And then the old hypocrite proceeded to lecture her as he once had lectured Deborah even while he was living in luxury. "Of all the dear things in this world, idleness is the dearest. . . . The spinning, I see, is laid aside, and you are to be dressed for the ball. . . . I therefore send all the articles you desire that are useful and necessary and omit the rest."[70]

Even as William atrophied in a stinking death cell in Connecticut — he had to wait another five months in solitary confinement for an answer from Trumbull — Temple drew for his aunt Sally a vividly contrasting picture of life with his grandfather in a fashionable Paris suburb. "I never remember to have seen my grandfather in better health. The air of Passy and the warm bath three times a week have made quite a young man of him. His pleasing gaiety makes everybody in love with him, especially the ladies, who permit him always to kiss them."[71] Franklin was at first closely watched by the French: the Sûreté detectives reported, after searching his rooms, how remarkably clean his underwear was. There were stories, too, of his amours with the wives of French noblemen, but they must have been highly fictitious. By then, Franklin was suffering increasingly from an inoperable kidney stone, and by the war's end, he moved only with considerable pain and had to be carried everywhere in a sedan chair. He was the darling of the entire French nation, his smiling face in scores of poses on medallions, prints and busts, rather than the darling of any one woman, or succession of women.[72]

Yet in his relations with British and French diplomats, he was brilliantly successful. His years of imperial agency in England gave him an enormous advantage, even against the comte de Vergennes, the masterful French foreign minister. Franklin knew that the King wanted to keep peace in Europe while restoring the French fleet and colonial empire, above all wanted to keep America from making peace with England. The entry of France into the war early in 1778 on the side of America was in many ways Franklin's greatest triumph. He had learned that Britain had decided, in the event of war with France, on a strategy of holding only the main American naval bases of New York, Charleston and Savannah, thereby enabling her to release a good proportion of her resources for worldwide combat against France and Spain. If America made peace with Britain, American corsairs would be turned loose on French shipping, and French divisions would be drained off to America.

Franklin played on Vergennes's fears that America would settle her differences with her natural ally, gain her independence as the price for remaining neutral, and no longer need France. In a secret memorandum to the King, Vergennes expressed this fear: "There is a numerous party in America which is endeavoring to fix as a basis of the political system of the new States that no engagement can be contracted with other European powers."[73] Dr. Franklin had assured him that Britain had made "definite offers" of peace, and that it was no longer a question of independence. As Franklin had pointed out, "The United States are in fact independent. They have in their hands all that constitutes sovereign power."[74] Further, Franklin was able to stress, after the American victory at Saratoga in October of 1777, that Britain was willing to grant independence rather than continue a war that was proving both costly and unpopular in England.

In February of 1778, when Franklin was summoned to Versailles to sign the treaty of alliance between France and America, his attire, usually dismissed as odd, this day horrified his aides. Why, he was asked, had he put on a faded, speckled old Manchester coat in which to be received by the King on such an occasion of state? The smile was more enigmatic than ever as Franklin recalled the morning four years earlier when he had worn the same clothes to the Cockpit on the day of his deepest humiliation. Turning to his aides, Franklin answered, "For a little revenge."[75]

The pressure to release William Franklin became a crusade involving the most unlikely people on both sides. For one, Francis Hopkinson, now a rebel congressman, tried to influence other members of the Congress on William's behalf. For another, James Kinsey, once the Quaker leader of the New Jersey Assembly, now the rebel chief justice, wrote to a moderate member of the Congress that the severity of William's treatment "probably will, if no relief is afforded, conduct him to his grave in a short time. . . . I am told that his situation is so exceedingly disagreeable that he has offered to comply with my terms for the liberty of a district [in New Jersey]." Kinsey did not "attempt to justify nor even palliate" William's "imprudence": after all, it was William who had once identified him in a dispatch to Lord Dartmouth as a "tool of faction." But Kinsey could not help reminding his revolutionary colleagues that because "he is the only son of a man to whom America owes so much, he seems to be almost entitled to some indulgence."[76]

But the treatment of prisoners of war depends primarily on political and military considerations. The British army had soundly defeated Washington's army at Brandywine and had foiled his predawn counterattack at Germantown. After the fall of Philadelphia in October 1777, thousands of rebel prisoners were crowded into the city's hospitals and overflowed into the State House and nearby churches. Some two thousand died in the ensuing months even as three thousand died of epidemic camp fever at Valley Forge. The surviving rebel soldiers huddled in snow-covered huts little more comfortable than William Franklin's cell. Bitterness against the Loyalists reached its peak in Philadelphia that winter. The Pennsylvania German and Quaker farmers refused to sell their crops and livestock for the worthless Continental paper money and they marched their provisions past Valley Forge into the city, where Loyalists and British, paying hard money, remained warm, well fed, even convivial, while Washington's army was driven to cattle rustling to survive.

William Franklin was not the only Loyalist prisoner to suffer inhumane treatment, of course. As the British approached Philadelphia, the rebels rounded up twenty-one leading Quakers, including Israel Pemberton, Benjamin Franklin's old political rival and a cousin of Deborah Read Franklin. Refused habeas corpus, they were at first held in the Masonic Lodge, then, surrounded by a mob, they were dragged into wagons and carried west. Stoned as they passed through the streets of rebel towns, they eventually were imprisoned in the mountains of Virginia. Two died.[77]

It was a chance visit by old friends from Philadelphia that finally brought to light the appalling condition into which William had sunk during the hot summer months and early fall of 1777. Two Continental officers traveling through Litchfield were told, apparently by a tavernkeeper, of the illness of the town's highest-ranking prisoner. They gained permission to visit William, and one of them was shocked enough to write Richard Bache immediately. Even as a commissary of prisoners, Captain Daniel Clymer was surprised at conditions in the Litchfield jail. At first, he said, he had been concerned only that William's "accommodations were suitable to his station," but he found William in a "small room in the jail without furniture. He requested me to write to you that he may be permitted to be confined in a private house in the town. . . . He complains of his loss of strength — he is very much emaciated and appears to me to be in a bad state of health. Dictates of humanity have induced me to write to you. . . . He desired his respects to you and his sister."[78]

But William had powerful enemies who still controlled his fate. Bache, a leading revolutionary by this time, could only write to his father-in-law for instructions, a woefully inadequate measure. So successful was the British blockade that letters sent across the Atlantic stood little chance of escaping interception, and even those that did took six months to reach their destination. William could appeal to the Board of War, but one of its most powerful members was William Duer, the man who had trapped him in his protections scheme.

It was Governor Trumbull who, rather than risk William's death in jail, finally granted his request to be moved to a private home in East Windsor, thirty-five miles northeast of Litchfield near the Massachusetts border. He was taken there, gravely ill, in an open carriage on December 31 after eight months of solitary confinement. In January 1778, when the British next offered to exchange a full American colonel for William, the British commissary writing to Washington was Henry Hugh Fergusson, who five years earlier had married Elizabeth Graeme, William's first love.[79] At the same time another ghost from William's past was working against him. Elias Boudinot of Elizabethtown was now the chief American commissary of prisoners. He reported to Washington that on January 5, rebel prisoners were so starved that when "one of their number seized and devoured [a piece of pork] with so much eagerness he immediately dropped down dead. . . . The Provost Marshal [William Cunningham] used to sell their provisions and leave them to starve, as he did their allowance of wood. Some of them being ill with dysentery, could scarcely walk and for not coming faster he beat them with his rattan [riding crop]." One man was in a privy "longer than the rest. . . . Cunningham gave him a blow" with a large jail key "which killed him on the spot."[80] The report left Washington in no mood to smile favorably on William Franklin's exchange. The request for exchange was denied.

A more desperate plan was soon conceived by William's old friend Galloway, who had returned to Philadelphia with the British army. Like many other rich Loyalists, he had raised his own private troop of cavalry. From his base at Trevose, he gathered intelligence reports for Major John André, the British adjutant general, who was living in Benjamin Franklin's house. Galloway obtained information in April 1778 that Governor William Livingston of New Jersey and his entire government — staff, judges, council of safety and assembly — were about to arrive unguarded in Burlington, just across the river. According to the Loyalist historian Thomas Jones, a close friend of Galloway's, he "weighed the information well and minutely inquired into every particular . . . through his friends in Bucks County the inhabitants of which were in general loyal." In that icy winter, troopers could cross the Delaware ice pack near Trenton. "He laid . . . every particular before Lord Howe, who gave it his hearty approbation and desired Galloway to get everything ready — But behold! To the great surprise of [Galloway] the day preceding . . . the General sent for Mr. Galloway and told him the expedition must be laid aside. The General told him a cartel was soon to be entered for exchange of prisoners. Had Galloway's plan succeeded," William Franklin "might have been immediately released in exchange for Livingston's captured government. . . . No cartel ever took place," wrote this Loyalist who was among those doomed to spend the rest of the war in prison because of Howe's blundering.[81]

After his move to East Windsor, William was allowed to resume writing to his sister Sally and her husband. Bache finally wrote to Benjamin in July 1779, "Governor Franklin is on the point of being exchanged. I have had two or three letters from him that he enjoys better health." William's hope and health had returned when he learned that a rebel governor, John McKinley of Delaware, who had been captured by the British and was on parole in British-held New York, had been allowed to return to Philadelphia to seek congressional approval of his exchange for William so that he could go home. A four-day debate over the exchange ensued in the Congress. The motion was not without opposition: the new rebel commissary of prisoners was John Witherspoon's son-in-law, and evidently the Witherspoon faction in secret session tried to have the motion tabled. Congressional radicals wanted to refuse McKinley's return to New York for exchange with William, even though McKinley, too, was in poor health. The vote against tabling was 7 to 5 against the Witherspoon faction. There immediately followed, late in the afternoon of September 14, 1778, a roll-call vote "respecting the exchange of William Franklin." The New England delegations, the Middle States, Virginia, and North Carolina voted aye. States suffering severely from Loyalist regiments — South Carolina and Georgia — voted nay. Only New Jersey abstained. The date of William's exchange was set for November 1, 1778.[82]

It had been just one month short of three years since Lord Stirling's troops had surrounded Proprietary House and scared Elizabeth nearly out of her wits. William had been held in solitary confinement for 250 days. On October 24, 1778, William said goodbye to his latest warders. In a gesture of appreciation, he wrote to the governor and people of Connecticut that "Capt. John Ellsworth and Mrs. Ellsworth his wife have treated me and other British prisoners with great civility and kindness. I do, therefore, though unsolicited on their parts, recommend them, their family and their property to the protection of all British officers and other His Majesty's loyal subjects."[83] On the first day of November, he reached the British outposts at New York City, ready to take his revenge.

20

I SHALL NEVER SEE YOU AGAIN

1778–1785

O N NOVEMBER 1, 1778, WILLIAM FRANKLIN WAS escorted to the outskirts of New York City, free after nearly three years' captivity. It had been five years since he had visited the city, now the center of the British war effort. As he crossed King's Bridge and entered the British lines, he could see all around him the consequences of civil war. The road passed between a Hessian strongpoint at Prince Charles Redoubt to his left and Fort Tryon, a Loyalist cavalry outpost on the Hudson River. For four miles to the east, William could make out nothing but British tents, gun implacements, walls and guard posts.[1]

By this time, New York City had been thoroughly transformed into a fortress crowded with forty thousand soldiers and sailors and nearly twenty thousand civilians, mainly Loyalist refugees. More than a thousand of its four thousand houses had been burned in a series of fires which Loyalists contended Washington had ordered set. In the latest fire, only three months before, the vast British military warehouses holding William's furniture, his library of priceless maps and historical documents, and all his account books had been destroyed. William had no money and no chance, now, to collect any, but he was past the point of despair. As his carriage passed the street where his wife had died, he could see, standing tall and charred above the ruins, the red spire of Trinity Church, where she was buried.[2]

While William recuperated with friends, he wrote a long narrative of his arrest and imprisonment and sent if off to Secretary of State George Germain. It brought a rapid response: a pension of five hundred pounds (half his governor's salary) and money to reimburse his outlays for himself and for the numerous British prisoners in Connecticut he had helped.[3] But William wanted to do more than sit out the war as a pensioner. He began meeting with other leading Loyalists and studied Loyalist problems.

His joy at release from his "horrible confinement" was dampened when he found that Joseph Galloway had already sailed for England. "I had almost determined to follow you," he wrote his old friend, "but for an unwillingness to quit the scene of action, where I think I might be of some service."[4] The next day he wrote again: "Everyone here expresses the greatest eagerness for action and only wishes that vigorous measures may be adopted."[5] William missed Galloway, who also had sacrificed much for his Loyalist views: his farm at Trevose had been sacked and confiscated, his Philadelphia mansion seized, his wife evicted bodily. Galloway was bitter about America and never returned, but William saw that his old friend would be a valuable spokesman in London for his plan to unite all the fragmented Loyalist groups and gain for them the right to fight as equals at the side of British and Hessian armies in an independent command.

William discovered that he was popular among the refugees — one jealous rival wrote Galloway that William "is much caressed."[6] Indeed, over the next four years he became at once one of the most respected and reviled figures of the Revolution. He became the living symbol of the Loyalist cause at a time when thousands were despairing of ever being saved by the British. He lost his influence only when he became enmeshed in a bloody round of local atrocities in rural Monmouth County, New Jersey, where the war had taken an ugly turn and become a long series of guerrilla raids and reprisals. By the time of his release in late 1778, British strategists were just beginning to take seriously the potential for Loyalist participation in the war, but they still overestimated Loyalist numbers and underestimated the hatred of the rebels for their former friends and neighbors. When the French had entered the war in February 1778 and the British decided they could not hold Philadelphia, they had shifted to a New York-based defensive strategy in the North, abandoning the Continental capital to the rebels. A few days before the British evacuation in June, Galloway had been told that the estimated six thousand Loyalist refugees crowded into Philadelphia should go out to Valley Forge and swear allegiance to Washington and all would be well. In the ensuing panic, three thousand refugees carried and dragged their belongings across New Jersey in one hundred–degree heat, closely pursued by the rebel army all the way to New York.[7] Caught between rebel fury and British ignorance, many Loyalist Philadelphians were unable to leave. Some were rounded up by Benedict Arnold, the new military governor sent to the city in part to punish the Tories who had collaborated with the British. As William recovered in New York, he and other Loyalists learned what they could expect when the British occupation of any sector was over.

Throughout the occupation, rebel committees had secretly assembled lists. Now, a blacklist of 490 names was published. Loyalists must either surrender and stand trial as traitors or have their properties confiscated and sold. Most chose to flee, leaving virtually everything behind. The gallows at Centre Square in Philadelphia was kept busy in the autumn of 1778. Two executions particularly shocked Loyalists. Abram Carlisle and John Roberts, both Quakers, were condemned to die despite a plea for mercy from 387 citizens, five clergymen and many of the leading revolutionaries. But the Pennsylvania Council was unmoved: the councillors considered it necessary to terrorize the Quakers into submission. "The executions have had a great effect on the minds of the people," one leading Loyalist wrote to Galloway.[8] An estimated four thousand Philadelphians nevertheless braved reprisals by marching behind the coffins of the executed Loyalists.

The British occupation of New York City, now entrenched, seemed to guarantee to the Loyalists a secure and permanent stronghold. Entire counties on Long Island had remained loyal to the King, and the island became a fortified refuge for Loyalists fleeing from upstate New York, Connecticut and New Jersey. Nearby Staten Island had become the base for the newly organized Loyalist provincial corps. At their wartime peak, there were more than ten thousand Loyalist troops in these corps and an equal number in regular British units, their numbers often exceeding the strength of Washington's Continentals. When New York City was threatened by a French fleet, an additional six thousand Loyalists volunteered as militiamen and formed sixty-two companies that drilled until the war's end.

The numbers were deceptive, however. In actuality, the British commander in chief, Sir Henry Clinton, rarely used Loyalist forces in the field, and never effectively. Like many of his officers, Clinton regarded the Loyalists as inferior provincials. Even though the British ministry considered them as the primary reason to prolong the fighting in America, Clinton ignored or feuded with Loyalist leaders. Using Loyalist regiments only for occasional raids, he relegated them to guard duty, to cutting firewood and rounding up provisions for his regular troops. The result was that at least twenty thousand Loyalists were bottled up in New York City and its environs by the time William Franklin was released from prison in November 1778.[9]

Although he described himself to Galloway as "considerably reduced in flesh" by his time in prison, William threw himself into the long-neglected task of helping the refugees. He helped old friends first. Reverend Jonathan Odell and his large family had suffered terribly. William talked Clinton into hiring Odell as a Loyalist propagandist. Together the two kept New York Loyalist newspapers filled with stories, songs and poems that heartened the refugees, taunted the rebels.[10]

But more systematic support was needed. By the third week of his freedom, William had drawn up a master plan to organize the refugees under their own board of directors with powers to conduct raids on rebel shipping and privateering ports, to free Loyalist prisoners in rebel jails, and to carry out reprisals that would discourage rebel depredations on refugee settlements on Long Island. He presented the plan to General Clinton, who ignored it.[11]

When he conferred with the British peace commissioners, who were visiting New York, he had no trouble winning their support: the commission secretary was none other than his old friend Adam Ferguson of Edinburgh. William made no secret of his distaste for Clinton's insensitivity, indeed open hostility, to the Loyalists. He asked the commissioners to present to Lord Germain a plan for "procuring, digesting and communicating intelligence of the motions of the enemy" to the British Secret Service.[12] He also put forward once again his master plan which Clinton had ignored and tentative plans for speeding up prisoner exchange. He buttressed his proposals with graphic descriptions of the conditions in Connecticut prisons, notably the Litchfield jail and the infamous Simsbury Mine. He also proposed a plan for encouraging Loyalist recruitment. No doubt to his surprise, he found that his ideas for organizing the Loyalists dovetailed neatly with the plans of the peace commissioners.

Lord Carlisle, Undersecretary of State William Eden and other members of the commission had failed in their primary mission: to open peace talks with the Congress. Rebuffed, they now were ready to urge the waging of political warfare, using the King's troops to subdue a district, raise the royal standard, offer amnesties, and invite Americans to set up Loyalist militia. At the same time, they urged the reestablishment of civil government and were openly sympathetic to the plight of the Loyalists: "In our present condition the only friends we have, or are likely to have, are those who are absolutely ruined for us," wrote Lord Carlisle.[13] The commission had no teeth. All it could do was make recommendations to the King, but it could show support for William's proposals. At its urging, Clinton turned over to William a house on King Street for his newly formed Refugees' Club, which began to hold almost daily meetings and rounds of inspection of Loyalist camps.[14]

In touring the camps on Long Island, where thousands of refugees lived in poverty and constant fear of nighttime rebel raids from across Long Island Sound, Governor Franklin soon devised a plan for an independent Loyalist organization, part military, part civilian, to relieve Loyalist sufferings and provide support and protection for the large number unwilling to join British or provincial corps. His popularity so impressed General Sir William Tryon, the former governor of New York who now commanded the provincial regiments, that Tryon soon was advancing Franklin as the leader of all the Loyalist forces in America. What also impressed militant Loyalists was the message Governor Franklin was preaching. The Loyalists, as he wrote Lord Germain on November 12, "ardently wish to see a respectable army of the King's force sent into their country, though their property would be destroyed with others, rather than live under such tyranny as they are compelled to at present."[15] To his old friend Joseph Galloway, Franklin wrote of growing Loyalist resentment at the British army and an unwillingness to leave the fate of their country entirely in the hands of professional soldiers. "Many of the Loyalists in America think they have reason to complain not only of slights and inattentions, but of ill-usage from those who ought to have favored and encouraged them. Good policy, if there was no other motive, would certainly have dictated a quite different conduct."[16]

While exhilarating many Loyalists, Franklin's words as well as his popularity annoyed a few prominent Loyalists who had been eclipsed by his arrival. One of them, Chief Justice William Smith, was an old enemy: he attracted others who shared his opinion that a retaliatory war was wrong. "If America prevails by the sword or obtains concessions to her contentment, the Tories are ruined. In either case, they must finally abandon the continent."[17] Franklin's call for a guerrilla war of vengeance led Smith's ally, Lieutenant Governor Andrew Elliott, to write to Lord Carlisle that only the British should be trusted. Raids on the seacoast in conjunction with regular forces "may be useful" to "annoy all the coast," but the talk of "burning of dwelling houses can answer no purpose, and excursions to Jersey, a country already destroyed by both sides, would only distress . . . country people and fill our jails with prisoners that Congress would never pay any attention to."[18]

Any wavering over William Franklin's leadership, however, was swept away in an episode that galvanized the Loyalist majority behind him. Within weeks of his arrival in New York, eight Loyalists were captured on Long Island while gathering firewood for the British army. Tried by a Connecticut court, they were convicted of treason and sentenced to death. Franklin and his Refugees's Club demanded that Sir Henry Clinton release eight rebel prisoners from the British Provost (prison) and place them in their custody. When Clinton complied, Franklin sent word through the lines that unless the Loyalist prisoners in Connecticut were released, his prisoners would be forced to dig a dungeon under the New York prison similar to Simsbury Mine, where they would be treated severely. If the Loyalists were harmed, his hostages would receive the same treatment. The Connecticut authorities relented. The prisoners were exchanged.[19]

Encouraged by Governor Franklin's exhibition of a "certain spirit that has been wanting," Loyalist militants from all the northern colonies gathered under his leadership and formulated one plan after another at the Refugees' Club.[20] They wanted to organize raids into Connecticut and Rhode Island. Clinton objected. He was opposed to any incursion into the prerogatives of his command or into his war chest.

Relations between Clinton and the Loyalists had never been good. "Having determined against a predatory war," Chief Justice Smith wrote, "and conceiving that the want of reinforcements would justify his not attacking the highland forts and penetrating the county, he resolved to do nothing, and yet hope for approbation."[21] Judge Thomas Jones was more direct: "Clinton was one of the most irresolute, timid, stupid and ignorant animals in the world. It is really surprising that a great king should have trusted such a man with the command of a great army to quell a great, a dangerous and a stubborn rebellion, in which the welfare of the nation and the honour of the Crown were so immediately concerned."[22]

Undaunted by Clinton's objections, Governor Franklin next collaborated with General Tryon in June 1779 on a comprehensive and militant "Regulation of Refugees." It proposed that the Loyalists place themselves under William's command as "commandant of the Associated Loyalists." His proposed army would operate, subject to Clinton's approval, from bases in Rhode Island, on Long Island and Staten Island, and at Sandy Hook, New Jersey. They would pay themselves from the plunder of rebels and take, keep and exchange their own prisoners. This plan, submitted in July 1779, was ignored for three months.[23] Then it was returned by Clinton's aide, Major John André, with the stipulation that Clinton have full control of all refugee activities. Franklin accepted the restriction reluctantly, but agreed to take the command. In writing his acceptance to André, he took a slap at Clinton: "Unless the refugees and other Loyalists are . . . put under the command of a person in whom they confide, and to whom they have an attachment . . . they can answer no valuable purpose."[24] Clinton responded by sailing off to South Carolina without activating the plan. The exasperated Loyalists decided to appeal over his head to London for a direct order from Lord Germain to Clinton.

In the late winter of 1779, Germain, eager to use the Loyalists, promptly endorsed the plan. His only modification was that the Loyalists be guided, not by a single commander, but by a board of directors. In the instructions Germain sent to Clinton, he named Franklin as chairman of the board. The directors and all their subordinates were to serve without pay or rank in the army, were to be free of British army discipline. The Associated Loyalists were to "annoy the seacoasts of the revolted provinces and distress their trade." Clinton was to supply them, but they were to "undertake no enterprise" without advising headquarters. All captured goods were to be divided among the Associators; each man who served for the duration was to receive at least two hundred acres of land. Germain stressed that the Association not only had his personal approval but that of the King. At the same time, Clinton was given control over the board and would be held personally responsible if this experiment in paramilitary organization backfired.[25]

Just how wide the gulf was between Clinton and the Loyalists was demonstrated as soon as Germain's instructions reached New York. As usual, Clinton sat on the plans. Franklin, on the other hand, was convinced that Germain had already given him an independent command. The Board of Associated Loyalists finally received its articles of association from Clinton in December 1780, more than two years after Franklin had proposed his first plan.[26]

By the time the Associators began to raid coastal counties in January 1781, a long series of clashes had already taken place in Monmouth County, New Jersey. When the British marched through en route from Philadelphia to New York in June, 1778, a large number of New Jersey Loyalists had joined them. Among them was Stephen Edwards of Eatontown, who left his wife and parents behind. Sometime in September of that year, Edwards reappeared. Rebel leaders were quickly informed: one of the tragedies of this sort of guerrilla warfare was that it pitted old friends and neighbors against each other. Captain Jonathan Forman of the Third New Jersey Militia Regiment led a contingent of cavalry to the Edwards family home. He did not have any trouble finding it.

The Edwards and Forman families were old friends. Entering the house late at night, the rebel party found the young Loyalist in bed with his wife. He was wearing a woman's nightcap. Mrs. Edwards said her husband was a serving girl. But Captain Forman spotted Edwards's clothes protruding from under the bed. In a pocket he found papers that allegedly linked Edwards's visit to a spying mission for the British. Edwards was taken to the Monmouth County jail in Freehold. The next day he was court-martialed and convicted of spying. The day after that, he was hanged from a tree near the county courthouse.[27]

One of the first raids authorized by the Board of Associated Loyalists apparently was in direct reprisal for this hanging. On April 30, 1780, Stephen Edwards's brother-in-law, Richard Lippincott, also a Loyalist refugee, returned to his hometown of Shrewsbury, Monmouth County, with a party of seven Associated Loyalists led by Captain William Gillian. They captured the privateer brig *Elizabeth* and several rebel officers. They then paid a visit to the home of a prominent rebel named John Russell. As they entered Russell's house, Russell fired, but missed. Captain Gillian shot and killed Russell, then seized him by his collar and was about to stab him in the face when, according to one rebel account, the fireplace flared up, distracting Gillian. Russell's son, who had been wounded by another of the raiders, had been lying, as if dead, on the floor. Now he fired, killing Gillian. Another Loyalist pointed his musket at the younger Russell, but Lippincott knocked up the gun with his sword. The man was dying, said Lippincott, who had married into the Russell family. No need to shoot him again. The Loyalist party, which included a refugee named Philip White, then ransacked the Russell house. On the way out, one of them shot and wounded Russell's five-year-old grandson. The boy and his father survived.[28]

Many of the episodes involving Associated Loyalists took place in seacoast towns like Shrewsbury. Between 1778 and 1782, at least fourteen British and Loyalist ships laden with valuable cargoes were seized by privateers based at the Monmouth County port of Toms River. Early in March 1782, a Massachusetts privateer captured a British sloop and sailed it into the harbor. The same Massachusetts privateer then attacked the Loyalist sloop *Lucy*. The captain of *Lucy* was William Dillon, who had organized a considerable privateering fleet after his escape from the Freehold jail four years earlier. Dillon escaped again, this time to New York, leaving his ship behind.[29] There, he undoubtedly met with the Board of Associated Loyalists, which suggested an immediate raid on Toms River, with Dillon as guide. British forces had, over the past two years, destroyed rebel privateering bases in New Jersey from Egg Harbor to New Brunswick. On March 24, a 120-man force of Associators sailed from the Loyalist fort at Lloyd's Neck, Long Island, in the armed brig *Arrogant*. According to *Rivington's Royal Gazette,* "about 12 o'clock on that night, the party landed near the mouth of Toms River and marched to the block house . . . and reached it just at daylight. . . . They found . . . twenty-five or twenty-six . . . militia . . . prepared for defense. . . . The post into which the rebels had thrown themselves was six or seven feet high, made with large logs, with loop holes between and a number of brass swivel guns on the top which was entirely open, nor was there any way of entering but by climbing over. They had, beside swivel guns, muskets with bayonets and long pikes for their defense. Lieutenant Blanchard [the Loyalist leader] summoned them to surrender, which they not only refused, but bid the party defiance. . . . He immediately ordered the place to be stormed. . . . The rebels had nine men killed in the assault and twelve made prisoners, two of whom are wounded. The captain of the twelve months' men stationed there is among the prisoners."[30]

Since the Loyalist view was that all loyal subjects had long ago fled Toms River and only, as the *Royal Gazette* put it, "a piratical set of banditti resided,"[31] the town as well as the fort was put to the torch. Only two houses, one belonging to William Dillon's niece and the other to the widow of a rebel officer killed by Loyalists three months earlier, were spared. The prisoners, including the manacled Captain Joshua Huddy, were taken to New York.

A week after this raid, commissioners for the British and the Americans met for the first time in Elizabethtown, New Jersey, to discuss a general exchange of prisoners of war. Five months had passed since Lord Cornwallis had surrendered his army of eight thousand at Yorktown. The Americans still held many of the fifty-seven hundred men who had surrendered at Saratoga nearly five years before. The issue of prisoners had finally reached the highest level of negotiation.[32]

That same day, as the commissioners exchanged credentials, a Loyalist schooner stood off Long Branch, thirty miles away, waiting to pick up two Associators. Ashore, a brief fight took place in which a rebel horseman was killed. Reinforced, the rebels captured Loyalist Philip White, who was taken off between two guards. They went about twelve miles and "halted until the commander of horse came up, then threatened and abused Philip White . . . that the rebels would murder him before they got to Freehold." At this point, Philip White's guard was changed. Three militiamen, one of them John Russell, Junior, left for dead in the Shrewsbury raid on the Russell house two years earlier, took charge of him and kept him far in the rear.[33] Philip White was never seen alive again.

News of Philip White's death reached New York shortly after Joshua Huddy arrived with his fellow prisoners from Toms River. Rumors flew that Philip White had been prodded by swords until he ran and then was cut down by John Russell, who hacked off his arms and legs and mutilated his body.[34] The rumors coincided with the growing anxiety of Loyalists over their fate at the hands of the British as well as the rebels, especially after Cornwallis had refused to protect Loyalist prisoners when he had surrendered at Yorktown. At George Washington's demand, Cornwallis had turned them over to Washington as prisoners of state, not war: they could therefore be tried and executed as traitors.[35]

Just who first got the idea that it was time to retaliate for the death of Philip White probably will never be known, but by April 8, 1782, Captain Richard Lippincott of the New Jersey Associators had apparently won the support of a number of the members of the Board of Associated Loyalists and possibly, as he later claimed, that of Sir Henry Clinton himself to take reprisal on the prisoner Captain Joshua Huddy. Lippincott knew that Huddy was not responsible for Philip White's death — Huddy had been taken prisoner four days before White's capture — but Huddy was guilty, by his own admission, of pulling the rope that strangled Stephen Edwards back in 1778. (Edwards had since come to be regarded as the Loyalist Nathan Hale.) Both Edwards and White were Lippincott's brothers-in-law.[36]

Documents among the British Headquarters Papers indicate that by April 8, 1782, Captain Lippincott had met with at least three members of the board to arrange for a set of covert orders to take Huddy to New Jersey under the guise of exchanging him but that they really intended to hang him in retaliation for Philip White's death. Moreover, as Lippincott wrote on a placard he intended to pin to Huddy's chest, the hanging was to initiate a policy of retaliatory hangings until rebel atrocities against Loyalists ceased. On April 8 Lippincott conferred with Daniel Coxe, vice president of the Board of Associated Loyalists, to ask for the necessary orders. Coxe undoubtedly told Lippincott that if he came to board headquarters the next day before the regularly scheduled meeting, he would have everything ready. According to sworn testimony given at Lippincott's subsequent court-martial, William Franklin and another member, Charles Stewart, arrived late for the meeting the next day. As William Franklin approached the board table, Lippincott came toward him with the placard in his hand and started to show it to Franklin and Stewart. Sampson Blowers, secretary of the board, testified: "Captain Lippincott came forward from his seat, took a paper from his pocket, and going towards Governor Franklin with a paper in his hands, said, 'This is the paper we mean to take down with us,' or words to that effect, and gave this paper either to the Governor or to Mr. Stewart. Governor Franklin just looked on that paper, and Mr. Stewart, discovering an inclination to look over his shoulder or take it from him, Mr. Coxe hastily said, 'We have nothing to do with that paper, Captain Lippincott. Keep your papers to yourself. The board do not wish to see them or hear them read.' The paper was then directly given back to Captain Lippincott by Mr. Stewart. He does not know the paper was read by anyone in the room." Blowers, a Harvard-educated Boston lawyer who had represented the British soldiers in the Boston Massacre case and later became chief justice of Nova Scotia, further testified that he had "no reason to suppose any of the members had been previously acquainted with the contents of it."[37]

By the time Lippincott left the meeting, he evidently had *two* sets of orders. Coxe gave him an order dated April 8 to the Loyalist commissary of prisoners, Walter Chaloner, to "deliver to Captain Richard Lippincott the three following prisoners: Capt. Joshua

Huddy, Lt. Daniel Randolph and Jacob Fleming to be taken down to the Hook to procure the exchange of Captain Clayton Tilton and two other Associated Loyalists in Freehold Jail." The order was signed by Blowers.[38] Lippincott also carried a letter from Coxe to Lieutenant Colonel Oliver DeLancey, Clinton's adjutant general, which stated the urgency of the case: "We have reason to believe Capt. Tilton will speedily fall a sacrifice to the resentment of the rebels, to whom he has rendered himself particularly obnoxious by his loyalty and activity unless he is relieved by the immediate exertions of the loyal refugees. To effect his relief a party of refugees propose to make an attempt to force the jail or to seize and bring off General Forman, a violent persecutor of the Loyalists in that county. We request you will be pleased to inform His Excellency the Commander in Chief of the above, and if he shall approve of the enterprise, give immediate orders to issue arms and supplies for thirty men for five days."[39]

The board minutes for April 9 reveal that Lippincott also was given explicit orders by President Franklin, who noted that Clinton's approval had been sought. In his orders, which Franklin apparently presumed to be the only orders issued by the board, he went on in great detail about Lippincott's mission, in no way even hinting at a retaliatory tone. Lippincott was "to proceed with the greatest dispatch and secrecy to Freehold" to free the Loyalist prisoners held there, including Clayton Tilton and Aaron White (White had actually already escaped). Significantly, Franklin closed: "On your return, you will report your proceedings to the board."[40]

Captain Lippincott followed none of his orders from President Franklin. In what appears on the face of it to be a carefully preconceived scheme, he took his three prisoners to the guard ship *Britannia* off Sandy Hook and arranged to leave them on board in irons for three days. He then went on a carefully planned, three-day mission, not to Freehold jail but to Shrewsbury, his hometown, to attack and seize a privateer's galley and sail it back to Sandy Hook. There, with a party of twenty-two men, he finally took Joshua Huddy ashore. Allowing him time only to dictate and sign a brief will, Lippincott ordered Huddy hanged, without the slightest pretense of a court-martial, from a gallows made of three fence rails and a barrel. Then he pinned to Huddy's chest the placard of retribution he had brought with him: "We, the refugees, having with grief long beheld the cruel murders of our brethren and finding nothing but such measures daily carrying into execution, we therefore determine not to suffer without taking vengeance for numerous cruelties and thus begin and have made use of Capn. Huddy as the first object to present to your views, and further *determine* to hang man for man as long as a refugee is left existing. Up goes Huddy for Philip White."[41]

On his return to New York with his valuable prize, Lippincott reported tersely in writing to the board that he had captured the vessel and then, verbally, to William Franklin that he was on his way back to New Jersey to conclude the prisoner exchange.[42] Back in Sandy Hook he sent a party of his men overland to Freehold with prisoners Randolph and Fleming, who were subsequently exchanged for Tilton. It was not until he returned to New York on April 19 that he reported more fully to President Franklin. In a letter dated April 27 from the board to Clinton, Franklin recounted the scene: Lippincott had mentioned "verbally to one or two members who happened to be at the board room before a full board had met, that Huddy was *exchanged* (laying an emphasis on the word) for *Philip White.*"[43] But by this time, Clinton had already learned of the hanging of Joshua Huddy from General Washington and was demanding some answers of his own.

As Franklin had gotten to know the British commander better, he liked him less and less. Modern historians still accept without contradiction his terse estimate of the man. Clinton was, Franklin wrote, "weak, irresolute, unsteady, vain, incapable of forming any plan himself, and too weak or rather too proud and conceited to follow that of another. If folly herself had [been placed] at the helm, she could not take more effectual measures to overturn everything we have been doing. Our present chief never continues in one mind from breakfast to dinner, or from dinner till bed-time, and he is as much above advice as his predecessor. He could have destroyed [military] stores, intercepted convoys, surprised parties, but the court style on all occasions is, *these are not the objects,* and what *are* his objects none can tell. Perhaps it can be doubted if he knows himself. We are fortifying this town and island and showing every sign of fear of invasion. This may be prudent, but we can do nothing besides?"[44]

William's open feud with Clinton and other British officers had deepened as British victory slipped farther away. He once again pressed for an expedition through the Middle States to arouse disillusioned Loyalists. Their numbers, he insisted, were doubtlessly multiplying as inflation undermined the rebel economy. Five hundred Loyalist Associators were making a desperate stand in the Pennsylvania German country. William wanted to reinforce them, to make them the core of a Pennsylvania German Loyalist army, but Clinton's field commander, Lord Cornwallis, had refused to release regulars for anything as frivolous as reinforcing Loyalists.[45] Instead, after incurring heavy losses in a confusing southern campaign, Cornwallis decided to reinforce himself inside a new British fortress at Yorktown. As the French fleet approached, Cornwallis kept sending messages to Clinton for more men, but Clinton ignored him. Franklin was horrified when he learned through his Loyalist spies that Washington, with a fifteen-thousand-man mixed forced of French and Continentals, was preparing to dash south to trap Cornwallis. But Clinton would not believe Franklin's information, and he would not allow Loyalist troops to try to intercept Washington in New Jersey.

Once a man of peace who had argued for two years to prevent a civil war, William Franklin was pressing for victory by any means, even if the success of his plans would have subjected the peaceful people he had once led to years more of brutal internecine warfare. All through the last two years of revolution, he had urged more aggressive tactics. Because the British had repeatedly deserted the Loyalists to rebel reprisals as they came and went, armies like that of Cornwallis received no new support from the Loyalists. The Loyalists indeed had already lost untold thousands of lives in battles with hard-riding, British-hating rebel partisans, who, time after time, had cut them off from rescue by the redcoats and slaughtered them piecemeal. At the worst debacle, King's Mountain, more than a thousand Loyalists had been killed or wounded in less than an hour. Eighteen Loyalist prisoners were lynched on the battlefield after they surrendered.[46] At Yorktown, in a disgraceful final scene to the tragic British southern campaign, hundreds of Loyalists rowed frantically after the crowded British sloop *Bonetta* as it sailed away sagging with British officers. Only fourteen Loyalists were allowed on board. The others were overtaken and hauled back by the rebels.[47]

When the *Bonetta* arrived in the Loyalist capital of New York City, despair swept over the crowded refugee camps. "It is scarcely possible to give your lordship an adequate idea of the surprise and distress," Franklin wrote Lord Germain, and demanded that the ship's captain be court-martialed. (Germain indeed acceded to the request.) Loyalists now saw clearly that they were "in fact considered in no better light than runaway slaves restored to their former masters." As his officers demanded whether they and their men "too are to be sacrificed,"[48] William was urged by the Board of Loyalists to go at once to England to petition Parliament for protection. General Clinton urged William to stay and agreed he would give "public orders that no distinction would ever be made" between Loyalists and "the King's troops."[49] But when William made the promise public, Clinton denied it and denounced William for breaching a confidence. William wrote of the entire episode to Lord Germain. His letter came too late. It arrived after Cornwallis's surrender became known in London.

For nearly two years, there had been mounting opposition to the King's war policies both in the streets of London and in the Houses of Parliament. "The American War had once been the favorite of the country," wrote Edward Gibbon, then a member of Parliament. "The pride of England was irritated by the resistance of her colonies, and the executive power was driven by national clamor into the most vigorous and coercive measures. But the length of a fruitless contest, the loss of armies, the accumulation of debt and taxes, and the hostile confederacy of France, Spain and Holland indisposed the public to the American war and the persons by whom it was conducted. The representatives of the people followed, at a slow distance, the changes of their opinion; and the ministers, who refused to bend, were broken by the tempest."[50]

In a rebuff to the King, the lawyer who had mutely stood beside his client Benjamin Franklin during the Cockpit ordeal nearly ten years earlier now found his tongue. He introduced a motion in the

House of Commons "that the influence of the Crown had increased, was increasing and ought to be diminished." Though John Dunning's resolve nearly carried the House — it lost only by a narrow margin — it launched an opposition campaign that contributed to the bloodiest riots in centuries.[51]

By the time word of Cornwallis's surrender reached Lord North, he had already tendered his resignation to the King. Even stubborn George III conceded: "At last the fatal day is come."[52] Finally ready to negotiate with the United States as an independent nation, the King bitterly accepted the resignation of his war ministers and sent a new commander in chief to New York with orders to stop all offensive operations while peace talks got under way. Word of the cease-fire did not arrive in time to prevent William Franklin and his Board of Associated Loyalists from embroiling themselves in one of the most acrimonious scandals of the long war.

George Washington had hanged many men throughout the long war, many of them Loyalists, but in his eyes Captain Huddy had committed no crime and was considered under the King's protection as a prisoner of war when he was killed. Washington was outraged. He quickly informed General Clinton that he wanted the man responsible sent through the lines to him for execution. Clinton, afraid to do anything that might bring on a general engagement until his replacement arrived, saw an opportunity to silence William Franklin. He ordered Lippincott's arrest for murder and, despite the fact that Lippincott and Franklin were technically civilians outside British army discipline, ordered an investigation by an army board of inquiry. The board recommended that Captain Lippincott alone stand trial for murder.[53]

Lippincott's court-martial, conducted from June to August of 1782, ended in acquittal for lack of evidence that he had acted from malice, and the outcome was rendered even murkier when the British prosecutor neither prosecuted members of the Board of Associated Loyalists nor allowed them to testify. The obvious whitewashing of Lippincott led Washington to fly into a rage and order the hanging of a British officer equal in rank to Captain Huddy unless William Franklin, the man Washington was sure had ordered the hanging, was turned over to him. On Washington's orders, ten captains among the British officers taken at Yorktown were instructed to draw lots. When they refused and demanded an appeal to Clinton, Washington ordered that lots be drawn for them. The lot fell to Captain Asgill of the Grenadier Guards. The British officers then demanded that William Franklin or Captain Lippincott or both be turned over to Washington, that no Loyalist was worth the life of a guardsman whose father was a member of Parliament. Washington resolutely ordered Asgill brought to his camp at Morristown and placed in solitary confinement.[54] As the guardsman waited, the Congress received the court-martial record demanded by Washington. Arriving at a conclusion opposite that of the British court on the same evidence, the Congress found, "that the prisoner acted under orders from the Board of Refugees of which Governor Franklin was president, and that though the prisoner might be entitled to the acquittal, that yet Governor Franklin was the culprit and should have been punished."[55]

As Washington prepared to carry out his threat, the British prisoner's mother wrote a personal letter to the Queen of France, appealing to her as a mother to intercede with the King to ask Washington to relent. The King and Queen immediately complied. The letter they wrote Washington was "enough to move the heart of a savage,"[56] and they instructed the French minister in Philadelphia to intercede with the Congress. As minister plenipotentiary to France, Benjamin Franklin was in charge of all American exchanges in Europe, and can be presumed to have been fully informed. He was mortified, he later wrote, to learn that his own son was implicated in the case.

Amid an uproar of international publicity, Washington was perturbed to find that he was being made to appear a brute for ordering the hanging of an innocent officer and gentleman. He bowed to the wishes of the Congress and the King of France and released Asgill. But he remained convinced that William Franklin had given Lippincott verbal orders, that the British command was covering up for him, and a number of congressmen, led by the ubiquitous Witherspoon, agreed with him. Elias Boudinot said that he never saw so much "ill blood" as during the three-day congressional debate over the Huddy affair.[57]

William came away from the episode probably the most notorious Loyalist with the single exception of Benedict Arnold. He himself blamed the entire controversy on General Clinton: "The truth of the matter is that the Board was an obnoxious institution to Sir Henry, and he thought this was a favorable opportunity to make an attack upon it, and to get rid of it altogether, as it was reported that though the Board did not give orders for the execution of Huddy, yet they had secretly encouraged the refugees to that act of retaliation."[58] William never managed to clear himself of the suspicion that he had ordered the Huddy hanging, partly because there was no tribunal in which he could attempt to vindicate himself. Since the adjutant general failed to produce enough evidence to warrant an indictment against him or against other members of the Board of Associated Loyalists, William could not be tried and was unable to testify under oath after he refused to participate in the Lippincott court-martial. During the British occupation, even if there had been the proper jurisdiction, no civilian courts remained open in New York. In the pandemonium of evacuating the city, the authorities showed little interest in beginning a new trial. If William hoped to clear his name once he reached England, he was to be disappointed. The English did not care to be reminded of their debacle in America. An American in London could expect scant sympathy.

Even as congressional radicals demanded that the "absconded" William Franklin be turned over to them, William sold his furniture and prepared to sail for England. He was disgusted with America, disheartened and disenchanted by British generals who made no secret of their scorn for all Americans. Twenty years after the King had appointed him a royal governor, he left New York on August 13, 1782, ostensibly to seek protection for the Loyalists in the peace negotiations. He had time for a letter to his sister before leaving:

> I writ to you some time in the autumn of last year and enclosed a letter from Benny [Benjamin Franklin Bache, his nephew, had written from Geneva], which had been brought here in a prize, since which I have not had the pleasure of hearing from you.
> When I was sending my dear Mrs. Franklin's clothes to her

niece, I observed among them a set of tambour ruffles which I believe to be your work. . . . As they have never been made up, I reserved them that I might, in case I should see you again, request your acceptance of them. But as I am now about to embark for England, and it will probably be some years before I can promise myself that pleasure, if ever, I embrace [this] opportunity to send them to you with my best wishes for your happiness. I have but just time to desire that you would present my affectionate regards to Mr. Bache and the children, and to assure yourself that I am, as ever,

> Your loving brother,
> William Franklin[59]

On the morning of November 26, 1782, three envoys to France from the Continental Congress assembled at the Hôtel du Roi in Paris for a breakfast strategy meeting. For more than six months, they had negotiated with British, French, Dutch, Spanish and Russian diplomats. Now they were only days away from signing a preliminary peace treaty. A new British ministry had sent a variety of emissaries, several personally unacceptable to the man who had emerged as the dominant American negotiator, Benjamin Franklin. Finally, Franklin decided he could deal successfully with a one-eyed Scottish merchant with American trading connections, Richard Oswald; with Caleb Whitefoord, his old wine-merchant neighbor from Craven Street and a confidant of Lord Bute, the King's friend; and with a starchy professional diplomat named Henry Strachey, who had met Franklin when he was aide to Lord Howe at the first peace parley on Staten Island six years earlier.[60]

The terms of the treaty were highly favorable to the Americans. The British were now ready to acknowledge American independence. As a result of Benjamin's negotiations, vast new western territories (including all of the Illinois country he and William had once tried to corner) were about to be added to the new nation. At first, the British had seemed most interested in securing for their creditors American debts owed them before the war, but in recent weeks, as William Franklin and Joseph Galloway lobbied for the Loyalists in London, the talks had virtually deadlocked over the most sensitive issue of all: what to do about the large number of

Americans who refused to acknowledge the need for a new American state: the Loyalists.[61]

The new prime minister, Benjamin and William's old friend Lord Shelburne, was now insisting that a new article be added to the treaty to provide for restitution of all estates, rights and properties confiscated during the war by the rebels. Ironically, Benjamin Franklin had created the impasse at the outset of the negotiations. Without consulting his colleagues in the American mission, he had met secretly with Oswald, giving him a confidential memorandum for the prime minister in which he offered compensation for Loyalists in exchange for English cession to the United States of all of Canada.[62]

Britain may have already effectively lost thirteen American colonies, but each month that the talks dragged on, British arms were triumphing again against the ancient rival France. Now the pendulum had swung: soon after the talks began, a brilliant British naval victory over the French in the Caribbean had steeled British resolve to work out an advantageous treaty. Oswald had new orders from London: "Lord Shelburne will never give up the Loyalists."[63]

Franklin's vindictive campaign against the Loyalists in the peace negotiations grew out of his personal experiences with Loyalists he felt had betrayed him. He was as relentless, as bitter, toward his old friend Galloway as he was toward William. Long after he had given up on his son, he had trusted Galloway, leaving the bulk of his personal papers in trunks for safekeeping at Trevose. When Galloway went over to the British, he left Franklin's belongings behind. They were pilfered by looters.[64]

The talks flagged: Franklin became more adamant that there could be no provision for the Loyalists in the treaty. The British briefly tried to defuse the issue by suggesting that reparations for war victims could be made out of the proceeds of sales of British-held Canadian frontier land. Franklin argued that *all* of Canada had to be ceded to the United States "without any stipulation" in exchange for compensating the Loyalists.[65] The weary British began to back down. They suggested that France and Spain give up Florida and New Orleans and turn them into Loyalist refuges. As if in a flash of prescience, the French complicated negotiations for their

American allies by insisting that the Loyalist refugees must be compensated: such provision was *de rigueur* in any peace treaty. No royal government could sit by without providing for the faithful adherents of a king![66]

The talks seemed on the edge of disintegrating when the three American envoys met at the Hôtel du Roi to form a final strategy. Franklin was annoyed, blaming much of their troubles on his own son. He was no doubt aware that William was at this very moment bombarding the British prime minister, his old superior from his days as governor of New Jersey, with petitions from the Loyalists appealing to British national honor and demanding full amnesty and compensation. Increasingly embarrassed by his son's activities, Franklin was, according to Adams's diary, "very staunch against the Tories." Franklin was not the only American emissary with sensitive feelings on the question. John Jay's brother, Sir James Jay, was a Loyalist refugee; Adams, of course, had Loyalist relatives and in-laws. But Franklin was "a great deal more decided on this point," Adams noted, "than Mr. Jay or myself."[67]

Franklin remained adamant on the Loyalists because he knew that his own personal case was fairly representative: during the British occupation of Philadelphia, his house had been plundered and even his portrait of Lord Bute had been dumped into John André's wagon and hauled off to New York.[68]

He now produced a document which the leading historian of the peace talks, Richard B. Morris, describes as "not only a brilliant propaganda weapon but diplomatic blackmail of the first order."[69] If the British and French continued to insist on Loyalist reparations, then the Congress and the new American states would itemize all damages by British, Hessians and Loyalists, every shingle of every shelled town, every pillaged farm and ear of corn, every dead horse and cow, and every raped woman and scalped frontiersman! Franklin suggested that both sides gather and exhibit accounts of their losses "and that if a balance appears in favor of the Loyalists, it shall be paid by us to you. If, on the other hand, the balance is found due to us, it shall be paid by you."[70] The process could take years, the war would go on meanwhile, thousands more would die. The man must be mad! As diplomatically as they could, Franklin's colleagues suggested that if he insisted on reading such a memorandum to the British and the French, he must make it clear that it contained only "his private sentiments."[71]

When the peace talks resumed that morning, a British negotiator requested either a large tract of land (what is now the state of Maine would be fine) or amnesty and "strong recommendations" to the states for compensation of the Loyalists. Benjamin set teeth to grating all around the table by declaring, "You will please recollect that you have not conquered us."[72] The British envoy nevertheless retorted that the King was concerned not only about active Loyalists but all the "persons terrified into submission."[73] Here Franklin could sense his son's fine hand, and he could not have appreciated it. Though no one was willing to submit to the preposterous process suggested by Franklin, he had impressed everyone with his resolve to fight on.

The treaty put an end to William's pretensions to a vast western empire. Of more immediate concern to him and the other Loyalists, however, was Article Five of the treaty. The American commissioners pledged the Congress to "earnestly recommend" to the state legislatures full restitution of the rights and property of the Loyalists. In fact, no state felt bound by this recommendation and Loyalists saw British accession to this wording as a complete sellout of Loyalist rights. A welter of wartime anti-Loyalist laws remained on the books after the peace treaty. Nine states had passed acts exiling prominent Loyalists and those who remained had to pay double and triple taxes. Five states had disenfranchised Loyalists and every state had barred Loyalists from office and from the practice of law and medicine. All of the states had passed laws confiscating Loyalist lands.

Months later, when William Franklin demanded of Richard Oswald how he could justify the surrender of all Benjamin territories in the West and the trading away of all Indian lands without consulting the Indians, Oswald replied, "Your father, Dr. Franklin, insisted on a boundary being drawn. . . . The Doctor ran his finger along the map to indicate the desired boundaries. And what could I object to a man of Dr. Franklin's influence and authority?"[74]

As the preliminary treaty was sped across the Atlantic for ratification by Congress, the first shiploads of Loyalist refugees began to clear New York and Charleston harbors for England, Nova Scotia and the Caribbean. A vast migration began of more than one hundred thousand Americans into exile, more than five percent of the population, probably the highest refugee rate of any revolution. In one day, April 26, 1783, more than seven thousand sailed from New York harbor. Before the British evacuation ended, rebel mobs surged through the streets of the coastal cities, avenging the ills of a war they blamed on their damned Tory brothers.

"No sooner had the evacuation taken place at Charleston," wrote the Loyalist historian Thomas Jones, "than the rebels, like so many furies, entered the town. The Loyalists were seized, shoved into dungeons, tied and whipped, tarred and feathered, dragged to horseponds and drenched till near death, carried about the town in carts with labels upon their breasts and back with TORY in capitals. All the Loyalists were turned out of their houses and obliged to sleep in the streets and fields. A universal plunder took place. A gallows was erected and twenty-four reputable Loyalists hanged in sight of the British fleet with the army and thirty-five thousand Loyalists looking on."[75]

Even if William Franklin had wished to return to America, he would have found Perth Amboy in ruins, Proprietary House burned. One of his friends tried to visit Elizabethtown nearby to collect bills. A crowd immediately surrounded him, yelling "Hang him up! Hang him up!" until a justice of the peace persuaded them to escort him to the New York ferry landing.[76]

For the next five years, as thousands of Loyalist refugees suffered and died from British bungling that left them without adequate housing, food or clothing in the Canadian wilderness, William was pushed as governor of Nova Scotia: many of his best friends had gone there. But William had decided that his primary usefulness was as the Loyalists' leading agent and lobbyist in London, pressing the cause of reparations for all Loyalists. Within five years, more than five thousand claims for compensation by the British government were honored.[77]

Despite all their protestations during the peace negotiations in Paris, Lord Shelburne's government had, by the terms of the treaty, in effect renounced all obligations to the Loyalists until there was an uproar in the House of Lords. The surrender of America was bad enough but, as the deposed Lord North put it,

England had to indemnify the losses of its loyal subjects "to keep the faith of the nation with them." He organized support for men like William Franklin who had been "sacrificed for their bravery and principles. . . . They have exposed their lives, endured an age of hardships . . . forfeited their possessions . . . ruined their families in our cause." It was Parliament's duty, he argued, to repay them for their lost lands, businesses, possessions, "to protect them from that state of misery with which the implacable resentment of the States has punished their loyalty to their sovereign. Never was the honor, the principles, the policy of a nation so grossly abused as in the desertion of those men."[78] The compromise finally reached was to appropriate the equivalent of the cost of one more year of war to compensate the Loyalists. A royal commission was set up to adjudicate claims and assign pensions and compensation.

The seven-year-long process of testifying for himself and his friends got under way as William settled into a modest house in London near his old haunts and began a thirty-year exile. He wrote to cousins and nephews, kept in touch with Sally. Nine months after the war ended, nine years after he had last seen or talked to or heard from his father, he got word that his father, still in Paris, was willing to receive a letter from him. On July 22, 1784, he wrote: "Dear and Honoured Father: Ever since the termination of the unhappy contest between Great Britain and America, I have been anxious to write to you and to endeavor to revive that affectionate intercourse and connection which, till commencement of the late troubles, had been the pride and happiness of my life."[79] William was still not sure, he said, whether Benjamin also wished to see or correspond with him because of "the decided and active part I took in opposition to the measures you thought proper." William was not apologizing, and he in fact noted "the cruel sufferings, scandalous neglects, and ill treatment which we poor unfortunate Loyalists have in general experienced." But he had hesitated to write his father before this time because he thought his father had "some political reasons for avoiding such correspondence while you retained your present employ under the Congress." But he needed to know "whether your inclination is likely to meet my wishes." He hated the awful family rift, the grand silence that had descended between them. He undoubtedly still remembered his father's injunction to him at the beginning of the struggle that no one would ever blame him if he did what he thought was right. "I can with confidence appeal not only to you but to my God," he now wrote, "that I have uniformly acted from a strong sense of what I conceived my duty to my king and regard to my country required. If I have been mistaken, I cannot help it. It is an error of judgment that the maturest reflection I am capable of cannot rectify, and I verily believe, were the same circumstances to occur again tomorrow, my conduct would be exactly similar to what it was."

He had no desire to argue again the old arguments with his father. The subject was "so disagreeable." He hoped "everything which has happened" could be "mutually forgotten." "I flatter myself that you are actuated by the same disposition and that my advance towards a renewal of our former affectionate intercourse will be as acceptable to you as . . . agreeable to myself." William went on to request a "private interview" with his father, either in London or in Paris. But he would not come without his father's "approbation."[80]

Three weeks later, William received his father's reply. Benjamin said he was "glad to find you desire to revive the affectionate intercourse that formerly existed between us. It would be very agreeable to me. Indeed, nothing has ever hurt me so much and affected me with such keen sensibilities as to find myself deserted in my old age by my only son; and not only deserted, but to find him taking up arms against me in a cause wherein my good fame, fortune and life were all at stake."

William had not sought forgiveness, nor had he blamed his father for all he had suffered at his instigation, and now Benjamin's letter held out little hope for peace or forgiveness. "You conceived, you say," Benjamin pressed on, "that your duty to your King and regard to your country required this. I ought not to blame you for differing in sentiments with me in public affairs. We are men, all subject to errors. Our opinions are not in our power. They are formed and governed much by circumstances that are often as inexplicable as they are irresistible. Your situation was such that few would have censored your remaining neuter, though *there are natural duties which precede political ones,* and cannot be extinguished by them. This is a disagreeable subject: I drop it."[81]

Father and son had cleared the air between them as much as they ever would, each having his say about the most unpleasant episode in lives that had once, long ago, been so inextricably interconnected. But Benjamin quickly barred the door on any closer contact. He did not want to see his son, not right now. "I will be glad to see you when convenient, but would not have you come here at present." William wanted reunion with his father and did not worry about "narrow illiberal minds" who might accuse them, if they became reconciled, to have been acting in collusion throughout the war. Benjamin said he would send Temple on any confidential family business. He was delighted, it seemed, to turn to his favorite subject, Temple: "I trust that you will prudently avoid introducing him to company that it may be improper to be seen with"—a cutting reference not to William's morals so much as his choice of Loyalists for friends. Temple should study law "as a necessary part of knowledge for a public man": just such legal studies had been part of William's plan for his son.[82] William was to relinquish to Temple lawbooks Benjamin had purchased for him some thirty years ago. Benjamin evidently did not yet know that everything of William's — every lawbook and many of his own books once willed to William — had burned.

Out of the wreckage, William Franklin grasped the chance to see Temple again, and for more than two months that summer they toured England together just as two other Franklins, father and son, had done so long ago. Indeed, William even offered Temple a half share in his Vandalia claim as an inducement to stay on with him. Benjamin, perhaps remembering that intimacy and camaraderie and jealous of anyone who might estrange Temple from him, began to write ever more strident notes to Temple to rejoin him at once. "I have not received a line from you now near a month," he chided Temple three weeks after the young man left Paris. "I have waited with impatience . . . but not a word. . . . Judge what I must feel. . . . What am I to think of such neglect."[83]

Actually, Temple had written his grandfather and their letters crossed on the Channel. When Temple's letter arrived, Benjamin, old, lonely now for the first time, was pathetically grateful. He wrote back immediately to "My Dear Child." Temple could stay in England another two weeks. But there was no word of greeting for

William, only an indirect order that he must, if he wanted to keep Temple a little longer, take him to see Benjamin's friend, the bishop of St. Asaph, at whose country house fifteen years earlier Benjamin had begun his autobiography with the words "Dear Son."

William saw his father only once more, in August 1785, when Benjamin was on his way back to America for the last time. Nearly eighty, Benjamin suffered from severe gout and obesity aggravated by years of inertia. He had to be taken slowly, carefully, to the French coast and put on a packet for England. William was there before him with Cortlandt Skinner.

They had reserved rooms for the Franklin party. Temple and Benny Bache were with Benjamin as he came up the dock. The greeting was stiff, cool, both men obviously glad the boys were there to ease things.

For four days the two men met, but there was little hope left for reconciliation. Benjamin was angry at William for inadvertently involving Temple in Loyalist politics when, at Benjamin's behest, he tried to transfer his last Pennsylvania lands from son to grandson. To their final meeting Benjamin brought all the warmth of a real estate settlement. He presented William with titles, deeds, bills of account. In the presence of witnesses, William signed over his farm at Rancocas (for one-third its value), his Burlington property and his last New York lands in exchange for the forgiveness of debts which Benjamin said William owed him. William was livid. His father was making him pay for clothes and pocket money all the way back to his schooldays. His anger deepened when he saw that he was giving up everything he had in America to Temple, but at the price he had paid fifteen years earlier, with no allowance for postwar inflation. At the same time, Benjamin required that Temple sign a note which documented that Benjamin had lent him the money to buy out his father.[84]

Benjamin spent most of their last days together apart from William, dining and reminiscing with old British friends who had come down to see him off. William evidently was not invited to the dinners with the editor of Benjamin's papers and the bishop of St. Asaph. He spent his time with his son and his nephew Benny, who had always adored his Uncle William.

Having extracted every possible penny from William, Benjamin Franklin waited, no doubt impatiently, for a favorable wind to carry his ship off for America. One morning the wind and the tide were right. He woke Temple but they did not wake William, and they slipped off to America without even saying goodbye.

21

MY SON KEEPS HIMSELF ALOOF

1785–1813

ALWAYS CONVINCED HE WAS SOON TO DIE, BENJAMIN Franklin lived another five years after returning to America. He returned to a hero's welcome in Philadelphia. Until his death he remained in many ways an enigma. Responsible as much as any man for the stunning diplomatic success at Paris, for the millions of livres in French loans that supported the American war effort, his political influence in the new capital was at such an ebb that he could not get a low-level secretaryship in the foreign service for his grandson and heir.[1]

His fondest ambition, to found a political dynasty to match those of the Adamses and the Lees, died long before he did. Capable of being callous and unfeeling to his immediate family, he nonetheless surrounded himself with grandchildren and even sent for the widowed Polly Stevenson and her children from England to live with him as she once had lived with him on Craven Street in London. Yet he treated his own daughter, Sally, now middle-aged, much as he had her mother: she was someone to keep his house, someone to wait on him. Visitors to Franklin Court for afternoon tea in the garden noted how plain, how servile Sally was.[2] For all his outward criticism of others' opulence, he returned to America amid criticism that he had lived lavishly in Paris when his countrymen were destitute from a long war. Unperturbed by such criticism, he built a sumptuous three-story wing on his house, devoting one story to the meetings and collections of his American Philosophical Society. As a poor young newcomer to Philadelphia, he had admired James Logan's fine library and had been allowed to read in it. Now, he turned two stories of the new wing into a handsome private library. He was immensely proud of his rare books, this once-poor printer's devil. A visiting Connecticut delegate to the Congress was shown the centerpiece of the Franklin collection: a priceless history of American horticulture with illustrations in color, one of only twelve copies printed.[3] He had been invited to subscribe to it when the Pope relinquished his right to a copy. Benjamin boasted that the King of Spain had intrigued to buy the book, but this man who had begun his lifelong rebellion by being cuffed around a printer's shop delighted in telling how he had refused a king.[4] He also proudly showed off a fine edition of *Don Quixote* he had bought in France, a first edition of Paine's *Crisis,* and another favorite entitled *Political Considerations on Coups d'Etat.* But the books were overshadowed, his visitor noted, by a large portrait of King Louis XVI, who had personally presented it to Franklin as a farewell gift. The visitor was dazzled by the 408 diamonds encrusted in the frame.

A man who had despised governors and worked against them half his life, Franklin now served as chairman of the Supreme Executive Council, the equivalent then of the governorship of Pennsylvania. A man who had once invested in ships engaged in the slave trade, who had sold advertisements in his newspaper for slaves to be purchased or auctioned at his printing office, Franklin was now elected president of the Pennsylvania Abolition Society — while he kept his slaves.

He did not die quickly. His last illness took two years, bringing him so much pain he was drugged with opium for long periods. Between bouts of gout, kidney stone and pleurisy, he rarely mentioned his son. They did not correspond, even though William stayed in touch with Sally and other relatives. Only once, apparently, did Benjamin write of William. An Austrian scientist inquired if he had a family. He had a daughter, Franklin replied, who "lives with me and is the comfort of my declining years, while my son is estranged from me by the part he took in the late war, and keeps aloof, residing in England, whose cause he espoused, whereby the old proverb is exemplified:

My son is my son till he take him a wife;
But my daughter's my daughter all the days of her life."[5]

His second greatest disappointment was his oldest grandson. Temple hated Philadelphia, was bored with republican life, his farm in New Jersey and the study of the law (which he abandoned) in that order. He had left a mistress and an infant son in Paris; he pined for them even as he made a brief attempt to turn Franklin Park into an estate in the French style: he imported French deer and hunting dogs, wooden shoes for his servants, vines and fruit trees. But he spent more time racing and dancing in Philadelphia than under his vine and fig tree, and when he quarreled with the tenant farmer, the farm grew over once again.

As Benjamin Franklin lay dying at the age of eighty-four on April 17, 1790, he was surrounded by his real family — Sally, her children, her husband — and his acquired family — Temple, Polly and her children. Only his son was not there at the end. In his will, which was published in the Philadelphia newspapers, he left to Temple all that he had once designated his son's portion, leaving to William only a worthless pre-Revolutionary War claim to Nova Scotia lands already settled by Loyalist refugees and forgiveness for some debts William said he had already paid. The will included a final public insult: "The part he acted against me in the late war, which is of public notoriety, will account for my leaving him no more of an estate he endeavored to deprive me of."[6]

Benjamin Franklin was buried beside Deborah Read Franklin in a corner of an Anglican churchyard. His heirs promptly began to dismantle his estate and all the visible symbols of his personal philosophy. His house was demolished eventually to make way for a wider street to a family real estate subdivision, but long before that, in 1792, a public auction took place in Franklin Court to dispose of "a variety of valuable furniture and plate." Benjamin's personal effects went under the gavel that day, including his harpsichord, his copying press, coal grates he had designed and insisted upon, Franklin stoves he had invented, his sedan chair.[7]

Years before, William had warned that Richard Bache was a fortune hunter. That opinion, unpopular like most of William's, now proved to be true. Despite Benjamin's wishes as expressed in his will, Bache chipped out the diamonds from around the King's portrait and took Sally on an extended and lavish tour of Europe in 1792. Temple had already left America, never to come back. After selling the Rancocas farm he sailed for England and moved in with his father and his father's new wife, a wealthy Irish gentlewoman. Soon there was another illegitimate Franklin. Temple fathered a daughter by the stepmother's younger sister. When the Baches arrived in England, there was a great reunion party, and all the Franklins were there except Benjamin.[8]

Bache had interceded for William's release from prison, and it was Bache who set off with William, the last Franklin *paterfamilias*, on a summer tour of England and Scotland in 1792. This time, it was William who pointed out the country houses he had once visited with his father, commenting on the changes of a generation and introducing Bache to old friends. "We were handsomely treated," Bache wrote Sally. Bache signed the letter "with Mr. Franklin's joint love," and they sallied off again on William's old familiar itinerary.[9]

This new family harmony was not to last. More and more, William became preoccupied with the forty thousand acres of property he had lost as a result of the Revolution. For thirty years he tried to regain a house and lands that George Croghan owed him but instead had left to his heirs and which William had always considered rightfully his. Over and over he tabulated the interest from the day in 1769 when he had mortgaged his New York lands to underwrite Croghan's activities. His letters to relatives in America became a pathetic litany of his case. As a Loyalist refugee in exile, he had no direct access to American courts and could only rely on the help of his sister and Bache and his cousin Jonathan Williams, Jr., whom he had last seen on shipboard with his father at Southampton, and in 1793 he began to pester them for help in gathering information to press his claims.

At first, William tried to foreclose on Croghan's riverfront estate in the Northern Liberties section of Philadelphia, but other creditors on the scene, old partners of William's in the Burlington Land Company, forced its sale and divided the receipts, excluding William.[10] William retained lawyers in New York City who specialized in Loyalist claims. They produced little but bills. Frustrated, he began to badger Sally. Her letters gave him "great pleasure," but typically William did not answer them for three and four months, and then he chastised her for not including the legal information he had requested. The United States government had just granted Croghan's heirs "a considerable tract of land" and William wanted his share: where were the pertinent details?[11] Sally's letters all but stopped.

William's relationship with his own son came to vex him even more than his financial losses. After living for several years in his father's house in London, Temple abandoned his mistress, William's sister-in-law, and his illegitimate daughter Ellen and went off to Paris. There he sired another daughter by the wife of the British ambassador. Preposterously, William, well past seventy, now pretended for all the world that Ellen was *his* child, and he doted on her. But Temple's desertion had wounded him deeply, as he finally confided to his cousin Jonathan on July 24, 1807. "All connection between him and me has been a long time broken. It is now upwards of 8 or 9 years since I have had any communication with him. The cause of it I am unwilling to write, but you may be assured that his conduct must have been offensive in no small degree to overcome the partial and affectionate regard I had ever manifested for him. In short, it hurt my feelings, and occasioned me more trouble of mind than I had ever before experienced, or can be expressed. He resides altogether in France, and I am told has a house in Paris, another in the country, lives genteelly, and keeps a female companion. But whether he has any child or children there I have not heard. He always expressed an aversion to matrimony." Temple knew, he went on, that "it was the earnest desire of his grandfather that he should marry in hopes of its being the means of his living a more regular life, and, I suppose, of perpetuating the family name in the male branch, which will otherwise probably become extinct at his death."[12]

Temple's estrangement had led William to rewrite his will in 1802, disinheriting him and leaving to Ellen and to his cousin Jonathan and Jonathan's children much of the fortune apparently brought to William by his second marriage. When he wrote Jonathan Williams of the legacy of £5,700 he was leaving his family,

William kept up the fiction of having a young daughter of his own. "She is now nine years old, very much like my father, and has every promise of making a fine sensible woman."[13]

William's unexpected generosity to his cousin, who was now the influential commandant of West Point, prompted a flurry of legal activity on the Illinois grant. Colonel Williams wrote to William's old partner Joseph Wharton, Jr., in Philadelphia, to Croghan's son-in-law, John Prevost, who now lived on William's old Otsego lands at Cooperstown, and to relatives and old friends in Philadelphia and promised to search through all of Benjamin Franklin's papers. The case soon took a strange twist: Prevost's lawyer on land dealings for many years had been Aaron Burr, now himself in exile. Colonel Williams wrote to William on April 6, 1808, that he dared not have anything to do with Burr, but that Burr would soon be in touch with him.[14]

Sally Franklin Bache also resumed writing William on April 29, 1808, offering to advance any legal fees to William's new lawyers in Philadelphia.[15] Soon William began transmitting long memoranda to Williams and his lawyers recounting every detail of his claims: some 102 pages of his correspondence, never before published, survive among Jonathan Williams's papers at Indiana University.

In his last years, William Franklin turned his attention to what remained of his family. He wrote of Ellen to Jonathan: "My dear little girl is very well, has a fine temper, and promises to make an accomplished woman." He had seen that she was better educated than any other Franklin woman. He sent her to a "genteel school" outside London where "every attention is paid to her morals and education."[16]

Whenever visitors came from America, he plied them with questions about his friends and relatives there. One of his dinner guests, on at least two occasions, was Aaron Burr. He, too, had attempted to recover lands and money owed by Croghan's estate. In his opinion, "nothing can be done in it." By 1808, William was growing tired of the "great deal of roguery" surrounding the case, and became reluctant to spend any more effort or money on it.[17] In early May of 1809, illness and death swept in around him. His wife became "extremely ill for upwards of two months [and was] confined to her chamber." It was at this time, too, that he learned of the death of his sister, Sally, "for whom I am now in mourning."[18] In October 1811, he wrote that, despite two years of visits by the King's physicians and "trying what traveling and change of air might effect," his wife "was at length taken so ill about Christmas last as to be confined to her bed until the time of her death."[19]

William Franklin had always hated to be alone almost as much as he despised family quarrels. Now he worked to reconcile the breach with his son. Temple stayed in France all through the Napoleonic Wars. In 1813, the year before William died, Temple suddenly wrote from Paris that he would soon come to England to begin the editing of his grandfather's papers. William was delighted. Their separation, he wrote Temple, had been "more trouble of mind than I had ever before experienced."[20]

During the years between the Revolution and the War of 1812, William had lived a clubman's life in London. Given a military half pension, he was called "The General" by his old friends, and British historians, apparently without substantiation, began to refer to him as "Sir William." He had been publicly apologetic about his relationship to Benjamin Franklin more than once: in an affidavit filed with the Lords of the Treasury in 1788, he claimed that, because of his last meeting with his father in order to settle accounts with him, "there have been base insinuations and suggestions of my having acted ... a preconcerted collusive part in conjunction with my father in the Revolution."[21] Probably as a consequence of such suspicions, he received only a token compensation from the Loyalist Claims Commission, the value of his lost furniture and books.[22]

But in 1802, when a long article about William in *Public Characters* magazine singled him out as one of the most noteworthy men in England, he was considered a "martyr to his principles and an honor to the country." The article, written with the help of Benjamin Franklin's old friend Joseph Priestley, found William not only "a man of engaging manners, amiable disposition and interesting conversation," but one who remarkably "resembles his father in a variety of particulars." William now suffered from gout. He was "cheerful, facetious, admirably calculated for telling a pleasing story." His role in his father's scientific experiments gave him access to the royal societies. The magazine reported that William had, during the Revolution, "remained undaunted before the storm," refusing to desert his British loyalty in the face of his father's claim to his personal loyalty. "So much was the Doctor attached to this, his only son," the author claimed, that he had "offered to make over all his possessions to him, and that, too, during his own lifetime," if only William "but declare for the American cause."[23] The statement remains unsubstantiated, but its language explained why William had become, on both sides of the Atlantic, the symbol of Loyalism.

The day before William Franklin died, he spent the day giving a final deposition about his Illinois grant at the United States consulate in London. He had just learned that the British army, its ranks swelled by the sons of Loyalist refugees, had beaten back the American invasion of Canada and had recaptured the Illinois country for the aged King George III. Born on an unpaved back street in Philadelphia the bastard of a journeyman printer, William died believing he was a rich lord of an incredibly vast manor in the American wilderness. For years, he had suffered from angina pectoris:[24] now the excitement proved too much for him.

On May 17, 1813, William Franklin sat down to write a letter to his friend Jonathan Williams. He did not have the strength to finish it. Halfway through, the handwriting changes, becomes light and fast: he had to ask Ellen to take the pen. "Since I began this letter, I have been very ill," he dictated, and went on to say that he had forgiven Temple, "not being able to bear the thoughts of dying at enmity with one so nearly connected." He hoped to see Temple once more but Temple did not come. There was only time left to make his peace with his American cousins. "My best wishes will ever attend every branch of our family."[25]

In his will, William bequeathed the bulk of his sizable estate to Ellen. She died childless. William was generous as ever to his servants. He left each of them a year's pay and other gifts. He had already arranged a Loyalist pension for Thomas Parke. To Temple, he left a half share of what he believed to be a fabulous fortune in the American West.[26] But it turned out to be worthless. Half of nothing is still nothing.

And when William Temple Franklin died ten years later — after haphazardly editing Benjamin's papers and leaving them scattered in a stable and a tailor shop — the fondest dream of the celebrated Doctor Franklin, the dream of a noble family dynasty suitable to his accomplishments, died with him — without legitimate issue.

CHAPTER NOTES

BIBLIOGRAPHY

INDEX

CHAPTER NOTES

Preceding the numbered notes in most of the chapters are background subjects, each with sources that were found especially valuable and pertinent.

Full particulars of each work cited are given in the bibliography.

The following abbreviations are used in the citations:

AA	Peter Force, ed., *American Archives*
ABF	*The Autobiography of Benjamin Franklin* (Labaree edn.)
APS	American Philosophical Society, Philadelphia
BF	Benjamin Franklin
BHQP	British Head Quarters Papers
CR and CRG	Catherine Ray and Catherine Ray Greene
DAB	*Dictionary of American Biography*
Dartmouth MSS	The Historical Manuscripts Commission, *The Manuscripts of the Earl[s] of Dartmouth*
DF	Deborah Franklin
EDF	Elizabeth Downes Franklin
GW	George Washington
HR	[Benjamin Franklin and William Franklin], *An Historical Review of the Constitution and Government of Pennsylvania* (1759)
HSP	Historical Society of Pennsylvania, Philadelphia
IHC	*Illinois State Historical Library Collections*
JCC	Continental Congress, *Journals . . . 1774–1783*
JM	Jane Franklin Mecom
JW	Jonathan Williams
JWP	Jonathan Williams Papers
LC	Library of Congress
LDC	Paul H. Smith and others, eds., *Letters of Delegates to the Congress*
Mecom	*Letters of Benjamin Franklin and Jane Mecom*, edited by Carl Van Doren

NEQ	*New England Quarterly*
NJA	*Archives of the State of New Jersey*
NJH	*New Jersey History*
NJMPC	State of New Jersey, *Minutes of the Provincial Congress*
NYHS	New-York Historical Society
NYHSQ	*New-York Historical Society Quarterly*
PA	*Pennsylvania Archives*
PAPS	*Proceedings of the American Philosophical Society*
PBF	*The Papers of Benjamin Franklin*
PCC	Papers of the Continental Congress
PCR	State of Pennsylvania, *Colonial Records*
PG	*The Pennsylvania Gazette*
PH	*Pennsylvania History*
PMHB	*Pennsylvania Magazine of History and Biography*
PMHS	*Proceedings of the Massachusetts Historical Society*
PNJHS	*Proceedings of the New Jersey Historical Society*
PRO	Public Record Office, London
PUL	Princeton University Library
SF and SFB	Sarah Franklin and Sarah Franklin Bache
TAPS	*Transactions of the American Philosophical Society*
WBF	*Writings of Benjamin Franklin,* edited by A. H. Smyth
WF	William Franklin
WFP	William Franklin Papers
WMQ	*William & Mary Quarterly*
WTF	William Temple Franklin

1. WE EXPECT THE ENEMY EVERY HOUR

The fort-building expedition: PBF, 6:307–396; L. W. Labaree, "Benjamin Franklin and the Defense of Pennsylvania"; W. A. Hunter, *Forts on the Pennsylvania Frontier.*

Quaker trade with the Indians: F. P. Jennings, "The Indian Trade of the Susquehanna Valley"; N. D. Wainwright, *George Croghan,* 207–217; N. Swanson, *The First Rebel.*

The Quaker dilemma over defense: J. H. Hutson, "Benjamin Franklin and Pennsylvania Politics," 303–371; T. Thayer, *Israel Pemberton,* 3–50; F. B. Tolles, "The Twilight of the Holy Experiment"; I. Sharpless, *A Quaker Experiment in Government,* 226–267; J. J. Zimmerman, "Benjamin Franklin and the Quaker Party."

The Walking Purchase: K. Thompson, *The Walking Purchase Hoax of 1737;* A. F. C. Wallace, *Teedyuscung;* C. A. Weslager, *The Delaware Indians.*

The Massacre at Gnadenhütten: W. C. Reichel, *Memorials of the Moravian Church,* 197–212; J. M. Levering, *A History of Bethlehem,* 253–259, 310–318; G. H. Loskiel, *History of the Mission of the United Brethren among the Indians of North America,* 164–169.

Anti-German prejudice: W. J. Bell, "Benjamin Franklin and the German Charity Schools," 381–387; BF, *Observations concerning the Increase of Mankind;* L. H. Gipson, *The British Empire,* 3:149–160.

The German march on Philadelphia: PBF, 6:257, 267–274, 279, 281–284; *PCR,* 6:729; *PA,* 2:524.

1. *PBF,* 6:382.
2. T. F. Gordon, *History of Pennsylvania,* 312–313.
3. Quoted in P. A. W. Wallace, *Conrad Weiser,* 379.
4. BF to Peter Collinson, Oct. 25, 1755, *PBF,* 6:229.
5. BF to Richard Partridge, Oct. 25, 1755, *PBF,* 6:231.
6. John Harris to BF, Oct. 31, 1755, *PBF,* 6:232–233.
7. W. Penn, *Letter to the committee of*
the Society of Free Traders, August 16, 1683.
8. Rev. William Smith, *A Brief State of the Province of Pennsylvania,* 40.
9. *ABF,* 212–214.
10. Hutson, 353.
11. "Reply to the Governor," Aug. 19, 1755, *PBF,* 6:151.
12. Ibid., 154.
13. T. Penn to Richard Peters, Mar. 30, 1748, quoted in *PBF,* 3:186.

2. OUR FATHER WAS A VERY WISE MAN

BF's childhood: ABF, 53–70; A. B. Tourtellot, *Benjamin Franklin . . . The Boston Years;* C. Van Doren, *Benjamin Franklin,* 3–33; R. H. Bremner, *Children and Youth in America,* 1:27–33; C.-A. Lopez and E. W. Herbert, *The Private Franklin,* 5–15.

The Puritan family: A. T. Vaughan and F. J. Bremer, eds., *Puritan New England,* 44–91; 232–249; E. S. Morgan, *The Puritan Family;* P. Miller, "Preparation for Salvation"; C. F. Adams, "Church Discipline in New England"; G. L. Haskins, *Law and Authority in Early Massachusetts,* passim.

History of the Franklin family: BF the Elder (1650–1727), "A Short Account of the Family of Thomas Franklin of Ecton in Northamptonshire"; *PBF,* 1:xlix–lxxvii. See also works listed under *BF's childhood* above.

The Folger family of Nantucket: A. Starbuck, *History of Nantucket,* 1:740–778; Tourtellot, *Benjamin Franklin . . . The Boston Years,* 99–107; *ABF,* 50–51.

1. *PBF,* 1:xiii, 3. According to the Julian calendar, which was in use at the time BF was born, the date was Jan. 6, Epiphany Sunday.
2. *PBF,* 1:lvi–lxii, 3; *ABF,* 52.
3. *ABF,* 50.
4. Tourtellot, 10–37, 52–53.
5. Starbuck, 1:53.
6. Ibid., 91–92.
7. Bremner, 1:7–28.
8. Ibid., 33.
9. *PBF,* 1:lvi.
10. Mecom, 126.
11. *ABF,* 55.
12. Mecom, 19.
13. Tourtellot, 141.
14. *ABF,* 53–54.
15. Mecom, 8.
16. *ABF,* 58–59.
17. *ABF,* 68. For an opposing view of James Franklin, see his entry in the *DAB.*
18. *ABF,* 60.
19. C. Mather, "Diary," 663. On the inoculation controversy, see R. P. Stearns, *Science in the British Colonies,* 417–423.
20. *ABF,* 70–71.
21. Josiah Franklin to BF, Mar. 21, 1738, quoted in *PBF,* 2:202–204.

3. I AM TOO INDULGENT A PARENT

BF in Philadelphia: C. Van Doren, *Benjamin Franklin,* 39–72; C.-A. Lopez and E. W. Herbert, *The Private Franklin,* 16–41; *ABF,* 81–184.

WF's illegitimate birth and education: W. Mariboe, "William Franklin," 1–48; Lopez and Herbert, 22–23, 26, 118.

Poor Richard's Almanack: W. J. Bell, Jr., ed., *The Complete Poor Richard's Almanacks,* 2 vols., passim.

BF's scientific experiments: *PBF,* v. 4, passim; J. Heilbron, *Electricity in the Seventeenth and Eighteenth Centuries,* 324–372; R. F. Stearns, *Science in the British Colonies,* 506–574, 601–641.

1. *PBF,* 1:53; *ABF,* 82.
2. *ABF,* 89.
3. Lopez and Herbert, 20.
4. *ABF,* 128.
5. "Notes," *PMHB* 38 (1924): 383.
6. The harsh laws against a woman in Deborah's predicament were spelled out in books BF himself printed, including *A Collection of All the Laws of the Province of Pennsylvania* (1729) and *The Charters of the Province of Pennsylvania and City of Philadelphia* (1743). See also Blackstone, *Commentaries,* 1:424, 430, 442; Coke, *Institutes,* 1:10–13; Danvers, *General Abridgement of the Common Law,* 1:728–729.
7. *ABF,* 129.
8. *PBF,* 11:370–371n.
9. *ABF,* 129.
10. *ABF,* 145.
11. *ABF,* 148–150.
12. Lopez and Herbert, 37.
13. Bell, 1:v–xxii.
14. *PBF,* 2:445.
15. *ABF,* 184.
16. BF to JM, June 1748, *PBF,* 3:302.
17. The author is indebted to the Princeton University Library for permission to use the inventory of WF's schoolbooks from the George Simpson Eddy Collection.
18. BF to Jane Mecom, June 1748, *PBF,* 3:302–303.
19. Lopez and Herbert, 61.
20. Fifteen articles on the Pennsylvania contingent in the northern campaign appeared in *PG* between June 12 and Sept. 14, 1746.

21. *PG,* Aug. 25, 1746.
22. BF to Abiah Franklin, Apr. 12, 1750, *PBF,* 3:474–475.
23. Quoted in J. Boyd, ed., *Indian Treaties, Printed by Benjamin Franklin,* 113.
24. P. A. W. Wallace, *Conrad Weiser,* 264–269; *Pa,* 2:12–15; R. G. Thwaites, *Early Western Journals,* v. 1, passim.
25. BF to Abiah Franklin, Apr. 12, 1750, *PBF,* 3:474.
26. *ABF,* 241.
27. BF to Peter Collinson, July 29, 1750, *PBF,* 4:9.
28. WF to BF, July 12, 1753, *PBF,* 5:4–7.
29. *Register of Admissions to the Honourable Society of the Middle Temple* (3 vols.; London, 1949), 1:343.
30. Daniel Fisher, "Diary," *PMHB* 17 (1893): 276–277.
31. BF to CR, Sept. 11, 1755, *PBF,* 6:182–183.
32. J. F. Sachse, *Benjamin Franklin as a Freemason,* 90–100. For the subscribers to Freemasons Hall, including BF and WF, see *PBF,* 5:235–237.
33. BF to CR, Sept. 11, 1755, *PBF,* 6:182–183.
34. CR to BF, June 28, 1755, *PBF,* 6:96–97.
35. BF to CR, Oct. 16, 1755, *PBF,* 6:225.
36. BF to CR, Mar. 1755, *PBF,* 5:535–537.

4. WE GOT FIVE SCALPS BUT THEY GOT NINE

March to Gnadenhütten: see sources listed under *The fort-building expedition* in the notes for chap. 1.

Frontier forts of Pennsylvania: W. A. Hunter, *Forts on the Pennsylvania Frontier;* J. B. Nolan, *General Benjamin Franklin,* 74–85.

1. *PG,* Dec. 18, 1755.
2. BF to James Read, Nov. 2, 1755, *PBF,* 6:234.
3. For a description of WF's circle, see T. W. Balch, *The Philadelphia Assemblies;* G. B. Warden, "The Proprietary Group in Pennsylvania"; J. M. Diamondstone, "Philadelphia's Municipal Corporation."
4. N. C. Hale, *Colonial Wars in Pennsylvania,* 11.
5. W. J. Bell, Jr., and L. W. Labaree, "Franklin and the Wagon Affair."
6. J. M. Levering, *History of Bethlehem,* 327.
7. Edward Shippen to Richard Peters, Dec. 5, 1755, quoted in P. A. W. Wallace, *Conrad Weiser,* 317.
8. William Parsons to James Hamilton and BF, Dec. 15, 1755, *PBF,* 6:293–294.
9. Nolan, 18.
10. James Hamilton to Thomas Penn, Dec. 29, 1755, *PCR,* 6:156.
11. BF to DF, Jan. 25, 1756, *PBF,* 6:364–365.
12. For the practice of sharing beds, see, for example, A. Carlyle's *Autobiography,* 318, and C. Van Doren, *Benjamin Franklin,* 558–559.
13. Quoted in Levering, 323.
14. Quoted in ibid., 325–326.
15. Ibid., 328–329.
16. BF to William Parsons, Dec. 5, 1755, *PBF,* 6:290–291.
17. *PCR,* 6:156–168. For conditions in Easton, see D. Chidsey, "Easton Before the French and Indian War"; Van Doren, 246–247; Nolan, 30–36.
18. Nolan, 35–37.
19. *PBF,* 6:313–314.
20. For instance, see BF, "Reply to the Governor," Aug. 19, 1755, *PBF,* 6:156; J. H. Hutson, "Benjamin

Franklin and Pennsylvania Politics," 358–359.
21. BF to Conrad Weiser, Jonas Seely and James Read, Dec. 30, 1755, *PBF,* 6:315.
22. BF to Peter Collinson, June 26, 1755, *PBF,* 6:86–87.
23. BF to R. H. Morris, Jan. 14, 1755, *PBF,* 6:359; W. C. Reichel, ed., *Memorials of the Moravian Church,* 1:203–204.
24. *PBF,* 6:237n.
25. Quoted in Nolan, 48.
26. BF to James Read, Nov. 2, 1755, *PBF,* 6:234.
27. BF to DF, Jan. 1, 1756, *PBF,* 6:339–340.
28. Nolan, 49–50; P. A. W. Wallace, 420–421.
29. W. Mariboe, "William Franklin," 54–55.
30. William Hays to R. H. Morris, Jan. 3, 1756, *PBF,* 6:340–342.
31. Levering, 328–331.
32. *PBF,* 6:348–349.
33. *PCR,* 6:771–772; *PBF,* 6:342–343. For the detailed plan of the forts, see Hunter, 187–191.
34. *PBF,* 6:343–348.
35. For WF's account of the march, see *PBF,* 6:357–360.
36. H. Cummings, *Richard Peters,* 151.
37. *PBF,* 6:348–349; 349–352; BF to R. H. Morris, Jan. 14, 1756, *PBF,* 6:357–360.
38. *PBF,* 6:357–359. The letter, drafted by WF, was signed by BF.
39. Levering, 334.
40. *PBF,* 6:353–354.
41. Nolan, 63–64.
42. BF to DF, Jan. 15, 1756, *PBF,* 6:360–361.
43. *ABF,* 231.
44. Thomas Lloyd to John Hughes, Jan. 30, 1756, *PBF,* 6:380–383.

45. Ibid., 381.
46. BF to the Provincial Council, Jan. 25, 1756, *PBF,* 6:365–366.
47. Ibid., 366.
48. *PBF,* 6:381.
49. BF to the Provincial Council, Jan. 25, 1756, *PBF,* 6:366–367.
50. Ibid., 366.
51. *ABF,* 233.
52. BF to the Provincial Council, Jan. 25, 1756, *PBF,* 6:367.
53. *ABF,* 235.
54. BF to DF, Jan. 30, 1756, *PBF,* 6:378–379.
55. BF to George Whitefield, July 2, 1756, *PBF,* 6:468–469.
56. *ABF,* 235–236; Nolan, 83–85.
57. J. T. Schaarf and T. Westcott, *History of Philadelphia,* 1:250.

5. The People Happen to Love Me

BF in Pennsylvania politics: J. H. Hutson, "Benjamin Franklin and Pennsylvania Politics," 303–373; Hutson, *Pennsylvania Politics, 1746–1770,* 1–60; R. L. Ketcham, "Conscience, War and Politics in Pennsylvania, 1755–1757"; W. S. Hanna, *Benjamin Franklin and Pennsylvania Politics.*

The Philadelphia Dancing Assembly: T. W. Balch, *The Philadelphia Assemblies;* J. P. Sims, ed., *The Philadelphia Assemblies, 1748–1948;* C. and J. Bridenbaugh, *Rebels and Gentlemen,* 149–163; J. T. Schaarf and T. Westcott, *History of Philadelphia,* 1:854–855, 877–890; G. B. Warden, "The Proprietary Group in Pennsylvania, 1754–1764"; W. Mariboe, "William Franklin," 45–48.

Elizabeth Graeme: J. J. Loeper, *Elizabeth Graeme Fergusson of Graeme Park;* Simon Gratz, "Some Material for a Biography of Mrs. Elizabeth Fergusson"; C. P. Keith, "The Wife and Children of Sir William Keith"; Mariboe, 49–67.

1. *ABF,* 240; for the row over commissions, see *PBF,* 6:409–412, 415–420.
2. Warden, 369–389.
3. Loeper, 9.
4. W. S. Hanna, *Benjamin Franklin and Pennsylvania Politics,* 47, 95.
5. Warden, 371–373.
6. Gratz, 267–268; Mariboe, 67; Loeper, 11.
7. Mariboe, 67–68.
8. *PBF,* 6:425n.
9. Quoted in T. F. Jones, *A Pair of Lawn Sleeves,* 35.
10. Mariboe, 67.
11. BF to Peter Collinson, June 15, 1756, *PBF,* 6:456–457.
12. Richard Peters to Thomas Penn, June 26, 1756, Penn Papers, 8: 123–125, HSP.
13. *ABF,* 246. BF was elected unanimously to the Royal Society in May 1756; *PBF,* 6:449.
14. William Allen to Ferdinand Paris, Oct. 25, 1755, L. B. Walker, ed., *The Burd Papers,* 24–25.
15. William Allen to Thomas Penn, Oct. 26, 1755, ibid., 25–26.
16. Thomas Penn to Richard Peters, Mar. 30, 1748, Penn Letter Book, II, 225, HSP.
17. Hutson, *Pennsylvania Politics,* 41–55. For Denny, see *PBF,* 6:489–490.
18. WF to Margaret Abercrombie, Oct. 24, 1758, WFP.
19. A. F. C. Wallace, *Teedyuscung,* 103–115, 126–136, 155–160; *PBF,* 6:487–489; P. A. W. Wallace, *Conrad Weiser,* 439–453.
20. BF to CR, Aug. 26, 1756, *PBF,* 6:494.
21. WF to Elizabeth Graeme, Apr. 11, 1757, WFP.
22. MS in Lilly Library, University of Indiana at Bloomington.
23. BF to DF, July 17, 1757, *PBF,* 7:243.

6. ONE GREAT SMOKY HOUSE

London in the mid-eighteenth century: G. E. Mingay, *Georgian London;* H. B. Wheatley, *London Past and Present;* W. L. Sachse, *Colonial Americans in Britain;* James Boswell, *London Journal, 1762–1763;* D. George, *London Life in the Eighteenth Century;* John Hancock, "Letters from London, 1760–1761"; A. S. Turberville, *Johnson's England;* J. B. Nolan, *Benjamin Franklin in Scotland and Ireland.*

The Inns of Court: the most comprehensive study is W. C. Richardson's *A History of the Inns of Court.* Since the traditions of the Inns were still handed down orally in the eighteenth century, studies of the Inns in that period are restricted for the most part to published after-dinner lectures. See the works by L. L. Macassey, D. P. Barton and H. Munroe listed in the bibliography. The early history of the Inns has been amply documented by W. R. Prest in *The Inns of Court Under Elizabeth I and the Early Stuarts.*

BF's London friends: D. W. Singer, "Sir John Pringle and His Circle"; V. W. Crane, "The Club of Honest Whigs"; W. J. Bell, Jr., " 'All Clear Sunshine': New Letters of Franklin and Mary Stevenson Hewson."

BF's expense account: G. S. Eddy, "Account Book of Benjamin Franklin, 1757–1762."

John Stuart, earl of Bute: J. Brewer, "The Misfortunes of Lord Bute"; L. B. Namier, *England in the Age of the American Revolution,* passim.

The enclosure movement: J. Addy, *The Agrarian Revolution,* 25–49; H. Habakkuk, "La Disparition du paysan anglais"; L. W. Moffit, *England on the Eve of the Industrial Revolution,* 55–68.

1. Horace Walpole to Horace Mann, Aug. 8, 1759, quoted in J. B. Nolan, *Benjamin Franklin in Scotland and Ireland,* 25.
2. The temperature on Aug. 8, 1759, was recorded in a weather journal by Thomas Gray, newly appointed director of the British Museum, who lived only a few blocks from the Franklins in Westminster. See his *Works,* 2:388.
3. BF to DF, Jan. 1758, *PBF,* 7:368–369.
4. WF to Elizabeth Graeme, Dec. 9, 1757, *PBF,* 7:289.
5. W. Blackstone, *Commentaries,* 1:6–8. For the evolution of this famous lecture, see W. Seagle, *Men of Law,* 198–199. For Blackstone's impact on the Tory resurgence of the 1760's, see Daniel Boorstin, *The Mysterious Science of the Law,* passim. That Blackstone intended legal reforms which would draw the nobility back to the law is argued convincingly by P. Lucas in "Blackstone and the Reform of the Legal Profession," *English Historical Review* 77 (1962): 456–489.
6. E. A. Jones, *American Members of the Inns of Court,* 78.
7. W. Strahan to DF, Dec. 13, 1757, *PBF,* 7:297.
8. Ibid., 296.
9. BF to Hugh Roberts, Feb. 26, 1761, *PBF,* 9:280.
10. *PBF,* 8:114–121.
11. WF to BF, Sept. 3, 1758, *PBF,* 8:132.
12. BF to DF, Feb. 19, 1758, *PBF,* 7:379–384.
13. BF to DF, June 10, 1758, *PBF,* 8:92.

14. [BF], "A Letter from Father Abraham to His Beloved Son," in W. Allen, *Extracts from . . . Allen's Letter Book,* 1:25–26.
15. Richard Peters to T. Penn, Jan. 31, 1757, from photostats in the Peters Papers, HSP.
16. Penn to Peters, May 14, 1757, Penn Papers, 5:109 (Penn Letterbook), HSP.
17. John Fothergill to Israel Pemberton, June 12, 1758, *PBF,* 8:100–101.
18. *ABF,* 261.
19. WF to Peter Schuyler, June 19, 1759, *PBF,* 8:308.
20. Quoted in *HR,* 440.
21. Ibid., 8.
22. Quoted in V. W. Crane, *Benjamin Franklin's Letters to the Press, 1758–1775,* xxvi.
23. BF to Isaac Norris, June 9, 1759, *PBF,* 8:402.
24. BF to Joseph Galloway, Feb. 17, 1758, *PBF,* 7:374.

25. BF to I. Norris, June 9, 1759, *PBF,* 8:402.
26. Her letter, written in Mar. 1758, did not reach William until October 23. He replied the next day: WF to E. Graeme, Oct. 24, 1758, *PMHB,* 39 (1916): 253–267.
27. Ibid.
28. Quoted in Namier, 88.
29. Ibid., 93.
30. *HR,* 7.
31. Alexander Carlyle, *Autobiography,* 98.
32. Eddy, 123–125.
33. BF to DF, Aug. 29, 1759, *PBF,* 8:431–432.
34. BF to J. Galloway, Sept. 6, 1758, *PBF,* 8:146.
35. WF to the *Citizen,* Sept. 16, 1757, quoted in *HR,* 440.
36. BF to DF, Sept. 6, 1758, *PBF,* 8:144.
37. BF to DF, Aug. 29, 1759, *PBF,* 8:431.

7. Six weeks of the densest happiness

Edinburgh in the eighteenth century: T. C. Smout, *A History of the Scottish People 1560–1830,* 53–87, 198–207, 229–239; J. D. Mackie, *A History of Scotland,* 293–310; J. McMillan, *Anatomy of Scotland,* 180–189; and L. H. Gipson, *The British Empire Before the American Revolution,* 1:154–184.

The Scottish Enlightenment: A. Chitnis, *The Scottish Enlightenment,* passim; J. Clive and B. Bailyn, "England's Cultural Provinces, Scotland and America"; E. C. Mossner, *The Life of David Hume,* 281–386; R. G. Cant, *The University of Saint Andrews,* 86–100.

1. J. B. Nolan, *Benjamin Franklin in Scotland and Ireland,* 43–44.
2. *PBF,* 8:431; Nolan, 46–52.
3. Quoted in M. Lee, "James VI, King of Scots," 156.
4. W. B. Sprague, *Annals of the American Pulpit,* 1:288.
5. A. Carlyle, *Autobiography,* 413.
6. A. Carlyle, *Plain Reasons for Removing a Certain Great Man.* See also his *Question Relating to a Scots Militia* (London, 1759).
7. WF to Peter Schuyler, June 19, 1759, *PBF,* 8:406–411.
8. A. Carlyle, *Autobiography,* 413–414.

9. *ABF,* 60.
10. W. Strahan to David Hall, Oct. 6, 1759, quoted in J. A. Cochrane, *Dr. Johnson's Printer,* 105.
11. A. Carlyle, *Autobiography,* 414.
12. H. G. Graham, *Scottish Men of Letters,* 147.
13. A full account is in J. Prebble, *Glencoe: The Story of a Massacre,* 185–264.
14. Quoted in Nolan, 76.
15. *PBF,* 7:277–280; Cant, *St. Andrews,* 91–98.
16. The visit is described in *PBF,* 8:440–445.

17. BF to Lord Kames, Jan. 3, 1760, *PBF,* 9:5–6. See also Smout, 196–198.

18. Ibid., 9.

19. *ABF,* 265–266.

8. I DISLIKE FAMILY QUARRELS

Resurgent Tory society: PBF, 9; E. B. Chancellor, *Private Palaces of London,* 50–57; H. B. Wheatley, *London Past and Present,* passim; L. B. Namier, *England in the Age of the American Revolution;* John Hancock, "Letters from London"; John Dickinson, "A Pennsylvania Farmer at the Court of King George"; A. Valentine, *The British Establishment,* vols. 1 and 2 passim; James Boswell, *Life of Samuel Johnson* and *London Journal.*

The Craven Street menage: PBF, vols. 9 and 10 passim; C. Van Doren, *Benjamin Franklin,* 294–299; C.-A. Lopez and E. W. Herbert, *The Private Franklin,* 147–155.

Judicial tenure controversy: L. W. Labaree, *Royal Government in America; NJA,* 9:345–381; J. F. Burns, *Controversies between Royal Governors and Their Assemblies;* L. R. Gerlach, *Prologue to Independence,* 82–86; J. J. Nadelhaft, "Politics and the Judicial Tenure Fight in Colonial New Jersey."

WF's appointment as royal governor: PBF, 10:146–155; C. Fennelly, "William Franklin of New Jersey"; W. S. Randall, "William Franklin: The Making of a Conservative"; *NJA,* 9:361–388.

1. Chancellor, 50–57; Wheatley, 1:604–605. Northumberland House was razed in 1870 to make way for Northumberland Street.

2. *PBF,* 9:364–365.

3. Quoted in Namier, 120.

4. J. Hancock to Daniel Perkins, Oct. 29, 1760, in J. Hancock, "Letters from London," 193.

5. Quoted in Namier, 128.

6. Quoted in Valentine, 2:693.

7. Boswell, *London Journal,* 70–71.

8. *PBF,* 1:lxii; W. Mariboe, *William Franklin,* 102; Van Doren, *Benjamin Franklin,* 290.

9. Mariboe, 100.

10. BF to DF, June 27, 1760, *PBF,* 9:174.

11. W. J. Bell, " 'All Clear Sunshine': New Letters of Franklin and Mary Stevenson Hewson," passim.

12. Quoted in Boswell, *Life of Johnson,* 2:275.

13. Hugh Roberts to BF, May 15, 1760, *PBF,* 9:113.

14. BF to DF, June 27, 1760, *PBF,* 9:174.

15. C.-A. Lopez and E. W. Herbert, *The Private Franklin,* 27.

16. Bell, 522.

17. V. Stumpf, "Who Was Elizabeth Downes Franklin?" *PBF,* 18:195; L. H. Gipson, *British Empire,* 2:216.

18. *PBF,* 9:231–232.

19. BF to Mary Stevenson, Aug. 10, 1761, *PBF,* 9:338.

20. WF to SF, Oct. 10, 1761, *PBF,* 9:364–368.

21. *NJA,* 9:361–364; D. L. Kemmerer, *Path to Freedom,* 270.

22. *PBF,* 10:76–78, 133.

23. See, for example, BF to JM, Nov. 25, 1762, *PBF,* 10:154–155.

24. Stumpf, 195–196.

25. WF to J. Galloway, June 16, 1760, *PBF,* 9:122–123.

26. Quoted in A. B. Tourtellot, *Benjamin Franklin,* 129.

27. WTF, *Memoirs ... of Benjamin Franklin,* 1:75.

28. BF to W. Strahan, July 20, 1762, *PBF,* 10:133.

29. James Hamilton to Jared Ingersoll, July 8, 1762, *PBF,* 10:113.

30. *PBF,* 10:108.
31. BF to Polly Stevenson, Aug. 11, 1762, *PBF,* 10:142–143.
32. C. H. Hart, "Letters from William Franklin to William Strahan," 421. The London *Chronicle* reported that the marriage took place on Sept. 2, 1762; *Gentleman's Magazine* had it Sept. 5; and *PBF* (10:146), on Sept. 4. Announcement of the marriage appeared in *PG* on Nov. 25.
33. Thomas Bridges to Jared Ingersoll, Sept. 30, 1762, *PBF,* 10:154n–155n.
34. Quoted in Mariboe, 117.
35. *PBF,* 10:147.
36. John Adams, *Diary,* 4:151; John Penn to Lord Stirling, Sept. 3, 1762, quoted in *PBF,* 10:147n.
37. BF to JM, Nov. 25, 1762, *PBF,* 10:154–155.
38. Elizabeth Graeme Fergusson correspondence, Gratz Collection, HSP.
39. *NJA,* 28:147; *PBF,* 10:235–236; Hart, 425.

9. Yours till Deth

BF's return to Philadelphia: C.-A. Lopez and E. W. Herbert, *The Private Franklin,* 92–113; *PBF,* vol. 10; C. Van Doren, *Benjamin Franklin,* 299–301.

The Paxton Boys' march: J. H. Hutson, *Pennsylvania Politics,* 86–113; B. Hindle, "The March of the Paxton Boys"; D. A. Sloan, " 'A Time of Sifting and Winnowing': The Paxton Riots and Quaker Non-Violence in Pennsylvania."

Burlington, N.J., in the eighteenth century: G. DeCou, *Burlington: A Provincial Capital;* G. M. Hills, *History of the Church in Burlington,* 276–304; W. Mariboe, "The Life of William Franklin," 129–149.

The Stamp Act riots: E. S. and H. M. Morgan, *The Stamp Act Crisis;* P. Maier, *From Resistance to Revolution,* 51–76; L. H. Gipson, *The British Empire Before the American Revolution,* 10:246–338; B. Knollenburg, *Origins of the American Revolution,* 221–237; R. Middlekauff, *The Glorious Cause,* 70–117; D. Kemmerer, *Path to Freedom,* 275–292; J. H. Hutson, "An Investigation of the Inarticulate: Philadelphia's White Oaks"; *PBF,* vols. 12 and 13, passim.

1. Pringle to BF, [May 1763], *PBF,* 10:269.
2. Strahan to BF, Aug. 18, 1763, *PBF,* 10:324–325.
3. Pringle to BF, [May 1763], *PBF,* 10:268.
4. Lopez and Herbert, 114–115.
5. WF to Strahan, Apr. 25, 1763, in C. H. Hart, "Letters from William Franklin to William Strahan," 423. For BF's new house, see *PBF,* 10:237n.
6. *PBF,* 10:276–279, 286–287, 290–291; Lopez and Herbert, 100–102.
7. *PBF,* 10:277n, 290n.
8. *PG,* June 7, 1763.
9. *PBF,* 11:42–69.
10. BF to J. Fothergill, Mar. 14, 1764, *PBF,* 11:103.
11. Ibid., 103–104.
12. *PBF,* 11:383.
13. *PG,* Nov. 5, 1764.
14. BF and WF to W. Strahan, Sept. 24, 1764, MS in the de Coppet Collection, PUL.
15. *NJA,* 25:391. See also *NJA,* 9:574–576; F. J. Esposito, "Indian-White Relations in New Jersey." According to Gregory E. Dowd of the History Department, Princeton University, these may be the only

executions of whites for the murder of Indians in eighteenth-century America.

16. W. S. Randall, *The Proprietary House at Amboy*, 5-13.
17. WF to W. Strahan, Apr. 25, 1763, in Hart, 425.
18. Mariboe, 149.
19. Hills, 239.
20. F. Hopkinson, "The Treaty," MS in the du Simitière Papers, Library Company of Philadelphia.
21. WF to Hopkinson, quoted in F. H. Hastings, *Francis Hopkinson*, 451.
22. WF to the earl of Halifax, Feb. 21, 1765, *NJA*, 9:488-490; W. S. Randall, "William Franklin," 60.
23. For BF's views on the Stamp Act, see *PBF*, 12:222, 365.
24. Quoted in Randall, "William Franklin," 63.
25. BF to Richard Jackson, June 1, 1764, *PBF*, 11:215.
26. WF to BF, Nov. 13, 1765, *PBF*, 12:366-369.
27. Lopez and Herbert, 125.
28. DF to BF, Sept. 22, 1765, *PBF*, 12:270-271.
29. BF to Daniel Wister, Sept. 27, 1766, *PBF*, 13:429.

30. The full text is in *PBF*, 13:124-159.
31. WF to BF, Nov. 13, 1765, *PBF*, 12:367-368.
32. SFB to BF, Mar. 23 [1766], *PBF*, 13:199.
33. WF to BF, Apr. 30, 1766, *PBF*, 13:256.
34. BF to DF, Apr. 6, 1766, *PBF*, 13:234.
35. BF to DF, June 13, 1766, *PBF*, 13:316.
36. BF to DF, Dec. 13, 1766, *PBF*, 13:519-520.
37. DF to BF, Oct. 6-13, 1765, *PBF*, 12:292-299.
38. DF to BF, Oct. 8, 1765, *PBF*, 12:300-304.
39. DF to BF, Apr. 20-25, 1767, *PBF*, 14:136.
40. WF to BF, May 1767, *PBF*, 14:174.
41. BF to DF, June 22, 1767, *PBF*, 14:192-195.
42. BF to Bache, Aug. 5, 1767, *PBF*, 14:220.
43. BF to SFB, Jan. 29, 1772, *PBF*, 19:46-47.
44. WF to BF, May 10, 1768, *PBF*, 15:123.
45. Lopez and Herbert, 143.

10. I STEER MY LITTLE BARK QUIETLY

BF's and WF's land speculations: C. W. Alvord, *The Illinois Country*, 288-292: Alvord and C. E. Carter, *The New Regime*, 247-257; G. Croghan, *Journal*, 31-47; W. Mariboe, "William Franklin," 277-344; P. Marshall, "Lord Hillsborough, Samuel Wharton and the Ohio Grant"; J. M. Sosin, *Whitehall and the Wilderness*, 128-150; *PBF*, vols. 13-20, passim.

WF's opulent lifestyle: W. Mariboe, "William Franklin," 121-128; W. S. Randall, "William Franklin"; C. H. Hart, "Letters from William Franklin to William Strahan"; N. Burr, *The Anglican Church in New Jersey*, 46-50, 493-498.

WF as royal governor: NJA, vols. 9, 10; L. R. Gerlach, *Prologue to Independence*, 37-144; Mariboe, 124-272; W. S. Randall, "William Franklin," 61-66.

The Illinois grant: W. Johnson, *Papers*, vol. 5, passim; *IHC*, vol. 11, passim; Sosin, *Whitehall and the Wilderness*, 181-210.

The Treaty of Fort Stanwyx: J. T. Flexner, *The Mohawk Baronet*, 323-331; *PBF*, vols. 15, 16, passim; N. D. Wainwright, *George Croghan*, 201-238; Sosin, 175-185.

WF's estate at Franklin Park: Mariboe, 148–149; Randall, *The Proprietary House at Amboy* and "William Franklin."

1. Wainwright, 212–225.
2. *PBF,* 14:235; Gerlach, *William Franklin,* 22.
3. *PBF,* 13:258, 322; Hart, 430–438.
4. E. G. Fisher, *The Province of New Jersey,* 42.
5. *PBF,* 13:443–444.
6. Quoted in Wainwright, 230.
7. Wainwright, 228–229, 240. For the intercolonial rivalry, see W. N. Franklin, "Pennsylvania-Virginia Rivalry for the Indian Trade of the Ohio Valley."
8. *PBF,* 13:192–199; 14:134–140, 230, 231; Newcomb, 330–331, 338–339; Grace G. Galloway, *Diary,* 33.
9. For the articles of incorporation, see C. Alvord, *The New Regime,* 203–204. For maps of the proposed grants at various stages, see *PBF,* 12:10; Sosin, opposite 170; H. T. Jackson and J. T. Adams, "Proclamation Line of 1763." The initial shareholders were WF, Croghan (for himself and for Johnson), John Baynton, Samuel Wharton, George Morgan, Joseph Wharton, Joseph Wharton, Jr., John Hughes and Joseph Galloway.
10. *IHC,* 43:203–204.
11. Croghan to Johnson, Mar. 30, 1766, quoted in Alvord and Carter, 205.
12. Johnson to WF, May 3, 1766, quoted in ibid., 224–225.
13. *IHC,* 43:248–257.
14. Johnson to WF, May 3, 1766, in W. Johnson, *Papers,* 5:196–198.
15. C. W. Alvord, *Illinois Country,* 289–290.
16. Johnson to BF, *PBF,* 13:330.
17. WF to BF, Dec. 17, 1765, *PBF,* 12:403–406.
18. WF to BF, *PBF,* 13:257.
19. BF to WF, Sept. 12, 1766, *PBF,* 13:415.
20. For the Nova Scotia grant, see *PBF,* 14:202–204, 291–292.
21. BF to Johnson, Sept. 12, 1766, *PBF,* 13:415.

22. BF to WF, Sept. 12, 1766, *PBF,* 13:416.
23. BF to WF, Sept. 27, 1766, *PBF,* 13:424.
24. *Journal of the Commissioners of the Board of Trade and Plantations . . . ,* quoted in *PBF,* 18:75n.
25. Sosin, 146–147.
26. "Plan for the Future Management of Indian Affairs," *PBF,* 13:435–441.
27. Ibid., 438.
28. BF's response to the plan, ibid., 438–439.
29. BF to WF, Oct. 11, 1766, *PBF,* 13:446.
30. BF to WF, Nov. 8, 1766, *PBF,* 13:486.
31. WF to BF, [Dec. 1766], *PBF,* 13:538–540.
32. BF to WF, Feb. 14, 1767, *PBF,* 14:40.
33. BF to WF, June 13, 1767, *PBF,* 14:180.
34. BF to Galloway, Aug. 8, 1767, *PBF,* 14:228–229.
35. WF to BF, Aug. 22, 1767, *PBF,* 14:235.
36. BF to WF, Dec. 29, 1767, *PBF,* 14:349–350.
37. BF to WF, Aug. 28, 1767, *PBF,* 14:242.
38. BF to WF, Oct. 9, 1767, *PBF,* 14:275.
39. BF to WF, Nov. 13, 1767, *PBF,* 14:302.
40. BF to WF, Mar. 13, 1768, *PBF,* 15:74.
41. In his copy of Charles Crawford, *An Essay on the Propagation of the Gospel* . . . (Philadelphia, 1801), Benjamin Rush wrote in the margin of p. 154 that WF had refused to eat venison broth with some maggots in it. I am indebted to Whitfield J. Bell, librarian of the APS, for this anecdote.
42. Tax Ratables Book, Willingboro Township, Burlington County, 1773–1774, MS in the New Jersey Archives, Trenton.

43. The description of Franklin Park is from the advertisement listing the estate for sale (*Pennsylvania Packet,* Jan. 31, 1774).
44. WF to BF, Jan. 31, 1769, *PBF,* 16:38.
45. *PBF,* 18:74–75. Copies of WF's accounting are in APS and the Eddy

Collection, Princeton University Library.
46. *PBF,* 16:163–168; 18:8, 97; T. P. Abernethy, *Western Lands,* 45; S. E. Slick, *William Trent and the West,* 141; Mariboe, 310–311.
47. BF to WF, July 14, 1773, *PBF,* 20:310.

11.   Government should have no passions

BF and Lord Hillsborough: P. Marshall, "Lord Hillsborough, Samuel Wharton and the Ohio Grant"; C. Van Doren, *Benjamin Franklin,* 318–352; *PBF,* 18:9–16; A. Valentine, *The British Establishment,* 1:453–454.

Riots in Boston: H. Zobel, *The Boston Massacre,* passim; J. Adams, *Legal Papers,* passim; B. Bailyn, *The Ordeal of Thomas Hutchinson,* 157–163; R. Middlekauff, *The Glorious Cause,* 70–93.

BF and colonial agencies: M. Kammen, "The Colonial Agents, English Politics, and the American Revolution"; J. M. Sosin, *Agents and Merchants; PBF,* vol. 18, passim.

1. BF to T. Cushing, June 10, 1771, *PBF,* 18:121–122.
2. *PBF,* 18:12–16.
3. BF to Cushing, Feb. 5, 1771, *PBF,* 18:25.
4. BF to John Ross, May 14, 1768, *PBF,* 15:129.
5. BF to WF, Mar. 13, 1768, *PBF,* 15:75–76.
6. See L. H. Gipson, "The American Revolution as an Aftermath of the Great War for the Empire, 1754–1763," *Political Science Quarterly* 70 (1950): 86–104.
7. Quoted in Middlekauff, 193.
8. Quoted in Zobel, 97.
9. BF to the Massachusetts House of Representatives Committee of Correspondence, May 15, 1771, *PBF,* 18:102–104.
10. BF to WF, Aug. 19, 1772, *PBF,* 19:259.
11. Quoted in BF to WF, Mar. 13, 1768, *PBF,* 15:77.
12. Hillsborough to WF, Aug. 16, 1768, *NJA,* 10:46.
13. WF to Hillsborough, Nov. 23, 1768, *NJA,* 10:64–95.
14. WF to Strahan, June 18, 1771, in C. H. Hart, "Letters from William

Franklin to . . . Strahan," 448–449.
15. Quoted in W. H. Mariboe, "William Franklin," 358.
16. Strahan to WF, Apr. 3, 1772, *PBF,* 18:65.
17. *NJA,* 10:301; *PBF,* 18:218, 260, 262.
18. WF to BF, Jan. 6, 1772, *PBF,* 19:3.
19. WF to BF, Oct. 13, 1772, *PBF,* 19:335–336.
20. Ibid., 336.
21. BF to WF, Dec. 2, 1772, *PBF,* 19:418.
22. WF to BF, Apr. 20, 1771, *PBF,* 18:74–75; WF to BF, June 30, 1772, *PBF,* 19:193.
23. BF to WF, July 14, 1773, *PBF,* 20:311n.
24. BF to SFB, Jan. 29, 1772, *PBF,* 19:46.
25. BF to WF, July 14, 1773, *PBF,* 20:300–313.
26. BF to WF, Aug. 17, 1772, *PBF,* 19:243.
27. BF to Joseph Galloway, Apr. 6, 1773, *PBF,* 20:149–150.
28. BF to WF, Nov. 3, 1772, *PBF,* 19:53.
29. WF to Lord Dartmouth, Jan. 5, 1773, *NJA,* 10:392.

30. WF to BF, Jan. 5, 1773, *PBF*, 20:12.
31. BF to WF, Apr. 6, 1773, *PBF*, 20:147.
32. BF to WF, July 29, 1773, *PBF*, 20:331.
33. C.-A. Lopez and E. W. Herbert, *The Private Franklin*, 147–155.
34. BF to John Winthrop, July 25, 1773, *PBF*, 20:329.
35. Quoted in V. W. Crane, "The Club of Honest Whigs," 218–219.
36. See, for example, *PBF*, 14:24; 19:278, 393, 439.
37. BF to WF, July 14, 1773, *PBF*, 20:307.
38. T. Hutchinson, *Diary and Letters*, 1:67–71.
39. BF to Thomas Cushing, May 6, 1773, *PBF*, 20:199–203.
40. WF to BF, July 29, 1773, *PBF*, 20:332.

12. A MAN OF LETTERS

The Hutchinson letters: B. P. Bailyn, *Ordeal of Thomas Hutchinson*, 221–254; *PBF*, vols. 20 and 21; C. Van Doren, *Benjamin Franklin*, 440–448; T. Hutchinson, *Diary and Letters*, vol. 1; L. H. Gipson, *British Empire Before the American Revolution*, 12:57–69; C.-A. Lopez and E. W. Herbert, *The Private Franklin*, 188–192.

Boston town meetings: Votes and Proceedings of the Freeholders and Other Inhabitants of the Town of Boston (London, 1773), i–vi; *PBF*, vols. 19 and 20.

The Boston Tea Party: Bailyn, 259–263; L. W. Labaree, *The Boston Tea Party;* T. Hutchinson, *History*, 3:262–266.

BF's Cockpit hearing: PBF, vols. 20 and 21; *Franklin Before the Privy Council* (London, 1877); A. Valentine, *British Establishment*, vols. 1 and 2 passim; D. Marshall, *England in the Eighteenth Century*, 414–443, 514–517.

1. The letters are reprinted in full in *PBF*, 20:539–580.
2. BF to Thomas Cushing, Feb. 2, 1772, *PBF*, 19:409–411.
3. Ibid., 411–412.
4. John Adams, *Diary*, entry dated July 1776, 2:81.
5. *PBF*, 20:xxxiii; Hutchinson to James Gambier, Feb. 19, 1773, *Massachusetts Archives*, 17:448–449; Hutchinson, *History*, 3:262–263, 266.
6. "Preface to the Declaration of the Boston Town Meeting," *PBF*, 20:82–84.
7. *PBF*, 20:389–399, 402–403, 413–418.
8. BF to WF, Nov. 3, 1773, *PBF*, 20:461.
9. BF to WF, July 14, 1773, *PBF*, 20:300–313.
10. BF to WF, Feb. 14, 1773, *PBF*, 20:63–64.
11. BF to WF, Apr. 6, 1773, *PBF*, 20:147.
12. BF to Thomas Cushing, May 6, 1773, *PBF*, 20:200–203.
13. WF to Lord Hillsborough, Nov. 23, 1768, *NJA*, 1st ser., 10:69.
14. WF to BF, July 29, 1773, *PBF*, 20:332.
15. BF to WF, Sept. 1, 1773, *PBF*, 20:385–388.
16. *PBF*, 20:xxxii–xxxiii, 514–515.
17. Ibid., 515–516.
18. *PBF*, 21:19–20, 37.
19. For Wedderburn, see *PBF*, 21:20, for Namier and Brooke, 3:618–620.
20. Valentine, 2:914–915.
21. *PBF*, 21:13–18. For BF's ostensible withdrawal from the Illinois venture,

see *PBF,* 21:31–33. That BF underestimated his predicament is revealed in BF's letter to Thomas Cushing, Feb. 15, 1774, *PBF,* 21:88.

22. W. T. Franklin, *Memoirs,* 1:358–359; R. M. Bache, "Franklin's Ceremonial Coat."
23. Valentine, 2:746.
24. BF to Thomas Cushing, Feb. 15, 1774, *PBF,* 21:89.
25. Transcript of Wedderburn's speech, *PBF,* 21:43–49.

26. William Bollan to the Massachusetts privy council, *Massachusetts Historical Society Collections,* 6th ser., 9 (1897): 338; London *Public Advertiser,* Feb. 2, 1774; Priestley quoted in WTF, *Memoirs,* 1:184–186.
27. BF to Thomas Cushing, Feb. 15, 1774, *PBF,* 21:92.
28. Quoted in A. O. Aldridge, *Benjamin Franklin,* 247.
29. BF to WF, Feb. 2, 1774, *PBF,* 21:75.

13. YOU ARE A THOROUGH COURTIER

The East Jersey treasury robbery: R. East and J. Judd, eds., *The Loyalist Americans,* 65–68; *PBF,* 18:135; 21:11–12, 259–261; L. R. Gerlach, "Politics and Prerogatives: The Aftermath of the Robbery of the East Jersey Treasury in 1768"; D. L. Kemmerer, *Path to Freedom: The Struggle for Self-Government in Colonial New Jersey,* 311–315; *NJA,* 1st ser., 17:295–296, 523–525.

William Livingston's return to politics: W. Livingston, *Papers,* 1:8–9, 365; M. Klein, "The Rise of the New York Bar: The Legal Career of William Livingston," 344; Klein, "The American Whig: William Livingston of New York," vol. 3 passim.

WF's move to Perth Amboy: W. S. Randall, *Proprietary House,* 10–17; *NJA,* 1st ser., 10:449.

Princeton as the center of Presbyterianism: P. V. Fithian, "Journals"; A. G. Olson, "The Founding of Princeton University"; L. Butterfield, *John Witherspoon Comes to America.*

Smuggling in New Jersey: W. S. Randall, "A Colonial Seaport"; M. Egnal, "The Changing Structure of Philadelphia's Trade with the British West Indies," 156–179; L. R. Gerlach, "Customs and Contentions," 69–92.

Galloway-Franklin plan of union: *NJA,* 1st ser., 10:473–475, 578; J. P. Boyd, *Anglo-American Union,* 28–41; B. F. Newcomb, *Franklin and Galloway,* 274.

1. BF to James Kinsey, Feb. 18, 1774, *PBF,* 21:111.
2. BF to WF, Feb. 18, 1774, *PBF,* 21:107–108.
3. WF to BF, Jan. 5, 1774, *PBF,* 21:11.
4. Quoted in J. Shy, "Quartering His Majesty's Forces in New Jersey."
5. *Minutes of the Board of Proprietors of the Eastern Division of the Province*

of New Jersey, Sept. 17, 1773. For the housing allowance, see *NJA,* 1st ser., 10:449.
6. I am indebted to William Pavlosky of the Proprietary House Association of Perth Amboy for sharing his research on WF's wallpaper drawings.
7. Randall, *Proprietary House,* 20.

8. WF to BF; Dec. 24, 1774, *PBF*, 21:404.
9. BF to WF, Oct. 6, 1773, *PBF*, 20:437.
10. T. Hutchinson, *Diary*, 1:219.
11. WF to BF, May 3, 1774, *PBF*, 21:207. The kind friend was Major Philip Skene of Skenesborough, New York.
12. WF to Lord Dartmouth, May 31, 1774, *NJA*, 1st ser., 10:457–459.
13. The manuscript draft of the Essex County resolves is in PUL.
14. WF to Lord Dartmouth, Sept. 6, 1774, *NJA*, 1st ser., 10:473–475.
15. Lord Dartmouth to WF, July 6, 1774, ibid., 468.
16. WF to BF, July 5, 1774, *PBF*, 21:238.
17. BF to WF, Sept. 7, 1774, *PBF*, 21:285–289.
18. BF to WF, Oct. 12, 1774, *PBF*, 21:332–333.
19. WF to BF, Dec. 24, 1774, *PBF*, 21:402–404.
20. BF to Jan Ingenhousz, Feb. 12, 1777, *PBF*, 23:310.
21. Witherspoon's lectures in moral philosophy for 1771 are in PUL.

22. John Hatton's ordeal as customs collector is detailed in Randall, "A Colonial Seaport," 21–22.
23. BF to Jonathan Shipley, Mar. 10, 1774, *PBF*, 21:138–140.
24. WF to Lord Dartmouth, June 28, 1774, *NJA*, 1st ser., 10:464–467.
25. WF to Lord Dartmouth, Sept. 6, 1774, ibid., 473–475.
26. Joseph Galloway to WF, Mar. 26, 1775, ibid., 579–586.
27. State of New Jersey, *Minutes of the Provincial Congress . . . of New Jersey*, 31–33.
28. Quoted in L. W. Sabine, *Biographical Sketches of Loyalists of the American Revolution*, 1:302–303.
29. WF to Lord Dartmouth, Dec. 6, 1774, *NJA*, 1st ser., 10:503–504.
30. WF's speech to the Assembly, Jan. 11, 1775, *NJA*, 1st ser., 10:538–541.
31. Ibid., 543–545.
32. Ibid., 575–577.
33. Ibid., 576.
34. WF to Lord Dartmouth, Mar. 12, 1775, *NJA*, 1st ser., 10:577.
35. *NJA*, 1st ser., 10:548.

14. The times are greatly altered

Makeup of the Continental Congress: LDC, vol. 1; E. A. Jones, *American Members of the Inns of Court;* J. L. Sibley, *Biographical Sketches of the Graduates of Harvard College;* F. B. Dexter, *Biographical Sketches of the Graduates of Yale College;* DAB.

William Temple Franklin: C.-A. Lopez and E. W. Herbert, *The Private Franklin,* 151–155, 199, 202–203; C.-A. Lopez, *Mon Cher Papa; PBF,* 19:52; 20:311; 21:266, 404.

Lord North's peace plan: A. Valentine, *Lord North,* 2:357–361; W. Knox, Papers, vol. 2, fol. 23, Feb. 20, 1775; *LDC,* 1:371–406; *NJA,* 1st ser., 10:590–638 passim.

1. WF to Lord Dartmouth, May 6, 1775, *NJA*, 1st ser., 10:591.
2. *PG*, Apr. 28, 1775.
3. Dartmouth MSS, 2:259.
4. Ibid.
5. WF to Dartmouth, May 6, 1775, *NJA*, 1st ser., 10:511.
6. BF to WF, May 7, 1775, *PBF*, 21:211. The editors of the Benjamin

Franklin Papers contend that the letter was written on May 8, 1774, a full year earlier. However, not only does the context call the latter date into question, but WF positively states that the letter was written on May 7, 1775, in his Loyalist claims petition. See also *PBF*, 22:32, for WF's reaction to BF's arrival.

7. WF to Dartmouth, May 6, 1775, *NJA*, 1st ser., 10:591–592.
8. William Smith, *Diary*, 1:223.
9. WF to Dartmouth, May 6, 1775, *NJA*, 1st ser., 10:591–592.
10. Quoted in C. Van Doren, *Benjamin Franklin*, 519.
11. *PBF*, 21:526–529, 539, 599; J. Priestley, *Autobiography*, 117.
12. *PBF*, 21:540–541.
13. BF to David Hartley, May 8, 1775, *PBF*, 22:34.
14. Jane Mecom to BF, Nov. 3, 1774, *PBF*, 21:349.
15. W. Smith, *Diary*, 1:224.
16. *PBF*, 22:32.
17. Quoted in L. R. Gerlach, ed., *New Jersey in the American Revolution*, 237–239.
18. Quoted in Wallace Brown, *The Good Americans*, 40.
19. BF to WTF, June 13, 1775, *PBF*, 22:65.

20. BF to Charles Thomson, July 11, 1765, *PBF*, 12:207; Thomson to BF, Sept. 24, 1765, ibid., 279.
21. Quoted in A. Aldridge, *Benjamin Franklin*, 261.
22. Lopez and Herbert, 201–203; W. S. Randall, *Proprietary House*, 21–24.
23. WF to Dartmouth, Mar. 12, 1775, *NJA*, 1st ser., 10:575–579.
24. Ibid., 620–623.
25. Ibid., 633–637.
26. Ibid., 638.
27. WF to Dartmouth, June 5, 1775, *NJA*, 1st ser., 10:603.
28. Ibid., 602–603.
29. Silas Deane, "Diary," May 23, 1775, quoted in *LDC*, 1:371.
30. R. H. Lee to F. L. Lee, May 21, 1775, *LDC*, 1:367–369.
31. *JCC*, May 15–18, 1775.
32. John Dickinson, memorandum, May 23, 1775, *LDC*, 1:371–383.
33. Silas Deane, Diary, *LDC*, 1:371.

15. A MATTER OF PUNCTILIO

The Franklins and Galloway at Trevose: PBF, 21:548–596, 22:32–36; W. Mariboe, "William Franklin," 431–450; T. Hutchinson, *Diary*, 2:237–238; R. M. Calhoon, "I Have Deduced Your Rights: Joseph Galloway's Concept of His Role."

Lord North's plan of reconciliation: PBF, 21:391–392; A. Valentine, *Lord North*, vol. 2 passim; *NJA*, 1st ser., 10:620–638.

The battle for Breed's Hill: C. Ward, *The War of the Revolution*, 1:74–84; A. French, *The First Year of the American Revolution*, 1:212–247; R. Middlekauff, *The Glorious Cause*, 282–292; G. F. Sheer and H. F. Rankin, *Rebels and Redcoats*, 55–64; B. Knollenburg, "Bunker Hill Reviewed."

1. Hutchinson, *Diary*, 2:287.
2. *PBF*, 21:546.
3. Ibid., 546–547.
4. Ibid., 548.
5. Ibid.
6. Ibid., 549.
7. Ibid.
8. Ibid., 552.
9. Ibid., 588.
10. Ibid., 561.
11. Ibid., 499–500.
12. Ibid., 569.
13. Ibid., 572.

14. Ibid., 581.
15. Ibid., 579.
16. Ibid., 583.
17. *NJMPC*, 126.
18. *NJA*, 1st ser., 10:632.
19. Ibid., 578, 628.
20. Ibid., 633.
21. Hutchinson, *Diary*, 2:287.
22. Ibid., 288.
23. WF to BF, Aug. 14, 1775, *PBF*, 22:169.
24. Hutchinson, *Diary*, 2:287.
25. *NJMPC*, 126–127.

26. C. Van Doren, *Benjamin Franklin,* 532–535; E. C. Burnett, *Continental Congress,* 60–79.
27. Ward, 1:73; French, 1:212–213.
28. Ward, 1:74–78.
29. Middlekauff, 282–284.
30. French, 1:221–222; Ward, 1:82–84.
31. Middlekauff, 289–292; Sheer and Rankin, 62–63; French, 1:247; J. Fortescue, ed., *Correspondence of George the Third,* 3:220–224.
32. BF to W. Strahan, June 1775, *PBF,* 22:85.

16. ADAM HAD HIS CAIN

WF and Lord Dartmouth: NJA, 1st ser., 10:599–671; B. D. Bargar, *Lord Dartmouth and the American Revolution,* 131–181; *PBF,* 22:33–273 passim.

BF's rise in the Continental Congress: PBF, 22:112–168; C. Van Doren, *Benjamin Franklin,* 527–547; E. C. Burnett, ed., *Letters of Members of the Continental Congress,* vol. 2 passim; P. H. Smith and others, eds., *Letters of Delegates to Congress,* vols. 1 and 2 passim.

The defense of Philadelphia: M. Balderston, "Lord Howe Clears the Delaware," *PMHB* 96 (1972): 326–346; J. W. Jackson, *The Pennsylvania Navy;* W. S. Randall, "Franklin Made Us What We Are."

Royalist Perth Amboy: W. Whitehead, *Contributions to the Early History of Perth Amboy,* 23–49, 59–120, 133–146; W. S. Randall, *Proprietary House,* 20–24; T. L. Purvis, "The New Jersey Councillors, 1702–1776."

1. WF to Dartmouth, Oct. 3, 1775, *NJA,* 1st ser., 10:665.
2. WF to Dartmouth, June 5, 1775, ibid., 10:602.
3. WF to Dartmouth, Aug. 2, 1775, ibid., 10:653.
4. WF to Gage, Aug. 5, 1775, Gage Papers, American Series, Clements Library, Ann Arbor, Mich.
5. Deposition of an anonymous officer, *NJA,* 1st ser., 10:608.
6. Unsigned intelligence report, ibid., 606.
7. WF to Dartmouth, June 5, 1775, ibid., 10:604.
8. Dartmouth to WF, June 7, 1775, ibid., 10:643.
9. WF to Dartmouth, July 4, 1775, ibid., 10:644.
10. Ibid.
11. Daniel Coxe to Cortlandt Skinner, July 4, 1775, ibid., 10:654–655.
12. Dartmouth to WF, July 5, 1775, ibid., 10:646.
13. WF to Dartmouth, July 5, 1775, ibid., 10:648–649.
14. Dartmouth to WF, July 5, 1775, ibid., 10:647.
15. *Dartmouth MSS,* 1:353.
16. WF to BF, Aug. 14, 1775, *PBF,* 22:169.
17. *JCC,* July 5, 1775.
18. BF to Joseph Priestley, July 7, 1775, *PBF,* 22:94–95.
19. *PBF,* 22:122–125.
20. BF, "Proposed Articles of Confederation" [July 21, 1775], *PBF,* 22:120–125.
21. WF to BF, Aug. 14, 1775, 22:169–171.
22. Ibid., 170.
23. Ibid.
24. Ibid.
25. L. Hunt, *Autobiography,* 8–9.
26. See W. Mariboe, "William Franklin," 324–327 and 343–344, for details of WF's financial condition at this time.
27. Post Office Ledger, Sept. 6, 1775, APS.
28. BF to Robert Morris, Aug. 29, 1775, *PBF,* 22:186–187.

29. W. Whitehead, 190.
30. Charles Pettit to Joseph Reed, Aug. 10, 1775, Reed Papers, 2:113, NYHS.
31. *ABF*, 71–73; Whitehead, 190.
32. *Public Characters of 1801–1802*, 195.
33. WF to BF, Sept. 6, 1775, *PBF*, 22:191–192.
34. Quoted in *Mecom*, 121–122.
35. WF to Dartmouth, Sept. 5, 1775, *NJA*, 1st ser., 10:658.
36. Ibid.
37. Ibid., 659–660.
38. Ibid., 662.
39. Dartmouth to WF, July 12, 1775, *NJA*, 1st ser., 10:668–669.
40. *Mecom*, 125.

17. WITH ALL DUE REGULARITY AND DECORUM

Lord Stirling: Alan Valentine, *Lord Stirling;* W. A. Duer, *The Life of William Alexander;* G. H. Danforth, "The Rebel Earl"; T. M. Doerflinger, "Hibernia Furnace During the Revolution."

Tarring and feathering: H. S. Commager and R. B. Morris, *The Spirit of 'Seventy-Six,* 341; K. Britt, "The Loyalists," 510–541.

1. WF to Dartmouth, Nov. 1, 1775, *NJA*, 1st ser., 10:669–674.
2. Ibid., 670.
3. Ibid., 676–681.
4. Wm. Smith, *Historical Memoirs, 1776–1778,* 224.
5. *NJMPC*, 287.
6. Ibid., 283–285.
7. Ibid., 286–287.
8. Ibid., 292–293.
9. Ibid., 290–291.
10. Ibid., 302.
11. Ibid., 309–312.
12. Ibid., 316–317.
13. Ibid., 314–318.
14. WF to Lord Stirling, Oct. 3, 1775, *NJA*, 1st ser., 10:689.
15. William Alexander Papers, vol. 4, NYHS.
16. Quoted in W. A. Duer, *Life of Stirling,* 113.
17. Notes of Dickinson speech before the Assembly, *NJA*, 1st ser., 10:689.
18. Ibid.
19. *NJMPC*, 317–318.
20. Duer, 121.
21. WF to Dartmouth, Jan. 5, 1776, *NJA*, 1st ser., 10:678.
22. Ibid., 679.
23. *AA*, 4th ser., 3:240–241.
24. WF to Dartmouth, Jan. 5, 1776, *NJA*, 1st ser., 10:679–680.
25. Ibid.
26. New York *Journal*, Jan. 10, 1776.
27. Quoted in L. Gerlach, ed., *New Jersey in the American Revolution,* 171.
28. Ibid., 156–157.
29. Ibid., 157.
30. Examples of the correspondence between Pettit and Reed are in *Dartmouth MSS*, 2:337, 345, 346, 351–354, 358, 362, 366, 367, 371–373.
31. W. Whitehead, *Early Contributions to the History of Perth Amboy,* 327–328.
32. WF to Dartmouth, Jan. 5, 1776, *NJA*, 1st ser., 10:676–698.
33. John Adams, Notes of debates, Oct. 6, 1775, *LDC*, 2:125.
34. *JCC*, Oct. 7, 1775.
35. *JCC*, Jan. 4, 1776.
36. Richard Smith, "Diary," Jan. 9, 1776, *LDC*, 3:98.
37. A. Valentine, *Lord Stirling,* 160.
38. R. Smith, "Diary," Jan. 9, 1776, *LDC*, 31:71–72.
39. Valentine, 160.

18. IT IS YOUR TURN NOW

John Witherspoon: his *Works;* W. B. Sprague, *Annals of the American Pulpit,* 2:289–300; H. W. Dodds, *John Witherspoon;* J. H. Nichols, "John Witherspoon on Church and State"; V. L. Collins, *John Witherspoon.*

1. WF to Lord Dartmouth, Jan. 8, 1776, *NJA*, 2d ser., 10:698–701.
2. WF to Lord Germain, Mar. 28, 1776, ibid., 702.
3. WF to WTF, Jan. 10, 1776, APS.
4. *NJMPC*, 327–330; John Hancock to Charles Lee, Feb. 2, 1776, *LDC*, 3:235; *JCC*, Jan. 2 and 10, 1776.
5. Richard Smith, "Diary," Jan. 9, 1776, *LDC*, 3:72.
6. WF to Germain, Mar. 28, 1776, *NJA*, 10:705–706.
7. W. Whitehead, *Early History of Perth Amboy,* 134–135.
8. M. Morris, *Diary,* 7–8; G. Hills, *History of the Church in Burlington,* 307–313; N. Burr, *Anglican Church in New Jersey,* 630.
9. "Schedule and Valuation of the Estate and of the Losses of William Franklin," Loyalist Claims Commission, PRO, AO 13/109.
10. Quoted in C.-A. Lopez and E. W. Herbert, *The Private Franklin,* 209.
11. *Pennsylvania Magazine,* Jan. 1776, 5–6.
12. Quoted in W. Mariboe, "William Franklin," 452–453.
13. WF to WTF, Jan. 22, 1776, APS.
14. WF to WTF, Mar. 14, 1776, *PBF,* 22:391–392.
15. EDF to SFB, Feb. 2, 1776, APS.
16. WF to WTF, Mar. 14, 1776, *PBF,* 22:391–392.
17. WTF to WF, Mar. 7, 1776, APS.
18. WF to WTF, May 8, 1776, APS.
19. Ibid.
20. WF to WTF, June 13, 1776, APS.
21. Mariboe, 457.
22. R. O. De Mond, *The Loyalists in North Carolina,* 94–97.
23. R. Middlekauff, *Glorious Cause,* 308–311; P. Mackesy, *The War for America,* 80; Esther C. Wright, *The Loyalists of New Brunswick,* 3–4.
24. Germain to WF, Dec. 23, 1775, *NJA*, 2d ser., 10:675.
25. WF to Germain, Mar. 28, 1776, ibid., 708–710.
26. R. Smith "Diary," Jan. 6 and 10, and Feb. 6, 1776, *LDC*, 3:50, 80, 211–212; William Livingston to John Hancock, Feb. 3, 1776, *LDC*, 3:190.
27. [John Witherspoon], "The Druid," *Pennsylvania Magazine,* May 1776, 3–13.
28. Receipts in the Witherspoon Papers, PUL.
29. See, for instance, N. Burr, *The Anglican Church in New Jersey:* WF was "the most friendly and generous governor" to the established church in his province (p. 158).
30. Witherspoon, *Works,* 4:307.
31. John Adams, "Diary" [Aug. 29–Sept. 5, 1774], quoted in *LDC*, 1:8.
32. Quoted in Dodds, 3.
33. Witherspoon, *Works,* 7:104.
34. Quoted in Collins, 1:202.
35. Witherspoon, "Thoughts on American Liberty," *Works,* 9:9.
36. E. Boudinot, *Journal,* 4–8.
37. Ibid., 6.
38. Witherspoon, *Works,* 9:80.
39. R. Smith, "Diary," Mar. 14, 1776, *LDC*, 3:378.
40. Witherspoon, *Works,* 2:441.
41. *JCC*, May 15, 1776.
42. *Pennsylvania Magazine,* June 1776, 295–296; *NJMPC*, 453; L. Gerlach, *Prologue to Independence,* 329.
43. Samuel Adams to Samuel Cooper, Apr. 30, 1776, *LDC*, 3:601.
44. WF to Germain, Nov. 10, 1778, PRO, AO/113.
45. *NJMPC*, 449–450.
46. WF to Germain, Nov. 10, 1778, PRO, AO/113.
47. Ibid.
48. E. Boudinot, "Thoughts on the Present State of Affairs," June 11, 1776, PUL.
49. Ibid.

50. *NJMPC*, 455.
51. WF to Germain, Nov. 10, 1778, PRO, AO/113.
52. *NJMPC*, 455.
53. Ibid.
54. T. Jones, *History of New York*, 1:108–110.
55. *NJMPC*, 461.
56. WF to Germain, Mar. 28, 1776, *NJA*, 2d ser., 10:707.
57. *AA*, 4th ser., 2:367.
58. Samuel Tucker to John Hancock, June 18, 1776, *AA*, 4th ser., 6:967–968.
59. BF to GW, June 21, 1776, *LDC*, 4:280–281.
60. Thomas Jefferson to BF, June 21, 1776, *LDC*, 4:286.
61. R. H. Lee to Landon Carter, June 2, 1776, *LDC*, 4:280–281.
62. William Whipple to John Langdon, June 17, 1776, *LDC*, 4:261.
63. Elbridge Gerry to Joseph Trumbull, June 19, 1776, *LDC*, 4:268.
64. William Livingston to Jonathan Trumbull, "The Trumbull Papers," *Collections of the Massachusetts Historical Society*, 5th ser., 9:251.
65. BF to GW, June 21, 1776, *LDC*, 4:280–281.
66. *JCC*, June 19, 1776; John Hancock to John Witherspoon, June 19, 1776, *LDC*, 4:270.
67. WF to the New Jersey Legislature, June 22, 1776, *NJA*, 2d ser., 10:719.
68. WF to Germain, Nov. 10, 1778, PRO, AO/113.
69. Ibid.
70. *NJMPC*, 482–483.
71. *Princetonians*, 1:437–440.
72. WF to the New Jersey Legislature, June 22, 1776, *NJA*, 2d ser., 10:730.
73. A. Green, *The Life of the Rev'd John Witherspoon*, 125.
74. *AA*, 4th ser., 6:1010.
75. Affidavit of Elias Brown, Sept. 1, 1856, Pension Claims, New Jersey Archives, Trenton.
76. WF to the New Jersey Legislature,

77. A. Green, 125.
78. E. Brown affidavit, New Jersey Archives.
79. A. Green, 128.
80. *AA*, 4th ser., 6:1010.
81. WF to the New Jersey Legislature, June 22, 1776, *NJA*, 2d ser., 10:731.
82. BF to WF, Aug. 16, 1784, *WBF*, 9:252.
83. *JCC*, June 24, 1776.
84. T. Jones, *History of New York*, 1:238.
85. WF to the New Jersey Legislature, June 22, 1776, *NJA*, 2d ser., 10:733.
86. WF to WTF, June 25, 1776, APS.
87. Anna Zabriskie to Richard Varick, June 30, 1776, Tomlinson Collection, NYHS.
88. WF to EDF, quoted in GW to Essex Committee of Safety, June 30, 1776, in GW, *Writings*, 5:204.
89. Quoted in Mariboe, 466–467. For the plot to kill Washington, see L. Lundin, *New Jersey: Cockpit of the Revolution*, 106–107; William Whipple to Joshua Brackett, June 23, 1776, *LDC*, 4:301; Francis Lightfoot Lee to R. H. Lee, June 30, 1776, *LDC*, 4:343; Thomas Jefferson to William Fleming, June 1, 1776, *LDC*, 4:366.
90. Quoted in F. Moore, *Diary of the American Revolution*, 1:352.
91. State of Connecticut, *Public Records, 1634–1776*, 15:457–460.
92. WF to Germain, Nov. 10, 1778, PRO AO/113; *AA*, 4th ser., 4:46, 240.
93. S. B. Webb, *Correspondence and Journals*, 1:70–71, 105–106.
94. Wallace Brown, *The Good Americans*, 141–143.
95. GW to Essex Committee of Safety, June 30, 1776, quoted in GW, *Writings*, 5:204.
96. Mariboe, 467; Jonathan Trumbull, Letter Books, 1775–1779, LC.

19. A LITTLE REVENGE

1. A. Serle, *American Journal,* 49.
2. C.-A. Lopez and E. W. Herbert, *The Private Franklin,* 205.
3. EDF to BF, Aug. 6, 1776, *PBF,* 22:551–552.
4. W. Mariboe, "William Franklin," 468.
5. EDF to BF, Aug. 6, 1776, *PBF,* 22:551–552.
6. EDF to WTF, July 16, 1776, quoted in Lopez and Herbert, 211.
7. Ibid.
8. Quoted in W. A. Whitehead, *Early History of Perth Amboy,* 329.
9. Quoted in L. C. Lundin, *New Jersey: Cockpit of the Revolution,* 119.
10. Whitehead, 330–331.
11. EDF to BF, Aug. 6, 1776, *PBF,* 22:552.
12. Whitehead, 332–333.
13. R. Middlekauff, *Glorious Cause,* 340–346; C. Ward, *War of the Revolution,* 1:213–214; M. Dix, ed., *History of the Parish of Trinity Church,* 387.
14. BF to WTF, Sept. 19, 1776, *PBF,* 22:612–613.
15. BF to WTF, Sept. 22, 1776, *PBF,* 22:622.
16. Ibid.
17. BF to WTF, Sept. 28, 1776, *PBF,* 22:634.
18. BF to RB, June 2, 1779, *WBF,* 7:345.
19. EDF to WFT, Oct. 11, 1776, quoted in Lopez and Herbert, 213.
20. Thomas Wharton, Letter Book, 1773–1784, Wharton Papers, HSP.
21. WF to EDF, Nov. 6, 1776, APS.
22. Minutes, Conn. Council of Safety, July 16, 1776, Conn. State Historical Society, Hartford.
23. Ralph Isaacs to WF, Aug. 7, 1776, reproduced in facsimile in J. Trumbull, *The Lebanon War Office.*
24. G. O. M. Trevelyan, *The American Revolution,* 4:47–49.
25. Issuance of the protections by WF was first authorized in a letter from Lord Howe to WF, June 20, 1776, written aboard the flagship *Eagle.*
    Howe had been given full power to grant protections on May 1, 1776, in letters patent from George III. Howe's letter to WF was sent ashore at Perth Amboy and forwarded by GW to the Congress, which ordered it printed in *PG,* July 24, 1776.
26. R. A. East, *Connecticut's Loyalists* (Chester, Conn., 1974), 16.
27. Connecticut Archives, Revolutionary War ser. 1, 432a, Connecticut State Historical Society, Hartford.
28. WF to EDF, Oct. 11, 1776, APS.
29. Serle, 221.
30. Mariboe, 456.
31. *JCC,* Dec. 3, 1776.
32. J. Hancock to GW, Nov. 24, 1776, *LDC,* 5:534.
33. J. Hancock to GW, Dec. 4, 1776, *LDC,* 5:572.
34. T. Jones, *History of New York,* 1:134–135.
35. Minutes, Connecticut Council of Safety, Jan. 6, 1777.
36. *JCC,* Apr. 18 and 22, 1777; William Livingston, *Papers,* 1:288–289; GW, *Writings,* 7:317.
37. Roger Sherman to Jonathan Trumbull, May 14, 1777, Massachusetts Historical Society, *Collections,* ser. 7, 2:46–48.
38. PCC, M247, reel 66, 63–64.
39. *JCC,* Apr. 18, 1777.
40. *JCC,* Apr. 22, 1777.
41. J. Hancock to J. Trumbull, Apr. 23, 1777, *LDC,* 6:639.
42. J. Trumbull to J. Hancock, May 5, 1777, PCC, M247, reel 80, 389.
43. WF to Germain, Nov. 10, 1778, PRO, AO/13.
44. W. Smith, *Historical Memoirs,* June 3, 1777, 146.
45. *Some Historic Sites in Litchfield,* 5–6; J. C. Connolly, "Governor Franklin in Litchfield Jail," *PNJHS,* 3 (1918): 45–48.
46. Minutes, Connecticut Council of Safety, May 1, 1777.
47. Serle, 221.

48. WF to Germain, Nov. 10, 1778, PRO, AO/109.
49. William Hick to WF, June 29, 1777, PCC, M247, reel 80, 389.
50. T. J. Wertenbaker, *Father Knickerbocker Rebels,* 131.
51. GW to WF, July 2, 1777, in GW, *Writings,* 8:476.
52. Ibid., 474.
53. *JCC,* July 28, 1776.
54. *Rivington's Royal Gazette,* Aug. 4, 1777.
55. WF to Germain, Nov. 10, 1778, PRO, AO/109.
56. W. S. Randall, *Proprietary House,* 14.
57. WF to J. Trumbull, quoted in Mariboe, 480–481.
58. WF to Germain, Nov. 10, 1778, PRO, AO/109.
59. T. Jones, *History of New York,* 1:280.
60. WF to J. Trumbull, quoted in Mariboe, 480–481.
61. Ibid.
62. W. Strahan to BF, Sept. 8, 1778, quoted in Mariboe, 528.
63. BF to Jan Ingenhousz, Feb. 12, 1777, *PBF,* 23:310.
64. BF to John Jay, Oct. 4, 1779, *WBF,* 7:386; *PBF,* 23:330–331.
65. BF to [SFB], Oct. 25, 1779, *WBF,* 7:406.
66. BF to SFB, June 3, 1779, *WBF,* 7:348.
67. Ibid.
68. *WBF,* 7:10, 201; BF to J. Witherspoon, Sept. 11 and Nov. 11, 1781, and WTF to J. Witherspoon, Sept.

13, 1781, de Coppet Collection, PUL. For WTF's attempts to help WF, see *WBF,* 7:348, and R. M. Bache to BF, Oct. 22, 1778, APS.
69. BF to CRG, Feb. 28, 1778, *WBF,* 7:112–113.
70. BF to SFB, June 3, 1779, *WBF,* 7:347.
71. WTF to SFB, Nov. 25, 1777, APS.
72. The best personal portrait of BF in Paris is in C.-A. Lopez, *Mon Cher Papa.*
73. Lopez and Herbert, *The Private Franklin,* 243.
74. Comte de Vergennes to Louis XVI, in B. F. Stevens, ed., *Facsimiles,* 13:1312
75. R. M. Bache, "Franklin's Ceremonial Coat," *PMHB,* 23 (1899): 444–452; "Rush Papers," *PMHB,* 29 (1905): 27–28.
76. James Duane Papers, Miscellaneous MSS, NYHS.
77. A. Ousterhout, "Controlling the Opposition in Pennsylvania During the American Revolution," *PMHB,* 105 (1981): 3–34.
78. Daniel Clymer to R. M. Bache, Oct. 11, 1777, PCC, M247, reel 93, 111.
79. Hugh Fergusson to Elias Boudinot, Mar. 6, 1778, PCC, M247, reel 91, 351.
80. E. Boudinot, *Journal,* 18.
81. T. Jones, *History of New York,* 2:227–228.
82. PCC, M247, reel 84, 655–659; *JCC,* Aug. 20 and Sept. 11–14, 1778.
83. Quoted in Mariboe, 485.

20. I SHALL NEVER SEE YOU AGAIN

The Paris peace talks: R. B. Morris, *The Peacemakers;* J. R. Dull, "Franklin the Diplomat"; G. Stourzh, *Benjamin Franklin and American Foreign Policy;* R. R. Crout, "The Diplomacy of Trade"; J. H. Hutson, "Intellectual Foundations of Early American Diplomacy"; R. B. Morris, ed., *John Jay: The Winning of the Peace.*

1. A. Flick, *Loyalism in New York,* 104–113.
2. M. Dix, ed., *Parish of Trinity Church,* 387–392.
3. WF to Germain, Nov. 10 and Nov. 12, 1778, PRO, AO/109; Germain to Treasury, Jan. 6, 1779, and Germain to WF, Jan. 5, 1779,

PRO, AO13/109, XL/7230:306–310.

4. WF to Galloway, Nov. 16, 1778, Balch Papers, NYPL.

5. WF to Galloway, Nov. 17, 1778, Balch Papers, NYPL.

6. Isaac Ogden to Galloway, Nov. 22, 1778, Balch Papers, NYPL.

7. T. Jones, *History of New York,* 2:718.

8. Ibid., 724–725. A. Ousterhout, in "Controlling the Opposition" (PMHB 105 [1981]: 23–34), lists twenty Loyalists who were executed by Pennsylvania on various charges during the Revolution.

9. P. H. Smith, *Loyalists and Redcoats,* 77.

10. L. Sabine, *Biographical Sketches,* 2:122.

11. I. Ogden to Galloway, Nov. 22, 1778, Balch Papers, NYPL; WF to Henry Clinton, Apr. 27, 1782, BHQP.

12. J. Berkenhout, "Dr. Berkenhout's Journal, 1778," *PMHB* 65 (1941): 79–82.

13. Earl of Carlisle to Lady Carlisle, July 21, 1778, quoted in R. G. Davies, ed., *Transcripts,* 131.

14. WF to Germain, Nov. 12, 1778, PRO, AO/109; I. Ogden to Galloway, Dec. 15, 1778, Balch Papers, NYPL; WF to Galloway, Feb. 6, 1779, Balch Papers, NYPL.

15. WF to Germain, Nov. 12, 1778, PRO, AO/109.

16. WF to Galloway, Nov. 16, 1778, PRO, AO/109.

17. William Smith, *Historical Memoirs, 1778–1783,* 39.

18. Andrew Elliott to the earl of Carlisle, Feb. 1, 1779, quoted in B. F. Stevens, ed., *Facsimiles,* 2:115.

19. WF to Clinton, Apr. 27, 1782, BHQP, item 4487(7); I. Ogden to Galloway, Nov. 22, 1778, Balch Papers, NYPL.

20. Ogden to Galloway, Nov. 22, 1778, Balch Papers, NYPL.

21. W. Smith, *Historical Memoirs, 1778–1783,* 151.

22. T. Jones, *History of New York,* 2:221.

23. PRO, CO5/82, 48–49.

24. WF to John André, Nov. 10, 1779, PRO, CO5/85, 52.

25. BHQP, 2694–2695; PRO, CO5/82, 135–136.

26. For the various proposals, see E. H. Tebbenhoff, "The Associated Loyalists," 115, 144.

27. E. Salter, *History of Monmouth and Ocean Counties,* 182–183.

28. Ibid., 170–171.

29. Ibid., 90–91.

30. Quoted in ibid., 204–207. R. P. McCormick, in *Experiment in Independence,* says that the raid was in reprisal for Monmouth Retaliator raids. Several of the Tory raiders identified by Salter (p. 14) had had their lands confiscated and sold by the revolutionary government. See also M. P. Riccards, "Patriots and Plunderers."

31. Quoted in Salter, 206.

32. BHQP, 4361–4367.

33. Aaron White's deposition, BHQP, 4490.

34. The rumors are set forth in L. K. Wroth, "Vengeance: The Court-martial of Captain Richard Lippincott," in H. H. Peckham, ed., *Sources of American Independence,* 2:499–610. See also F. B. Weiner, *Civilians Under Military Justice,* 95–121.

35. Deposition of Lt. Josiah Parker, BHQP, 4456; deposition of Capt. John Tilton, BHQP, 4439.

36. For Lippincott's relatives, see Sabine, 2:17–18.

37. Testimony of Sampson P. Blowers, June 9, 1782, quoted in Peckham, 2:563.

38. Blowers to Walter Chaloner, Apr. 8, 1782, BHQP, 4368.

39. D. Coxe to Oliver DeLancey, Apr. 9, 1782, BHQP, 4374.

40. WF to Richard Lippincott, Apr. 9, 1782, BHQP, 4375.

41. Undated MS, GW Papers, microfilm reel 84, LC.

42. R. Lippincott to WF, BHQP, 4387.
43. WF to Clinton, Apr. 27, 1782, BHQP, 4487(7).
44. Quoted in W. B. Willcox, *Portrait of a General*, 452–453.
45. G. M. Kyte, "Some Plans for a Loyalist Stronghold."
46. J. W. dePeyster, "The Affair at King's Mountain," *Magazine of American History* 5 (1880):351.
47. Mariboe, 527–528; Esther C. Wright, *Loyalists of New Brunswick*, 24–25; Tebbenhoff, 140.
48. WF to Germain, Nov. 6, 1781, PRO, CO5/175.
49. Minutes, Board of Associated Loyalists, Nov. 8, 1781.
50. E. Gibbon, *Memoirs of My Life*, edited by G. A. Bonnard (London, 1966), 163.
51. R. B. Morris, *The Peacemakers*, 67–87.
52. George III to Lord North, Mar. 27, 1782, in J. Fortescue, ed., *Correspondence of King George III*, 5:421.
53. GW, *Writings*, 25:217–231; BHQP, 4525, 16–20; D. S. Freeman, *Washington*, 5:412–414, 419, 425.
54. L. Van Closen, *Revolutionary Journal*, 199–200, 272.
55. *JCC*, Aug. 19, 1782.
56. W. Stryker, *Block House at Toms River*, 24–31.
57. *JCC*, Oct. 15, 1782.
58. WF to Galloway, May 11, 1782, Balch Papers, NYPL.
59. WF to SFB, Aug. 13, 1782, APS.
60. Morris, 374–375.
61. WF to Shelburne, Nov. 12, 1782, PRO, FO95/511; Loyalist petition to the House of Commons, Jan. 1783, PRO, CO5/8:3; Loyalists to

Shelburne, Feb. 12, 1783, Ledgers of Parliament, 67:1–4.
62. Morris, 263.
63. Ibid., 270.
64. R. Bache to BF, Mar. 10, 1777, *PBF*, 23:455–456.
65. Morris, 375.
66. Ibid., 308–310.
67. Quoted in John Jay, *Diary*, 3:77.
68. Inventory in G. S. Eddy Collection, PUL.
69. Morris, 375.
70. BF to Oswald, Rodney MSS, Clements Library, University of Michigan, Ann Arbor.
71. John Jay, *Diary*, 3:375.
72. Quoted in W. A. S. Hewins, ed., *Whitefoord Papers*, 188.
73. Benjamin Vaughan to Shelburne, Apr. 10, 1782, Lansdowne Papers, Clements Library, University of Michigan, Ann Arbor.
74. WF to Richard Oswald, undated, bundle 13, Rodney MSS, Clements Library.
75. T. Jones, *History of New York*, 2:783.
76. McCormick, 189.
77. M. Norton, *British-Americans*, 202.
78. Quoted in J. Galloway, *The Claims of American Loyalists*, 5–6.
79. WF to BF, July 22, 1784, APS.
80. Ibid.
81. BF to WF, Aug. 16, 1784, *WBF*, 9:252–254.
82. Ibid.
83. BF to WTF, Aug. 25, 1784, *WBF*, 9:268.
84. *PBF*, 23:19–20, lists BF's accounts for WTF's expenses in France. They are initialed as paid by WF in return for his American lands. See also *WBF*, 10:469, and WTF, *Memoirs*, 2:165.

21. MY SON KEEPS HIMSELF ALOOF

1. C. Van Doren, *Benjamin Franklin*, 765.
2. W. P. Cutler and J. Cutler, *Life . . . of Manasseh Cutler*, 1:267.
3. Ibid., 270.
4. BF to Jane Mecom, May 30, 1787, *Mecom*, 295.
5. BF to Jan Ingenhousz, 1788, quoted in WTF, *Memoirs*, 78.
6. BF, "Last Will and Testament," *WBF*, 10:493–510.
7. Auction notice in the G. S. Eddy Collection, PUL.
8. BF, "Last Will," *WBF*, 10:497;

C.-A. Lopez and E. Herbert, *The Private Franklin,* 307.

9. R. Bache to SFB, Sept. 7, 1792, PUL.
10. WF memorandum, Mar. 29, 1783, JWP.
11. WF to SFB, July 8, 1803, JWP.
12. WF to JW, July 24, 1807, JWP.
13. Ibid.
14. JW to WF, Apr. 6, 1808, JWP.
15. SFB to WF, Apr. 29, 1808, JWP.
16. WF to JW, May 26, 1808, JWP.
17. WF to JW, Nov. 22, 1808, JWP.
18. WF to JW, May 2, 1809, JWP.
19. WF to JW, Oct. 28, 1811, JWP.
20. WF to WTF, June 13, 1813, APS.
21. WF, sworn affidavit, Loyalist Claims Commission, PRO, AO 12/17.
22. Ibid.
23. *Public Characters of 1801–1802,* 189–202.
24. WF to JW, May 17, 1813, JWP.
25. Ibid. The letter was apparently not sent until June (the date of June 13 was appended to it).
26. WF, "Last Will and Testament," APS.

BIBLIOGRAPHY

Abernethy, T. P. *Western Lands and the American Revolution,* New York, 1937.

Adams, Charles Francis. "Church Discipline in New England." *PMHS,* 2d ser., 4 (1891): 477–516.

Adams, John. *Diary and Autobiography of John Adams.* Edited by Lyman H. Butterfield. 4 vols. Cambridge, Mass., 1961.

———. *Legal Papers of John Adams.* Edited by L. Kinvin Wroth and Hiller B. Zobel. 3 vols. Cambridge, Mass., 1965.

Adams, Randolph G. *Political Ideas of the American Revolution.* Rev. ed. Intro. by Merrill Jensen. New York, 1958.

Addy, John. *The Agrarian Revolution.* London, 1972.

Adye, Stephen P. *A Treatise on Courts-martial.* 2d ed. London, 1778.

Albemarle, George Thomas, earl of. *Memoirs of the Marquis of Rockingham and His Contemporaries.* 2 vols. London, 1852.

Alberts, Robert C. *Benjamin West.* Boston, 1978.

Alden, John R. *The American Revolution.* New York, 1962.

Aldridge, Alfred Owen. *Benjamin Franklin: Philosopher and Man.* Philadelphia, 1936.

Alexander, William [known as Lord Stirling]. *Lord Stirling Papers, 1759–1773.* MSS in the New-York Historical Society, New York City.

Allen, William. *Extracts from Chief Justice William Allen's Letter Book.* Vol. 1: *The Burd Papers.* Edited by L. B. Walker. Pottsville, Pa., 1897.

———. Letter Book. MS in the Historical Society of Pennsylvania, Philadelphia.

Alvord, Clarence W. *The Illinois Country, 1673–1818.* Springfield, Ill., 1920.

———. *The Mississippi Valley in British Politics.* 2 vols. Cleveland, 1917.

Alvord, Clarence W., and C. E. Carter. *The New Regime, 1765–1767.* Springfield, Ill., 1916.

Anburey, Thomas. *Travels Through the Interior Parts of America.* London, 1789.

Archives of the State of New Jersey. See New Jersey, State of.

Aries, Philippe. *Centuries of Childhood: A Social History of Family Life.* New York, 1962.

Axtell, James. "The Unkindest Cut." In *The European and the Indian.* Oxford, 1981.

Bache, Richard M. "Franklin's Ceremonial Coat." *PMHB* 23 (1899): 444–452.

Bailey, Kenneth P. *The Ohio Company of Virginia and the Westward Movement, 1748–1792.* Glendale, Calif., 1939.

Bailyn, Bernard P. *Ideological Origins of American Independence*. Cambridge, Mass., 1967.

——. *The Ordeal of Thomas Hutchinson*. Cambridge, Mass., 1974.

Balch, Thomas Willing. *The Pennsylvania Assemblies*. Philadelphia, 1916.

——, ed. *The Examination of Joseph Galloway, Esq., by a Committee of the House of Commons*. Philadelphia, 1855.

——. *Letters and Papers Relating Chiefly to the Provincial History of Pennsylvania*. Philadelphia, 1855.

Barber, J. W., and Henry Howe. *Historical Collections of the State of New York*. New York, 1841.

Barch, Oscar T. *New York City During the War for Independence*. New York, 1931.

Bargar, B. D. *Lord Dartmouth and the American Revolution*. Columbia, S.C., 1965.

Barton, Dunbar P. *The Story of Our Inns of Court*. London, 1924.

Beck, Henry C. *The Jersey Midlands*. New Brunswick, N.J., 1962.

Bell, Whitfield J., Jr. " 'All Clear Sunshine': New Letters of Franklin and Mary Stevenson Hewson." *PAPS* 100 (1956): 521–535.

——. "Benjamin Franklin and the German Charity Schools." *PAPS* 100 (1956): 381–387.

——. "Some American Students of That Stunning Oracle of Physic, Dr. William Cullen of Edinburgh." *PAPS* 94 (1950): 275–281.

——, ed. *The Complete Poor Richard's Almanacks*. 2 vols. Philadelphia, 1971.

Bell, Whitfield, J., Jr., and L. W. Labaree. "Franklin and the Wagon Affair." *PAPS* 101 (1957): 551–558.

Bentham, Jeremy. *Works*. 11 vols. Edinburgh, 1843.

Benton, William A. *Whig-Loyalism: An Aspect of Political Ideology in the American Revolution*. Teaneck, N.J., 1969.

Berkenhout, John. "Dr. Berkenhout's Journal, 1778." *PMHB* 65 (1941): 79–82.

Bill, Alfred H. *New Jersey and the Revolutionary War*. New Brunswick, N.J., 1964.

Blackstone, William. *Commentaries on the Laws of England*. 4 vols. Oxford, 1765.

Blake, J. B. "The Inoculation Controversy in Boston." *NEQ* 25 (1952): 489–506.

Bliven, Bruce. *Battle for Manhattan*. New York, 1956.

——. *Under the Guns: New York, 1775–1776*. New York, 1972.

Boldt, David R., and W. S. Randall, eds. *The Founding City*. Philadelphia, 1976.

Bolles, Albert S. *Pennsylvania, Province and State: A History from 1690 to 1790*. Philadelphia, 1899.

Bolton, Reginald P. *Relics of the Revolution*. New York, 1916.

Bonomi, Patricia U. *A Factious People: Politics and Society in Colonial New York*. New York, 1971.

Boorstin, Daniel J. *The Americans: The Colonial Experience*. New York, 1958.

——. *The Mysterious Science of the Law*. Cambridge, Mass. 1941.

Boston, City of. *A Report of the Record Commissions of the City of Boston . . . 1660 to 1701*. 39 vols. Boston, 1876–1909.

Boswell, James. *Boswell's London Journal, 1762–1763*. Edited by F. A. Pottle. New Haven, 1950.

——. *The Journal of a Tour to the Hebrides*. Rev. ed. Edited by L. F. Powell. London, 1958.

——. *The Life of Samuel Johnson*. 4 vols. Oxford, 1826.

[Boucher, Jonathan.] *Letter from a Virginian to the Members of the Congress to be held at Philadelphia . . . New York*, 1774.

Boucher, Jonathan. *Reminiscences of an American Loyalist, 1738–1789*. Boston, 1925.

——. *A View of the Causes and Consequences of the American Revolution*. 1797. Reprint: New York, 1967.

Boudinot, Elias. *Journal, or Historical Recollections of American Events during the Revolutionary War.* Philadelphia, 1894.

———. *A Journey to Boston, 1809.* Princeton, 1955.

———. "Thoughts on the Present State of Affairs . . ." MS in the de Coppet Collection, Princeton University Library, Princeton, N.J.

Bowen, Catherine Drinker. *John Adams and the American Revolution.* Boston, 1948.

———. *Miracle at Philadelphia: The Story of the Constitutional Convention.* Boston, 1967.

Bowman, Larry. "The Court-martial of Captain Richard Lippincott." *NJH* 89 (1971): 23–36.

Boyd, George A. *Elias Boudinot, Patriot and Statesman, 1740–1821.* Princeton, 1952.

Boyd, Hugh. *Genuine Abstracts from Two Speeches of the Late Earl of Chatham.* London, 1879.

Boyd, Julian P. *Anglo-American Union: Joseph Galloway's Plans to Preserve the British Empire, 1774–1788.* Philadelphia, 1941.

———. "Silas Deane: Death by a Kindly Teacher of Treason?" *WMQ*, 3d ser., 16 (1959): 319–342.

———, ed. *Indian Treaties, Printed by Benjamin Franklin, 1736–1762.* Introduction by Carl Van Doren. Philadelphia, 1938.

Bremner, R. H. *Children and Youth in America: A Documentary History.* 3 vols. Cambridge, Mass., 1970–74.

Brewer, John. "The Misfortunes of Lord Bute: A Case-Study in Eighteenth-Century Political Argument and Public Opinion." *The Historical Journal* 16 (1973): 3–43.

———. *Party Ideology and Popular Politics at the Accession of George III.* New York, 1976.

Bridenbaugh, Carl and Jessica. *Rebels and Gentlemen.* New York, 1942.

Brigham, Clarence S. "An Account of American Almanacs and Their Value for Historical Study." 1925. MS in the American Antiquarian Society, Worcester, Mass.

Brissot de Warville, J. P. *New Travels in the United States of America.* 1792. Translated by M. S. Vamos and Durand Echeverria. Cambridge, Mass., 1964.

British Head Quarters Papers. MSS in the William L. Clements Library, University of Michigan, Ann Arbor, Mich. Referred to as BHQP.

Britt, Kent. "The Loyalists, Americans with a Difference." *National Geographic* 147 (1975): 510–540.

Brooke, John. *George III.* London, 1972.

Brown, Richard D. "The Confiscation and Disposition of Loyalists' Estates in Suffolk County, Mass." *WMQ*, 3d ser., 21 (1964): 534–550.

Brown, Wallace. *The Good Americans: Loyalists in the American Revolution.* New York, 1969.

———. *The King's Friends: The Composition and Motives of the American Loyalist Claimants.* Providence, 1966.

———. "The View at Two Hundred Years: The Loyalists of the American Revolution." *Proceedings of the American Antiquarian Society* 80 (1970): 25–47.

Brown, Weldon C. *Empire or Independence.* University, La., 1941.

Brunhouse, Robert L. *The Counter-Revolution in Pennsylvania, 1776–1790.* Harrisburg, 1942.

Burke, Edmund. *Correspondence.* Edited by T. W. Copeland and others. 4 vols. Cambridge, 1958–1970.

———. *Speeches and Letters on American Affairs.* London, 1956.

Burnaby, Andrew. *Travels Through the Middle Settlements in North America, 1759–1760.* London, 1775.

Burnett, Edward C., ed. *Letters of the Members of the Continental Congress.* 8 vols. Washington, D.C., 1921–36.

Burns, John F. *Controversies Between Royal Governors and Their Assemblies*. Boston, 1923.

Burr, Nelson R. *The Anglican Church in New Jersey*. Philadelphia, 1954.

Bushman, Richard L. *From Puritan to Yankee: Character and the Social Order in Connecticut, 1690–1765*. Cambridge, Mass., 1967.

Butler, Ruth L. *Doctor Franklin, Postmaster General*. Garden City, N.Y., 1928.

Butterfield, Lyman H. *John Witherspoon Comes to America*. Princeton, 1953.

Buxbaum, Melvin. *Benjamin Franklin and the Zealous Presbyterians*. Philadelphia, 1968.

Cable, Mary. *The Little Darlings: A History of Childrearing in America*. New York, 1973.

Calhoon, R. M. "I Have Deduced Your Rights: Joseph Galloway's Concept of His Role, 1774–1775." *PH* 35 (1968): 375–378.

———. *The Loyalists in Revolutionary America, 1760–1781*. New York, 1973.

Callahan, North. *Flight from the Republic: The Tories of the American Revolution*. New York, 1967.

Campbell, Alexander. *A Journey from Edinburgh Through Parts of North Britain*. London, 1811.

Canfield, Cass. *Sam Adams's Revolution*. New York, 1976.

Cant, R. G. *The University of St. Andrews: A Short History*. Edinburgh, 1970.

[Carlyle, Alexander.] *An Argument to Prove that the Tragedy of Douglas Ought to be Publicly Burnt by the hands of the Hangman*. Edinburgh, 1757.

Carlyle, Alexander. *Autobiography of the Rev. Dr. Alexander Carlyle*. Edinburgh, 1860.

———. *Plain Reasons for Removing a Certain Great Man from His Majesty's Presence and Councils Forever*. London, 1759.

[———.] *The Question Relating to a Scots Militia*. London, 1759.

Chancellor, Edwin B. *The Private Palaces of London Past and Present*. London, 1908.

Chidsey, A. Donald, Jr. "Easton Before the French and Indian War." *PH* 25 (1958): 156–168.

Chitnis, Anand. *The Scottish Enlightenment*. London, 1976.

Christie, Ian. *The Earl of North's Ministry, 1780–1782*. London, 1958.

Clark, George L. *Silas Deane: A Connecticut Leader in the American Revolution*. New York, 1913.

Clinton, Sir Henry. *The American Rebellion*. See Willcox, William B.

Clive, John, and Bernard P. Bailyn. "England's Cultural Provinces: Scotland and America." *WMQ*, 3d ser., 11 (1954): 200–213.

Coad, Oral S. *New Jersey in Travelers' Accounts, 1524–1971*. Metuchen, N.J., 1972.

Cobbett, William, and Thomas C. Hansard, eds. *The Parliamentary History of England*. 36 vols. London, 1806–20.

Cochrane, J. A. *Dr. Johnson's Printer: The Life of William Strahan*. Cambridge, Mass., 1964.

Cohen, I. Bernard. *Franklin and Newton*. Philadelphia, 1956.

Cohen, Sheldon S., and Larry Gerlach. "Princeton in the Coming of the American Revolution." *NJH* 92 (1974): 69–92.

Colden, Cadwallader. *The Letters and Papers of Cadwallader Colden, 1711–1775*. 9 vols. New York, 1917–35.

Collins, Varnum L. *President Witherspoon*. Princeton, 1925.

Commager, Henry S., and Richard B. Morris. *The Spirit of 'Seventy-Six*. New York, 1967.

Connecticut, State of. *Public Records, 1634–1776*. 15 vols. Hartford, 1850–1890.

———. *Public Records, 1776–1919*. 17 vols. Hartford, 1894–1919.

Connolly, James C. "Quit-Rents in Colonial New Jersey as a Contributing Cause for the American Revolution." *PNJHS* 7 (1922): 13–20.

————. "The Stamp Act and New Jersey Opposition to It." *PNJHS* 9 (1924): 137–150.

Continental Congress. *Journals of the Continental Congress, 1774–1783.* 10 vols. Philadelphia, 1775–1785. Referred to as *JCC.*

————. Papers of the Continental Congress, 1774–1789. 204 reels. U.S. National Archives, microfilm ed., 247.

Cook, Fred J. *The New Jersey Colony.* New York, 1969.

Corner, Betsy C. "Day Book of an Education: William Shippen's Student Days in London, 1759–1760." *PAPS* 94 (1950): 132–136.

Corner, Betsy C., and Christopher C. Booth. *Chain of Friendship: Selected Letters of Dr. John Fothergill of London, 1735–1780.* Cambridge, Mass., 1971.

Cowie, Donald. *Scotland: The Land and the People.* South Brunswick, N.J., 1973.

Crane, Verner W. *Benjamin Franklin, Englishman and American.* Baltimore, 1936.

————. "The Club of Honest Whigs." *WMQ,* 3d ser., 23 (1966): 210–233.

Crary, Catherine S. "Guerrilla Activities of James DeLancey's Cowboys in Westchester County." In Robert A. East and Jacob Judd, eds., *The Loyalist Americans: A Focus on Greater New York.* Tarrytown, N.Y., 1975.

————. *The Price of Loyalty.* New York, 1973.

Creighton, Donald. *Dominion of the North: A History of Canada.* Boston, 1944.

Croghan, George. *George Croghan's Journal of His Trip to Detroit in 1767.* Edited by Howard H. Peckham. Ann Arbor, 1939.

Crout, Robert R. "The Diplomacy of Trade: The Influence of Commercial Considerations on French Involvement in the Angloamerican War of Independence, 1775–1778." Ph.D. diss., University of Georgia, 1977.

Cummings, Hubertis. *Richard Peters.* Philadelphia, 1944.

————. *Scots Breed and Susquehanna.* Pittsburgh, 1964.

Cunningham, Peter, ed. *The Letters of Horace Walpole,* 9 vols. London, 1858.

Cunningham, Timothy. *The History and Antiquities of Our Inns of Court . . .* London, 1780.

Cutler, William P., and Julia P. Cutler. *The Life, Journals, and Correspondence of Manasseh Cutler . . .* 2 vols. Cincinnati, 1888.

Danforth, George H. "The Rebel Earl." Ph.D. diss., Columbia University, 1955.

D'Anvers, Knightley. *General Abridgement of the Common Law.* 2 vols. London, 1705–1713.

Dartmouth, earls of. Papers. *See* Historical Manuscripts Commission.

Davidson, Philip. *Propaganda and the American Revolution.* Chapel Hill, N.C., 1941.

Davies, R. G., ed. *Documents of the American Revolution: Colonial Office Series, Transcripts, 1770–1783.* 21 vols. Dublin, 1972–1981.

Davies, Samuel. *The Reverend Samuel Davies Abroad: The Diary of a Journey to England and Scotland, 1753–1755.* Edited by George W. Pilcher, Urbana, Ill., 1967.

Davis, William W. *A Genealogical & Personal History of Bucks County, Pennsylvania.* New York, 1905.

DeCou, George, *Burlington: A Provincial Capital.* Philadelphia, 1945.

Defoe, Daniel. *Tour Through Great Britain.* Edited by Samuel Richardson. 2 vols. New York, 1975.

Del Papa, Eugene M. "The Royal Proclamation of 1763: Its Effect upon Virginia Land Companies." *VMHB* 83 (1975): 406–411.

De Mond, Robert O. *The Loyalists in North Carolina During the Revolution.* Durham, N.C., 1940.

dePeyster, Arent S. *Miscellanies by an Officer.* Edited by J. W. dePeyster. New York, 1888.

Dexter, F. B. *Biographical Sketches of the Graduates of Yale College.* 4 vols. New York, 1885–1919.

Diamondstone, Judith M. "Philadelphia's Municipal Corporation." *PMHB* 95 (1966): 183–201.

Dickinson, John. "A Pennsylvania Farmer at the Court of King George: John Dickinson's London Letters, 1754–1756." Edited by H. T. Colborne. *PMHB* 86 (1965): 417–453.

Dickson, R. *Ulster Emigration to Colonial America, 1718–1775.* London, 1966.

Dillon, Donald R. *The New York Triumvirate,* New York, 1949.

Dix, Morgan, ed. *A History of the Parish of Trinity Church in the City of New York.* New York, 1898.

Dodds, Harold W. *John Witherspoon.* Princeton, 1944.

Doerflinger, T. M. "Hibernia Furnace During the Revolution." *NJH* 90 (1972): 97–114.

Donoughue, Bernard. *British Politics and the American Revolution: The Path to War, 1773–1775.* London, 1964.

Donovan, A. L. *Philosophical Chemistry in the Scottish Enlightenment.* Edinburgh, 1975.

Donaldson, Gordon. *The Scottish Reformation.* Cambridge, Eng., 1960.

[Dove, David James.] *The Quaker unmask'd, or Plain Truth: Humbly address'd to the Consideration of all Freeman of Pennsylvania.* Philadelphia, 1764.

Drake, Samuel Adams. *Old Landmarks and Historic Personages of Boston.* Boston, 1876.

Drake, Samuel G. *The History and Antiquities of Boston.* Boston, 1856.

Drake, William, ed. *Letters to Benjamin Franklin from His Family and Friends, 1751–1790.* New York, 1859.

Duane, James. Papers. MSS in the New-York Historical Society, New York City.

Duer, William Alexander. *The Life of William Alexander, Earl of Stirling.* New York, 1847.

Dull, Jonathan R. "Franklin the Diplomat: The French Mission." *TAPS* 72 (1982): 1–72.

Eardley-Wilmot, John. *Historical View of the Commission for Enquiring into the Losses, Services and Claims of the American Loyalists.* 1815. Reprint: Boston, 1972.

Earle, Alice Morse. *Stage-Coach and Tavern Days.* New York, 1900.

East, Robert A., and Jacob Judd, eds. *The Loyalist Americans: A Focus on Greater New York.* Tarrytown, N.Y. 1975.

Eddis, William. *Letters from America.* Edited by Aubrey C. Land. Cambridge, Mass., 1969.

Eddy, George Simpson. "Account Book of Benjamin Franklin, kept by him during his First Mission to England as Provincial Agent, 1757–1762." PMHB 55(1931): 97–133.

Egnal, Marc. "The Changing Structure of Philadelphia's Trade with the British West Indies." *PMHB* 99(1975): 156–179.

Einstein, Lewis. *Divided Loyalties: Americans in England during the War of Independence.* London, 1933.

Eiselen, Malcolm R. *Franklin's Political Theories.* Garden City, N.Y., 1928.

Ellis, Kenneth. *The Post Office in the Eighteenth Century.* London, 1958.

Elmer, Lucius Q. C. *Reminiscences of New Jersey.* New York, 1876.

Esposito, Frank J. "Indian-White Relations in New Jersey." Ph.D. diss., Rutgers University, 1976.

Farrand, Max. *The Records of the Federal Convention of 1787.* Rev. ed. 4 vols. New Haven, 1937.

Faÿ, Bernard. *Franklin: The Apostle of Modern Times.* Boston, 1929.

Fennelly, Catherine. "Riots of 1742." *PMHB* 92 (1968): 306–319.

———. "William Franklin of New Jersey." *WMQ,* 3d ser., (1949): 362–382.

Ferguson, Adam. *An Essay on the History of Civil Society.* 1767. Edited by Duncan Forbes, Edinburgh, 1966.

Ferling, J. E. *The Loyalist Mind: Joseph Galloway and the American Revolution.* University Park, Pa., 1977.

———. *Joseph Galloway and the Philosopohy of Loyalism.* Morgantown, W. Va., 1971.

Fingerhut, Eugene P. "Uses and Abuses of the American Loyalists' Claims: A Critique of Quantitative Analysis." *WMQ,* 3d ser., 25 (1968): 245–258.

Fisher, Edgar J. *The Province of New Jersey.* New York, 1911.

Fithian, Philip Vickers. Journals. 1767–1773. MS in Princeton University Library. Princeton, N.J.

Fitzpatrick, John C., ed. *Writings of George Washington.* 38 vols. Washington, D.C., 1931–1944.

Flanagan, Vincent, and Gerald Kurland. "Stephen Kemble: New Jersey Loyalist." *NJH* 90 (1972): 5–26.

Fleming, Thomas. *The Forgotten Victory: The Battle for New Jersey, 1780.* New York, 1973.

Flexner, James Thomas. *George Washington: The Forge of Experience (1732–1775).* Boston, 1965.

———. *Mohawk Baronet: Sir William Johnson of New York.* New York, 1959.

Flick, Alexander C. *Loyalism in New York During the American Revolution.* New York, 1901.

Flower, Milton E. *John Dickinson, Conservative Revolutionary.* Charlottesville, Va., 1983.

Force, Peter, ed. *American Archives: Consisting of a Collection of Authentic Records, State Papers, Debates, and Letters . . .* Fourth ser.: Mar. 7, 1774–July 4, 1776; 6 vols. Fifth ser.: July 4, 1776–Sept. 3, 1783; 3 vols. Washington, D.C., 1837–1846 and 1848–1853. Referred to as *AA.*

Ford, Paul L. *Who Was the Mother of Benjamin Franklin's Son?* New York, 1889.

Ford, Worthington C. "Franklin's *New England Courant.*" *PMHS* 57 (1923–24): 336–353.

Fortescue, John, ed. *The Correspondence of King George the Third, from 1760 to December 1783.* 6 vols. London, 1927–28.

Fox, R. Hingston, M.D. *Dr. John Fothergill and His Friends: Chapters in Eighteenth-Century Life.* London, 1919.

Franklin, Benjamin. *The Autobiography of Benjamin Franklin.* Edited by Leonard W. Labaree. New Haven, 1965. Referred to as *ABF.*

———. *Benjamin Franklin's Letters to the Press, 1758–1775.* Edited by V. W. Crane. Chapel Hill, N.C., 1950.

———. *Benjamin Franklin's Memoirs.* Edited by Max Farrand. Parallel text ed., comprising the texts of Franklin's original manuscript, the French translation by Louis Guillaume le Veillard, the French translation published by Buisson, and the version edited by William Temple Franklin, his grandson. Berkeley, 1949.

———. *A Dissertation on Liberty and Necessity, Pleasure and Pain.* London, 1725.

[———.] "A Letter from Father Abraham to His Beloved Son." *New England Magazine* 1 (Aug. 1758): 20–28.

———. *Letters and Papers of Benjamin Franklin and Richard Jackson, 1753–1785.* Edited by Carl Van Doren. Philadelphia, 1947.

———. *The Letters of Benjamin Franklin and Jane Mecom.* Edited by Carl Van Doren. Princeton, 1950. Referred to as *Mecom.*

———. *A Narrative of the Late Massacres, in Lancaster County, of a Number of Indians, Friends of This Province . . .* Philadelphia, 1764.

——. *Observations concerning the Increase of Mankind . . .* Boston, 1755. Reprinted in *PBF,* 4:225–234.

——. *The Papers of Benjamin Franklin.* Edited by Leonard W. Labaree, William B. Willcox, and others. 23 vols to date. New Haven, 1959–83. Referred to as *PBF.*

——. *Poor Richard's Almanack.* See Bell, Whitfield, J., Jr., ed., *The Complete Poor Richard's Almanacks.*

——. Post Office Ledger. MS in APS, Philadelphia.

——. *Works.* Edited by John Bigelow. 10 vols. New York, 1887–88.

——. *The Writings of Benjamin Franklin.* Edited by Albert H. Smyth. 10 vols. New York, 1905–1907. Referred to as *WBF.*

[Franklin, Benjamin and William]. *An Historical Review of the Government and Constitution of Pennsylvania.* London, 1759. Referred to as *HR.*

Franklin, Benjamin, the Elder. "A Short Account of the Family of Thomas Franklin of Ecton in Northamptonshire." MS in the Yale University Library, New Haven, Conn.

Franklin, W. Neil. "Pennsylvania-Virginia Rivalry for the Indian Trade of the Ohio Valley." *Mississippi Valley Historical Review* 20 (1934): 463–480.

Franklin, William. Papers. MSS in the Gratz Collection, Historical Society of Pennsylvania, Philadelphia. Referred to as WFP.

——. "Reasons for Establishing a Colony in the Illinois." *Illinois Historical Collections* 11 (1916): 248–257.

——. "Schedule and Valuation of the Estate and of the Losses of William Franklin." Submitted to the Loyalist Claims Commission, London, 1787. MS AO13/109 in the PRO, London.

Franklin, William Temple, ed. *Memoirs of the Life and Writings of Benjamin Franklin . . .* 3 vols. London, 1818.

Freeman, Douglas Southall. *George Washington: A Biography.* 7 vols. New York, 1948–57.

French, Allen. *The First Year of the American Revolution.* Boston, 1934.

Frost, J. *The Art of Swimming.* New York, 1818.

Fuller, Wayne E. *The American Mail.* Chicago, 1972.

Galloway, Grace Growden. *Diary.* Edited by R. C. Werner. New York, 1971.

Galloway, Joseph. *Claims of American Loyalists Reviewed and Maintained.* London, 1788.

——. "Letters of Joseph Galloway from Leading Tories in America." *The Historical Review* 5 (1861): 271–301.

George III, King. *Correspondence.* See Fortescue, Sir John, ed.

George, Dorothy. *London Life in the Eighteenth Century.* London, 1925.

Gerlach, Larry R. *The American Revolution: New York as a Case Study.* Belmont, Calif., 1972.

——. "Anglo-American Politics in New Jersey on the Eve of the Revolution." *Huntington Library Quarterly* 39 (1976): 291–316.

——. "Customs and Contentions: John Hatton of Salem and Cohansey." *NJH* 89 (1971): 69–92.

——. "Politics and Prerogatives: The Aftermath of the Robbery of the East Jersey Treasury in 1768." *NJH* 90 (1972): 133–168.

——. "Princeton in the Coming of the American Revolution." *NJH* 92 (1974): 69–92.

——. *Prologue to Independence: New Jersey in the Coming of the American Revolution.* New Brunswick, N.J., 1976.

——. *William Franklin: New Jersey's Last Royal Governor.* Trenton, 1975.

——, ed. *New Jersey in the American Revolution: A Documentary History.* New Brunswick, N.J., 1976.

Gipson, L. H. *The American Revolution as the Aftermath of the Great War for Empire.* Bethlehem, Pa., 1950.

———. *The British Empire Before the American Revolution.* 15 vols. New York, 1966–1970.

———. *The Coming of the Revolution, 1763–1775.* New York, 1954.

Glubok, Shirley, ed. *Home and Child Life in Colonial Days.* New York, 1969.

Goebel, Julius, and T. Raymond Naughton. *Law Enforcement in Colonial New York.* New York, 1944.

Gordon, Thomas F. *The History of Pennsylvania.* Philadelphia, 1829.

Graham, H. G. *Scottish Men of Letters in the Eighteenth Century.* London, 1908.

Gratz, Simon. "Some Material for a Biography of Mrs. Elizabeth Fergusson, nee Graeme." *PMHB* 39 (1915): 257–321.

Gray, Thomas. *Works.* Edited by John Mitford. 3 vols. London, 1816.

Green. A. W. *The Inns of Court and Early English Drama.* New Haven, 1931.

Green, Ashbel. *The Life of the Rev'd. John Witherspoon . . .* New Brunswick, N.J., 1973.

Greene, Evarts. *Religion and the State.* New York, 1941.

Greene, Jack P. "The Plunge of Lemmings: A Consideration of Recent Writings on British Politics and the American Revolution." *South Atlantic Quarterly* 67 (1968): 141–175.

Habakkuk, H. "La Disparition du paysan anglais." *Annales E.C.S.* 20 (1965): 649–663.

Hale, Edward E., and Edward E. Hale, Jr. *Franklin in France.* 2 vols. Boston, 1888.

Hale, Nathaniel C. *Colonial Wars in Pennsylvania.* Wynnewood, Pa., 1971.

Hall, Alice J. "Benjamin Franklin, Philosopher of Dissent." *National Geographic 148* (1975): 93–123.

Hamilton, Alexander. *The Papers of Alexander Hamilton.* Edited by Harold C. Syrett. Vols. 1–4. New York, 1961–1962.

Hamilton, Kenneth G. *The Bethlehem Diary.* Bethlehem, Pa., 1971.

Hanna, William S. *Benjamin Franklin and Pennsylvania Politics.* Stanford, Calif., 1964.

Hancock, John. "Letters from London, 1760–1761." *PMHS* 43 (1909–10): 193–200.

Hans, Nicholas. *New Friends in Education in the Eighteenth Century.* London, 1966.

Harlan, Robert D. "William Strahan's American Book Trade, 1744–1776." *Library Quarterly* 31 (1961): 235–244.

Hart, Charles H. "Letters from William Franklin to William Strahan." *PMHB* 35 (1911): 415–462.

———. "Who Was the Mother of Franklin's Son?" *PMHB* 35 (1911): 308–314.

Haskins, George L. *Law and Authority in Early Massachusetts.* New York, 1960.

Hastings, G. *Life and Works of Francis Hopkinson.* Chicago, 1926.

Heilbron, J. L. *Electricity in the Seventeenth and Eighteenth Centuries.* San Francisco, 1979.

Heimert, Alan, and Perry Miller, eds. *The Great Awakening.* Indianapolis, 1967.

Hewins, W. A. S., ed. *The Whitefoord Papers . . .* Oxford, 1898.

Hills, George M. *History of the Church in Burlington [N.J.].* Trenton, 1876.

Hinman, Royal R. *A History . . . of . . . Connecticut During the Revolution.* Hartford, 1842.

Hindle, Brooke. "The March of the Paxton Boys." *WMQ,* 3d ser., 3 (1946): 461–486.

Historical Manuscripts Commission, The. *The Manuscripts of the Earl[s] of Dartmouth.* Eleventh Report, Part 5; Fourteenth Report, Part 10; Fifteenth Report, Part 1. 3 vols. London, 1887–96. Referred to as *Dartmouth MSS.*

Hoerder, Dirk. *Crowd Action in Revolutionary America.* New York, 1977.

Hofstadter, Richard. *American Violence.* New York, 1970.

Horowitz, Gary S. "New Jersey Land Riots, 1745–1755." Ph.D. diss., Ohio State University, 1966.

Hough, Franklin B. *History of St. Lawrence and Franklin Counties, N.Y.* Albany, 1970.

Hume, David. *Letters of David Hume.* Edited by John Y. T. Greig. 2 vols. Oxford, 1932.

Hunt, Leigh. *Autobiography.* Edited by Roger Ingpen. London, 1903.

Hunter, William A. *Forts on the Pennsylvania Frontier, 1753–1758.* Harrisburg, 1960.

Hutchinson, Thomas. *The Diary and Letters of His Excellency Thomas Hutchinson, Esq.* Edited by P. O. Hutchinson. 2 vols. London, 1883, 1886.

———. *History of the Province of Massachusetts Bay.* London, 1767.

Hutson, James H. "Benjamin Franklin and Pennsylvania Politics, 1751–1755 . . ." *PMHB* 93 (1969): 303–371.

———. "Intellectual Foundations of Early American Diplomacy." *Diplomatic History* 1 (1977): 1–19.

———. "An Investigation of the Inarticulate: Philadelphia's White Oaks." *WMQ,* 3d ser., 28 (1971): 3–25.

———. *Pennsylvania Politics, 1746–1770: The Movement for Royal Government and Its Consequences.* Princeton, 1972.

Illinois State Historical Library Collections. 34 vols. Springfield, Illinois, 1903–1959. Vols. 5, 10, 11, 16.

Indian Treaties Printed by Benjamin Franklin, 1736–1762. See Boyd, Julian, ed.

Ingpen, Roger. *Life of Samuel Johnson.* 3 vols. Oxford, 1925.

Jackson, Henry T., and James T. Adams. "Proclamation Line of 1763, Indian Cessions and the Land Companies." In *Atlas of American History.* New York, 1978. Pp. 70–71.

Jackson, John W. *The Pennsylvania Navy, 1775–1781: The Defense of the Delaware.* New Brunswick, N.J., 1974.

Jackson, Richard. *Letters and Papers.* See Franklin, Benjamin.

Jacob, Margaret. *Newtonians and the English Revolution, 1689–1720.* Ithaca, N.Y., 1976.

Jacobson, David L. "John Dickinson and Joseph Galloway." Ph.D. diss., Princeton University, 1959.

James, W. St. G. Walker. "Blacks as American Loyalists: The Slaves' War for Independence." *Historical Reflections* 2 (1975): 51–67.

Jamieson, J. Franklin. *The American Revolution as a Social Movement.* Princeton, 1926.

Jay, John. *Diary During the Peace Negotiations of 1782.* Edited by Frank Monaghan. 3 vols. New Haven, 1934.

———. *Some Conversations of Dr. Franklin and Mr. Jay . . . in Paris, 1783–1784.* New Haven, 1936.

Jeaffreson, J. C. *A Book About Lawyers.* London, 1867.

Jefferson, Thomas. *The Papers of Thomas Jefferson.* Edited by Julian P. Boyd, 20 vols. to date. Princeton, 1950–1983.

Jennings, Francis P. "The Indian Trade of the Susquehanna Valley." *PAPS* 110 (1966): 406–424.

———. *Invasion of America.* Chapel Hill, N.C., 1973.

Jensen, Arthur L. *Maritime Commerce of Colonial Philadelphia.* Madison, Wis., 1963.

Jensen, Merrill. *Tracts of the American Revolution, 1763–1776.* Indianapolis, 1967.

———. *The Founding of a Nation: A History of the American Revolution, 1763–1776.* New York, 1968.

[Johnson, William]. *Deed Executed at Fort Stanwyx, New York, November 5, 1768.* n.p., n.d. A copy is in the Princeton University Library.

Johnson, William. *Papers.* Edited by J. Sullivan and others. 13 vols. Albany, N.Y., 1921–1965.

Jones, Alice H. *Wealth Estimates for the American Middle Colonies.* Chicago, 1969.

Jones, E. Alfred. *American Members of the Inns of Court.* London, 1924.

———. *The Loyalists of New Jersey.* Newark, N.J., 1927.

Jones, E. L. *Agricultural and Economic Growth in England, 1650–1815.* New York, 1967. Introduction and ch. 7.

Jones, R. V. "Benjamin Franklin." *Notes and Records of The Royal Society, London,* 31 (1977): 201–225.

Jones, Thomas. *History of New York during the Revolutionary War.* 2 vols. New York, 1879.

Jones, Thomas Firth. *A Pair of Lawn Sleeves.* Philadelphia, 1971.

Jordan, John W. *Colonial Families of Philadelphia.* 2 vols. New York, 1911.

Kalm, Peter. *Travels in North America.* 1753–1761. Reprint: 2 vols. New York, 1937.

Kammen, Michael G. "The Colonial Agents, English Politics, and the American Revolution." *WMQ* 22 (1965): 244–268.

———. *A Rope of Sand: The Colonial Agents, British Politics and the American Revolution.* Ithaca, N.Y., 1968.

Keescy, Ruth M. *Loyalty and Reprisal: the Loyalists of Bergen County, N.J., and Their Estates.* New York, 1957.

Keith, C. P. *The Provincial Councillors of Pennsylvania.* Philadelphia, 1883.

———. "The Wife and Children of Sir William Keith." *PMHB* 56 (1932): 1–8.

Kemmerer, Donald L. *Path to Freedom: The Struggle for Self-Government in Colonial New Jersey, 1703–1776.* Princeton, 1940.

Kemp, Franklin W. *A Nest of Rebel Pirates.* Atlantic City, 1966.

Kennedy, Archibald. *The Importance of Gaining and Preserving the Friendship of the Indians to the British Interest, considered.* London, 1752.

Ketcham, Ralph L. "Conscience, War and Politics in Pennsylvania, 1755–1757." *WMQ,* 3d ser., 20 (1963): 416–439.

Ketchem, Richard M. *Winter Soldiers.* New York, 1972.

Kinnan, Peter. *Order Book Kept by Peter Kinnan, July 7–Sept. 4, 1776.* Edited by M. E. Kinnan. Princeton, 1931.

Klein, Milton. "The American Whig: William Livingston of New York." Ph.D. diss., Columbia University, 1958.

———. "Rise of the New York Bar: Legal Career of William Livingston." *WMQ,* 3d ser., 15 (1958): 334–358.

Klingelhofer, Herbert E. "Matthew Ridley's Diary During the Peace Negotiations of 1782." *WMQ,* 3d ser., 20 (1963): 95–133.

Knollenburg, Bernhard. "Bunker Hill Reviewed: A Study in the Conflict of Historical Evidence." *PMHS* 72 (1963): 84–100.

———. *Growth of the American Revolution.* New York, 1975.

———. *Origin of the American Revolution.* New York, 1960.

Knox, William. Papers. MSS in the William L. Clements Library, University of Michigan, Ann Arbor, Mich.

Koke, R. J. "War, Profit and Privateers Along the New Jersey Coast." *NYHSQ* 41 (1957): 279–337.

Konkle, Burton A. *Benjamin Chew, 1722–1810.* Philadelphia, 1932.

———. *The Life of Andrew Hamilton, 1676–1741.* Philadelphia, 1941.

Kouwenhoven, John A. *The Columbia Historical Portrait of New York: An Essay in Graphic History.* New York, 1953.

Kraybill, Richard L. *The Story of Shrewsbury, New Jersey.* Shrewsbury, 1964.

Kuntzleman, Oliver C. *Joseph Galloway, Loyalist.* Philadelphia, 1941.

Kyte, George M. "An Introduction to the Periodical Literature Bearing upon Loyalist Activities in the Middle States, 1775–1783." *PH* 18 (1951): 104–118.

———. "A Projected British Attack Upon Philadelphia in 1781." *PMHB* 76 (1952): 379–398.

———. "Some Plans for a Loyalist Stronghold in the Middle Colonies." *PH* 16 (1949): 177–190.

Labaree, Leonard W. "Benjamin Franklin and the Defense of Pennsylvania." *PH* 29 (1962): 7–28.

———. *The Boston Tea Party.* New York, 1964.

———. *Conservatism in Early American History.* Ithaca, N.Y., 1948.

———. "The Nature of American Loyalism." *Proceedings of the American Antiquarian Society* 54 (1944): 15–58.

———. *Royal Government in America.* New Haven, 1930.

Land, Aubrey C. *The Dulanys of Maryland.* Baltimore, 1955.

Lea, Henry Charles. *Studies in Church History: The Rise of the Temporal Power.* Philadelphia, 1883.

Lee, Maurice, Jr. "James VI, King of Scots." *History Today* 6 (1956): 155–164.

Leiby, Adrian C. *The Revolutionary War in the Hackensack Valley.* New Brunswick, N.J., 1962.

Lemay, J. A. Leo. *Ebenezer Kinnersley: Franklin's Friend.* Philadelphia, 1964.

———. "Franklin and the 'Autobiography': An Essay on Recent Scholarship." *Eighteenth-Century Studies: A Journal of Literature and the Arts* 1 (1967): 185–211.

Leonard, Sister Joan de Lourdes, C.S.J. "The Organization and Procedure of the Pennsylvania Assembly, 1682–1776." *PMHB* 72 (1948): 215–239.

Levering, Joseph M. *A History of Bethlehem, Pennsylvania, 1741–1892.* Bethlehem, 1903.

Lewis, George E. *The Indiana Company.* Glendale, Calif., 1941.

Livingston, William. *The Independent Reflector.* Edited by Milton Klein. Cambridge, Mass., 1963.

———. *Papers.* Edited by C. E. Prince and others. 3 vols. Trenton, 1979.

Lockard, Duane. *The New Jersey Governor.* Princeton, 1964.

Loeper, John J. *Elizabeth Graeme Fergusson of Graeme Park.* Philadelphia, 1974.

Lopez, Claude-Anne. *Mon Cher Papa: Franklin and the Ladies of Paris.* New Haven, 1966.

Lopez, Claude-Anne, and Eugenia W. Herbert. *The Private Franklin: The Man and His Family.* New York, 1975.

Loskiel, G. H. *History of the Mission of the United Brethren Among the Indians in North America.* London, 1794.

Love, William D. *Colonial History of Hartford.* Chester, Conn., 1974.

Lundin, Leonard C. *New Jersey: Cockpit of the Revolution.* Princeton, 1940.

Lynd, Staughton. "Who Should Rule at Home? Dutchess Country, New York, in the American Revolution." *WMQ*, 3d ser., 17 (1961): 330–359.

Macassey, Lynden L. *The Middle Temple's Contribution to the National Life.* London, 1930.

McBarron, H. Charles, Jr. "The American Regiment, 1740–1746." *Military Collector and Historian* 21 (1969): 84–87.

McClelland, William S. *Smuggling in the American Colonies at the Outbreak of the Revolution.* New York, 1912.

McCormick, Richard P. *Experiment in Independence: New Jersey in the Critical Period, 1781–1789.* New Brunswick, N.J., 1950.

McEvoy, John G. "Joseph Priestley: Philosopher." Ph.D. diss., University of Pittsburgh, 1976.

McHugh, Thomas F. "The Moravian Mission to the American Indian." *PH* 33 (1966): 412–431.

McKenzie, Robert T. *British Political Parties.* Melbourne, 1955.

Mackesy, Piers. *The War for America.* Cambridge, Mass., 1964.

Mackie, John D. *A History of Scotland.* London, 1964.

——. *The University of Glasgow, 1451–1951.* Glasgow, 1954.

McMillan, James. *Anatomy of Scotland.* London, 1969.

Maier, Pauline. *From Resistance to Revolution: Colonial Radicals and the Development of American Opposition to Britain, 1765–1776.* New York, 1972.

Main, Jackson Turner. *The Sovereign States, 1775–1783.* New York, 1973.

Malcolmson, R. *Popular Recreations in English Society, 1700–1850.* Cambridge, Eng., 1973.

Mariboe, William H. "The Life of William Franklin, 1730–1813." Ph.D. diss., University of Pennsylvania, 1962.

Marshall, Dorothy. *Eighteenth-Century England.* London, 1962.

Marshall, Peter. "Lord Hillsborough, Samuel Wharton and the Ohio Grant." *English Historical Review* 80 (1965): 721–722.

Mason, Thomas, Jr. "Child Abuse and Neglect." *North Carolina Law Review* 50 (1972): 293–343.

Mather, Cotton. "The Diary of Cotton Mather." Edited by C. Worthington Ford. Massachusetts Historical Society *Collections,* 7th ser., vols. 7 and 8. Boston, 1911–1912.

——. *The Diary of Cotton Mather, 1681–1724.* Edited by Worthington C. Ford. 2 vols. Boston, 1911–1912.

Mathieson, William Law. *The Awakening of Scotland: A History from 1747 to 1797.* Glasgow, 1910.

——. *Scotland and the Union: A History of Scotland from 1695 to 1747.* Glasgow, 1905.

Mauduit, Israel. *The Letters of Governor Hutchinson . . .* 2d ed. London, 1774.

Mayo, Katherine. *General Washington's Dilemma.* New York, 1938.

Mecom, Jane. Letters to Benjamin Franklin. *See* Franklin, Benjamin.

Mellick, Andrew J. *The Story of an Old Farm.* Somerville, N.J., 1889.

Metzger, C. H. *Catholics and the American Revolution.* Chicago, 1962.

——. *The Quebec Act: A Primary Cause of the American Revolution.* New York, 1936.

Middlekauff, Robert. *The Glorious Cause: The American Revolution, 1763–1789.* New York, 1982.

Miller, Perry. "Preparation for Salvation in Seventeenth-Century New England." *Journal of the History of Ideas* 4 (1943): 253–286.

Mingay, G. E. *Georgian London.* London, 1975.

Mitchell, Edwin V. *It's an Old Pennsylvania Custom.* New York, 1947.

Mittleberger, Gottlieb. *Journey to Pennsylvania.* London, 1756.

Moffitt, Louis W. *England on the Eve of the Industrial Revolution.* London, 1963.

Montgomery, Thomas H. *History of the University of Pennsylvania.* Philadelphia, 1900.

Moore, Frank. *Diary of the American Revolution from Newspapers and Original Documents.* 2 vols. New York, 1860.

Moravian Church. *Memorials of the Moravian Church.* Edited by William C. Reichel. Philadelphia, 1870.

Morgan, Edmund S. *The Puritan Family: Essays on Religion and Domestic Relations in Seventeenth-Century New England.* Boston, 1944.

——. *Visible Saints: The History of a Puritan Idea.* New York, 1963.

Morgan, Edmund S., and Helen M. Morgan. *The Stamp Act Crisis: Prologue to Revolution.* Rev. ed. New York, 1962.

Morren, N., ed. *Annals of the General Assembly of the Church of Scotland.* Edinburgh, 1838.

Morris, Margaret. *Her Journal.* John W. Jackson, ed. Philadelphia, 1949.

Morris, Richard B. *The American Revolution Reconsidered.* New York, 1967.

———. *The Peacemakers: The Great Powers and American Independence.* New York, 1965.

———, ed. *John Jay: The Winning of the Peace.* New York, 1980.

Mossner, Ernest C. *The Life of David Hume.* Austin, Tex., 1954.

Munroe, H. *The Barrister and His Inn.* London, 1966.

Murdock, David H., ed. *Rebellion in America: A Contemporary British Viewpoint.* Oxford, 1979.

Murray, James. *Letters from America, 1773 to 1780.* Edited by Eric Robson. New York, 1951.

Murtagh, William J. *Moravian Architecture and Town Planning.* Chapel Hill, N.C., 1967.

Nadelhoft, J. J. "Politics and the Judicial Tenure Fight in Colonial New Jersey." *WMQ,* 28 (1971): 52–58.

Namier, L. B. "Country Gentlemen in Parliament, 1750–1784." In *Crossroads of Power.* New York, 1963.

———. *England in the Age of the American Revolution.* London, 1950.

Nash, Gary P. *Quakers and Politics.* Princeton, 1968.

Nelson, William H. *The American Tory.* Boston, 1961.

Nevins, Allan. *American States During and After the Revolution, 1775–1789.* New York, 1924.

Newcomb, Benjamin F. *Franklin and Galloway: A Political Partnership.* New Haven, 1972.

New Jersey, State of. *Archives of the State of New Jersey.* Edited by W. A. Whitehead and others. Series 1 and 2. Newark and elsewhere, 1880–. Referred to as *NJA.*

———. *Minutes of the Provincial Congress and the Council of Safety of the State of New Jersey, 1774–1777.* Trenton, 1879. Referred to as *NJMPC.*

New York Journal; or General Advertiser. Edited by Hugh Gaine. Published Oct. 16, 1766, to Aug. 29, 1777.

Nichols, J. H. "John Witherspoon on Church and State." *Journal of Presbyterian History* 42 (1964): 166–176.

Nolan, J. Bennett. *Benjamin Franklin in Scotland and Ireland, 1759 and 1771.* Philadelphia, 1938.

———. *General Benjamin Franklin: The Military Career of a Philosopher.* Philadelphia, 1936.

Norton, Mary Beth. *The British Americans: The Loyalist Exiles in England, 1774–1789.* Boston, 1972.

Oaks, Robert F. "The Impact of British Western Policy in the Coming of the American Revolution." *PMHB* 101 (1977): 171–189.

———. "Philadelphians in Exile: The Problem of Loyalty During the American Revolution." *PMHB* 19 (1972): 298–325.

Oberholtzer, Ellis. *The Literary History of Philadelphia.* Philadelphia, 1906.

Oberholzer, Emil. *Delinquent Saints: Disciplinary Action in the Early Congregational Churches of Massachusetts.* New York, 1956.

O'Callaghan, E. B., ed. *Documents Relative to the Colonial History of the State of New York.* 14 vols. Albany, 1856–83.

Olson, Alison G. "The British Government and Colonial Union." *WMQ*, 3d ser., 17 (1960): 22–34.

———. "The Founding of Princeton University: Religion and Politics in Eighteenth-Century New Jersey." *NJH* 87 (1969): 133–150.

Olson, Richard. *Scottish Philosophy and British Physics, 1750–1880.* Princeton, 1975.

Oswald, John Clyde. *Benjamin Franklin, Printer.* New York, 1917.

Ousterhout, Anne M. "Controlling the Opposition in Pennsylvania during the American Revolution." *PMHB* 105 (1981): 3–35.

Paine, Thomas. *Common Sense.* Philadelphia, 1776.

———. Complete Writings. 2 vols. New York, 1945.

Pares, Richard. *King George III and the Politicians.* Oxford, 1952.

———. *Yankees and Creoles: The Trade between North America and the West Indies Before the American Revolution.* London, 1956.

Pargellis, Stanley M. *Lord Loudoun in North America.* New Haven, 1933.

Parton, James. *Life and Times of Benjamin Franklin.* 2 vols. New York, 1864.

Pearson, Michael. *Those Damned Rebels: The American Revolution As Seen Through British Eyes.* New York, 1972.

Peckham, H. H., ed. *Sources of American Independence.* 2 vols. Chicago, 1978.

———. *The Toll of Independence: Engagements and Battle Casualties of the American Revolution.* Chicago, 1974.

———. *The War for Independence: A Military History.* Chicago, 1958.

Pencak, William. *War, Politics and Revolution in Provincial Massachusetts.* Boston, 1981.

Penn, William. *A Letter to the Committee of the Society of Free Traders, August 16, 1683.* London, 1685.

Pennsylvania, State of. *Colonial Records.* 16 vols. Harrisburg, 1838–53. Includes *Minutes of the Provincial Council of Pennsylvania; Minutes of the Council of Safety; Minutes of the Supreme Executive Council.* Referred to as *PCR.*

———. Senate. *Votes and Proceedings of the House of Representatives* . . . Vol. 4, beginning Oct. 15, 1744. *Philadelphia, 1774.*

Pennsylvania Archives. Edited by Samuel Hazard and others. 9 series. Philadelphia and Harrisburg, 1852–1935. Referred to as *PA.*

Pennsylvania Gazette, The. 1728–1789. Reprint edition: 25 vols.: Philadelphia, 1968. Referred to as *PG.*

Pepper, William. *The Medical Side of Benjamin Franklin.* Philadelphia, 1911.

Peters, Richard. Diary. MS in the Historical Society of Pennsylvania, Philadelphia.

Pettit, Norman. *The Heart Prepared: Grace and Conversion in Puritan Spiritual Life.* New Haven, 1966.

Phillips, Hugh. *Mid-Georgian London: A Topographical and Social Survey* . . . London, 1964.

Pierce, Arthur D. *Smugglers' Woods.* New Brunswick, N.J., 1960.

Pinchbeck, Ivy, and Margaret Hewitt. *Children in English Society.* London, 1969.

Pitt, William. *Correspondence.* Edited by W. S. Taylor and J. H. Pringle, 4 vols. London, 1838–40.

Pope, Robert G. *The Halfway Covenant: Church Membership in Puritan New England.* Princeton, 1969.

Powell, Sumner C. *Puritan Village: The Formation of a New England Town.* Middletown, Conn., 1963.

Pownall, Thomas. *The Administration of the British Colonies.* 2 vols. 5th ed. London, 1774.

Prebble, John. *Glencoe: The Story of the Massacre.* London, 1966.

Prest, Wilfred R. *The Inns of Court Under Elizabeth I and the Early Stuarts, 1590–1640.* London, 1972.

Priestley, Joseph. *Autobiography*. 1806. Edited by J. Lindsay. Bath, 1970.

———. *The History and Present State of Electricity, with Original Experiments*. London, 1767.

———. *Memoirs of Dr. Joseph Priestley, to the Year 1795 . . .* London, 1806.

Princetonians: A Biographical Dictionary. Edited by James McLachlan and others. 3 vols. to date. Princeton, 1976–.

Public Characters of 1801–1802. Edited by [Sir Richard Phillips]. London, 1802.

Purvis, Thomas L. "The New Jersey Councillors, 1702–1776." In Bruce C. Daniels, ed., *Power and Status: Essays on Officeholding in the American Colonies*. Middletown, Conn., forthcoming.

———. "Origins and Patterns of Agrarian Unrest in New Jersey, 1735 to 1754." *WMQ*, 3d ser., 39 (1982): 600–627.

Quincy, Josiah. *Memoir of the Life of Josiah Quincy . . .* Boston, 1825.

Rae, John. *Life of Adam Smith*. New York, 1895.

Randall, W. S. "A Colonial Seaport." In David Boldt and W. S. Randall, eds., *The Founding City*. Philadelphia, 1976.

———. "Penn's Dream Dissolves." In David Boldt and W. S. Randall, eds., *The Founding City*. Philadelphia, 1976.

———. *The Proprietary House at Amboy*. Trenton, N.J., 1975.

———. "William Franklin: The Making of a Conservative." In Robert A. East and Jacob Judd, eds., *Loyalist Americans: A Focus on Greater New York*. Tarrytown, N.Y., 1975.

Raymond, William O., ed. *The Winslow Papers*. St. John, N.B., 1901.

Records of the Presbyterian Church in the U.S.A. Philadelphia, 1841.

Reed, Joseph. Papers. MSS in the New-York Historical Society, New York City.

Reed, William B. *Life and Correspondence of Joseph Reed . . .* 2 vols. Philadelphia, 1847.

Reichel, William C., ed. *Memorials of the Moravian Church*. Philadelphia, 1870.

Reid, H. M. B. *The Divinity Professors in the University of Glasgow, 1640–1903*. Glasgow, 1923.

Reid, John Philip. *In a Rebellious Spirit . . .* University Park, Pa., 1979.

Reubens, Beatrice G. "Pre-emptive Rights in the Disposition of a Confiscated Estate: Philipsburg Manor, New York." *WMQ*, 3d ser., 22 (1965): 435–456.

Riccards, Michael P. "Patriots and Plunderers: Confiscation of Loyalist Lands in New Jersey, 1776–1786." *NJH* 86 (1968): 14–28.

Richardson, Walter C. *A History of the Inns of Court*. Baton Rouge, La., 1972.

Ricord, Frederick W., and William Nelson, eds. *Documents Relating to the Colonial History of the State of New Jersey*. Newark, N.J., 1886.

Riley, Edward M. "Franklin's Home." In *Historic Philadelphia . . .* Issued as pt. 1, *TAPS* 43 (1953): 148–160.

Rivington's New York Gazette. 1773–1783.

Roach, Hannah B. "Benjamin Franklin Slept Here." *PMHB* 84 (1960): 127–174.

Roelker, William Greene, ed. *Benjamin Franklin and Catharine Ray Greene: Their Correspondence, 1755–1790*. Philadelphia, 1949.

Rosenberg, Leonard B. "William Paterson: New Jersey's Nation-Maker." *NJH* 85 (1967): 7–40.

Rosengarten, J. G. "Franklin in Germany." *Lippincott's Monthly Magazine* 71 (1903): 128–134.

Rossiter, Clinton. *Seedtime of the Republic*. New York, 1953.

Rothermund, Dietmar. "The German Problem of Colonial Pennsylvania." *PMHB* 84 (1960): 3–21.

Royster, Charles. *A Revolutionary People at War: the Continental Army and American Character, 1775–1783.* Chapel Hill, 1979.

Rudé, George. "The Gordon Riots: A Study of the Rioters and Their Victims." *Royal Historical Society Transactions,* 5th ser., 6 (1956): 93–114.

Russell, Carl P. *Guns on the Early Frontier.* Berkeley, Calif., 1962.

Rutt, John T. *Life and Correspondence of Joseph Priestley, LL.D., F.R.S.* 2 vols. London, 1831–32.

Ryan, Dennis P. *New Jersey's Loyalists.* Trenton, 1975.

Ryerson, Egerton. *The Loyalists of America and Their Times.* 2 vols. Toronto, 1880.

Ryerson, Richard A. *The Revolution Is Now Begun.* Philadelphia, 1978.

Sabine, Lorenzo. *Biographical Sketches of the Loyalists of the American Revolution.* 2 vols. Boston, 1864.

Sabine, William H. W. *Historical Memoirs from 26 August 1778 to 12 November 1783 of William Smith.* New York, 1971.

Sachse, Julius F. *Benjamin Franklin as a Freemason.* Philadelphia, 1906.

———. "Roster of the Lodge of Free Masons Which Met at Tun Tavern." *PMHB* 20 (1896): 116–121.

Sachse, William. *Colonial Americans in Britain.* Madison, Wis., 1956.

Salter, Edwin. *History of Monmouth and Ocean Counties.* Bayonne, N.J., 1890.

Salter, Edwin, and George C. Beekman. *Old Times in Old Monmouth: Historical Reminiscences of Old Monmouth County.* Freehold, N.J., 1887.

Schaarf, John T., and Thompson Westcott. *History of Philadelphia.* 3 vols. Philadelphia, 1884.

Schermerhorn, William E. *The History of Burlington, New Jersey.* Burlington, 1927.

Schlesinger, Arthur M., Sr. *Colonial Merchants and the American Revolution, 1763–1776.* New York, 1918.

Schlesinger, Arthur M., Jr. *Prelude to Independence: The Newspaper War on Britain, 1764–1776.* New York, 1958.

Schoenbrun, David. *Triumph in Paris: The Exploits of Benjamin Franklin.* New York, 1976.

Schonbach, Morris. *Radicals and Visionaries: A History of Dissent in New Jersey.* Princeton, 1964.

Scott, Kenneth. "The Tory Associators of Portsmouth," *WMQ,* 3d ser., 17 (1960): 507–515.

———, ed. *Rivington's New York Newspaper: Excerpts from a Loyalist Press, 1773–1783.* New York, 1973.

Seagle, William. *Men of Law from Hammurabi to Holmes.* New York, 1948.

See, Geoffrey. "A British Spy in Philadelphia, 1775–1777." *PMHB* 85 (1961): 3–37.

Sellers, Charles C. *Benjamin Franklin in Portraiture.* New Haven, 1962.

Serjeantson, R. M., and W. R. D. Adkins, eds. *Victorian History of the County of Northampton. London,* 1902.

Serle, Ambrose. *The American Journal of Ambrose Serle, 1776–1778.* Edited by E. H. Tatum, Jr. San Marino, Calif., 1940.

Seybolt, Robert F. *The Town Officials of Colonial Boston.* Cambridge, Mass., 1939.

Sharpless, Isaac. *A Quaker Experiment in Government.* Philadelphia, 1898.

Sheer, George F., and Hugh F. Rankin. *Rebels and Redcoats.* Cleveland, 1957.

Shepard, William R. *History of Proprietary Government in Pennsylvania.* New York, 1896.

Shurtleff, Nathaniel B. *A Topographical and Historical Description of Boston.* Boston, 1871.

Shy, John. "A New Look at Colonial Militia." *WMQ,* 3d ser., 20 (1963): 175–185.

————. *A People Numerous and Armed.* New York, 1976.

————. "Quartering His Majesty's Forces in New Jersey." *PNJHS* 78 (Apr., 1960): 82–94.

Sibley, J. L. *Biographical Sketches of the Graduates of Harvard College.* 17 vols. Cambridge, Mass., 1881–1975.

Siebert, Wilbur H. *Loyalists in East Florida, 1774–1785.* DeLand, Fla., 1929.

Simcoe, John Graves. *Military Journal.* New York, 1844.

Simon, Grant Miles. "Houses and Early Life in Philadelphia." *TAPS* 43 (1953): 280–288.

Sims, J. P., ed. *The Philadelphia Assemblies, 1748–1948.* Philadelphia, 1948.

Singer, Dorothea W. "Sir John Pringle and His Circle." *Annals of Science* 6 (1949–50): 127–180.

Slick, Sewell E. *William Trent and the West.* Harrisburg, 1947.

Sloan, David A. " 'A Time of Sifting and Winnowing': The Paxton Riots and Quaker Non-Violence in Pennsylvania." *Quaker History* 66 (1977): 3–22.

Sloan, Douglas. *The Scottish Enlightenment and the American College Ideal.* New York, 1971.

Smith, Adam. *Theory of Moral Sentiments.* London, 1759.

Smith, Edward Owen, Jr. *Thomas Penn, Chief Proprietor of Pennsylvania: A Study of His Public Governmental Activities from 1763 to 1775.* Bethlehem, Pa., 1966.

Smith, Matthew. "Narrative of Matthew Smith . . ." *Lancaster* (Pa.) *Intelligencer and Journal,* May 16, 1843.

Smith, Paul H. "The American Loyalists: Notes on Their Organization and Numerical Strength." *WMQ,* 3d ser., 25 (1968): 259–277.

————. *Loyalists and Redcoats: A Study in British Revolutionary Policy.* Chapel Hill, N.C., 1964.

————. "New Jersey Loyalists and the British 'Provincial' Corps in the War for Independence." *NJH* 87 (1969): 69–78.

Smith, Paul H., and others, eds. *Letters of Delegates to Congress.* 9 vols. to date. Washington, D.C., 1976–. Referred to as *LDC.*

Smith, Rev. William. "Account of the College and Academy of Philadelphia." *The American Magazine . . .* 1 (Oct., 1757, to Oct., 1758), and supplement (Oct., 1758): 630–640.

[————.] *A Brief State of the Province of Pennsylvania.* London, 1755.

Smith, William [chief justice of the province of N.Y.] *Historical Memoirs from 12 July 1776 to 25 July 1778.* Edited by W. H. W. Sabine. New York, 1958.

————. *Historical Memoirs of William Smith, 1778–1783.* Edited by W. H. W. Sabine. New York, 1971.

Smith, William. "The Colonial Post Office." *American Historical Review* 21 (1915): 258–275.

Smout, T. Christopher. *A History of the Scottish People, 1560–1830.* Glasgow, 1977.

Sosin, Jack M. *Agents and Merchants: British Colonial Policy and the Origins of the American Revolution, 1763–1775.* Lincoln, Neb., 1965.

————. *The Revolutionary Frontier, 1763–1783.* New York, 1967.

————. *Whitehall and the Wilderness: The Middle West in British Colonial Policy, 1760–1775.* Lincoln, Neb., 1961.

Sprague, William B., ed. *Annals of the American Pulpit.* 9 vols. Philadelphia, 1858.

Starbuck, Alexander. *History of Nantucket.* 2 vols. Boston, 1924.

Stearns, Raymond P. *Science in the British Colonies.* Chicago, 1972.

Stephen, Leslie. *History of English Thought in the Eighteenth Century.* New York, 1876.

Steumph, Vernon. "Who Was Elizabeth Downes Franklin?" *PMHB* 94 (1970): 533–534.

Stevens, Benjamin F., ed. *Facsimiles of Manuscripts in European Archives Relating to America, 1773-1783* . . . 25 vols. London, 1889-1898.

Stewart, Gordon, and George Rawlyk. *A People Highly Favoured of God.* Toronto, 1972.

Stone, Lawrence. "Literacy and Education in England, 1640-1900." *Past and Present* 42 (1969): 69-139.

Stourzh, Gerald. *Benjamin Franklin and American Foreign Policy.* Chicago, 1954.

Strahan, William. "Correspondence between William Strahan and David Hall, 1763-1777." *PMHB* 10 (1886) and 11 (1887).

Stryker, William S. *Capture of the Block House at Tom's River.* Trenton, 1883.

———. *The New Jersey Volunteers.* Trenton, 1887.

Swanson, Neil H. *The First Rebel.* New York, 1937.

Tebbenhoff, Edward H. "The Associated Loyalists: An Aspect of Militant Loyalism." *NYHSQ* 63 (1979): 115-144.

Tesser, Charles H., ed. *The Sinews of Independence: Monthly Strength Reports of the Continental Army.* Chicago, 1976.

Thayer, Theodore. *As We Were: The Story of Old Elizabethtown.* Elizabethtown, N.J., 1964.

———. *Israel Pemberton, King of the Quakers.* Philadelphia,1943.

———. *Pennsylvania Politics and the Growth of Democracy, 1740-1770.* Harrisburg, 1953.

Thomas, Isaiah. *The History of Printing in America* . . . 2d ed. 2 vols. Albany, 1874.

Thompson, Kay. *The Walking Purchase Hoax of 1737.* Philadelphia, 1973.

[Thompson, William]. *A Tour in England and Scotland in 1785.* London, 1788.

Thomson, John. *An Account of the Life, Lectures, and Writings of William Cullen* . . . 2 vols. Edinburgh, 1859.

Thwaites, Reuben G. *Early Western Journals.* 22 vols. Cleveland, 1904-1912.

Thwing, Annie H. *The Crooked and Narrow Streets of the Town of Boston, 1630-1882.* Boston, 1920.

Tolles, Frederick B. "Benjamin Franklin's Business Mentors: The Philadelphia Quaker Merchants." *WMQ*, 3d ser., 2 (1945): 60-69.

———, ed. "The Twilight of the Holy Experiment: A Contemporary View." *Journal of the Friends Historical Society* 48 (1956): 30-37.

Tourtellot, A. B. *Benjamin Franklin: The Shaping of Genius.* Vol. 1: *The Boston Years.* New York, 1977.

Trevelyan, George O. M. *The American Revolution.* 6 vols. London, 1895.

Trinterud, Leonard J. *The Forming of an American Tradition: A Reexamination of Colonial Presbyterianism.* Philadelphia, 1949.

Trumbull, Jonathan. Letter Books, 1775-1779. MSS in the Library of Congress, Washington, D.C.

———. *The Trumbull Papers.* Massachusetts Historical Society Collections, ser. 5, vols. 9 and 10; ser. 7, vols. 2 and 3. Boston, 1885-1902.

Trumbull, Jonathan, ed. *The Lebanon War Office.* Hartford, Conn., 1891.

Tully, Alan. *William Penn's Legacy: Politics and Social Structure in Provincial Pennsylvania, 1726-1755.* Baltimore, 1978.

Turberville, A. S. *Johnson's England: An Account of the Life and Manners of His Age.* 2 vols. Oxford, 1940.

Turner, G. B. "Colonial New Jersey, 1703-1763." *PNJHS* 70 (1952): 229-245.

Turner, M. *English Parliamentary Enclosures.* London, 1980.

Upton, L. F. S. *The Loyal Whig: William Smith of New York and Quebec.* Toronto, 1969.

Valentine, Alan. *The British Establishment.* 2 vols. Norman, Okla., 1970.
―――. *Lord North.* 2 vols. Norman, Okla., 1967.
―――. *Lord Stirling.* New York, 1969.
Van Closen, Ludwig. *The Revolutionary Journal of Ludwig Van Closen.* Translated by Evelyn M. Acomb. Chapel Hill, N.C., 1958.
Van Doren, Carl. *Benjamin Franklin.* New York, 1938.
―――. *Secret History of the American Revolution.* New York, 1941.
Van Tyne, Claude H. *The Loyalists in the American Revolution.* New York, 1902.

Wainwright, Nicholas D. *George Croghan, Wilderness Diplomat.* Chapel Hill, N.C., 1959.
Walker, James W. *The Black Loyalists.* Dalhousie, N.S., 1976.
―――. "Blacks as American Loyalists: The Slaves' War for Independence." *Historical Reflections* 2 (1975): 51–67.
Wallace, Anthony F. C. *King of the Delawares: Teedyuscung.* Philadelphia, 1949.
Wallace, Paul A. W. *Conrad Weiser, 1696–1760: Friend of Colonist and Mohawk.* Philadelphia, 1945.
Walpole, Horace. *The Last Journals of Horace Walpole . . .* Edited by A. F. Steuart. 2 vols. London, 1858.
Ward, Christopher. *The War of the Revolution.* 2 vols. New York, 1952.
Warden, G. B. "The Proprietary Group in Pennsylvania, 1754–1764." *WMQ,* 3d ser., 21 (1964): 367–389.
Washington, George. *Writings.* Edited by J. C. Fitzpatrick. 38 vols. Washington, D.C., 1931–44.
Watson, Elkanah. *Men and Times of the Revolution; or, Memoirs of Elkanah Watson.* Edited by W. C. Watson. New York, 1856.
Watson, John Fanning. *Annals of Philadelphia and Pennsylvania in the Olden Time . . .* 2 vols. Philadelphia, 1844.
Weaver, Glenn. "Benjamin Franklin and the Pennsylvania Germans." *The Social Studies* 46 (1955): 227–235.
Webb, Samuel B. *Correspondence and Journals.* Edited by Worthington C. Ford. 3 vols. New York, 1893–94.
Webb, Sidney, and Beatrice Webb. *The King's Highway.* London, 1913.
Webster, Eleanor B. "Insurrection at Fort Loudoun in 1765: Rebellion or Preservation of Peace?" *PH* 47 (1964): 125–139.
Wedgwood, Josiah. *Selected Letters of Josiah Wedgwood . . .* Edited by Ann Finer and George Savage. 2 vols. London, 1965.
Weiner, Frederick B. *Civilians Under Military Justice.* Chicago, 1967.
Weiss, Harry B., and Grace M. Weiss. *Some Legislation Affecting Rural Life in Colonial New Jersey.* Trenton, 1957.
Wertenbaker, Thomas J. *Father Knickerbocker Rebels.* New York, 1946.
Weslager, Charles A. *The Delaware Indians.* New Brunswick, N.J., 1972.
Wharton, Francis, ed. *The Revolutionary Diplomatic Correspondence of the United States.* Vol. 5. Washington, D.C., 1889.
Wharton, Thomas. Letter Book, 1773–1784. MS in the Wharton Papers, Historical Society of Pennsylvania, Philadelphia.
Wheatley, Henry B. *London Past and Present.* 3 vols. London, 1891.
Whitehead, William A. "Biographical Sketch of Governor William Franklin." *PNJHS* 3 (1849): 137–159.
―――. *Contributions to the Early History of Perth Amboy.* New York, 1856.
Wickwire, Franklin B. *British Subministers and Colonial America, 1763–1783.* Princeton, 1966.
Wigmore, John H. *A Treatise on the Anglo-American System of Evidence.* Boston, 1940.

Willcox, William B. *Portrait of a General: Sir Henry Clinton in the War of Independence.* New York, 1964.

———, ed. *The American Rebellion: Sir Henry Clinton's Narrative of His Campaigns, 1775–1782.* New Haven, 1954.

Willis, William. "Doctor Franklin, Charles Thompson and Mrs. Logan." *The Historical Magazine . . . ,* 2d ser., 4 (1868): 280–282.

[Witherspoon, John]. "The Druid." *Pennsylvania Magazine* (May, 1776).

Witherspoon, John. *Works.* 9 vols. Edinburgh, 1804.

Woodward, Carl Raymond. *Ploughs and Politicks: Charles Read of New Jersey and His Notes on Agriculture, 1715–1774.* New Brunswick, N.J., 1941.

Woody, Thomas. *Educational Views of Benjamin Franklin.* New York, 1931.

Wright, Esmond. *Benjamin Franklin and American Independence.* London, 1966.

Wright, Esther C. *The Loyalists of New Brunswick.* Moncton, N.B., 1972.

Wykoff, George S., ed. "Peter Collinson's Letter concerning Franklin's 'Vindication': Notes and Documents — II." *PMHB* 66 (1942): 99–105.

Young, Henry J. "The Treatment of Loyalists in Pennsylvania." Ph.D. diss., Johns Hopkins University, 1955.

Yates, W. Ross, ed. *Bethlehem of Pennsylvania: The First One Hundred Years.* Bethlehem, 1965.

Young, Chester Raymond. "The Evolution of the Pennsylvania Assembly." *PH* 25 (1958): 147–168.

Zimmerman, John J. "Benjamin Franklin and the Quaker Party." *WMQ,* 3d ser., 25 (1968): 291–313.

Zobel, Hiller. *The Boston Massacre.* New York, 1971.

INDEX

Academy of Philadelphia. *See* Philadelphia Academy for the Education of Youth

Adams, John: quoted on WF as governor of N.J., 183; and the Hutchinson letters, 259; on John Witherspoon, 402; negotiates with Lord Howe, 433

Adams, Samuel, 291, 292; distrusts BF, 310–311, 312; at Burlington, 377

Albany Plan of Union (1754), 18, 97, 293–294, 356, 362

Allen, Ethan: seizes Ft. Ticonderoga, 324

Allen, William (chief justice of Pa.): BF's mentor, 66; opposes BF, 106, 112

Anglicans: and BF, 89; WF supports, 102, 207, 402; in East Jersey, 289; beset by Presbyterian mobs, 311; priests flee, 311, 394; Witherspoon opposes, 401–402; missionaries, 402; aid Loyalists in prison, 439

Arnold, Benedict: seizes Ft. Ticonderoga, 324; invades Canada, 348; is attacked from Canada, 440

Asgill, Charles: in Huddy affair, 478

Assembly, the Philadelphia (dancing), 102–105

Association, the (Pa. militia): and Indian raids, 72–74, 87, 91; attacked at Gnadenhütten, 87; Presbyterian makeup, 91

Bache, Richard (BF's son-in-law): WF disapproves of, as husband for SF, 202, 203, 492; BF's advice to, 203, 244; as Continental postal official, 366; mentor of WTF, 396, 397; and WF's treatment in prison, 458, 459; disposes of BF's property, 492; tours England and Scotland with WF, 493

Bache, Sarah (Sally) Franklin (BF's daughter): birth, 51; and WF, 53, 186, 198, 451, 495; portrait by Benjamin West, 76; BF's treatment of, 132, 172, 187, 199–200, 202–204, 490; travels with BF, 186–187; described, 187, 313, 490; quoted, 199; marries R. Bache, 202–204; nurses BF, 313; friendship with EDF, 395–396; dies, 496

Beatty, Rev. Charles, 92, 96

Bentham, Jeremy; attends Cockpit hearing with BF, 269

Bethlehem, Pa., 3, 77–78, 99; BF's defense of, 89–92

Blackstone, Sir William, 262; quoted, 127

Boston, Mass.: mobs in, 253–254, 256, 257, 258, 261 (*see also* Boston Tea Party); radicals of, 255, 256–257, 262; British occupation of, 256, 399. *See also* Boston Massacre; Declaration of the Boston town meeting

Boston Massacre, 236–237

Boston Port Act, 292–293

Boston Tea Party, 267–268, 282, 312; WF's and BF's views on, 285–286

Boudinot, Elias: rebuts WF, 299; opposes Witherspoon, 405; urges neutrality, 409; and WF's release, 458

Braddock, Edward, 3, 8, 66

Breed's Hill, battle of, 341–346

British army: in Boston, 235–237, 300, 399; invades New Jersey, 441–443; captures Philadelphia, 457; evacuates New York, 484

Bullman, John: defies radicals in Charleston, 311

Bunker Hill, battle of. *See* Breed's Hill

Burke, Edmund: attends Cockpit hearing with BF, 270

Burlington, N.J.: provincial capital, 191, 275, 279, 370; WF builds house in, 191; last royal Assembly at, 370–381; provincial congress in, 409–411, 417–420; WF arraigned in, 417–423

Burr, Aaron, 400; confers with WF in London, 495

Bute, Lord: and George III, 140–143; appoints WF governor, 178–180, 182; BF and, 185

Canada: Quebec Act, 291–292; invasion from feared, 325, 396, 440; BF demands in Paris talks, 481; Loyalists land in Nova Scotia, 484

Carlyle, Alexander, 143; meets the Franklins, 156; on foreign policy, 156; on rift between BF and WF, 158; describes Elphinstone Academy, 316

Catholicism. *See* Roman Catholicism

Chandler, Rev. Thomas Bradbury: writes *What Think Ye of Congress Now?*, 311; flees America, 311

Chatham, Lord (William Pitt): negotiates with BF, 330–334. *See also* Pitt, William

Christ Church, Philadelphia, 15, 73, 102

Clinton, Sir Henry: as British commander, 464–479; criticism of, 467, 474; WF and, 474–479

Common Sense (Paine), 394–395, 397, 399

Continental Congress, First, 293–308; delegates appointed, 293; Franklin-Galloway Plan of Union defeated, 295; endorses ban on imports, 296; draws up list of grievances, 300

Continental Congress, Second, 309–312; makeup, 312; secrecy of proceedings, 323; votes on independence, 407; orders WF jailed, 421–422; policy on Loyalist prisoners, 426; and the Huddy affair, 478

Coxe, Daniel: councillor to WF, 351; and the Huddy affair, 471–473

Connecticut: prisons for Loyalists in, 411, 426; WF held in, 412, 422, 436–460; is one-fourth Loyalist, 439

Croghan, George, 205, 208, 358; WF's partner in Illinois scheme, 208; defaults, 223; WF's partner in New York lands, 225

Dartmouth, Lord: appointed colonial secretary, 247; receives petition of Mass. assembly, 258–259; BF presents Boston declaration, 264; letters to WF, 282, 284–285, 349, 352, 365, 366; letters from WF to, 248, 282–283, 283–284, 295, 296, 300, 302, 347, 349, 350; orders radicals arrested, 303–304

Deane, Silas, 324, 326

Declaration of the Boston town meeting, 259–261, 264–265

Declaratory Act of 1766, 265; and Parliamentary authority, 233–234; Lord Mansfield on, 265

Delaware Indians: raids, 7–9; and Walking Purchases, 10–11, 79; and Lehigh Valley, 11

Denny, Francis (deputy governor of Pa.): offers BF bribe, 111–112; scorned by the Indians, 114

Dickinson, John: author of *The Farmer's Letters*, 233; drafts Olive Branch Petition, 324; in the Continental Congress, 325; addresses N.J. Assembly, 377–379

Downes, Elizabeth. *See* Franklin, Elizabeth Downes

Dunning, John (BF's attorney): defends BF at the Cockpit, 269; his parliamentary resolution to curb royal power, 476–477

Easton, Pa.: Indians attack, 75; fortified, 79–80; peace talks at, 115

Ecton, Northamptonshire, 25–27, 131

Edinburgh, 151–152, 155–156, 162–163

Ferguson, Adam (Scottish soldier and philosopher), 156, 464

Ft. Allen, construction of, 94–95

Ft. Duquesne, 3, 8, 85

Ft. Stanwyx: Six Nations cede land to WF and partners at, 221–222

Ft. Ticonderoga, seized, 324

Franklin, Abiah Folger (BF's mother), 24, 29, 31

Franklin, Benjamin:

PERSONAL LIFE

Appearance, 4, 130, 315; ancestry, 25–30; parents (*see* Franklin, Abiah, and Franklin, Josiah); childhood, 31–36; religious beliefs, 24, 102; education, 33–34, 36–37, 49; apprenticeship, 36–38; youthful amours, 41–45; courts and marries Deborah Read, 40–45; marital fidelity questioned, 172; travels in England and Scotland, 121–165 *passim;* in Europe, 175–176, 200; as clubman, 130–131, 252; in old age, 490–492; disinherits WF, 492

BUSINESS CAREER

Printer in Philadelphia, 40, 42–43; printer in London, 41; founds *Pennsylvania Gazette*, 42; publishes *Poor Richard's Almanack*, 47, 59; his retirement, 59

PUBLIC CAREER

Enters politics, 5; as Pa. assemblyman and defense commissioner, 8, 21, 23, 64, 72–99, 190; appointed deputy postmaster general for North America, 64; commands militia against French and Indians, 4, 88–91, 94–96, 112; ousts Gov. Morris, 100–101; as Pa. Assembly agent to England, 114, 190; lobbying tour through England and Scotland, 121–165 *passim;* as Mass. agent, 229–232, 256–274; as N.J. agent, 240, 300, 307; as Ga. agent, 307; arranges theft of Hutchinson letters, 257–259; his humiliation at the Cockpit, 267–273; dismissed as deputy postmaster general, 274; talks with Lord North's emissaries, 330–335; in the Second Continental Congress, 309–310, 354; drafts Articles of Confederation, 356; mission to Canada, 396–399; and WF's arrest and imprisonment, 412–414, 422, 441; minister to France, 453–456; and the Paris peace talks, 480–484;

chairman, Pa. Executive Council, 491

SCIENTIFIC WORK AND HONORS

Inventor of Franklin stove, 50; electrical experiments, 59–63; elected to the Royal Society, 111–112; honorary degrees, 145, 161–162, 178; controversy over lightning rods, 145, 237–238; designs chevaux-de-frise, 355–356

OPINIONS

On Indian warfare, 8; on Pa. Germans, 17, 189; on the Quakers, 18–19, 111; on Gov. Morris, 19; of his electrical experiments, 61; on thrift, 45–46, 202–203; on lawyers, 64–65; on liberty, 137; on disputation, 157; on his daughter's wedding, 202; on the King's right to own America, 262; on the authority of Parliament, 280–281

LETTERS

To DRF, 91, 96, 116–117, 123, 132, 149, 172, 200, 201, 202–203; to Catherine Ray Greene, 115, 454; to Joseph Galloway, 138, 247; to Mary Hewson, 175, 181; to William Strahan, 180, 345; to Jane Mecom, 183; to Richard Jackson, 196; to WF, 214, 215, 216, 219, 220–221, 233–234, 237, 243, 244–245, 247, 248, 253, 261, 262, 263, 265, 274, 275, 280, 283, 285, 286, 305, 309, 486; to Sir William Johnson, 215; to Thomas Cushing, 229–232; to SFB, 244; to Joseph Priestley, 354; to George Washington, 412–413; to EDF, 431; to WTF, 431–432, 433–434, 487

Franklin, Deborah Read (BF's wife): letters to, 91, 96–97; common-law marriage to BF, 6, 43–45, 72–73, 84, 96; assists him in business, 45–46; relations with WF, 65, 96–97; refuses to cross ocean, 185–186; melancholy, 200–202; BF berates, 201; and SFB's wedding, 202; dies, 287

Franklin, Elizabeth Downes (WF's wife): WF courts, 173–175; BF visits, 181; first lady of N.J., 192; refuses to leave Perth Amboy, 349; ill, 388; writes SFB, 396; and WF's arrest, 416; BF helps, 429; writes Washington, 430; dies, 446–449

Franklin, Ellen (WTF's illegitimate daughter): WF brings up, 494–495; WF leaves estate to, 497

Franklin, Francis Folger (BF's legitimate son), 47, 51

Franklin, Jane (BF's sister). See Mecom, Jane Franklin

Franklin, Josiah (BF's father), 24–39 passim

Franklin, Sarah (BF's daughter). See Bache, Sarah Franklin

Franklin, William (BF's illegitimate son):

PERSONAL LIFE

Appearance, 5, 129, 450, 464, 496; birth and parentage, 43–45; early schooling and legal studies in Philadelphia, 20–21, 51; joins Masons, 59; studies law at the Inns of Court, 64, 124–129; courtship of Elizabeth Graeme, 104–114, 138–140; named BF's heir and executor, 114; travels with BF, 123, 132–165, 175–176; admitted to the bar, 129; marries Elizabeth Downes, 181–182; builds house in Burlington, 191; acquires Franklin Park, 223–224; debts to BF, 224, 243; buys N.Y. lands, 248–249; moves to Perth Amboy, 275, 279–280; meets BF for last time, 488; dies, 496–498

MILITARY CAREER

Captain in Canada expedition, 54–56; on expedition to the Ohio, 56–59; aide-de-camp to BF, 3–6, 68, 88, 91–92; organizes defense of Easton, 80, of Bethlehem, 90–91; leads march to Gnadenhütten, 92; builds frontier forts, 95–96

SCIENTIFIC WORK

Assists BF in electrical experiments, 61–63, 178; physical courage in experiments, 62; independent observations, 63; awarded honorary degree from Oxford, 63, 178

PUBLIC CAREER

Pa. Assembly clerk, 5, 19, 20; Philadelphia postmaster, 5, 20, 64; comptroller of post office, 64; secretary to Pa. defense commission, 68; BF's assistant in England, 114; royal governor of N.J., 177–184; Indians name him "Dispenser of Justice," 191; relations with N.J. Assembly, 194, 241, 276–277, 291, 297, 299–300, 317–319, 370–379; as royal governor, 207–208, 238–242, 410, 427; Illinois land scheme, 211–213; and Lord Hillsborough, 238–242; argues North Plan with BF, 335–340; imprisoned in Connecticut, 436–461; exchanged as prisoner, 440–441, 443, 452–453, 456–460; and parole violations, 442–445; organizes Loyalists in N.Y., 462–468; exile in England, 479–480; Loyalist lobbyist, 480–483

LETTERS

To Elizabeth Graeme, 116, 138–140; to BF, 131–132, 200, 202, 214, 241, 242, 243, 249, 254, 265, 276, 280, 281, 285, 287–288, 353, 356–358, 485–486; to Joseph Galloway, 138, 179, 317, 462, 466; to SFB, 175–176, 479–480; to William Strahan, 182, 186, 239–240, 281; to Francis Hopkinson, 194; to Lord Hillsborough, 238–239, 240; to Lord Dartmouth, 282–283, 283–284, 293, 295, 296, 300, 302–307, 347, 349, 350, 364, 369–370; to Lord Germain, 380–382, 389, 390, 462, 476; to Lord Stirling, 389; to WTF, 395, 396, 422; to EDF, 435, 436, 440; to Jonathan Trumbull, 436, 452; to Jonathan Williams, 494–495, 497

OTHER WRITINGS

Tit for Tat, 68; "Mild Advice for a Certain Parson," 109; his defense of Quakers in the London Citizen, 137; An Historical Review of the Consti-

tution and Government of Pennsylvania (with BF and R. Jackson), 137–138; "Reasons for Establishing a Colony in the Illinois," 212–213; "Regulation of Refugees," 467

Franklin, William Temple (WF's illegitimate son): mother unknown, 169–170; WF's support of, 170, 208, 224; comes to America, 308; visits Perth Amboy, 315, 397, 428–429; education, 315–317; writes WF, 395–396, 422; writes BF, 433; leaves for France with BF, 435; writes SFB, 454; visits WF in London, 487; hates Philadelphia, 492; lives with WF in London, 494; illegitimate daughter, 494; WF disinherits, 494; WF leaves Illinois claim to, 497–498

Freemasonry in Philadelphia, 59. *See also* Masons

French and Indian War (1754–1760), 11. *See also* Braddock, Edward; Gnadenhütten; Indians; Walking Purchases

Gage, Thomas: sent to arrest radicals, 303–304; ignores Privy Council, 304; WF writes, 347

Galloway, Grace Growden (Mrs. Joseph), 327

Galloway, Joseph, 314, 463; WF visits often, 192; in land scheme, 210; his Plan of Union, 293–294; resigns from the Congress, 295; and the Presbyterians, 314; confers with BF and WF at Trevose, 326, 327–340; helps EDF, 446–451; Loyalist spokesman in England, 462, 480, 481

George II, 113, 140, 143, 166

George III: under the tutelage of Lord Bute, 127, 140–143, 167; appoints WF royal governor of N.J., 179–180, 182, 479; his cabinet changes, 215–216, 221, 232; his hatred of republicanism, 233, 254–255; WF's loyalty to, 241, 283, 323, 349, 390; and Lord Hillsborough, 245–246, 247; and Locke's theory of a social contract between king and subject, 259–260; and royal prerogatives, 260, 313, 319–320, 476–477; BF criticizes, 261; WF petitions for estab-

lishment of a colonial congress, 284, 377, 378; resolves to crush American rebellion, 352, 353, 381–382; WF criticizes policy of, 364; reads WF's letter to Dartmouth, 370; approves N.J. currency, 374, 375, 379: as viewed by T. Paine, 394; called a tyrant by Witherspoon, 402; approves creation of Board of Associated Loyalists, 468; British opposition to his war policies, 476; move to restrict his power, 476–477; concedes defeat in America, 477

Germain, Lord George, 374, 380–382, 389, 390, 462, 468

Germans of Pa.: march on Philadelphia, 15–18, 22–23; customs, 16; political power, 17; prejudice against, 17. *See also* Moravians

Gibbon, Edward: quoted on the American Revolution, 476

Gnadenhütten (Moravian mission): first massacre at, 12–15, 68; killed at (Gottlieb Anders, Johanna Anders, George Fabricius, John Gattermeyer, Martin Kiefer, Martin Nitschmann, Susanna Nitschmann, Martin Presser, George Schweigert, Anna Sensemann), 14–15; survivors of (John Mack, Susanna Partsch, Joachim Sensemann, Joseph Sturgis, Peter Worbas), 15; second attack, 86–87; fort built, 88; BF's march to, 91–95; garrison routed, 115

Goldsmith, Oliver, 129

Graeme, Elizabeth (Betsy), 103, 104, 105, 107; learns Greek and Latin, 105; WF's courtship of, 104–111; their engagement, 113–114, 115, 138–140; married to H. Fergusson, 458

Graeme, Thomas: father of Elizabeth, 104–109; member of Pa. Council, 105; cofounder of Pennsylvania Hospital, 106; opposes BF, 107; outraged by the writings of Humphrey Scourge (WF), 109; and Graeme Park, 109–111

Grand Ohio Company (successor of Illinois Company): formed by BF, 225; scheme approved by Board of Trade, 245–246

Granville, Lord: berates BF, 133–134

Greene, Catherine Ray. *See* Ray, Catherine

Halifax, Lord: president of Board of Trade, 113, 133; opposes WF's appointment, 180

Hamilton, James: leads relief expedition, 72–77; member, American Philosophical Society, 76; at Easton, 79; advocates grand army, 79–80; commands militia, 87; questions BF as Assembly agent, 181; decries WF's appointment as N.J. governor, 182–183

Hancock, John: elected president of the Continental Congress, 341; and WF's arrest, 412–414

Heard, Nathaniel: as "Tory hunter," 411; arrests WF, 412–419

Hillsborough, Lord, 233, 304; opposes Illinois land scheme, 216; appointed secretary of state, 221; outraged by Ft. Stanwyx treaty, 225; encourages Grand Ohio Company, 225; refuses to honor BF's credentials as agent, 229–232; orders troops to Boston, 235; accuses WF of misconduct, 238; BF visits in Ireland, 244; rebuffs BF in London, 245; resigns, 246

Hopkinson, Francis: composer, 193–194; writes poetry, 194; WF writes to, 194; clashes with WF, 374–375

Howe, Lady (wife of Richard): negotiates with BF, 332

Howe, Lord Richard (admiral), 332; negotiates with BF, 432–433; issues amnesty proclamation, 438–439, 443

Howe, Sir William (general): commands British at Breed's Hill, 342; at battle of Long Island, 432; issues amnesty proclamation, 438–439, 443; and WF's exchange, 441

Huddy, Joshua: commander at Toms River, 470; prisoner in N.Y., 470–473; hanged, 473

Hume, David, 129; meets BF and WF, 155–156

Hutchinson, Thomas, 254; petition to remove him as governor, 255, 268; and his purloined letters, 256–259; upholds WF to the British ministry, 281; burned in effigy, 282

Illinois Company: WF drafts articles of agreement, 211; expanded into Grand Ohio Company, 225; during Revolutionary period, 356–358

Indians: trade with Quaker merchants, 7–8; cheated by the Penn sons (*see* Walking Purchases); attack settlers, 8–9, 12–15; tortured, scalped by whites, 85–87; massacred by Scotch-Irish, 187–189. *See also* Braddock, Edward; Delaware Indians; French and Indian War; Shawnee Indians

Jackson, Richard ("Omniscient"): described, 134–135; befriends WF, 134–135; BF hires, 135; coauthor of *An Historical Review*, 135–138; supports Illinois land scheme, 218; joins Grand Ohio Company, 225; with BF in Ireland, 244

Jay, John: at Paris peace talks, 377, 482

Johnson, Samuel, 129; quoted on Ecton, 26; on Americans, 171

Johnson, Sir William, 208; WF's partner in Illinois Company, 210–212, 217; BF writes to, 215; convenes Ft. Stanwyx Indian conference, 221–222; partner with WF in N.Y. land deal, 225

Jonson, Ben: quoted, 64–65

Junto, BF's discussion group, 49, 52, 60; WF revives, 68

Kames, Lord: entertains BF and WF, 163–164

Kinnersley, Ebenezer, 59–60; assists BF in electrical experiments, 63

Kinsey, James: BF letter to, 275; as N.J. Assembly speaker, 299; WF calls him a tool, 317, 456; seeks WF's release from prison, 456

Land speculation: BF and WF form Illinois Company, 205–226; BF's Grand Ohio Company, 225, 244–247; quashed by the British, 292; WF presses claims, 495–497

Lehigh Gap, 12, 23, 78, 87

Lehigh River, 3, 13, 87, 92, 94

Lexington, battle of, 302–303, 309; WF gathers intelligence on, 348

Lippincott, Richard: in Shrewsbury

raid, 469; hangs Joshua Huddy, 471–474; court-martial, 477–479

Livingston, William: and N.J. treasury robbery, 278; delegate to First Continental Congress, 293; rebuts WF speech, 299; letter to, 310

Lloyd, Thomas, 77; diary of Gnadenhütten expedition, 91, 92, 93–94

Locke, John: on William Penn, 9; on children, 31; on relation of king to subjects, 259

Logan (Six Nations chief): quoted on Walking Purchase, 7

Long Island, battle of, 432; Loyalist refugee camps on, 463–467

Louis XVI, 477, 478

Loyalists, 400, 407; flee America, 311, 387, 398, 484; mobbed, 358–359; armed, 382, 398, 424, 463–464, 475; disarmed, 384, 400, 411; imprisoned, 426, 436, 451; persecuted, 463; refugee camps on Long Island, 463–467; British treatment of, 475–477; and peace talks, 480–484; claims for compensation, 485

Mansfield, Lord: BF and WF visit, 161; settles Penn tax dispute, 164

Masons, 66–67, 102–103; WF joins, 59; BF's role in, 66; first lodge hall dedicated, 66; WF merges three lodges, 102

Mecom, Jane Franklin (BF's sister): BF writes to, 52–53; on WF's marriage, 183; seeks refuge in R.I., 310; visits WF in Perth Amboy, 363–366; son killed at Breed's Hill, 363

Militia, Pa. See Association, the

Monmouth County, N.J.: guerrilla warfare in, 468–479

Moores Creek Bridge (N.C.), battle of, Loyalists lose, 398

Moravians of Pa., 11–15, 77–78, 187; fortify Bethlehem, 78; march with BF, 92; oppose revolution, 310; barred from voting, 407. See also Germans of Pa.; Gnadenhütten

Morris, Robert Hunter, 18–23; attacked in print by WF, 68; opposes BF's defense plans, 74; Moravian appeal to, 77–78; and Reading conference, 81–82, 85–88; and arms deals, 82; offers bounty on scalps, 87; ig-

nores Reading plan, 98–99; BF ousts, 100–101; commissions BF colonel, 101; resigns, 102; dies, 193

New Jersey, College of (later Princeton University): WF *ex officio* president, 289–290; student unrest, 290; students enlist, 306; students escort GW to New York City, 350. See also Witherspoon, John

New Jersey provincial congress: origins in Essex County, 283–284; rejects Boston Port Act, 292–293; Witherspoon takes control of, 365; debates independence, 409; deposes WF, 410–411

New York (City): radicals raid, 306–307; Washington orders fortification of, 400; as Loyalist base, 463–467

Norris, Isaac, 22, 138

North, Lord: spurns BF, 253; as prime minister, 303; BF negotiates with, 308, 332–333; proposes peace plan, 318–323; rejected by the Congress, 340–341, 356; advocates Loyalist compensation, 484–485

Northumberland House: WF attends parties at, 166–169; James Boswell describes, 169

Odell, Rev. Jonathan (Loyalist poet, propagandist), 193, 394; WF aids, 464

Ohio Company. See Grand Ohio Company

Parke, Thomas (WF's steward), 425–460 *passim;* WF arranges pension for, 497

Paterson, William: secretary of N.J. provincial congress, 417

Paxton Boys: murder Moravian Indians, 187–189

Peale, Charles Willson: sketches BF and woman, 172

Pemberton, Israel: opposes militia bill, 20–21; negotiates with the Indians, 106; imprisoned as Loyalist, 457

Penn, Thomas (son of William Penn), 21, 102; leader of proprietary party, 7; BF's vendetta against, 112–113, 165, 171, 179; scorns BF's influence in England, 133. *See also* Walking Purchases

Penn, William, 7, 9, 10, 21; his *Frame of Government*, 9; critics of: John Locke, 9, Algernon Signey, 9

Penn, William, Jr., beats constable, 10

Pennsylvania: founding of, 9–10; charter, 9–10; dissension among religious sects, 16–17; political dissension in, 16–17, 100–101, 111–115

Pennsylvania Gazette, 21, 72, 89, 185, 289, 302, 303, 306, 307; BF founds, 42–43

Percy, Lady Elizabeth Seymour: entertains WF at Northumberland House, 167–169

Perth Amboy, N.J.: provincial capital, 306, 347, 349; WF moves to, 275, 279–280; addresses Assembly there, 297; Loyalists in, 351; BF visits, 359–363, 366; WF and BF confer at, 361–363; rebels seize barracks, 369; WF under house arrest in, 387; EDF describes, 396, 429; WTF visits, 396; petitions against independence, 410; becomes American "flying camp," 429; Loyalists leave, 430; in ruins, 484

Pettit, Charles (WF's secretary), 384; letter to Joseph Read, 384–385

Philadelphia Academy for the Education of Youth: BF a founder and trustee, 50, 316; besieged by Franklin troops, 101; BF ousted from the board, 106

Pitt, William (later, earl of Chatham): spurns BF, 140, 167, 216, 233. *See also* Chatham, Lord

Plans of union. *See* Albany Plan of Union; Franklin-Galloway Plan of Union

Poor Richard's Almanack (BF), 47–49

Presbyterians: New Light, 102; in Scotland, 155; in New Jersey, 289; persecute Anglicans, 311; Philadelphia group led by Charles Thomson, 314; ministers killed by British, 444. *See also* Witherspoon, Rev. John

Priestley, Joseph: BF finds job for, 251–252; witnesses Cockpit hearing, 269; BF's tearful farewell to, 308–309; on WF, 496

Princeton, N.J., 283; Committee of

Safety meets in, 382–389; as provincial capital, 400, 405; plundered by British and Americans, 443–444

Pringle, Sir John: physician to George III, 144–145, 307; accompanies BF to Germany, 200

Proprietary House, Perth Amboy, N.J.: WF moves to, 275, 279–280; described, 279–280; WF under arrest in, 388–416; Skinners move in, 429; burned, 484

Puritans: and Sabbath, 24, 28; views on Catholic Canada, 291–292

Quakers: in Pa. Assembly, 7; pacificism of, 7–9, 20, 97, 187; and sale of guns to the Indians, 8; quit the Assembly, 111; BF derides, 111; oppose revolution, 310; barred from voting, 407

Quebec Act, 291–292; BF denounces, 292

Ray, Catherine (Caty): friendship with BF, 68–71, 187; BF's letters to, 69, 115; hers to BF, 69–70; and Jane Mecom, 310

Read, Deborah. *See* Franklin, Deborah Read

Read, James (DRF's cousin): militia officer, 75; feuds with BF, 82–84

Read, John (DRF's brother): Braddock's wagonmaster, 73; BF's wagonmaster, 84

Reading, Pa.: defense conference at, 81, 84–88

Reed, Joseph (GW's secretary), 384; report from C. Pettit, 385–386

Roman Catholicism: Franklin family opposes, 26; Puritan views on, 291, 313

Roosevelt, John: sells wallpaper for Proprietary House, 280

St. Andrews University: confers degrees on BF, 145, 161–162

Scotch-Irish, the, in Pa.: immigration, 9, 12, 16; resented by Germans, 16; prejudice against Moravians, 78; refugees, 78–79, 89; BF confronts, 89–90, 188; in N.J., 276; volunteers join GW, 350; on march to Quebec, 392. *See also* Paxton Boys

Scottish Enlightenment, 155–159

Scourge, Humphrey: WF's pseudonym, 68; insults Rev. William Smith, 109

Seven Years' War. *See* French and Indian War

Shawnee Indians, 11; and Gnadenhütten massacre, 13–15

Shelburne, Lord: BF enlists in Illinois land scheme, 216; BF lobbies, 217–218; prime minister during Paris talks, 481; defends Loyalists, 481–483

Six Nations Indians, 221–222; and Pa. frontier, 7; Delawares defy, 85

Skinner, Cortlandt: and Stamp Act, 195; flees to British, 387; house searched, 389; seeks aid for WF, 440; with WF at Southampton, 488

Skinner, Stephen: and robbery of N.J. treasury, 276–279; and WF's arrest, 391

Smith, Adam, 158–159

Smith, William (chief justice of N.Y.): distrusts BF, 310; opposes guerrilla warfare, 466

Smith, Rev. William: as provost of Philadelphia Academy, 66; ousts BF from board, 106; accused of seeking Anglican bishopric, 109; blackballs BF to Oxford dons, 145

Smollett, Tobias, 129, 143

Smuggling: Hancocks of Boston involved in, 234; and Whartons of Philadelphia, 234; in New Jersey, 291; WF cracks down on, 300

Smyth, Frederick (chief Justice of N.J.), 390–391

Spangenburg, Augustus, 77–78, 87

Stamp Act: passed by Parliament, 195; reaction in American colonies, 195–196; WF and, 196–197; riots in Philadelphia, 198; and DRF, 198; BF's testimony before Parliament on, 199

Stevenson, Mary (Polly), 123, 204; BF exchanges 130 letters with, 172; WF declines to marry, 179; BF wanted as daughter-in-law, 181; BF sends for, 490

Stevenson, Margaret, 123, 132, 251, 308

Stirling, Lord, 193, 379; resigns from N.J. Council, 375; appointed colonel, 376; orders WF's arrest, 387; letter to WF, 388; WF's opinion of, 392; defends New York City, 400

Stockton, Richard, appointed by WF to N.J. Council, 282; home sacked by British, 443

Strahan, William: foremost London publisher, 129–130; describes WF, 129; writes to DRF, 130; cares for WTF, 183; partner in Grand Ohio Company, 225; warns WF of BF's political disfavor, 241; chastises BF on son's treatment, 452–453. *See also* Gibbon, Edward; Goldsmith, Oliver; Hume, David; Johnson, Samuel; Smollett, Tobias

Tarring and feathering: in Boston, 253–254; in Philadelphia, 291; in N.J., 383–384

Thomson, Charles: secretary of Second Continental Congress, 324; BF befriends, 313–314

Tories, *See* Loyalists

Trumbull, Jonathan: WF turned over to, 422; WF arraigned before, 424–426; censors WF's mail, 433–434; writes Congress in behalf of WF, 444–445; and WF's transfer from Litchfield jail, 451–452, 455, 458

Tryon, Sir William, 350; supports WF's advancement as Loyalist leader, 465–466

Tucker, Samuel: presides at WF's arraignment, 417

Vergennes, comte de, 455

Wagons, Conestoga, 4, 16–18, 21, 74

Walking Purchases: first, by William Penn, 10; second, by the Penn sons, 10–11; Delawares seek revenge for, 79; as the cause of the French and Indian War, 115

Washington, George: visits WF in Burlington, 193; land speculator, 206, 210; in the Second Continental Congress, 310; plans defense of New York City, 325, 400; plot to assassinate, 423; and treatment of prisoners, 426; refuses furlough to WF, 448; in Huddy affair, 478

Wayne, Anthony: drummer boy on Gnadenhütten march, 93

Wedderburn, Alexander: denounces BF at the Cockpit, 268–273; burned in effigy, 282; prepares warrant for BF's arrest, 308

Weiser, Conrad: on expedition to Ohio with WF, 56–59; militia colonel at Reading, 84–85; spies on Indians, 85

West, Benjamin: portrait of James Hamilton, 76; of SFB, 76

Whately, Thomas (British undersecretary of state): corresponds with T. Hutchinson, 256

Whately, William (member of Parliament): fights duel with John Tem-ple, 266–267; sues BF in chancery, 269

Whitefield, George: BF writes on westward expansion, 97–98; and Great Awakening, 289

Whitefoord, Caleb, 144, 480

Williams, Jonathan, Jr., 493, 494

Witherspoon, Rev. John, 409; denounces Anglicans, 155; recruited by College of New Jersey, 290; WF sponsors for American Philosophical Society, 290; and student revolutionaries, 400; as revolutionary leader, 401–407; attacks WF at hearing, 417–420; son killed at Brandywine, 454; second son captured by British, 454